NEW JERSEY

LAURA KINIRY

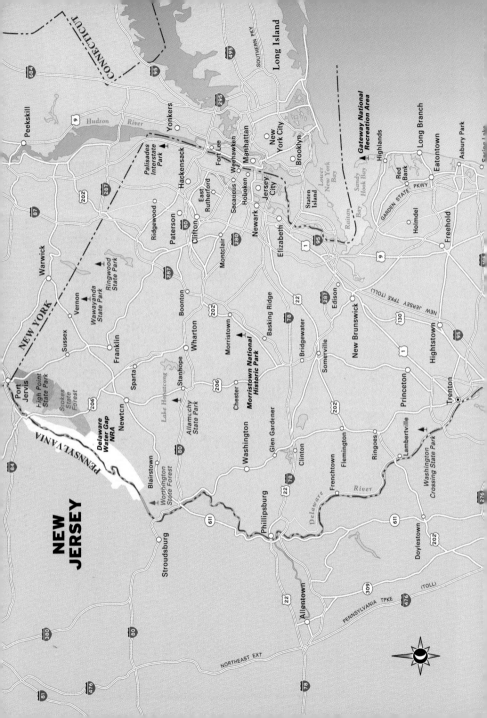

DISCOVER NEW JERSEY

Iconic and misunderstood, individual and resilient,
New Jersey is one of America's best known and most misrepresented states. Away from the grays and browns of its chugging smokestacks, the notorious toll roads, and the tarnished rainbow of freight cars, visitors may be surprised to find a place of stunning beauty and expansive wilds.

Benjamin Franklin is cited as describing New Jersey like "a barrel tapped at both ends," and indeed the state is often considered a throughway between New York City and Philadelphia. In reality, however, it's an accessible getaway with plenty of state parks, dazzling lakes, bed-and-breakfasts, and farmland. Emerge from the highways, and you may pass cranberry bogs and blueberry thickets, apple and peach orchards, occasional silos, 24-hour chrome-and-neon diners, and colonial homes graced with herringbone design.

Images of New Jersey, seemingly at odds with each other, show an atmosphere unattainable elsewhere. Roadside flea markets and

nothing but huge greetings at Cowtown Rodeo and Flea Market

drive-in eateries with car-hops stand in the next town over from high-rise apartments and urban-style boutiques. Desolate beaches where shorebirds feast on eggs laid by horseshoe crabs lie south of an African drive-through safari along a busy highway.

After years of shielding jokes, the state has finally begun to grow comfortable in its own skin. Historic towns have regained new life, and urban centers like Jersey City, Newark, and Atlantic City are reinventing themselves – modernizing to keep up with a changing world. River towns like Lambertville and Frenchtown and the downtown stretches of Collingswood and Haddonfield have finally come of age.

The urban landscape so readily associated with New Jersey is merely a glimpse into this wonderfully varied state. The region itself is a cultural haven – brimming with restaurants, boutiques, nightlife, and populations from Brazil, Spain, India, Japan, Korea, Cuba, Italy, and the Middle East, to name a few. But venture beyond, and you'll easily stumble into mountain towns and old mining villages, horse farms and open hillsides home to black bear, deer, squirrel, and

Ritz Theatre, Oaklyn

beaver, wetlands where blue heron, Canada geese, and osprey fly, and miles and miles (and miles) of coastline.

To get unintentionally lost in New Jersey is difficult. All you have to do is drive for a few hours, and eventually you'll hit water – the Delaware River, the Delaware Bay, the Atlantic, or the Hudson. Only along a small sliver north will you continue into New York. But if you're looking to disappear, well, that's another story. You'll find miles of hiking trails within the Kittatinny Mountains, unmarked back roads that wind along the Delaware Bayshore, and over a million miles of virtually untouched forest in the center of Central and South Jersey – heavy with Atlantic cedar, scrub, oak, pine, and three roaring rivers. Even to many of its residents, the scope of the state remains a mystery as loyalists stick close to home.

New Jersey sustains its place in the nation's forefront with its fair share of drama – most recently with the almost farcical resignation of its outed gay governor, its longstanding debate over the hunting of black bears, and of course, the claim to Jimmy Hoffa's body tucked well beneath the Meadowlands. Although it lost its Miss

Tony's Freehold Grill, "Boss" territory

America pageant in 2005 after 85 years and a couple of its sports teams are searching for new digs, this state knows better than to keep its eggs in one basket, and its inherent diversity has long sustained its livelihood.

In a place where the Devil is legendary, Muffler Men tower over roadways, gigantic wine bottles blend into the scenery, and an elephant makes her home along the shoreline, one may think that New Jersey's oddities have run amok. But it's the state's iconic image – its overwhelming place in the hearts of its musicians and its leading role in TV and films such as *The Sopranos* and Kevin Smith features – that in part draws the masses in search of its allure. Dozens of books have been written about New Jersey's bizarre past and present. Once the world's silent movie capital, it's regaining its place as a movie picture locale.

New Jersey is relatively small, traditionally losing many of its residents to out-of-state colleges, but numbers are returning, lured by lucrative job growth, revived townships, and the prime locale on the Great Northeast Corridor. Its people are both brash and

a late spring afternoon on the Ocean City boardwalk

© LAURA KINIRY

opinionated, while also big hearted and proud. Years of defending themselves have given residents a hard-bitten sense of unity tough to come by elsewhere, and Jersey girls have earned themselves a spot in the books and in the American psyche. Many who arrive begrudgingly in New Jersey discover a state far more green, accommodating, pleasant, and exciting than the reputation that precedes it.

Historians, outdoor enthusiasts, art collectors, pop culture fanatics, beach dwellers, shoppers, antique buyers, families, artists, musicians, gamblers, and Sunday drivers will find much to do here, as New Jersey is at once beautiful and inspiring, quirky and kitsch, tough and uninhibited. It's a state too often disregarded and just begging to be discovered. Shouldn't you be the one to do it?

Madame Marie's Temple of Knowledge, Asbury Park

Contents

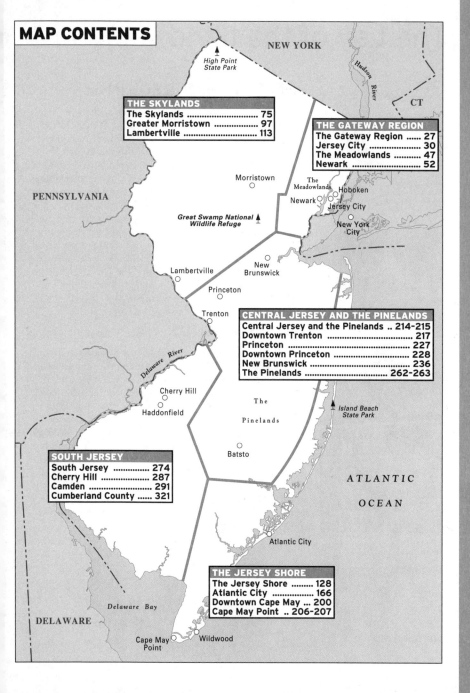

MAP CONTENTS

NEW YORK

High Point
State Park

CT

PENNSYLVANIA

Morristown

The
Meadowlands Hoboken
Newark Jersey City

New York
City

Great Swamp National
Wildlife Refuge

Lambertville

New
Brunswick

Princeton

Trenton

Delaware River

Cherry Hill

Haddonfield

The

Pinelands

Island Beach
State Park

Batsto

ATLANTIC

OCEAN

Atlantic City

Delaware Bay

DELAWARE

Cape May Wildwood
Point

The Lay of the Land

THE GATEWAY REGION

Although it's the most readily associated with New Jersey, the Gateway is also the least encompassing of the state's vast geographic diversity. It's New Jersey's smallest, most densely filled region and a worthy alternative to the dining, shopping, and nightlife of New York City. Its residents come from a many backgrounds, as a visit to Union City's Little Havana, Jersey City's Little India, and Newark's Portugal Avenue will show. Entertainment is a regional stalwart, especially in the Meadowlands, which host everything from sports and concerts to medieval jousting matches. When the urban cityscape becomes too much, you can take to the Meadow's wasteland for a pontoon boat trip or a bicycle ride along Palisades Interstate Park's Henry Hudson Drive. The Newark Museum and the suburban outskirts of Montclair, South Orange, and Summit also offer convenient escapes.

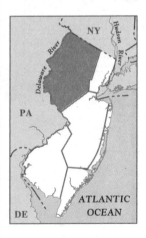

THE SKYLANDS

West of the state's urban enclave lay the Skylands, a mountainous expanse filled with old canal and mining towns, antique hubs, river villages, and an excess of nature. This is New Jersey's recreation center, chock-full of state parks, mountains, lakes, and rivers. The possibilities are numerous: you can cycle along many of the region's roads, float down the Delaware in an inner tube, cross-country ski in High Point State Park, fly-fish in Big Flat Brook, or soar in a hot air balloon above Hunterdon County. There are still pockets of urban life, though nothing like the Gateway Region, in Lambertville and surrounding towns. A car is a must for much of the region, especially the most remote areas. Accommodations here can range from exquisite B&Bs to luxury hotels and camping resorts.

THE JERSEY SHORE

Heading "down the Shore" is synonymous with New Jersey and an absolute must when visiting the state. From the casinos of Atlantic City to the Victorians of Cape May, there is so much to do along this 127-mile narrow expanse running the length of the lower east coast that it's impossible to experience it all in one trip. Shore towns range from classy to tacky, and cuisines from fine dining to fried feasts. Accommodations are just as varied, with quaint bed-and-breakfasts, historic hotels, modern digs, and angular motels decked out in neon. Salty air, five-and-dimes, boardwalks, casino arcades, T-shirt shops, pizza stands, amusement rides, skeeball, outdoor bars hosting cover bands, festivals, antique shops, birding, fishing, and lighthouses are all easy to come by along New Jersey's Atlantic Coast. And if that's not enough—well, there's always the beach.

CENTRAL JERSEY AND THE PINELANDS

Stretching west to east across New Jersey's midriff and south running vertically along the coast is a region of Revolutionary sites, historic villages, orchards, woodlands, and rivers. Within this convenient crossroads are easily accessible sights, including Princeton University, the museums of Trenton, and the nearby Grounds for Sculpture. Not least of the region's many attractions is Great Adventure, a mega–amusement park situated smack in the state's center. Nature lovers will find plenty to do in this section of the Garden State. Horseback riding outside New Brunswick and canoeing through the Pinelands, an area plentiful with bogs, thickets, forest, and folklore, are just two options. Those with urban leanings will be happy with Red Bank, one of New Jersey's most cosmopolitan boroughs and home to interesting shops, restaurants, and great people-watching.

SOUTH JERSEY

Lining the Delaware River across from Philadelphia and expanding to the marshes and beaches of the bay, South Jersey is a blend of small town, suburb, country, and fishing village—with a few cities tossed in for variety. Activities range from shopping along Haddonfield's Kings Highway, browsing the antiques in Mullica Hill, and dining on Collingswood's Haddon Avenue, to exploring the historic sites of Burlington City, Mount Holly, and Salem. While in the area, a stop by Camden's waterfront is a must. Cumberland County, with its Bayshore region and Millville's rejuvenated Glasstown Arts District, is close enough to the Cape to warrant an excursion from the shore. Some of the state's best birding opportunities are found along the Wild and Scenic Maurice River, an area also home to numerous fishing villages and back roads ideal for cycling.

Planning Your Trip

New Jersey is ideally located for a day trip or weekend excursion from New York, Philadelphia, and many places along the Atlantic Seaboard. Each of the state's five regions differ exponentially from one another, and all require some time to get a complete overview of the state. With such a wide array of sights, attractions, and geography, some forethought should be given to the activities you're interested in pursuing before arrival. Ironically, the state's Gateway Region, which draws to mind the average Jersey image, is the one where many are inclined to spend the least amount of time. Outdoor enthusiasts will find bountiful opportunity in the Skylands, Central Jersey's Pinelands, and South Jersey's Bayshore region, as well as the shore's Sandy Hook, Island Beach State Park, and Cape May Point. Nightlife seekers will find plenty to do in Hoboken and Atlantic City and seasonally in Belmar and Sea Isle City.

New Jersey is about 150 miles long (240 km) and 69 miles (110 km) wide at its widest point. It takes about 1.5–2 hours to drive across the state, and 2.5–3 hours to travel from top to bottom. Although public transport is viable for exploring smaller stretches such as the Gateway's Gold Coast and South Jersey's Camden–Burlington City area, a car is essential if you're planning to travel between regions or through some of the state's more remote areas, such as Warren and Salem Counties and the Pinelands. Note that toll roads are the bane of New Jersey drivers, and you'll experience fees galore along the New Jersey Turnpike, Garden State Parkway, Atlantic City Expressway, and between many of the shore towns.

Although no singular event transforms the state, there's little doubt that New Jersey springs to life Memorial Day–Labor Day, and it seems as though the entire Mid-Atlantic population has climbed into their cars to head down the Shore. This mass exodus usually makes traffic traveling west–east across the state and in either direction along the Parkway unbearable on Friday evenings and Saturday mornings throughout summer, and in the opposite direction Sunday afternoons. That being said, a visit to the Shore during July or August is essential for complete immersion into New Jersey culture, especially on weekends and holidays when festivals, parades, art shows, and concerts are usually held. No trip to the state is complete without a visit to the Shore, a stop at a diner, a Muffler Man sighting, and a canoe trip along one of its many rivers.

WHEN TO GO

New Jersey is a four-season locale offering numerous season-specific activities and plenty of year-round attractions, although the ideal time for a general visit is May and June or September and October, when temperatures are cooler, most sights remain open (at least on weekends), and crowds have vacated in lieu of school and work. For nature enthusiasts, this is the best time for bird-watching, as migrating warblers, raptors, songbirds, and shorebirds make their way through the state along the Atlantic Flyway, and mosquitoes and green flies have dissipated with the heat and humidity. Summer is essential for a true shore experience, when boardwalks are in full swing, lifeguards are watching over beaches, bars and restaurants have been restored to life, and sand sculpting contests, pavilion concerts, and outdoor movies are prevalent. This is also the season of sticky air, soaring temperatures, massive crowds, and unattainable parking spaces. Luckily, water-based activities, including canoeing, tubing, swimming, and numerous waterparks are available statewide to offer reprieve from the heavy temperatures. Rain can occur at any time throughout the year, with frequent thunder and lighting storms during summer; the skies may be blue over Haddonfield, but they can easily be hazy over Beach Haven.

Expect snowstorms in winter, usually with

added accumulation in the state's northern half. Anything more than a few inches, and towns will often shut down—a nuisance if you're planning on shopping or museum hopping, but for snowboarders, cross-country skiers, and snowmobilers, it's pure delight. The state really comes to life during the holiday season, with village festivals and an abundance of colorful lights and decor. During this time, a dusting of snow can easily transform a local town into a winter wonderland.

In the fall, many farms throughout South and Central Jersey and the Skylands brew apple cider, offer hayrides among pumpkin patches, and host the occasional corn maze. Autumn is also a great time to enjoy antiquing and Pineland bog excursions and for taking in the magnificent burnt oranges and fiery reds so prevalent throughout the state.

Most New Jersey accommodations offer discounted rates outside summer, and visitors can save more than half the price by booking a room at the Shore in the shoulder season rather than July or August. Some Shore properties remain open throughout the year, but many beach towns are absolutely deserted (and quite peaceful) in the winter. An exception is Cape May, where December brings horse-drawn carriage rides, heated trolley tours, and candlelight walkthroughs of decorated Victorians. New Jersey's many state parks are mostly free in winter, with a fee common June–August. A way to beat this is to arrive after 5 P.M. after the staff has gone home but the scenery remains.

WHAT TO TAKE

Casual is the way to go in most of New Jersey. You should feel comfortable in your everyday attire—though many restaurants are "casual elegant" or "proper attire," and some establishments, especially in cities such as Atlantic City and Trenton, don't allow sneakers, headwear, or baggy clothes.

If traveling in winter, be sure to pack a warm coat, gloves, hat, scarf, and waterproof shoes, and it's always a good idea to bring along an umbrella.

During summer, a swimsuit is essential no matter where you are, and shorts, tanks, and tees are the norm. If you're heading down the Shore, it tends to be a few degrees cooler and often windy, so bring a jacket and a pair of long pants for the evening. Typical Shore attire consists of swimsuit, flip-flops, a beach towel, and, if you like, a shirt and shorts to throw on for a walk down the beach. You'll often see beach goers lugging a makeshift living room onto the sand: folding chairs, a beach umbrella, a beach bag packed with suntan lotion, iPod, bottled water, lunch, and a novel. This may not be a mandatory set-up, but it's the norm and well worth it if you plan on spending your entire day near the ocean. Bug spray keeps away the biting green flies, a problem during sticky summer months when the breeze blows east off the bay. There's a noticeable shift in temperature come autumn, and the air gets crisp. A jacket is definitely a good idea.

Explore New Jersey

THE BEST OF NEW JERSEY

New Jersey is packed with so many historic sights, urban enclaves, recreational regions, shore towns, diners, and quirky attractions that at least a few weeks are required to really delve into most of the sights and scenery. Unfortunately, most visitors have only 10 days to devote, but not to worry—that's plenty of time to get a good overview of the state and allow brief stopovers in places you may want to concentrate on in future visits. New Jersey's relatively small size works to its advantage, making a trip through each of its five regions easily possible (though a fair drive between sights) and essentially required for a true portrayal of this diverse place. The best time of year to enjoy this tour is late spring, early summer, or fall, when prices are lower, crowds are at a minimum, most establishments are open for at least limited business hours, and temperatures are generally pleasant. Though this tour begins in the Gateway Region, it can easily be started from Philadelphia, Trenton, or even from Cape May, arriving to the city from Delaware aboard the Cape May–Lewes Ferry. In addition to your usual suitcase necessities, you may want to bring camping gear to enjoy the recommended outdoor sleeps.

DAY 1

Begin at **Ellis Island,** catching the ferry from Liberty State Park. Spend the afternoon touring the immigration museum and maybe searching for the names of your ancestors. Afterward, hop over to **Hoboken's Washington Street** for dinner. Spend your evening at one of the Meadowlands' hotels.

DAY 2

Take I-80 west across the state to the **Delaware Water Gap.** Take the day to explore this naturally scenic region, heading north to visit **High Point State Park** and the state's highest peak. Stay at the **Inn at Millrace Pond** in Hope, or if it's summer, set up camp at one of the numerous resorts in the area.

DAY 3

South along Route 519 will carry you along a winding path of rolling hills and open farmland, through lower Warren County into **Milford.** Take time to explore the town before continuing

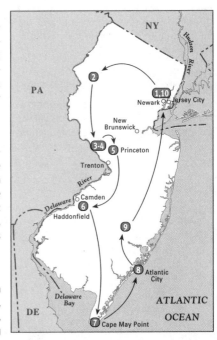

into **Frenchtown,** where you'll rent a bike at Freeman's Bicycle Shop for easy cycling south along the **D&R Canal** towpath, stopping in Stockton and on to Lambertville. Return to Frenchtown by way of Route 29 (equipped with a wide shoulder), and spend the evening in the borough's National Hotel.

DAY 4

Head south again – this time in your car. **Trenton** is the destination to spend the day exploring its fine museums.

DAY 5

From Trenton, head east to Princeton. Walk around the **Princeton University** campus, browse the shops, and enjoy pub-style dining at the Yankee Doodle Tap Room.

DAY 6

Make a stop at **Grounds for Sculpture,** in nearby Hamilton Township, where you'll want to wander for a few hours before heading south along I-295 to Camden County. Check into the Haddonfield Inn, and enjoy an Italian dinner along Haddon Avenue in **Collingswood.**

DAY 7

Beeline southeast to **Cape May,** where you can meander the Washington Street Mall, take a trolley tour, or simply relax on the beach. For a relaxing evening, choose one of the many Victorian bed-and-breakfasts and spend your time on the porch with a book. If it's entertainment you're after, head north to **Wildwood,** where you can cruise the boardwalk, let loose on the rides, and spend the night in one of the city's famed and endangered Doo Wop motels.

DAY 8

Enjoy a leisurely car ride north along Ocean Drive, passing through residential stretches and downtown centers of Stone Harbor, Avalon, and Sea Isle City, before arriving in **Ocean City,** where you may want to stop for a slice of Mac and Manco's pizza along the boards. Continue on to **Atlantic City** and enjoy late afternoon shopping at **The Quarter,** taking a ride in one of the Boardwalk's rolling chairs, or playing your cards at the blackjack table. Stay the night in the Tropicana's Havana Tower.

DAY 9

Hop on the Garden State Parkway heading north, and exit at Route 72 west for an afternoon of **Pinelands canoeing.** Camp at one of the nearby resorts.

DAY 10

Back on the Garden State Parkway heading north, stop off for lunch in **Red Bank** before returning to the Gateway Region.

EIGHT-DAY POP CULTURE TOUR

There's no doubt that when it comes to weird and wacky sights and roadside oddities New Jersey is king. In a state where attractions are abandoned as quickly as they're built, partially swallowed by barren, windy landscapes and rusted over time, and crumbling facades pay homage to the fame that once passed behind their walls, a pop culture tour is an absolute must. There's no better place to get lost in folklore and legend, park your car by a plastic palm tree and go searching for the remains of once famed "haunted castles" and long-forgotten amusement parks, or make pilgrimages to the sights obviously marked and bizarrely alluring. If you want pop culture, you'll find it: in the museums, along the highways, on bus tours, around campfires, and in every one of the state's five regions. So grab a roadmap, fill the tank, and tack on your sense of adventure—it's going to be one strange trip!

DAY 1

Begin your tour in the **Meadowlands,** where you can ditch the car for the three-hour **Soprano Sue's Tour** (weekends only) that covers the favorite family's numerous area haunts. If it's a weekday, try finding the Bada Bing and Satriale's Pork Store on your own. Finish off your evening with the frolicking knights and a hearty meal at **Medieval Times.**

DAY 2

Begin with a breakfast blintz at Clifton's **Tick Tock Diner** – all shiny color and chrome, this favorite New Jersey hangout was completely renovated in the 1990s by Kullman Industries, a pioneer in diner design. Afterward, hop on Route 23 West to cross the northern part of the state, briefly detouring if you wish to see Hamburg's **Gingerbread Castle** – a cakelike structure with dome-topped turrets – before continuing on to **Space Farms Zoo & Museum** in Beemerville. Spend the afternoon visiting with Goliath (the stuffed grizzly), browsing such displays as the miniature circus and antique rifle collection, and getting friendly with Space Farms' snake pit occupants. Spend the night in nearby **Vernon.**

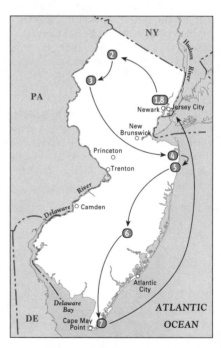

among stagecoach robbers and shoot-ups before driving southwest to **Blairstown** to visit the original *Friday the 13th* filming locale.

DAY 3

Route 206 will bring you south to **Wild West City,** where you'll spend the afternoon

DAY 4

South through Hunterdon County will bring you into the Capital Region, where you'll want to stop at Grover's Mill just outside of Princeton (look for Einstein's former abode) to snap photos of the **War of the Worlds monument.** From here, travel along backroads through Middlesex County cutting straight across to **Red Bank,** where you can engage in a self-guided Kevin Smith tour, including Jack's Music Shoppe and the Galleria.

DAY 5

From Red Bank, hit the Shore and head south to the still-crumbling facades of **Asbury Park,** the birthplace of Jersey Shore music and home to the one-time Palace Amusements. (Tillie the Clown – the city's pop-culture icon – has been rescued from the Palace wall and currently remains in an undisclosed location.) Stay in nearby **Ocean Grove,** and make sure to have a look at **Tent City** – one of the most architecturally unique communities in the state – before taking off.

DAY 6

Drive along the shoreline south to **Seaside Heights,** where in September you might catch the Clownfest parade. If its summer, head to the boards for a bit of '80s rejuvenation at the Flashback Arcade, and don't miss the two big-eared Muffler Men or a go at Stillwalk Manor, one of the state's only haunted amusement castles.

Before night falls, drive inland into the heart of the **Pinelands** to search for the Jersey Devil. If Russ Juleg isn't hosting one of his infamous devil hunts and campfires, you're on your own.

DAY 7

Back at the Shore, grab a sub like Sinatra liked 'em at **Atlantic City's** White House Sub Shop before a stop at the Boardwalk's Historical Museum, where you'll be greeted by a life-size replica of Mr. Peanut and given a free Heinz pickle pin to go. Drive south into **Ocean City,** where Grace Kelly spent her childhood summers, before making your way to **Wildwood.** This is the epitome of pop, with its gaudy boardwalk, airbrushed half-tees, and neon-lit strip of concrete motels with exotic names and oversized signs. For old school, stay at the Lollipop or the Caribbean motel. If modern retro is more your thing, the Starlux is your place.

DAY 8

Return north on the Garden State Parkway.

RECREATIONAL NEW JERSEY

New Jersey's outdoor opportunities are varied and plentiful, and whether you're into birding, cycling, hiking, canoeing and kayaking, scuba diving, or winter sports, you'll find something to suit your tastes. The state has a multitude of rivers, lakes, and streams where water activities abound, and if you're looking for mountainous terrain, scenic and winding roads, sheer bluffs, and mellow marshlands, New Jersey's got you covered.

CYCLING

For recreational sports, there's no better place in the state than the Skylands. The Highlands' **Ringwood State Park** and the Ridge and Valley Region's **Jenny Jump State Forest** are excellent places for mountain biking, and during summer months Vernon's **Mountain Creek** resort transforms into a downtown two-wheel haven. The roads near Morris County's **Great Swamp** and the **Delaware Water Gap's** Old Mine Road are ideal for road cycling. The casual cyclist will find that the **D&R Canal** towpath, along with the 5.5-mile **Edgar Felix Bike Path** in Central Jersey, and the **Henry Hudson Bike Trail** running from Keyport to the Atlantic Highlands suit their purposes. For something more challenging try the Gateway's **Henry Hudson Drive,** lined by the sheer cliffs of Palisades Interstate Park.

HIKING

Short day hikes are plentiful in the Garden State, and a number of longer, more strenuous routes challenge even experienced hikers. For something easy but scenic, try South Jersey's **Belleplain State Forest** and **Parvin State Park,** Central Jersey's **Washington Crossing Park,** or Morris County's **Jockey Hollow.** The Pinelands' **Batona Trail** is 50 miles traveling through a few area forests, but its flat terrain and numerous entry points make it accessible to even casual hikers. Lengthy, somewhat strenuous trails include the Skylands' incongruent **Highland Trail,** the 20-mile **Sussex**

Branch Trail, and the 27-mile **Paulinskill Valley Trail,** and the many trails that can be conjoined within the Gateway's **Palisades Interstate Park.** All offer rewarding views coupled with vast expanses of changing scenery.

BEACHES

New Jersey's 127 miles of Atlantic coastline offer some of the finest beaches in the Mid-Atlantic. Those looking for quiet solitude will enjoy Cape May Point's **Higbee Beach** and **Island Beach State Park's** northern and southern natural areas. Cape May Point's **Sunset Beach** is the only beach in the state where you can watch the sun both rise and set over water, and its also the only spot to go hunting for the region's infamous Cape May diamonds – small pieces of quartz crystal that, when polished, resemble jewels.

For an excess of sand you can't beat the **Wildwoods** – these free beaches are undoubtedly the state's widest, and you'll have no trouble finding a place to plant your beach blanket and umbrella. **Belmar's** beach is a beautiful white stretch of sand lined by a semi-commercial boardwalk, while Sandy Hook's **North Beach** is likely New Jersey's only beach where you can swim with a Manhattan backdrop. For those looking to go au naturel, the Hook's **Gunnison Beach** is the state's only clothing-optional beach.

BIRDING

New Jersey is a major migratory route along the Atlantic Flyway and an excellent venue for birding. Some of the best spots in the state are Morris County's **Great Swamp,** where you'll also find the **Raptor Trust,** and the Brigantine division of the **E. B. Forsythe National Wildlife Refuge** – both are best visited during spring and fall. **Cape May Point** and **Cumberland County** are exceptional birding locales, and May's World Series of Birding and February's Winter Raptor Festival each take place in this region. L.B.I.'s **Island Beach State Park** and **Sandy Hook** are additional birding favorites and great places to spot waterfowl, raptors, and osprey. The marshes of the **Meadowlands** are a good place to do a bit of birding from the comfort of a canoe or kayak.

WINTER SPORTS

Skiing and snowboarding opportunities are plentiful in New Jersey's Skylands, where the Vernon Valley hosts both **Hidden Valley,** a ski resort ideal for families, and **Mountain Creek,** the perfect place for downhill skiers to get some time on the slopes and a favorite spot for hardcore snowboarders. Those who enjoy cross-country skiing will find trails scattered throughout the state, most notably in the Ridge and Valley Region's **High Point State Park,** as well as South Jersey's **Belleplain State Forest,** Central Jersey's **Washington Crossing** and **Monmouth Battlefield State Parks,** and the Pinelands' **Brendan T. Byrne State Forest.**

ADVENTURE ACTIVITIES

Now this is no New Zealand, mind you, but New Jersey does host a couple of adventure activities. **Skydiving** is offered in the Skyland's Sussex County, near Central Jersey's Allaire State Park, and just outside South Jersey's Washington Township in Williamstown. If you're looking for an adrenaline rush on water, Wildwood hosts the **Silver Bullet speedboat.**

FIVE-DAY FAMILY VACATION

A wide range of historical parks, living-history farms, museums, educational facilities, boardwalks, aquariums and zoos, natural sights, oddball attractions, and pleasant shore towns make New Jersey a wonderful state for a family to explore together. There is no shortage of things to do or activities that will please all age groups. Some destinations, such as the Cape May Zoo, are free, while others offer exceptional discounts for kids.

DAY 1

Begin your trip in South Jersey with a visit to Camden's **Adventure Aquarium** and adjacent **Children's Garden,** before heading north to **Mount Laurel** for an evening in a hotel. **The Falls** entertainment center, full of rides and games, and **PAWS Farm Nature Center,** where kids will be learning without even knowing it, are both located nearby.

DAY 2

Hop on I-295 north en route to Trenton, where you'll explore the **Old Barracks Museum** and pay a visit to the **State House** for a fun history and civics lesson. Or during summer, try the **Howell Living History Farm** in nearby Titusville for agricultural demonstrations that will interest young and old.

DAY 3

Take a drive east to the state's center for a visit to **Great Adventure** theme park for a safari drive and a day at the amusements. Stay at a nearby hotel, or continue east to the Shore.

DAY 4

Head south along the Garden State Parkway to **Storybook Land,** just west of Atlantic City. Although it really is fun for all ages, teens may prefer checking out the unique specialty shops at nearby **Smithville.** Afterward, make the trip into **Ocean City** for an evening of boardwalk strolling, mini golf, and skeeball.

DAY 5

Spend the morning searching for shells along the beach before taking Route 9 south to Stone Harbor's **Wetlands Institute,** where you can explore marshes outside or the aquarium inside, or the Cape May Zoo, where animals from reptiles to lions are gathered. Scour the beach at **Cape May Point** for "diamonds" before driving onto the **Cape May–Lewes Ferry,** heading back toward Philadelphia via Delaware.

WEEKEND EXCURSIONS

There is perhaps no better state as well suited for a weekend getaway than New Jersey, since it's sandwiched between New York City and Philadelphia, and easily accessible from Delaware and Pennsylvania's Brandywine and Lehigh Valleys. Depending on how far you'd like to venture and the type of activities you enjoy, there are a number of possibilities for weekend travel. The following trips are reasonable from any of these major points, and at most require an extra tank of gas and a few additional hours driving time.

FROM NEW YORK CITY

On Friday, drive two hours west to the Skyland's Hunterdon County and spend two nights at the romantic **Chestnut Hill on the Delaware** in Milford. Enjoy dinner at the **Milford Oyster House,** and later, a nightcap on the bed-and-breakfast's veranda overlooking the Delaware River before turning in for the evening.

The following morning, have breakfast in the countryside at the **Café at Rosemont** before heading to **Frenchtown** for a bit of window-shopping and a walk over the bridge into Pennsylvania. If it's summer, you have the option nearby of renting an inner tube for a leisurely float along the Delaware River. Afterward, drive down to **Stockton** to enjoy a snack by the railroad tracks, and perhaps a 20-minute carriage tour, before continuing south to Lambertville.

There's plenty to do in **Lambertville** – here you'll find antique shops, art galleries, specialty stores, a brewery, numerous restaurants, and south of the city center on Route 29, a wonderful weekend flea market. Stop for a late lunch at downtown's **49 North Main,** then return north with a brief stop at Bull's Island for a scenic view and some information on the D&R Canal.

The evening is reserved for a **balloon ride** over Hunterdon County with Alexandria Balloon Flights, complete with champagne and hors d'oeuvres. If the day's events have left you feeling overexerted, spend another quiet night on the B&B's veranda, listening to the crickets and the peaceful river sounds. If they've left you hungry, you may want to head into Milford business district for a late-night snack and a beer at the **Ship Inn.**

The following morning travel east to **Clinton** for an early breakfast and a walk across the Raritan River along Main Street, maybe stopping at the **Red Mill Museum Village** or at the **Hunterdon Museum of Art,** before continuing on to **Round Valley Recreation Area** for a couple of leisurely hours and heading back to New York.

FROM PHILADELPHIA

Take the Atlantic City Expressway to Route 9 and travel north to the village of **Smithville,** where you'll spend two nights at the **Colonial Inn Bed & Breakfast.** If you arrive early, take some time to explore the historic village and shops before having dinner at the **Smithville Inn.** Afterward, stop off for a drink at **Fred & Ethel's Lantern Light Tavern.**

The following morning, grab a simple bite to eat at the **Colonial Coffee Café,** adjacent to the B&B, and drive north along Route 9 to New Gretna, taking Route 542 east into the **Pinelands.** Here you can spend an afternoon **canoeing** or hiking in the greater **Wharton State Forest.** Later, head over to the nearby **Sweetwater Casino,** where you can fill up on "Casino cheese" and live entertainment. Return to Smithville for the evening.

On Sunday morning take some additional time to walk around Smithville, if you didn't have time before, then head west to Egg Harbor City for brunch at the **Renault Winery.** Explore the grounds and enjoy a bit of wine tasting, before traveling north along Route 563 back into the Pinelands.

Stop in for a look at **Batsto,** a restored mining and glass-making village, and tour the mansion before continuing north to Route 72 West and connecting with Route 70 West. Take this road back toward Philly. If hunger sets in before reaching home, you can stop off for a bite at Cherry Hill's **King of Pizza** or, for something more sit-down, **Caffe Aldo Lamberti.**

FROM TRENTON

Travel across the state's center to **Red Bank,** where you've reserved a two-night stay at the **Oyster Point Hotel.** After checking in, head downtown for dinner at **Teak** or **Red,** and remain around Broad Street for a few after-dinner cocktails before turning in.

Start your Saturday morning at **No Ordinary Café** and afterward browse the shops along Broad and Monmouth Streets before taking a drive down Rumson Road toward Sea Bright. Upon reaching the Shore, turn north toward **Sandy Hook,** and spend your afternoon along the beach and enjoying a snack at the **Sea Gull's Nest.** Afterward, travel west into the Highlands and the nearby Atlantic Highlands, and take in the views from the **Twin Lights of Navesink** and **Mount Mitchell.** Return to Red Bank for another evening of dining and nightlife, and perhaps a show at the **Count Basie Theatre.**

Spend a leisurely morning before departing toward Freehold, where you'll enjoy a late breakfast or early lunch at **Tony's Freehold Grill** (check out the signed Springsteen photo on the wall) before continuing west along Route 537, stopping at **Jackson Outlet Village** for a bit of shopping before returning home.

THE GATEWAY REGION

When some people think of New Jersey, they think of the great urban northeast—a congested conglomeration of highways and high density, smoke stacks and smog—an area many say is trying to imitate New York City—but the Gateway Region is so much more. Along with Manhattan, this part of New Jersey represented the "Gateway to Freedom" for millions of New World immigrants who arrived at Ellis Island. The German, Italian, and Irish, striving for a better life in the new world, took up residence in the Gateway's Hoboken and Union City, with brownstones filling the neighborhoods, and mom-and-pop stores occupying commercial space. Newark became one of the world's leading manufacturing cities, and Paterson became America's first planned industrial town. The suburban Oranges and mountainside Montclair swelled with the overflow of people spilling from these riverfront cities.

Today this "mirror of Manhattan" remains highly populated, but there is no mistaking you're in New Jersey. This small area is bursting with activity, and is easily more diverse than any other of the state's regions: It's here that you'll find Jersey's City's "Little Bombay," the "Little Havana" of Union City, Newark's Spanish and Portuguese Ironbound district, Hoboken's Irish pubs, and the Middle Eastern shops throughout Paterson. The Gateway Region also packs a punch with some of New Jersey's best shopping, from the boutiques of Hoboken's Washington Street and the specialty shops of Ridgewood, to the great mall of Short Hills and the outlets of Secaucus. Sports are also a big deal in the Gateway Region, with

© LAURA KINIRY

HIGHLIGHTS

(Ellis Island: This new-world welcoming place stands in the Upper New York Harbor and belongs to not only New York and New Jersey, but also to the millions of immigrants who first arrived on its shores (page 32).

(Hoboken: Once down-and-out, this mile-square city has sprung back to life tenfold, most notably along the 14-block thoroughfare of Washington Street, where boutiques and specialty shops, cafés, bars, and superb people-watching are the norm (page 37).

(Palisades Interstate Park: New Jersey's contribution to a joint state recreational palace is 12 miles of sheer cliffs and wooded canopies. It's easy to forget you're right across the Hudson from the United States' largest city and in the center of the most densely populated portion of the entire country (page 45).

(Eco-Tours in the Meadowlands: It may seem like a stretch, but this region long known as a dumping ground has cleaned up its act to promote eco-tourism. Bring along the binoculars, and keep your eyes peeled for shore birds — as well as Jimmy Hoffa's remains (page 49).

(The Newark Museum: The Garden State's largest museum is jam-packed with art and science exhibits that include world-renowned sculpture, hungry piranhas, Red Planet star shows, and one of the greatest Tibetan collections in the western hemisphere (page 55).

(Tick Tock Diner: There's no better place to begin a tour of New Jersey's famous diners than the Tick Tock — a shiny chrome space with booth and counter seating, A.M. hours, and the juiciest burgers in town (page 65).

LOOK FOR **(** TO FIND RECOMMENDED SIGHTS, ACTIVITIES, DINING, AND LODGING.

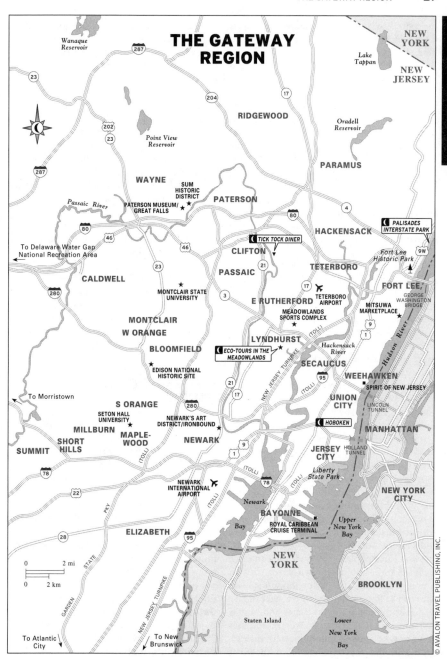

THE GATEWAY REGION

Wanaque Reservoir

NEW YORK

NEW JERSEY

Lake Tappan

RIDGEWOOD

Oradell Reservoir

Point View Reservoir

PARAMUS

WAYNE

SUM HISTORIC DISTRICT

PATERSON MUSEUM/ GREAT FALLS

PATERSON

Passaic River

HACKENSACK

PALISADES INTERSTATE PARK

To Delaware Water Gap National Recreation Area

TICK TOCK DINER

CLIFTON

Fort Lee Historic Park

FORT LEE

TETERBORO

CALDWELL

PASSAIC

MONTCLAIR STATE UNIVERSITY

E RUTHERFORD

TETERBORO AIRPORT

GEORGE WASHINGTON BRIDGE

MITSUWA MARKETPLACE

MEADOWLANDS SPORTS COMPLEX

MONTCLAIR

W ORANGE

LYNDHURST

Hackensack River

BLOOMFIELD

ECO-TOURS IN THE MEADOWLANDS

EDISON NATIONAL HISTORIC SITE

SECAUCUS

Hudson River

To Morristown

S ORANGE

WEEHAWKEN

SPIRIT OF NEW JERSEY

SETON HALL UNIVERSITY

NEWARK'S ART DISTRICT/IRONBOUND

UNION CITY

LINCOLN TUNNEL

MILLBURN

MAPLE-WOOD

NEWARK

HOBOKEN

MANHATTAN

SHORT HILLS

SUMMIT

JERSEY CITY

HOLLAND TUNNEL

Liberty State Park

NEWARK INTERNATIONAL AIRPORT

NEW YORK CITY

ELIZABETH

Newark Bay

BAYONNE

ROYAL CARIBBEAN CRUISE TERMINAL

Upper New York Bay

NEW YORK

BROOKLYN

0   2 mi

0   2 km

To Atlantic City

To New Brunswick

Staten Island

Lower New York Bay

© AVALON TRAVEL PUBLISHING, INC.

the centralized hub of the Meadowlands Sports Complex, where big-name concerts are also held. To escape the density, there's Palisades Interstate Park, offering excellent cycling and hiking opportunities.

When you think of the region's geography, it's hard not to picture highways, but the Gateway Region features not only the mountainous urban outskirts, but also the sheer Palisades cliffs. Rivers run through the area, and the wetlands and marshes composing the 30-mile Meadowlands region are once again becoming home to various non-mutant wildlife.

So, the next time you watch the opening credits of *The Sopranos* and see Tony embark on that turnpike, you'll know that he should take a different exit—there's so much more to see.

PLANNING YOUR TIME

Most visitors arriving in the Gateway Region by way of Newark International Airport are simply passing through with little time to spend, while others cross the Hudson for an afternoon, day, or weekend excursion. The overall land area of the Gateway is actually quite small, and sans traffic, can be covered fairly easily in a relatively short time. It makes sense to visit the region for a day or weekend, and add an extra day or two if you want a more complete feel for the area. Accessible from a number of places along the East Coast, the Gateway Region is an easy place to come back to, and public transport is perhaps better here than anywhere else in the state.

A day trip from New York City might begin with a ferry ride into Hoboken where you can enjoy breakfast and shopping along Washington Street, with a visit to the Hoboken Historical Museum or the city's Sinatra-related spots afterward.

From the Hoboken Terminal you can catch a PATH train into downtown Jersey City for a stop at the Jersey City Museum. Or stay on the train to Journal Square, where you can take a tour of the old Stanley Theatre and sample Indian treats along Newark Avenue. You may want to take the PATH into Newark instead, for a walk down Ferry Street, also known as

Portugal Avenue and a many-hour visit to the Newark Museum. Settle on your evening meal—perhaps back on Ferry Street—sit back, and enjoy. Don't worry if you've missed the ferry: You can catch a PATH train back into Manhattan from Newark, Jersey City, or Hoboken until approximately midnight.

If you are planning a weekend trip and you're traveling by car, spend the evening at one of Jersey City's waterfront hotels and take a drive up the Gold Coast the following day. Afterward, continue into Palisades Interstate Park and drive north to search for the remnants of millionaire's mansions or go hiking along the scenic cliffs.

An extra day in the Gateway might be spent in the Urban Northeast, perusing the shops of Ridgewood, stopping for a look at Paterson's Great Falls, and heading south into Clifton for a meal at the Tick Tock Diner. If you're in the mood for a museum, make a stop at the Montclair Art Museum, or continue on into West Orange for a visit to the Turtle Zoo. If shopping's your thing, drive over to Short Hills to do a bit of spending at New Jersey's most fantastic mall.

INFORMATION AND SERVICES

There are a couple of convenient welcome centers in the Gateway Region, beginning with the **Liberty State Park Welcome Center** (NJ Turnpike exit 14B, 201/915-3401). Despite its name, the center provides information on accommodations and attractions throughout the area and is conveniently located close to Newark Liberty International Airport and New York City. The **Montvale Welcome Center** (201/391-5737) is situated at the state's northern border on the Garden State Parkway by mile marker 172 and works best for those entering New Jersey from New York State.

For additional information concerning the entire Gateway Region, contact the **Gateway Tourism Council** (P.O. Box 2011, Bayonne 07002, 201/436-6009 or 888/428-3930). Gateway Welcome Centers include the **Satellite Information Center** (Newark Liberty International Airport, Terminal B, International Arrivals, Door 11, 973/623-5052) for those arriving from overseas by plane, and the New Jersey Turnpike's **Vince Lombardi Travel Plaza & Information Center** (Mile Marker 116 N. and S., Ridgefield, 201/943-8757).

GETTING THERE AND AROUND

The **Lincoln Tunnel** travels between Weehawken and Manhattan's Midtown, and the **Holland Tunnel** between Jersey City's Newport neighborhood and New York City's Canal Street. The bicycle-friendly **George Washington Bridge** connects Fort Lee to the Bronx. Tolls for both the bridge and tunnels run $6 for autos; E-Z Passholders get a discount.

NY Waterway operates ferry service between New York City and numerous New Jersey Gold Coast cities, including Weehawken, Edgewater, Hoboken, and Jersey City. **Newark Liberty International Airport** (888/EWR-INFO or 888/397-4636, www.panynj.com) is the region's major out-of-state transport hub, and is connected by train to Newark's Penn Station and downtown New York City.

Newark Penn Station (800/772-2222, http://nycsubway.org/nyc/newark) is a hub for NJ Transit and Amtrak trains, as well as Greyhound and interstate transit buses. **PATH** (800/234-PATH or 800/234-7284, www.pathrail.com) trains and the **Hudson-Bergen Light Rail** (800/772-2222, www.njtransit.com) connect Gold Coast cities, as well as Newark, to one another and New York City.

NJ Transit (800/772-2222, www.njtransit.com) runs commuter trains throughout the Gateway Region, with stops in most major towns; major transfer points are at Hoboken Terminal and Secaucus Junction.

Major auto routes that run through the area include I-280 (the Urban Outskirts), I-80 (the Urban Northeast), the New Jersey Turnpike, and the Garden State Parkway. Routes 17 and 3 connect most Meadowland towns. A good way to enter the Gateway Region is from the north, taking Palisades Interstate Parkway south from New York State into New Jersey, and slowly being introduced to the waterfront towns of Fort Lee, Edgewater, Weehawken, and Hoboken, before culminating with Jersey City.

Jersey City and the Gold Coast

As New Yorkers may snarl, "It's New Jersey," but this primo locale along the Hudson River has views that just aren't possible in Manhattan, as well as excellent dining and nightlife options, exciting culture, and boutique and specialty shopping without the hordes of tourists. It's North Jersey's own financial center and home to much of New York City's overflow, a dense population of people, commerce, business, and backgrounds where you'll find some of the best alternatives to the Big Apple around.

Situated on a peninsula between the Hackensack and Hudson Rivers and the Newark and New York Bays is the sprawling 14.8-square-mile Jersey City, located so close to Manhattan's downtown district that it's often

referred to as "the sixth borough." From all accounts Jersey City has vastly improved from what it was a decade ago. The city has completely revamped its waterfront, adding mixed-use townhouse properties and glass-walled towers, including the 40-story Goldman Sachs building, the largest structure in the Garden State. In downtown, new life is evident in the million-dollar brownstones previously occupied by squatters.

Once a great transportation and manufacturing hub, Jersey City remains a convergence point for many of the region's major routes and train lines. It's a good thing, because Jersey City is not a walkable place—neighborhoods are scattered, connected by potholed streets with faded lane dividers and lax traffic

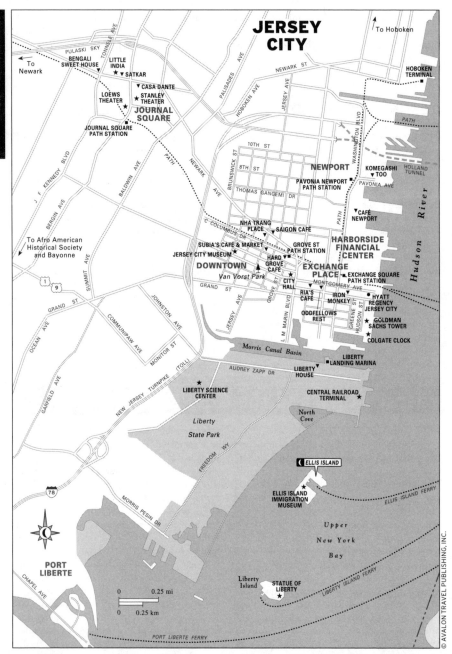

the Colgate Clock, a Jersey City landmark

© LAURA KINIRY

rules. Rather than a definitive center, the city has many small enclaves and boasts dozens of nationalities, including Irish, Italian, Puerto Rican, Russian, Indian, and Asian.

SIGHTS
The Financial Waterfront

Easily visible from New York City, Jersey City's waterfront is a few miles of coastline stretching from the **Newport** neighborhood south of the Holland Tunnel down through Liberty State Park and onto **Port Liberte,** a mixed-use residential space and one of Jersey City's newest neighborhoods. The city's financial hub, known as **Exchange Place,** stands tall along the waterfront center, directly across the Hudson from New York City's Wall Street. Jersey City's revitalization efforts are most notable here, with a new hotel and New Jersey's tallest structure—the **Goldman Sachs Tower**—soaring high on the end of Hudson Street. Across the street in an otherwise empty lot stands the octagon-shaped 55-foot diameter **Colgate Clock,** a Jersey City icon that once

topped the former Colgate-Palmolive building and a reminder of prosperous days past, something the city is looking to re-create, and with notable success.

Like many financial centers, Exchange Place turns into a ghost town after 5 P.M. weekdays, but occasional festivals and fairs keep things lively on weekends throughout the year. There's not a ton to see here, but the recent development explosion makes this a pleasant place to walk around.

Van Vorst Park

Van Vorst Park is a Jersey City historic district and one of the city's nicest neighborhoods. Central to downtown, it's only a short PATH ride west of the Financial Waterfront and easily explored from the Grove Street station. Its streets are lined with cafés, restaurants, and restored brownstones like those along York Street, and in the center is the neighborhood's namesake community park (Montgomery St. and Jersey Ave.), complete with hot dog vendor. The **Jersey City Free Public Library** (472 Jersey Ave., 201/547-4500, 9 A.M.–8 P.M. Mon.–Thurs., until 5 P.M. weekends) and City Hall (280 Grove St.) provide good reference points for navigating the area.

It's in this neighborhood that you'll find one of the city's finest art museums, the **Jersey City Museum** (350 Montgomery St., 201/413-0303, www.jerseycitymuseum.org, $4 adults, $2 seniors), a modern space hosting a permanent collection of 19th- and 20th-century fine art and historic objects, as well as a changing display of contemporary works that include furniture, paintings, mixed media, pen and ink, and sculpture. The museum's crisp, white interior is a direct contrast to the historic structures outside. Admission hours are 11 A.M.–5 P.M. Wednesday–Friday, noon–5 P.M. Saturday and Sunday, 5–8 P.M. Thursday.

Liberty State Park

Created in 1976 for the U.S. Bicentennial, the 1,200-acre Liberty State Park (www.liberty statepark.com) is one of the most popular recreational facilities around. It's a massive place,

© LAURA KINIRY

Statue of Liberty as seen from Liberty
State Park

though much of it is closed to the public. Fortunately, the prime waterfront stretch remains accessible and on a weekend afternoon every inch gets packed with all walks of life, tossing Frisbees, picnicking, or hopping on a ferry to nearby Ellis Island. Facilities include a high-tech museum, restaurant, numerous trails, and plenty of open space, and in the northeast corner the **Central Railroad of New Jersey Terminal** or CRNJT (201/915-3440), once the main transportation center for thousands of immigrants arriving to America. Today it hosts special events and a welcome center and features changing displays, some that relate to the immigrants' journey.

Along the waterfront the two-mile **Liberty Walk** connects the park's north and south portions with a bench-lined walkway, perfect for viewing Ellis Island, Manhattan, and a profile of the Statue of Liberty. Boats can be launched from the **Liberty Landing Marina,** where you can also catch a **water taxi** (201/985-1164) for a unique view of the bay, or a trip over to New York City.

In the park's northwest corner is the **Liberty Science Center** (251 Phillip St., 201/200-1000, www.lsc.org), an interactive museum with three floors of themed exhibits, centered around health, environment, and invention. Kids will enjoy the 100-foot-long touch tunnel and an indoor climbing wall. The center is home to one of the world's largest Hoberman spheres—a collapsible sphere that expands to gargantuan proportions—and the state's largest **IMAX theater,** as well as an observation platform and café. Beginning in November 2005, the museum is in a temporary location in the CRNJT while the main building undergoes major renovation and expansion, expected to continue until mid-2007. During this time the IMAX theater will remain closed.

Hours for Liberty State Park Riverside are 10 A.M.–4 P.M. weekdays, until 5 P.M. weekends, and admission is $3.

Circle Line (866/STATUE-4 or 866/782-8834, www.statueoflibertyferry.com) offers ferry service ($11.50 adult, $9.50 seniors, $4.50 children 4–12) to Ellis Island and the Statue of Liberty from Liberty State Park and is available 9:30 A.M.–3:30 P.M. daily throughout the year, except Christmas. Expanded service is available most holiday weekends. The last ferry leaves the Statue of Liberty at 5 P.M., stopping at Ellis Island, and arrives back to the park at 5:25 P.M.

The Hudson–Bergen Light Rail line stops at the park's northwest corner, and from here you can catch NJ Transit bus 305 to various points within the park.

〖 Ellis Island

In 1998 the U.S. Supreme Court ruled that the bulk of 27-acre Ellis Island does, in fact, belong to New Jersey. This includes former hospital wards and the home of the superintendent. Once you've arrived, there's no reason not to cross state boundaries and make a day of it.

The **Ellis Island Immigration Museum** (201/435-9499, www.ellisisland.com) opened in 1990 and pays tribute to the thousands of immigrants who first stepped foot in America on these grounds—people like Bob Hope and the von Trapp family, and many of our grandparents and relatives. Inside you'll find items that belonged to these people, accompanied by their black and white images. One of the museum's highlights is the Family Immigration History Center, where you can trace your ancestors by reviewing the records of steamship passengers who arrived between 1892 and 1924. You can then get a picture of the ship they sailed on, as well as a copy of the original passenger list. For the full museum experience, take the $6 audio tour, narrated by Tom Brokaw, and interspersed with personal accounts from those who know the story best, the immigrants who arrived here.

Ferry rides (866/STATUE-4 or 866/782-8834, www.statueoflibertyferry.com) to Ellis Island cost $11.50 adult, $4.50 child, and parking is available at Liberty State Park. There is no admission fee to visit the island (9:30 A.M.–5:30 P.M. daily, with extended hours during summer), only for audio tours of the immigration museum ($6). A "food court" within the museum provides snacks for those without picnic provisions.

Journal Square

To reach Journal Square (www.thenewjournalsquare.com) from downtown, drive west through bail bond central, or hop on a PATH train. Once a vibrant center, the neighborhood is in the process of reinventing itself. Beneath the awnings among the garage-door storefronts there are some retail shops, but the area's main draws are its two famous movie theaters and the dense stretch of Indian shops and eateries along Newark Avenue.

Loews Theater (54 Journal Square, 201/798-6055, www.loewsjersey.org) escaped a 1987 scheduled demolition and has since been glamorously restored. The theater celebrated its 75th anniversary in 2004. It's said that Frank Sinatra attended a performance of Bing Crosby here in the 1930s, leading him to want to be in show business. Loews was once partitioned into a multiplex, but has been returned to true form as a single theater showing independent flicks and classic films, and hosting live music, drama, kids' plays, and jazz and swing shows. The grand 1928 **Stanley Theater** (2932 Kennedy Blvd.,

DINNER AND A SHOW

It used to be that a night on the town in Jersey City meant a picture show at Journal Square's Loews Theater accompanied by dinner at the Canton House, also known as Canton Casino or Canton Tea Garden to locals. Situated a few doors up from the movie house along Bergen Avenue, this second-floor Chinese restaurant opened in 1930 as the Hudson Royal and grew along with the theater during the days of the Depression and World War II. It sailed through the prosperous '50s and turbulent '60s and remained steadfast even when Loews declined in the '70s and finally shut its doors in the late '80s. (It reopened again in 2002.) But in 2004, a year before the Canton was to celebrate its 75th anniversary, it locked its doors for renovations and never reopened. Information about the restaurant's mysterious closing later emerged: The death of owner Tommy Tang in 2003 marked the beginning of the Canton's demise, and soon after it closed for renovations, those handling its finances declared bankruptcy.

The Canton was a true Jersey City landmark. Perched atop a long flight of stairs, the spacious restaurant evoked a film noir setting, with its saturating red tint and red-jacketed waiters, wooden booths and angular tables, dim lighting, paper lanterns, and a dance floor that stood only for show. Over the years, the restaurant earned a reputation as the establishment of choice for baby showers, wedding receptions, and office parties, and even gained a bit of national recognition when it appeared in the 1995 film *To Wong Foo, Thanks for Everything, Julie Newmar*. Its traditional Cantonese cuisine (later embellished with regional spices) was no culinary feast, but the decor was unbeatable.

201/377-3100) has been acquired and restored by the Jehovah's Witnesses. You'll recognize it by its gorgeous marquee, in bronze copper like a roller coaster going up the hill. Drop-in tours are given daily 8 A.M.–5 P.M., and admission is free.

South of Journal Square in the city's Greenville neighborhood is the **Afro-American Historical Society Museum** (1841 Kennedy Blvd., 201/547-5262, 10 A.M.–5 P.M. Mon.–Sat., closed Sun.). Located on the second floor of the **Greenville Public Library,** it's New Jersey's only museum dedicated solely to African American history. Civil rights posters advertising marches, a large quilt collection, and a display of memorabilia belonging to the Pullman porters, an African American labor union, are some of the treasures found here along with more than 800 artifacts.

Just north of the square is a few-block stretch of Newark Avenue known as "Little Bombay," a colorful enclave of Indian eateries, markets, and retail shops selling silk saris and diamonds. Signs that hang above the sidewalk say "India Square," though there'll be no mistaking it.

Farmers Markets

The **Journal Square Farmers Market** (Journal Square, 201/798-6055, 11 A.M.–7 P.M.) takes place outdoors on Wednesday afternoons, mid-July–late November. Jersey Fresh fruits and veggies as well as a variety of baked goods are up for grabs, and it's definitely worth a stop if you're in the neighborhood. Other local markets include the waterfront's **Newport Pavonia Farmers Market** (Pavonia East St., 973/236-1875, 11:30 A.M.–6:30 P.M. Tues. and Thurs., late June–late Nov.) and downtown's **Van Vorst Market** (Jersey Ave. and Montgomery St., 201/433-5127, 8 A.M.–1 P.M. Sat., mid-June–late Nov.).

FESTIVALS

Jersey City hosts over a dozen ethnic festivals, many of which take place at **Exchange Place** along the waterfront, near the Colgate Clock. These include the annual July **Jersey City West Indian/Caribbean Festival,** and September's **Greek Festival, Irish Festival,** and **Chinese Festival.** For more information, call the Division of Cultural Affairs at 201/547-6921.

Jersey City's annual day-long **St. Patrick's Day Festival** begins in the early A.M. with a breakfast, followed by a morning mass and an afternoon parade along Kennedy Boulevard that culminates at Journal Square. The party continues into the evening hours with lots of song and drinking in good ol' Irish fashion.

ACCOMMODATIONS

Jersey City is home to a few waterfront hotels that are conveniently located near transit lines and ferry ports, and ideally situated as jumping-off points for exploring the city's various neighborhoods, or in a couple of cases, the rest of the Gold Coast region. Since each of the hotels cater primarily to business travelers, rates drop substantially on weekends.

$150-200

Right across the river from New York City and within walking distance to the Pavonia-Newport PATH station, the **Courtyard by Marriott Jersey City** (540 Washington Blvd., 800/346-8357) is a 10-story hotel with clean rooms, an indoor pool, and a free breakfast buffet. Guest rooms feature high-speed Internet, and an on-site café serves three meals daily.

$200-250

The nearby, all-suite **Doubletree Club Suites Jersey City** (455 Washington Blvd., 201/449-2400) offers amenities that include living room, fridge, microwave, and room service. A restaurant and bar are located off the lobby.

$250-300

You'll have a superb view of the Manhattan skyline from the 14-story **◖ Hyatt Regency Jersey City on the Hudson** (2 Exchange Pl., 201/469-1234 or 800/233-1234, www .hyatt.com), located at the city's waterfront financial center. Modern rooms are equipped with refrigerator, in-room safe, and both wired and wireless Internet access, and the *New York Times* is delivered to your door daily. Downstairs you'll find a gift shop selling convenience items and an ATM. This is a great place for exploring downtown Jersey City, and even the heated indoor pool has an awesome backdrop.

FOOD AND NIGHTLIFE
The Financial Waterfront

Each of the waterfront enclaves has its own eateries and bars, and with so much construction, new places continue to open. Newport is a good neighborhood to try for a meal, and a fairly new waterfront bar seems to be paving the way for a financial center trend.

Situated within the Newport Complex is **Komegashi Too** (99 Pavonia Ave., 201/533-8888, www.komegashi.com, noon–2:30 P.M. and 5–10:30 P.M. Mon.–Fri., 5–10:30 P.M. weekends, $8–23), a Japanese and sushi restaurant with more excellent views and a stylish bar area. Try the Whatever Roll, with tuna, eel, and avocado, rolled in tobiko and topped with spicy sauce ($8.50), or go wild with the King-Komegashi, a fish-lover's frenzy with tuna, salmon, yellowtail, and king crab, finished with asparagus and a dollop of avocado ($15.95).

Close to Exchange Place is the **Hearts & Horns Bar & Grill** (101 Hudson St., 201/333-6500, $14–28), a swanky waterfront space with dim lighting, intimate tables, and a bottom-lit bar. It's easy to snag an available stool even on the weekends, though I'd say not for long. Southwestern-inspired cuisine is served 11 A.M.–11 P.M. daily.

Downtown

On the corner of Columbus and Grove Streets across from the PATH station is the fun **Hard Grove Cafe** (319 Grove St., 201/451-1853, www.hardgrovecafe.com, 11 A.M.–11 P.M. Mon.–Fri., 8 A.M.–midnight weekends, $7–12), a Cuban-American eatery decorated in palm trees and neon. In the summer grab a seat under one of the sidewalk umbrellas resembling Mexican blankets, and sip a glass of *té frío* while watching the crowds pass by.

You'll find two of the city's best Vietnamese restaurants along Newark Avenue. At **Nha Trang Place** (249 Newark Ave., 201/239-1988, 10 A.M.–10:30 P.M. Mon.–Thurs. and Sun., until 11 P.M. Fri. and Sat., $6–12) reasonable prices and phenomenal cuisine more than make up for the absent decor. It's been rumored that the *real* Village People hang out at **Saigon Café** (188 Newark Ave., 201/332-8711, 11 A.M.–10 P.M. Mon.–Thurs., until 11 P.M. Fri. and Sat., 2–10 P.M. Sun., $5–17), where *pho* is the specialty, but the tamarind soups come highly recommended.

For fresh juices, vegan dishes, or a healthy snack-to-go, try the organic **Subia's Café and Market** (506 Jersey Ave., 201/432-7639, 8 A.M.–8:30 P.M. Mon.–Fri., until 7:30 P.M. Sat., 6:30 P.M. Sun., $5–7.75), owned by two local sisters who will also accommodate your java craving.

Ria's Cafe (135 Montgomery St., 201/915-0045, 8 A.M.–3 P.M. Mon. and Tues., until 10 P.M. Wed.–Sat., 10 A.M.–4 P.M. Sun., $15–22) serves freshly prepared Dominican dishes and a popular Sunday brunch. Known for their frittatas, the service receives mixed reviews.

Iced cappuccino doesn't get much better than at **Beechwood Café** (290 Grove St., 201/985-2811, $5–12), where the selection of sandwiches, salads, soups, and sweets are just as tasty. Go for the garden veggie sandwich with olive tapenade ($8), or head to the adjoining market to browse their kitchenware selection. Hours are 7 A.M.–11 P.M. Monday–Friday, 8 A.M.–11 P.M. Saturday, and 8 A.M.–8 P.M. Sunday, with brunch served 9 A.M.–4 P.M. weekend mornings. They are closed 4–5 P.M. daily to set up for dinner.

◖ **The Iron Monkey** (97 Green St., 201/435-5756, noon–2 A.M. Mon.–Fri. and Sun., 7 P.M.–2 A.M. Sat., $12–20) is a classic pub housed in a converted brownstone. Live jazz and rock play upstairs, and entrées are selected from an American-European menu that locals rave about. When the weather heats up head for the rooftop patio. Food is served until 10 P.M.

Oddfellows Rest (111 Montgomery St., 201/433-6999, $8.95–16.95) is the place for New Orleans–inspired nightlife. Tangy specialty drinks, a good brew selection, and Creole cuisine begin the party—Tuesday night karaoke sees it through. Oddfellows serves food 11:30 A.M.–10:30 P.M. Sunday–Wednesday,

4–11 P.M. Thursday–Saturday, and 11:30 A.M.–4 P.M. Sunday. The bar is open 11:30 A.M.–2 A.M. Sunday–Thursday, and until 3 A.M. Friday and Saturday.

Liberty State Park

The **Liberty House** (Liberty State Park, 76 Audrey Zapp Dr., 201/935-0300, www.liberty houserestaurant.com, $19–36) serves American eats and features both a sushi and raw bar. Gorgeous glass windows afford excellent waterfront views, though there's no doubt this place is touristy. Lunch is served noon–3 P.M. and dinner from 5 P.M. Tuesday–Saturday. The restaurant is open 11 A.M.–8 P.M. Sunday, with brunch hours 11 A.M.–3 P.M.

Journal Square

Journal Square is not especially known for its dining options, though there is one exception: **Casa Dante** (737 Newark Ave., 201/795-2750, $16–40). Just a couple of blocks northeast of the square, it's classic Southern Italian that can do no wrong. Hours are 11:30 A.M.–10 P.M. Monday–Friday, 4–11 P.M. Saturday, and 2–9 P.M. Sunday.

However, if Indian cuisine is what you're after, there's no better place in the city than the nearby stretch of Newark Avenue known as "Little India," beginning at Kennedy Boulevard and continuing west to Tonnele Avenue. The area is overflowing with Indian markets and over a dozen food vendors to choose from, and by all accounts, it's hard to go wrong. Both vegetarian and vegan snacks, also known as *chaats,* are easy to come by. These flavorful concoctions vary in texture, sweetness, and ingredients and are topped with yogurt or other sauces. The **Bengali Sweet House** (836 Newark Ave., 201/798-9241, www.bengalisweet.com) is a good place to sample these treats, as well as dozens of sweets that represent regions from throughout India. The vegetarian **Satkar** (806 Newark Ave., 201/963-6309, 10:30 A.M.–9:30 P.M. daily, closed Mon.) is one of the city's most beloved Indian restaurants, while **Dosa Hut** (777 Newark Ave., 201/420-6660, 11 A.M.–10 P.M. daily,

$4–10) serves South Indian cuisine and an expansive *dosa* (the Indian version of a crepe) selection. For North Indian eats, a full bar, and a vegetarian-friendly buffet try **Rasoi** (810 Newark Ave., 201/222-8850), open 5–10 P.M. Monday, 11:30 A.M.–10 P.M. Tuesday–Thursday, until 11 P.M. Friday–Sunday. A buffet lunch is available 11:30 A.M.–3 P.M. Tuesday–Friday, until 4 P.M. weekends.

Diners

Not to be mistaken for the White Manna (notice the extra "n") in Hackensack, **White Mana** (470 Tonnele Ave., 201/963-1441, $3–11) in Jersey City is a 24-hour space-age circular diner originally built for the 1939 World's Fair, and selling burgers "since 1946." Also in Jersey City is the 1950s **Miss America Diner** (322 West Side Ave., 201/333-5468, $5–14), a quintessential American diner and one of New Jersey's best. Hours are 5:30 A.M.–9:30 P.M. Monday, until 9 P.M. Tuesday–Friday, 8 P.M. Saturday, and 4 P.M. Sunday.

GETTING THERE AND AROUND

Jersey City is seven miles east of Newark and is easily reachable by car from Newark Liberty International Airport via I-78. If traveling from Manhattan, take the Holland Tunnel from Canal Street, which enters the state by way of Jersey City's northeastern waterfront. The city is a 10-minute train ride from Manhattan's Wall Street, and **PATH** (800/234-PATH or 800/234-7284, www.pathrail.com, $1.50 one-way, $3 round-trip) trains connect Jersey City with New York, Hoboken, and Newark. Both **NJ Transit** (800/772-3606, www.njtransit.com) and **Amtrak** (www.amtrak.com) run trains from Newark Liberty International Airport to Newark's downtown Penn Station, where you can transfer to a PATH train with numerous stops in Jersey City. If arriving from other points along the Gold Coast, the **Hudson-Bergen Light Rail** (800/772-2222, www.njtransit.com) travels north from Bayonne through Jersey City and onto Weehawken.

NY Waterway (800/53-FERRY or 800/533-3779, www.nywaterway.com) operates commuter ferries ($5.50 one-way) between midtown Manhattan and Jersey City's Colgate Center (Hudson St. near Exchange Place), and between midtown Manhattan and Newport, 6:30 A.M.–9 P.M. weekdays only. Another weekday ferry ($5.50 one-way) operates between New York's Wall Street and midtown, and Jersey City's Harborside (end of 2nd Street), 6:30 A.M.–9 P.M.

Unless you are planning on focusing on a particular neighborhood, having a car or making use of Jersey City's public transport is essential. **PATH** stations are located at Pavonia-Newport, Grove Street (downtown district), Exchange Place, and Journal Square. **Hudson-Bergen Light Rail** has stops at Pavonia-Newport, Harborside Financial Center, Exchange Place, Essex Street, and Liberty State Park, and trains appear approximately every 10 minutes.

In Liberty State Park, ferries run from Liberty Landing Marina (201/985-8000) to nearby Ellis Island, and to the Statue of Liberty.

BAYONNE

South of Jersey City on the peninsula's southern tip is Bayonne, a 5.39-square-mile city that in 2004 became home to Royal Caribbean Cruise Lines, the only cruise ship to dock in New Jersey.

Bayonne has also succeeded in attracting the motion picture industry. Numerous TV shows and films have been filmed here over the last few years, including *War of the Worlds,* HBO's *Oz,* and the movie version of *Strangers with Candy,* and plans are in negotiation to build the state's first full-service motion picture studio and back lot on an old military terminal. Still, there's little reason to visit unless you're stalking a celebrity or taking to the seas. In either case, be sure to have a look at the architecturally powerful steel-arch **Bayonne Bridge** while you're here. Completed in 1931, it connects the city to Staten Island's Port Richman.

Royal Caribbean Terminal

Cape Liberty Cruise Port (the Peninsula, Rte. 440, 866/562-7625) is the "New York" terminal for **Royal Caribbean Cruise Line** (www.royalcaribbean.com), which runs cruises to Canada and the Caribbean.

Getting There and Around

Bayonne has numerous **Hudson-Bergen Light Rail** (800/772-2222, www.njtransit.com) stops that connect it to Jersey City, Hoboken, and Weehawken. The Light Rail connects with PATH trains and transit lines in numerous locations along the Gold Coast.

◖ HOBOKEN

Known as the "Mile Square City," this once down-and-out waterfront town is now living large with luxury housing, classy bars, elegant restaurants, and fashionable boutiques. Like much of New Jersey it's a predominately Irish/Italian town, isolated by the Hudson River to the east, the Palisades to the west, and separated from Jersey City by railway yards, and it takes full advantage of its tiny space. Squint, and you may glimpse the ghosts of the longshoremen who once worked the shipyards and see the corruption that plagued the town in earlier days. Today Hoboken is filled with twenty- and thirty-something hipsters who treat their home as a Manhattan alternative, a smaller, Jersey version of the "city that never sleeps."

One of the beautiful things about Hoboken is the life that exudes from its brownstone walls—exteriors now painted in varying shades of gray, blue, white, maroon, yellow, and green. Along Hudson Street, closest to the river, you'll find three- and four-story structures with hand-railed stoops, jutting windows, basement units, small courtyards, usually a bike locked outside—and up until recently, superb views of the New York Harbor, now replaced with waterfront condos, townhouses, and shopping plazas. It's a city of one-way streets and brick-laid crosswalks that changes form from gentrified to industrial as you make your way west.

Washington Street is the city's undisputable hub—a wide, ultra-bustling thoroughfare with endless shops, Irish bars, and in the summer, railed-off sidewalk seating—and is one of the city's main draws. Hundreds of attractively colorful brownstones line the street's 14 blocks. The already-bustling street picks up even more as you continue south, into a conglomeration of cafés, boutiques, and hard-to-find parking spaces.

In 2005 the city celebrated its 150th anniversary.

History

The area now known as Hoboken was purchased by Colonel John Stevens in 1784 for $90,000, intended as a place New Yorkers could travel as a "home away from home." Before World War I the city had a large German population, but when the war began these citizens were forced to flee, abandoning shops and businesses and creating a financial downward spiral for Hoboken. During the years of Prohibition, River Street was lined with saloons, and organized crime ran rampant during the middle of the 20th century. The docks were occupied with shipping yards where longshoremen arrived each day in the hope of finding work, an image accurately depicted in 1954's *On the Waterfront*. The city didn't begin to recover until the 1980s, when New Yorkers came lured by cheaper rents and the city's close proximity. A Hudson River ferry that had stopped all service years before was up and running again, boutiques and restaurants moved in, and the city was reborn.

Hoboken is home to a number of firsts, including the first organized baseball game at Elysian Fields—an area along the waterfront—and the country's first brewery, opened in 1642.

Sights

Housed within the former machine shop of the Bethlehem Steel Shipyard, the **Hoboken Historical Museum** (1301 Hudson St., 201/656-2240, www.hobokenmuseum.org, 2– 9 P.M. Tues.–Thurs., 1–5 P.M. Fri., noon–5 P.M.

Hoboken's Washington Street

© LAURA KINIRY

Sat. and Sun., $2 adult, children free) pays tribute to this proud city's fascinating history. Displays include a 12-foot-tall coffee drop, once part of a Maxwell House "Good to the Last Drop" sign that hung above the company's downtown coffee plant, and images from the filming of *On the Waterfront*. While you're here, be sure and pick up a copy of the Hoboken self-guided tour map, or for fans of Ol' Blue Eyes, a Sinatra-centric map highlighting the city's many crooner-related spots.

Frank Sinatra was born in Hoboken and resided at **415 Monroe Street,** west of Washington in the city's former "Little Italy" section, until he was 12. Though the original four-story home no longer remains, a bronze star plaque commemorating the legend exists along the sidewalk, a gift from the Historical Society. Just off of Hudson Street along the waterfront is **Sinatra Drive,** where you'll find some amazing views of the Manhattan skyline. Along the drive you'll pass a skate park and a riverfront walkway, complete with benches and a little gazebo. Sinatra Park, where *On the Waterfront* was filmed, is situated at the south side of the bend, and hosts various festivals throughout the year. Frank left town in 1939, bought his mother a house in nearby Fort Lee, and never played another show here, but his name remains synonymous with the city—on its streets, in its parks, and always at its restaurants.

Festivals and Events

Hoboken's **First Sunday's Artists' Open Studio Days** (201/795-3767, www.monroe center.com) are held the first Sunday of every month, noon–5 p.m. throughout the city.

The **Hoboken Italian Festival** (www .hobokenitalianfestival.com) is held annually for four days in September the weekend after Labor Day. Derived from Italy's Feast of the Madonna Dei Martiri, the festival is over 75 years old and takes place in Sinatra Park—food (including a cannoli-eating contest), fireworks, music, and an evening procession of the Madonna statue are part of the highlights. **Saint Ann's Feast** is another popular Italian festival, held in July and occurring annually for nearly a century. Celebrations begin with a mass at St. Ann's Church and continue for seven days.

Hoboken's **Farmer's Market** (Newark St. between Hudson and River Sts., 3–7:30 p.m. Tues., late June–late Oct.) features local fresh fruits and veggies, organic produce, and baked goods. It's been going strong since 1996.

Shopping

Fourteen blocks may seem like a long stretch, but **Washington Street** makes full use of the space with no shortage of shops and boutiques.

For True Religion jeans and Allison Burns handbags, **Peper Inc** (1028 Washington St., 201/217-1911) is your place. This established boutique sells fashionable women's clothing with a small men's selection.

Looking for that perfect gift? **The Wishing Tree** (706 Washington St., 201/420-1136) sells the ultimate in candles, soaps, and artsy jewels.

Sea Monkeys live on at **Big Fun Toys** (602 Washington St., 201/714-9575, www.big funtoys.com), along with whoopee cushions, potato guns, and pocket air hockey. There are plenty of goods for tots and teens as well. **Down to Earth** (527 Washington St., 201/656-7766) sells the best in denim and unique styles for women and men.

It's all about the shoes and eveningwear at **Via Mode** (404 Washington St., 201/217-6727), where shoppers can complement a Betsey Johnson dress with a stylin' bag.

At **Aaraa** (106 Sixth St., 201/386-0101) you'll find Indian-inspired shawls, scarves, jewelry, handbags, embroidery, and accessories like pillows, table linens, and bedspreads that can be custom-tailored to suit your home.

Recreation and Entertainment

Movies Under the Stars (201/420-2207) are shown on Wednesday evenings throughout the summer at **Pier A Park,** situated at the southern end of Sinatra Drive. Rental kayaks are available at nearby **Sinatra Park,** which also has a soccer field, café, and plenty of waterfront benches.

Accommodations

A stay at one of Jersey City's hotels is an excellent option for a visit to Hoboken. As this book goes to press, plans are underway to construct a 25-story **W Hotel** and residential space along the Hoboken waterfront between 2nd and 3rd Streets. This luxury property is scheduled to open in late 2006.

Casual Eateries

Hoboken is a great spot for enjoying a casual bite, especially during summer when dining goes hand in hand with people-watching while seated along Washington Street at one of dozens of sidewalk tables.

Occupying the first floor of a five-story brownstone is the corner **Elysian Café** (1001 Washington St., 201/798-5898, $15–23), a French bistro with an upscale bar and attractive bistro decor. Score a seat next to one of the wall-length windows to enjoy the afternoon light, and don't leave without trying the French onion soup. The café does a mean weekend brunch (10 A.M.–3 P.M.), and features a just-as-popular bar. Lunch hours are noon–3 P.M. Monday–Thursday, 11 A.M.–3 P.M. Friday, and dinner is served 5–10 P.M. Sunday–Thursday, until 11 P.M. Friday and Saturday. Don't worry if you miss the entrée boat; a bar menu is available for an hour after the dining room closes.

For coffee, shakes, or waffles and ice cream any time of the day there's the **Frozen Monkey Café** (526 Washington St., 201/222-1311, www.frozenmonkeycafe.com, $3–8). This casual space is ideal for milling through your afternoon under the hippest of contemporary artwork. Hours are 8 A.M.–11 P.M. Monday–Thursday, until midnight Friday, 9 A.M.–midnight Saturday, and 9 A.M.–11 P.M. Sunday.

Pizza is king at the cozy **Margherita's Pizza & Café** (440 Washington St., 201/222-2400, $10–17), but large pasta portions are just as well-received. The café features an outdoor patio for those sweltering nights. Hours are 11:30 A.M.–10:30 P.M. Tuesday–Thursday, until 11:30 P.M. Saturday, 12:30 P.M.–9:30 P.M. Sunday.

For Malaysian try the enjoyable **Satay** (99 Washington St., 201/386-8688, $7–16), housed in a white brownstone at the south end of Washington. Open 11:30 A.M.–11 P.M. daily.

On the corner of Third and Willow Avenue is **Zafra** (301 Willow Ave., 201/610-9801, $5–23), a fun BYOB place serving flavorful Nuevo Latino fare amid inspired, brightly colored decor. For $10 they'll turn your bottle of wine into a delicious pitcher of sangria. The restaurant is open 8 A.M.–10 P.M. Monday–Thursday, until 11:30 P.M. Friday, and 10 A.M.–10 P.M. Saturday and Sunday.

Leo Grandevous grew up with Sinatra, and though neither man is still around, both remain immortalized at **Leo's Grandevous** (200 Grand St., 201/659-9467, www.leosgrandevous.com, $7–16), a casual corner Italian joint that opened in 1939. Inside you'll find a strictly swing decor, including a curving, turquoise bar, a Sinatra-tributed jukebox, and dozens of old Frank photos adorning the walls. Lunch is served 11:30 A.M.–2 P.M. weekdays. The restaurant is open for dinner 5–11 P.M. Saturday, and 4–10 P.M. Sunday.

Originally known as the 14th Street Diner, Hoboken's only 24-hour diner was remodeled and renamed **Malibu Diner** (257 14th St., 201/656-1595, $5–13) in 1984. A black-and-white checkered border running beneath its windows makes it easily recognizable.

Fine Dining

It seems like whenever a new restaurant opens in Hoboken, people claim it's "trying to be Manhattan." Is that so bad? New York's got many of the country's best restaurants, and with this Mile Square City following suit, you're in for a culinary experience.

For the best porterhouse in town head to **Frankie & Johnnie's** (163 14th St., 201/659-6202, www.frankieandjohnnies.com, $21–37), a 140-seat steakhouse with a piano player on weekends. The building dates back to the late 19th century and has retained its original tile floor and tin ceiling. Valet parking is offered at this swanky establishment, open for dinner 5–10 P.M. Monday, until 11 P.M. Tuesday–Thursday, 5–11:30 P.M. Friday and Saturday, and 4–9 P.M. Sunday.

Named for the United States' food-loving third president, **The Jefferson** (1319 Washington St., 201/386-9955, www.thejefferson.net, $18–25) is currently Hoboken's hotspot. A limited menu of well-executed Italian entrées that change seasonally receives high praise from returning customers. Service is impeccable, and with a dimly lit, cozy dining area and a three-way chocolate dessert on the menu, you can't help but feel the love. The restaurant offers a three-course special, selected from the set menu or the daily selections, 5–10 P.M. Monday, 5–7 P.M. Tuesday–Friday, Sunday, and a late-night menu is available until 1 A.M. Monday–Thursday and Sunday, until 2 A.M. Friday and Saturday. The Jefferson is open 11:30 A.M.–1 A.M. Tuesday–Thursday, until 2 A.M. Friday and Saturday,

3 P.M.–1 A.M. Sunday (closed for private parties 10 A.M.–3 P.M. Sunday).

The crowds never cease at **Lua** (1300 Sinatra Dr. N., 201/876-1900, $19–28), a large and boisterous 150-seat restaurant and bar with exceptional riverfront views and cuisine described as "Latin-influenced American eclectic." Come here for tapas, margaritas, and to be seen, but not for conversation. Lua's is open for dinner 6–10 P.M. Sunday, until 11 P.M. Monday–Wednesday, and midnight Thursday–Saturday. Brunch is served 11 A.M.–2:30 P.M. weekends. The bar opens at 5:30 P.M. and last call is usually 1:30 A.M. weekdays, and 2:30 A.M. weekends. Housed in an old brownstone diagonal from its sister property Elysian Café, **Amanda's** (908 Washington St., 201/798-0101, www.amandasrestaurant.com, $20–32) is a top pick for romance and a wonderful wine selection. Arrive for the 5–5:30 P.M. seating to order from the fixed-price, three-course menu (Mon.–Sat., $28 for two). Boutique-bought blue jeans are not out of place. The restaurant is open for dinner 5–10 P.M. Monday–Thursday, until 11 P.M. Friday and Saturday, and 5–9 P.M. Sunday, and for brunch 11 A.M.–3 P.M. weekends.

For flavorful entrées, lively atmosphere, and an outstanding decor, there's no beating ◖ **Cucharamama** (233 Clinton St., 201/420-1700, $12–25). Start with the calamari and move on to the fish of the day, accompanied by your preferred Spanish wine or one of the best *mojitos* in town. Meals are cooked on a wood-fired oven, but a clay-tiled floor keeps things cool, and in the summer door-like windows open out onto sidewalk seating.

Nightlife

Often seen as an evening alternative to New York City, Hoboken is brimming with neighborhood watering holes, Irish pubs, and swanky bar/restaurants. Many of the spots showcase live music, and food is a standard complement to the plethora of available drafts and martini concoctions.

Trendy **Madisons Bar and Grill** (1316 Washington St., 201/386-0300, www.madisonbarandgrill.com, 11:30 A.M.–10 P.M. Mon., until 11 P.M. Tues.–Fri., 11 A.M.–11 P.M. Sat., 10 A.M.–10 P.M. Sun.) is famous for its Tuesday night martini party—and the crowds pack in for half-price specials. The classy decor is spiced with black and white photos, hanging fringed lampshades, a long bar, and a wood floor. For meals, the Sunday jazz brunch comes highly recommended. **Tonic Bar & Lounge** (1300 Park Ave., 201/653-2583) is all that a lounge should be, with black pleather couches, tables, and a dance floor, and a 1980s-induced Saturday night spin, with a bit of rock, R&B, and hip-hop to keep the vibe flowing. Widescreen tellies and an acoustic night round out the deal. Hours are 6 P.M.–2 A.M. Tuesday–Saturday, until 3 A.M. Friday and Saturday.

Maxwell's (1039 Washington St., 201/653-1703, www.maxwellsnj.com, 5 P.M.–midnight Sun.–Thurs., until 1 A.M. Fri. and Sat., 11:30 A.M.–4 P.M. Sun.) is *the* place for live music in Hoboken. This suave city institution offers plenty of seating, and leopard-print curtains protect from sidewalk eyes, allowing local and big-name bands to rock out their alternative ways in full force.

Toward the south side of Washington is the **Mile Square Bar & Grill** (221 Washington St., 201/420-0222, www.themilesquare.com), a loud, casual space with international brews on tap. Live acts and DJs are featured throughout the week, though karaoke reigns on Sundays. Grab one of the straight-back booths for an internationally infused meal. Hours are 11:30 A.M.–10 P.M. Monday–Wednesday, until midnight Thursday and Friday, noon–midnight Saturday, and 11 A.M.–10 P.M. Sunday.

Though Irish pubs abound in Hoboken, you'll find no finer than **O'Donoghues on First** (205 First St., 201/798-7711, 4 P.M.–2 A.M. Mon.–Fri., noon–2 A.M. Sat. and Sun.). This fun bar is both a cover band and DJ venue and a laid-back sports bar, with a couple of large-screen TVs, a pool table, and a dartboard. Beer pong tournaments take place on Sundays, and half-price martinis draw trendsetters on Tuesdays.

For true individuals there's the **Gold Hawk** (936 Park Ave., 201/420-7989, www.the goldhawk.com, 5:30 P.M.–2 A.M. Sun.–Thurs., until 3 A.M. Fri. and Sat.). This hipster hangout hosts Fiesta Fridays with chips, salsa, and half-price margaritas. The Hawk's a mix between pub and lounge, with a bar menu available.

Services

Steven's Park at 4th and Hudson Streets is Hoboken's first free public wireless Internet park. Information on how to connect to the network can be found on the city's official website, www.hobokennj.org.

Getting There and Around

Hoboken lies between Jersey City and the Holland Tunnel to the south and the Lincoln Tunnel to the north, along the Hudson River waterfront. **PATH** trains traveling from New York City or Jersey City stop in Hoboken at the **Hoboken Terminal** (1 Hudson Pl.), and run 6 A.M.–11 P.M. Monday–Friday, 9 A.M.–7:30 P.M. weekends. The **Hudson-Bergen Light Rail** connects at Hoboken Terminal and continues north with stops at Second and Ninth Streets along the city's western side before reaching Weehawken.

Hoboken's **Crosstown Bus** runs through the city 7 A.M.–7 P.M. weekdays approximately every half hour, and stops at Hoboken Terminal.

NY Waterway operates a commuter ferry ($4 one-way) between Hoboken South (near the transit terminal) and Manhattan's Wall Street (6 A.M.–9 P.M. daily), and another between New York's Midtown and Hoboken's 13th Street (6 A.M.–11 P.M. weekdays, 10 A.M.–9 P.M. weekends), with a stop at Hoboken South.

WEEHAWKEN

Atop the Palisades cliffs north of Hoboken is Weehawken, a small, working-class town where you'll find the west end of the Lincoln Tunnel. There are two sections to Weehawken—the low-level waterfront and the original downtown district, residing on the cliffs above. The borough's claim to fame is as the site of a July 11, 1804, standoff between Alexander Hamilton and Aaron Burr, during which Hamilton was fatally wounded.

Though Weehawken's waterfront resembles other Gold Coast communities with its mixed-use residences and endless construction, the borough's upper portion is reminiscent of a 1950s neighborhood, with narrow side streets and spacious two-story homes. A paved walkway offers scenic overhead views of the area below, as well as the Hudson River and the Empire State Building. But just a block or two west this borough adopts a city-like feel, and **Park Avenue**—once the main thoroughfare—quietly stands, lined by four- and five-story brick buildings with rusted front fire escapes and service businesses occupying bottom floors.

Water Excursions

The **Spirit of New Jersey** (866/211-3809, www.spiritcitycruises.com) offers year-round lunch ($29 and up) and dinner ($53 and up) cruises along the Hudson and East Rivers, past the Statue of Liberty and the Brooklyn Bridge.

One of New Jersey's tall ships, the over-a-century-old **Richard Robbins** (Lincoln Harbor Yacht Club, 973/966-1684, www.classicsail.com) sets sail a few times a month, and trips range in price from $65 for a champagne brunch excursion to $199 for a two-day Hudson River cruise.

The **New York Waterway** (800/53-FERRY or 800/533-3779, www.nywaterway.com) offers cruises along Hudson Bay from the Weehawken waterfront.

Accommodations

$200-250: The ten-story ◖ **Sheraton Suites on the Hudson** (500 Harbor Blvd., 201/617-5600) is situated on the shores of the Hudson by the dock of New York Waterway. There's a grill and lounge with full bar on-site, as well as an indoor heated pool and gift shop, and room prices include a morning buffet and often a superb view of midtown Manhattan. Because of its accessibility, the hotel makes a great alternative to a New York stay.

Food

If you're craving Italian try **Paula at Rigoletto** (3706 Park Ave., 201/422-9500, 5–10 P.M. Tues.–Thurs., until 11 P.M. Fri. and Sat., $13–20), a small decorative BYO located in the borough's downtown district. Paula once worked as Springsteen's chef.

Arthur's Landing (1 Pershing Circle, 201/867-0777, $19–35) serves New American cuisine with phenomenal views of the Manhattan skyline. The restaurant is located on the Hudson River waterfront and has huge, plate glass wall-like windows. Arthur's offers a pre-theater package that includes an early dinner (5–6:30 P.M.), a round-trip ferry into New York City (six minutes one-way), and a shuttle to the theater district. The restaurant is open for dinner 5–10 P.M. Sunday–Thursday, until 10:30 P.M. Friday and Saturday, and 11:30 A.M.–2:30 P.M. weekends for brunch.

Getting There and Around

Weehawken is 10 minutes north of Hoboken by car. The **Hudson-Bergen Light Rail** stops at Weehawken's Lincoln Harbor, and continues south through Hoboken, Jersey City, and into Bayonne. One-way fares are $1.75 adult, $0.85 child.

UNION CITY

The United States' most densely populated city, Union City has earned the name "Havana on the Hudson" due to its large Latino population, making up 80 percent of the city's residents and including Cubans, Colombians, Ecuadorians, and Dominicans. The city is located atop the Palisades cliffs just west of Hoboken, and its downtown has been declared an Urban Enterprise Zone, with three percent sales tax.

Bergenline Avenue, a narrow one-way street packed with two- and three-story brick and clapboard buildings, is the centerpiece to Union City's "Little Havana." Ground-level storefronts are filled with Latin eateries, religious shops, and family-owned bodegas, and sidewalks overflow with activity and people even on a weekday afternoon. If you're looking for an authentic Cuban experience and a reason

why New Jersey is the most densely populated state, this is the place to come.

Food

One standout of the eateries along Bergenline Avenue is the **Latin American Restaurant** (4317 Bergenline Ave., 201/863-9280, 7 A.M.–10:30 P.M. daily, closed Wed.), where you can get a cubano—a traditional Cuban sandwich filled with ham, Swiss, and *lechón asado* (Cuban pork roast)—served piping hot.

On Park Avenue is one of the state's best Turkish restaurants, **Beyti Kebab** (4105 Park Ave., 201/865-6281, www.beytikebab.com, 11:30 A.M.–10 P.M. Sun.–Fri., until 11:30 P.M. Sat., $10–20). This large restaurant has been serving the masses for over two decades, and features a belly dancer on Saturday nights after 9 P.M.

Getting There

Union City is situated on the Palisades cliffs above Hoboken. In 2005 the Hudson-Bergen Light Rail had plans to expand its service to Union City, but for now public transport is limited.

EDGEWATER

There's so much new construction along the waterfront in Edgewater borough it's almost ridiculous. Luxury apartment units like Avalon at Edgewater and Mariners Cove have appeared seemingly overnight, helping to turn an architecturally nondescript town into a modern conglomeration of high-rise, townhouse, and shopping center. The borough is home to a notable Asian population, including a high percentage of Japanese residents, and one of the region's most popular food and shopping centers—a Japanese marketplace—is located here.

Mitsuwa Marketplace

A great way to spend your afternoon is a visit to Mitsuwa Marketplace (595 River Rd., 201/941-9113, www.mitsuwa.com, 9:30 A.M.–8 P.M. Sun.–Fri., 9:30 A.M.–9 P.M. Sat.), an Asian shopping center with a food court, supermarket, make-up counter, home furnishing shop (www.littlejapanusa.com), and waterfront restaurant, among others. A highlight is the Borders-like **Kinokuniya Bookstore** (www.kinokuniya.com), with stock that includes teen books, celebrity mags, videos, posters, novels, stationary, and anime—all in Japanese. The marketplace is not your ordinary mall, and all shops have their own outside entries.

Food

Get yourself in line at **Mitsuwa Supermarket** for freshly made spring rolls and cream crab cakes to enjoy outdoors along one of the few riverfront benches, or snag a table at the popular food court—Sunday mornings fill up quickly. Across the parking lot along the waterfront is **Matsushima Restaurant** (595 River Rd., 201/945-9450, $20–30), a two-story Japanese restaurant that's a standard favorite. The restaurant opens for lunch at 11 A.M. daily, and again at 5 P.M. for dinner.

Nestled along a cute little artsy stretch of Old River Road is **Rebecca's** (236 Old River Rd., 201/943-8808, www.rebeccasedgewater.com, 5:30–10 P.M. Tues.–Sat., 4–9 P.M. Sun., closed Mon., $18–28), a cozy BYO serving Cuban-Caribbean fare within a three-story former home. The eatery has a seasonal backyard garden.

FORT LEE

Fort Lee is an affluent borough that lies on a steep incline from the river, working its way up the Palisades cliffs in a hodge-podge of architectural styles including brick buildings, Victorian clapboards, and plenty of high-rises. The heart of Main Street stands at the summit, where you'll find many of the Asian eateries—most notably Korean—that the borough is known for.

Fort Lee played an important role in the American Revolution, and housed a portion of the Palisades Amusement Park (www.palisadespark.com) for over 80 years, but perhaps its largest starring role was as America's "silent movie capital," from 1905 to 1920 (Fort Lee Film Commission, www.fortleefilm.org). Many of the borough's streets have been re-

named to honor the nearly three dozen movie studios that once operated here, as well as famous actors and actresses like Theda Bara, who shares her name with Linwood Avenue. Silent movies filmed in the area include *Robin Hood* (1912), *The Vampire* (1913), and *Poor Little Rich Girl* (1917).

The George Washington Bridge connects Fort Lee to the Bronx, and is a strong downtown presence.

Fort Lee Historic Park

On the southern tip of Palisades Interstate Park is 33-acre Fort Lee Historic Park (Hudson Terrace, 201/461-1776), a site used by American soldiers during the Revolution to defend against British troops. On the property today is a bi-level visitors center with numerous displays relating to the fort's wartime role—some look shoddily handmade while others, such as a small-scale model depicting the Palisades before development, are quite interesting. Outside you'll find short nature trails, a couple of overlooks, and artillery and hut reproductions. The park is open 8 A.M.–sunset, and the visitors center 10 A.M.–5 P.M. Wednesday–Sunday, closed January and February. A $5 parking fee is charged during special events.

Food

According to North Jersey's *Bergen Record,* Fort Lee borough is "fast becoming the leading destination for Asian food in North Jersey," with dozens of Asian restaurants and eateries. You'll find the bulk of restaurants toward the top of Main Street, and many establishments remain open 24 hours.

Gammiok (485 Main St., 201/242-1333, $13) is a 24-hour Korean eatery famous for its oxtail soup and kimchi—a country staple.

Silver Pond Seafood Restaurant (230 Main St., 201/592-8338, $9–20) serves Hong Kong–style dim sum daily throughout the week, and a large though somewhat dreary setting doesn't stop this place from packing crowds. Hours are 11:30 A.M.–10:30 P.M. Monday–Thursday, until 11 P.M.

Friday, 11 A.M.–11 P.M. Saturday, and 11 A.M.–10:30 P.M. Sunday.

The upscale **Hiura** (400B Main St., 201/346-0110, closed Wed.) is a Japanese BYO known for its sushi. They cater to a large Japanese clientele.

Coffee, pastries, and Korean-style cakes are served at the popular **Parisienne Bakery & Cafe** (250 Main St., 201/592-8878, 8 A.M.–8:30 P.M. Mon.– Sat., opens at 8 A.M. Sun.), on the corner of Main and Center.

Customers flock to **Restaurant So Kong Dong** (130 Main St., 201/585-1122) for *soon-dooboo jigae* ($7), or "soft-tofu stew," a gurgling egg-topped soup that comes in nearly a dozen varieties (some that will even please meat eaters) and is accompanied by rice and a handful of side dishes.

For Vietnamese try **Mo Pho** (212 Main St., 201/363-8886) a 50-seat BYO praised for its *pho,* with both meat and vegetarian versions available.

Getting There

Fort Lee is just north of Edgewater and stands on the western side of the George Washington Bridge, connecting New Jersey to the Bronx. The bridge has a bike path leading into Fort Lee.

◖ PALISADES INTERSTATE PARK

Lined by sheer cliffs to the west and Hudson River shorefront to the east, and heading north into New York, is Palisades Interstate Park (201/768-1360, www.njpalisades.org). Twelve miles long and no more than a half-mile wide on its Jersey side, it's part of a greater collection of parks and historic sites that together make up over 100,000 acres. Here you'll find some excellent hiking and cycling opportunities, as well as options for cross-country skiing, picnicking, and perhaps most importantly, urban retreat.

Historic Sights

Mansions that once stood atop the Palisades cliffs are long gone, but it's still possible to spot their remains in the area that lies between Route 9W and Palisades Interstate Highway. **Millionaire's Row,** as it was known, included the estates of John Ringling (of circus fame) and George A. Zabriskie, the New York director of Pillsbury Flour. Today there's little more than stone ruins and a pillar of two, but it's fun to have a look, especially if you're accompanied by a knowledgeable guide. Tours are sometimes given by the Palisades Park Commission—call 201/768-1360 to find out more or check the Palisades website (www.njpalisades.org) for an updated schedule of events.

Hiking

New Jersey's portion of Palisades Interstate Park features over 30 miles of hiking trails, including the **Shore Trail,** which follows along the banks of the Hudson north before eventually ascending the cliffs, and the **Long Path,** a higher-elevation trail that runs the length of the park's Jersey portion before continuing into New York. The two trails range from easy to strenuous depending on direction, and a handful of smaller trails intersect them to offer various hiking opportunities. Each trail is marked by a different color blaze, and in the winter, skiing is allowed.

Henry Hudson Drive

One of the Gateway Region's best spots for cycling is the park's seven-mile Henry Hudson Drive, a north–south scenic route open to bicyclists and motor vehicles mid-April–mid-November. On any weekend afternoon throughout summer you're sure to spot dozens of cyclists taking advantage of the uphill challenge and the shade provided by dense tree stands lining the road's eastern side, isolating visitors from the river and the city across it and creating a canopy over the roadway. The Park Commission requires that bikes must have "at least 24-inch tires" and that cyclists wear a helmet and be over 14 years of age.

An old stretch of Route 9W runs through the northern portion of the park's Jersey side near the **State Line Lookout** (201/750-0465), a year-round snack stand and book shop. The road is closed to autos, but open to cyclists.

THE GATEWAY REGION

The Meadowlands

The so-called "Armpit of America" is going to great lengths to clean up its image. At 30 square miles, the Meadowlands consist of wetlands, estuaries, marshes, and lots of development, and have long been a dumping ground for trash, toxins, and bodies. Buried somewhere beneath are the remains of New York City's original Penn Station and, legend has it, organized crime leader Jimmy Hoffa, last seen in Michigan in 1975. Incinerated trash heaps, mosquito infestations, and mercury-polluted rivers seem to be synonymous with this giant landfill, but these days a new item has been added: eco-tourism. The Meadowlands are said to host over 250 bird types and 60 fish and shellfish species, and 8,400 acres of the region are being touted as a wildlife preserve. Boat tours and canoe trips are two of the activities now offered, and efforts seem to be working—people are booking months in advance, perhaps hoping to catch a glimpse of a bygone legend or two.

In addition to its wetlands, the Meadowlands consist of 14 towns, including East Rutherford and Rutherford (where you'll find the mega–sports and entertainment complex that the region is famous for), Lyndhurst, Teterboro, and Secaucus, a former pig farm that's now known for its outlets and train station.

Restoration efforts aside, development in the Meadowlands continues, and a new upscale retail entertainment plaza is currently in the works to accompany the sports arenas, as is a mixed-use residential facility with golf courses that will incorporate portions of several towns, including Rutherford and Lyndhurst.

MEADOWLANDS SPORTS AND ENTERTAINMENT COMPLEX

In the late 1970s and early 1980s, the Meadowlands (www.meadowlands.com) became the new home for a handful of professional sports teams. The first to arrive was basketball's New

© LAURA KINIRY

the "real" Meadowlands at the Meadowlands Environmental Center

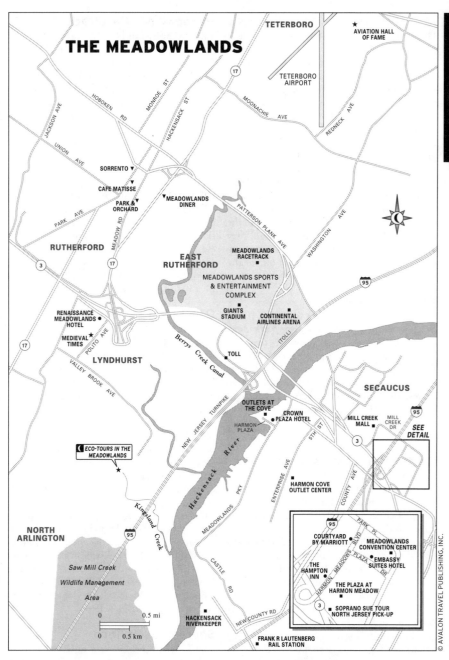

THE MEADOWLANDS

TETERBORO

★ AVIATION HALL OF FAME

TETERBORO AIRPORT

JACKSON AVE

HOBOKEN RD

MONROE ST

HACKENSACK ST

17

MOONACHIE AVE

REDNECK AVE

UNION AVE

WASHINGTON AVE

SORRENTO ▼

CAFE MATISSE ▼

PARK & ORCHARD ▼

▼ MEADOWLANDS DINER

PATTERSON PLANK AVE

PARK AVE

MEADOW RD

RUTHERFORD

3

17

EAST RUTHERFORD

MEADOWLANDS RACETRACK ■

MEADOWLANDS SPORTS & ENTERTAINMENT COMPLEX

95

RENAISSANCE MEADOWLANDS HOTEL ●

MEDIEVAL TIMES ★

POLITO AVE

GIANTS STADIUM ■

CONTINENTAL AIRLINES ARENA ■

LYNDHURST

VALLEY BROOK AVE

Berrys Creek Canal

TOLL ●

(TOLL)

SECAUCUS

95

MILL CREEK MALL ■

MILL CREEK DR

SEE DETAIL

NEW JERSEY TURNPIKE

OUTLETS AT THE COVE ●

CROWN PLAZA HOTEL ●

HARMON PLAZA ●

5TH ST

3

COUNTY AVE

☾ ECO-TOURS IN THE MEADOWLANDS

★

Hackensack River

ENTERPRISE AVE

HARMON COVE OUTLET CENTER ■

MEADOWLANDS PKY

Kingsland Creek

NORTH ARLINGTON

95

Saw Mill Creek Wildlife Management Area

CASTLE RD

95

COURTYARD BY MARRIOTT ■

PARK PL

MEADOWLANDS CONVENTION CENTER ■

HARMON MEADOW BLVD

EMBASSY SUITES HOTEL ■

THE HAMPTON INN ■

THE PLAZA AT HARMON MEADOW ■

3

SOPRANO SUE TOUR NORTH JERSEY PICK-UP ●

| 0 | 0.5 mi |
| 0 | 0.5 km |

HACKENSACK RIVERKEEPER ■

NEW COUNTY RD

FRANK R LAUTENBERG RAIL STATION ■

© AVALON TRAVEL PUBLISHING, INC.

Jersey Nets, followed by ice hockey's Jersey Devils, and football's New York Giants and New York Jets. The now-infamous sports and entertainment complex also includes a race-track, and in more-recent years has acquired pro soccer's MetroStars, but big changes are in the works. Before leaving office in 2004, Governor Jim McGreevey signed off on a plan to build **Xanadu** (www.meadowlandsxanadu.com), a retail and entertainment wonderland on the grounds of the Meadowlands Complex, while the Nets are in negotiations to relocate to Brooklyn, and a new stadium is being built for the Devils in Newark. The football teams have their own issues, with the Jets looking to get themselves a stadium in New York and the Giants asking for a new stadium should they stay in New Jersey. Regardless of the turning wheels, the Meadowlands remain one of the region's largest draws.

Giants Stadium
Home to the NFL's **New York Giants** (201/935-8111, www.giants.com) and **New York Jets** (516/560-8200, www.newyorkjets.com), as well as major league soccer's **MetroStars** (201/583-7000, www.metrostars.com), Giants Stadium (201/935-3900) is the Meadowlands' largest showcase, with a seating capacity of more than 80,000. The stadium also plays host to dozens of entertainment events throughout the year.

Continental Airlines Arena
Continental Airlines Arena (201/935-3900) opened in 1981 with six sold-out Bruce Springsteen shows and has since hosted hundreds of concerts, skating performances, circuses, and so on. The 20,000-seat arena is home venue to basketball's **New Jersey Nets** (201/935-8888, www.njnets.com) and ice hockey's **New Jersey Devils** (201/935-6050, www.newjerseydevils.com), and also hosts Seton Hall University's men's basketball team.

The recent addition of **The Theater of Continental Airlines Arena** follows a statewide trend of introducing more intimate performing venues; seating ranges from 4,000 to 9,000.

Meadowlands Racetrack
The Meadowlands Racetrack (50 Rte. 120, East Rutherford, 201/THE-BIGM or 201/843-2446, www.thebigm.com) hosts live harness and thoroughbred racing. General parking is free and admission to the grandstand and paddock is only $1 ($1.50 for reserved seating). Admission to the club-house is $3, and the grandstand has a seating capacity of up to 40,000. Races take place throughout the year—check the website for a current schedule.

Information and Services
The Meadowlands Event Information Hotline (201/935-3900) offers current information on scheduled and upcoming games and events at both Giants Stadium and the Continental Airlines Arena. Ticket purchases can be made through Ticketmaster (201/507-8900, 212/307-7171, www.ticketmaster.com).

OTHER SIGHTS AND RECREATION
The Meadowlands Environmental Center
At the Meadowlands Environmental Center (2 DeKorte Park Plaza, 201/460-8300, www.njmeadowlands.gov/ec/index.cfm, free) you can pick up information on local tours and birding ops, and meander a marsh discovery trail. The center is primarily an administration building; although it has a classroom and a couple of short boardwalk walkways, tourism hasn't quite caught on here. While eco-trips run by the center get a lot of attention, there's little inside the building to see and you may receive some strange looks for being here if you're not on, or leading, a school trip. Try to forget the awkwardness and instead take in the interesting view of the Manhattan skyline, serving as a backdrop for the Meadowlands marshes and tall grass. The Environmental Center is a collaboration between The New Jersey Meadowlands Commission and Ramapo College of New Jersey.

Soprano Sue's Tour
The TV show *The Sopranos* tossed Jersey back

into the spotlight—what better way to pay homage than taking Soprano Sue's Tour (212/209-3370, www.sopranosuessightings.com)? After all, they're family. Sue leads three-hour bus tours that'll take you to Satriale's, the Bada Bing strip club, and many of the Meadowlands and Newark locales used in filming. So make like a Moltisanti and follow in Tony's footsteps; just be careful not to get too close. Tours leave from Secaucus's Meadow Plaza off Route 3 at 2:20 P.M. Sunday, and from New York City at 2 P.M. at Seventh Avenue by 39th Street, in front of the Garment District "Button." Reservations are required; be sure to specify your pick-up location.

C Eco-Tours

The New Jersey Meadowlands Commission (201/460-4640, www.njmeadowlands.gov/ec) leads a variety of excursions including **pontoon boat tours and canoe trips** along the waters of the Meadowlands. Keep your eyes peeled for waterfowl and Jimmy Hoffa's remains as you weave through this delicate region. Guided pontoon boat trips ($15 per person) last about two hours and leave from Carlstadt Marina, and guided canoe trips ($15 per person) last approximately three hours, with each canoe holding up to three people.

Captain Bill Sheehan is in large part responsible for the transformation of the Meadowlands and its image over the last decade, so it's little wonder why his **Hackensack Riverkeeper** (231 Main St., 201/968-0808, www.hackensackriverkeeper.org, $10 adult, $5 child) eco-tours are extremely popular. Beginning from Secaucus's Laurel Hill County Park, a 15-seat pontoon vessel floats down the Hackensack River and its tributaries, making its way toward Jersey City. Every tour includes a trip to the wildlife-infested **Sawmill Creek Wildlife Management Area.** The water remains polluted (do NOT eat the fish), but as long as you stay put, there's a possibility of heron and bald eagle sightings. Tours last about 2–3 hours—book ahead.

Teterboro Airport and Aviation Hall of Fame

Teterboro Airport is the region's oldest operating airport, located 12 miles from Manhattan and run by the Port Authority of New York and New Jersey. Here you'll find the **New Jersey Aviation Hall of Fame Museum** (400 Fred Wehran Dr., 201/288-6344, www.njahof.org, 10 A.M.–4 P.M. Tues.–Fri., $6 adult, $4 child), a showcase of vintage airplanes and various aviation-themed exhibits, including military and space flights. The airport is situated within a larger residential area and its two runways have recently seen an increase in traffic, leading to a plethora of problems within the community.

Medieval Times

Just west of Giants Stadium and Continental Airlines Arena is Medieval Times (149 Polito Ave., 888/WE-JOUST or 888/935-6678, www.medievaltimes.com, $49.95 adult, $39.95 child), where two-hour dinner shows come complete with jousting matches, valiant knights, shining armor, and succulent old-world fare. Have your photo taken with a court jester and cozy-up in the stadium seating for a frolicking good time.

Medieval Times, a "dinner theatre" from the Middle Ages

SHOPPING

Outlet-shopping is synonymous with Secaucus, and all are located in the section of town known as **Harmon Meadow** (off Rte. 3 and NJ Turnpike, 201/392-8700, www.harmonmeadow.com), a retail center littered with individual outlets, discount indoor shopping plazas, food courts, hotels, all-in-one centers, and a regular mall. Individual outlets scattered about include the Burlington Coat Factory (201/866-1665) and Levi's Outlet Store (201/867-6040), both on Hartz Way; Tommy Hilfiger (Emerson Ln., 201/863-5600); and Gucci (American Way, 201/392-2670).

The Plaza at Harmon Meadow (700 Plaza Dr., 201/392-8700) features such stores as Pier 1 Imports (201/319-1110) and European Man (201/866-9777), as well as numerous fast-food and chain restaurants, and two modern multiplex theaters. Nearby are the **Meadowlands Exposition Center** (www.mecexpo.com) and a number of hotels.

The enclosed two-story **Harmon Cove Outlet Center** (20 Enterprise Ave., 201/348-4780) is billed as the area's "largest enclosed outlet center" and is the nicest of the bunch. Inside are a food court and bargain branches such as Samsonite (201/863-1366), Bed Bath & Beyond (201/864-1360), Aeropostale (201/864-8900), and a Lenox Factory Outlet (201/319-1980).

Outlets at the Cove (45 Meadowlands Parkway, 201/348-4780 or 877/668-5382) is an indoor outlet center with only a handful of stores, among them Nine West Outlet (201/864-5335) and Van Heusen Factory Outlet (201/617-7799).

The **Mill Creek Mall** (3 Mill Creek Dr., 201/392-8700) offers everyday shopping ops, including Modell's Sporting Goods (201/392-9500), A. C. Moore, Big and Tall Casual Male (201/223-1330), and Kohl's (201/553-9143).

ACCOMMODATIONS

Though the Meadowlands host a bevy of hotel and low-budget accommodations, most of the "preferred" establishments are centered around the Sports Complex and within Secaucus's Harmon Meadow.

$100-150

The **Crowne Plaza Meadowlands Hotel** (2 Harmon Plaza, Secaucus, 877/898-1721) is conveniently located within walking distance to the outlets and right across the Hackensack River from the Meadowlands Sports and Entertainment Complex. It's 14 stories with views of New York City, an on-site restaurant and lounge, and an outdoor pool. Located just off the New Jersey Turnpike, it's a good place to stay if you're coming to one of the shows or games.

$150-200

For a bit of luxury try the ❰ **Renaissance Meadowlands Hotel** (801 Rutherford Ave., Rutherford, 201/231-3100), a nine-story space with heated indoor pool, valet parking, high-speed Internet in guest rooms, and wireless Internet access in public areas. An on-site steakhouse is open all day and has an extensive wine menu.

Situated in Harmon Cove, next to the Plaza at Harmon Meadow and the Meadowlands Exposition Center, is the standard **Courtyard by Marriott** (455 Harmon Meadow Blvd., Secaucus, 201/617-8888, www.marriott.com), where rooms come equipped with a large, roomy desk and high-speed Internet.

The nine-story **Embassy Suites Hotel** (455 Plaza Dr., Secaucus, 201/864-7300) is ideally situated within Harmon Cove and has both a restaurant and lounge. All rooms include refrigerator, microwave, and separate living area.

FOOD

The Meadowlands has a few wonderful "sit back and enjoy" fine dining establishments. Of course, fast food and diners are well-represented.

One of the state's most revered restaurants is East Rutherford's classy **Park & Orchard** (240 Hackensack St., 201/939-9292, www.parkandorchard.com, $15.95–22.95), where healthy eclectic dishes, large portions, and a well-fleshed wine list keep patrons coming. Lunch is served noon–4 P.M. weekdays, and dinner 4–10 P.M. Monday–Friday, 4:45–10 P.M. Saturday, and 2–9 P.M. Sunday.

Known for its amorous atmosphere and eye-catching design, ◖ **Cafe Matisse** (167 Park Ave., Rutherford, 201/935-2995, www .cafematisse.com, 5:30–9 P.M. Tues.–Thurs., until 10 P.M. Fri. and Sat., and 5–8:30 P.M. Sun., closed Mon.) is an eclectic BYO that leaves you feeling as though you stepped into a color-soaked Impressionist painting. Three- and four-course fixed-price meals ($65/$85) are the norm, though à la carte entrées ($38) are available every evening but Saturday. An outdoor garden opens for dining in the spring.

For traditional Italian, a local favorite is **Sorrento** (132 Park Ave., East Rutherford, 201/507-0038, $17–25), a BYO open for dinner only beginning at 5 P.M.

A visit to the Meadowlands isn't complete without a trip to the diner. Why not go for the namesake at the 24-hour **Meadowlands Diner** (320 Rte.17, 201/935-5444, $5–15),

an easily recognizable stone structure with blue trim.

GETTING THERE AND AROUND

The newly constructed Frank R. Lautenberg Rail Station (100 Laurel Hill Dr.), better known as **Secaucus Junction,** links 10 of NJ Transit's 11 train lines, and from here trains head to Rutherford (Orient Way and Park Ave.) and Teterboro (Williams Ave. and Rte. 17).

Route 17 runs north–south between numerous Meadowland towns, but be prepared for traffic any time of the day. Taking neighborhood back roads or hopping on the Turnpike is an alternative, but Route 17 remains the most direct route to the northern towns. Secaucus, the Rutherfords, and Lyndhurst are accessible to one another by way of Route 3.

Newark and Vicinity

If you've only experienced Newark on the way to and from the airport, chances are good that you'll never want to go back. But New Jersey's largest city has much more to offer than traffic, shipping crates, smog, and smokestacks. It's home to a vibrant downtown arts district, housing the state's largest museum; a bustling ethnic neighborhood; and some of the area's choicest restaurants and eateries. Construction is underway throughout downtown Newark, and over the last decade the city has already seen a complete revamping of its center, with the addition of a minor league ballpark and a state-of-the-art entertainment center.

Of course Newark still has its problems. Nicknamed the "Brick City" because of the large number of brick housing units once located here, litter is strewn about the streets, rundown homes are prominent in outlying areas, traffic is difficult to navigate as stop signs and corner crossings seem not to apply, and a stench rising from the Passaic River has the city smelling like an urban ocean on a

hot, humid day. Sounds appetizing—but in the end, it's not so bad to be Newark. While jokes are being cracked, the city is reinventing itself, and you may be surprised at what you find. There's plenty of signage pointing the way to tourism sites and neighborhoods, and *The Sopranos* fans may notice a number of recognizable sights. The city has good transportation and is a major hub, connecting New York City, Trenton, and Philly, as well as many of the state's outlying areas.

Newark is home to five colleges and universities, including a branch of Rutgers and a prominent jazz school, and was the childhood home of Frankie "Castelluccio" Valli, Queen Latifah, and Philip Roth, the Pulitzer Prize–winning author who sets many of his short stories and novels in his childhood town.

To Newark's south is Elizabeth—an older, industrial city that survived Revolutionary attacks by the British and has retained many of its original structures. Today it's known for its shopping and is an easy afternoon excursion—

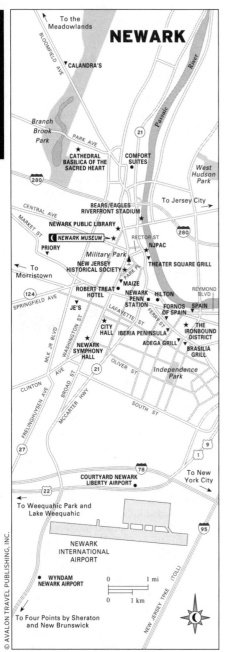

nearly half of Newark Liberty International Airport lies within Elizabeth's boundaries.

History

Robert Treat settled Newark with a group of puritans who'd made their way down from Connecticut in search of free religious practice. Treat purchased the land from the Hackensack Indians for a bartering fee including guns, swords, blankets, and beer, totaling approximately $750.

The city's first hotel opened in 1670 on the present site of Grace Episcopal Church, and the College of New Jersey—later Princeton University—made its home in Newark for nearly a decade, from 1747 to 1756. The puritans ruled the community until one Sunday in 1733, when Colonel Josiah Ogden disobeyed the Sabbath to harvest wheat. He was chastised and left the church, turning to the Episcopalian missionaries, and in 1746 the First Episcopal Church—now known as Trinity—was built.

Newark grew into one of the world's manufacturing capitals, and became a hotspot for invention. Samuel Whitehead, the town's first shoemaker, arrived in the 1680s, and Azariah Crane opened the first leather tannery in 1698. Newark's Thomas Cort invented the tennis shoe and Seth Boyden made patent leather, starting a trend that includes over 150 manufacturers. Though shoes would later move north, the tannery business exploded because of a plethora of tamarack trees in the area, where tannin could be obtained for Russian and Moroccan leather production. Other notable moments in history are Thomas Edison's invention of the ticker-tape machine, the founding of Newark's Prudential Insurance in 1875, and the city's massive production of hats.

One of Newark's major sources of revenue came from breweries, and the Ballantine Brewery, founded in 1840, became America's sixth-largest brewery. Pabst Blue Ribbon also maintained a presence here, and the massive amber bottle that identified the building is still in existence today.

As Newark's population soared, the city's

infrastructure was not being updated to handle such large growth. From the late 19th century through World War II, thousands of African Americans had arrived from the South looking for factory work at a time when Newark was playing its card as a defense center. With an unemployed and booming population, things were starting to get out of hand. By the 1960s police brutality was a common occurrence, and the leveling of the Central Ward—a primarily black neighborhood torn down to make space for the University of Medicine and Dentistry—coupled with the arrest of an African American cab driver, broke the city's back and four days of riots began.

Though riots took place in 125 U.S. cities in 1967, the two most notorious were in Detroit and Newark, and on the third day in Newark the National Guard was called in, and state troopers opened fire on rioters. Urban flight began and continued through the 1970s, and Newark caved in upon its breaches. In 1970 the city elected its first black mayor, Kenneth Gibson, who was beat out in 1986 by now five-term mayor Sharpe James, responsible for the building of the New Jersey Performing Arts Center, and for the city's valiant efforts at reconstruction.

Neighborhoods

Newark consists of five wards—districts used for orientation and political purposes—each containing a number of smaller neighborhoods. Though visitors tend to stick mostly within the city's Downtown Arts District, the Ironbound, and Branch Brook Park, a brief description of Newark's wards goes a long way when trying to get your bearings within the city.

West of the Garden State Parkway is Newark's aptly named West Ward, home to **Vailsburg,** a traditionally Irish, Italian, and German neighborhood that was once considered the city's political capital. Two of Newark's most revered movie theaters—the Stanley, now a church, and the Mayfair—were also found here.

Newark's South Ward contains Weequahic, the once Jewish neighborhood of Philip Roth

that's immortalized in many of his short stories and novels. The area has changed completely since the 1967 riots, and is now home to a large black community.

The city's East Ward is the most commonly visited district, home to the culturally diverse Ironbound, Newark Penn Station, and the Downtown Arts District. This is where you'll find most of Newark's sights, center-city accommodations, and dining options, as well as the city's 21-block historic district known as **James St. Commons,** which includes portions of James, Bleeker, and Warren Streets.

The North Ward is home to Branch Brook Park, as well as **Ahavas Shalom Synagogue,** the last remaining synagogue in the city.

Newark's fifth ward is the Central Ward, located to the west of the city's downtown center.

SIGHTS AND RECREATION

Most activity in Newark takes place in the East Ward, and requires a decent but comfortable walk from Newark Penn Station. To reach those sights located within the North Ward, hop on the Newark City Subway at the station.

Military Park

The six-acre Military Park (Broad St. between Rector St. and Raymond Blvd., 800/843-6420) is a small park located at the center of downtown. While in the area, pick up a pretzel from one of the street vendors and stop by and have a look at the **Wars of America Monument,** created by Mount Rushmore artist Gutzon Borglum. The statue has been a part of the park since 1926.

Newark Penn Station

Besides being a major transportation hub, Newark Penn Station (Market St. and Raymond Plaza, 800/772-2222, http://nycsubway.org/nyc/newark) is architecturally significant. Built in the art deco and neoclassical styles, it's the second Penn Station to stand at this spot, and was dedicated in 1935. While waiting for your connection, be sure and have a look around at the sculptured ceilings and transportation medallions along the walls.

© LAURA KINIRY

Newark's Arts District

Cathedral Basilica of the Sacred Heart

Cathedral Basilica of the Sacred Heart (89 Ridge St., 973/484-4600, www.cathedralbasilica.org) is the fifth-largest cathedral in the United States. Throughout the year this French Gothic church, known for its stained glass, hosts a variety of vocal and instrumental concerts known as the **Cathedral Concert Series** (check the cathedral's website for an updated schedule). The church can be seen in the opening credits of *The Sopranos,* and is located just east of Branch Brook Park and south of Park Avenue.

New Jersey Historical Society

Founded in 1845, the nonprofit New Jersey Historical Society (52 Park Pl., 973/596-8500, www.jerseyhistory.org, 10 A.M.–5 P.M. Tues.–Sat.) is a three-floor statewide museum focusing on the people of New Jersey and what it means to be from here, as well as the factors that go into making New Jersey "New Jersey." It's free to enter the museum, and walking tours of various parts of the city are scheduled

throughout the year. For Garden State history, this place can't be beat. The on-premise library opens at noon Tuesday–Saturday.

Newark Symphony Hall

Built originally as a temple in 1925, Newark Symphony Hall (1020 Broad St., 973/643-4550, www.newarksymphonyhall.org) is a grand site, its exterior flanked by Ionic columns and its interior patterned by Greek and Egyptian design. The hall is home to the 3,500-seat **Sarah Vaughan Concert Hall,** a main auditorium named to honor the late locally born jazz singer.

Newark Public Library

New Jersey's largest public library, the Newark Public Library (5 Washington St., 973/733-7784, www.npl.org), is currently undergoing some renovations, but exhibits are still featured throughout the year, including the recent "Newarks of the World." The library plays a secondary role in Philip Roth's short story "Goodbye, Columbus."

Bears and Eagles Riverfront Stadium

Bears and Eagles Riverfront Stadium (450 Broad St., 973/848-1000, www.newarkbears.com, $7–9) or "the Den," as it's also known, is named for the city's original minor league baseball teams, the Newark Bears, who played during the 1930s and '40s, and the Newark Eagles, a Negro League team that played until 1950. The Bears is also the name of the present ball club, a member of the Atlantic League and not associated with any major league team. The stadium was built in 1999 and includes a concert stage; during every Sunday game kids get to run the bases. The Newark Subway runs directly from Penn Station to the 6,200-seat ballpark.

New Jersey Performing Arts Center (NJPAC)

Credited as the spark that has sent Newark on an upward spiral, the redbrick New Jersey Performing Arts Center (1 Center St., 888/GO-NJPAC or 888/466-5722, www.njpac.org)

opened in 1997 and remains the jewel of the Downtown Arts District. The center consists of two theaters—the 2,750-seat **Prudential Hall** and the more intimate 500-seat **Victoria Theatre**—and is home to the **New Jersey Symphony Orchestra.** Performances range from jazz acts to dance parties to concerts by *American Idol's* Fantasia. During summer months you can catch free musical events at the center's outdoor **Theatre Square.**

(Newark Museum

With 80 galleries dedicated to both the arts and science, the Newark Museum (49 Washington St., 973/596-6550, www.newarkmuseum.org, noon–5 P.M. Wed.–Fri., 10 A.M.–5 P.M. weekends, $7 adult, $3 child) is the state's largest, a nearly century-old space housing sculpture gardens, a fire museum, and a schoolhouse, among many other exhibits. In addition to African clothes, Native American pottery, and landscapes painted by the Hudson River School, the museum's main collection includes Hiram Power's 1847 neoclassical statue *The Greek Slave* and an exquisite five-paneled painting titled *Voice of New York Interpreted* (1920–1922) by Joseph Stella. One of the most prolific exhibits, however, is the museum's Tibetan art collection, which occupies eight permanent galleries and is the largest such compilation in the western hemisphere. Its centerpiece is a true-to-size Tibetan Buddhist altar consecrated by the 14th Dalai Lama in 1990; a hands-on display of Tibetan culture and a mural depicting Tibetan life and scenery are other standouts.

Adjacent to the main museum is the **Ballantine House** (49 Washington St., 973/596-6550), a restored 1885 brick and limestone mansion that once housed members of one of Newark's prominent brewing families. Today the property is a National Historic Landmark and two floors depicting period life are open to the public.

You can literally spend hours exploring the museum's exhibits, and a must-stop is the mini-zoo, where over 100 domestic and exotic animals are cared for, including red-bellied piranhas, cotton-top tamarins, dwarf mon-

the enormous Newark Museum

© LAURA KINIRY

gooses, and boa constrictors. I also recommend a visit to **The Alice and Leonard Dreyfuss Planetarium** ($3 adult, $2 child), which features rotating astronomy programs throughout the year.

If you're traveling by car, there's a $6 secure parking lot adjacent to the museum.

The Ironbound

Newark's Ironbound District (www.goironbound.com) receives its name from the railway tracks that run a loop around the neighborhood. A few blocks southeast from Newark Penn Station, this vibrant district is home to the largest Portuguese population in the United States, as well as large numbers of Spanish and Brazilians. Even on weekday afternoons the streets are packed—trucks packed with boxes of fruit deliver to sidewalk groceries, sidewalks are filled with people coming and going, and numerous dialects drift through the air. The Ironbound is its own urban center, a seemingly independent community filled with homes, clothing stores, fabric shops, nail centers, bars, restaurants, and a large supermarket. **Ferry Street** is the district's commercial hub—dubbed "Portugal Avenue" by brightly colored signs hanging above the street—and its architecture ranges from factory to brick, with plenty of medieval turrets, fortress-style features, and international flags.

During the day, this tourist hot spot may seem run down, with curbside litter, cracked sidewalks, and rusted grates, but it shouldn't stop you from browsing the shops, touring the markets, and stopping at one of the dozens of restaurants, bars, and cafés for a leisurely afternoon.

Branch Brook Park

The best time to head to four-mile Branch Brook Park (973/268-2300, www.branchbrook park.org), designed by Central Park architect Frederick Law Olmsted, is for the annual April Cherry Blossom Festival. This display of approximately 3,500 white and pink cherry trees is larger than Washington D.C.'s, and coincides with the famous festival in Japan. For two weeks the park hosts traditional music and dance celebrations and demonstrations in Japanese traditions like origami and bonsai.

Branch Brook Park is located within Newark's North Ward. To get here from the Downtown Arts District, take Broad Street north to Bloomfield Avenue, and turn left onto Park Avenue. The Newark City subway, accessible from Newark Penn Station, also has a stop here.

SHOPPING

Regardless of its big city status, Newark doesn't have a lot of notable shopping ops. Nearby Elizabeth hosts the bulk of the region's retailers.

Elizabeth

Just south of Newark is Elizabeth, a nearly 12-square-mile city often associated with its northern neighbor. A large portion of Newark Liberty International Airport and a number of hotels that cater to Newark lie within this smaller industrial center's borders. Since its opening in 1999, **Jersey Gardens** (651 Kapkowski Rd., 908/354-5900, www.jerseygardens.com) has reigned supreme as New Jersey's largest outlet mall, a two-story indoor structure with over 200 combined shops, eateries, and entertainment centers, including a Loews multiplex movie theater and an indoor theme park with kiddie rides, arcade games, and a makeshift fossil dig. You can spend hours shopping for discounted goods at Old Navy, Filene's Basement, Samsonite, and Off 5th (the Saks 5th Avenue's outlet store), among dozens of other name-brand stores.

The first of New Jersey's two **IKEA** (1000 IKEA Dr., 908/289-4488, www.ikea.com) stores is conveniently located off exit 13A of the New Jersey Turnpike (along with Jersey Gardens) and offers an admirable view of the state's most famous toll route from the cafeteria windows. There's nothing better than bumper-to-bumper traffic when you're enjoying Swedish meatballs from above.

ACCOMMODATIONS

The city's accommodations range from no-nonsense airport hotels to convenient downtown locales, though there are none that particularly stand out. For something away from the urban bustle without going the distance, nearby Plainfield offers a wonderful bed-and-breakfast option.

$100-150

In the center of the city's Downtown Arts District is the 170-room **Robert Treat Hotel** (50 Park Place, 973/622-1000, www.rthotel.com), a historic structure serving Newark for over a century. Rooms are small, but cozy, with complimentary chocolates, coffee, and toiletries, and room service and take-out menus are provided for those who'd like to dine in-room. A popular continental restaurant is also located on the first floor.

The 86-room **Comfort Suites** (1348 McCarter Hwy., 973/481-5200) features free continental breakfast and a 24-hour airport shuttle. The hotel is clean and close to the minor league ballpark, but seemingly endless construction and its distance from Newark's restaurants and Arts District make the locale less than ideal.

$150-200

The 2001 **Wyndham Newark Airport** (1000 Spring St., Elizabeth, 800/346-8357) is located just across the street from a NJ Transit station, and amenities include a computer room, regularly operating airport shuttle, and a notable steak restaurant on-site. The hotel's entry is off a service road and easy to miss without close attention.

Free high-speed Internet and 24-hour airport transport are available at **Courtyard Newark Liberty Airport** (Rtes. 1 and 9 S., 973/643-8500), which also features a café, ATM, and front-desk safety box.

$200-250

Approximately 20 miles west of Newark Airport is the **C Pillars of Plainfield Bed & Breakfast** (922 Central Ave., 908/753-0922, www.pillars2.com), an 1870 Victorian-colonial mansion that makes for the perfect urban escape. Four guestrooms and two suites each come with TV, telephone, data port hook-up, and daily Swedish breakfast, and guests can lounge by one of four public fireplaces while sipping complimentary sherry. Outside you'll find a covered veranda and plenty of flowers and trees, including dogwoods and cherry, and pet owners take note: Dogs are welcome. For directions, check the website.

$250-300

Downtown Newark's **Hilton Newark Gateway at Penn Station** (1 Gateway Center, Raymond Blvd., 973/622-5000) is ideally located with a connecting walkway to Newark Penn Station, and features an on-premise bar and grill and a fine-dining restaurant. For additional eateries, the city's Ironbound District is right outside its doors. Still, at over two decades old, the hotel is beginning to show wear, and it's not quite up to typical Hilton standards.

FOOD
Arts District

On the first floor of the Robert Treat Hotel is **Maize** (50 Park Pl., 973/639-1200, $19–27), a posh eatery serving continental cuisine. Maize is stylishly decorated with a number of blown-glass pieces and plush bench seating along the side, and the space has been used as a filming location for *The Sopranos*. The restaurant's open for breakfast, lunch, and dinner, and features live jazz every Thursday and Friday evening. Breakfast is served 7–10:30 A.M., lunch 11:30 A.M.–3:30 P.M. Monday–Friday, dinner 5–10 P.M. Saturday, closed Sunday.

The **Theater Square Grill** (NJPAC, 1 Center St., 973/642-1226, www.njpac.org, $23–29) is located within the NJPAC complex, serving New American cuisine and featuring a special fixed-price menu on nights when there's a show. During the summer the restaurant is only open on performance evenings, so for the remainder of the week, try the affiliated **Calcada**, a seasonal outdoor eatery with wrought iron tables and strewn lights throughout, and seating that pours onto the walkway. Hours for Calcada are 11:30 A.M.–2:30 P.M. Monday–Friday, and 5–9 P.M. Tuesday–Sunday, May–September. On weekends meals are served in conjunction with Prudential Hall performances. The Grill keeps the same hours the remainder of the year.

Surrounding Downtown

South of the central Arts District you'll find **Je's** (260 Hasley St., 973/623-8848, 8 A.M.–8 P.M. daily, closed Mon., $7–15), a corner eatery where you can load up on soul food and family-style comfort cooking. Devout customers include Queen Latifah and Shaquille O'Neal.

A couple of blocks west of the Ironbound is **Priory** (233 W. Market St., 973/242-8012), a Gothic church-turned-restaurant serving a daily lunch buffet, as well as a Tuesday and Thursday soul food menu and an exquisite Creole Sunday brunch. Jazz, piano, and gospel performances are scheduled throughout the week. Lunch is served 11:30 A.M.–3 P.M. Monday–Friday, and dinner 5–10 P.M. Wednesday–Saturday. Brunch is available 10 A.M.–5 P.M. Sunday.

For over 30 years, **Calandra's** (204 First Ave., 973/484-5598, 6 A.M.–9 P.M. daily) has been serving the community with donuts, cannoli, cakes, lemon meringue pie, and more. This Italian and French bakery, situated just west of Branch Brook Park, sells fresh bread daily from opening to close.

The Ironbound

It's hard to go wrong in the Ironbound—your only quandary should be which to choose.

Fornos of Spain (47 Ferry St., 973/589-4767, www.fornosrestaurant.com, $13–34) is a classic Spanish eatery serving large portions in a romantic space, with seasonal garden seating, and private parking. The restaurant is open 11:30 A.M.–10:30 P.M. Monday–Friday, noon–11 P.M. Saturday and Sunday.

The name means "wine cellar" in Portuguese, and **⟨ Adega Grill** (130 Ferry St., 973/589-8830, www.adegagrill.com, $17–39) does not disappoint, with a castle-like setting where guests choose from over 180 wines. Spanish and Portuguese fare is served amid a cool, upscale decor that includes stone pillars, wrought iron gates, and roaring fires. For something a bit sleeker try the restaurant's **One Thirty-Two,** a low-ceilinged lounge furnished in plush art deco style. Adega serves lunch 11:30 A.M.–3 P.M. Monday–Friday, dinner 3–10 P.M. Monday–Thursday and Sunday, until 11 P.M. Friday and Saturday.

Behind the velvety curtains of **Brasilia Grill** (132 Ferry St., 973/465-1227, www.brasilia grill.com, 11:30 A.M.–11 P.M. daily) you'll find a spacious dining area, a cozy bar, and endless *rodizio* ($20.95 weekday, $22.95 weekend)—an all-you-can *carnes* fest. The grand **Iberia Peninsula** (63–69 Ferry St., 973/344-5611 or 973/344-1657, www.iberiarestaurants.com, $16–32) and the original **Iberia Tavern & Restaurant** (80–84 Ferry St., 973/344-7603, $16–32) share a massive brick exterior and a parking lot. Both have breathtaking interiors—the Peninsula with cathedral ceilings and the Tavern with beamed ceiling and brick walls, and mounted sconces throughout. The restaurants serve similar Portuguese/Spanish cuisine, and make pitchers of sangria for $16. Hours are 11 A.M.–2 A.M. Monday–Wednesday, until 3 A.M. Thursday–Saturday, noon–2 A.M. Sunday. The Tavern is closed Monday and the Peninsula on Tuesday.

Casual **Spain** (419 Market St., 973/344-0994, www.spainrestaurant.com, 11:30 A.M.–10 P.M. Mon.–Thurs., until 11 P.M. Fri. and Sat., noon–10 P.M. Sun., $10–16) is a popular corner space on the Ironbound's edge, featuring Spanish eats and a fun, boisterous atmosphere.

INFORMATION

Newark is home to the *Star-Ledger* newspaper (www.nj.com/starledger).

GETTING THERE AND AROUND

Newark Liberty International Airport (888/EWR-INFO or 888/397-4636, www.panynj.com) is located south of Newark's business district, three miles outside of the city and partially within the borders of Elizabeth. From here you can hop a NJ Transit train for an easy ride into the city's downtown, or to connect with the **Newark City Subway** at Newark Penn Station. The subway runs nearly four miles north along a former portion of the Morris Canal, with a stop at Branch Brook Park. The PATH train traveling from downtown Jersey City and Manhattan also connects at Newark Penn Station.

For drivers, Newark is easily reached by way of the New Jersey Turnpike, and, traveling from the east, via the **Pulaski Skyway** connecting the city to Jersey City. Once here, the city's downtown district is walkable, though it may be a stretch for some. Parking garages are plentiful around the Ironbound, and run $1 every half-hour, $10 a day.

The Upper Northeast

Above the Meadowlands and west of the Gold Coast the state's urbanized northeast corridor continues, petering out into a variety of landscapes including maximum-built suburban stretches, crowded city centers, and upscale village enclaves with walkable downtown districts and spacious surrounds. The area's best dining options are found in Ridgewood, with a few standouts in Paramus and Hackensack, while accommodations seem to center around the Route 17 thoroughfare.

Information

The **Bergen County Record** (www.bergen .com) is the local newspaper.

Getting There and Around

I-80 travels through the Upper Northeast from east to west and is easily accessible from both the New Jersey Turnpike and Garden State Parkway. Though traffic may be unpleasant on any of these roads, they all beat the oft-harrowing stretch of Route 17 carrying traffic north from the Meadowlands into Hackensack and Paramus before exiting into Ridgewood.

HACKENSACK AND PARAMUS

North of the Meadowlands you'll find plenty of congestion and build-up in the city of Hackensack and the nearby town of Paramus, a typical suburb filled with traffic lights and shopping malls. Route 17—an unpleasant and dated stretch of roadway but the main vantage point for reaching most of the area's sights and shops—connects the two towns. Blue laws are in effect throughout all of Bergen County, banning the sale of almost all non-food and non-drug-related items on Sunday and affecting both Hackensack and Paramus. The Sunday purchase of clothing, furniture, home appliances and home furnishings, and building supplies is prohibited—translation: No IKEA on Sunday.

Sights

The **New Jersey Naval Museum** (Court and River Sts., Hackensack, 201/342-3268, www .njnm.com) is permanent home to the **USS Ling,** a 312-foot-long, 2,500-ton BALAO class submarine open for tours ($7 adult, $3 child). The museum houses a collection of photos and personal items, and German Seahund torpedoes and a Patrol Boat Riverine once used in Vietnam are on display in the outer grounds. Hours of admission are 10 A.M.–4 P.M. weekends only, with the last submarine tour beginning at 3:15 P.M. Poor weather may cause the grounds to close, so call ahead.

South of Paramus in the town of River Edge is one of New Jersey's newest state parks, **Historic New Bridge Landing** (1201 Main St., 201/343-9492). Situated along the banks of the Hackensack River, the landing was granted state park status in 2004 but has long been a favorite for class trips and history buffs. It's home to three Dutch colonial sandstone structures—the 1774 **Campbell-Christie House,** the 1794 **Demarest House,** and the 1752 **Steuben House** (1209 Main St., 201/487-1739), a "Washington slept here" locale and the only building of the three that remains in its original location. Both the Campbell-Christie House and the Steuben House are property of the **Bergen County Historical Society** (201/343-9492, www.bergencountyhistory.org), which operates the latter as a museum 10 A.M.–noon and 1–5 P.M. Wednesday–Saturday (the Campbell-Christie House usually holds an open house 2–5 P.M. the second Sunday of the month). Admission to both the park and the museum are free.

The Hermitage (335 N. Franklin Turnpike, Hackensack, 201/445-8311, www.the hermitage.org, $5 adult, $3 child) is a National Historic Landmark that began as an 18th-century home, hosting the wedding of Aaron Burr and welcoming General George Washington. It was later restructured into a 19th-century Greek Revival mansion, integrating parts of the original building into its walls. The Hermitage museum is open 9 A.M.–5 P.M. Monday–Friday, year-round, with tours offered 1–4 P.M. Wednesday–Sunday; the last tour begins at 3:15 P.M. A museum shop is open during tour hours.

Within Paramus's Van Saun County Park is the **Bergen County Zoological Park** (216 Forest Ave., Paramus, 201/262-3771, 10 A.M.–4:30 P.M. daily), a small zoo with an interesting array of reptiles, birds, and mammals found only in the Americas, including bison, elk, alligator, boa constrictors, and the endangered Andean condor. Admission ($2 adults, $1 students and seniors, children under 12 free) is only charged Wednesday–Sunday and holidays, May–October; the remainder of the year is free.

Located on the lower level of the Bergen Mall is the **The Bergen Museum of Art & Science** (Rte. 4 E., Paramus, 201/291-8848, 10 A.M.–5 P.M. Tues.–Thurs., and Sat., $5 adult, $3 child under 12), a collection of exhibits highlighting the unique art, culture, and scientific contributions of Bergen County. The museum's highlight is a Mastodon skeleton (the museum owns two) discovered in the 1960s during the construction of a nearby highway. Juried displays are hosted throughout the year.

The **New Jersey Children's Museum** (599 Valley Health Plaza, Paramus, 201/262-5151, www.njcm.com, 10 A.M.–6 P.M. daily, $8) is divided into dozens of cubicle-style rooms fit for a kid, each home to a different interactive theme that include a life-size dollhouse, play TV station, and climbable helicopter. The museum closes an hour early on weekends during summer.

Shopping

In true Jersey fashion, Bergen County is plentiful with chain stores and shopping malls—though a few retail places warrant their own mention.

There's no need to make a trip across the Hudson when you have **The Shops at Riverside** (One Riverside Square, Hackensack, 201/489-2212, www.shopriverside.com) for your New York finds. Saks Fifth Avenue, Tiffany & Co., and Bloomingdale's are all represented at this two-story shopping mall, but

the county's blue laws manage to keep most stores closed on Sunday (Barnes & Noble remains open).

Westfield Garden State Plaza (One Garden State Plaza, Paramus, 201/843-2121, www.westfield.com/gardenstateplaza/) houses five department stores including Lord & Taylor, Nordstrom, and Neiman Marcus, and over 100 retail shops such as J.Crew, Jessica McClintock, Kenneth Cole New York, and Louis Vuitton.

New Jersey is home to two **IKEA** stores, both within the Gateway Region. This location (100 IKEA Dr., 201/843-1881) is situated just off the hellish Route 17 in Paramus.

Known for their simple, newspaper-like catalogs sent by mail to loyal customers throughout the country, **Campmor** (810 Rte. 17 N., 201/445-5000, www.campmor.com) has their home base in Paramus, with a showroom that features a ton of outdoor gear and accessories, including packs, tents, canoes and kayaks, and ski, snowboard, and cycling equipment.

Accommodations

$100-150: Many visitors to the area prefer to stay in the nearby Meadowlands or even around the Newark Airport for easy highway accessibility and convenience. For something a bit closer, try the **Howard Johnson Inn & Suites** (393 Rte. 17 S., Paramus, 201/265-4200). It's nothing special, but it is centrally located along Route 17 and the rooms are clean. A complimentary continental breakfast is included with your overnight stay, and all suites contain a fridge and microwave.

Food

Between Paramus and Hackensack you'll have no trouble finding fast food, chain restaurants, or diners, but for a standout experience a handful of places do exist.

White Manna (358 River St., Hackensack, 201/342-0914, 8 A.M.–9:30 P.M. Mon.–Sat.) is cousin to the diner that shares its name (minus an "n") in Jersey City. This tiny diner is a true atmospheric experience, and is known for its "sliders," small onion-topped burgers as greasy as they come.

For delicious Thai try **Wondee's Fine Thai Food Noodle** (296 Main St., Hackensack, 201/883-1700, $8.50–15), a foodie favorite. Hours are 11 A.M.–10 P.M. Tuesday–Friday, 11:30 A.M.–10 P.M. Saturday, noon–8:30 P.M. Sunday and holidays.

Solari's (61 River St., Hackensack, 201/487-1969, www.solarisrestaurant.com, 10 A.M.–2:30 P.M. Mon.–Fri., until 10 P.M. Sat., $17–25) is an area classic offering standard Northern Italian eats (pastas and sauces) and great service. The restaurant often hosts live music and dinner shows, and with its oval bar and bright, spacious dining area, it feels somewhere between upscale banquet hall and classy supper club.

For a true night out you can't beat the massive **Chakra** (W-144 Rte. 4, Paramus, 201/556-1530, www.chakrarestaurant.com, $19–34), featuring New American cuisine in a dimly lit dining area, accented by sconce-lit brick walls and including pillowed booths with sheer silk curtains that can be pulled taut for privacy. With lots of white candles, towering palms, and plenty of seating, it's both uber-romantic and oddly conspicuous. The restaurant is open for lunch 11:30 A.M.–2:30 P.M. Monday–Saturday, and dinner 6–10 P.M. Monday–Thursday, until 11 P.M. Friday and Saturday, closed Sunday. A bar/lounge is open 5 P.M.–2 A.M. Monday–Saturday. Jazz plays Tuesday evenings.

Services

A new addition to the fabulous Shops at Riverside is **The Fountain European Spa** (Rte. 4, West Hackensack, 201/327-5155, www.fountaineuropeanspa.com), a 12,500-square-foot full-service day spa featuring whirlpool tubs for couples and home to more than 20 treatment rooms. The spa offers manicures ($20 and up) and pedicures ($40 and up), as well as special massages and facials for athletic and acne-prone teens.

Hackensack University Medical Center (30 Prospect Ave., Hackensack, 201/996-2000, www.humc.com) is one of New Jersey's largest and highest-rated hospitals.

The 24-hour **Oradell Animal Hospital** (580 Winters Ave., Paramus, 201/262-0010, www.oradell.com) is one of the United States' largest animal hospitals and the Gateway's premier pet-care facility. A variety of surgeons are on hand, and treatments are available in dentistry, dermatology, and acupuncture.

Getting There and Around

NJ Transit's Pascack Valley line has stops in Hackensack at Essex and Anderson Streets, where you can catch the **Hackensack Shuttle** (5:53 A.M.–7 P.M. Mon.–Fri., 10 A.M.–4 P.M. Sat.) to access various points throughout town. Paramus is best explored by car.

PATERSON

At 8.73 square miles, Paterson is New Jersey's third-largest city, created in 1791 by Secretary of State Alexander Hamilton, who wanted to utilize the waters of its Great Falls for textile manufacturing. Along with investors, he founded the Society for Establishing Useful Manufactures (S.U.M.), and America's first planned industrial city began. This ethnically diverse "Silk City," which at one time housed over 800 silk operations in addition to handgun manufacturers and rail cars producers, is today filled with industrial sites, volcanic rock quarries with fossilized dinosaur footprints, and old warehouses. Much of the city's commercial district was destroyed by fires in the early 20th century, and replaced with massive beaux arts buildings, including City Hall. Today a battle ensues over whether to preserve these structures or tear them down to make way for more modern units, at the same time that landlords have been covering their historical properties with cheap facades, damaging what might be a key to the city's successful revitalization.

Paterson is the country's most strike-ridden city, with over 137 strikes from 1880 to 1900. When businesses moved south to escape the unions, Paterson suffered a blow from which it has never quite recovered. Still, the city touched the hearts of its residents deeply, including poets William Carlos Williams and Allen Ginsberg. Williams, who won a Pulitzer Prize posthumously in 1963, wrote the epic poem *Paterson*

© LAURA KINIRY

locomotive display in front of the Paterson Museum, Paterson

here, while Ginsberg penned his "Paterson" from New York City. As a side note, his friend Jack Kerouac depicted *On the Road*'s main character Sal as a resident of this urban maze.

Architecture and history buffs may be drawn to Paterson, but others try and avoid it. The city is crowded and filled with people on a weekday afternoon, and Market Street is storefront after storefront in structures several stories high atop each other. Buildings all have huge signs and front fire escapes, and you'll see faded awnings, heaved sidewalks, and plenty of litter and parking meters. After visiting some of the outlying areas, the center of Paterson hits the tourist like a shockwave, and there is no denying the grittiness. If you decide to come for the downtown sites, try not to take the Market Street exit (head for Main Street instead), and definitely don't do it at night. The main reasons to come here are the architecture and the falls, and if you stick close to these areas you'll be fine.

Great Falls/S.U.M. Historic District

The Great Falls of Paterson are the natural

attribute around which the city was formed. Once used to supply energy for manufacturing, it is the second largest waterfall by volume east of the Mississippi. The falls and over 100 surrounding acres were declared one of New Jersey's newest state parks in 2004. Known as **Great Falls State Park,** it encompasses the S.U.M. Historic District (973/225-0826, www.patersongreatfalls.com), filled with old brick buildings and the Silk Machinery Exchange Building, which is an excellent example of historic preservation. The names of various textile machines are found above first-floor windows, and the name of the exchange still cries out from the top of the building (16 Spruce St.). You can take a self-guided tour of the 77-foot falls, which feature a footbridge above the water. As of this writing the park has little more than a few picnic tables and a memorial statue of Lou Costello, who was born here. It doesn't feel like the safest area, but then again, no portion of the city does.

Paterson Museum

The standout of the city's historic district is

the Paterson Museum (2 Market St., 973/881-3874, 10 A.M.–4 P.M. Tues.–Fri., 12:30–4:30 P.M. weekends, $2 adults, children free), easily recognizable by the locomotive parked out front. Inside you'll find exhibits that highlight Paterson's reign as Silk City, a collection of Colt firearms, and a Wright aeronautical display, as well as a friendly and helpful staff.

Lambert Castle

West of Paterson, within the mountain-top **Garret Mountain Reservation County Park,** is Lambert Castle (3 Valley Rd., 973/247-0085, www.lambertcastle.org), the home of the **Passaic County Historical Society.** During the early 20th century this Medieval Revival–style castle was the home of Catholina Lambert, an antique and art collector and owner of one of Paterson's silk mills, and has since been restored to its turn-of-the-20th-century motif, housing a number of Lambert's original belongings. The castle and its collection are open to the public 1–4 P.M. Wednesday–Sunday, while the Historical Society's library is open 1–4 P.M. Wednesday–Friday, and 1–4 P.M. the second and fourth Saturdays of the month. Admission is $5 adults, $3 children for entrance into either the museum or library, which grants access to the adjoining property for free. The museum is always closed for two months from mid-October to mid-December.

Wayne

The nearly 24-square-mile township of Wayne was inspiration for the pop group Fountains of Wayne, who supposedly named themselves after a decades-old lawn furnishings and garden center on Route 46. Wayne is a sprawling township with no downtown center, but it is home to **William Paterson University** (300 Pompton Rd., 973/720-2000, ww2.wpunj.edu) and **Dey Mansion** (199 Totowa Rd., 973/696-1176, www.passaiccountynj.org/ParksHistorical/Historical_Attractions/deymansion.htm, $1 adult, children free), a colonial estate situated within Preakness Valley Park that was used by George Washington as his Revolutionary War headquarters in July, October, and November

1780. Tours of the mansion take place 1–4 P.M. Wednesday–Friday, and 10 A.M.–noon and 1–4 P.M. on weekends; the park is open 8:30 A.M.–4:30 P.M. Wednesday–Sunday.

Getting There and Around

Paterson's transit station is located at Market and Ward Streets and can be reached by riding NJ Transit's Bergen County line from Hoboken Terminal or Secaucus Junction. Though the station is within distance to the Paterson Museum and Great Falls, driving instead by way of I-80 west, exiting at Main Street, is recommended. This may require a bit of backtracking depending on your starting point, but it beats an unnecessary and somewhat uncomfortable drive through downtown Paterson. To reach Wayne from Paterson, take I-80 west for about 4.5 miles to Route 23 north (exit 53—Wayne, Butler, Verona).

RIDGEWOOD

Known for its unique shopping opportunities, plentiful restaurants, and spacious and walkable downtown, the upscale village of Ridgewood is definitely worth a trip. Ridgewood Avenue is the main street, filled with one- and two-story brick, black, and white buildings that house a good mix of chain, independent, and service establishments. The village's train station is conveniently located downtown, but a slight decline toward the shops may make the walk back a bit of a challenge for some. Surrounding the village center are large, old homes—including a number of craftsman-style—that merit a look.

Shopping

Ridgewood's downtown consists of both retail stores and independent boutiques.

Leapin' Lizards (250 Ridgewood Ave., 201/444-1300, www.shopleapinlizards.com, 10 A.M.–6 P.M. Mon.–Fri., until 5 P.M. Sat., closed Sun.) sells the Easter egg–colored ensembles of Lilly Pulitzer clothing for men, women, and children, as well as Lilly signature jewelry and home furnishings.

Bookends (232 E. Ridgewood Ave., 201/445-0726, www.book-ends.com, 9:30 A.M.–6 P.M.

Mon.–Sat., until 8 P.M. Thurs., 11 A.M.–4 P.M. Sun.) is a wonderful local bookstore hosting a bevy of author events, including such well-known names as Oliver North, Chuck Norris, and Goldie Hawn. Besides an excellent selection of new books the store has begun its own publishing venture, allowing aspiring authors to put their words into print without need of an agent. Many of these books are then sold in-store.

Mango Jam (41 N. Broad St., 201/493-9911, www.mangojamonline.com, 10 A.M.–6 P.M. Mon.–Sat., closed Sun.) specializes in unique home decor items like swanky magnets and decorated dinnerware, as well as perky garden scents and treats for your pooch.

For the expectant mama who's all about style there's **9 Months Boutique** (24 S. Broad St., 201/652-8100).

You can't help but feel good when you walk into **Happy Tuesday** (210 E. Ridgewood Ave., 201/447-0074, www.happytuesday.com), a bright specialty store whose stock includes handmade greeting cards and journals, crafted candles, and distinctive jewelry, among other items.

Day Spas

Ridgewood is a wonderful place to get pampered, especially after a long day perusing the shops. The day spa **Araya Rebirth** (10 Garber Square, 201/445-7005, www.araya-rebirth.com, 10 A.M.–8 P.M. Tues. and Thurs., until 6 P.M. Wed. and Fri., 9 A.M.–5 P.M. Sat., closed Sun. and Mon.) features custom facials, a variety of massage techniques including reflexology and deep-tissue, and specialized treatments like "ear candling," a technique to help rid clients of extraneous ear wax.

Services at **Ridgewood European Day Spa** (30 Franklin Ave., 201/447-1600) include seaweed body wraps, self-tanning treatments, facials (including one for acne management), and massage. The spa is open 10 A.M.–4 P.M. Monday, 9 A.M.–9 P.M. Tuesday and Wednesday, noon–9 P.M. Thursday, and 9 A.M.–5 P.M. Friday and Saturday, closed Sunday.

Food

Ridgewood's many restaurants range from casual coffeehouses to fine dining, with a number of smaller chain eateries strewn about.

Situated along a side street just off Ridgewood Avenue is **Village Green** (36 Prospect St., 201/445-2914, $23–39), a reputable restaurant offering internationally inspired American entrées amid tastefully understated decor. This BYO is known for its use of fresh ingredients. Lunch is served 11 A.M.–3 P.M. Monday–Saturday, and dinner 5:30–9:30 P.M. Tuesday–Thursday, until 10 P.M. Friday and Saturday.

Jumbo portions of every kind of pancake imaginable are up for grabs at the cash-only **Country Pancake House** (140 E. Ridgewood Ave., 201/444-8395, 7 A.M.–9:30 P.M. Mon.–Thurs., until 10 P.M. Fri.–Sun., $4.95–8.50), as well as an expansive menu of American eats. This boisterous establishment is hopping even on a Monday morning and pancakes are a staple all day long.

Natalie's Cafe (17 S. Broad St., 201/444-7887, 8:30 A.M.–9 P.M. Sun.–Thurs., until 10 P.M. Fri. and Sat., $6.95–11.95) is a bustling and cozy Italian/American eatery serving fresh soups, salads, sandwiches, and focaccia pizzas. Inside is both comfortable and casual, with a chalkboard menu, pastry counter, and plenty of espresso drinks, and during warmer weather a couple of tables grace the sidewalk out front.

Situated next to the train station, elegant **Latour** (6 E. Ridgewood Ave., 201/445-5056, $21–29) is a Modern French restaurant graced with high ceilings, crisp white tablecloths, and dark wood floors. This BYO offers a five-course prix fixe tasting menu during dinner hours Tuesday–Thursday and Sunday ($42.50). Lunch is served 11:30 A.M.–2:30 P.M. Tuesday–Friday, and dinner 5–10 P.M. Tuesday–Thursday, until 11 P.M. Friday and Saturday, and 4–9 P.M. Sunday.

Getting There

Ridgewood's transit station is at Garber Square and West Ridgewood Avenue. Ridgewood is reached by riding NJ Transit's Bergen County line from Hoboken Terminal or Secaucus Junction.

The Urban Outskirts

West of the Gateway's densely packed urban center are the Watchung Mountains, where affluent and interesting suburban towns stand within commuting distance to New York City. This is a good place to escape the often-overbearing madness to the east with a leisurely drive or a lengthy meal. You'll find plenty of restaurants in both Summit and Montclair, the latter offering an excellent selection of cuisine choices and, it seems, an influx of new restaurants monthly. Accommodation choices in the area are slim, though West Orange and Summit both have recommendable options. Visitors may choose to stay at one of the many hotels near Newark Airport, only a short distance away. Some of the state's best shopping ops exist in Montclair and Short Hills, which houses perhaps New Jersey's finest mall, and as suburban communities go, you'll find a wonderful array of sights and entertainment, including an art museum in Montclair, a famous historical laboratory in West Orange, a New York–caliber theater in Millburn, and two well-known universities.

UPPER MONTCLAIR AND CLIFTON

Residing high above downtown Montclair and separated by Watchung Road, Upper Montclair's centerpiece is the Spanish-style **Montclair State University,** a commuter campus with its own diner and thousands of students, which spreads into nearby Clifton and Little Falls.

【 Tick Tock Diner

The epitome of New Jersey diner culture is the Tick Tock Diner (281 Allwood Rd. and Rte. 3, Clifton, 973/777-0511, $5–15), a shiny, spacious, sunny place with plenty of counter space, a separate mini-bar, and a roomy dining room in addition to its original meal car. Burgers come huge at this 24-hour institution, packed onto a plate with steak fries, pickles, *and* slaw, and clientele include suits, thirtysomethings,

late-night chatterers, and senior couples who cozy into a booth to reminisce about meals past at their favorite establishment.

Yogi Berra Stadium and Museum

On the campus of Montclair State University is Yogi Berra Stadium (Valley Rd. and Norman Ave., Upper Montclair, 973/655-8009, $4–9), the state's smallest minor league ballpark and home to the **New Jersey Jackals** (www.jackals.com). This 1998 hillside stadium, named in honor of former Yankees catcher Lawrence "Yogi" Berra (a Montclair resident), has 3,800 seats and a general-admission lawn in the outfield that can accommodate an additional 4,000.

Adjacent to the stadium is the Yogi Berra Learning Center and Museum (8 Quarry Rd., Little Falls, 973/655-2378, www.yogi berramuseum.org, $6 adult, $4 student), an educational facility and exhibit space stressing sports as an essential learning tool. Recent displays have included "Jersey Girls," an exhibit highlighting the history of Garden State females and sports. Berra's signature and hand prints are preserved in the cement out front. The museum is open noon–5 P.M. Wednesday–Sunday, and until 7 P.M. during New Jersey Jackals games. It's closed major holidays.

Other Sights

The **Montclair Hawk Lookout** is the perfect place for watching the region's annual fall hawk migration. The platform is a project of the New Jersey Audubon Society and is located atop Upper Montclair's First Watchung Mountain, along Edgecliff Road a couple blocks west from Upper Mountain Avenue. It's open to the public September–November.

For approximately three weeks each year **Presby Memorial Iris Gardens** (Mountainside Park, Upper Montclair Ave., Upper Montclair, 973/783-5974) opens its grounds to the public to witness the blooming of over 4,000 iris varieties. The bloom period usually begins around the middle of May and stretches into the first week of June, but varies each year; visitors are welcome from dawn to dusk daily.

The **Mount Hebron Cemetery** (851 Valley and Mt. Hebron Rds., Upper Montclair, 973/744-1380) plays final earthly resting place to a few somewhat well-known historic and entertainment figures, including John Charles Barclay (1856–1934), inventor of the electric telegraph, and the actress Shirley Booth (1898–1992).

Getting There

There's a NJ Transit commuter station at Montclair State University, about a 40-minute ride from New York City, but trains only stop here during the week. To get here, board the Montclair–Boonton line and exit at the Montclair State University Station. Watchung Avenue separates Upper Montclair from Montclair to the south, and if traveling west on Watchung, a right turn onto Upper Mountain Avenue will carry you into town.

MONTCLAIR

Known for its colorful diversity and eclectic ways, Montclair is a desirable urban suburb less than 14 miles west of New York City. Its downtown centers along Bloomfield Avenue, a long, heavily trafficked stretch that stems from nearby Bloomfield and continues west into Caldwell and Verona, the centerpiece for a great mix of bookstores, movie theaters, boutiques, retail shops, cafés, galleries, and restaurants—even an art museum. Montclair's sloping landscape to the north of the downtown center provides it the appeal of a Rocky Mountain town, with some of the highest property values in New Jersey. Though a commuter bus does stop downtown and NJ Transit has numerous stations in the outlying township, it's not an easy place to explore without a car.

Montclair Art Museum

Housed in a Greek Revival structure is the nearly century-old Montclair Art Museum (3 S. Mountain Ave., 973/746-5555, www.montclairart.org, 11 A.M.–5 P.M. Tues.–Sun., $8 adult,

$6 child), an excellent museum with a diverse collection that includes original work by Andy Warhol, as well as Hudson River School paintings, sculpture, works on paper, and Native American artifacts. The expanded museum includes both an art school and an art library with over 14,000 books. Admission is free to everyone 11 A.M.–1 P.M. Fridays.

Grover Cleveland Birthplace

In nearby Caldwell you'll find the Grover Cleveland Birthplace (207 Bloomfield Ave., Caldwell, 973/226-0001, free), the first home of the only U.S. president elected to two non-consecutive terms. It's open to the public Wednesday–Sunday, though hours vary so call ahead.

Entertainment

Cafés and old-style movie theaters are both part of Montclair's quasi-urban streetscape.

Originally opened as a stage venue in 1922, the brick-front **Wellmont Theater** (5 Seymour St., 973/783-9500) is today a multi-screen art-house theater with two cozy, somewhat worn screening rooms, and a larger upstairs balcony. Fortunately, bite-sized screens translate to discount ticket prices and a unique snack selection, including truffles and complimentary java.

Situated along Bloomfield Avenue's prime stretch, the **Montclair-Claridge Cinemas** (486 Bloomfield Ave., 973/470-CLVW or 973/470-2589, press #574) is a converted sixplex specializing in first-run features and art-house films. The theater is operated by Clearview Cinemas, who run many of the former single screens in the Gateway Region.

Café Eclectic (444 Bloomfield Ave., 973/509-9179, www.cafeeclecticnj.net) is a comfortable couch-filled coffeehouse serving Cuban sandwiches, sorbet, and free wireless Internet to a clientele heavy with Montclair undergrads and local teens. Live music and karaoke are featured evenings throughout the week. The café is open 11 A.M.–midnight Monday, 9 A.M.–midnight Tuesday–Thursday, 9 A.M.–2 A.M. Friday, noon–2 A.M. Saturday, and 1 P.M.–midnight Sunday.

About a 10-minute drive from downtown Montclair, **The Remedy** (401 Broad St., Bloomfield, 973/566-0404) opened in July 2005 to rave reviews. Live music and an expanded sandwich menu are in the works to round out this café's fine selection of espresso drinks and herbal-based "cures," and a seasonal and spacious outdoor patio ideally complements the stylish decor. Hours are 9:30 A.M.–11 P.M. Tuesday–Saturday, until 8 P.M. Sunday, closed Monday.

Shopping

Much of Montclair's shopping ops are found along lengthy Bloomfield Avenue and nearby Church Street, a short and narrow stretch that lies diagonal to the south, somewhat hidden behind the main street's storefronts. Following its angle north will put you on Glenridge Avenue, where the shopping continues.

For all your party supplies and pop-culture gifts head to **Copabananas** (44 Church St., 973/655-8844). This colorful and kid-friendly shop stocks both Ugly Dolls and piñatas. **Milk Money** (76 Church St., 973/744-0504) is a children's clothing consignment store.

The nature lover's fave is **Where the Wild Bee Wings** (217 Glenridge Ave., 973/223-9464). Three-story **Montclair Book Center** (219–221 Glenridge Ave., 973/783-3630, www.montclairbookcenter.com) has been operating in the community for over twenty years, selling new, rare, and collectible books in an authentic stamped-tin-ceiling space. Look for the red and white awning and the sidewalk rack of books. **Watchung Booksellers** (54 Fairfield St., 973/744-7177) is a small-spaced venue specializing in new books. The shop features a well-stocked children's room.

Euro Glass Art LLC (27 S. Park St., 973/744-4004, www.euroglassart.com) promotes the selling and distribution of European-crafted glassworks, including fused-glass plates, etched vases, and hand-blown Murano glass.

Food

Montclair's ever-fluctuating restaurant scene is as eclectic as its people, with most dining options centered around Bloomfield Avenue.

For Mediterranean eats—and gyros in particular—the restaurant of choice is **Greek Delights** (14 Park St., 973/783-9100, www.greekdelightsnj.com, 11 A.M.–9:40 P.M. Mon.–Thurs., until 10:40 P.M. Fri. and Sat., noon–8:40 P.M. Sun., $4.50–14.95), which knowledgeable foodies call the best around.

Montclair hosts a number of Thai restaurants, including **Tuptim Thai Cuisine** (600 Bloomfield Ave., 973/783-3800, www.tuptimthaicuisine.com, $11.95–16.95), a BYO with a nice selection of vegetarian dishes and authentic Thai decor. Lunch hours are 11:30 A.M.–2:30 P.M. Tuesday–Friday, and dinner is served 5–10 P.M. Monday–Thursday, until 11 P.M. Friday and Saturday, and 3:30–10 P.M. Sunday.

◖ Nouveau Sushi (635 Bloomfield Ave., 973/746-0399) serves high-end sashimi that can only be described as outstanding, even outside the New Jersey market. They're open for dinner only 5:30–10:30 P.M. Monday–Wednesday, until 11 P.M. Thursday–Saturday, closed Sunday.

A Montclair transplant from nearby Nutley and one with a loyal following, **Little Saigon** (19 Elm St., 973/783-3914, 11 A.M.–9 P.M. Tues.–Thurs., until 10 P.M. Fri., 10 A.M.–10 P.M. Sat., 10 A.M.–9 P.M. Sun., closed Mon., $7.95–25) is a BYO that tempts the palate with Vietnamese fare, though service can be spotty.

Located in nearby West Caldwell, **Wazwan Indian Restaurant** (691 Bloomfield Ave., 973/226-3132, www.wazwan.net, noon–9 P.M. Tues.–Thurs., until 10 P.M. Fri. and Sat., closed Mon. and open only by special arrangement Sun., $14–22) serves exquisitely spiced Kashmiri cuisine with a selection of vegetarian-friendly entrées and mouth-warming chai.

For kid-friendly atmosphere and cuisine nothing beats the Southwestern Tex-Mex of **Mexicali Rose** (10 Park St., 973/746-9005, 11:30 A.M.–10:30 P.M. Sun.–Thurs., until 11 P.M. Fri. and Sat., $12–20). This festive BYO is colorful and casual, decked with mariachi frog figurines and offering sidewalk seating during summer months.

A new addition to the Montclair restaurant

scene is **Le Carousel** (700 Bloomfield Ave., 973/746-5699, $12.95–19.95), a New American multi-level space with an intimate first-floor lounge and a bright and inviting upstairs dining area. Upon entry you'll spot muraled walls done by local artists, and a grand piano to provide evening entertainment. Lunch is available 11 A.M.–3 P.M. daily and dinner starting at 5 P.M.

The popular **Montclair Farmers Market** (8 A.M.–2 P.M. Sat., late June–Nov.) takes place at the Walnut Street train station and features an array of locally grown fruits and vegetables, many organic, as well as a fine selection of breads and cheeses.

For a healthy on-the-go alternative, stop by **Whole Foods** (701 Bloomfield Ave., 973/746-5110).

Nightlife

Montclair hosts a few nightlife options that range from collegiate clientele to SoHo-style hangout, and food always comes with the territory.

Billed as Montclair's only dance club, the **Diva Lounge** (373 Bloomfield Ave, 973/509-3000, www.divalounge.com, 6 P.M.–2 A.M. Wed.–Sun.) is a multi-room locale heavy with velvet and dim with lights, suspended somewhere between Gothic and Medieval decor. The lounge features a full bar and steak, chicken, and seafood menu, and music varies from Latin to hip-hop to soul, depending on the evening. Dress codes and cover charges vary, so call ahead.

Reputed for its Sunday jazz brunch, **Trumpets Jazz Club-Restaurant** (6 Depot Sq., 973/744-2600, www.trumpetsjazz.com, $11.95–23.95) is also the swankiest supper club in town, and has been for over 20 years. Dinner is served during shows ($8–15), which take place throughout the week (except Mon.) beginning at 7:30 P.M. Tuesday–Thursday and Sunday, and 8:30 P.M. Friday and Saturday. Hours are 6 P.M.–12:30 A.M. Tuesday–Thursday, until 1:30 A.M. Friday and Saturday, 11:30 A.M.–3 P.M. and 7 P.M.–midnight Sunday; closed Monday year-round and Sunday–Tuesday July and August.

Popular with the Montclair State crowd,

Just Jake's Bar & Restaurant (30 Park St., 973/655-8987, $7–20) specializes in live music, drink specials, and casual American cuisine, with a bar menu that extends late-night for post-dinner stragglers. Jake's is open for lunch and dinner 11:30 A.M.–10 P.M. Tuesday–Saturday, and until 9 P.M. Sunday. Brunch ($4.50–12) is served 11 A.M.–2:30 P.M. Sunday.

Getting There

Montclair lies 14 miles west of New York City. NJ Transit's Montclair–Boonton line runs through town from New York City, Secaucus Junction, and Hoboken Terminal, with several stops in the area (including one on Watchung Ave.), none of which are convenient for accessing the downtown area on foot. **DeCamp** (101 Greenwood Ave., 973/783-7500, www.decamp.com) runs a commuter bus (Rte. #33) from New York City with a stop in downtown Montclair (Gates and Bloomfield Aves.), about a 35-minute ride. Call or check the website for updated fares and schedules—bus runs are limited on the weekends.

WEST ORANGE

West Orange is a large suburban hilltop town with a couple of attractions and some fine eateries. It's home base to the office of Mark Sceurman and Mark Moran, the "Weird NJ" boys who have been going strong writing about New Jersey oddities for over a decade (www.weirdnj.com).

Edison National Historic Site

Thomas Edison opened his West Orange manufacturing plant while in his 40s, and operated it until his death in 1931. Now known as the Edison National Historic Site (Main and Lakeside Ave., 973/243-9122), it also encompasses **Glenmont** (12 Honeysuckle Rd., 973/736-0551, www.nps.gov/edis/home.htm), Edison's home estate and burial site. The expansive laboratory is made up of nearly a dozen sites, including an exact replica of Black Maria, the world's first motion picture studio. Other buildings include a chemistry lab, a physics lab that operates as a visitors center, and a main laboratory that includes Edison's personal library. This is by far the much larger of the two Edison sites located in New Jersey (the other is in the Menlo Park section of aptly named Edison Township), and thousands of artifacts are on hand here, such as motion picture projectors and phonographs. In 2005 the laboratory complex is undergoing extensive restoration and is closed to the public—work is expected to continue through 2006.

South Mountain Reservation

Situated upon the Watchung Mountain Range is 2,048-acre South Mountain Reservation (973/268-3500), a multiuse recreation area once traversed by George Washington that doubles as a watershed and nature preserve. Spread between West Orange, Millburn, and Maplewood, and touching the South Orange border, it features numerous hiking trails, as well as the **South Mountain Arena** (560 Northfield Ave., West Orange, 973/731-3828), a large indoor venue housing two ice hockey rinks. Also within the perimeters of the reservation is the **Turtle Back Zoo** (560 Northfield Ave., 973/731-5800, www.turtlebackzoo.com, 10 A.M.–4:30 P.M. Mon.–Sat., 11 A.M.–5:30 P.M. Sun., $7 adult, $3 child and senior), home to both domesticated animals and wild creatures like wolves, wallabies, bobcats, and bears, in addition to a wide array of birds, including penguins, eagles, owls, doves, peacocks, and a toucan. The zoo also features a petting zoo, train, and pony rides at no extra cost. There are also events throughout the year, including a guided night tour during summer. The property has recently been revamped to include extra space for its occupants, including an environmentally integrated black bear habitat.

Accommodations

$200-250: Opened in 2002, the **Residence Inn West Orange** (107 Prospect Ave., 973/669-4700) is a three-story hotel with an indoor pool and tennis courts, wireless Internet in public areas, and wired high-speed Internet in rooms. A safe is available at the front desk, and for an extra $75 pets can be guests too. Rooms include studios, one- and two-bedroom suites, and presidential suites.

Food and Nightlife

What began during the Great Depression as a hot dog stand has evolved into **Pal's Cabin Restaurant** (265 Prospect Ave., 973/731-4000, www.palscabin.com, 7:30 A.M.–11 P.M. Mon.–Fri., 11 A.M.–11 P.M. weekends, $8–27), a rustic, family-owned American restaurant with wood booths and high ceilings.

A favorite spot for dim sum is **China Gourmet** (468 Eagle Rock Ave., 973/731-6411 or 800/652-6688, 11 A.M.–10 P.M. Sun.–Thurs., until 11 P.M. Fri. and Sat.), which also features live jazz monthly.

To get into the groove sensation, try **Cecil's Jazz Club** (364 Valley Rd., 973/736-4800, www.cecilsjazzclub.com, noon–2 A.M. daily), with live performances of jazz, blues, Latin, and swing throughout the week. A weekly jazz jam session takes place on Tuesdays, beginning at 9 P.M., and food is served daily from noon to 2 A.M. Shows run about $10.

SOUTH ORANGE

Downtown South Orange resembles a Swiss alpine village, especially when you approach it from the western residential hillside. The train station has the look of a miniature castle, surrounded by chalet-style buildings with chocolate-brown accents, and on the outer streets, Craftsman-style homes. A sign reading Village Hall and an elevated transit platform add to the ambience, as do the fairytale houses with curvy pitched roofs and large-stone facades that ascend through the village above. The 2.7-square-mile village of South Orange separated from South Orange Township in 1977. It's the home of **Seton Hall University** (400 S. Orange Ave., 973/761-9000, www.shu.edu) and lies 15 miles from New York City.

Festivals and Events

Held annually in the Tulip Springs Section of nearby South Mountain Reservation (accessible by South Orange Ave.), weekends throughout July and August, the **New**

Jersey Renaissance Fair (732/271-1119, www.njkingdom.com) offers admittance into a costumed world of fair maidens and dashing knights. A makeshift village provides plenty of shopping ops, including some wonderful handmade crafts and clothes. Browsing is just as fun, as is dining on medieval-inspired fare while mingling with peasants and nobles. Cost is $15 adults, $7 children under 12, or $22 for a Two-Day Pass.

Somewhat surprisingly, the Urban Outskirts are a haven for jazz musicians, and the **Giants of Jazz Festival** ($25–35) is an annual October one-night gathering that celebrates this amazing art. This performance is put on by South Orange's Department of Recreation and Cultural Affairs (Baird Community Center, Mead St., 973/378-7754, http://southorange.org/CulturalAffairs), which also hosts a monthly jazz concert January–May.

Food and Entertainment

South Orange's status as a university town makes casual food, drink, and shows easy to come by.

Since 1998 the family-owned and operated **Gaslight Brewery & Restaurant** (15 S. Orange Ave., 973/762-7077, www.gaslightbrewery.com, 3 P.M.–midnight Mon. and Tues., 11:30 A.M.–midnight Wed.–Sun., $7.50–28.95) has been drawing in the college crowd with tasty beers, good food, and a bevy of entertainment. Housed in a former bank, it's now set up for live music (Friday nights) and shuffleboard, and menu items include freshly prepared burgers, wraps, and pizzas, as well as more formal entrées and Bavarian cuisine.

The easygoing **Dancing Goat Café Gallery** (21 S. Orange Ave., 973/275-9000, www.thedancinggoat.com, $5.50–8) is part eatery, part art gallery, and part entertainment venue, with *panini,* wraps, and salads on the menu and shows ranging from open mic to flamenco dance—there's even a musical story hour for kids (11:30 A.M. Thurs.). Admission is charged on evenings when there's a show and ranges $5–10, depending on the performance. The Café opens at 9:30 A.M. and usually closes

between 10 P.M. and midnight, Sunday–Saturday. It's closed Mondays.

Tucked beneath downtown's railway overpass, the **Blue Moon Diner** (1 Sloan St., 973/761-6666, 8 A.M.–9:30 P.M. daily, $6–8) is a casual coffee shop/café staffed mostly by undergrads from nearby Seton Hall.

Getting There

South Orange's transit station is conveniently located downtown at 19 Sloan Street, and is accessible from New York City, Secaucus Junction, or Hoboken Terminal on NJ Transit's Morris & Essex Morristown line.

MAPLEWOOD, MILLBURN, AND SHORT HILLS

Maplewood is an upscale residential community of charming hillside homes centered around a curvy downtown main street lined by service and specialty shops and a movie theater. The train station features its own concierge (973/763-7155), and in 2004 the town came under fire with its attempt to ban Christmas caroling. Nearby is Millburn, another upscale enclave with an outstanding musical theater and, in the township's **Short Hills** section, one of the state's most luxurious shopping centers.

Shopping and Entertainment

With five anchor stores including Bloomingdale's, Nordstrom, and Saks Fifth Avenue, the two-story **Mall at Short Hills** (Rte. 24 and JFK Parkway, 973/376-7350, www.shopshorthills.com) is easily the grand dame of New Jersey indoor shopping complexes. This is not your typical mall selection—Betsey Johnson, Nicole Miller, Diesel, and Anthropologie are all represented—and with no sales tax on clothes and shoes in New Jersey, you've got New York shopping, Garden State–style.

Millburn's **Paper Mill Playhouse** (Brookside Dr., 973/379-3636, www.papermill.org) is New Jersey's answer to Broadway. Founded in 1934 and named for a paper mill that once operated in its place, the playhouse is the state's official theater, running top-caliber productions of musicals and children's theater throughout the year. For those pressed for time, gourmet sandwiches are sold on-site before shows and during intermission.

Food

For true pub and grub try **St. James's Gate Publick House** (167 Maplewood Ave., Maplewood, 973/378-2222, www.stjamesgatepub.com, 11:30 A.M.–2 A.M. daily, $7–13), an Irish establishment serving bangers and mash ($11.50)—translated that's sausage and potatoes—and eight-ounce blue-cheese Dublin burgers to be enjoyed in front of the fire with a pint of Guinness in hand.

Getting There

NJ Transit has stops in Maplewood (between Dunnell Rd. and Maplewood Ave.), Millburn (35 Essex St.), and Short Hills (25 Chatham Rd.). All three stations are accessible on the Morris & Essex Morristown line from New York City, Secaucus Junction, and Hoboken Terminal.

SUMMIT

The city of Summit received its name when the first train arrived here to the "Summit of Short Hills" in the early half of the 19th century. Located along the Passaic River, it later became a resort getaway for those looking to escape the urbanity of Manhattan. Bulbous trees and grid-laid streets occupy the city's downtown, where you'll find attractive two- and three-story red, brown, and white brick buildings housing numerous shops and restaurants. Summit's train station is conveniently located in the city center, making for an easy stroll around a downtown that has vibrantly survived where others could not.

New Jersey Center for the Visual Arts

Since 1933 the New Jersey Center for the Visual Arts (68 Elm St., 908/273-9121, www.njcva.org, 10:30 A.M.–4:30 P.M. Mon.–Fri., noon–4 P.M. Sat., closed Sun., $1 donation) has been part of the Summit community. It's a nonprofit school hosting an array of classes and workshops for all

© LAURA KINIRY

downtown Summit

ages in a variety of media that includes photography, ceramics, and digital design. Indoor and outdoor exhibit spaces host changing displays of contemporary art throughout the year.

Accommodations

$200-250: Since the late 19th century the stately brick **Grand Summit Hotel** (570 Springfield Ave., 908/273-3000, www.grandsummit.com) has been serving as Summit's accommodation of choice. Inside are 150 elegantly designed guestrooms garnished with chocolate chip cookies and bottled water. High tea and pastries are the norm on weekday afternoons, and a complimentary morning meal at the hotel's grill accompanies all overnight stays. Additional perks include an outdoor pool, on-site Avis car rental, and a downtown locale.

Food

Summit offers numerous dining opportunities, ranging from diner food to Italian to sushi. You'll have little trouble finding something that suits your needs, and most restaurants are within walking distance to one another and the train station.

In this state where the diner is royalty, the ◖ **Summit Diner** (Summit Ave. and Union Pl., 908/277-3256, 5:30 A.M.–8:00 P.M. daily, $5–10) stands as king. It's compact, clean, and cozy, lined with booths and counter space, and the state's diner expert, Peter Genovese, touts it as the best diner in New Jersey to "bring a newcomer to." This is the place to come for exceptional morning meals and grilled favorites.

Northern Italian cuisine is served amid mural-painted walls in a spacious setting at **Fiorino Ristorante** (38 Maple St., 908/277-1900, www.fiorinoristorante.com, 11:30 A.M.–10 P.M.

Mon.–Thurs., until 11 P.M. Fri., 5–11 P.M. Sat., closed Sun., $16–32), an inviting establishment visited by the Trumpster himself.

New Italian is the specialty at **Adagio Ristorante** (401 Springfield Ave., 908/277-1677, www.adagioristorante.net, $16.95-34.95), a four-room space that includes a chef's tasting room, a superbly sophisticated dining area, and a more casual Tavern with wonderful high-back booths. Lunch is served 11:45 A.M.–2:45 P.M. Monday–Friday, and dinner 5–10 P.M. Monday–Thursday, until 10:30 P.M. Friday and Saturday, closed Sunday.

New York City's **Monster Sushi** (395 Springfield Ave., 908/598-1100, www.monster sushi.com, $13.95–25.95) has found its way into the streets of Summit, where vegetarian-friendly "monster rolls" are the norm, and entrées include teriyaki, tempura, steak, and a special kid's menu. Hours are 11:30 A.M.–10 P.M. Monday–Friday, noon–11 P.M. Saturday, and 3–10 P.M. Sunday.

Specializing in steak and seafood, the Grand Summit Hotel's **Hunt Club Grill** (570 Springfield Ave., 908/273-7656, $20–34) serves a popular Sunday champagne brunch and features seasonal outdoor patio seating, and live music on the weekends. Lunch is served 11:30 A.M.–2 P.M. Monday–Saturday, and dinner hours are 5–10 P.M. daily. Brunch is served 11:30 A.M.–2:30 P.M. Sunday.

Getting There

Summit is located west of Millburn. The town's transit station stands at Union Place, near the intersection of Broad and Elm Streets. If riding public transit, take the Morris & Essex Morristown line from New York City, Secaucus Junction, or Hoboken Terminal.

THE SKYLANDS

For those looking to experience New England without leaving the Mid-Atlantic region, the Skylands has you covered. A world away from the nearby Gateway Region, the Skylands is packed with mountainous terrain, riverfront towns, state parks, bed-and-breakfasts, and plenty of recreational opportunities. This is where you'll find New Jersey's largest lake, its most naturally scenic areas, odd mining towns, ski resorts, and the state's highest point standing tall in the northwest corner. As in areas further south, the Skylands is filled with farmland, though instead of flatlands there are miles and miles of rolling hills where deer, black bear, and cattle are the most prominent residents. This is also where you'll find some of New Jersey's best cycling, as well as opportunities for fishing, tubing, swimming, and hiking—more than anywhere else in the state.

The Skylands also has its fair share of history. The country's first national historic park was created in Morristown in the 1930s, honoring the place where General Washington and his men spent two long winters, and the Lindbergh baby kidnapping trial, a follow-up to the "crime of the century," took place in Central Piedmont's Flemington. The region is also home to some of the state's best oddities, including the Space Farms Zoo & Museum and the Gingerbread Castle. In the Ridge and Valley Region you'll find historic villages like Hope, where the Moravian religious sect lived for a brief but significant time, and Blairstown, the original filming locale for *Friday the 13th*.

© LAURA KINIRY

THE SKYLANDS

HIGHLIGHTS

◖ **Mountain Creek:** With half-pipes, water-slides, and downhill mountain biking, this re-made ski mountain is all action winter, spring, summer, and fall (page 80).

◖ **High Point State Park:** This home to New Jersey's highest point offers a panoramic mountain view, as well as a stretch of the Appalachian Trail and some of the state's best cross-country skiing (page 88).

◖ **Delaware Water Gap National Recreation Area:** New Jersey shares this gorgeous attribute with Pennsylvania, and there's no better place for hiking, cycling, and exploring (page 90).

◖ **Great Swamp:** This 7,500-acre refuge is a great spot for seeing wildlife, especially birds. The roads around the swamp are good for bicycling, too (page 100).

◖ **Shopping in Lambertville:** This artsy little riverfront city is a walkable spree of antique stores, art galleries, and specialty shops, and one of the most attractive places around (page 114).

◖ **Ballooning the Skylands:** Soar over the countryside in New Jersey's most picturesque region and you'll easily forget that you're in the country's most densely populated state (page 123).

LOOK FOR ◖ TO FIND RECOMMENDED SIGHTS, ACTIVITIES, DINING, AND LODGING.

For shopping, the antique stores and art galleries of Lambertville, Frenchtown, and Chester are some of the best around, and you won't drive far without reaching another state park. As for nightlife, just grab a seat at one of the many outdoor eateries and linger the night away.

The area also offers terrific camping spots, excellent bed-and-breakfasts, and in Hunterdon County, which locals like to refer to as "the other shore," you'll find some of the region's top restaurants. A world-class ski and snowboard resort has been resurrected in the north, and cross-country skiing is popular throughout the region. For those who don't

think New Jersey is alluring, or who believe it's nothing but flatland and highways, they haven't seen the Skylands.

PLANNING YOUR TIME

The Skylands makes the perfect weekend escape from the nearby Gateway Region or an excellent weeklong vacation from New Jersey's more suburban areas located to the south. Filled with recreational opportunity, it's well suited to the outdoor enthusiast, but the many bed-and-breakfasts and picturesque landscapes make the region just as popular with visitors who prefer to enjoy nature from the comfort of a covered veranda. If you plan to devote your time to a

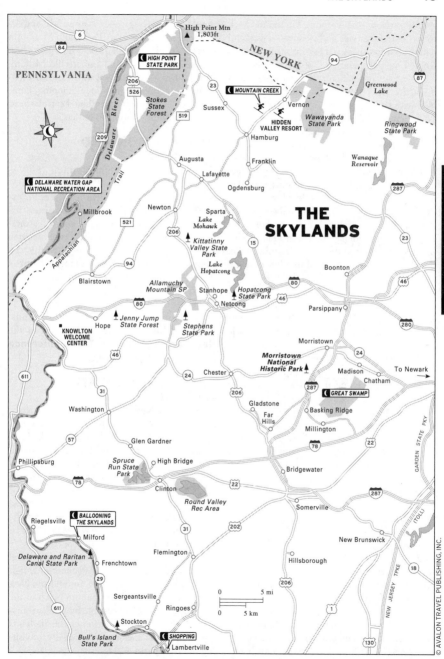

specific section—say Vernon's Mountain Creek Resort or Lambertville and vicinity—a weekend will do, but to really get a feel for the region as a whole I suggest spending five days or a week.

Unless you're a winter sports enthusiast (and if you are, the Highlands' Vernon Valley, coupled with the Ridge and Valley Region's High Point State Park, are the places to be), I recommend beginning a weekend trip in the Lambertville area. The best B&Bs in the region are located in Lambertville, Stockton, Frenchtown, and Milford, and make a good base for exploring farther north. Get an early start Saturday morning for a drive along Old Mine Road in the Delaware Water Gap National Recreation Area, a hike in the Jenny Jump State Forest, or a stop at the Golden Nugget Antique & Flea Market just south of downtown Lambertville. For those who are interested in a bit more action, canoeing, kayaking, and tubing trips along the Delaware are possible from the Ridge and Valley Region and the area around Frenchtown. On Sunday, make your way east by way of Morristown to visit Morristown National Historic Park or one of the town's many museums.

If you'd rather spend your evenings camping, there are a few wonderful campgrounds located in the vicinity of Hope, in the Ridge and Valley Region. Head to High Point State Park via the Delaware Water Gap the next day—there are a couple of campgrounds on the northern tip of the recreation area, as well as in the Highlands region to the east. Set up camp, and spend your evening with a couple of lawn chairs and a camp stove cookout under the evening stars. On Sunday you can return to the Northeast Corridor via Ringwood State Park, with a possible stop at one of the area's mining museums before heading home.

A weeklong trip to the Skylands should include stops in the sights mentioned above, as well as Allamuchy Mountain State Park, with visits tailored to interests. History buffs will want to take in Waterloo Village and the mining towns of Franklin and Ogdensburg. Nature-lovers can visit the Great Swamp, in addition to the Delaware Water Gap, Jenny Jump State Forest, and Wawayanda State Park. Mountain bikers should head to Ringwood, Wawayanda, and Allamuchy Mountain State Parks, and Mountain Creek's Diablo Freeride Park. The region's best options for dining are in Lambertville, Milford, Frenchtown, Morristown, and Central Piedmont's Somerville. For antique shopping, Lambertville, Frenchtown, and Chester can't be beat, and Flemington is home to outlets.

INFORMATION AND SERVICES

The **Skylands Tourism Council** (800/4-SKYLAND or 800/475-9526, www.skylands tourism.org) offers excellent resources for exploring New Jersey's northwest corner, including brochures, a website, and a seasonal magazine available for free at numerous area locations, or by subscription through the website. The **Knowlton Welcome Center** (908/496-4994) lies along I-80 East, milemarker 7, in Columbia, along the bottom stretch of the Ridge and Valley Region.

For more information on the Skylands' parks and hiking opportunities, contact the **New York–New Jersey Trail Conference** (201/512-9348, www.nynjtc.org).

GETTING THERE AND AROUND

Tucked into New Jersey's northwest corner, the Skylands may seem like one of the state's most inaccessible regions, but towns like Phillipsburg, Flemington, and Frenchtown are all easily reachable from Pennsylvania's **Lehigh Valley International Airport** (3311 Airport Rd., Allentown, PA, www.lvia.org), about an hour or less by car. Those towns located along the eastern portion of the Skylands lie within close proximity to **Newark Liberty International** (www.newarkairport.com).

NJ Transit (www.njtransit.com) lines travel as far west as Morristown, Gladstone, and High Bridge (three miles north of Clinton) from New York City before ending, making much of the southeast Skylands accessible by public transport. A thorough exploration of the Skylands region makes a car essential, especially for visiting the state parks and forests.

Major roads that run though the area include east–west I-80, traveling from the Gateway's Meadowlands toward Allamuchy Mountain State Park and on to the lower tip of the Delaware Water Gap; Route 23, heading from the Urban Outskirts west into the Upper Highlands where you'll find mining towns and Vernon Valley; Route 46, an old thruway carrying visitors from the Gateway west into stretches of country and following the Pequest River for a portion; and to the south, I-78, a direct route from Newark Airport south through the Central Piedmont—an easy alternative for reaching Bridgewater, Somerville, Morristown, and all of the Delaware River towns—continuing on past Clinton en route to Phillipsburg and Easton, Pennsylvania.

Major north–south routes include Route 206, which travels from South Jersey continuing north to access Chester, Allamuchy State Park, and Augusta, as well as Stokes State Forest and High Point State Park, before crossing the Delaware into Milford, Pennsylvania; and I-287, easily accessible by way of I-78 west from Newark Airport, heads south into Bridgewater and Somerville, and north into Morristown before intersecting with I-80 and Route 23.

Traffic can be heavy on all of the roadways, but none are particularly daunting save for the possibility of wildlife (namely deer) darting onto the roads. Always be on the lookout— "deer in the headlights" is not just an idiom in these parts. As roadways go, Routes 23 and 46 tend to be older and more built-up, while I-287 is lined with exits.

The Highlands

As a travel destination, the Highlands is said to attract more annual visitors than Yellowstone National Park. New Jersey's portion of the greater Reading Prong—a northern extension of the Blue Ridge Mountains—is heavily coated with forest and sheer cliffs, funneling out into open areas of lakes and streams. It's an area once heavily mined and now filled with the remains of old mining towns, and its ecosystem supplies a natural water source for much of the Northeast Corridor. The Highlands begins to the east at Ringwood State Park, typically considered part of the Gateway Region due to its location in Passaic County, and travels west to the Vernon Valley, and south, where you'll find glacial lakes and remnants of the former Morris Canal. Highlights of the region include Ringwood State Park, where you'll find New Jersey's only botanical gardens; Vernon Township, home to the state's best downhill skiing and snowboarding; the mining towns of Franklin and Ogdensburg; and the Central Highlands' Allamuchy Mountain State Park. The Highlands offers few dining options other than chain eateries; your best bets are around Sparta and in the central region. Vernon and the nearby resorts, and the central lake region, are your best bets for lodging, with B&B selections and a campground or two nearby.

Getting There and Around

The Upper Highlands is accessible from the Gateway Region by way of Route 23, which intersects with Route 94 for travel north into Vernon and the resort area, and Route 517 South leading through Ogdensburg to Sparta, and continuing through to Route 206 where you'll find the bulk of the Central Highlands state parks, and sights such as Wild West City. Running west from New York City, I-80 carries visitors directly to the central state parks, including Allamuchy Mountain and Stephens State Parks.

RINGWOOD STATE PARK

Situated within Bergen and Passaic Counties below the New York State border and along the foothills of the Ramapo Mountains is 4,034-acre Ringwood State Park (304 Sloatsburg Rd., 973/962-7031, www.state.nj.us/dep/parksand forests/parks/ringwood.html, free, $5 parking fee on weekends Memorial Day–Labor Day). Here you'll find two historical mansions and New Jersey's official botanical garden, as well as excellent mountain biking trails. Boating, kayaking, swimming, hiking, cycling, horseback riding, fishing, and hunting can be enjoyed as well, making Ringwood easily one of the state's most desirable parks.

Skylands Manor and New Jersey Botanical Garden

Skylands Manor is a 1920s Tudor Revival mansion partially built with granite from the Ramapo Mountains. This grand estate plays centerpiece to the 96-acre New Jersey Botanical Garden (Morris Ave., 973/962-7527, www.njbg.org, 8 A.M.–8 P.M. daily), where you'll find over 400 varieties of lilac from around the world, including Asia and the Middle East. These exquisite gardens stand at the mountain foothills, and you can easily spend a couple of hours strolling along the Magnolia Walk and through Crabapple Vista, among many other areas. At the **Carriage House Visitors Center,** open weekdays and some Sundays May–September, self-guided tour maps are available, or you can catch one of the guided tours that take place 2 P.M. Sunday, May–October.

Guided tours of the Manor take place on the first Sunday of each month, March–December.

Ringwood Manor

Just north of the botanical garden on the west side of Sloatsburg Road is Ringwood Manor (973/962-7031, www.ringwoodmanor.com), built to house the region's most prominent iron masters. This Gothic Revival mansion is surrounded by gardens with stone fences and statues. A small footbridge traverses a nearby creek, and benches are scattered throughout. You'll also find an old blacksmith shop, and inside 19th-century period furniture and paintings. Ringwood Manor is open to the public year-round, 10 A.M.–3 P.M. Wednesday–Sunday.

Sports and Recreation

South of Skylands Manor is the turn-off for

Shepherd Lake, a 74-acre spring-fed lake open for swimming and boating. A lifeguard is on duty Memorial Day–Labor Day, and kayaks and rowboats can be rented from the seasonal boathouse (973/962-6999). Bathhouses, a concession stand, and picnic tables are located nearby. The park offers a couple of opportunities for fishing—**Ringwood Brook** is annually stocked with trout, and at Shepherd Lake anglers can also cast for sunfish, pickerel, largemouth bass, and catfish.

Ringwood State Park features over a dozen hiking and multi-use trails ranging from simple to difficult, and varying in length 0.5–5 miles—all are well-marked with a colored blaze. For something a bit challenging, one to try is the five-mile **Crossover Trail,** denoted by a white blaze and beginning in the park's Skylands Manor section. This trail can be combined with numerous others in the vicinity, including the **Ringwood Ramapo Trail,** for a half-day loop. For an in-depth description of this and other hiking trails, visit the New York–New Jersey Trail Conference website at www.nynjtc.org.

Ringwood is one of the best locations instate for mountain biking, partially due to the efforts of the **Ramapo Valley Cycling Club** (www.rvccmtb.com), which maintains many of the park's trails. Here you'll find a large number of single tracks for experienced riders, and double tracks suitable for all levels. A 7.5-mile mountain bike trail begins at Shepherd Lake.

Getting There

Ringwood is about one hour and 40 minutes by bus from New York City. To reach the park, take I-287 to exit 57, and follow the signs.

WAWAYANDA STATE PARK

Wawayanda State Park (885 Warwick Turnpike, Hewitt, 973/853-4462, $5 weekdays, $10 weekends, Memorial Day–Labor Day) is 18,235 acres of wild mountain forest and swampland, straddling the borders of Passaic and Sussex Counties. Though not one of the Skylands' most picturesque, this massive park is known for exceptional views from atop **Wawayanda Mountain,** and once here visitors will find sloping terrain, over 60 miles of hiking trails ranging from casual to challenging (including 20 miles of the Appalachian Trail), three natural areas, and a 225-acre lake ideal for enjoying a wide range of watersports—you may even spot a black bear or two. Mountain biking is common along the park's fire roads, though both single and double track trails do exist. Wawayanda is also a good place for winter recreation; cross-country skiing and snowshoeing are both popular park activities. Recently, the park acquired new land to be used for horseback riding, hiking, birdwatching, and canoeing. Group camping sites are available April–late October.

Lake Wawayanda

The 225 acres of **Lake Wawayanda** are ideal for activities year-round, including swimming, boating, ice fishing, snowmobiling, and ice skating. A lifeguard is on duty (Memorial Day–Labor Day), and you'll find both restrooms and a concession stand in the area. Rowboats, paddleboats, and canoes are available for rent throughout the summer, and fishing opportunities include perch, pickerel, trout, and largemouth and smallmouth bass.

Getting There

The park's proximity to Vernon Township is somewhat deceiving. The main entrance to Wawayanda is on the east, accessible by Warwick Turnpike. To get there, follow Route 23 (north from New York City) to Union Valley Road (Rte. 513) and head north through West Milford, where the road turns into White Road (but also remains Rte. 513) and bears left, eventually intersecting Warwick Turnpike. Make a left and the park entrance is about four miles down on the left.

VERNON

It may be hard to believe, but New Jersey does a good winter sports business, and at the heart of it is Sussex County's **Vernon Township,** also known as Vernon Valley. Ski tourism came to

the valley in 1964, but it wasn't until recently that it began taking on a life of its own. Sure, the longest vertical drop may be no more than 1,040 feet, but close proximity to Manhattan, a revived world-class ski resort, and a multitude of new real estate have turned Vernon into a sought-after resort community. During winter months skiing and snowboarding share equal spotlight, and in the summer water rides, and golfing at the township's Crystal Springs Resort, take over. The region is a hard mix between development and nature, and you're still likely to see deer, black bear, and hawks swooping overhead. With no official "Main Street" to speak of, Vernon's downtown centers around Routes 94 and 515. Here you'll find mostly service-oriented stores and a fast-food chain or two, with the best dining options at nearby Crystal Springs.

Bobolink Dairy

A nice break from the recreational activity offered by the township is a visit to Bobolink Dairy (42 Meadow Burn Rd., Vernon, 973/764-4888, www.cowsoutside.com), a working sustainable farm raising grass-fed cattle and producing homemade breads and cheeses (Apr.–Nov.). In addition to offering tastings of their wares (noon–6 P.M. Wed.–Fri., 9 A.M.–5 P.M. weekends), the farm offers 1–3 day internships (with off-site housing), as well as longer apprenticeships. Workshops in cheese- and bread-making ($40) are held in the morning every other Sunday throughout the year, but tend to fill up way in advance, so plan ahead—a listing of upcoming courses is occasionally posted on their website.

Sports and Recreation

The smaller of Vernon's two ski locales (the other, Mountain Creek, is described below), **Hidden Valley** (44 Breakneck Rd., 973/764-4200, www.hiddenvalleynj.com, 9 A.M.–9 P.M. Mon.–Thur. and Sat., until 10 P.M. Fri., until 5 P.M. Sun.) is a family-oriented ski resort with 12 slopes, 3 lifts, and a 620-foot vertical drop. There's a 0.5-mile slope fit for beginners, and six black diamond trails for the adventurous.

The resort also features a snowboard park, snow tubing, and night skiing, and includes its own ski school. If you drive up the mountain to the second entryway, you'll find a restaurant, cafeteria, and the **Breakneck Bar** (973/764-4200, 4 P.M.–closing weekdays and Sat., noon–10 P.M. Sun.), a casual space with jukebox and pool table where you can unwind after a day on the slopes. Hidden Valley transforms into an area park in the summer, complete with tennis courts, badminton, and volleyball. This small-scale place is perfect for kids. Full-day weekend lift tickets are $45 adult, $35 child and senior.

Saddle up at **Legends Riding Stable** (Rte. 94, 973/827-8332, www.saddleupatlegends.com, 9 A.M.–3:45 P.M. Sat.–Mon., $30), which features extensive riding trails for riders of all levels. The ranch is located right across Route 94 from Crystal Springs Mineral Hotel. Credit cards are not accepted.

Accommodations

A few wonderful bed-and-breakfasts are scattered throughout the area, but book early; space is limited (especially during cold winter months—Vernon's high season).

$100-150: Closest to the resorts is the two-story **Alpine Haus Bed & Breakfast Inn** (217 Rte. 94, 973/209-7080 or 877/527-6854, fax 973/209-7090, www.alpinehausbb.com), a Federal-style structure with a cozy indoor fireplace and a second-floor covered porch, where guests can enjoy daily country breakfast during summer months. Antique furnishings decorate each of the eight guestrooms; all are equipped with private bath, TV, telephone, and data port. Two suites, including one that is accessible to guests with disabilities, are available in a separate guesthouse behind the main inn.

The 1831 **Apple Valley Inn Bed & Breakfast** (967 Rte. 517, Vernon, 973/764-3735, www.applevalleyinn.com) is a country inn with a wraparound second-story veranda and a long family-style dining table where daily breakfast is served. Gardens surround the home—there's even a creek and a small footbridge. Eight

guestrooms are equipped with TV/DVD, and a few have private bath and fireplace.

$150-200: With only two guestrooms and two suites, its important to book ahead for the ((**Glenwood Mill Bed & Breakfast** (1860 Rte. 565, Glenwood, 973/764-8660, www.glenwoodmill.com), a 200-year-old inn in a former gristmill just south of the New York State border. All guest accommodations have private bath, sitting area, and a gas fireplace, and the main common area, known as the Great Room, features exposed wood beams and a brick fireplace. The 18-foot-high waterfall once supplying power to the mill remains on the property. TV, telephone, data port, and air-conditioning are included.

((MOUNTAIN CREEK

New Jersey's premier ski and snowboarding resort is Vernon Valley's Mountain Creek (200 Rte. 94, 973/827-2000, www.mountaincreek.com), a once underwhelming destination since purchased and completely remade by Canadian-based IntraWest. Part of what makes Mountain Creek special is its devotion to snowboarding: Approximately half of the park is dedicated to the sport, including an Olympic-size half-pipe and five terrain parks. Mountain Creek also features 11 lifts, including an eight-person open-air gondola, and 46 trails on four mountains. South Peak is where you'll find most of the intermediate and black diamond slopes, while Vernon Peak is best-suited for beginners. Snow tubing is also available, and there's a snow sports school featuring top-notch ski instruction.

In summer months downhill runs give way to mountain bikers enjoying Diablo Freeride Park, and the resort's mountainside water park draws plenty of crowds.

Skiing

Centered around South Peak is what's known as the Main Park—an area designated for advanced skiers and requiring a $5 park pass to enter. For those still working on their turns and jumps, Vernon Peak and Half Peak provide numerous "training opportunities" and are open to all. An all-day lift ticket costs $53/$35 on weekends, and $40/$32 weekdays. Twilight skiing is available throughout winter, 3–10 P.M., for $35 weekends, $29 weekdays. Cost for snow tubing is $14 for one hour, $20 for two; these fees apply to anyone older than five.

Mountain Creek Waterpark

Mountain Creek Waterpark (200 Rte. 94, 973/827-2000, www.mountaincreekwaterpark.com, $26.99 adult, $17.99 child) has chiseled its space into the mountainside as a replacement for the old-school favorite Action Park with over two dozen rides, including a High Tide Wave Pool and a four-story High Anxiety tubing ride. Competitive types can race side by side down the mat-equipped Sidewinder, and tykes will have plenty to do at Half Pint Harbor. The park is open daily Memorial Day–Labor Day.

Diablo Freeride Park

The state's only downhill mountain bike park, Diablo Freeride Park (200 Rte. 94, 973/209-3388, www.diablofreeridepark.com) fills up nearby campgrounds with weekend warriors gearing up for a heart-thumping adrenaline rush. Ski lifts carry riders to the top, two wheels thrust them back down. Diablo boasts nearly 40 freeride and mountain bike trails, and is open 9 A.M.–4 P.M. weekends, mid-May–late October. Downhill bike rental with equipment runs $79, and a full-day lift ticket $28. If you bring your own bike, equipment is available for separate rental.

Accommodations

In addition to Mountain Creek lodging, Vernon's bed-and-breakfasts and Crystal Springs Mineral Hotel offer convenient overnight alternatives.

$200-250: A world-class resort needs upscale accommodation, and Mountain Creek has this sufficiently covered with **Black Creek Sanctuary** (200 Rte. 94, 973/209-7080, www.mountaincreekrealty.com/BlackCreek/blackcreek.htm), a gated array of Adirondack-style townhouses. Each overnight space is equipped with a full kitchen, gas fireplace, and

outdoor deck, as well as wireless Internet connection, and TVs in the common area and each bedroom (ranging from one to three). As of early 2006, Mountain Creek is also in the process of constructing the **Appalachian Grand Lodge.**

Getting There

Mountain Creek is about an hour-and-a-half drive from New York City. Take the George Washington Bridge and follow Route 23 to Route 94, where you'll turn north. The resort is just south of the Route 94 and 515 intersection of "downtown" Vernon.

CRYSTAL SPRINGS RESORT

Another addition to the local resort community is the exclusive Crystal Springs (100G Port Royal Dr., Vernon, 973/827-5996, www.crystalgolfresort.com). Spread between Vernon and Hamburg, this upscale golf resort and spa features six golf courses, numerous restaurants, a hotel, spa facility, and townhouses, to name just a few of its amenities. There's a golf school on the premises, and the courses range in difficulty from fairly straightforward to challenging. The main golfing hub, where you'll find the **Crystal Springs Country Club** set back on the mountainside, is located along Route 94 in northern Hamburg; the **Minerals Hotel and Elements Spa** is found three miles north in Vernon Township. The resort offers the region's best fine-dining restaurant, as well as a couple of eateries that are some of the only dining choices around. This resort is a great place for those who love the game or want to enjoy the day spa, but may be a bit too much for others who prefer coziness and variety.

Golf Courses

There's no doubt this is a golfing resort, with carts more commonplace than cars, and six golf courses within five miles of each other. These include **Ballyowen** (105–137 Wheatsworth Rd., Hamburg, 973/827-5996), which has received top ratings as the state's number one public course from a number of publications, including *Golfweek;* and **Black Bear** (128 Rte. 23, North Franklin, 973/827-5996), site of the

David Glenz Golf Academy. Other courses are **Minerals, Wild Turkey, Great Gorge,** and **Crystal Springs.** Call 973/827-5996 to schedule a tee time at any of the six courses.

Elements Spa

From Crystal Springs Resort, continue north along Route 94 three miles and turn right into Great Gorge Resort to reach the Elements Spa (2 Chamonix Dr., Vernon, 973/827-5996, www.crystalgolfresort.com), a day spa offering golfer-designed pedicures, and salt body scrubs chased with a tropical-inspired bath. Even the spa's exterior—light green and yellow clapboard interspersed with stone—is soothing.

Accommodations

$200-250: For an overnight visit there's the Great Gorge Resort's **Minerals Hotel** (2 Chamonix Dr., Vernon, 973/827-5996), a 175-room space where rooms range from luxury to presidential suites, and all come decorated in Aspen-style decor. The hotel can get loud in the evening, though you won't see many kids, and beds tend to be on the hard side. Still, one perk is complimentary use of the Minerals Sports Club, where you'll find a running track, whirlpool tubs, and more than a handful of heated pools—if you plan on being active and sticking close to the resort, this is the place to stay.

Food

Crystal Springs has only a small handful of restaurants. The casual **Kites Restaurant** (973/864-5840), located at the Great Gorge Resort, serves casual American fare in an average space that can get somewhat rowdy on the weekends. The restaurant opens for à la carte breakfast 7 A.M.–11 A.M. Monday–Friday, and buffet-style 7 A.M.–11 A.M. weekends. An all-day lunch and dinner menu is featured 11:30 A.M.–9 P.M. Sunday–Thursday, until 10 P.M. Friday and Saturday.

For something more refined try **Latour** (Crystal Springs Country Club Clubhouse, 1 Wild Turkey Way, Hardyston, 973/827-0548, 5–9 P.M. Thurs.–Sat., 3–7 P.M. Sun., closed Mon.–Wed.), a posh and intimate space with

an expansive wine cellar. Here the servers wear white gloves, the men wear jackets, and a three-course internationally inspired American meal, heavy on the French influence, runs $52–70.

Open only during golf season is the Irish **Owen's Pub** (Wheatsworth Rd., Hamburg, 973/827-5996), with an Irish pub setting and Celtic cuisine.

Getting There and Around

It takes about an hour-and-a-half to reach Crystal Springs from New York City, and Vernon's downtown center at the intersection of Routes 94 and 515 is five minutes away from the resort.

HAMBURG, FRANKLIN, AND OGDENSBURG

Travel Route 94 south from Vernon and you'll pass through the borough of Hamburg, known to many as Children's Town because of the now-defunct pink and peach cake-like castle that stands grandly deserted on the east end of town. Continue on and you'll enter Franklin and Ogdensburg, collectively known as "mining country," and home to some of the world's rarest fluorescent rocks. These downtowns aren't much to look at, but the beauty lies in the history, and geology, that can still be explored today.

The Gingerbread Castle and Frank's Castle Grille

Though no longer open to the public, the Gingerbread Castle (www.thegingerbreadcastle.com) remains, a pastel place will all the makings of a giant cupcake, graced with gingerbread men and an arched black cat standing atop one of the swirly domes, and flanked by two stone pillars on either side of the entrance. The castle, a magical world based on the Brothers Grimm fairytales that opened to the public in the 1930s, was the creation of F. H. Bennett. It's really something to see.

Across the street is **Frank's Castle Grille** (50 Gingerbread Castle Rd., 973/827-2303, www.frankscastlegrille.com, $4.95–7.95), a ranch-style American grill and music venue that holds benefits to raise money for the castle's

© LAURA KINIRY

Beaver Hill Campground, Hamburg

restoration. Frank, who owns the grill, is also the castle's owner.

Mining Museums

Iron, zinc, and quarry mines were all prominent in Franklin borough, and fluorescent rocks found nowhere else on earth are plentiful here. Often referred to as the world's "fluorescent minerals capital," Franklin's legacy is well-represented at the **Franklin Mineral Museum** (32 Evans St., 973/827-3481, www .franklinmineralmuseum.com), an unassuming brick building standing alongside an 1879 engine house and tucked along the back streets. This nonprofit museum was created as an aid in public education in the fields of mineralogy, geology, and paleontology, and inside is a cool space staffed by passionate rock geeks who are more than happy to share their knowledge. A display room on the main floor is dedicated to local rocks, and there's a gift shop with books and fluorescent goods—such as polished, magnificently colored rock slices—for sale (one of my favorite items is a bag that'll hold as many

rocks as you can fit for $5, the only catch being the bag must close). A two-story mine replica that is the museum highlight, and tours are given hourly, $6 adult, $4 child. The museum is open 10 A.M.–5 P.M. Saturday and 11 A.M.– 5 P.M. Sunday in March, and 10 A.M.–4 P.M. Monday–Friday, until 5 P.M. Saturday, 11 A.M.– 5 P.M. Sundays, April–November.

Nearby at the **Buckwheat Dump** visitors can dig their own rocks from a variety of rock specimens discarded here by mid-1800s zinc miners. Rock-collecting is $1 per pound, and museum tours and rock-collecting combo tickets are available: $11 adult, $6 child.

Ogdensburg's specialty is sterling zinc mining, and at the **Sterling Hill Mining Museum** (30 Plant St., 973/209-7212, www.sterlinghill.org, $9.50 adult, $7 child) you'll see exhibits of real mining equipment and dynamite casings, and can take a tour into an actual mine that closed in 1986. There is no mistaking your surroundings as you pull into the parking lot—sheer cliffs of slated rock stand 50–75 feet high to your right, and around the grounds are statues of men holding mining picks and explosive guns. The small museum, which opened in 1990, houses the Workman's Lunch Box, filled with picnic tables and a small snack shop, and a gift shop (10 A.M.–3 P.M. daily Apr. 1–Nov. 30) selling fool's gold, petrified wood, and locally mined rocks. You can't go much further without a guide, and tours of the mine are offered once daily at 1 P.M. April 1–November 30, other times by chance or appointment. Regardless of the outside weather, it can get quite cold underground, and warm dress is recommended.

Camping

Spacious **Beaver Hill Campground** (Big Spring Rd., 973/827-0670, 800/229-CAMP or 800/229-2267, May–mid-Nov., $33 water and electric) has plenty of RV and tent sites, though only one facility for restrooms and showers. If you wake up early, this shouldn't be a problem, and the showers make up for the lack of amenities by having some of the warmest water around. The area is quiet scenic and draws a lot of families with small kids, many who like to ride their bicycles all over the campground and stay up late—for the most part this is a loud, fun place.

SPARTA

For a South Jersey native like myself, Sparta is one of those cool little places that you stumble upon and think, "Who knew this was in New Jersey?" In actuality, Sparta is far from small—this nearly 39-square-mile township encompasses 11 private communities, the largest of which surrounds man-made **Lake Mohawk** and was created as a summer resort in the 1920s. From the community's inception there was a mandate that every house must be different, and this included its lakeside downtown known as **White Deer Plaza,** whose unique architecture dubbed "Lake Mohawk Tudor" is a blend of English Cottage, Tudor, and German styles. It's so unique, in fact, that the plaza has earned its place on the State and National Registers of Historic Places because of it. The whole area has a "shore away from shore" feel, even

featuring a small, curvy boardwalk belonging to the **Mohawk Country Club,** a large reception hall with an exterior reminiscent of a medieval castle. Though the walkway is private, you should have little trouble scoring a seat on one of its lakeside benches as long as you're not reckless and wild. Motorboats and water-skiers are common sights during summer months, and while Lake Mohawk offers limited access to the outside visitor, it's still a sight to see.

Tomahawk Lake

From White Deer Plaza, take Stanhope Road for a few miles and turn left onto Tomahawk Trail to reach Tomahawk Lake (Tomahawk Trail, Sparta, 973/398-7777, www.tomahawklake.com). This 20-acre family operated water park and beach is replete with shaded picnic tables as well as waterslides that a sign claims are the "longest in New Jersey." Try out the Rampage Watercoaster, the Apache Plunge speed slide, or the Black Snake enclosed tube slide, or take out one of the bumper, paddle, and rowboats available for rental. For land-lovers there are horseshoes, volleyball, and table tennis, or you can while away the afternoon in the beer garden. The lake is open seasonally, 9:30 A.M.–6 P.M. Monday–Friday June–July, until 5:30 P.M. August–September, 9 A.M.–7 P.M. weekends and holidays. Tomahawk Lake accepts cash only, and admission fees are $8 adult, $7 child on weekdays, $10 adult, $8 child on weekends.

Food and Nightlife

White Deer Plaza has a handful of eateries, including **Krogh's Restaurant and Brew Pub** (23 White Deer Plaza, 973/729-8428, www.kroghs.com, 11:30 A.M.–10 P.M. Mon.–Sat., noon–9 P.M. Sun.), housed in the Plaza's first-ever commercial establishment. Live music is featured on the weekends—a perfect accompaniment to the homemade beers and New American cuisine. The bar stays open until 2 A.M. daily. Across the street, **Casa Mia** (20 White Deer Plaza, 973/729-6606, $3–16.50) fills with locals who come for pepperoni pizza pies and delectable baked ziti slices.

A few hundred yards east of Tomahawk Lake is (**Zoe's by the Lake** (112 Tomahawk Trail, 973/726-7226, www.zoesbythelake.com, $23–31), a classy restaurant with bright walls and large windows, situated on the bank of Seneca Lake and serving a selected menu of country French cuisine and exceptional desserts (go for the warm upside-down chocolate soufflé). The restaurant offers a three-course dinner ($29) with a weekly changing menu Tuesday–Thursday, and Sunday brunch is offered once monthly. Lunch hours are noon–2 P.M. Tuesday–Friday. Dinner is served 5–9 P.M. Tuesday–Thursday, until 10 P.M. Friday and Saturday, 4–8 P.M. Sunday.

ALLAMUCHY MOUNTAIN STATE PARK

The 8,461-acre Allamuchy Mountain State Park (800 Willow Grove St., Hackettstown, 908/852-3790, free) is a haven for anglers and hikers, filled with ponds, lakes, and a portion of the Musconetcong River, as well as numerous marked and unmarked multiuse trails. The park contains the Allamuchy Natural Area, a nearly 2,500-acre reserve made up of a variety of fields maintained to show the progression of hardwood forests. This is where you'll find many of the park's marked trails (approximately 14 miles of them). Some of these trails travel around Deer Park Pond. Hunting is permitted within park boundaries, and boats can be taken out on **Cranberry Lake** where during summer months a concession stand rents rowboats daily. Canoes, kayaks, and rowboats can also launch by the lake and follow a three-mile water trail along the Musconetcong, ending at the Saxton Falls Dam. Allamuchy is also home to Waterloo Village, one of the last remaining features of New Jersey's Morris Canal.

Waterloo Historic Village

Waterloo Village (525 Waterloo Rd., 973/347-0900, www.waterloovillage.org, $9 adult, $7 child) was an active inland port along the Morris Canal during the late 19th and early 20th centuries, and is today a restored town where costumed guides re-create life during the canal's

working days. Situated upon Waterloo Lake—which leads into the Musconetcong River—the village includes an operating gristmill and blacksmith shop, a Lenape Indian village, and the **Rutan Farm,** an 1825 farmhouse with livestock. Canal-related artifacts, photos, and a short video are on display in the village museum, and classes and events, including knitting workshops and a summer beer festival, take place throughout the year. Waterloo is open 11 A.M.–5 P.M. weekends mid-May–October, as well as 11 A.M.–4 P.M. Wednesday–Thursday throughout July and August.

Hiking

Trails include a three-mile portion of the Sussex Branch Trail, a 20-mile trail whose bulk is within nearby Kittatinny Valley State Park. The trail begins at Waterloo Road and continues on to Branchville. Ten miles of the **Highland Trail,** a still-in-development combination of new and established trails and roads that when finished will connect New York's Storm King Mountain to the Delaware River's Phillipsburg, run from the northern tip of the park through to Stephens State Park, and is one of the park's more difficult trails.

Fishing

The Musconetcong River runs through the park and offers some of New Jersey's best trout fishing. The park provides year-round ops and the river is stocked with brown, rainbow, and brook trout. Other bodies of water available for in-park fishing include Cranberry Lake and Deer Park Pond, where you'll find warm species like largemouth bass, sunfish, and pickerel.

Camping

Camping is available at nearby 805-acre **Stephens State Park** (800 Willow Grove St., Hackettstown, 908/852-3790), with 40 primitive sites for tents and pop-up trailers ($20/night Apr.–Oct.). Situated east of Allamuchy State Park, Stephens State Park is located 7.5 miles south of Route 206 along Waterloo Road (Route 604), which eventually turns into Willow Grove Street.

KITTATINNY VALLEY STATE PARK

The 3,348-acre Kittatinny Valley State Park (4 Lake Aeroflex Rd., Newton, 973/786-6445, www.state.nj.us/dep/parksandforests/parks/kittval.html, dawn–dusk, free) is an excellent spot for outdoor enthusiasts, with 8 miles of mountain bike trails, and a portion of the wooded **Paulinskill Valley Trail** showcasing 27 miles for hiking, biking, and horseback riding. You can also try the 20-mile **Sussex Branch Trail,** used for hiking, horseback riding, biking, cross-country skiing, and dog sledding, that continues on southward through Allamuchy Mountain State Park (and north through to Branchville). Both the Paulinskill Valley Trail and the Sussex Branch Trail are former railroad tracks. The park also includes the 119-acre **Lake Aeroflex** and the **Aeroflex-Andover Airport** (973/786-5100), used by the New Jersey fire service. This relatively small park is a favorite for mountain bikers, hikers, anglers, and hunters.

STANHOPE, NEWTON, AND NETCONG
Wild West City

Wild West City (Rte. 206 N., Netcong, 973/347-8900, www.wildwestcity.com, $11.50 adult, $11 child) is a "city running wild," according to its theme song—and that claim is hard to dispute. This family-owned makeshift western town, inspired by 1880s Dodge City, Kansas, has been shootin' 'em up and roundin' up doggies since 1956. It may sound out of date, but the City strives to be PC by offering firearm-free programs to school and church groups with advance notice. Either way you're in for a hootin' and hollerin' time, with 22 live-action shows scheduled along Main Street throughout the day, always a bit different. You may see dancing Can Can girls, a Big Bang Hold-Up, or a good ol' fashioned gun fight at the O.K. Corral, though a definite highlight is the "interactive stagecoach hold-up." Live western music is performed throughout the day.

With plenty of extra on-site activities at additional costs, including a train ride, miniature golf, and a candy store, prices can add up. The City is open 10:30 A.M.–6 P.M. daily mid-June–early September, 10:30 A.M.–6 P.M. weekends early September–Columbus Day.

Accommodations

$100-150: The **Wooden Duck Inn** (140 Goodale Rd., Newton, 973/300-0395, www.woodenduckinn.com) is a two-story country and carriage house located on 10 acres. This bed-and-breakfast includes 10 guestrooms that are clean, spacious, and modernly equipped with high-speed Internet, TV, air-conditioning, telephone, and private bath. The inn is located in Newton, just north of Kittatinny State Park. There's an in-ground pool, and a classic game room and snug fireplace for all to enjoy. Full country breakfast is served daily.

Situated along a downtown street in the quiet town of Stanhope is the **Whistling Swan Bed & Breakfast** (110 Main St., Stanhope, 973/347-6369, www.whistlingswaninn.com), a three-story Victorian B&B offering bright guestrooms, 24-hour soft drinks and sherry, wireless Internet, and a gourmet breakfast selection that includes orange marmalade French toast. The inn is centrally located between Allamuchy State Park and Wild West City, though a large wraparound porch decked with comfy chairs and a couple of hammocks may inspire you to never leave the property.

Camping

Panther Lake Camping Resort (6 Panther Lake Rd., Andover, 973/347-4440, 800/543-2056, Apr.–Oct.) features 435 tent and RV sites, a 45-acre lake open for fishing, swimming, and boating (paddle boats available for rent), and a small beach. Additional highlights include shuffleboard and a heated pool, though hot showers have an additional fee. All sites feature water and electric and run $32/night for two people.

With 250 sites available for tents and RVs, the seasonal **Green Valley Beach Campground** (68 Phillips Rd., Newton, 973/383-4026, May–mid-Oct.) is a nice overnight option for exploring the Highlands and nearby lower

Ridge and Valley Region. The grounds include a huge heated pool and a private lake for fishing and boating (paddle boat rentals available). Fee is $30/night for a site with water and electric.

Food

On Route 206 heading toward Wild West City is **Black Forest Inn** (249 Rte. 206, Stanhope, 973/347-3344, $17–26). Lunch is served 11:30 A.M.–2 P.M. Monday–Friday, and dinner 5–10 P.M. Monday–Saturday, 1–9 P.M. Sunday, closed all day Tuesday. It's a multi-room space for fine dining, as well as a casual pub. Cuisine is "light" German and the atmosphere is heavy and dark, with brick and carved wood walls, white tablecloths, and maroon seats.

Ridge and Valley Region

THE SKYLANDS

The Kittatinny Mountains line New Jersey's northwest corner, isolating sprawling valleys and giving way to one of the state's most prominent features—the Delaware Water Gap. The entire region is a haven for outdoor enthusiasts, with opportunities for hiking (including a portion of the Appalachian Trail), cross-country skiing, fly-fishing, canoeing and kayaking, and camping. Dining and indoor overnight options are limited, though they do exist, but for greater options visitors may also want to explore the nearby Highlands region.

AUGUSTA

Part of the larger Franklin Township, Augusta is home to Culver's Gap—the only opening through the Kittatinny Mountains for 30 miles. Within the area are a few notable shopping and entertainment venues.

Olde Lafayette Village

East of Augusta is Olde Lafayette Village (75 State Rte. 15, 973/383-8323, www.lafayette villageshops.com), a quaint planned village of factory outlets, antique stores, cafés, candy shops, and even a yoga studio. The village is a bit nicer than the outlet centers in Flemington, but it's not really a high quality selection. Look for **Lafayette Clayworks** (22 Wantage Ave., 973/948-3987, www.lafayetteclayworks.com), which showcases pottery and offers classes in wheel-throwing. The antique shops include

Craftsmans Antiques, Country Floors and Antiques, and clothing stores feature Bass, Geoffrey Beene, Uptown Girl, and Maidenform. The central restaurant is the **Lafayette House** (973/579-3100, www.thelafayettehouse.com), serving standard American fare and drinks in a convenient, if not touristy, setting. The Lafayette House is also a tavern and banquet hall.

Entertainment and Events

Head out to a ballgame at **Skylands Park** (94 Championship Pl., 973/579-7500, www .njcards.com, $5–10), a 4,258-seat minor league stadium built in 1994 upon former cropland, and home to the New Jersey Cardinals, a class-A affiliate of the St. Louis Cardinals. The team's mascots are both a live "rally cow" and a plush cardinal named Claudia.

A couple of big-name events take place annually at the **Sussex County Fairgrounds** (37 Plains Rd., Augusta), including the June **Michael Arnone's Crawfish Festival** (www.crawfishfest.com, $25 advance, $30 gate, under 14 free with parent), a three-day fest that's good ol' Louisiana fun, with camping sites and plenty of po-boy sandwiches and swamp tunes. Known for many years as the Sussex County Horse and Farm Show, the **New Jersey State Fair** (www.newjerseystatefair.org) features rides, crafts, food, horse shows, a livestock competition, and plenty of scheduled events and exhibits.

SPACE FARMS
ZOO & MUSEUM

The quirky Space Farms Zoo & Museum (Rte. 519, Beemerville, 973/875-5800, www.spacefarms.com, 9 A.M.–5 P.M. daily May 1–Oct. 31, $11 adult, $6.50 child) was begun by the Space family in the late 1920s as a small store and wildlife center, and has since grown to 100 acres. It's an odd museum and zoo of sorts where you'll find an assortment of exhibits and animals, including antique cars, rifles, a miniature circus, snake den, and hyena, leopards, lemurs, jaguars, lemurs, llamas, and "retired circus bears." The farm's most celebrated resident was a 2,000-pound, 12-foot-tall Alaskan Kodiak bear named Goliath who lived on the complex from 1967 to 1991, and whose stuffed upright figure remains on display. An August Teddy Bear Day is held annually in his honor.

◖ HIGH POINT STATE PARK

High Point State Park (1480 Rte. 23, Sussex, 973/875-4800, www.state.nj.us/dep/parksand-forests/parks/highpoint.html, $5 weekdays, $10 weekends, Memorial Day–Labor Day) is seven miles north of Sussex borough, along the crest of the Kittatinny Mountains in Sussex County and due south of the New York State line. This 15,654-acre park is home to New Jersey's highest point, as well as an 18-mile portion of the Appalachian Trail that leads south into Stokes National Forest. It's a great all-season park, in the summer offering opportunity for mountain biking, horseback riding, swimming, hiking, and fishing (lakes are stocked with largemouth bass and trout), and during winter months cross-country skiing, ice fishing, dogsledding, and snowshoeing. It's actually considered one of New Jersey's prime ski resorts, using artificial snow to cover trails and housing the **High Point Cross Country Ski Center,** where snowshoes, cross-country skis, and other winter sports equipment are available for rent.

The park has three natural areas, including the 1,500-acre **Dryden Kuser Natural Area,** named for the park's land donors and containing what is thought to be the highest Atlantic white cedar swamp in the world.

© LAURA KINIRY

High Point Monument at High Point State Park

High Point Monument

High Point State Park is the site of New Jersey's highest elevation, rising 1,803 feet above sea level. Atop this peak stands 220-foot **High Point Monument,** a 1930s structure that was built as a memorial to war veterans and calls to mind a smaller Washington Monument. Visitors can climb to its top (9 A.M.–4:30 P.M. daily Memorial Day–Labor Day, noon–4 P.M. weekends the rest of the year,) for an exceptional view of the surrounding region, including New Jersey's Wallkill Valley, Pennsylvania's Pocono Mountains, and New York's Catskill Mountains. Nearby is a snack stand selling ice cream, hot dogs, soda, and water.

Sports and Recreation
SUMMER RECREATION

High Point's spring-fed, 20-acre **Lake Marcia** is open for swimming during summer months. Lifeguards are on duty, and there's a snack bar and bathhouse nearby. The lake is also open to fishers, along with the park's Sawmill and Steenykill Lakes, and the catch between the three includes trout, bass, and catfish.

High Point hosts more than 50 miles of multiuse trails also intended for hiking, mountain biking, and horseback riding. These trails vary in length 0.5–18 miles and include a portion of the Appalachian Trail. Most are well marked with colored blazes. If you're a casual hiker, one to try is the 1.5-mile **Cedar Swamp Trail,** an easy loop trail that lies within the park's Dryden Kuser National Area to the north. For autos, the park has a "scenic drive" that begins near Lake Marcia—it's a short one-way route with plenty of rocks on view, but nothing too exciting.

SKYDIVE SUSSEX

For views unattainable on New Jersey's highest point, try Skydive Sussex (53 Rte. 639, Sussex, 973/702-7000, www.skydivesussex.com). Trips begin at the Sussex Airport, and cost $175 for the first tandem jump.

WINTER SPORTS

High Point State Park (www.xcskihighpoint.com) has 9.3 miles of groomed cross-country ski trails,

as well as a 5-mile trail for snowshoeing. Skis ($20 adult, $18 child weekend full-day; $17 adult, $15 child weekend half-day) and snowshoes ($17 adult, $15 child weekend full-day, $15 adult, $13 child weekend half-day) can both be rented at the park's **High Point Cross Country Ski Center** (973/702-1222, 9 A.M.–4 P.M. Mon.–Fri., 8 A.M.–4 P.M. weekends mid-Nov.–Apr.). Trail passes are required and run $16 adult, $14 child for a full weekend day, and $12 adult, $10 child for a weekend half-day. The ski center hosts group lessons for cross-country skiers 10 A.M.–2 P.M. daily.

High Point's **Center at Lake Marcia** sells hot soup and comfort meals, and features a fireplace for guests to relax by after a hard day on the trails.

Accommodations

$200-250: About a half-hour drive from High Point State Park on the Pennsylvania side of the Delaware River is the **Cliff Park Inn** (155 Cliff Park Rd., Milford, PA, 570/296-6491 or 800/225-6535, www.cliffparkinn.com), where you'll find 14 well-appointed rooms in a variety of sizes, all with wireless Internet, TV, DVD, down bedding, and complimentary breakfast. The inn has its own nine-hole golf course as well as numerous nature trails and an on-site dining facility.

Additional overnight options in the vicinity of High Point State Park can be found in Vernon Township, about a 30–40 minute drive east.

Camping

There are 50 tent sites, each with fire ring and picnic table, situated along 20-acre Sawmill Lake. They're available April–late October, and flush toilets are nearby. High Point also hosts two family cabins and a group cabin, all with running water, full bathroom, and a full kitchen, available mid-May–mid-October. The family cabins can accommodate six, the group cabin up to 28. Tent sites are $20/night, cabins are $65/night, and the group cabin is $155/night, with a two-night minimum. For reservations, contact the park office at 973/875-4800.

Food

In nearby Sussex, stop by the **The Holland American Bakery** (246 Rte. 23, Sussex, 888/ 401-9515, 6 A.M.–6 P.M. Tues.–Sat., until 9 P.M. Friday) for tasty *speculaas* (traditional Dutch biscuits) and almond tarts—just keep your eyes peeled for the miniature windmill on the front lawn.

For breakfast try the **Sussex Queen Diner** (289 Rte. 23, Sussex, 973/702-7321, $5–16), a brick and stucco landmark that gets packed on weekends.

Information and Services

Right before the park entry there's parking for the Appalachian Trail. A visitors center (Route 23) is open 9 A.M.–4 P.M. daily.

STOKES STATE FOREST

South of High Point is 15,996-acre Stokes State Forest (1 Coursen Rd., Branchville, 973/948-3820, www.state.nj.us/dep/parksandforests/parks/stokes.html). Known for its scenic mountain views and natural area, it contains an attractive stretch of the Appalachian Trail. Rugged terrain makes the forest a good spot for mountain biking, but it's just as popular for hiking, fishing, and a plethora of winter sports. Stokes features the 525-acre **Tillman Ravine Natural Area,** home to a number of endangered species, including the cream and brownish-gray colored barred owl. Admission to the forest is $5 weekdays, $10 weekends, Memorial Day–Labor Day.

To get here, take Route 206 four miles north from Branchville.

Camping

Stokes State Forest has 77 sites suitable for tents or trailers, all with picnic table and fire ring ($20/night), and a few sites are available year-round. You'll also find seasonal group sites, 10 lean-tos with similar amenities ($30/ night), and seven lakeside cabins ($45/night) with electricity, kitchen, a working fireplace, half-bath, and beds for four people. There are two additional cabins ($85/night) that sleep eight and include shower facilities, and another sleeps 12 and has two full baths ($125/night).

All the cabins are available April–November. To reserve a campsite or cabin, call the park office at 973/948-3820.

◖ DELAWARE WATER GAP NATIONAL RECREATION AREA

Encompassing 70,000 acres and 37 riverfront miles, the Delaware Water Gap National Recreation Area (570/588-2452, www.nps .gov/dewa) is a sight to behold—an expanse of greenery and river that's easily one of the most breathtaking spots in the Mid-Atlantic region of the country. Culminating to the south at a 1,400-foot-deep, 900-foot-wide gap that cuts between New Jersey's 1,527-foot Mount Tammany and Pennsylvania's 1,463-foot Mount Minsky, this is a mountainous haven idyllic for backpackers, hikers, cyclists, nature lovers, and wildlife enthusiasts, filled with brooks, streams, and a curving blue river enjoyed by canoeists, kayakers, snorkelers, divers, and fishers.

Though it's on the recreation area's Pennsylvania side that you'll find the bulk of hiking trails, as well as a designated cycling trail, the Jersey side offers its own array of natural trails, driving excursions, hikes, and cycling opportunities, as well as the chance for numerous wildlife sightings including white-tailed deer, red fox, gray squirrels, bats and flying squirrels, black bear, groundhog, beaver, and otter.

Sights

Located along Route 615 is the **Peters Valley Craft Education Center** (19 Kuhn Rd., Layton, 973/948-5200, www.pvcrafts.org), a small village-style campus offering summer workshops in numerous disciplines, including fiber arts, metal working, and photography. The center hosts an annual craft fair the last weekend in September at the Sussex County Fairgrounds in Augusta, and has a retail store and gallery highlighting the works of both local and countrywide artists, open 11 A.M.–5 P.M. Thursday–Tuesday.

Situated on the southern stretch of Old Mine Road is **Millbrook Village** (908/841-

9531, www.millbrooknj.com, 9 A.M.–5 P.M. weekends), a 19th-century re-created farming community filled with old wood structures that could use a little TLC. Spangenberg Cabin serves as the village information center, though it's only open on summer weekends, and while interpreters are on hand in custom dress to demonstrate skills of the era, this is not one of New Jersey's better living-history museums. Still, there are more than two dozen buildings of historic significance that some may find fascinating, and a number of short hiking trails can be accessed in the vicinity.

Sports and Recreation

One of New Jersey's best spots for fly-fishing is **Big Flat Brook,** which runs through the Water Gap beginning in the north to the east of Layton, outside the boundaries of the recreation area, and flowing downstream through the Walpack Valley and into Flatbrookville, where it joins with the Delaware River. A fly-fishing-only area runs from the Route 206 bridge east of Layton south for about four miles, outside of the recreation area, but the river can also be accessed from points along Route 615, within Water Gap boundaries. The Delaware Water Gap offers opportunities for both cold- and warm-water fishing.

The Appalachian Trail runs from Pennsylvania through the southern portion of the recreation area, crossing the Delaware at the Kittatinny Point Visitor Center and continuing north into Worthington State Forest, along the western side of the Kittatinny Mountain Range. Camping facilities located along the trail within the recreation area are limited to through-hikers who are planning to travel two or more days. Around Millbrook Village are numerous trails that provide access to the Appalachian, including the steep **Coppermine Trail,** which begins on Old Mine Road across from the Coppermine Parking Area and continues for nearly two miles before reaching the trail at Camp Road. An easier access route is the White-Blaze Trail from the parking lot on Route 602, a mile south of Millbrook Village. This trail is one mile long and climbs 300 feet to a fire lookout. Another good spot for hiking is the area around **Blue**

Mountain Lakes (Flatbrook–Stillwater Rd.), 2.5 miles north of Millbrook Village. Parking is available along Route 627.

With its rolling terrain, heavy woods, and limited traffic, Old Mine Road is a wonderful route and a quiet reprieve for cyclists, especially the long expanse of roadway between Millbrook Village to the south and Route 206 to the north, with sights that include the Walpack Inn (see Food below) and Peters Valley Craft Education Center.

In addition to fishing, other water-based activities in the Water Gap region include snorkeling and diving, both permitted along the Delaware. Law requires that you don't come within 50 feet of a boat or canoe launch. According to the Water Gap's website, the Point of Gap (the actual water gap), on the southern end of the park, is a preferred diving area. Canoes and kayaks are allowed on the river, and there's a boat launch near Kittatinny Point in the recreation area's southern section. **Kittatinny Canoes** (102 Kittatinny Ct., Dingmans Ferry, PA, 800/FLOAT-KC or 800/356-2852) runs canoe and kayak trips down the Delaware from seven locations within the upper tri-state region, including **River Beach Campsites** (378 Rtes. 6 and 209) in Milford, Pennsylvania, 3.5 miles over the bridge from Montague on the northern tip of the recreation area.

Camping

Situated along Old Mine Road within the southern portion of the recreation area is **Worthington State Forest** (908/841-9575), home to about 70 campsites ($20/night, Apr.–Dec.) with access to flush toilets and showers.

The Water Gap hosts a number of Appalachian through-way campsites, as well as river sites for those exploring the region by kayak or canoe. For a list of sites currently open, check the website (www.nps.gov/dewa) or call park headquarters at 570/588-2452.

Situated near the northern tip of the Delaware Water Gap National Recreation Area, the year-round **Cedar Ridge Family Campground** (205 River Rd., Montague, 973/293-3512, 800/813-8639, wwww.cedarridgecampground.com) features a swimming pool and its own lake for fishing and boating (paddle boat rentals available), and hosts scheduled activities according to season. The campground is a popular stop for Appalachian Trail through-hikers, and is located five minutes from I-84. A tent or RV site with water and electric runs $25/night.

Food

For a true backcountry dining experience you can't beat the **Walpack Inn** (Rte. 615, Walpack Center, 973/948-3890, www .walpackinn.com, $19–40), a large country restaurant that seemingly appears out of nowhere along Route 615. Cuisine is full-on American, with a brief children's menu and a limited selection of meat, chicken, and seafood, and decor is decidedly rustic, with walls graced by mounted deer head and a Native American wall painting. Eighteenth-century tools hang in the inn's entryway, and a greenhouse dining area provides extensive views of the Walpack Valley, and, quite often, deer grazing in the field. A pig roast takes place 6–8 P.M. Friday evenings. The inn is open weekends only, 5–10 P.M. Friday and Saturday, 3–8 P.M. Sunday all year long, and the bar opens one hour earlier.

Information and Services

The **New Jersey Ranger Station** (973/948-7761) is located within Walpack Valley along Old Mine Road. New Jersey's **Kittatinny Point Visitors Center** is indefinitely closed due to flood damage, though the recreation area has a second visitors center (9 A.M.–5 P.M. weekends and holidays) located further north on the Pennsylvania side, across Dingmans Ferry Bridge and off Route 209 along Johnny Bee Road. The bridge is a privately owned structure that costs $0.75 to cross; you pay an older gentleman standing between oncoming lanes. Public restrooms are available on the Pennsylvania side.

Getting There and Around

The Delaware Water Gap National Recreation Area is accessible by following River Road/Old Mine Road north from I-80, or taking Millbrook Road from Blairstown. In the north, Route 206 connects with Delaware Mine Road, which becomes Old Mine Road further south.

BLAIRSTOWN

East of the lower Delaware Water Gap is Blairstown, a small rural mountainside town that served as the shooting locale for the original *Friday the 13th*. Rectangular buildings, many with tall columns and second-floor covered porches, line the picturesque Main Street, and serve as home to various shops and eateries. The sidewalks have retained their original brick, and a tunnel carved through an old stone mill stands at the foot of a neighborhood park, picture-perfect with a waterfall and towering steel footbridge.

Sports and Recreation

Mill Brook Road out of Blairstown is a good cycling road because it's a wide road with plenty of shoulder space, light on traffic, and there are things to see. It is a constant climb north of Blairstown but the road will eventually take you down into the Delaware Water Gap National Recreation Area.

To the northwest of Blairstown's downtown center is the **Mohican Outdoor Center** (50 Camp Rd., 908/362-5670, www.mohican outdoorcenter.com), the southernmost branch of the Appalachian Mountain Club and a good base for exploring the Delaware Water Gap National Recreation Area. You can access a number of shorter hikes from here in addition to the Appalachian Trail (0.25 mile away). The center offers guided nature hikes and weekend skill courses, including rock climbing and whitewater kayaking, as well as opportunities for swimming, canoeing, and cross-country skiing.

Blairstown's **Double D Guest Ranch** (81 Mt. Herman Rd., 908/459-9044, www.doubled guestranch.com) claims to offer the most horseback riding trails in New Jersey. Two-hour guided rides tackle a portion of the Paulinskill Trail, and cost $60. The ranch is open 9 A.M.–6 P.M. daily spring and summer, and

9 A.M.–4 P.M. daily fall and winter, closed on Mondays year-round.

Food

If you're looking for an inexpensive and satisfying meal, try the **Forge Restaurant** (Hwy. 94, 908/362-5858, $4.95–14.95) just outside of town. It comes locally recommended, and I ate the largest, juiciest barbecued chicken sandwich I've ever had in my life here, complete with thick steak fries, for $4.95. The restaurant is virtually empty at midday, and the food is nothing fancy, but man—is it good.

HOPE

Part of the much larger area of Hope Township, Hope Village was founded by the Moravians, a religious sect of Bohemian Protestants who stayed on the land for 39 years, from 1769 to 1808, deserting after smallpox killed off many of the inhabitants. Like South Jersey's Burlington City, Hope was one of America's first planned communities, and today many of its 16 original buildings remain in their authentic state or have been restored, including a gristmill that was built in 1769 and now operates as a restaurant and inn. The tiny downtown is only a few blocks, filled by limestone colonials with steeply pitched roofs and dual brick fireplaces, and houses a handful of antique stores, though the village is far from being a consumer hotspot. At the bottom of the main street's hill is **Trout Alley,** known to the Moravians as "Locust Alley," a historic trail that makes for a pleasant stroll, and on the opposite side of town is the **Moravian Cemetery,** where you'll find a small plot dedicated to original Moravian settlers.

Historic Sights

For a better sense of Moravian history visit the **Hope Historical Society Museum** (Rte. 519, 908/459-4268, 11 A.M.–1 P.M. Sat., June–Oct.), housed within an aged cottage thought to have been the home of a bridge toll collector. The society provides a free self-guided map of Hope's Moravian structures.

Ninety-minute walking tours of Hope Village, which is on both the New Jersey and National Register of Historic Places, are given by **Help Our Preservation Effort,** or H.O.P.E. (908/459-9177), beginning along Route 519—the village's main thoroughfare—in front of the Inn at Millrace Pond. Tours take place at 10 A.M. on the first and second Saturdays of the month, June–October, and cost $8.

Land of Make Believe

A mile from Hope's village center is the Land of Make Believe (354 Great Meadows Rd., Rte. 611, 908/459-9000, www.lomb.com, $16.50 adult, $18.50 child), a children's wonderland that's home to an **Enchanted Christmas Village** and a water park containing the "largest wading pool in the U.S." and numerous waterslides. This is the type of place that kids love, and parents can have fun, too. Ride the carousel, visit the petting zoo, hide from the talking scarecrow, or dress in costume at the **Middle Earth Theater** and become a play participant. The Land of Make Believe is one of those rare finds where parents get a cheaper deal. Hours are 10 A.M.–6 P.M. weekends in June, daily late June–Labor Day.

Lakota Wolf Preserve

On the grounds of the Camp Taylor Campground, west of Hope and along the Delaware River, lies the Lakota Wolf Preserve (89 Mt. Pleasant Rd., Columbia, 908/496-9244 or 800/SEE-WOLF, www.lakotawolf.com, $15 adult, $7 child), an outdoor setting where visitors are provided the opportunity to witness wolves in their natural habitat. From the preserve's entrance, it's a 0.5-mile walk to the observation deck (bus transport is also available), which stands between the roaming areas of four wolf packs, including arctic, tundra, and timber wolves. Visitors may also catch glimpses of resident bobcats and foxes.

The preserve is a favorite spot among wildlife photographers, who can book either a half-day ($300) or whole-day ($500) shoot. Regular viewing hours take place 10:30 A.M.–3 P.M. Tuesday–Sunday fall and winter, and 10:30 A.M.–4 P.M. Tuesday–Sunday spring and summer, closed

THE SKYLANDS

Monday year-round. The preserve is cash only, and reservations are required weekdays, although walk-ins are allowed on weekends.

Accommodations

$150-200: The ◖ **Inn at Millrace Pond** (313 Johnsonburg Rd., 908/459-4884, www .innatmillracepond.com) operated in the 1770s as a gristmill, and still contains its original waterwheel. Inside is an upscale eatery ($25–30) serving American-continental cuisine by candlelight, and featuring a full wine menu and a basement tavern with a huge walk-in fireplace. The restaurant is open 6–8 P.M. Monday–Thursday, 5–9 P.M. Friday and Saturday, 4–7:30 P.M. Sunday.

In addition to the restaurant, the inn has 17 guestrooms spread between three buildings—the grist mill, the Millrace House, and a two-room wheelwright's cottage. All rooms have a colonial theme and feature wood floors and space rugs, and many are decorated with white walls and linens that contrast beautifully with the dark wood of the furniture and ceiling beams. Each room has private bath, and some are equipped with TV.

Camping

Located on a working farm, **Triple Brook Family Camping Resort** (58 Honey Run Rd., 908/459-4079, www.triplebrook.com, Apr.–Oct.) features 200 open and shaded sites suited for tents and RVs. The resort is an ideal jumping-off point for exploring Hope and nearby Blairstown, and the southern portion of the Delaware Water Gap. Amenities include Olympic-size pool, adults-only lounge, camp store, shuffleboard, and horseshoes. Basic sites run $30/night for two people, $35/night with water, electric, and sewer.

Four-hundred-acre **Camp Taylor Campground** (85 Mount Pleasant Rd., Columbia, 908/496-4333, 800/545-9662, www.camp taylor.com, mid-Apr.–late Oct.) features tent sites and seasonal RV sites, as well as a few cabins ($60/night two adults) and RVs ($90/night two adults) available for rent. Many sites are wooded and the grounds feature numerous

hiking trails, in addition to being home to the Lakota Wolf Preserve. Hot showers are available for an additional fee. A basic tent site costs $21/night, $27/night with water and electric.

Food

For casual dining try the **Village Cafe** (1 Millbrook Rd., 908/459-4860, 11 A.M.–9 P.M. Mon.–Fri., 8 A.M.–9 P.M. weekends, $12–17), a white clapboard converted home with low ceilings—it has the feel of dining in someone's tea room. Outside there's seating among manicured gardens. Breakfast is served on the weekends, 8–11:30 A.M.—two eggs, home fries, and toast go for $3.95.

Getting There and Around

Hope is 15 miles west of the Delaware Water Gap, situated along Route 521 at the junction of Route 519, just a few minutes south of I-80, which travels east from the Gateway Region. If arriving from Blairstown, take Route 521 south for 6.5 miles—this will bring you to the center of town.

JENNY JUMP STATE FOREST

Just outside Hope Village is Jenny Jump State Forest (330 State Park Rd., 908/459-4366, www.state.nj.us/dep/parksandforests/parks/jennyjump.html, free), 4,244 acres of mountainous, wooded terrain marked with ancient moraines resulting from moving glaciers and noted for its inspiring views. The forest is home to a number of black bears and is a popular hiking, camping, hunting, and mountain biking locale. Fishers can choose from the trout-stocked waters of Mountain Lake or Ghost Lake's plentiful supply of sunfish, catfish, and bass.

Greenwood Observatory

Located within Jenny Jump State Forest is Greenwood Observatory (908/459-4366), home to the United Astronomy Clubs of New Jersey (www.uacnj.org). The venue has a retractable roof and a 16-inch Newton telescope, and hosts free summer stargazing on Saturday evenings April–October, beginning with an astronomy presentation at 8 P.M.

Recreation

Jenny Jump hosts six miles of hiking-only trails, and three additional miles of multiuse trails. The 1.5-mile **Summit Trail** climbs upward for awesome views, joining the 1.3-mile **Ghost Lake Trail,** which carries hikers on a descending path to Ghost Lake. At 3.7 miles, the **Mountain Lake Trail** is the park's longest, forming two loops through heavy woodlands. It's also open to mountain bikers.

Camping

There are a number of public campsites within the forest, including 22 sites equipped for tents and trailers ($20/night, Apr.–Oct.). Showers and toilets, though not in pristine condition, are located nearby. The forest also hosts two group sites ($1/night per person, Apr.–Oct.), and eight mountain-top shelters ($10/night per person, year-round) with four bunks each. For reservations, call the park office at 908/459-4366.

BLACK BEAR AMOK IN NEW JERSEY

It seems odd that the country's most densely populated state is also home to a thriving black bear population – but it's true. The number of black bears in New Jersey is estimated to be somewhere between 1,600-3,400 with more than half residing in the state's northwest corner of Sussex, Warren, Passaic, and Morris Counties. Since 1980, their once-dwindling numbers have increased dramatically, fueled by the restoration of forest habitat, their increasing comfort with humans, and many argue, a lack of sufficient population control. This increase has created tension between local and state authorities, as well as among New Jersey residents.

In the last few years, black bears have been spotted in all of the state's 21 counties, and reports of human-related incidents have become more common. Most reports are generally minor and include bears rifling through trash, stealing food, and occasionally harassing farm animals. But they've also gone so far as to kill house pets, and in October 2004, one even attacked two Boy Scouts outside Blairstown. The state's bear situation has become so notable, in fact, that it was included as a storyline in season five of HBO's Jersey-based mob drama The Sopranos.

Cited as a response to an increase in black bear numbers, encounters, and their expanding territory, New Jersey's Department of Environmental Protection allowed the state's first black bear hunt in 33 years in 2003, amid

vibrant opposition from environmental groups and animal rights activists who promote viable methods of population control, including increasing public education and awareness, possible relocation, and the use of contraception to stabilize bear numbers. The six-day hunt resulted in the issuing of 5,000 permits and the killing of 328 bears.

The New Jersey Fish and Wildlife Division's proposed 2004 bear hunt was successfully blocked by Department of Environmental Protection Commissioner Bradley M. Campbell, who declared it an unnecessary means of population stabilization. The state's Supreme Court sided with Campbell, ruling that a bear hunt could only be reinstated if and when New Jersey's bear policy was brought up to date. As of 2005, a new five-year plan has been proposed and includes dividing the state into six bear-hunting zones with permits issued in correlation to the zone's bear population, establishing a seven-day hunting season set to expand to nine days in forthcoming years, permitting farmers to shoot bears that have attacked their livestock, and capturing and killing bears who wander into "bear exclusion zones," especially those regions close to New York City and Philadelphia, as well as the entire Jersey Shore.

Although the 2005 bear hunt was permitted, the inevitable controversy surrounding the animals continues to rage, and the future of the bears remains uncertain.

Morristown and Vicinity

Morristown is one of New Jersey's most historic cities, site of two winter encampments by George Washington, and though no Revolutionary battles were fought here, the American army, led by Washington, was able to survey the Brits across the Hudson in New York City from this vantage point. The town is less than three square miles, but its downtown gives the impression of an endless stretch. Along South Street lies a nice mix of independent shops, restaurants, and chain retailers, most housed in colonial brick buildings, also home to apartment rentals. The seat of Morris County, Morristown's courthouse is an old Williams-style building—two-story brick with a white bell tower—and, similar to New Brunswick, its downtown "high rises" hover around 10 stories. Perhaps the downtown's best-known attribute, the Morristown Green is a 2.5-acre town square filled with benches, walkways,

and a central fountain. On Thursday evenings throughout the summer, movies play here.

MORRISTOWN NATIONAL HISTORIC PARK

America's first national historic park is here in Morristown, the site where General George Washington and his troops spent two long winters during the Revolutionary War, 1777–1778 and 1779–1780. The park encompasses four distinct areas, including Ford Mansion and Jockey Hollow, and is scattered throughout the town.

Washington's Headquarters Museum and Ford Mansion

North of Morristown's downtown center are the Washington's Headquarters Museum and Ford Mansion, the General's Revolutionary headquarters during the brutal winter of 1779–1780. Washington was allowed use of the Ford

Washington statue in front of Ford Mansion, Morristown

© LAURA KINIRY

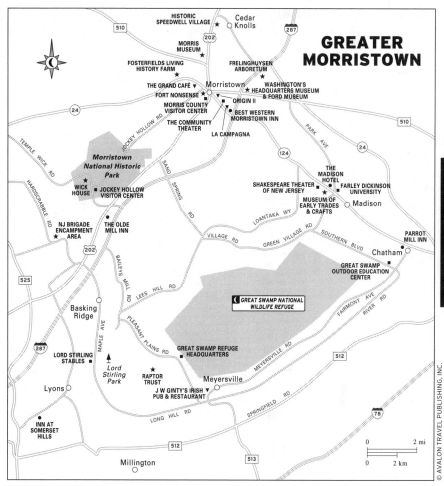

GREATER MORRISTOWN

HISTORIC SPEEDWELL VILLAGE ★
Cedar Knolls
510
202
287

MORRIS MUSEUM ★

FOSTERFIELDS LIVING HISTORY FARM ★

FRELINGHUYSEN ARBORETUM ★

THE GRAND CAFÉ ▼   Morristown   WASHINGTON'S ★ HEADQUARTERS MUSEUM & FORD MUSEUM

FORT NONSENSE ★
MORRIS COUNTY VISITOR CENTER ■   ORIGIN II ▼
BEST WESTERN MORRISTOWN INN ■

THE COMMUNITY THEATER

LA CAMPAGNA ▼

24

510

124

Morristown National Historic Park

24

THE MADISON HOTEL ■

WICK HOUSE ■
■ JOCKEY HOLLOW VISITOR CENTER

SHAKESPEARE THEATER OF NEW JERSEY ■
FARLEY DICKINSON UNIVERSITY ●
● Madison

MUSEUM OF EARLY TRADES & CRAFTS ○

TEMPLE WICK RD

HARDSCRABBLE RD

SAND SPRING RD

LOANTAKA WY

NJ BRIGADE ENCAMPMENT AREA ■
THE OLDE MILL INN ■

VILLAGE RD
GREEN VILLAGE RD
SOUTHERN BLVD

PARROT MILL INN ■

202

Chatham ■

525

BAILEY'S MILL RD

LEES HILL RD

GREAT SWAMP OUTDOOR EDUCATION CENTER ●

GREAT SWAMP NATIONAL WILDLIFE REFUGE

FAIRMONT AVE
RIVER RD

Basking Ridge ○

287

MAPLE AVE

PLEASANT PLAINS RD

PLEASANT PLAINS RD

GREAT SWAMP REFUGE HEADQUARTERS ■

MEYERSVILLE RD

512

LORD STIRLING STABLES ■
Lord Stirling Park
RAPTOR TRUST ★

Meyersville ○

Lyons ○

J W GINTY'S IRISH PUB & RESTAURANT ▼

LONG HILL RD

SPRINGFIELD RD

78

INN AT SOMERSET HILLS ●

512

513

Millington ○

0   2 mi
0   2 km

PARK AVE

© AVALON TRAVEL PUBLISHING, INC.

THE SKYLANDS

Mansion and its 200-acre estate by the widow of Jacob Ford Jr., enabling him to keep a close watch on British movements in nearby New York City. While the widow and her four children set up house in half of the mansion, Washington occupied the other, and guests to the estate included Martha Washington and Marquis de Lafayette, the French soldier and statesman. Though the Jacob Ford Mansion survived over time, other buildings on the property did not—only their foundations. Ford Mansion is easily viewed from Morris Street.

Washington's Headquarters Museum (230 Morris St., 973/539-2016, www.nps.gov/morr) is temporarily closed for renovations, with a scheduled 2007 reopening. Tours of Ford Mansion continue to be held throughout construction and take place hourly 10 A.M.–4 P.M. from the visitor services trailer.

Jockey Hollow

Five miles south of Ford Mansion is Jockey Hollow, home to 10,000 of Washington's troops during the winter of 1779–1780. Though none of their original huts still exist, five reproductions have been placed on the property. Here you'll also find the **Wick House** (9:30 A.M.–4:30 P.M.), a farmhouse used by officers including General Arthur St. Clair.

With 27 miles of hiking trails and a two-mile auto tour, there's plenty to explore within Jockey Hollow's sloping and spacious wooded terrain. The **Jockey Hollow Visitor Center** (Tempe Wick Rd., 973/543-4030) is open 9 A.M.–5 P.M. daily, and roads into and out of the park are open dawn–dusk.

OTHER SIGHTS

For a blend of historical and educational sites in the Skylands, Morristown can't be beat.

Historic Speedwell Village

The Historic Speedwell Village (333 Speedwell Ave., 973/540-0211, www.speedwell.org) pays homage to Speedwell Ironworks and its proprietor, Stephen Vail. Little of the actual 19th-century complex still remains, but a collection of Vail's personal belongings, including photos, diaries, and maps, helps illustrate a major contributor to New Jersey's industrial past. Present-day Speedwell Village encompasses 7.5 acres, including the **Vail House,** the proprietor's home, and the factory used by Samuel F. B. Morse and Vail's son Alfred to "perfect and demonstrate" the nation's first telegraph. Tours of the Vail House and factory are given 10 A.M.–5 P.M. Wednesday–Saturday, noon–5 P.M. Sunday April–October, $4 adult, $3 senior, $2 child (4–16).

Fosterfields Living History Farm

Living history is big in New Jersey, and Morristown is no exception. The Fosterfields Living History Farm (73 Kahdena Rd., 973/326-7645, www.morrisparks.net, $5 adult, $3 child) re-creates 19th-century farm life with period-dressed interpreters engaging in daily activities like traditional crop raising and tending to livestock. Charles Foster's Gothic Revival home remains on the property, and extracurricular events are held on the farm throughout the year. Fosterfields is open 10 A.M.–5 P.M.

Wednesday–Saturday, noon–5 P.M. Sunday, April–October.

Morris Museum

A visit to the Morris Museum (6 Normandy Heights Rd., 973/971-3700, www.morris museum.org, $7 adult, $5 child) is rewarded with a unique art and science display that includes vintage costumes, dolls, fire trucks, New Guinea artifacts, and a stuffed grizzly, but the highlight is the Mechanical Musical Instrument Collection of New Yorker Murtogh Guinness, a member of the Guinness brewing family. One of the world's largest such sets (though only a portion of the 700 are on display), its pieces range from early 16th- to late 20th-century, life-size to miniature, and take the forms of jesters, clocks, jewelry boxes, and peacocks. It is said that before his death, Guinness would host late-night parties at his house where the instruments would be played. The museum offers its own live performance a couple of times weekly—call ahead for schedule. The Museum is open 10 A.M.–5 P.M. Tuesday and Wednesday, Friday and Saturday, 10 A.M.–8 P.M. Thursday, and 1–5 P.M. Sunday, with free admission on Thursdays 1–8 P.M.

Frelinghuysen Arboretum

Frelinghuysen Arboretum (53 Hanover Ave., Whippany, 973/326-7600, www.arboretum friends.org, free) is 127 acres of themed gardens and succulent smells. Listed on the National Register of Historic Places, the wheelchair-accessible arboretum includes a rock garden, vegetable garden, and a Braille Trail for the vision-impaired. The grounds are open dawn–dusk daily, with guided tours available on weekends.

The Stickley Museum at Craftsman Farms

In the early 20th century, Gustav Stickley, a pioneer of the arts and crafts movement, acquired 650 acres of land for the purpose of operating a self-sufficient school for boys. Stickley and his family resided on the property until 1915 in a log home that he designed. Although the school never fully came to fruition, the home, which now operates as a museum (Rte. 10 W., 973/540-1165, www.stickleymuseum.org, $7 adult, 4 child), and 26 acres of the land original from the property—known as Craftsman Farms—remain. Tours of the museum take place 12:15 and 2:45 P.M. weekdays April–November, 11:15 A.M.–3:15 P.M. hourly at quarter past on weekends April–November and the first three weekends in December. During these months Craftsman Farms is open to the public dawn–dusk daily.

NIGHTLIFE AND ENTERTAINMENT

Many of Morristown's restaurants feature full bars, and often entertainment. The following locales place nightlife first.

The **Funky Monkey** (13 South St., 973/267-5890, www.funkymonkeybar.com, $11–18) is an indoor/outdoor venue with live bands, DJ grooves, plenty of dance space, and a saucy young crowd. A menu of southwest-inspired cuisine is available throughout the day.

For something a bit fancier, try **The Side Bar** (14 Washington St., 973/540-9601), a classy piano bar made to resemble a library, where proper dress is required and 25 is the minimum age. It's located to the rear (around the corner) of the Famished Frog (see Food below), and a selection of appetizers are served. Entertainment takes place on weekends. The bar opens at 4 P.M. Tuesday–Friday, and at 5 P.M. Saturday, closed Sunday and Monday.

Watch performances such as comedians, Shakespeare, traditional dancers, and Vanessa Williams at **The Community Theatre** (100 South St., 973/539-0345, www.communitytheatrenj.com), a former movie theater now home to the **Colonial Symphony** (www.colonialsymphony.org).

ACCOMMODATIONS
$100-150

Though it's a chain, the ◖ **Best Western Morristown Inn** (270 South St., 973/540-1700 or 800/688-7474, fax 973/267-0241, www.bestwestern.com) does well to fit in with its historic surroundings. The hotel offers high-speed wireless Internet and the usual amenities. Housed in a colonial-style structure, it boasts an antique-filled lobby with a framed print of Washington himself above the fireplace. The rooms are more modern, with high-speed Internet and satellite TV. Pets are allowed for an additional $10/night, plus a $75 non-refundable cleaning fee. The hotel is located one mile from downtown.

The **Parrot Mill Inn** (47 Main St., Chatham, 973/635-7722, fax 973/635-0620, www.parrotmillinn.com) is a small bed-and-breakfast located in nearby Chatham. It features 10 tasteful and cozy rooms with private bath, telephone, and TV. Continental breakfast is served daily in a spacious dining area.

$150-200

Situated in a convenient locale at the intersection of Route 202 and North Maple Avenue is **The Olde Mill Inn** (225 Rte. 202, Basking Ridge, 908/221-1100, www.oldemillinn.com,), a hotel with spacious rooms and an onsite piano bar and outdoor courtyard. Across the parking lot is the inn's popular Grain House Restaurant.

$200-250

The massive ◖ **Inn at Somerset Hills** (80 Allen Rd., Basking Ridge, 908/580-1300 or 800/688-0700, www.theinnatsomersethills.com) can be found in ritzy Basking Ridge. There are 120 large, country-elegant guestrooms, an on-site restaurant and pub, and a library equipped with laptop stations. Room amenities include high-speed Internet, complimentary breakfast, and a *USA Today* delivered weekday mornings. This hotel was built in 2000 and is a sister property to Somerset Hills Hotel in Warren. It caters to cooperate clients, so rates are significantly cheaper on the weekends ($150–200).

FOOD

Washington and South Streets make up Morristown's main dining arena, one long stretch filled with restaurants and casual eateries, with an option or two scattered beyond.

THE SKYLANDS

Named for a mountain range in Central Asia, **Pamir** (85 Washington St., 973/605-1095, www .pamirrestaurant.com, 10 A.M.–10 P.M. daily, $12–20) is an Afghan BYO decorated in rich colors and tapestries, serving bowls of mildly flavored entrées complete with a yogurt-dressed salad and a side of Afghan bread.

For a special occasion head to **The Grand Café** (42 Washington St., 973/540-9444, www.thegrandcafe.com, $22.50–39), a fancy French bistro that'll make you feel as though you've arrived in Paris, with pink and gold decor, ornate Victorian accents, and plenty of fine wine. Lunch is served 11:45 A.M.–2 P.M. Monday–Friday, and dinner 5–9 P.M. Monday–Friday, until 10 P.M. Saturday, and Sunday is reserved for private parties.

The casual atmosphere of **The Famished Frog** (18 Washington St., 973/450-9601, www.famishedfrog.com, $7.99–25.99) falls somewhere between "diner" and "rainforest." Meals are simple, with signature eats that include Onion Straws ($4.49) and Sizzling Fajitas ($15.49–18.49). The Frog is open for lunch 11 A.M.–4 P.M. Monday–Saturday, and dinner 4–10 P.M. Monday–Thursday, until 11 P.M. Friday and Saturday, noon–9 P.M. Sunday.

For sleek, stylish Thai fusion try **Origin II** (10 South St., 973/971-9933, www.originthai.com, $8–12), a long and lean restaurant with a fish tank up front, and basement seating. Open for lunch and dinner.

Provesi (50 South St., 973/993-1944) is an Italian BYO frequented by baby boomers and young couples. The restaurant is open 11:30 A.M.–10 P.M. Monday–Thursday, until 11 P.M. Friday, 4:30–11 P.M. Saturday, closed Sunday.

Regional favorite 〔 **La Campagna** (5 Elm St., 973/644-4943, $18.95–25.95) serves superb Italian dishes in a lively BYO old-world setting, occupying two storefronts and a scattering of sidewalk seating. The restaurant is open for lunch 11:30 A.M.–3 P.M. Monday–Friday, and dinner 5–10 P.M. Monday–Saturday.

Both a comedy club and eatery, **The Calaloo Café** (190 South St., 973/993-1100, www.calaloocafe.com, $8.95–14.95) features Caribbean-American cuisine amid fun, bright decor with a plethora of outdoor tables perfect for people-watching. The café hosts live Jamaican music and houses real palm trees (returned to Florida during winter). Hours are 11:30 A.M.–10 P.M. Monday–Thursday, until 11 P.M. Friday, noon–11 P.M. Saturday, and 11 A.M.–10 P.M. Sunday.

Sharing a parking lot with the Olde Mill Inn in nearby Basking Ridge is the historic **Grain House Restaurant** (225 Rte. 202, Basking Ridge, 908/221-1150, $10–27), an 18th-century barn that today specializes in serving country American cuisine. Alongside a small creek is the restaurant's seasonal outdoor garden, complete with umbrella tables, while inside you'll find the Coppertop Pub, a full bar showcasing live music on Thursdays (6–10 P.M.). Hours are 11:30 A.M.–10 P.M. Monday–Thursday, until 11 P.M. Friday and Saturday, 10 A.M.–9 P.M. Sunday.

INFORMATION AND SERVICES

The **Morris County Visitor Center** (973/631-5151, www.morristourism.org) is located at 6 Court Street. On the north side of town is the NJ Transit train station.

〔 GREAT SWAMP

New Jersey's Great Swamp (241 Pleasant Plains Rd., 973/425-1222 or 973/425-7309, www.greatswamp.org, http://greatswamp .fws.gov/, dawn–dusk daily, free) would have become an airport had it not been for a group of locals bent on saving this marshland, considered little more than a royal "nuisance" during Revolutionary years. Today the 7,500-acre swamp is run by the U.S. Fish and Wildlife Service and is a "resting and nesting" place to hundreds of bird species; mammals such as white-tailed deer, coyote, and muskrat; and dozens of reptiles, amphibians, and fish. Walk along some of the 8.5 miles of trails and boardwalks and you may see beavers, storks, blue herons, snakes, bullfrogs and wood frogs, the evasive blue-spotted salamander, numerous turtles like the rarely seen Eastern mud and more common snapping and stinkpot turtles, and fish like smallmouth bass and redbreast sunfish, among so many others. The region is filled with mountain laurel, ferns, and oak trees, and encompasses a number of smaller parks, including the Raptor Trust, the refuge bookstore, and the education center.

The best time to visit the Great Swamp is during spring and fall, morning or late afternoon when the sun is not at its peak. During these seasons, mosquitoes and ticks are at a minimum and wildlife is at a premium. Summer on the other hand, with its sticky heat and many insects, can be unbearable.

Birding

The **Great Swamp Outdoor Education Center** (247 Southern Blvd., Chatham, 973/635-6629) is known to be an excellent place for birdwatching. The center is to the east of the Great Swamp and features a reference library, natural history displays, and nature trails.

The **Friends of Great Swamp National Wildlife Refuge Bookstore and Gift Shop** (197 Pleasant Plains Rd., 973/425-9510) is open 11 A.M.–5 P.M. daily. Closed July and August.

The **Raptor Trust** (1390 White Bridge Rd., Millington, 908/647-2353, www.theraptor trust.org, free, $2 donation accepted), a privately funded 15-acre facility, contains barnlike cages that hold about 100 injured birds of prey, including broad-winged hawks, peregrine falcons, turkey vultures, golden eagles, and snowy owls (my favorite). Guests are invited to meander the wooded grounds and visit the cages, all of which are adorned with plaques highlighting pertinent information about their residents, including Latin name, size, habitat, diet, migratory pattern, and the status of the species in New Jersey. Even those birds without a usual presence in the state have found a home here, shipped to the facility for care, while others were injured nearby on their migratory journey. Those birds that cannot be released are often used as foster parents, and for breeding and education. The Raptor Trust is open to the public daily, dawn–dusk.

Lord Stirling Park

Lord Stirling Park (190 Lord Stirling Rd., Basking Ridge, 908/766-6471) is less than a half-mile down a dirt road from the Raptor Trust. Stirling was once surveyor general of New Jersey and a major general during the Revolutionary War. Inside the park, **Lord Stirling Stables** (256 S. Maple Ave., Basking Ridge, 908/766-5955) is a gorgeous area that offers moonlight rides.

Recreation

Anyone with binoculars and a hankering for the outdoors will enjoy the region, and there are a number of good roads for cyclists (you'll enjoy the ride more if you come prepared with plenty of water and some bug spray). For a free cycling map to the Great Swamp area, visit the New Jersey Department of Transportation at www.state.nj.us/transportation/commuter/bike/freeinfo.shtm.

Food and Entertainment

A short drive southwest of the Great Swamp National Wildlife Refuge is **JW Gitney's Irish Pub & Restaurant** (632 Meyersville Rd., Meyersville, 908/647-6302, $7–22), formerly known as the Olde Meyersville Inn. Continental cuisine with a touch of Irish is the specialty, along with occasional live music and a popular Sunday brunch (11 A.M.–3 P.M.). Hours are 11:30 A.M.–10 P.M. Monday–Thursday, until 11 P.M. Friday and Saturday, 11 A.M.–10 P.M. Sunday.

Getting There and Around

Just south of Morristown, the Great Swamp is 25 minutes by train from New York City (35 miles by car). To get here from Morristown, take Route 202 south to North Maple Avenue and turn left, following the road south through Basking Ridge, where it then become South Maple Avenue, and continuing on to Lord Stirling Road. Make a left onto Lord Stirling Road, and after about two miles, the Raptor Trust Center will be on your left. Continue just past the center, and you'll come to Pleasant Plains Road. Make a left to reach the refuge headquarters.

MADISON

Nicknamed "Rose City" after the rose-growing industry that once flourished here, the four-square-mile borough of Madison is an attractive university town—home to both **Fairleigh Dickinson's Florham Campus** (285 Madison Ave., 973/443-8500, www.fdu.edu) and **Drew University** (36 Madison Ave., 973/408-3000, www.drew.edu).

Museum of Early Trade & Crafts

The non-profit Museum of Early Trade & Crafts (9 Main St., 973/377-2982, www.rosenet.org/metc, 10 A.M.–4 P.M. Tues.–Sat., noon 4 P.M. Sun., $3.50 adult, $2 child) displays unique handcrafted artifacts, including toys, furniture, tools, and musical instruments, as well as a number of rotating exhibits, and focuses on the works of New Jersey tradespeople. Housed within a unique 1900 Romanesque revival former library, a glimpse at the museum's interior—with vaulted ceilings, rounded archways, and detailed walls—is worth a visit of its own.

Shakespeare Theatre of New Jersey

For nearly half a century the Shakespeare Theatre of New Jersey (www.ShakespeareNJ.org, June–Dec.) has been entertaining local audiences with their interpretations of works by the prolific playwright, and since 1990 have held performances at Drew University's **F. M. Kirby Shakespeare Theatre** (36 Madison Ave., 973/408-5600, www.drew.edu), the company's main stage. During summer, a select performance takes place at the **Greek Theatre** (2 Convent Rd., 973/236-2954), an outdoor venue located at nearby Morristown's College of St. Elizabeth campus.

Food and Entertainment

Shanghai Jazz (24 Main St., 973/822-2899, www.shanghaijazz.com, $15.95–29.95) is an Asian cuisine and music hotspot. A cover is not charged, but there is a food and drink minimum per person ($15 Wed. and Thurs., $20 Fri. and Sun., $30 Sat.). There's a full bar and live music five nights a week. Reservations are recommended. Hours are 10:30 A.M.–10:30 P.M. Tuesday–Thursday, until midnight Friday, noon–midnight Saturday, and 1–10 P.M. Sunday, closed Monday.

At the **Garlic Rose Bistro** (41 Main St., 973/822-1178, www.garlicrose.com, $13.50–21.95), there are a few sidewalk tables and a non-spectacular dining area, but the draw of this place is in the taste and scent—a plethora of garlic. Start with the baked brie and garlic ($8.95) and make your way to the Garlic Rose Crab Cakes ($19.95). Lunch is served 11:30 A.M.–3 P.M. Monday–Friday, and dinner 5–10 P.M. Monday–Thursday, until 11 P.M. Friday and Saturday, 4–9 P.M. Sunday.

A great place to try essential Garden State fare is **Pop's Bar-B-Q** (42 Lincoln Pl., 973/301-0101, 11 A.M.–9 P.M. Mon.–Thurs., until 9:30 P.M. Fri., noon–9:30 P.M. Sat., closed Sun.), advertising the "best rack in town." Come here for the pulled-pork dinner along with a side of jalapeño corn bread.

Getting There

NJ Transit's Morris & Essex Line stops at the Madison Train Station. To reach Madison from Morristown, take Route 124 southeast just over 4.5 miles (about a 10 minute drive).

The Central Piedmont

Situated between New Jersey's urban east and the hard-to-reach western Skylands border, the Central Piedmont is a mix of office parks and attractive downtown centers that are still accessible from New York City by way of NJ Transit, but far enough away to feel as though you're in the middle of remote countryside. The region offers plenty of dining options, and although it's not heavy on the B&B front, it does provide a nice mix of overnight accommodations. Visitors will find numerous shopping options, including the antiques of Chester and the famed outlets of Flemington, as well as numerous recreation facilities that offer opportunities for hiking, boating, and camping. The region is a popular spot for hot air ballooning and hosts an annual hot air balloon festival in July. The Central Piedmont is easily accessible by way of Routes 22 and 202.

CHESTER

Founded in 1736, historic Chester is a charming borough filled with colonial and Victorian buildings housing antique and specialty shops, many with front porches where wares for sale are displayed. In the warmer months these goods spill down the front steps and onto the sidewalks, always heavy with foot traffic on weekend afternoons.

Shopping

Most of Chester's shops are along East Main Street, where you'll find everything from antique furnishings to vinyl collectibles.

Ferret for Kids (10 Main St., 908/879-8446) sells kid-centric furniture, linens, and clothing for special occasions like christenings and communion. For blankets, rugs, and quilts (some even depicting Chester), try **Chester Country Furnishings** (60 Main St., 908/879-4288). **Hollyberries** (92 Main St., 908/879-8995) features authentic antique and reproduction furniture, including tables, cabinets, and armoires. Housed within the 1844 Old Factory building is the **Stained Glass Boutique** (76 Main St., 908/879-7351), home to colorful glass sunflowers, sailboats, cats, and hot air balloons, as well as stained glass window hangings waiting to be refurbished.

The **Chester Carousel Antiques and Gifts** (125 Main St., 908/879-7141) features a varied selection of antiques including bird cages, dolls, even a carousel horse. The shop also sells *Byers' Choice Carolers.* For everything nature, try **Nature's Visions** (71 Main St., 908/879-9700, www.natures-visions.com), where you'll find an assortment of blankets, photos, frames, jewelry, and lawn ornaments all related to the outdoors. Occupying the basement space of a large mansard-roof Victorian is **Penny Lane Music** (87 Main St., 908/879-5540), featuring a sweet selection of vinyl, CDs, vintage posters, and rockin' music memorabilia.

Food

Popular with families, **Benito's Trattoria** (44 Main St., 908/879-1887, 11:30 A.M.–10 P.M. Tues.–Fri., 5–10 P.M. Sat., 1–9 P.M. Sun., $17–24) is a BYO serving Italian fare.

Getting There

By car, take Route 206 south to Chester.

GLADSTONE-PEAPACK AND FAR HILLS

From Chester take Old Chester–Gladstone Road (Rte. 512), a narrow and windy route, past set-back mansions into Gladstone-Peapack, a scenic borough with a local market and brick storefronts scattered throughout. Both the borough and neighboring Far Hills are filled with oversized homes, some ranch-style, others newly built with white shingles and black shutters, and a few enormous estates set on undulating acres with stone or natural wood fences, surrounded by dense forest. It's a lovely area and the road is ideal for cycling, hilly with plenty to see and light on traffic, though the shoulder is virtually non-existent.

The USGA Museum and Archives

The USGA Museum and Archives (Liberty Corner Rd., Far Hills, 908/234-2300, www .usga.org) is *the* museum for the United States Golf Association. An extensive library and archives on everything golf is open by appointment during weekday business hours. As of August 2005 the museum is closed indefinitely for repairs, but the library remains open.

U.S. Equestrian Team Headquarters

The U.S. Equestrian Team, now known as the USET Foundation (1040 Pottersville Rd., 908/234-1251, www.uset.org), makes its official home at Gladstone's Hamilton Farm. Visitors are welcome to explore these Olympic training grounds, which include a trophy room and oversized stable, during weekday office hours (8:30 A.M.–4:30 P.M.) and on weekends when an event is held. Events take place throughout the year, but the highlight is June's annual **Festival of Champions,** in which horses and riders complete in three Olympic-style events.

Accommodations

$200-250: The grand **Somerset Hills Hotel** (200 Liberty Corner Rd., Warren, 908/647-6700, www.shh.com) features 111 stylish guestrooms, an on-site Italian restaurant, and a bar. The bocce court is the hotel's standout, but the outdoor pool, complimentary breakfast, and shuttle service to the surrounding area are nice perks as well. Pets can accompany you for a $25/night fee. The hotel offers a rate reduction on weekends.

BRIDGEWATER

Bridgewater is just north of Somerville, and the two towns are often associated together. There are a number of office parks in the area.

Commerce Bank Ballpark

Commerce Bank Ballpark (1 Patriots Park, 908/252-0700, www.somersetpatriots.com, $5–12) was built in 1999 and seats 6,100, with additional general admission lawn seats along the right-field line ideal for stretching out under the stars. The stadium is home to minor league baseball's **Somerset Patriots.**

United States Bicycling Hall of Fame

Located across from the ballpark, the United States Bicycling Hall of Fame (941 E. Main St., 732/356-7016, www.usbhof.com, 10 A.M.– noon and 1–4 P.M. Tues.–Fri.) is loaded with jerseys, bikes, trophies, medals, and tons of photos and article clippings featuring America's cycling greats. The center hosts an annual induction ceremony honoring road, BMX, and mountain bikers, as well as outside contributors to the sport.

Bridgewater Commons

For modern shopping, head to Bridgewater Commons (400 Commons Way, 908/218-0001, www.bridgewatercommons.com), New Jersey's first three-floor shopping mall. Bloomingdale's and Lord & Taylor are the anchors, and smaller shops include American Eagle, Esprit, Coach, Eddie Bauer, and Vans. The mall also features a multiplex AMC Theater (908/725-1161).

Accommodations

$200-250: Bridgewater Summerfield Suites (530 Rte. 22, 908/725-0800) is a Wyndham property featuring one- and two-bedroom suites, 24-hour convenience store, and an on-site video rental. The hotel caters to business travelers with a complimentary weekday happy hour (Mon.–Thurs.) and full kitchens and living rooms in all units. Rates (and added amenities) are reduced on weekends.

SOMERVILLE

Somerville serves as the county seat of Somerset, and the borough features a massive beaux-arts style courthouse—a stately white structure with Greek columns and rounded dome, topped with a gold statue of Justice, holding scales and a sword. Somerville's expansive downtown has numerous restaurants, plenty of service shops, and a pretty, castle-like train station, and while shopping exists, it's nothing spectacular. The area is in the midst of revitalization—signs reading "Shop, Dine, and Discover" dress the main street—though with such a long stretch of downtown, it seems a difficult undertaking. Nineteenth-century homes of Gothic, Victorian, and Greek Revival designs line the borough's side roads, and are large in this middle class town, but they're kept in varying states of repair.

Wallace House

The Wallace House (38 Washington Pl., 908/725-1015) served as George Washington's 1779–1780 winter and spring headquarters. This 1776 clapboard colonial is a nice spot for history buffs, and surrounding grounds host an interpretive center and a short walking path, as well as the historic Old Dutch Parsonage House. Candlelight tours of both buildings are given Wednesday–Friday evenings throughout the winter. Tours of the Wallace House are held 10 A.M.–noon and 1–4 P.M. Wednesday–Saturday, 1–4 P.M. Sunday year-round.

Duke Farms & Gardens

The 2,700-acre Duke Farms & Gardens (Rte. 206 S., 908/722-3700, www.dukefarms.org, noon–4 P.M. Oct.–June, $10 adult, $8 child) belonged to tobacco heiress Doris Duke (the same Duke family as the university) until her death in 1993. On land she'd inherited from her father, Duke created a gorgeous garden setting that she first opened to the public in 1964, and today visitors can take an hour-long guided tour of 11 internationally themed greenhouses, with display gardens that include Japanese, English, and American desert. Three other tours are offered within the property, including an estate and nature park tour of the farm's "core" 700 acres. The environment on the Duke estate is heavily controlled, and reservations are a must.

The greenhouse gardens are only open October–May, but the rest of the farm is open throughout the summer. Guided tours are given 11 A.M., 2 P.M., and 3:30 P.M. Wednesday–Sunday April–November.

The estate is easily reachable by traveling south on Route 206 from Somerville—look for the low stone wall and two castle-like pillars on either side of a roadway and you've found Duke Parkway West.

Festivals and Events

On Memorial Day weekend, Somerville hosts the annual four-day **Tour of Somerville** (www.tourofsomerville.org), the United States' oldest bike race. Events include a criterium (lap race) and a cycling classic, and culminate with Monday's namesake event. Entertainment takes place in downtown Somerville the day of the Tour, and all events are free to attend.

The **Quick Chek Festival of Ballooning** (800/HOT-AIR-9 or 800/468-2479, http://quickchk.balloonfestival.com, $17 adult, $7 child) is an annual three-day event held in late July at Solberg Airport in Readington. More than 125 international hot air balloons ascend twice daily (weather permitting) at this popular festival, which also includes alligator wrestling, fireworks, and live music.

Food

Somerville has a fine selection of dining choices, including three Thai restaurants. **Thai Chef** (24 E. Main St., 908/253-8300, $9.95–18.50) is the largest of these and offers an excellent menu of French-inspired Thai dishes, as well as a small selection of sushi. Lunch hours are 11:30 A.M.–3 P.M. Monday–Saturday, and dinner 5–10 P.M. Monday–Thursday, until 11 P.M. Friday and Saturday, 3–9:30 P.M. Sunday. For a trendy dining atmosphere, there's **Origin** (25 Division St., 908/635-1444, www.originthai.com, $10–23), another BYO offering French Thai cuisine and with a second location in Morristown. Lunch is served 11:30 A.M.–3 P.M. Tuesday–Saturday, and dinner 5–9:30 P.M. Tuesday–Thursday, until 10 P.M. Friday and Saturday, and 3–9 P.M.Sunday, closed Monday. **Chao Phaya** (9 Davenport St., 908/231-0655) is the most authentic of the three Thai restaurants, serving traditional fare in an intimate space situated away from Main Street. Hours are 11:30 A.M.–9:30 P.M. Monday–Thursday, until 10 P.M. Friday, noon–10 P.M. Saturday, and 4–9 P.M. Sunday.

Verve (18 E. Main St., 908/707-8655, www .vervestyle.com, 5–10 P.M. Mon.–Thurs., until 11 P.M. Fri. and Sat., Sun. by special appointment, $18–36) is one of Somerville's prized establishments, a restaurant, bar, and lounge serving an eclectic menu of New American entrées, as well as a fine variety of wines and martinis. The dining area is cheerfully bright, while the lounge still has a black and white tile floor left over from Prohibition days. Verve is known for its Halloween costume party, and live jazz plays on weekends.

Martino's (212 W. Main St., 908/722-8602, 11:30 A.M.–10 P.M. Tues.–Sun., closed Mon., $10.95–16.95) is a casual BYO serving popular authentic Cuban fare, known for its excellent service and lively owner.

For Northern Italian cuisine, try **La Scala** (117 N. Gaston Ave., 908/218-9300, www.lascala fineitalian.com, $14.95–21.95) a neighborhood-style BYO whose signature dishes include homemade lobster ravioli and grilled ostrich steak. Lunch is served 11:30 A.M.–2:30 P.M. Tuesday–Thursday, and dinner 5–10 P.M. Tuesday–Thursday, until 11 P.M. Friday and Saturday, 4–9 P.M. Sunday. **Alfonso's** (99/101 W. Main St., 908/526-0616, www.alfonsosfamilypizzeria.com, 11 A.M.–10 P.M. Mon.–Sat., 11:30 A.M.–9 P.M. Sun., $5.95–19) is the place to go for pizza. Other offerings include an array of pastas, parmigianas, seafood, and a variety of hot and cold sandwiches.

CLINTON

The scenic town of Clinton is situated along the Raritan River, its downtown lined by late-19th-century two-story brick and clapboard buildings, with doorways level to the sidewalk and stained glass blocks surrounding many of their rectangular windows. Along Main Street an 1870 flat iron bridge crosses the river, accommodating both foot and auto traffic and passing next to a 200-foot-wide waterfall, flanked on either side by two historic mills—the town's most notable structures. Clinton is a fine place to spend an evening.

Historic Mills

One of New Jersey's most recognizable structures is the circa-1810 Red Mill that graces the western bank of the waterfall in downtown Clinton. Once a processor of wool, plaster, and graphite, and later used to generate electricity for limestone quarry mines, today it's home to the **Hunterdon Historical Museum** (56 Main St., 908/735-4101, $6 adult, $4 child). It's also part of the **Red Mill Museum Village** (www.theredmill.org), a handful of restored buildings, including a schoolhouse, and the 19th-century Mulligan Limestone Quarry, which still includes a stone crusher, dynamite shed, and lime kilns. The museum displays changing exhibits such as vintage toy soldiers and dollhouses, and local rock and fossil finds, and historic reenactments are occasionally held on the property. The museum and village are open 10 A.M.–4 P.M. Tuesday–Saturday, noon–5 P.M. Sunday, early April–mid-October.

Directly across the waterfall is the **Hunterdon Museum of Art** (7 Lower Center St., 908/735-8415, fax 908/735-8416, www.hunterdonartmuseum.org, 11 A.M.–5 P.M. Tues.–Sun., $3 adult), a contemporary art museum housed in an 1836 gray stone gristmill that operated until 1952. Inside visitors will find modern prints, paintings, photographs, and sculpture, as well as a low-ceilinged gift shop selling colorful items like jewelry and paper stars, cards, toys, and tees. Lectures and workshops take place throughout the year.

Recreation

Just west of Clinton you'll find **Sky Sweeper Balloon Adventures** (launch site off Rte. 78, 800/462-3201, www.skysweeper.com), offering two-person ($495) or group ($195 per person) flights in hot air balloons. Price includes a "hands-on set up and inflation," an hour in the air, and complimentary champagne and hors d'oeuvres afterward. Sky Sweeper is open, weather permitting, all year. **In Flight Balloon Adventures** (888/301-2383, www.balloonnj.com) offers hour-long flights concluding with champagne and treats.

Cost is $225 per person, $175 per person for groups more than two.

Paddle down the Raritan in a boat from **Clinton Canoe & Kayak** (9 Lower Center St., 908/735-6767). The shop is situated on the eastern riverbank just above the waterfall. Boats run $25 for up to two hours.

Spruce Run Recreation Area
Four miles north of Clinton is the Spruce Run Recreation Area (68 Van Syckel's Rd., 908/638-8572, www.state.nj.us/dep/parksandforests/parks/spruce.html), which features New Jersey's third-largest reservoir at 2,012 acres. With 15 miles of shoreline, the reservoir is a perfect spot for swimming and a popular sailing locale, and fishing opportunities include largemouth bass, catfish, carp, and stocked trout. Boats are also rented in the summer. In the winter Spruce Run remains open for ice fishing, boating, and cross-country skiing, and camping sites are available April–October 31, with toilets and showers located nearby ($20/night). The park is open year-round dawn–dusk, with an access fee (Memorial Day–Labor Day) of $5 weekdays, $10 weekends. Cyclists and walk-ins are $2 daily throughout the season.

Shopping
Clinton has some fun shops along Main Street, definitely worth an inside peek.

Pick up a new sleeper for your schnauzer at **Well Bred** (18 Main St., 908/730-7977), and grab yourself a pair of canine-covered socks. At the **Clinton Book Shop** (33 Main St., 908/735-8811, http://clinton.booksense.com), shoppers can score a copy of *Weird NJ* along with new releases and classic favorites. And there's always the occasional book signing. For greeting cards and specialty gifts, stop by **The Write Touch** (41 Main St., 908/713-9595). **Things We Like** (20 Main St., 908/730-9888) is a small, cozily crowded store filled with clothes, cups, pins, and German spring toys—a smorgasbord of selection.

Near Clinton in Pittstown is **Chia-Sin Farms** (215 Quakertown Rd., 908/730-7123, 10 A.M.–6 P.M.), a 40-acre pick-your-own farm featuring Chinese vegetables and East Asian herbs, as well as seasonal fresh flowers and Christmas trees.

Accommodations
$50-100: The **Holiday Inn Select** (111 W. Main St., 908/735-5111) is situated within walking distance to Clinton's downtown shops and restaurants. Free wireless Internet is featured throughout the hotel, and rooms include fridges and bathrobes. Families are catered to with homemade cookies in the rooms and a special kid package ($150) that includes poolside movies, an ice cream sundae bar, and a disposable waterproof camera. For the adults, wine and cheese is served in the lobby daily.

$100-150: Along I-78 you'll find the attractive **Courtyard Lebanon** (300 Corporate Dr., 908/236-8500), a new hotel with clean, spacious rooms, a small heated pool, and a complimentary deluxe breakfast. The hotel is just a couple miles distance from both Clinton and Round Valley Recreation Area.

Camping
Camp Carr Campground (144 W. Woodschurch Rd., 908/782-1030, Apr.–Oct.) is a small camp with 30-odd RV and tent sites, run by the wonderful John and Sandy Nagles. Although the grounds are used as a YMCA kids camp during the summer months and set-ups for tents are limited, the prime locale along the Raritan riverbank, convenience to nearby Clinton and Flemington, and gracious hosts make scoring a space here worthwhile (as long as you don't plan on sleeping in). Sites run $30/night for a family of four.

Food
The dining selection is not terribly varied in Clinton, but you will find some wonderful American eats, as well as a couple of good ethnic restaurants.

The Old River House (51 Main St., 908/735-4141, www.oldriverhouserestaurant.com) is the ideal place to unwind after a day of tackling New Jersey's highways. This truly scenic spot has both indoor fireside dining and expansive outdoor waterside dining, complete with waddling ducks and a Spanish-guitar player during summer months, and the view of the bridge, Red Mill, and waterfall are fantastic. Try the salmon sandwich with capers ($9.45) or the sautéed crab cake sandwich ($9.95). Breakfast is also served. Hours are 8 A.M.–9 P.M. Monday–Friday, 7 A.M.–9 P.M. weekends (closes at 8 P.M. Sun.).

Wasabi (5 Main St., 908/238-9300) is highly recommended by locals, a tiny place with only a handful of tables and an L-shaped sushi bar. For Thai food try **Pru Thai** (6 E. Main St., 908/735-0703); its orange and deep-red interior feels worlds away from the shops across the Raritan River.

For standard American eats head to the **Towne Restaurant** (31 Main St., 908/735-7559, 5:30 A.M.–4:30 P.M. Mon.–Sat., 7 A.M.–2 P.M. Sun.), a neighborhood gathering spot with ice cream.

Across the bridge and around the bend from the downtown center is **The Clinton House** (2 W. Main St., 908/730-9300, $15.50–35.50), a massive, white, 1743 historic inn reminiscent in appearance to the grand hotels of Michigan's Mackinac Island. The restaurant features numerous colonial-inspired dining rooms and an on-site bakery and bar, and meals are traditional American with a small vegetarian selection. The Clinton House is open 11:30 A.M.–2:30 P.M. Monday–Saturday, 5–9:30 P.M. Monday–Friday, 5–10 P.M. Saturday, noon–8:30 P.M. Sunday.

Midway between Clinton and Bridgewater is the **Ryland Inn** (Rte. 22, Whitehouse, 908/534-4011, www.therylandinn.com), highly regarded as one of the state's top dining establishments. This award-winning restaurant, located within an 18th century farmhouse, features a seasonally changing tasting menu ($90–120) of French-American dishes made with organic ingredients grown in the outside garden. Dinner is served nightly, beginning at 5 P.M. Monday–Saturday, and 5:30 P.M. Sunday. Reservations are recommended in the restaurant, although more casual meals ($12–22) can be had in the bar.

Getting There and Around

From the Bridgewater/Somerville area, Route 22 West carries you to Clinton. **Trans-Bridge Lines, Inc.** (www.transbridgebus.com) runs buses from New York City's Port Authority Bus Terminal (212/564-8484) to Clinton, departing weekday afternoons and evenings and all day on weekends. Buses arrive at Clinton's Park & Ride, at Route 31 and Center Street, in a little over an hour. Return buses run throughout the day daily. Tickets are $26.90 adult, $13.45 child round-trip if purchased from an agent, $20 one-way if purchased on board.

ROUND VALLEY RECREATION AREA

Four miles east of Clinton is the 3,369-acre Round Valley Recreation Area (1220 Lebanon-Stanton Rd., 908/236-6355, www.state.nj.us/dep/parksandforests/parks/round.html), home to a more than 2,000-acre reservoir that, at 180 feet, is the state's deepest body of water. Swimming is allowed during summer months in a day-use-only section separate from the main reservoir, and lifeguards are on duty daily. The recreation area itself is absolutely stunning, surrounded by rolling green hills and marked with tall trees and the seemingly endless reservoir at its center. This is a popular spot for fishing—the reservoir hosts 19 species and is stocked annually with trout—and a good place for freshwater scuba diving (Apr.–Oct., divers must be certified).

Round Valley hosts a number of multiuse trails accessible to mountain bikers and horseback riders as well as hikers and a couple of short nature trails easy enough for casual strollers. This is one of the few areas in New Jersey where you'll find backcountry camping, accessible only to those on foot or traveling by boat. The region surrounding the Recreation Area is ideal for cyclists, who can obtain a free map of the Round Valley Roundabout ride from the New Jersey Department of Transportation (www.state.nj.us/transportation/commuter/bike/freeinfo.shtm).

Round Valley is open year-round dawn-dusk and is free to enter during the off-season.

© LAURA KINIRY

Round Valley Recreation Area

From Memorial Day to Labor Day, admission is $5/vehicle weekdays, $10/vehicle weekends, and $2 for walk-ins and cyclists daily.

Recreation

The recreation area's shining star is the nine-mile **Cushetunk Trail,** rising to 500 feet above the shoreline and traversing both wooded stretches and exposed areas. The trail leads the way to Round Valley's backcountry sites (along the lower Cushetunk portion) and ranks as moderate to difficult. Easy hikes include the one-mile **Pine Tree Trail** and the 0.5-mile **Family Hiking and Biking Trail,** both popular tracks for birding, and possible sightings include osprey, blue jays, and woodpeckers. Cross-country skiers can make use of the trails in the winter.

Backcountry Campsites

Round Valley hosts 85 backcountry tent sites ($17/night, Apr.–Oct.), and eight group sites ($1/person, Apr.–Oct.) that can accommodate 7–25 each. All are accessible by way of the somewhat difficult nine-mile **Cushetunk**

Trail. They're located on the eastern end of the reservoir. Sites are pretty rustic, but there is drinking water available.

FLEMINGTON

Flemington is a spacious borough filled with steep-roof and front-porch Victorians, traffic circles, and plenty of outlet shopping. Downtown is known for its Greek Revival architecture and along Main Street grandiose columns are interspersed with brick buildings in orange, brown, and red. The town has a slightly industrial feel, and most of its shops are closed on Sundays.

Greek Revival Courthouse

Flemington is the seat of Hunterdon County and its towering white Greek Revival Courthouse (although no longer in use as a courthouse) stands along Main Street at the center of town. With tall Doric columns, the 19th-century building is itself quite impressive, although the architecture is not what earned it a place as a National Historic Landmark. The courthouse was the site of the 1930s

the Black River & Western Railroad, Ringoes

Lindbergh baby kidnapping trial, and it is here that Bruno Hauptmann was sentenced to death for the kidnapping and murder of Charles Lindbergh's son, who was taken from the Lindberghs' Hopewell, New Jersey home. The structure has since been restored to its 1935 trial-era appearance, and annually on weekends throughout October a play called *Trial of the Century* is performed inside, re-enacting the famous courtroom event. Visitors can even sit in the jury box to watch the performance. To find out more, visit www .famoustrials.com or call 908/782-2610.

Schaefer Farms
Schaefer Farms (1051 Rte. 523, 908/782-2705, www.schaeferfarms.com, 9 A.M.–6 P.M. daily) is a kid-friendly farm with fall haunted hay rides and a maize maze.

Northlandz
Just north of the Flemington Circle is North-landz (Rte. 202, 908/782-4022, www.north landz.com, $13.75 adult, $9.75 child), a ware-house-like museum with an extensive and quite impressive miniature train display. Guinness calls Northlandz "the largest model railroad ever"—a basement set gone awry with mountains, mining towns, amusements parks, train wrecks, graveyards, and outhouses. Known as "The Great American Railway," this awesome creation is the work of Bruce Williams Zaccagnino, who, along with his wife Jean, continues to operate Northlandz daily. Inside you'll also find a doll museum with a 94-room doll mansion, an organ chamber, and a snack bar. Just for the sheer feat, this place should not be missed, but keep in mind that it may be too much stimulation for young kids to handle. Northlandz is open 10 A.M.–4 P.M. Monday–Friday, 10 A.M.–6 P.M. Saturday and Sunday throughout the year.

Black River & Western Railroad
Why not take a ride of your own aboard the Black River & Western Railroad (908/996-3300, www.brwrr.com, $10 adult, $5 child), which runs a one-hour, 11-mile round-trip

© LAURA KINIRY

between Flemington's Liberty Village Outlets and Ringoes aboard steam and diesel locomotives. Special excursions include Haunted Trains in October, the North Pole Express in December, and the occasional Great Train Robbery. The railroad operates afternoons on weekends May–December, and some summer weekdays.

Recreation

Miniature golf aficionados will love **Pine Creek Miniature Golf** (394 Rte. 31, West Amwell, 609/466-3803, www.pinecreek.com), featuring two 18-hole courses in a "country-club-like setting." You won't find any mechanical mice or creaky dice as obstacles here, but you will be challenged—better practice your putt!

Enjoy more hot air ballooning at **Hunterdon Ballooning Inc.** (111 Locktown–Flemington Rd., 908/788-5415, www.hunterdonballooning.com).

Shopping

Flemington is New Jersey's outlet capital, though it seems to be losing a bit of its hype. While you won't find the finest store selection, you will find a unique blend of shops definitely worth a few hours' visit. Most are scattered throughout the borough and require a bit of highway and traffic-circle navigation.

Established in 1965, **Turntable Junction** (Church and Fulper Rd., 908/782-1919) resembles a miniature, somewhat outdated, village, home to a couple of children's clothing shops and a cellular phone store. Across the street, however, is **Liberty Village Premium Outlets** (1 Church St., 908/782-8550, www.premiumoutlets.com), cited as the United States' first outlet mall. Here you'll find Tommy Hilfiger, Ralph Lauren, Cole Haan, and the L. L. Bean Factory Store, as well as dish and pottery retailers such as Royal Doulton and Le Creuset. A brick walkway connects the shops, and a gurgling fountain stands at the village center. Nearby, a café selling coffee drinks and a delicious s'mores fondue platter keeps energy pumping.

A small stretch of outlet shopping along one of the borough's infamous circles, **Dansk Plaza** (Rte. 202/31, 908/782-7077, www.dansk.com) is virtually empty, housing only a Lenox Outlet, a Cookware & More, and a restaurant. I was told that the vacant storefronts will soon be occupied, but the state's trend in abandoned centers doesn't make it look promising.

Along downtown's Main Street is **Flemington Cut Glass** (156 Main St., 908/782-3017), featuring a wide selection of glassware and candles, and serving as the exclusive outlet for both Riedel Crystal and The Wilton Armetale Company. The cut glass company was founded nearly 100 years ago and in 1920 became one of the country's first outlet centers.

Accommodations

$100-150: Just off Route 202, one mile west of Flemington's downtown center, is the **Hampton Inn** (14 Royal Rd., 908/284-9427), a standard space with heated indoor pool, high speed Internet (wireless access in public areas), and continental breakfast. The hotel also features a complimentary snack bar, open to guests 24-hours.

$150-200: Centrally located along downtown's Main Street is the **Main Street Manor** (194 Main St., 908/782-4928, www.mainstreetmanor.com), a Queen Anne Victorian bed-and-breakfast with five bright guestrooms, each decorated in floral wallpapers and featuring private bath, air-conditioning, and cable TV. First floor common areas include Victorian furnished parlors and an arts and crafts–style dining room where homemade breakfast is served daily. The inn was built at the turn of the 20th century for the Schenk family, who has long held a place in Flemington history.

Food

Flemington is not known for its dining options, though you will find a couple of respected choices within the borough. For fine dining, venture outside Flemington.

California Grill (Dansk Plaza, Rtes. 202/31 Circle, 908/806-7141) is the shining star in a half-abandoned outlet strip, specializing in large specialty salads and gourmet pizzas with inventive names like The Mad Hungarian, combining hot wings and cheese slices. An average decor is made up for by a doting staff and a long list of specials, each vegetarian dish marked by a symbol. Lunch hours are 11:30 A.M.–3 P.M. daily. Dinner is served 5–9 P.M. Tuesday–Saturday, until 8 P.M. Sunday and Monday. The cute and kitschy **Shaker Café** (31 Main St., 908/782-6610, www.shakercafe.com, $3.95–12) is a local favorite. This BYO serves up simple American meals throughout the day, such as omelets (breakfast only), salads, and sandwiches. Dinner is a changing menu of affordable entrées, and Saturday evenings are often reserved for special events, like a live music and meal combo ($25). The café is open for breakfast and lunch 7 A.M.–3 P.M. Monday–Friday, and dinner 6–9 P.M. Tuesday–Saturday, breakfast only on Sunday 9 A.M.–noon.

Across from the courthouse is the 1772 **Union Hotel Restaurant & Bar** (76 Main St., 908/788-7474, www.unionhotelrestaurant.com, 11 A.M.–midnight daily, $16.50–27.50), a monstrous four-story historic brick inn serving as the town centerpiece and serving American entrées along a seasonal front veranda.

In nearby Ringoes, the **Harvest Moon Inn** (1039 Old York Rd., Ringoes, 908/806-6020, www.harvestmooninn.com) serves monstrous portions of New American cuisine in a breathtakingly traditional setting, with a fleshed-out wine list. The restaurant is housed in a former educational academy, a Federal stone and clapboard structure, and is the perfect spot for celebrating a special occasion. Lunch is served 11:30 A.M.–2:30 P.M. Tuesday–Friday. Dinner hours are 5–9:30 P.M. Tuesday–Thursday, until 10 P.M. Friday and Saturday, and 1–8 P.M. Sunday. The restaurant is closed Monday.

SERGEANTSVILLE

Part of the larger Delaware Township, Sergeantsville is situated at the intersection of Routes 604 and 523, a small village with an old-fashioned **General Store** (609/397-3214)

that has a sign hanging in the window that reads "bikers welcome." With its open farmland and plentiful hills the area resembles Pennsylvania's Amish country, and is home to the state's last pre-20th-century covered bridge.

Green Sergeant's Covered Bridge

Though Green Sergeant's Covered Bridge (570 Rosemont–Ringoes Rd., 609/397-3240) is New Jersey's only remaining pre-20th-century covered bridge, it's no longer the original structure—that had to be widened when automobiles were introduced. Today's bridge was remade with recycled material and is situated along Route 604 west of Sergeantsville, handling westbound traffic only.

Accommodations

$100-150: Between Flemington and Sergeantsville is the **Silver Maple Organic Farm and B&B** (483 Sergeantsville Rd., www.silvermaplefarm.net), a pet-friendly place with more than 20 acres that are home to chickens, pigs, ducks, and goats. The property's 200-year-old farmhouse includes four guestrooms and one suite, and an outdoor pool that's popular with kids. Full country breakfast is served daily, making fine use of the farm's organic veggies and freshly laid eggs.

Food

Across the street from the General Store is the circa-1734 **Sergeantsville Inn** (1 Rosemont-Ringoes Rd., 609/397-3700, www.sergeantsvilleinn.com, $19–28), a historic space with stone-laid walls and low ceilings. It was built as a private residence and used as a grain shop and ice cream parlor before its present incarnation as a restaurant. American entrées are accompanied by both an eclectic martini menu and an international wine selection. Lunch hours are 11:30 A.M.–3 P.M. Tuesday–Saturday, and dinner is served 5–9 P.M. Tuesday, until 10 P.M. Wednesday and Thursday, 4:30 –11 P.M. Friday and Saturday, noon–9 P.M. Sunday, closed Monday.

Lambertville and Vicinity

Hunterdon County's only city, Lambertville (www.lambertville.org) is known for its art galleries, antiques and specialty stores, dining opportunities, and open-mindedness. Located along the Delaware River directly across from New Hope, Pennsylvania, the two places are linked by a free auto- and footbridge to make up one of the region's most alluring tourism spots. Lambertville, however, is not nearly as traveled as New Hope, and continues to retain much of its charm. Along the streets are brick, stucco, and clapboard Federal row homes in shades of colonial blue and brown, maroon, and turquoise, built for factory workers in the 1800s and now in various stages of repair—aged, unfinished, and perched on the edge of the sidewalk, adding to the city's allure. This hotspot was abandoned in the 1960s when a lack of industry and a polluted river caused residents to search elsewhere for their creature comforts, and that's ultimately what kept Lambertville's structural integrity intact. Its five-block downtown stretch is extremely inviting for strollers and window shoppers, though the closer you get to the bridge the more touristy it gets.

The city also has some historic significance. Washington and his men visited Lambertville at least three times—in 1776, 1777, and 1778—and on his final trip through, the General set up headquarters in the **John Holcombe House** (260 N. Main St.), now a private residence. The D&R towpath runs through the city, connecting Lambertville to smaller towns further north, with Stockton a short three-mile walk, and the city's waterfront plays hosts to a number of activities, including rafting, tubing, kayaking, canoeing, and river trolleys.

SIGHTS

The **Lambertville Historical Society** (1–4 P.M. weekends, Apr.–Oct.) is housed in the **Marshall House** (62 Bridge St., 609/397-0770), the boyhood home of James Wilson

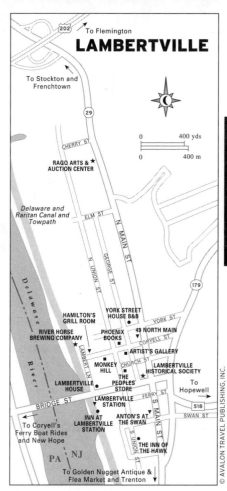

Marshall, who was first to discover California's gold in 1848 (along with partner Augustus Sutter). The society gives guided walking tours of Lambertville at 2 P.M. every first Sunday of the month, and holds an annual tour of local homes in October.

The slightly hidden **River Horse Brewing Company** (80 Lambert Ln., 609/397-7776,

downtown Lambertville

www.riverhorse.com) is a small two-story brew house offering tastings (noon–5 P.M. daily, $1) and self-guided tours. It occupies an old-brick factory down Lambert Lane behind Lambert Square on the Delaware. The "hippo"—another word for River Horse—is sold in eight different Northeast states.

ENTERTAINMENT AND EVENTS

Coryell's Ferry Boat Rides (22 S. Main St., New Hope, PA, 215/862-2050, www.spirit of76.biz) take guests on half-hour excursions upon the Delaware in an open pontoon craft. Rides board across the river in New Hope and leave every 45 minutes, 10 A.M.–5:30 P.M. May–September.

The annual **Shad Festival** is a two-day fish extravaganza celebrating the return of shad to the Delaware River. Craft and food vendors and live music fill the event, which traditionally takes place in April.

◖ SHOPPING
Art Galleries and Specialty Shops

In Lambertville, the line between gallery and shop is often blurred. It's possible to find anything from functional sculptures to $1,000 oil paintings in this eclectic downtown, and if you can't find what you're looking for, look again— it's bound to be created in the meantime.

Amid the historic district's row homes, brick sidewalks, and former movie house turned apartment complex is **The Coryell Gallery at the Pork Yard** (8 Coryell St., 609/387-0804). If you're looking for pieces by local artists, this is the place to come. **Phoenix Books** (49 N. Union St., 609/397-4960) is an independent bookstore for rare, used, and out-of-print books, stocking a quality selection from genres including art, ancient history, and nature. The shop is a maze of stacks, and the staff both helpful and unobtrusive. A fairly new addition to this riverfront city, **Monkey Hill** (6 Coryell St., 609/397-3332, www.monkeyhill.net) is a great place. Its collection of folk art and antiques includes purses styled from vintage album covers, candles offering "Greetings from NJ," and sculpted pigs. Inside is an Artomat machine—pop $6 into this converted cigarette machine and you've bought yourself an original work of art. Bravo!

For truly functional folk art, shop at **A Mano Inc Contemporary Craft** (42 N. Union St., 609/397-0063, www.amanogalleries.com). Here, coffee tables come graced with painted-on chess and backgammon boards, complete with whimsical playing pieces. Wearable art and kaleidoscopes are also sold. The shop is located in Lambertville's old Five & Dime, and the sign still hangs above the door.

Greca LTD (16 Church St., 609/397-4565) sells hand-painted wallpaper depicting historic and exotic mural-like scenes.

The artist-owned and -operated **Artist's Gallery** (32 Coryell St., 609/397-4588, www.lambertvillearts.com) hosts changing monthly exhibits and features a wide array of artistic genres. Hours are limited—11 A.M.–6 P.M. Friday–Sunday or by appointment.

At **Antick** (54 N. Union St., 609/773-0287), Master Craftsman David Wilson creates gorgeous replicas of antique furniture in natural, dark wood, and painted shades.

Greene & Greene Gallery (32 Bridge St., 609/397-7774, www.greeneandgreene gallery.com) displays functional blown glass and fiber arts, as well as a selection of jewelry, furniture, and ceramics. For ethnic designs and faraway fabrics, there's **Sojourner** (26 Bridge St., 609/397-8849, www.sojourner.biz). At the **Belenikin Fine Art Gallery** (5 Lambert Ln., 609/397-5855, www.belenikin.com), oil and canvas works portray exquisitely illustrated persons and scenes by contemporary narrative painter Valeriy Belenikin.

Antique Stores

South of downtown is the **Golden Nugget Antique & Flea Market** (Rte. 29, 609/397-0811, www.gnmarket.com, 8 A.M.–4 P.M. Wed., Sat., and Sun.), an indoor/outdoor venue with 40 permanent shops and up to 200 outdoor tables—some covered—whose wares include vinyl, coins, baseball cards, and Pepsi glasses. Inside browse through shops crowded with old pinball games, Beanie Babies, and autographed celebrity posters. There are a few food stalls along one of the dirt paths, including a kettle-corn shop and a little café.

At the center of downtown is **The Peoples Store** (28 N. Union St., 609/397-9808), a three-story co-op stuffed with secretaries, drop-leaf tables, vintage swimsuits, silver, jewelry, oil paintings, and more. Continue north on Main Street from downtown to reach **Rago Arts & Auction Center** (333 N. Main St., 609/397-9374, www.ragoarts.com). This large-windowed warehouse was once the Jockey underwear factory, and its proprietor has been an appraiser on *Antiques Roadshow*. The center is home to both a private art gallery featuring 20th-century crafted wares including glass and tiles (call 609/397-1802 for showings) and an auction house that holds approximately 15 events annually, usually during spring and fall. Depending on the auction, items for sale may include arts-and-crafts furnishings, Tiffany blown glass, perfume bottles, and estate jewelry. For an up-to-date schedule, refer to the website.

ACCOMMODATIONS
$200-250

Set back from Bridge Street near the bank of the Delaware River, the **Inn at Lambertville Station** (11 Bridge St., 609/397-8300, www.lambertvillestation.com) is the city's largest bed-and-breakfast, with 45 spacious guestrooms and a spaciously cozy antique-filled lobby. Lodgings range in size from standard to suite, and an on-site champagne buffet brunch is held every Sunday. It's also the most family friendly of the bunch (though some kids may find it a bit too Victorian). Perks include river views from all rooms, and continental breakfast delivered to your door daily.

The colonial-style **York Street House B&B** (42 York St., 609/397-3007 or 888/398-3199, www.yorkstreethouse.com) stands on a spacious lot with a garden and seat-swing, and its front porch is graced with wooden rocking chairs. Six individually styled and amply sized guestrooms are adorned with period features (Room 3 has a speaking tube connecting to the kitchen), and some are updated with modern amenities like hot tub and flat-screen TV. Coffee, tea, and freshly baked sweets are always on hand in the common area, and morning breakfast is served by candlelight.

The Federal brick **Martin Coryell House B&B** (111 N. Union St.) is a three-story property once owned by the descendents of Lambertville's original founder. Guestrooms come equipped with coffeemaker, air conditioning, desk, TV, telephone, private bath, and a fireplace or stove, and personal touches are featured throughout the inn, including a hand-painted dining room ceiling. Weeknight discounts are offered to corporate travelers.

$250-300

Built in 1812, the ◖ **Lambertville House** (32 Bridge St., P.O. Box 349, 888/867-8859, www.lambertvillehouse.com) once served as a stagecoach stop and today is a guesthouse and restaurant, with 26 antique-filled rooms, some with balconies. Amenities include morning papers, bathrobes, and lighted make-up mirrors, and business travelers are accommodated with a number of meeting rooms and high-speed Internet. Complimentary continental breakfast is offered. It's a smoke-free and pet-free space. The hotel is situated at the foot of the bridge into New Hope, Pennsylvania.

The most romantic of Lambertville's lodgings is the **Chimney Hill Estate & Old Barn** (207 Goat Hill Rd., 609/397-1516 or 800/211-4667, www.chimneyhillinn.com), situated on eight acres of property outside the downtown proper. This 1820 country inn—popular with wedding parties—features 12 guestrooms and suites, many with fireplace and all with private bath, although smaller rooms are without TV and telephone (some would consider this a plus). Downstairs features an open-floor common area and a dining room where homemade breakfast is served daily. Saturday stays require a two-night minimum.

FOOD AND NIGHTLIFE

Lambertville has a wonderful variety of dining options, most located within the city's downtown center.

At the foot of the New Hope Bridge is **Lambertville Station** (11 Bridge St., 609/397-8300, www.lambertvillestation.com, $19–26), a large, touristy, converted railway house with a basement bar and seasonal dining along the train tracks. American food is served in a split-level space, colonial-themed with a lax dress code. A "sunset menu" is offered 4–6:30 P.M. weekdays, and a "Sunday casual" selection is available as well. Lunch is served 11:30 A.M.–3 P.M. Monday–Saturday, and dinner 4–9:30 P.M. Sunday–Thursday, until 11 P.M. Friday and Saturday. Brunch is offered 10 A.M.–3 P.M. Sunday, with a buffet 10:30 A.M.–2:30 P.M.

Across the street is the casual **Full Moon** (23 Bridge St., 609/397-1096, $15.95–26.94), a breakfast and lunch café serving American eats and a fine selection of egg dishes ($9). Dinner is only served on the full moon of every month. The café is open 8 A.M.–3 P.M. Monday, Wednesday–Friday, 9 A.M.–4 P.M. weekends, closed Tuesday.

BYO **Manon** (19 N. Union St., 609/397-2596, $18–25) is a colorfully painted French bistro with a small specials menu, and daily selections that include *poisson du jour* and bouillabaisse. Tables are dressed with sunflower cloths; antiques and a *Starry Night*–inspired ceiling round out the decor. Manon is open for lunch noon–2:30 P.M. Saturday, and for dinner 5:30–9 P.M. Wednesday and Thursday, until 10 P.M. Friday and Saturday, and 5–8 P.M. Sunday. Brunch is served 11:30 A.M.–2:30 P.M. Sunday.

Hidden behind the Coryell Gallery at the Pork Yard, **Hamilton's Grill Room** (8 Coryell St., 609/397-4343, www.hamiltonsgrillroom.com, 6–10 P.M. Mon.–Sat., 5–9 P.M. Sun., $23.50–30) serves Mediterranean cuisine in a gorgeous little space above the D&R Canal, with a warm tile floor, white linen, and door-like windows that offer an excellent view of the footpath and stream below, not to mention a no cell-phone policy. Drinks are BYO, or you can enjoy a round at the bar across the courtyard while waiting for a table.

⬥ 49 North Main (49 N. Main St., 609/397-5990) is a wonderful BYO with intimate indoor seating and an outdoor garden, where the "high table" stands available for walk-ins on a busy Saturday night. New American entrées are lovingly prepared with a homemade touch—I highly recommend the crab cake ($23) and the delectable mac and cheese ($12). Hours are 11 A.M.–8 P.M. Monday–Thursday, until 9 P.M. Friday and Saturday, closed Sunday.

Along downtown's southern outskirts is the romantic **Anton's at the Swan** (43 S. Main St., 609/397-1960, www.antons-at-the-swan.com, $25–32), where guests enjoy a changing menu of innovative American dishes amid rich colonial decor. Anton's is open 6–9 P.M. Tuesday–Thursday, until 10 P.M. Friday and Saturday, 4:30–8 P.M. Sunday, closed Monday. The bar stays open an hour later.

On the basement floor of Lambertville Station is the **Station Pub** (609/397-8300), a cozy and intimate space decorated in dark wood and green leather and equipped with wireless access for those who like to linger with their brew. Live entertainment is featured throughout the weekend, including Thursday night performances by local acts. A casual dining menu ($7.95–16.95) is available.

Nestled within the brownstone courtyard across from Hamilton's Grill Room is the **Boat House** (8½ Coryell St., 609/397-2244), a small bar adorned with old photos and paintings. Outdoor seating is available when weather permits. The bar opens at 4 P.M. Monday–Saturday, beginning at 2 P.M. Sunday.

GETTING THERE AND AROUND

To reach Lambertville from Flemington or Sergeantsville, take Route 523 southwest to Stockton and travel south along Route 29 for nearly four miles. Lambertville is 15 miles north of Trenton, 70 miles southwest of New York City, and 40 miles northeast of Philadelphia. Buses are available from Trenton, as well as numerous

other points. Once here, visitors will have little trouble finding their way around the downtown area, where there is ample signage for shops and eateries. Lambertville's downtown streets have four-hour metered parking.

Trenton, Lambertville, and the Delaware River towns to the north are connected by Route 29, a pleasant drive except for the stretch between Central Jersey's Capital City and Lambertville. This is a busy two-lane roadway with hardly a shoulder and plenty of road kill. I recommend taking Route 31 north from Trenton and connecting with Route 518 west, which will carry you in to the riverfront city. While a bit out of the way, it's worth it to forgo the anxiety.

STOCKTON

Just north (10 minutes) of Lambertville is the much smaller Stockton, a charming little river community connected to Pennsylvania by a free bridge with footpath. Bridge Street and Main Street (Route 29) are the main cross streets, and downtown you'll find a few shops and eateries that serve up excellent meals. Cyclists often stop here en route from Lambertville to Frenchtown along the D&R towpath, running right through town.

If you're looking for a break from more-touristy Lambertville, Stockton's the kind of place where you can take off your shoes, put your feet up, and have a drink while watching the sun set over the water. Parking is free, but public restrooms are hard to find. The entire downtown district is about two blocks long, surrounded by separated single-family and duplex Victorian stone and clapboard structures in faded green, white, and country yellow with peaked roofs. Stockton is definitely worth a visit.

Recreation

Enjoy a 20-minute carriage ride throughout the valley with **Stockton Carriage Tours** (609/397-9066, www.stocktoncarriagetours.com, $5/person). Carriages seat up to 12, and schedules and tour times change—so call ahead.

Route 29 north from Lambertville and past Stockton has a large shoulder for cyclists.

© LAURA KINIRY

Prallsville Mills, Stockton

Prallsville Mills

North of Stockton's town center is Prallsville Mills (Rte. 29 N., 908/397-3586), a 19th-century mill complex once operated as part of the Delaware and Raritan Canal. Included as part of the D&R State Park, the property features an old grain silo, gristmill, and sawmill, and the original machinery used to operate them. Today the site doubles as an antique and art showcase, hosting various events throughout the year and housing an indoor gallery for local artists.

Accommodations

$150-200: Situated upon a hillside east of downtown Stockton is the ◖ **Woolverton Inn** (6 Woolverton Rd., 609/397-0802, www .woolvertoninn.com), a 1792 stone manor estate located on 300 acres of woodlands, gardens, and farmland—with nothing behind it but countryside and rolling hills. Seven guestrooms, five cottages, and a loft are available, all with private baths, and a country breakfast greets visitors daily (served in bed upon request). Covered porches adorn the manor's first and second floors. If you're looking to escape, this is the place.

Food

Once a stagecoach stop, the huge, three-story stone **Colligan's Stockton Inn** (1 Main St., 609/397-1250, $20–25) stands atop Bridge Street along Main, keeping watch over the small downtown center. The inn is filled with interesting features—hardwood floors and fireplaces, wall murals and a low-ceilinged tavern, and on the back outdoor patio, a waterfall and wishing well that inspired the theatrical tune "There's a Small Hotel with a Wishing Well." The front veranda is an excellent place to unwind during warmer months. American cuisine is well-prepared, but from most accounts the inn's reputation comes from its historic significance, rather than its cuisine. Reporters from the famous Lindbergh baby kidnapping trial would congregate here, and Dorothy Parker, F. Scott Fitzgerald, and members of the Algonquin Round Table used the inn as a country meeting place. Unfortunately, as of January 2006, the Stockton Inn is closed indefinitely due to earlier floods.

For good old-fashioned comfort food, try **Meil's** (Bridge and Main Sts., 609/397-8033,

8 A.M.–9 P.M. Sun.–Thurs., until 10 P.M. Fri. and Sat.), an eat-in/take-out BYO serving meals three times daily. Grab a seat by the baked goods display and admire the collection of Shad Fest posters decorating the wall while you wait for your Pennsylvania Dutch–style chicken potpie ($13). If you're looking to splurge, try the Thanksgiving dinner ($22), complete with mashed potatoes *and* stuffing.

If you're in need of a newspaper, breath mints, or a picnic lunch head to **Errico's Market & Deli** (12 Bridge St., 609/397-0049), where you'll find a mini-market, deli, and a few outdoor tables that line the towpath. The cool thing about this place is that people pull up on their bikes and sit on the pavement along the D&R, enjoying their morning snack and coffee. What could be better?

Just northeast of Stockton is the village of Rosemont, where you'll find the **Cafe at Rosemont** (88 Kingwood–Stockton Rd., 609/397-4097), a homey and casual place perfect for weekend brunch, with a menu that includes a sun-dried tomato and spinach omelet ($9) and granola with fruit and yogurt ($7.50). Cyclists can grab a seat at the counter to savor their morning brew ($1.50). Brunch hours are 9 A.M.–2 P.M. weekends. Lunch is served 11 A.M.–3 P.M. Tuesday–Friday and dinner until 9 P.M. Wednesday–Sunday.

Shopping

Family-owned and -operated **Phillips' Fine Wines** (Bridge St., 609/397-0587, www.phillips finewines.com) has an extraordinary stock and a seemingly endless selection of vodkas, liqueur, beer (including the Lambertville-brewed River Horse), and, of course, wine.

DELAWARE AND RARITAN CANAL STATE PARK

The Delaware and Raritan Canal State Park (732/873-3050, www.dandrcanal.com) is made up of nearly 70 miles of the original Delaware and Raritan Canal (a.k.a., D&R Canal), including 22 miles of feeder canal located in the Skylands region. The canal was created in the early 1800s as a transport route for freight-car-

riers between New York and Pennsylvania— the work of thousands of Irish immigrants, dozens of whom perished from cholera and are said to be buried along the hillsides. Most active in the 1860s and '70s, the canal lost much of its business to the railroads and closed for good in 1932. Its remains were placed on the National Register of Historic Places in 1973, and the entire V-shaped expanse was declared a state park in 1974. It stretches from Central Jersey's New Brunswick west to Trenton (where a portion has been filled), and the feeder canal travels north from Trenton to Frenchtown. One of the park's most popular attractions is a towpath that runs along this portion, west of Route 29 and parallel to the Delaware River. This multiuse path is heavily used by casual cyclists, strollers, joggers, and inline skaters, and makes a wonderful alternative to traveling by auto between Hunterdon County's riverfront towns.

Sights along the canal include bridge tender houses, locks, and occasional fossil finds. Canoes for use on the water are for rent in Princeton and Central Jersey's Griggstown.

Camping

Just west of Stockton, **Bull's Island** (2185 Daniel Bray Highway/Rte. 29, 609/397-2949, Apr. 1–Oct. 31, $15) provides the D&R's only camping facilities, with 69 tent and trailer sites and restrooms with showers. Picnic tables are plentiful, and a modern information center stocked with brochures is located nearby. In April 2005 a two-day storm caused major damage to the campground, closing it for the remainder of the year. Check the park's website at www.dandrcanal.com for a current update.

Information and Services

The D&R's **Feeder Canal Office** (Rte. 29, 609/397-2949) is located by the lock near Bull's Island, and the **Main Canal Office** (625 Canal Rd., 732/873-3050) is in Somerset. The D&R is open daily sunrise to sunset.

There's a footbridge across to Pennsylvania at Bull's Island, and there are 30 access points along the canal with parking—some include

Trenton, New Brunswick, Lambertville, and Princeton. Delaware River access points (for electric motorboats) can be found in Lambertville and at Bull's Island. Boats, including canoes and kayaks, have to portage at all locks and at some bridges.

FRENCHTOWN

Don't let the name fool you—Frenchtown is not actually French. The town is named for Paul Henri Mallet-Prevost, "a French-speaking man from Switzerland," who built what is now the Frenchtown Inn at the foot of the Pennsylvania Bridge. The town boomed during the railroad era but declined with the Depression, and like Lambertville to its south, the fact that it was overlooked for many years is what ended up preserving its architecture and overall appeal. Today Frenchtown remains a hidden gem inhabited by many artists, though others are beginning to find their way here, and its small downtown is brimming with art galleries, antique stores, specialty shops, clothing boutiques, and restaurants. Many of its buildings are three-story bricks and Victorians with gingerbread attributes, painted in shades of purple velvet and colonial blue.

For such a small town there are plenty of art events going on, and true to form, the town does celebrate the French Bastille Day with an annual weekend-long event in July.

Shopping

Tucked within Bridge Street's little brick-paved corner is the **Stone and Company Antiques** (8 Race St., 908/996-4840), where you'll find country-style antiques like a bird cage. **Philip W. Pfeifer Antiques** (19 Bridge St., 908/996-0166) is stocked with such "scientific and nautical antiques" as globes, model ships, weather vanes, and telescopes. Open weekends only. **Brooks Antiques** (24 Bridge St., 908/996-7161) features hooked rugs, ceramic dishware, hand-stitched dolls, dressers, and folk art paintings.

Art galleries include **Kissimmee River Pottery** (One 8th St., 908/996-3555, www.kissimmeeriverpottery.com), a pottery studio and gallery filled with functional ceramic pieces. **Decoys and Wildlife Gallery** (55

Frenchtown storefronts

Bridge St., 908/996-6501, http://decoyswildlife.com) is packed with paintings, bird and fish carvings, and plenty of bronze sculpture. For glass art try **Mendham Gallery** (33 Bridge St., 908/996-2243), where you'll find blown-glass vases, stained glass butterflies, and glass teapots with stainless steel attributes designed by Paul Counts. The gallery displays the work of over 100 artists, and also features jewelry, pottery, and worked iron, among other items.

Clothing boutiques include **Blue Fish at Barclay Studio** (62 Trenton Ave., 908/996-3720, www.barclaystudio.com). Founded locally in 1985, the store features hand-printed fashions and loose-flowing organic cotton wear, and is located just south of the downtown center. **Alchemy Creative Clothing and Gallery** (17 Bridge St., 908/996-9000, www.alchemyclothing.com) features the work of over 50 designers of women's clothing, scarves, bags, shoes, and jewelry. The selection ranges from casual to glamorous, and clothing can be individually custom-suited. Housed within the historic Gem Building—the first storefront in

Frenchtown—is **Race Street Kids** (15 Race St., Suite 4, 908/996-6787), selling fun and colorful children's clothing and specialty items.

Pets are welcome to snoop around at **Fifi Pet Boutique** (36 Bridge St., 908/996-0066) and help owners pick out outfits, treats, and grooming products for their "best friend's" harried life.

Try **Minette's Candies** (33 Race St., 908/996-5033) for all your truffles and fudge needs. **Moonlight Botanicals** (43 Bridge St., 908/996-0009) sells organic and handmade natural beauty products and home and animal goods, like car freshener and "smelly dog spray" to keep those canine odors at bay.

Beasley's Bookbindery (106 Harrison St., 908/996-9993, www.beasleysbookbindery.com) is a well-kept shop selling stationary and binding books in the classic style, and hosting occasional art events. Housed in a lovely blue Victorian, the **Book Garden** (28 Bridge St., 908/996-2022, www.bookgarden.biz) is a cozy, multi-room bookstore decorated with throw rugs and two comfortable window-side chairs to while away the afternoon. Proprietor Esther Tews began the store after "retiring" in 1999, and her book sales contribute to the *New York Times* bestseller list.

European Country Designs (35 Bridge St., 908/996-7463) stocks linens, furniture, rugs, and hand-painted ceramics reminiscent of the Mediterranean countryside. Housed within an Italianate Victorian, **The Studio** (12 Bridge St., 908/996-7424) displays a varied collection of glass art, rugs, mirrors, and furniture upon two floors. For country decor try **Thistle** (38 Bridge St., 908/996-7080), where you'll find a fine selection of cupboards and cabinets.

Sports and Recreation

For water-filled fun there's **Delaware River Tubing, Inc.** (2998 Daniel Bray Hwy., 908/996-5386, www.delawarerivertubing.com), located along Route 29 south of Frenchtown. Tubing excursions run up to four hours in length daily during summer, and rafting trips are also available. Cost includes a meal from the "River Hot Dog Man" (www.riverhotdogman.com)—a vendor selling snacks, sweets, sodas, and simple meals from a floating stand along the river. Tubing begins at 10 A.M. weekdays, and 9 A.M. weekends, and costs $15.95 adult, $14.95 child. Two-person rafts are $21.95 adult, $19.95 child weekends.

About seven miles south across the river is **Bucks County River Country** (2 Waters Ln., Point Pleasant, PA, 215/297-5000), which features canoeing and kayaking in addition to rafting and tubing. "Snuggle tubes" are available for lovebirds or parents traveling with kids, and a "full moon splash" is occasionally offered for boaters 18 and over. The cost of weekday tubing is $18, a two-person raft $48, six miles in a two-person canoe $50, and in a two-person kayak $68.

For a day of cycling stop by **Freeman's Bicycle Shop** (52 Bridge St., 908/996-7712), the perfect starting point for enjoying the towpath along the D&R Canal. Choose between a mountain bike, tandem, or recumbent (similar to a lounge chair on wheels). For those with small kids, the shop rents both trailers and attachments. An hour on the mountain bike costs $6.50, $24 for the day, while tandem and recumbent bikes go for $10/hour, $40/day. Additional child attachments are $6.50/hour.

Yogis will find refuge at downtown's **Yoga Loka** (34 Bridge St., Suite #2, 908/268-7430, www.yoga-loka.com, $15 drop-in).

Accommodations

$100-150: Enjoy a relaxing stay at the **Widow McCrea Bed & Breakfast** (53 Kingwood Ave., 908/996-4999, www.widowmccrea.com), an 1878 Italianate Victorian offering four antique-filled guestrooms and a cottage. A gourmet candlelit breakfast is served each morning, and afternoon tea and a bottle of wine are complimentary. Private bath, air-conditioning, and telephone are standard amenities.

The **National Hotel** (31 Race St., 908/996-4500, www.frenchtownnational.com) resembles something straight out of a Hemingway novel—an absolutely stunning decor of leopard print and camel color, contrasted with dark wood beams and beds draped in mosquito netting. Rooms include a continental breakfast, along with high-speed Internet and central air, and some with whirlpool tub and balcony. A wide veranda beckons onlookers inside.

$150-200: Away from the town center is the **Guesthouse at Frenchtown** (85 Ridge Rd., 908/996-7474, www.frenchtown guesthouse.com), a two-story 18th-century colonial that's available for overnight stays or long-term rentals. You'll have the home and its surrounding 70 acres all to yourself, and the property includes a hiking trail and a small outdoor dining area. Inside is a living room, fully equipped kitchen stocked with basic breakfast items, two bedrooms each with queen bed, air-conditioning, cable TV, and bath. There's a two-night minimum stay on weekends, and weekly rates run $1,100 during the high season.

Food and Nightlife

Frenchtown has a few wonderful restaurants with a bit of variety tossed in.

At the foot of the Pennsylvania Bridge is the three-story **Frenchtown Inn** (7 Bridge St., 908/996-3300, www.frenchtowninn.com, $21–29), an 1805 historic inn serving French-inspired continental cuisine. Inside you'll find high ceilings, brick walls, and large round tables, and a long bar and grill for a more casual meal. Hours are noon–2 P.M. Tuesday–Saturday for lunch, and 6–9 P.M. Tuesday–Friday, 5:30–9:30 P.M. Saturday, and 5–8 P.M. Sunday for dinner. Brunch is served noon–2:15 P.M. Sundays. Closed Monday.

Across the street from the inn is the **Bridge Café** (8 Bridge St., 908/996-6040, www.bridgecafe.net, 7 A.M.–5 P.M. Sun.–Thurs., until 9 P.M. Fri. and Sat.), where you'll find simple meals, coffee drinks, and friendly service. The café, housed in Frenchtown's original train depot, also sells ice cream.

Local residents can't say enough about **Cocina Del Sol** (10 Bridge St., 908/996-0900, closed Tues., $9–15) a superb BYO serving California-Mexican cuisine and the oldest such restaurant—and one of the few—in the region. Lunch is served noon–3 P.M. weekends and dinner 5–9 P.M. Tuesday–Thursday, until

10 P.M. Friday and Saturday, and 4–8 P.M. Sunday, closed Mondays. **Race Street Cafe** (2 Race St., 908/996-3179, 11 A.M.–3 P.M. weekends, 5–9 P.M. Thurs.–Sat., until 8 P.M. Sun., $15–25) is a tiny BYO with a reasonably priced menu and a fairytale facade, serving favored eclectic cuisine and homemade desserts.

Situated within the National Hotel, **Lila** (31 Race St., 908/996-4871) features made-to-order innovative American dishes like mixed-herb polenta cakes with sun-dried tomatoes ($15), and tapas-size plates that include French fries with pesto mayo ($4). Lunch is served 11:30 A.M.–3 P.M. Monday–Thursday, and dinner 5–9 P.M. Sunday–Thursday, until 10 P.M. Friday and Saturday. Also within the hotel is the **Rathskellar Pub** (11:30 A.M.–10 P.M. Mon.–Fri., until 2 A.M. Saturday, noon–8 P.M. Sunday), a classy, warm-toned space, where you'll find a menu of decadent martinis and specialty drinks.

Getting There and Around

Frenchtown is approximately 90 minutes from New York City and 90 minutes from Philly. Buses run from New York City's Port Authority Bus Terminal and take an hour and forty-five minutes.

Route 29 between Stockton and Frenchtown is deer central—remain very alert while driving, especially at dusk and during evening hours. Sheer cliffs line the road to the east in this area, and you'll see a few homes that seem as though they've been carved from rock.

Information

A great source for up-to-date Frenchtown information is www.frenchtowner.com, a wonderfully designed site filled with listings, articles, and a blog describing local news and happenings.

MILFORD

Just north of Frenchtown is Milford, a suburbanized river town situated at the foot of a tree-covered bluff. Like the towns to its south, Milford has a bridge that crosses over into Pennsylvania, and **Bridge Street** serves as the area's main thoroughfare. Larger than Stockton but smaller than Frenchtown, Milford is a bit sharper around the edges—it could be the service industries that occupy Bridge Street, or that its buildings are spread wide rather than packed tightly in a row. Milford looks as though it should exist somewhere along the Oregon Coast, but it's a unique Mid-Atlantic property with a few excellent restaurants and the perfect B&B.

Ballooning

Ready for more ballooning? Try **Alexandria Balloon Flights** (Sky Manor Airport, 42 Sky Manor Rd., Pittstown, 888/HOT-AIR-7 or 888/468-2477, www.njballooning.com). Advance notice is recommended. A standard two-person balloon flight runs $165. Flights last about an hour, and evening flights are followed by hors d'oeuvres and champagne. Do not wear sandals or open-toed shoes. On the ground at the Balloon Loft you'll find a gift shop.

Accommodations

$150-200: Removed from the Bridge Street bustle is **Chestnut Hill on the Delaware** (63 Church St., 908/995-9761, www.chestnuthillnj.com,), a tranquil and romantic Victorian bed-and-breakfast situated upon the Delaware. Innkeepers Rob and Linda begrudgingly moved to New Jersey on a corporate assignment in 1982, and a three-year stint lasted over twenty. Only the third family to own the inn, they have poured themselves into it, with a strictly Victorian living area and a completely modernized kitchen. A large veranda looks out over the water, and homemade cookies are available throughout the day. Lovely guestrooms are sizable enough for two, and all but one enjoy private bath and TV. High-speed Internet is available.

Food and Entertainment

Milford is home to New Jersey's first brew pub, **The Ship Inn Restaurant and Brew Pub** (61 Bridge St., 908/995-0188, www.shipinn.com), established in 1985. The building itself has been around since the late 1800s and has functioned as both a bakery and an ice cream parlor before its present incarnation. The Ship Inn's owners are British, and the cuisine is authentic pub grub like fish-and-chips and London broil. The dining room has window seats that look out over **Milford Creek,** and wireless

THE SKYLANDS

bustling Bridge Street, Milford

© LAURA KINIRY

Internet is offered throughout. Lunch is served daily noon–3 P.M. and dinner from 4–10 P.M. A late-night menu is available 10 P.M.–close (midnight weekdays, 1 A.M. Saturday).

A great place for dinner is the **Milford Oyster House** (92 Rte. 519, 908/995-9411, www.milfordoysterhouse.com, 5–9 P.M. Wed.–Mon., until 10 P.M. Fri. and Sat., $18–24). A bit north of the town center, this restaurant specializes in seafood, but serves a selection of meat, pasta, and poultry dishes as well.

Getting There
Milford is located 5 miles north of Frenchtown and 35 miles north of Lambertville on Route 29.

PHILLIPSBURG
Rural Warren County's largest town, 3.2-square-mile Phillipsburg—or "P-Burg," as the locals say—has long been a major transportation hub, and in 1998 the town was chosen as the future site of the New Jersey Transportation Heritage Center, a "theme park" to honor the state's transportation history. The town already has a couple of railway centers, two bridges into Pennsylvania (one free and one toll), and runs a scenic steam train throughout the year. To an outsider, P-Burg looks like an industrial river town filled with two- and three-story red, brown, and green brick and Victorian buildings, some with Queen Anne turrets and mansard roofs, but insiders claim the town is undergoing a resurgence, with artists moving in and some notable restaurants beginning to set up shop. In the meantime, the downtown area is a designated Urban Enterprise Zone, and includes Union Square, the entry to the town's historic business district east of the free bridge (the Easton–Phillipsburg Toll Bridge is a few blocks north).

If you're a transportation or a train buff I highly recommend a visit, and while walking around, keep your eyes open for the **Bullman Street Stairway,** a set of 100 steps leading clear up the hillside from the waterfront, just south of Union Square. This cast iron stairway has been a part of downtown Phillipsburg since the early 1900s.

Transportation Museums
Three railway centers currently operate within Phillipsburg. The **Phillipsburg Railway Historians** (www.prrh.org, 10 A.M.–3 P.M. Sun.) run a small, recently renovated museum that's open to the public once a week on Sundays during the summer. They also operate a miniature railway on summer weekends. Admission is free to ride the train and enter the museum, though donations are accepted. The museum is located atop the hill on South Main Street. The **New York Susquehanna and Western Technical and Historical Society** (908/454-4433, www.nyswths.org) operates Delaware River Railroad Excursions aboard open-window steam trains between P-Burg and Carpentersville, 11 A.M.–3 P.M. weekends (May–October, $10 adult, $5 child). A train nicknamed The Turtle Car operates on Thursday and Friday nights in July and August, and Santa and Easter Bunny trains pull out of the station at appropriate times during the year.

The **Friends of New Jersey Transportation Heritage Center** (178 S. Main St., 908/689-0472, www.njthc.org, 11 A.M.–4 P.M. Sat. and Sun.) runs a small exhibit space where you'll find a model train display and numerous photos of P-Burg during its transportation heyday. A site designated to house the future Transportation Heritage Center has instead been ceded for residential units, delaying construction indefinitely.

Festivals and Events
The fourth weekend in July Phillipsburg hosts the annual **Ole Town Festival,** featuring food, crafts, music, and carnival rides over two days, and concluding with a fireworks display. The **Riverside Festival of the Arts** takes place in September, and includes entertainment, arts, and crafts. Over the last few years it has operated in conjunction with a similar festival in Easton "Crayola" Pennsylvania, across the river. Two juried events are the highlight of the festivals—a juried craft show in Phillipsburg and a juried art show in Easton.

The town also hosts a **Criterium Bike Race** in September.

TIBETAN CULTURE IN THE GARDEN STATE

New Jersey and Tibet share a unique connection. The state's Newark Museum houses the largest collection of Tibetan artifacts in the western hemisphere, the first U.S. Lhasa Apso – a small Tibetan dog that was only permitted out of country as a gift – made its home at Gladstone's Hamilton Farm, and neatly tucked away along a residential back road in Warren County is the **Tibetan Buddhist Learning Center** (93 Angen Rd., Washington, 908/689-6080), or Labsum Shedrub Ling, the site where the 14th Dalai Lama gave his first lecture to a U.S. audience and where he has since visited more than a handful of times.

Geshe Ngawang Wangyal, a Kalmyk-Mongolian lama, originally founded the center in 1958 as the Lamaist Buddhist Monastery of America in Central Jersey's Howell Township. It moved to Washington when it became evident that a growing number of Westerners were interested in learning the teachings of Tibetan Buddhism and an educational facility was needed. Under the direction of the Dalai Lama, recognized as the center's spiritual teacher, the monastery's name was changed to its present incarnation in 1984.

Although Geshe-la passed away in 1983, his room is much as he'd left it. A photo highlighting his jovial nature hangs on the wall, as does one showing Robert Thurman, father of actress Uma Thurman and the first Westerner ever to be ordained as a Buddhist monk. By request of Geshe-la and the Dalai Lama, the center is run today by husband and wife Joshua and Diana Cutler, who each arrived here in the 1970s and have since remained fully committed as instructors, translators, and caretakers. The center's 32 acres consist of a prayer room, classroom, lodging quarters, and plenty of open space, as well as a simple apartment for the Dalai Lama to use during his regional visits.

A prayer and meditation session takes place every Sunday 11 A.M.-noon, followed by a class on Tibetan Buddhism. Neither is offered on weekends when the center is hosting a seminar, an occasional occurrence throughout the year. Donations are requested for classes, room, and board. For further information, visit the center's website at www.labsum.org.

THE SKYLANDS

Sports and Recreation

For an upward experience try **Balloonatics and Aeronuts** (7 Harmony-Brass Castle Rd., 908/454-3431, 877/4-FUN-FLY or 877/438-6359, www.aeronuts.com) or **Have Balloon Will Travel** (57 Old Belvidere Rd., 908/454-1991, www.haveballoonwilltravel.com).

Food

Not your typical P-Burg place, **Sugar: The Patisserie** (140 S. Main St., 908/387-6777, www.eatatsugar.com, $15–27) is the city's foray into fine dining. Continental cuisine is served in a warm and inviting space where you'll also find shelves of baked, custard-filled, and powered goods and espresso drinks. Dessert is key. Hours are 11 A.M.–9 P.M. Wednesday and Thursday, until 11 P.M. Friday and Saturday, 8 A.M.–4 P.M. Sunday, closed Monday and Tuesday.

For something easy and cheap there's **Jimmy's on the Delaware** (7 Union Square, 908/454-2999, 11 A.M.–10 P.M. daily, $1–5), serving up hot dogs, burgers, soft drinks, and milkshakes daily. It's named for a hot dog stand that once stood in its place years ago.

THE JERSEY SHORE

For nearly two centuries, New Jersey's 127-mile Atlantic coastline has been a favorite vacation spot for northeast travelers, and more recently for Canadians and Europeans, looking to spend their summers "down the Shore." There's no doubt about it—the Shore is where it's at. Pennsylvanians and New Yorkers clog the state's highways along with New Jersey's own "shoobies" and "bennies," all heading toward sun, surf, and fun that can only be found along the boardwalks and in the casinos, restaurants, bars, and bays of the Shore. Ladies slick back their locks in an effort to prevent the inevitable frizz, and guys dump their work suits for Bermudas and flip-flops. A week's worth of attire can fit into a weekend tote bag—it doesn't take much to cover up in the sticky Shore heat. Once along the

beaches, the blankets come out, accompanied by striped umbrellas and starfish-patterned chairs; the lotion is slapped on; and the bodysurfing, Frisbee tossing, and trashy-novel-reading begins. Kids break out their buckets and shovels to dig their way to China as banner planes fly low overhead, advertising the local bar's latest surf-and-turf special.

The Jersey Shore is made up of mostly low-lying barrier islands surrounded by back bays and wetlands, though a few towns exist on the mainland. Along the water you'll find fine sandy beaches, scrubs, dunes, and plenty of beach erosion. Beaches are constantly being artificially replenished, only to be washed away with the next big storm. Though Lenape Indians were known to enjoy the Shore, it became the stretch of seaside resort that it's known

HIGHLIGHTS

🌙 **Sandy Hook:** Where else in New Jersey can you swim in the ocean (naked, if you like) and bask in the backdrop of Manhattan (page 132)?

🌙 **Spring Lake:** The Jersey Shore of the past is alive in the grandeur of Spring Lake. Revel in the days gone by in this elegantly classic beachfront town (page 147).

🌙 **Barnegat Lighthouse State Park:** This park is home to one of the state's endeared lighthouses. Climb the 217 steps to the top of Old Barney and enjoy a much-earned picnic on the nearby jetty afterward (page 158).

🌙 **Atlantic City's Casinos:** Move over Vegas, the AC is back and she's "Always Turned On." With a new slew of beach bars, restaurants, and shopping additions, there's nowhere to go but up (page 169).

🌙 **Lucy the Elephant:** This multi-story pachyderm has weathered well over a century standing along Margate's coast, having spent days as both a tavern and hotel before her current stint as a museum. With a new coat of paint and freshly painted toenails, she has no plans to retire her trunk (page 181).

🌙 **Ocean City:** The best little Shore town this side of America. My nephew thinks his granddad owns the boardwalk because of all the time my father spends there. Oh, how I wish he did (page 183).

🌙 **Wildwood's Boardwalk:** Packed with amusement rides, stuffed prizes, fried-food stands, tacky T-shirt shops, and one of the surliest tram cars around, this two-mile waterfront stretch is as wonderful as they come. Pair it with the neon lights and plastic palms of the surrounding Doo Wop motels, and you've got yourself the kitschiest place along the Jersey Shore (page 193).

🌙 **Cape May's Bed-and-Breakfasts:** Spend the night in one of the dozens of B&Bs

LOOK FOR 🌙 TO FIND RECOMMENDED SIGHTS, ACTIVITIES, DINING, AND LODGING.

in this wonderfully Victorian Shore town and you'll be transported to a world of gas-lit streets, wide verandas, horse-drawn carriages and all the gingerbread accents you could wish for. And unlike much of the Jersey Shore, Cape May enjoys an event-filled 10-month season (page 203).

THE JERSEY SHORE

THE JERSEY SHORE

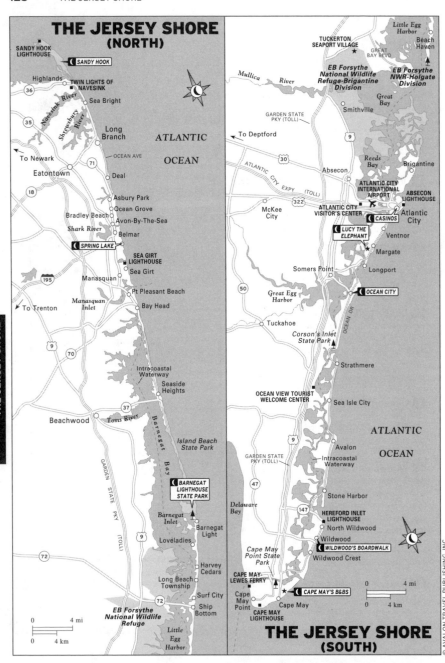

as today in the 1850s, when railways made it easy for city folk to escape to these "far away" beaches. At the same time religious groups founded Shore towns as camp meeting places. Towns like Ocean City and Ocean Grove still retain much of this religious history, and the effects are felt on their downtown streets.

The Shore has had its fair share of hardships. Two centuries ago hundreds of shipwrecks occurred off the coast, in 1916 a series of shark attacks terrorized the central coast, and in the 1980s hypodermic needles washed up on Shore. Most recently the Shore has earned a reputation as an unfriendly place, outsiders citing the "Jersey" (the local attitude) rather than the Shore itself as the main problem source.

But mind you, the Shore's a big place. And as every Shore-tripper knows, the town you go to says as much about who you are as does your name. There are the party towns of Belmar, Seaside, and Wildwood; the family boardwalks of Ocean City and Point Pleasant Beach; the desperate glory of Asbury Park; the nightlife of Atlantic City; and the upscale bed-and-breakfast resort communities of Spring Lake and Cape May. You've got the New Yorkers to the north and Philadelphians to the south—they meet somewhere around Long Beach Island.

The boardwalks, though existent, are not "real" boardwalks (i.e., with amusements, fried foods, souvenir shops) until you reach Point Pleasant heading south. But don't be deterred—most of the towns without beachfront strips offer plenty of recreational activities to keep you occupied. Most of the coastal beaches are loaded with shells—clam, conch, oyster—as well as horseshoe crabs and, during the hottest months, the vicious green fly.

And remember—you don't have to be born at the Jersey Shore to belong here. Sure, locals may roll their eyes at weekenders who clog up the beaches and steal parking spaces, but anyone can adopt a Shore town if they like. There's no denying—the Shore becomes you—it's almost inevitable. And at that first break of summer light, that first summer day, when the salty sea smell lies low in the air and the ocean breeze blows, you know where you're going: down the Shore.

BEST OF THE JERSEY SHORE

With so much to experience along the Jersey Shore, planning a visit can be a daunting task. It's nearly impossible to take everything in on one trip, so what's a person to do? To make things easier, here's a list of the best the Jersey Shore has to offer, from the perfect place to enjoy a rainy afternoon to the most romantic towns along the coast. Use it to narrow down the ideal spot for you.

Best amusements: Wildwood (page 192)

Best beaches: Belmar (page 145), Cape May Point (page 207)

Most tempting boardwalk eats: Jenkinson's Boardwalk at Point Pleasant Beach (page 151) and Ocean City Boardwalk (page 184)

Best family towns: Ocean City (page 183), Point Pleasant (page 151)

Best nightlife: Atlantic City (page 174), Asbury Park (page 140)

Best shopping: Atlantic City (page 175), Spring Lake (page 147)

Best bird-watching: Cape May (page 208), Island Beach State Park (page 156), Stone Harbor (page 191), Brigantine (page 178)

Best outdoor recreation activities: Sandy Hook (page 132), Island Beach State Park (page 156)

Best bargains: the bed-and-breakfasts of Ocean Grove (page 143), the free beaches of Atlantic City (page 169) and Wildwood (page 194)

Best on a rainy day: Atlantic City (page 165)

Best year-round town: Cape May (page 199)

Most romantic getaways: Cape May (page 199), Spring Lake (page 147)

Best seasonal haunts: Beach Haven (page 162), Surf City (page 160)

Best food: Cape May (page 204), Atlantic City (page 177)

Best tacky shore experience: Wildwood (page 192)

Best boardwalks: Ocean City (page 184), Wildwood (page 193), Atlantic City (page 167), Seaside Heights (page 154)

PLANNING YOUR TIME

The Shore is such an expansive place with so many different personalities that it's not one of those places you can, or should try to, cover in one visit. Most travelers stick to a particular town or region, though it is possible to drive down the coast and cover the highlights in a week's time. The Shore is a wonderful place because it makes for the perfect day trip, weekend, or seasonal excursion. If you do have a limited time—say a day or weekend—choose a section that's near your starting destination.

If you are traveling from New York City, stick to the Northern Shore or Barnegat Peninsula. Sandy Hook makes a good carless day trip: it's accessible by ferry from the city (summers only) and a bus can carry you to various points around the peninsula. A car gives you more range, allowing you to add to your trip with a drive down the coast from Sea Bright through the various Shore towns. To extend your trip into a weekend, Spring Lake is an ideal place to spend the night, but if it's high season I recommend backtracking to Ocean Grove, where accommodations are less expensive. The following morning, continue down the coast to Point Pleasant Beach for a walk on Jenkinson's Boardwalk, which a lot tamer than other boards and offers a good feel for the Shore without being overwhelming. Depending on your preference, afterward you may want to take a walk along the Shore or venture further south to experience the boardwalk of Seaside Heights, definitely the Northern Shore's craziest and most oddly interesting stretch of sand. If you're in a hurry to get back, you can hop on the Garden State Parkway for a quick drive (as long as it's not the height of the summer season) north.

From Philadelphia, your best bets are Cape May and the greater Cape region or Long Beach Island. On a day trip, your one stop should be Cape May. Get there early for breakfast, and afterward book a spot on one of the many tours available at the Washington Mall Information Booth. Peruse the nearby shops, venturing out into the nearby historic district if you have time, before returning for your afternoon excursion. After the tour you have numerous options: Drive out to Sunset Beach to search for Cape May Diamonds, then on to nearby Cape May Lighthouse; walk along the beachfront promenade and explore the city; or take Ocean Drive north to the Wildwood boardwalk for an evening of cotton candy and amusements. Extend your trip into the weekend and you can do it all, and stay at one of Cape May's numerous Victorian bed-and-breakfasts (highly recommended).

If visiting in the off-season (past October and before April), many places will be closed down: Cape May and Atlantic City are your two best bets for year-round entertainment. Atlantic City is a place that is worth a weekend unto itself—visiting the casinos, walking the Boardwalk, shopping and dining at the Quarter, and venturing out into the greater Atlantic City vicinity for a visit to Lucy the Elephant and a stop at one of the nearby wineries.

During the height of the summer season, many Shore accommodations require a 2–3 night minimum stay, usually on weekends. If possible, it's best to plan an overnight trip midweek—accommodations are at their cheapest Tuesday–Thursday evenings. Be aware that many dining establishments, especially along the boardwalks, are cash-only.

Weekly and seasonal rentals are common in many Shore towns, including Belmar, Bradley Beach, Point Pleasant Beach, Beach Haven, Ocean City, Sea Isle, and the Wildwoods, and local realtors specialize in summer tourism. The best time to search for accommodation is in the off-season, January–March, when you'll have the highest selection of choices—rentals tend to go quickly.

Take note: The sand gets extremely hot in the summer and can be unbearable to walk on without shoes—bring your flip-flops.

INFORMATION AND SERVICES
Beach Tags

Almost all of New Jersey's beaches—with the exception of Atlantic City and the Wildwoods—require the purchase of daily beach tags Memorial Day–Labor Day. You can usually purchase them at boardwalk kiosks or from beach tag checkers at beach entryways. More than a few dollars can be saved by purchasing a weeklong or (if you're planning a long trip) seasonal pass. If there's nobody around to check payment, don't be fooled into thinking you've escaped a fee. At many of the Shore's beaches, tag checkers walk up and down the sand, stopping at your blanket just as you're about to take a bite out of your gritty PB&J sandwich and making you lay down cash for yourself and your family on-site. Sure, the fee's a nuisance, but the money goes toward restoring the beaches for our future use. Still don't want to pay? Wait until after 5 P.M., when the lifeguards go off duty, or head to the Wildwoods or Atlantic City, where the beaches are free.

Visitors Centers

The Shore's two welcome centers are located along the region's southern stretch. The **Atlantic City Welcome Center** (Atlantic City Expressway Mile Marker 3.5, Pleasantville, 609/383-2727) can be found upon entry to the city by way of the Atlantic City Expressway, and the Cape's **Ocean View Tourist Welcome Center** (Garden State Parkway Mile Marker 18.3 N/S, 609/624-0918) is situated along the Garden State Parkway west of Sea Isle City. Both centers provide brochures, maps, and a variety of information regarding the surrounding regions. For Shore points further north, contact the town or city's chamber of commerce. Also, most welcome centers in the outlying greater New Jersey regions provide information on Shore attractions and accommodations since the area is the state's top travel destination.

Parking

Finding parking on a weekend during the height of the summer season can be a nightmare, especially in towns with boardwalks. Private lots are found most places, but prices can be steep ($10–15), and in most downtown areas, meters are the norm. The best thing to do is to get to town early, find a cush spot away from the action, and stay put for a while.

GETTING THERE AND AROUND

Travelers to the Jersey Shore have a number of options for getting here, depending on the town or city they're visiting. **NJ Transit's** (www.njtransit.com, 800/772-3606) North Jersey Coast Line runs trains daily as far down the coast as Bay Head, with stops in Long Branch, Asbury Park, Bradley Beach, Belmar, Spring Lake, Manasquan, and Point Pleasant Beach. **SeaStreak** (732/872-2600, 800/BOAT-RIDE or 800/262-8743, www.seastreak.com) runs a daily commuter ferry from New York City to the Northern Shore's Highlands, and on weekends throughout summer runs a ferry from Manhattan to Sandy Hook Gateway National Recreation Area.

Charter and tour buses running from both New York City and Philadelphia are a popular way to reach Atlantic City, although the city can also be reached from downtown Philadelphia by way of the **PATCO Speedline** (www.drpa.org/patco/index.asp), a transit line run by the Delaware River Port Authority. Another way to reach the region is to fly to **Atlantic City International Airport** (609/645-7895, www.acairport.com/contact.html). To reach the Jersey Shore Cape without having to deal with cross-state traffic, catch the **Cape May-Lewes Ferry** (800/64-FERRY or 800/643-3779, www.capemaylewesferry.com) in Lewes, Delaware. You'll be dropped off—car and all—just outside Cape May city.

If you are arriving to the Shore by car, the Garden State Parkway travels west of the coastline, remaining pretty much parallel from the Northern Shore all the way down to the Cape. Heading north, the Parkway continues straight into New York State and is easily accessible from many points in the Gateway Region, including by way of the New Jersey Turnpike from New York City. The Parkway is a toll road and traffic can get pretty bad during rush hours and summer weekends, but it does provide easy access to every town along the Shore.

Another option from New York is to take Route 9 (which begins as Route 1-9 in the

Gateway Region) south. The road travels west of the Parkway until the Barnegat Bay region, where the two routes cross over one another. Route 9 hugs the shoreline at this point and remains this way, for the most part, until the Cape region where they cross over each other once again.

Those traveling from Philadelphia can reach the southern Shores by way of the Atlantic City Expressway, an extremely straightforward toll road accessible from Route 42 that, on a good day, will get you to the slots in an hour. Heavy weekend traffic and an extreme lack of scenery are two reasons to look for other options. Route 55, also accessible by way of Route 42 and eventually turning into Route 47, leads visitors straight into Wildwood.

With so many barrier islands and inlets, it's impossible to drive a straight route through the Shore towns north–south, although it is possible to explore the individual regions in clus-ters. Route 36 travels from the Highlands east toward Sandy Hook and into Sea Bright, turning south toward Long Branch where it connects with a number of local avenues straight through to Manasquan. Here you can hop on Route 35 South and continue south through Seaside Heights straight into Island Beach State Park. This is the tricky park, because although you can see Long Beach Island from the southern tip of Island Beach, you have to catch Route 37 west from Seaside Heights to Route 9 or the Garden State Parkway and travel south to Route 72, turning east and crossing the Causeway Bridge to enter Long Beach Island—a trip that can take about an hour. The greater Atlantic City region and the southern Shore's Cape are connected by way of Ocean Drive, definitely the best route along the Shore. Ocean Drive is actually a series of local roads and bridges that make straight-through travel between Brigantine and Cape May not only possible, but extremely fun.

The Northern Shore

From Sandy Hook to Manasquan, New Jersey's Northern Shore is a conglomeration of stately mansions, recovering cities, late-night parties and romantic B&Bs. It's a decidedly New York and North Jersey hangout where you'll find great clubs and good surfing locales, and some of the best shopping ops along the Shore. Beach erosion has reduced the size of the northernmost beaches, leading to the development of private beach clubs from Sea Bright (south of Sandy Hook) straight through to Long Beach. As you continue south, numerous lakes and inlets dress the landscape, separating beach towns and lending postcard views. This northern strip of Shore is wider than those down south, creating a blend of beach town and residential suburb throughout many of the cities and boroughs, until reaching its southern point at Point Pleasant Canal.

Information and Services

Upstage Magazine (www.upstagemagazine .com) is a free publication listing shows and music events along Jersey's Northern Shore.

If you're looking for a weekly or seasonal beach house rental try **Diane Turton, Realtors** (www .dianeturton.com). This agency has locations in Sea Bright, Ocean Grove, Avon-By-The-Sea, and Spring Lake. You can find **The Mary Holder Agency** (www.maryholder.com) in Bradley Beach, Sea Girt, and Manasquan.

Getting There and Around

NJ Transit's **New Jersey Coast Line** runs from New York's Penn Station, Hoboken Terminal, and Newark's Penn Station with stops in Long Branch, Asbury Park, Bradley Beach, Belmar, Spring Lake, and Manasquan, continuing on to the Barnegat Peninsula.

◖ SANDY HOOK AND THE HIGHLANDS

On the northern portion of a barrier split protruding 11.2 miles from the city of Long Branch is the seven-mile Sandy Hook Peninsula. Often mistaken for a town, Sandy Hook is actually part of the greater 26,000-acre New Jersey/New York **Gateway National Recreation Area,** and at 1,665 acres, the Hook is a natural formation of salt marshes, coves, forest, and beaches dividing the Raritan Bay from the Atlantic. In 1974 Sandy Hook's southern portion—already a state park—was joined with its northern half, home to a decommissioned U.S. defense fort, and the two became part of the vast recreation facility.

Today Sandy Hook's visitors will find plenty to do. Numerous ocean and bay beaches are perfect for swimming, sunbathing, bird-watching, and water sports, and a multi-use trail runs the peninsula's entire length. The Hook's North Beach provides a backdrop of the Manhattan skyline, and just south of it stands the remains of the former fort and military batteries. A mile inland is the country's oldest continuously operating lighthouse, and farther south you'll find the Atlantic Coast's highest density of holly forest, and the state's only clothing-optional beach.

Most visitors combine a trip to Sandy Hook with the nearby Highlands, a seafaring town located just over the Highlands Bridge on the mainland. It's only natural—looking west from the Sandy Hook Peninsula, the Highlands greet you like a European city rising up on a waterfront hillside, and it's easy to be drawn here. Besides, this is where you'll find the area's B&Bs, as well as a few wonderful dining choices.

Sights

The bulk of the area's sights are in Sandy Hook, though the Highlands has a magnificent twin lighthouse that's worth a see.

In service since 1764, the **Sandy Hook Lighthouse** (Gateway National Recreation Area) remains the country's oldest operating lighthouse. It is also one of the states smaller ones, a two-and-a-half story white octagonal tower topped with a red lantern and located more than a mile inland from Sandy Hook's northern tip. Free tours are conducted by the New Jersey Lighthouse Society, noon–4 P.M. weekends April–November. Visitors must be taller than 48 inches to climb to the top.

BENNIES VS. SHOOBIES

So you haven't spent every summer day since birth at the Shore, your folks didn't inherit a beach home from their parents, you don't recognize your seasonal neighbors or the people who own the upstairs flat, and you've never worked on the boards. You're obviously not a local – so which are you, a benny or a shoobie?

Benny is the name adopted for day trippers along New Jersey's northern coast – an acronym for those arriving from the Great Northeast. The exact origin is unclear, but the word is a possible stand-in for "Bayonne, Elizabeth, and Newark," or even "Bergen, Essex, and New York." Along New Jersey's Cape and southern coast, shoobie is the designation of choice, a name based on the day travelers who used to arrive down the Shore with their lunches secured firmly in shoeboxes. Although both terms may be taken as derogatory, they're often viewed lightheartedly – in Sea Isle City there's even a restaurant named Shoobies. Still, if you'd rather not be mistaken for either, wear the sunscreen, lose the socks, and don't spend an hour on your 'do before hitting the sticky, salty air.

On the northern half of Sandy Hook are the remains of **Fort Hancock,** a U.S. coastal fort built to assist in the protection of New York Harbor. Army personnel employed to test military artillery at the Sandy Hook Proving Ground resided here, where there was also a hospital, school, bakery, and bowling alley. Battery defenses fortified with disappearing guns soon gave way to Nike missiles, and later Intercontinental missiles, before the fort was declared surplus in 1974 and all but abandoned. Today a battle ensues between preservationists and environmentalists over the future of these structures—should they be restored for use or the land given back to nature? A number of the buildings are now occupied for research and education purposes, and there are plans

THE JERSEY SHORE

© LAURA KINIRY

the Twin Lights of Navesink, Highlands

bird-watching locales: Over 340 bird species make their way through the region, including numerous waterfowl, raptor, and songbirds. The Hook is also a good spot to view butterflies, especially June–early October.

On the mainland hillside 200 feet above sea level, overlooking the Raritan Bay, are the **Twin Lights of Navesink** (Lighthouse Rd., Highlands, 732/872-1814, http://twin-lights.org/home.htm), two brownstone medieval-style turrets connected by a low-lying base. From the parking lot and the rear of the structure that's been designated a State Historic Site it all looks ordinary, but walk around front and you're greeted with a magnificent piece of architecture situated with a superb view of Sandy Hook and, on a clear day, a glimpse of the Manhattan skyline. The current lighthouse was built in 1862 and featured two lights—one stationary and one blinking—to make the area distinguishable to sailors. Both lights were decommissioned in 1949, though a commemorative light was placed in the north tower in 1962. Visitors can take a self-guided tour of this tower 10 A.M.–5 P.M. daily Memorial Day–Labor Day, Wednesday–Sunday the remainder of the year. Admission is free, and there's a small museum and gift shop on the premises.

Beaches

Sandy Hook has miles of ocean beaches that are open to swimmers and sunbathers. The best spots for swimming include the south beaches near Areas C and D, and **North Beach,** where you can jump the waves under the watch of the Manhattan skyline and marvel at low-flying planes as they make their descent into JFK Airport. One of the state's best-known beaches is also located along this stretch of Atlantic. Situated a little more than midway along the Hook, **Gunnison Beach** is New Jersey's only clothing-optional beach. A great sign pointing the way reads "Beyond this point you may encounter nude sunbathers."

Sandy Hook's beaches are open to the public all year, though there's a $10-per-vehicle parking fee to enjoy them during summer months.

to renovate a few dozen more for use as office space, labs, and lodging. Nearby still stand the decayed and weather-torn remnants of the old battery defenses.

Visitors can learn more about the history of Fort Hancock by stopping by the **Fort Hancock Museum and History House** on the bayside **Officer's Row.** The museum is open 1–5 P.M. weekends through July and August. Call the visitors center (732/872-5970) for additional hours.

The 20-inch **Rodman Gun** is located on the north end of Officer's Row. This huge canon is a Sandy Hook landmark, and the largest smooth bore muzzle loader ever made.

The New Jersey Audubon Society opened the **Sandy Hook Bird Observatory** (20 Hartshorne Dr., 732/872-2500, 10 A.M.–5 P.M. Tues.–Sat., 10 A.M.–3 P.M. Sun.) in 2001, and inside you'll find a small bookstore and gift shop, as well as information on bird sightings and the best viewing spots on the peninsula. Sandy Hook is considered one of the state's best year-round

Sports and Recreation

The one-mile **Old Dune Trail,** beginning at Area D near the visitors center, offers a nice overview of Sandy Hook and winds along the coast through a densely populated 200-year-old holly forest. Before starting off, stop by the center to pick up an information packet describing possible flora sightings. A paved six-mile multiuse path opened in 2004 and runs the length of the peninsula. It's almost entirely flat—making for easy use—though wind exposure can be a nuisance.

Surf fishing is a popular activity along the Hook's Atlantic side, and a beach dedicated to the sport lies just north of Area D. Proper license is required. Windsurfing, kayaking, and sailing are all easily enjoyed bayside, where you'll find a couple of small coves.

Accommodations

$150-200: The pet-friendly **SeaScape Manor B&B** (3 Grand Tour, Highlands, 732/291-8467, www.seascapemanorbb.com) features four country-elegant guestrooms, each with private bath. Gourmet breakfasts are served in the dining room or seasonally on the outdoor deck, and complimentary wine is available throughout the day. One of SeaScape's perks is the option of an in-room Thai massage; another is the complimentary use of Sandy Hook beach passes.

Grand Lady by the Sea (254 Rte. 36, Highlands, 732/708-1900, www.grandladybythesea.com) is a 1910 brick Victorian located along Route 36, featuring five guestrooms and one suite. Antique furniture is subtly displayed in each of the rooms, and organic coffee is served mornings along with a continental breakfast. A full breakfast menu (including cheese blintzes) is available on weekends for an extra $10.

Food and Entertainment

Sandy Hook's only dining establishment is located above the refreshment stand next to the visitors center. The **Sea Gull's Nest** (Area D, Hartshorne Dr., 732/872-0025, $6.50–10) is an outdoor bar and restaurant serving casual American cuisine against an unbeatable backdrop of the Atlantic Ocean. This 1962 establishment stays open from dawn till dusk during summer months, closing out each day with a recorded rendition of "God Bless America" played at sunset.

In the Shore town of Sea Bright just south of the peninsula you'll find **Donovan's Reef** (1171 Ocean Ave., 732/842-6789, www.donovansreefseabright.com), a beachfront bar and grill and an area mainstay since 1976. Donovan's Reef attracts a diverse crowd of twenty- and thirtysomethings and baby boomers, all who like to gather at the outdoor tiki bar and enjoy live music, dance on the open deck, or swim at the establishment's private and guarded beach. The grill serves typical American fare (11 A.M.–8 P.M., $4–6.75) daily throughout summer, with bar hours continuing on into the night. Hours are limited during the off-season—call ahead.

Highlands offers a number of dining options to choose from, ranging from casual American cuisine to ethnic-inspired eats.

Doris & Ed's (348 Shore Dr., Highlands, 732/872-1565, www.dorisandeds.com) serves a mix of classic and contemporary dishes to a diverse and loyal clientele. The seafood-heavy menu includes such entrées as lobster tails ($30) and fillet of flounder—your choice, broiled or fried ($22). Hours are 5–10 P.M. Wednesday–Friday, until 11 P.M. Saturday, and 3–10 P.M. Sunday, September–June; 5–10 P.M. Tuesday–Friday, until 11 P.M. Saturday, and 3–10 P.M. Sunday, July and August; closed Monday year-round.

A local staple since 1917, **Bahrs Landing Restaurant** (2 Bay Ave., Highlands, 732/872-1245, www.bahrs.com, $17–30) is known for its fresh seafood and excellent waterfront views. Head indoors for fine dining or try the seasonal outdoor deck for kid-friendly chalkboard platters and picnic seats. Bahrs is open 11:30 A.M.–10 P.M. Monday–Thursday, until 10:30 P.M. Friday and Saturday, until 9 P.M. Sunday throughout the summer. Hours slightly vary the remainder of the year.

Information and Services

The **Sandy Hook Visitor Center** (732/872-5970,

10 A.M.–5 P.M.) is located two miles from the park entrance on the right, at Area D, and is housed in a former 1894 U.S. Lifesaving Station. Public restrooms are available, and a refreshment stand is open April–October. Alcohol is allowed within park boundaries—just no glass containers.

Getting There and Around
SeaStreak (732/872-2600, 800/BOAT-RIDE or 800/262-8743, www.seastreak.com) runs a 30-minute Beach Excursion ferry ($29 adults, $14 child round-trip) from New York City to Sandy Hook and back on weekends throughout the summer. A free shuttle for ferry riders operates from Area D to designated stops throughout the park. The company also runs ferries between the Highlands (Conner's Ferry Landing) and New York City's Wall Street or 34th Street daily throughout the year (6 A.M.–10 P.M.), with a limited schedule on weekends. Round-trip fares are $37 adult (no child's fare is offered) during peak weekday hours (before 9:30 A.M.); $33 adult, $18 child on weekends

A daily shuttle bus ($1) operates around Sandy Hook during summer months, making various stops around the peninsula.

LONG BRANCH
What began as an elitist gambling resort and became a vacationing spot for seven U.S. presidents, including Ulysses S. Grant, Rutherford B. Hayes, and James A. Garfield, has emerged from a period of economic blight in an upward attempt to regain its niche as an upscale resort community. In recent years "The Friendly City" has wiped out much of its beachfront to rebuild from the ground up, and towering high rises and condos now occupy prime oceanfront real estate. Signs of construction are everywhere along the water, but head west down Broadway and the city's faltering past is evident. Wild West legends Annie Oakley and Buffalo Bill both spent time in the city, as did the Gould and Astor families, but with so much progress, finding a hint of their history can be difficult.

Sights
Long Branch's non-commercial concrete **boardwalk** does offer unbeatable views, thankfully because it's on the waterfront side of the city's recent construction boom. Level with the street, it rises above the sand about six or so feet, with a dedicated bike path that runs beside it. Along the walkway there's a monument honoring James A. Garfield, the country's 20th president, who died in Long Branch after suffering an assassination attempt in Washington, D.C.

St. James Historic Chapel was built in 1881 as a house of worship for the visiting presidents. It's today known as the **Church of Presidents** and serves as home to the **Long Branch Historic Museum** (1260 Ocean Ave., 732/229-0600). This is the place to come if you're interested in learning about the city's unique history, and inside you'll find the church's original altar. Call for hours.

One of the city's newest projects, **Pier Village** (732/528-8509, www.piervillage.com) is a residential/retail complex being constructed along the shoreline. It's set to feature over 100,000 square feet of restaurants, shops, and boutiques. As of 2005, tenants are already moving in, and include a contemporary furniture showroom, a day spa, and a surf shop.

In nearby Oceanport is the **Monmouth Park Racetrack** (Oceanport Ave., 732/222-5100, www.monmouthpark.com, 11:30 A.M.–5 P.M., $2 adult, child free), where you can catch live thoroughbred horse racing throughout the summer and shoulder seasons. Event attire ranges from grandstand casual to luxury-box formal, with dress or jacket as the norm. The racetrack is a favorite filming locale for television, with cameos in both *The Sopranos* and *Law & Order*. You'll find ATMs and a gift shop on the first floor, as well as a handful of restaurants and eateries throughout.

Beaches
Much of Long Beach's oceanfront land is considered private, so for sunbathing and salty sea swimming head to **Seven Presidents Oceanfront Park** (Ocean Ave. at Joline Ave., 732/229-7025, 732/229-0924 in summer, $5),

which also features volleyball courts and a skate-board park. There are a handful of other public beaches scattered throughout, including the North Bath Avenue Beach and West End Avenue I and II. For an additional list of the city's public-access beaches, call the **Greater Long Branch Chamber of Commerce** at 732/571-1833.

Daily beach tags cost $5 adult and $3 teen. Seniors and those 13 and under are free.

Accommodations

$150-200: In the city's West End district close to Monmouth Park Racetrack you'll find the spacious **Cedars and Beeches Bed & Breakfast** (247 Cedar Ave., 800/323-5655, www.cedarsandbeeches.com), a 12-room, two-suite Victorian with a variety of guestroom sizes. All rooms include a private bath, air-conditioning, TV, telephone, and complimentary breakfast.

$200-250: The **Ocean Place Resort and Conference Center** (1 Ocean Blvd., 800/411-6493, www.oceanplaceresort.com) is an upscale oceanfront hotel with indoor and outdoor swimming pools, an on-site spa, and exceptional views from many of its tastefully designed rooms. Amenities include private balcony, in-room safe, and wireless Internet, and the resort boasts a private beach fit for bonfires, and a second floor that's pet friendly.

Food and Nightlife

Hidden amongst the city's recent development, **Rooney's Ocean Crab House** (100 Ocean Ave., 732/870-1200, www.rooneysocean.com, $19.95–32.95) is a gem worth finding. Oceanfront property provides sweeping area views, especially from the bi-level outdoor deck, and the changing seafood specials and large wine selection are standouts. Dress varies from casual to stiff, though you'll probably want to forgo the shorts and flip-flops. The restaurant is open 11:30 A.M.–10 P.M. Monday–Thursday and Sunday, until 11:30 P.M. Friday and Saturday.

Joe and Maggie's Bistro (591 Broadway, 732/571-8848, www.joeandmaggiesbistro.com, $19–27) is a beloved establishment serving New American cuisine year-round. A "twilight menu" is offered 4–6 P.M. Monday–Thursday, and Fridays feature chocolate fondue nights. The restaurant is a bit of a hike from the beach in a less-than-desirable neighborhood, but from all accounts it's worth the trek. Parking is available in back. Lunch hours are 11:30 A.M.–2:30 P.M. Tuesday–Friday, and dinner is served 4–10 P.M. Tuesday–Thursday, 5–11 P.M. Friday and Saturday, and 4–9 P.M. Sunday. Hours are usually extended during summer months.

It may look like a dive, but **Brighton Bar** (121 Brighton Ave., 732/229-9676, www.cojack productions.com) has been a favorite live music venue for over 20 years. The bar showcases local acts including rock, jazz, and poetry for those 18 and older. Weekday performances are $6, weekend shows $7.

Getting There and Around

Long Branch is located off exit 105 of the Garden State Parkway.

NJ Transit runs the North Jersey Coast line from New York Penn Station with a stop at **Long Branch train station** (approx. 1.5 hrs one-way), located at 3rd Avenue between North Bath Avenue and Morris Avenue, just south of the **Monmouth Medical Center.** The station is a hike from any of the city's sights, but if you bring along a bike you'll have little trouble getting around. Round-trip fare costs $22 adult, $5 child.

ASBURY PARK

All the crumbling and abandoned buildings, the weather-beaten facades, and an overall sense of desolation may have some people asking, "What's the allure?," but there's no doubt that there is one. Whether it be the actualization of Springsteen's songs or what lies beneath the grimy exterior is hard to say—but the truth is, people love this town. Once the queen of the Jersey Shore during the early half of the 20th century, the "City by the Sea" was left alone when the Garden State Parkway paved the way to further Shore towns, and the grand gal was taken over by motorcycle men and music. What remained of the city was gone for good after racial riots occurred in the 1970s.

the now-empty Carousel House, Asbury Park

© LAURA KINIRY

Luckily, years of abandonment have left many of the city's grand structures still standing (sans the Palace Amusements), and concerned citizens are aiming to preserve. There's no doubt that Asbury Park has seen better days, but rarely does a city put up such a heartfelt fight to bring those days back. True, it's been "up and coming" for a while, and last decade went through an ugly period when all assets were frozen—but results are finally starting to show. A notable gay population has discovered the city and has breathed new life into Asbury Park, in the form of a hotel, a club, and some restaurants, and along Cookman Avenue revitalization efforts are evident in building exteriors and the abundance of new shops and galleries. The brand new boardwalk reestablishing access to nearby Ocean Grove is a giant leap forward.

Ocean Avenue may still be riddled with potholes and crime does occur, but there are reasons to come here. Not to linger on the boards after dark, mind you, but for the history, the muffled beauty, and surely the music. In the end, though, come for the people.

Sights

In 2004 a new million-dollar mile-long **boardwalk** opened as part of Asbury's new look. A few new boardwalk shops have since appeared (nothing that's worth its own trip), and the partially restored Casino at the walkway's southern end has reopened passage into neighboring Ocean Grove. You won't be mistaking these boards for Seaside Heights' or Wildwood's anytime soon, but they're definitely worth a stroll or bike ride. Much of the time you'll have them practically to yourself, though come July 4th and the place will be packed.

Just off the boards the architectural mama of **Howard Johnson's** (1213 Boardwalk at Fifth Ave., 732/988-3434) remains open for lunch, and you can still down a giant dog at the **Mayfair Boardwalk and Grill** (1009 Boardwalk, 732/774-3441); both places are seasonal. **Madame Marie** (732/775-5327), the infamous seer who made an appearance in the lyrics of Springsteen's "4th of July, Asbury Park (Sandy)" continues to work her boardwalk magic. After a seven-year hiatus she reopened

MUSIC OF THE JERSEY SHORE

Although not as well known as Motown and bluegrass, the Jersey Shore Sound – a rock blend with hints of jazz, soul, and R&B that came from New Jersey's Atlantic coastline in the late 1960s and throughout the '70s – is a major contributor to the history of music. The epicenter of this movement was Asbury Park, a city isolated from New York and Philadelphia, where songwriters and musicians would take to the stage and the streets, inspired by the local setting, the Shore, and undoubtedly the salty air. Notable musicians such as Gary U. S. Bonds, Joe Grushecky and the Houserockers, Bill Chinnock, and Southside Johnny and the Asbury Dukes came from this scene, as did Little Steven (of E Street and *Sopranos* fame), Bruce Springsteen – a Monmouth County native who captured the movement in his lyrical poetry and sound – and, in later years, Jon Bon Jovi.

The clubs where these bands, singers, and songwriters performed were as important to the movement as the musicians, and included Asbury Park venues the Upstage (a second-floor space on the corner of Cookman Avenue and Bond Street where Springsteen got his start), The Fastlane (recognized for putting Bon Jovi on the map), and perhaps best known of all, The Stone Pony.

In 2004, Gary Wien, author of *Beyond the Palace,* a book about the history of Asbury Park, and Carrie Potter, granddaughter of former Upstage owner Tom Potter, got together to form the **Jersey Shore Music Association** (www.jsma.org). Working with the city of Asbury Park, they announced plans for a **New Jersey Music Hall of Fame** (732/774-8877, www.njmusic.org), tentatively scheduled to open in summer 2006. Although the museum will feature music-related memorabilia crossing genres and county lines, at its heart will be Jersey Shore music and the Asbury Park scene.

---

the Temple of Knowledge in 2004, and now shares psychic time with her granddaughter and daughter-in-law.

Asbury Park is the birthplace of Asbury Park music, and there's little doubt that the christener is non other than Brother Bruce. What's considered to be the largest collection of Boss memorabilia is at home in the **Asbury Park Public Library** (500 First Ave., 732/774-4221, www.asburyparklibrary.org/Bruce.htm, 11 A.M.–8 P.M. Mon.–Wed., 9 A.M.–5 P.M. Fri. and Sat., noon–5 P.M. Sun.), a gift from the long-running fan magazine *Backstreets.* An appointment is suggested if you'd like to access the collection, and the library's current holdings list is available on their website at www.asburyparklibrary.org/springsteen_collection_holdings.htm.

Stephen Crane, author of *The Red Badge of Courage,* spent his childhood years in Asbury Park in a family of 14 children. His first short story was penned in his family home at 508 Fourth Avenue, now designated the **Stephen Crane House** (732/775-5682, www.stephencranehouse.org). Though currently not open to the public, future plans are to establish a library and use the home to host ongoing literary events.

Beaches

Asbury Park's daily beach tags run $4 weekdays, $5 weekends. Because of the city's relative desolation you'll have no trouble finding a spot to lay your blanket, but if you're looking for a true beach experience I suggest heading into nearby Ocean Grove. For quiet reprieve, Asbury does have you covered.

Shopping

Showing the greatest sign of the city's revitalization efforts with an emergence of art galleries, antique stores, and a growing number of shops is **Cookman Avenue.** Colorful pastel storefronts are ponying up to large brick department stores and from Bond Street north to Madison, the improvements are evident.

Antic Hay Books (721 Cookman Ave., 732/774-4590, www.antichay.com) carries new, used, and rare books. Inside you'll find prints, maps, and plenty of Jersey Shore merchandise. Springsteen held his only book signing here.

Wish You Were Here (612 Cookman Ave., 732/774-1601) is both a café and gift shop specializing in Asbury Park memorabilia.

At **APeXgallery** (611 Cookman Ave., 732/776-7746, www.apexgalleryasburypark.com) you'll find an assortment of contemporary photography, woodwork, pottery, painting, graphic design, and more. Rotating exhibits include a notable display of Asbury-centric pieces. **Sulli Studios** (605 Mattison Ave., Suite 3100, 732/775-9980, www.sullistudios.com) showcases artist Kelly Sullivan's colorfully psychedelic portraits and innovative "finger smears"—large canvases created when hundreds of people add their touch and signature to an original sketch. Past contributors have included the Rolling Stones, Bruce, and New York Yankee Jason Giambi.

The spacious **Wesley Lake Gallery** (608 Cookman Ave., Unit 6, 732/774-8680, www.wesleylakegallery.com) features fine art, photography, and sculpture. You'll find some superb black-and-white still lifes along with stunning nature shots.

Antique Emporium of Asbury Park (646 Cookman Ave., 732/774-8230) houses over 60 antique vendors, including the arts and crafts–era furniture of **Tristan's Antiques LLC,** and the 20th-century paintings of **Larkspur Gallery.** The 5,000-square-foot **Studebakers–Antiques and Collectibles Mall** (1201 Main St., 732/776-5565) is home to 30 antique and collectible dealers. At its center you'll find the **Rumble Seat Tea Room,** an ideal spot to stop and savor your purchase of cherished kitchen wares or Civil War finds.

Entertainment and Nightlife

The 3,600-seat **Convention Hall** and the more intimate 1,600-seat **Paramount Theatre** (1300 Ocean Ave., www.asburyparkconventionhall.com) are open for business, hosting musical acts, shows, festivals, and conventions. These two structures, high-society ladies of the 1930s that are both listed on the National Register of Historic Places, stand on the boardwalk's north end and are joined by a Grand Arcade that extends over the walkway. Jutting out onto the beach, the art deco Convention Hall has hosted numerous well-known acts throughout its history, including a couple of Springsteen's pre-tour performances. The acoustically superior Paramount is home to more intimate performances.

Made famous by the Boss, the **The Stone Pony** (913 Ocean Ave., 732/502-0600, www.thestonepony.com) opened in 1974 as a disco bar called The Magic Touch. The club's first house band was Southside Johnny & the Asbury Jukes—described by many as one of the world's greatest bar bands, and who still occasionally perform here. Today the Pony, after a number of wayward stints, is back in the city's forefront and seems to be growing in popularity as the years go on. Seeing a show at the Pony is like dining on rock and roll.

Its exterior painted as a tribute to the former Palace Amusements—complete with bumper cars and Tillie the clown's smiling face—the **Wonder Bar** (Ocean and Fifth Ave., 732/502-8886, www.wonderbarnj.com) hosts live bands and solo artists. There's a darkened dance floor and outdoor picnic-table seating.

Live bands take the stage at **The Saint** (601 Main St., 732/775-9144, http://saint.jerseynetworks.com, $7–15) 5–7 days a week. Since 1994, this 200-capacity club has been the place to see up-and-comers, including Jewel and Stereophonics. There are 20 brews on tap and all-age matinee shows on weekend afternoons. **The Asbury Café** at The Saint features seated shows ($10) that are "listening room only," meaning if you'd like to talk, head elsewhere. The café serves alcohol as well as coffeehouse treats, and independent rock bands jam here.

One of New Jersey's largest gay clubs is situated on the bottom floor of the renovated Empress Hotel. **Paradise** (101 Asbury Ave., 732/988-6663, www.paradisenj.com, 4 P.M.–2 A.M. Wed. and Thurs., opens at noon Sat. and Sun.) features two dance floors, two stages, and an in-ground pool flanked by two outdoor bars. Poolside happy hours take place on weekday afternoons throughout the summer.

Accommodations

Of the two hotel choices in Asbury Park, neither is ideal: One has received sub-standard ratings, and the other, while sparkling clean with modern amenities, is located above a pulsating gay bar that shares the hotel's pool and lounge. For a quiet and comfortable stay, my recommendation is to spend the night at one of nearby Ocean Grove's numerous bed-and-breakfasts.

Food

Sunset Landing (1215 Sunset Ave., 732/776-9732, $6–9) is a favored Asbury breakfast stop. Get yourself an order of Nestlé Crunch and banana pancakes, and afterward head out for a spin in one of this surf shack's canoe or rowboat rentals. Also open for lunch. Hang beside the tree-painted walls of **Be Green Juice Bar & Cafe** (609 Cookman Ave., 732/775-2633, www.begreenjuicebar.com, 10 A.M.–7 P.M. Tues.–Sun. year-round, $6.60–7.50) and sip on a smoothie with your sandwich or wrap, or go the organic coffee route—this place is as casual as they come.

In 2004 **Moonstruck** (517 Lake Ave., 732/988-0123, www.moonstrucknj.com, 5–10 P.M. Wed.–Thurs. and Sun., until 11 P.M. Fri. and Sat., $17–26) relocated from Ocean Grove to its current three-story, three-bar home overlooking Wesley Lake on the south end of town. This much-loved Mediterranean restaurant continues to draw crowds, who spill out onto the wraparound porches during summer months. No reservations taken.

Asbury's Main Street still has a ways to go, but a good start is **Bistro Olé** (230 Main St., 732/897-0048, www.bistroole.com, $10–20). This boisterous BYO serves Spanish-Portuguese cuisine upon colorful tableware, including tapas dishes like meaty plantains ($8) and mussels bathed in spicy sauce ($8). Olé is open for lunch 11:30 A.M.–2:30 P.M. Tuesday–Friday, and dinner 5–10 P.M. Tuesday–Sunday. Closed Monday.

Getting There and Around

Asbury Park is 40 miles south of Manhattan, and can be reached from exit 100A northbound or exit 102 southbound of the Garden State Parkway. The **Asbury Park train station** is at the south end of Cookman Avenue, an easy walk to the shops.

OCEAN GROVE

Founded in the late 19th century as a Methodist summer camp, "God's Square Mile" has managed to retain its roots. Strict blue laws—such as the forbiddance of car use on Sundays—have been lifted, though others (restricted beach use until after noon on Sunday) remain. From its central auditorium, where religious revivals are still held, spread narrow streets jam-packed with two-, three-, and four-story Victorians in various weathered conditions. You'll see fading clapboards accentuated with brightly colored gingerbread design, and long porches piled atop one another to savor the ocean breeze. To the right of the auditorium the historic canvas tents of the original settlers still stand, each with its pitched roof and porch-covered awning.

The Grove—which since the 1980s has been part of the larger Neptune Township—has an attractive downtown district and a non-commercial boardwalk. There are many affordable bed-and-breakfasts throughout town—though often without TV or telephone and seeming almost like youth hostels for solitary visitors. A release of mental patients from an area hospital in the 1980s and an influx of gays from neighboring Asbury Park have added a whirlpool blend to the population—one that, by most accounts, nobody seems to mind.

Sights

Ocean Grove's **boardwalk** connects with Asbury Park's through the Casino Building. It's a non-commercial wooden walkway built strictly for leisure, and a great place for an afternoon stroll while taking in the expansive ocean views.

You can't miss **The Great Auditorium** (21 Pilgrim Pathway, 732/775-0035 or 800/773-0097), a 6,500-seat house of worship and entertainment venue that's been around for over

THE JERSEY SHORE

© LAURA KINIRY

Tent City, Ocean Grove

a century and is located smack in the center of town. Inside this massive wood structure run performances by such family-friendly acts as the Smothers Brothers, and shows like the skirt-swaying Doo Wop Revue. Across the street toward the beach is the Auditorium Pavilion, an open-air gazebo hosting book sales and a weekly contemporary church service.

Situated at the center of town next to the Great Auditorium is **Tent City,** over 100 canvas tents originally leased to members of the Methodist church—the Grove's founders—in the late 19th century. Today they continue to be owned by the Ocean Grove Camp Meeting Association, though you don't have to belong to the church to rent one. You do, however, have to sign your name to an extremely long list of prospective tenants—a waiting list of more than 20 years. Regardless, they're just as fun to view from the outside—stretching for entire blocks with colorfully striped awnings over their doorways, and bicycles and beach chairs hanging from their sides. Almost all have been extended over the years with

additions and add-ons, and if you take a peek inside you'll see they're set up just like any other home—quilt-covered beds, comfy couches, and knick-knacks. They're a sight as unique to Ocean Grove as the Golden Gate Bridge to San Francisco.

Beaches

Ocean Grove's daily beach tags are $6. On Sundays the beach doesn't open until noon. It's a pleasant, mid-sized beach intended for public use.

Events

The **Ocean Grove Historical Society** (732/774-1869, www.oceangrovehistory.org) hosts a number of events, including annual summer and Christmas **House Tours,** and **Guided Historic District Walking Tours,** held at 1 P.M. Wednesday and Friday, and 11 A.M. Saturday, June–mid-September. The historic tours include a visit to Tent City and the Great Auditorium, and leave from in front of the Society museum at 50 Pitman Avenue.

Shopping

Ocean Grove's Main Street is worth a stop for its shops, eateries, and pleasant atmosphere.

There are numerous collectible shops along Main Street, including the Victorian-housed **Favorite Things** (52 Main St., 732/774-0230, www.1800foragift.com), where you'll find hand-painted furniture, period lace, quilted bags, and an old-fashioned candy counter all set amongst comfortable country decor. **The Loft** (60 Main Ave., 732/774-8507) sells Byers Choice Christmas Collectibles. **Kitsch and Kaboodle** (76 Main Ave., 732/869-0950) is a funky specialty shop where you'll find products by Smart Women and Burt's Bees, as well as retro Barbies and vintage tableware.

Located within the Majestic Hotel, the **Aloha Grove Surf Shop** (19 Main Ave., 732/869-1001, www.alohagrove.com) is a retro surf shop stocking clothing, boards, and accessories. Surf lessons are held during shop hours (9 A.M.–7 P.M. daily, summer). Be sure and call ahead to schedule, and check online for a 24-hour surf report.

Accommodations

The central area of Ocean Grove is the prettiest and it's also where you'll find a good portion of the bed-and-breakfasts. Rooms tend to be small and many lack modern amenities, though this keeps prices down. Establishments along Ocean Avenue usually offer the best views and get the ocean breeze.

$50-100: One of Ocean Grove's newer B&Bs, the four-story **Henry Richard Inn** (16 Main Ave., 732/776-7346, www.henryrichard inn.com) features mostly single and double units with in-room sink and shared bath.

$100-150: The 36-room **Manchester Inn** (25 Ocean Pathway, 732/775-0616, www.the manchesterinn.com) is a white four-story clapboard structure located at the center of town. Once two separate buildings, the current bed-and-breakfast is the first New Jersey inn to receive approval for installing solar power. Decorative halls lead to homey rooms, some of which rely on ocean air and ceiling fans for cooling. A long, covered front porch with rocking chairs provides afternoon relief from the Jersey heat, and a full complimentary breakfast is available at the on-site restaurant.

Half a block from the ocean, the imposing **Lillagaard Hotel** (5 Abbot Ave., 732/998-1216) is a 22-guestroom Victorian bed-and-breakfast with uniquely themed rooms and a cozy feel. The inn has both an English Garden Breakfast Room, where continental cuisine is offered each morning, and a newly added Victorian Tea Room. Guestrooms are decorated with hand-painted murals, and all feature air-conditioning, fan, and individual sink. Private baths accompany most.

The seasonal **House by the Sea** (14 Ocean Ave., 732/774-4771) gets great ocean breezes and provides a gorgeous beachfront view from its porch. It's three stories of simple living—no telephones or TVs (except for common areas) and a limited number of private baths.

$150-200: The three-story **Shawmont Hotel** (17 Ocean Ave., 732/776-6985, www .shawmont.com) is a seasonal establishment overlooking the ocean. Some rooms have TV and air-conditioning, and all rooms include private bath. There's a common library for guests to enjoy. A two-night minimum stay is required on weekends.

The year-round Victorian **(** **Ocean Plaza** (18 Ocean Pathway, 732/774-6552, www.ogplaza .com) features expansive wraparound porches and 18 guestrooms, each with new bathrooms, TV/VCR combos, and central air—amenities that are hard to come by at many of the Grove's other B&Bs. A continental breakfast is served daily, and during warmer months guests can enjoy their meals from the second-floor balcony that affords sweeping views of the ocean (which lies across the street) and the surrounding town.

One of the town's smallest B&Bs, **The Carriage House** (18 Heck Ave., 732/998-9441, www.carriagehousenj.com) features eight renovated rooms in a century-old Victorian, each with cable TV, private bath, and air-conditioning, and some with balconies. A full breakfast is complimentary with an overnight stay, and free wireless Internet is available.

THE JERSEY SHORE

Food

You'll find the bulk of Ocean Grove's eateries along Main Street or within the many bed-and-breakfasts. Most tend to keep it casual, catering to the Shore appeal.

Start your day at **The Starving Artist at Days** (47 Olin St., 732/988-1007, 8 A.M.–3 P.M. Mon.–Sat., until 2 P.M. Sun., closed Wed.), serving breakfast and lunch throughout the week, except Wednesday. The Artist also dishes out theatrical entertainment in the Outdoor Victorian Garden, such as the musical *Godspell*. Afterward, finish up with a hand-scooped cone at **Day's Ice Cream** (48 Pitman Ave., 732/988-1007, noon–10 P.M. Sun.–Thurs., until 11 P.M. Fri. and Sat., Memorial Day–Labor Day) and relax at one of the outdoor tables.

The brightly decorated **Captain Jack's** (68 Main Ave., 732/869-0770, $15–25) serves appetizing American eats with a focus on seafood. A large tank with tiny fish greets patrons upon entry to this BYO, and live music plays Wednesday and Thursday evenings. Jack's is open for lunch 11:30 A.M.–3 P.M. Tuesday–Sunday, and dinner 5–9 P.M. Tuesday–Thursday, until 10 P.M. Friday–Sunday. Brunch is served 11 A.M.–3 P.M. Sunday.

The century-old **Nagles Apothecary Cafe** (43 Main St., 732/776-9797, 8:30 A.M.–9 P.M. daily, closed Tues., $5–10) is a former pharmacy that's evolved into a classic American eatery, complete with soda fountain and ice cream (go for the peanut butter swirl). The café includes indoor and outdoor seating, and a takeout window that's popular even on rainy days.

Within the Majestic Hotel you'll find the small **Oceania** (19 Main Ave., 732/988-9198, www.oceaniarestaurant.com, $14–24), serving a brief Northern Italian menu that includes veal scallopini ($7.95) and ricotta gnocchi ($13.95). It's open for lunch 11:30 A.M.–2:30 P.M., and dinner 5–9 P.M. Tuesday–Thursday and Sunday, until 10 P.M. Friday and until 11 P.M. Sunday.

Getting There and Around

From the Garden State Parkway, take exit 100 to reach Ocean Grove. NJ Transit's North Jersey Coast line has a stop at Asbury Park, and Ocean Grove is just a half-mile south.

BRADLEY BEACH

South of Ocean Grove is the pleasant borough of Bradley Beach, a small community filled with one- and two-story homes that are seemingly passed down through generations. This Shore town was founded by middle-class Philadelphians and New Yorkers, and zoning laws have since protected it from excess build up. A couple of beachfront brick buildings seem misplaced, but it's otherwise attractive, quite neighborly, and without pretense. You'll find a series of Italian restaurants downtown, and a short block of Mexican shops and eateries catering to a significant Hispanic population. Along the beach is a non-commercial promenade lined with benches and gazebos, and a few casual food stands. Most of this Shore town's downtown restaurants are open all year.

Beaches

Daily beach tags cost $7, those 13 and under are free.

Accommodations

$100-150: Located across the street from the beach, the **Bradley Beach Inn** (900 Ocean Ave., 732/774-0414, www.thebradleybeachinn.com) is a simple three-story Victorian with eight guestrooms, two that feature an extra full-size bed. Amenities include individual air-conditioning and fridge, and a variety of ocean views, though some bathrooms are shared. A continental breakfast is provided.

$150-200: The renovated **Sandcastle Inn** (204 Third Ave., 732/774-2875, www.sandcastleinn.us) offers eight guestrooms and one suite, all charmingly decorated in soothing pastels that offset their dark wood floors. Private bath, cable TV, and both fan and air-conditioning are included with each room.

Food

La Nonna Piancone's Cafe (800 Main St., 732/775-0906, www.piancone.com, 11:30 A.M.–10 P.M. Mon.–Sat., 3–10 P.M. Sun.)

serves enormous family-style portions ($29.95 per person) of Italian eats in an always-bustling setting. Additional perks include a sizeable bar and the restaurant's on-site market.

Two-story **Giamano's** (301 Main St., 732/775-4275, www.giamanos.com, $15–25) receives high-ratings for its Italian cuisine, and menus feature both vegetarian and children's selections. Downstairs is the main dining area—the second floor hosts a live music lounge where you can relax to blues, jazz, R&B, and other types of music. Lunch is served 11:30 A.M.–3 P.M. Tuesday–Saturday. Dinner hours are 5–10 P.M. Tuesday–Thursday, Sunday, until 11 P.M. Friday and Saturday. The restaurant is closed Monday. Open all year.

Vic's (60 Main St., 732/774-8225, www.vics pizza.com, 11:30 A.M.–11 P.M. Sun.–Thurs., until midnight Fri. and Sat., closed Mon., $11–17) has been a Bradley Beach staple for great pizza and Italian eats since 1947. This old-school institution has paneled walls and still uses a number board to announce an order up. The joint gets packed, even early on a summer evening, but plenty of indoor and outdoor seating make for a quick turnaround. Prices are good, pizzas are thin crusted, and the sauce is homemade. Open year-round.

Getting There and Around

You can reach Bradley Beach by taking exit 100 off the Garden State Parkway and traveling east on Route 33 to Ocean Grove. It's the next town south.

BELMAR

Belmar is an outgoing borough with a lively nightlife and an active social calendar. Long-known as a retreat for high school grads and college keg-tappers, the town is taking strides to change this image, and regulations on the number of renters in summer units and noise restrictions at area clubs and bars are evidence of the town's shifting population. Still—while there's plenty of daylight activity to enjoy—nightlife remains a primary attraction in the borough and its southern counterpart, **Lake Como.** Belmar is strategically situated between the Shark River

and the Shore, with Silver Lake at the north of town and Lake Como to the south, and it's home to the state's largest commercial marina.

Belmar offers an attractive beachfront, a mile-long semi-commercial boardwalk, and a downtown plentiful with bars and restaurants, many of which remain open throughout the year. Most houses are two-story standard Victorians, easily mistaken for single-family homes if it weren't for the borough's rowdy reputation. High-turnout festivals and events take place throughout the year. With so much going on, it's no surprise that the legendary Captain Kidd is said to have abandoned his treasure here (no doubt after a long night at the pub).

Beaches

Daily beach fees are $6.

Events

Belmar and Lake Como together play host to the state's largest **St. Patrick's Day Parade** (www.belmarparade.com). Marching bands and bagpipes pave the way for an all-day event, and traditional Irish fare can be found throughout the boroughs.

The annual two-day **New Jersey Seafood Festival** (732/774-8506, www.belmar.com) is held the second weekend in June, highlighting fresh local catch and prepared dishes from area restaurants. There's a wine tent, and activities for the kids.

Anyone can participate in early July's annual **New Jersey Sand Castle Contest** (732/681-3700, www.belmar.com), with prizes given to the Most Creative and Most Elaborate sculptures. Even if you don't plan on building, it's well worth a visit to watch these sometimes-spectacular shapes take form.

The **AVP Volleyball Tournament** (732/681-3700, www.belmar.com) is a three-day professional open that takes place annually on the beach in July. They'll be plenty of bleacher seats and nearly as many pro volleyball players.

Sports and Recreation

The area is a big spot for sportfishing and the **Belmar Marina** (Rte. 35 and 10th Ave.,

732/681-5005) is the state's largest commercial marina, with dozens of charter boats and party vessels available. **Suzie Girl** (732/988-7760) and **Capt. Cal** (732/892-7816, www.captcal2.com) are both large vessels that provide opportunities for deep-sea fishing, while **Teri Jean II** (732/280-7364, www.terijean.com) is a much smaller six-person sportfishing boat. For diving and fishing excursions try **Fisherman's Den** (Rte. 35, 732/681-5005, www.fishermansdennj.com).

Belmar features designated beaches for each of its water sports. Surfing is allowed south of the 16th Avenue jetty and on both sides of the 19th Avenue jetty. Kayaks are permitted south of 20th Avenue, and for boogie boarding, the best ocean beaches are between 13th and 19th Avenues.

During summer months, bicycles are only permitted on the boardwalk before 8 A.M. and after 8 P.M.

Nightlife

The following spots are known for their nightlife, but all serve food during the day and early evening. Like most of Belmar's downtown restaurants, these establishments remain open throughout the year.

Bar Anticipation (703–705 16th Ave., Lake Como, 732/681-7422, www.bar-a.com, 10 A.M.–2 A.M. daily), or Bar A as it's called, may be open throughout the year, but the party really picks up during summer, when DJs and live bands make music nightly both indoors and out, and a large deck and sand-filled volleyball court keep the party rocking. Drink specials and theme nights like Beat the Clock and Dueling Pianos are all the rage. A menu includes pizza, sandwiches, and burgers.

The **Boathouse Bar & Grill** (1309 Main St., 732/681-5221, www.boathousebarandgrill.com, 11 A.M.–2 A.M. Mon.–Sat., noon–2 A.M. Sun.) features 30 TVs (including two large-screen), a pool table, dart board, pub and dinner menu, and live entertainment throughout the summer season.

Patrick's Pub (711 Main St., 732/280-2266) is rumored to cook some of the best steaks at the Jersey Shore. This tavern also features TVs, live entertainment, and a wraparound bar. Food is served daily from 11 A.M. to 11 P.M. ($3.95–13.95).

Accommodations

Overnight accommodations in Belmar include hotels, bed-and-breakfasts, and a couple of guesthouses, though the borough's reputation as a party town keeps many places average at best. The following accommodations are the borough's standouts.

$150-200: The eight-room **Morning Dove B&B** (204 Fifth Ave., 732/556-0777, www.morningdoveinn.com) is an 1890s inn with a year-round solarium. Guestrooms are pleasantly decorated in a country-suburban antique style, and all feature private bath and air-conditioning. Use of beach badges is included in the overnight fee and a full breakfast is served each morning. There's a three-night minimum stay in July and August, and a two-night minimum during the shoulder season (extending May–Oct.).

Across the street from Belmar's Silver Lake is **(The Inn at the Shore** (301 Fourth Ave., 732/681-3762, www.theinnattheshore.com), a lovely Victorian with 11 individually styled guestrooms, a spacious sit-down dining area with writing nook, and a complimentary breakfast that ranges from pancakes with vanilla cream syrup to granola and yogurt. Amenities differ from room to room at this family-friendly establishment, but some include private bath, down pillows, and fireplace. Most rooms with shared bath feature an in-room sink and vanity and offer considerably lower overnight rates. The inn offers various specials throughout the year, including massage packages, Romance Weekends, and even a Murder Mystery Weekend, in which clues are planted throughout the house and downtown.

Food

You can easily find a light snack or American eats along Belmar's boardwalk, but for something a bit more like fine dining, head away from the ocean, toward downtown and along the Shark River.

For a quick breakfast treat stop into **Freedman's Bakery** (803 Main St., 732/681-2334), a large classic bakery—you'll recognize it from the retro exterior sign. Take a seat at the counter for a morning bagel and fresh brewed coffee, or go straight for the sweet stuff—this is, after all, the Shore. Freedman's opens its doors for breakfast and lunch at 6 A.M.

Carrying over a loyal clientele from the former Veggie Works, the reincarnated **Kaya's Kitchen** (817 Belmar Plaza, 732/280-1141, $8–16) remains a favorite with a streamlined menu of vegetarian-only cuisine. This BYO is vegan-friendly as well. Lunch hours are 11:30 A.M.–3 P.M. Tuesday–Friday, and dinner 4:30–10 P.M. Tuesday–Saturday, until 9 P.M. Sunday. A brunch menu is offered 10 A.M.–1 P.M. Sunday, summer only. Kaya's is closed Monday.

The BYO **Brandl** (703 Belmar Plaza, 732/280-7501, www.brandlrestaurant.com, $28–37) serves a seasonally changing menu of New American cuisine amid warm and stylish decor. Enjoy the chef's signature crab cakes ($14) on the heated outdoor patio, and if it's Friday, stay on for the live jazz. This is some of the best fine dining at the Jersey Shore. Brandl is open for dinner only 5–10 P.M. Monday–Thursday, until 11 P.M. Friday and Saturday, 5–9 P.M. Sunday, throughout the year.

Situated along the Shark River, **Klein's Fish Market and Waterside Cafe** (708 River Rd., 732/681-1177, www.kleinsfishmkt.com, 11:30 A.M.–9 P.M. daily, until 10 P.M. Fri. and Sat., $11–20) is one of Belmar's most beloved eateries. Choose a seat at the grill or outdoors along the waterfront, and be sure to loosen your belt for all-you-can-eat sushi Mondays ($26.95). Sunday brunch (11 A.M.–3 P.M., $18) also receives top ratings. Klein's is open year-round.

For seasonal dining with oceanfront views try **Matisse** (13th and Ocean Aves., 732/681-7680, www.matissecatering.com, $23–33), a Grecian-style eatery serving continental cuisine. Situated along the boardwalk, it's open 5:30–10 P.M. nightly July and August, closed Tuesdays in June.

Getting There

To reach Belmar by car take exit 98 from the Garden State Parkway. The borough's train station is located downtown at Belmar Plaza between 9th and 10th Avenues, in the same locale as some of the restaurants.

◖ SPRING LAKE

The affluent and elegant community of Spring Lake is one of the last remaining authenticities of the grand ol' Shore. It's a peaceful and picturesque borough filled with Victorian homes, stately hotels, and bed-and-breakfasts that line the streets and surround the lake after which the town is named. Downtown's Third Avenue hosts some of the Shore's best shopping. The borough is primarily a year-round residential community, and most visitors stay at one of the over a dozen accommodation options around town. Along the beach is a two-mile non-commercial boardwalk made from recycled plastic, perfect for taking in the ocean views and salty air.

Beaches

Spring Lake's daily beach fee is $7. During summer months no food or drink is permitted on the beach, but *New Jersey Monthly* suggests leaving a cooler filled with goodies along the boardwalk until you're ready to chow down.

Events

The **Spring Lake Chamber of Commerce** (304 Washington Ave., 732/449-0577, www.springlake.org) sponsors an annual **Bed & Breakfast Christmas Candlelight Tour** in early December.

Shopping

Downtown Third Avenue is the borough's main shopping district. Though a bit of a walk from the beach, it's a pleasant one, and once here you'll find plenty in the way of specialty shops, boutiques, candy stores, and a gallery or two.

BOUTIQUES AND SPECIALTY SHOPS

Camel's Eye (1223 Third Ave., 732/449-3636) stocks funky designer fashions and Crocs wide-toed shoes, bright bags by Hobo and Kipling, and an assortment of distinguishing hairclips. The tiny **Teddy Bears by the Seashore** (1306 Third Ave., 732/449-7446) is packed with Jersey-centric hats, sweats, and tees, in addition to Jersey Girl dolls and a teddy bear collection. Shop hours are sporadic. Girls are queen bee at **Splash** (1305 Third Ave., 732/449-8388, www.splashofspringlake.com), a favorite clothing boutique for hip moms and daughters. Be sure and pick up a "Jersey Girl: Enough Said" T-shirt. **The Purse Peddler** (1304 Third Ave., 732/449-0804) carries ultra-stylish Vera Bradley bags. For a bit of city chic, try **The Spot** (1221 Third Ave., 732/974-1696), where you'll find dresses by Nicole Miller.

For men who prefer plaid, there's **Village Tweed** (1213 Third Ave., 732/449-2723). **Third Avenue Surf Shop** (1206 Third Ave., 732/449-1866, www.3rdavesurf.com) is a skate, surf, and clothing shop for men, women, and kids. Designer names include Oakley, O'Neill, and EMU footwear.

Having moved to its present location in 2005, the independent **Landmark Books** (306 Morris Ave., 732/449-0804, www.landmarkbks.com) is spacious enough for hosting author events but retains a cozy feel. The shop features a front-of-the-store reading area, an antiquarian section, and a nice selection of new and used New Jersey books. **Urban Details** (1111 Third Ave., 732/282-0013, www.urban-details.com) sells soothing spa items and uniquely crafted home decor items, including blown glass, metalware, and sculpted light fixtures. The shop displays an Artist of the Month.

GALLERIES AND ANTIQUES
Located just north of the main shopping strip, **Thistledown Gallery Framing** (1045 Third Ave., 732/974-0376) showcases fine artwork, including acrylics, watercolors, and lithographs, of local and national artists. The gallery specializes in framing, and limited edition prints are available for purchase. **Evergreen Gallery** (308 Morris Ave., 732/449-4488) is a photography, fine art, and mixed media gallery dedicated to the works of New Jersey artists.

Allison's Attic (1317 Third Ave., 732/449-3485) carries a fun selection of 20th-century antiques. Items include a Yankee Stadium blueprint with Mickey Mantle's signature, and a framed dinner menu from Spring Lake's former Monmouth Hotel.

CANDY STORES
At **Jean Louise Candies** (1025 Third Ave., 732/449-2627), chocolate comes in all shapes and sizes. The chocolate-covered strawberries are magnificent, or choose from chocolate seashells, baseball gloves, or elves. For your saltwater taffy or ice cream fix try **Third Avenue Chocolate Shoppe** (1138 Third Ave., 732/449-7535).

Accommodations
Hotels, inns, and B&Bs are all plentiful in this upscale resort borough.

$200-250: White Lilac Inn (414 Central Ave., 732/449-02 11, www.whitelilac.com) features nine uniquely designed guestrooms and one suite. Choose from the woodsy decor of the Vermont Cabin room, or the rich red hues of The Studio, reminiscent of a box of Valentine chocolates. Amenities include cable TV and air-conditioning, and some rooms feature old-fashioned soaking tubs. The inn is closed in January.

Close to Spring Lake's downtown shopping and train station is the **Chateau Inn and Suites** (500 Warren Ave, 732/974-2000, www.chateauinn.com), a 37-room boutique hotel. Built in 1888, the Chateau has been elegantly updated to feature modern amenities, including high-speed Internet and a plasma TV in every room. Soothing tones and marble bathrooms accentuate the decor.

At **La Maison Inn** (404 Jersey Ave., 732/449-0969, www.lamaisoninn.com) guests are treated to a gourmet candlelit breakfast and an afternoon helping of fruits and cheese. Use of the innkeeper's private library is welcome, and all guestrooms feature air-conditioning, cable TV, and telephone. A century-old backyard cottage accommodates up to four.

$250-300: The 1888 **Normandy Inn** (21 Tuttle Ave., 732/449-7172, www.normandy inn.com) offers 16 rooms and two suites, each decorated in a classic Victorian style. This Italianate villa is the borough's only bed-and-breakfast to be listed on the National Register of Historic Places. All rooms have private bath, telephone, TV/VCR, high-speed Internet, and air-conditioning.

Occupying prime oceanfront property is the 73-room **Breakers Hotel** (1507 Ocean Ave., 732/449-7700, www.breakershotel.com), a large white clapboard inn over a century old. Guests can enjoy a meal along the outdoor heated pool, or head to the ocean to catch some waves at the hotel's private beach. Size and location make Breakers an ideal host for wedding receptions and conferences, and noise can sometimes be a problem—requesting a room away from the banquet hall may help. The hotel is open year-round and standard rooms feature fridge and high-speed Internet, and many offer stunning ocean views.

A block from the beach is **Ashling Cottage B&B** (106 Sussex Ave., 732/449-3553, www.ashlingcottage.com), an 1877 Victorian with 11 guestrooms and a glass atrium where complimentary full morning meals are served. Make use of the inn's bicycles, or spend your day snoozing in the hammock. A covered front porch offers afternoon reprieve. Closed January.

Housed in a circa-1888 dark-wood Victorian, the 🎧 **Spring Lake Inn** (104 Salem Ave., 732/449-2010 or 800/803-9031, www.springlakeinn.com) offers 16 spacious guestrooms, each vividly painted in rich hues that complement their themes. Personal touches such as a telescope in the Moonbeam room, a sleigh bed in the Tower View, and the windowed tower of the Turret room make this bed-and-breakfast a must. Across the first floor stretches an 80-foot covered porch where guests can linger in rocking chairs. Beach badges, chairs, and towels, and gym passes are available for use, and additional amenities include private bath, air-conditioning, TV/HBO, and full breakfast daily.

$350-400: For a truly romantic evening, there's no better place than **Sea Crest by the Sea** (19 Tuttle Ave., 732/449-9031, www.seacrestbythesea.com). This 1885 Queen Anne Victorian features three guestrooms and

five suites, all of which enjoy individual fireplaces and whirlpool tubs for two. Guests arrive at their Victorian-themed rooms to find chocolates, robes, and slippers, and a complimentary bottle of wine, and modern amenities include wireless Internet, air-conditioning, TV/VCR, and a fully stocked fridge. Baked goods are available throughout the day, and a full breakfast is served daily.

Food

Spring Lake features a wonderful array of dining choices, both downtown along Third Avenue and within a few of the inns.

The BYO **Island Palm Grill** (1321 Third Ave., 732/449-1909, www.islandpalmgrill.com, $18–24) features a changing menu of Latin and American entrées and a gracious staff to help with your selections. The restaurant is open 11 A.M.–3 P.M. and 5:30–9 P.M. Tuesday–Saturday, 10 A.M.–2 P.M. and 5:30–9 P.M. Sunday, though hours may change seasonally.

Whispers (200 Monmouth Ave., 732/974-9755, www.whispersrestaurant.com, 5:30 P.M.–midnight daily, $26–33) offers a select menu of internationally inspired American entrées in an elegant and intimate Victorian space. The restaurant is located within the lakefront Hewitt-Wellington Hotel (www.hewittwellington.com).

Beneath the historic Sandpiper Inn is **Black Trumpet** (7 Atlantic Ave., 732/449-4700, www.theblacktrumpet.com, $18–29), a trendy and top-rated year-round BYO. Chef Mark Mikoljczck conjures up creative American cuisine with flair and seafood is the specialty, but the desserts are just as fabulous—if you like you can walk them off on the nearby beach afterward. Lunch for the summer season begins in May, 11:30 A.M.–2 P.M. daily. Regular dinner hours are 5–9 P.M. Monday–Thursday, until 10 P.M. Friday and Saturday, 4–8 P.M. Sunday.

Families head to **Who's on Third?** (1300 Third Ave., 732/449-4233, $5–21), a downtown deli and grill serving breakfast and lunch, and dinner in-season. Grab a stool at the lunch counter and devour a pork roll sandwich amid the photographed and framed images of baseball's greats.

Getting There

Spring Lake is located off exit 98 of the Garden State Parkway. The borough's train station is within walking distance to Third Avenue—about a two-hour ride from New York City.

SEA GIRT AND MANASQUAN

Just south of Spring Lake is Sea Girt, an affluent suburb with sizable homes, manicured lawns, and plenty of Mercedes parked in the driveways—it doesn't feel much like your typical Shore community. Nearby is Manasquan, a cozy borough filled with funky little beach shacks and bungalows, and plenty of jeep-driving residents carting around longboards on their roofless back seats. Downtown frizzy-haired teens (and there's plenty of them) ride beach cruisers on the sidewalk, no doubt on their way to the bike path that travels west to Allaire State Park. Manasquan enjoys both ocean and inlet beaches, and has some of the best surfing in the state.

Sea Girt Lighthouse

Built in 1896 to bridge the 40-mile gap between the Twin Lights and the Barnegat Light, this brick Victorian lighthouse (Ocean and Baltimore Blvd.)—the last live-in lighthouse to be built on the Atlantic Coast—no longer operates, but is open for tours (2–4 P.M. Sun.) through late November. Inside you'll find historic maps, local photos, and lighthouse memorabilia, among other items. For more info, call the lighthouse message line at 732/974-0514.

Beaches

Sea Girt's daily beach tags are $6. Use of the beach is free for those 12 and under. Daily beach tags for Manasquan cost $6 weekdays, $7 weekends, free for those 12 and under.

One of New Jersey's best spots for surfing is Manasquan's **Inlet Beach.** It's also a favorite fishing locale, and one of the state's most easily accessible beaches. There's lots of handicapped parking, and a wooden walkway that crosses the sand to a viewing area.

Accommodations

$200-250: Situated amid Manasquan's small but bustling downtown is the **Inn on Main** (152 Main St., 732/528-0809, www.inn onmainmanasquan.com), a 2004 boutique hotel featuring 12 unique and contemporary rooms, with some that offer gas fireplaces and balconies. Guests may use the inn's kitchen—stocked with refreshments, snacks, and breakfast eats—24 hours a day.

Food

Between Sea Girt and Manasquan you'll find a handful of dining choices, the more casual of which tend to be along Manasquan's waterfront, while fine-dining establishments are found in Sea Girt and within downtown Manasquan, a distance from the ocean beach, along Main Street.

Drive through downtown Sea Girt on a summer evening and you'll come upon ◖ **The Parker House** (1st and Beacon Ave., Sea Girt, 732/449-0442, www.theparkerhouseonline .com, $8.95–21.95), strung with white lights and looking absolutely magnificent with its raised wraparound veranda packed with dining tables, and a wide staircase leading the way to the host's stand, which towers like a clergyman's pulpit high above its congregation. This seasonal restaurant serves steak, seafood, burgers, and sandwiches and features an outdoor raw bar and a Wednesday night lobster special ($12.95) during summer. Happy hour specials, and live music and DJ spins over the weekend, put this one on the map as a one-stop extravaganza.

Just south of Sea Girt on the way into Manasquan is **Surf Taco** (121 Parker Ave., 732/223-7757, www.surftaco.com, 11 A.M.–9 P.M. Sun.–Thurs., until 9:30 P.M. Fri. and Sat., $2.95–9.95), a local semi-chain serving Mexican eats in a brightly painted surf shack. This is a popular place with the local teen crowd.

Across the street from the Manasquan beach where the inlet and ocean meet, the flip-flop casual **Riverside Café** (425 Riverside Dr., 732/223-2233, $5–10) sells burgers, grilled sandwiches, and a mean chocolate shake ($5). For fine dining in Manasquan try the stylish

Mahogany Grille (142 Main St., 732/292-1300, 5–10 P.M. Mon.–Thurs., until 11 P.M. Fri. and Sat., 4–9 P.M. Sun., $22–30), a white linen restaurant occupying a corner space along downtown's Main Street. The Grille serves a menu of eclectic entrees and requires proper dress at all times.

For a cup of coffee and a bit of Wi-Fi Internet there's Main Street's eclectic **Green Planet Coffee Co.** (78 Main St., Manasquan 732/772-8197), where you'll also find a small selection of pastries. Local artwork adorns the walls.

Getting There and Around
The Manasquan train station is just east of Main Street.

The Barnegat Peninsula

Known as the Barnegat Peninsula from its days before the addition of the Point Pleasant Canal, this stretch of land begins north at Point Pleasant and continues through to the southern tip of Island Beach State Park. The best boardwalks in North and Central Jersey are found here, along with one of the most pristine extensions of white sand beach along the entire Jersey Shore.

© LAURA KINIRY

Fun House, Jenkinson's Boardwalk

POINT PLEASANT BEACH
Not to be mistaken for the Boro of Point Pleasant, Point Pleasant Beach is a family-oriented fishing community that grew in popularity with the arrival of the railroad and later the opening of the Garden State Parkway. Unfinished Cape Cod houses with grassy lawns are the town's typical residence, and the downtown section hovers around Arnold, Bay, and Richmond Streets—where you'll find a coffeehouse and a few scattered bars and eateries. Still, it's the boardwalk that's the highlight of most evenings—especially for kids and teens.

In 2005 a short-lived Fox television show was loosely set in Point Pleasant Beach, though it bore little resemblance to this charming seafaring town.

Sights
It may not be the longest walkway, but **Jenkinson's Boardwalk** (300 Ocean Ave., 732/892-0600, www.jenkinsons.com) really packs a punch. Its end portions are casual walking venues, but get to the middle and the fun really begins—a double-sided build-up of custard stands, pizza places, carnival games, and casual bars, and all of it vibrating in colors of sea green, marine blue, and pink. There's a boardwalk aquarium and **Jenkinson's Amusement Park South** (www.jenkinsons.com/rides.cfm, opens noon daily during summer), an outdoor venue geared toward kids, but one of the best attractions is the old-fashioned **Fun House** ($5), complete with laughing clowns, lots of darkness, and a hall of mirrors.

THE JERSEY SHORE

Open year-round, **Jenkinson's Aquarium** (300 Ocean Ave., 732/899-1212, www.jenkinsons.com, $8 adult, $5 child) is a favorite for class trips. On the first floor you can visit with tropical fish, sharks, gators, and underwater penguins, while the second floor has a rainforest exhibit that includes macaws, hissing cockroaches, poison dart frogs, and the newest addition, pygmy marmosets—the world's smallest monkeys. Scheduled shark feedings are open to the public throughout the year. Aquarium hours are 9:30 A.M.–5 P.M. Monday–Friday, 10 A.M.–5 P.M. weekends.

Beaches

Daily beach passes are $5.50 weekdays, $6.50 weekends. No alcohol is allowed on Jenkinson's Beach, though coolers are allowed.

Entertainment and Events

The Southern-style **River Belle** (732/892-3377, www.riverboattour.com) riverboat takes visitors on two-hour sightseeing tours along the Barnegat Bay and Point Pleasant Canal. Tours ($15 adult, $8 child) run daily, except Sunday, through July and August, and advanced ticket purchases are recommended. The riverboat is docked along the canal and leaves from Broadway Basin.

Each February, drop your scarf and ear muffs and pull on your skimpiest swimsuit to get ready for the **Polar Bear Plunge** (732/213-5387), an annual frolic in the ocean that raises money for the Special Olympics.

Day-long amateur **beach volleyball tournaments** take place weekends throughout summer at Jenkinson's Inlet Beach, beginning the end of June.

Movies on the Beach are featured on scheduled summer evenings in front of Jenkinson's Boardwalk. Bring a blanket to lounge on the sand in front of the oceanfront screen—a screening of *Jaws* seems inevitable.

Since 1975 the September **Festival of the Sea** (www.pointpleasantbeach.com/seafoodfestival.htm) has called an end to summer in Point Pleasant Beach with craft vendors, local eats, antiques, and plenty of entertainment.

Free shuttles run from the boardwalk to the downtown festival grounds.

Sports and Recreation

Diversion II (www.diversion2.com) is a charter operation that takes professional divers to explore many of New Jersey's over 2,000 shipwrecks, both intentional (to act as makeshift reefs) and unintentional (the majority). For more info, contact Captain Steve Naglewicz by email at steve@njscuba.com.

The **New Jersey Sailing School** (1800 Bay Ave., 732/295-3450, www.newjerseysailingschool.com) holds sailing classes from basic cruising ($300–350) to advanced navigation ($130). Lessons are held during summer months, but a couple of seminars are available during the off-season. Contact them for a complete schedule.

The Point Pleasant Inlet is home to numerous fishing charters. Two to try are **Lady Diana** (Crystal Point Yacht Club, 908/769-3932), which offers inshore, canyon, and wreck sportfishing aboard a 50-foot Viking boat, and **Purple Jet Sportfishing Fleet** (Canyon River Club, 407 Channel Dr., 732/996-2579 or 800/780-TUNA, www.purplejet.com), a six-person charter vessel.

Take to the skies with **Point Pleasant Parasail** (Ken's Landing, 30 Broadway, 732/714-2FLY or 732/714-2359), which offers oceanfront flights, solo or in tandem, 500 feet above the sea.

Accommodations

$150-200: Within walking distance to the boardwalk is the **Carousel Inn** (1301 Ocean Ave., 732/892-5415, www.thecarouselinn.com), a remodeled guesthouse featuring cozy, individually styled rooms and efficiencies. Units are spacious and come equipped with air-conditioning, TV, private parking, and the use of beach passes. According to one of the employees, two doors in use at the inn were intentioned for use on the Titanic. Only a couple of standard rooms are offered, the remainder are one-, two-, and three-bedroom apartments that charge a higher fee, and a two-night minimum stay is required during high season.

In Point Pleasant Beach Inlet is the family-owned **Surfside Motel** (101 Broadway, 732/899-1109, www.surfside-motel.com), a two-story motel with clean, standard rooms complete with TV, telephone, fridge, and complimentary beach passes, and there's a heated in-ground pool roadside.

$200-250: The **White Sands Oceanfront Resort & Spa** (1205 Ocean Ave., 732/899-3370, www.thewhitesands.com) features both an oceanfront motel and a newer upscale hotel across the street. The 74-room motel is the more family-friendly of the two and houses two outdoor pools, while a highlight of the 56-room hotel is an adults-only spa. Shared amenities include an Italian steakhouse, fitness club, martini and frozen-drink bar, and a liquor store.

Food and Nightlife

The seasonal **Jenkinson's Inlet Bar and Restaurant** is a good place to grab a burger and a beer. It's situated on the north end of the boardwalk, and features an open-air bar decorated with surfboards and lighted beer signs. Located at the hub of boardwalk action, **Martell's Tiki Bar** (312 Boardwalk, 732/892-0131, www.tikibar.com) is part of a larger complex that hosts a few casual bars, a sushi stand, and an always-crowded fast-food line (732/892-3548) where you can pick up an exceptional slice of pepperoni pizza ($3.50). The open-air Tiki Bar is located at the rear of the complex toward the ocean and is a wonderful spot for enjoying a frozen daiquiri or margarita during sticky summer evenings while listening to live musical performances. Summer hours vary so call ahead. The bar is occasionally open for weekend events throughout the year.

For gourmet pizza slices try the nearby **Joey Tomatoes** (Central Avenue and Boardwalk, 732/295-2624, $3–15, open daily throughout summer) where you can get a chicken parm pizza slice and veg out at one of their boardwalk tables.

(Co-op Seafood (57 Channel Dr., 732/899-2211, $8.50–15) serves excellent quality fish fresh off the boat. Just a few tables line the inside windows of this small, no-frills establishment—the rest are located out front beneath a covered awning. Portions are large and the staff is knowledgeable and friendly. Owned by local fishers, this bayside eatery is open all year, 10 A.M.–6 P.M. during the off-season, until 9 P.M. in summer months.

Just off Route 35 by the Manasquan River is the Italian **Tesauro's** (401 Broadway, 732/892-5694, www.tesaurosrestaurant.com, $8.50–27.95), a long-time area favorite that came under new ownership in 2004. Dishes are heavy on the seafood at this family-friendly place, which also features a varied wine list and frozen drink specialties. Lunch is served 11:30 A.M.–3 P.M. Monday–Friday, and dinner 5–10 P.M.Monday–Thursday, until 11 P.M. Friday and Saturday.

Getting There

Point Pleasant Beach is located off exit 98 (southbound) or exit 90 (northbound) of the Garden State Parkway.

BAY HEAD

Often called the New England of the Jersey Shore, Bay Head is a charming hamlet filled with one- and two-story wood-shingled homes in shades of browns, grays, and blues. Barnegat Bay passes under the tiny downtown stretch of Bridge Avenue, where you'll find a handful of specialty shops, and just north along Lake Avenue, a number of bayside decks where you can sit to watch Canada geese and ducks frolic in the water. For those who enjoy quiet and reprieve, this is the place to come. The entire town is easy walking distance to the beach.

Beaches

Bay Head's daily beach passes cost $5.

Shopping

Most of Bay Head's shops are found along Bridge Avenue, with a couple more scattered about town.

The **Bay Head Cheese Shop** (91 Bridge Ave., 732/892-7585) is an old country shop selling a wide variety of cheese, including large blocks of English and Wisconsin brands. Its shelves are stocked with spreads and sauces. Old-fashioned **Mueller's Bakery** (80 Bridge Ave., 732/892-0442) is permeated with the smells of cherry-topped butter cookies and cheese-filled, vanilla-dripped pastries. Get in line at this often-busy, no-nonsense place.

If you're looking for matching beach blanket and tote bag combos, or your own handmade Jersey Girl plaque, **Cobwebs** (64 Bridge Ave., 732/892-8005) is the place to come. For specialty writing paper and hand-carved decoys there's **The Jolly Tar** (56 Bridge Ave., 732/892-0223), a gift shop and art gallery that's known for its bridal department.

The facades of shops inside the **Shopper's Wharf** (70 Bridge Ave., www.shopperswharf .com) are made to resemble a village exterior, and within this makeshift town you'll find the pet-lover's **Pet~Iquette,** a fashion and fine-dining stop for your dogs and cats; and a tiny tea and coffee shop called **Bay Head Blends** (732/295-4333), with a porch for seating.

The Victorian-housed **Fables of Bay Head** (410 Main Ave., 732/899-3633) sells antique quilts and contemporary American furniture. It's also an old-fashioned ice cream fountain.

Accommodations

$200-250: The Bentley Inn (694 Main Ave., 732/892-9589 or 866/423-6853, www .bentleyinn.com,) is an 1886 Victorian with covered porches and a dining solarium. The majority of the inn's 19 brightly colored guestrooms have shared bath (considerably less expensive), though all include TV/VCR, air-conditioning, phone, and sitting areas. Enjoy Belgian waffles for breakfast and go for a ride on the complimentary bicycles. For those traveling with laptops, wireless Internet access is available.

The **Conover's Bay Head Inn** (646 Main Ave., 732/892-8748, www.conovers.com) features nine guestrooms and three suites—all with private bath, TV/VCR, and air-conditioning. Fresh baked goods are available daily, to enjoy in the English garden or with afternoon tea.

Food

The **Historic Grenville Hotel** (345 Main Ave., 732/892-3100, www.thegrenville.com) is an 1890 remodeled Victorian with a superb fine-dining restaurant. New American entrées are served in a Queen Anne–style dining room or on the front porch, and the seasonally changing menu includes only fresh ingredients. The restaurant is open daily for lunch and dinner during July and August.

Getting There

Bay Head is located off exit 98 (southbound) or exit 90 (northbound) of the Garden State Parkway. You can also catch the NJ Transit North Jersey Coast Line from New York City—Bay Head will be the last stop.

SEASIDE HEIGHTS

It's been less than a decade since Seaside Heights played host to MTV's summer beach house, and if this gives any indication of what the town was like, things haven't changed. Sweaty late-night dance clubs, seedy motels advertising prom-night specials, and an ultra-tacky boardwalk with big-eared Muffler Men and Bon Jovi blaring from overhead speakers all add to the image—Seaside is a place to be seen. Want to fit the mold? Get to the boardwalk early, and buy yourself a "What Happens in Seaside Stays in Seaside" T-shirt, or one that reads "Not only am I cute, but I'm Italian, too." Then primp for the numerous security cameras, and hit the piers for one long carnival ride. You'll have a story to tell.

The boardwalk and amusement piers are the true reason to visit Seaside, along with a few bars and clubs, if the above describes your style. Dining and accommodations are not area highlights, though a couple of bars offer a decent food selection and you can always grab a snack on the boardwalk. There are a few motels in town that while not luxury palaces are okay choices if you decide to stay. But if you don't mind the drive, it's worth it to book a room in Bay Head to the north and visit Seaside for the day.

Boardwalk

The entire eastern border of Seaside Heights is

lined with boardwalk, and if there would be a Southern Shore comparison, it would be Wildwood—though I'd say it's really more like Santa Cruz, California. Amid the bright colors of the amusement rides you'll find bars, babes, and games of chance, and both sides of the walkway are built to oblivion—there are men in muscle shirts hawking tees, and piers jutting out onto the beach and into the crashing waves. Along the stretch of boards are miniature golf courses, casino arcades, and retail shops selling Yankee's paraphernalia, and above it all is a mile-long skyway advertising cool breezes from its open-air seats. Goth teens hang where the boardwalk narrows, connecting to the south with the recycled plastic planks of Seaside Park.

On the south side of the boardwalk **Casino Pier** (800 Ocean Terrace, 732/793-6495, www.casinopiernj.com) rises above the sand and sea with a plethora of amusement rides including a log flume, human slingshot, and hall of mirrors. This is where you'll find the Alfred E. Neuman Muffler Man towering over the course of **Rooftop Wacky Golf,** as well as one of the boardwalk's best attractions, the Gothic-style **Stillwalk Manor** haunted ride. The pier is open every day in July and August and through most of June, and weekends during the shoulder seasons, beginning mid-March and ending mid-September. A three-hour admission to the rides costs $18.95 adult, $13.95 child. All-day admission ($23.95/$18.95) is available.

A boardwalk highlight is the **Flashback Arcade,** located within the Casino Arcade behind the carousel house. This place is packed with everything old school: Centipede, Ms. Pac Man, Track and Field, and sit-down Pole Position. Continuing with the yesteryear theme, most of the games play for $0.25. Oh—the joy! It's the kind of place you could stay for hours if only it were properly ventilated.

The carousel house at Casino Pier is home to one of two American carved antique carousels that remain in New Jersey. The **Floyd Moreland Carousel** (732/793-6489, www.magicalcarousel.com, $2) features over 2,000 bulbs, nearly 20 paintings, and a Wurlitzer Band organ with 105 wooden pipes.

At Jenkinson's **Breakwater Beach** (800 Ocean Terrace, 732/793-6488, www.casinopiernj.com, $18.95 adult, $13.95 child all-day admission) at Casino Pier, you'll find water-slides that wiggle, shoot, and loop around turns, two hot-springs pools, a lazy river, and a considerably sized children's play area. As of 2005 the water park is in the midst of a multi-year renovation, but remains open every day through July and August.

Funtown Pier (1930 Boardwalk, 732/830-PIER or 732/830-7437, www.funtownpier.com) features over 40 rides and plenty of snack-food stands. Costumed characters like Wiggle the Wave roam the grounds while adults escape to the giant Ferris wheel and the 225-foot **Tower of Fear.** The majority of rides are for kids, but the Tilt-A-Whirl and bumper cars belong to anyone. The Pier is open throughout the summer, and unlimited rides on weekdays run $14.95, $10.95 for kiddie rides only.

Beaches

Daily beach tags are $5, free for those 12 and under. On Wednesdays and Thursdays the beaches are free.

In nearby Seaside Park a day at the beach is $8, free for 11 and under.

Events

Casino Pier hosts free fireworks Wednesday nights throughout the summer, beginning at 9 P.M.

Giant shoes take to the streets in September for the annual **Clownfest** convention (www.clownfest.com). Although the five-day event consists mostly of classes and competitions, a traditional Clownfest parade takes place along the Seaside Heights boardwalk at 2 P.M. on the final Sunday, before participants pack 12-deep into their buggies to drive home.

Accommodations

Motels are the primary form of accommodation in Seaside Heights, and while there are plenty of them, the majority are not recommendable. The following are your best options for spending the night in Seaside, although you

THE JERSEY SHORE

may also decide to book a room in Bay Head or Point Pleasant Beach to the north, where there's a better selection to chose from and you can leave the party of Seaside behind for a good night's sleep.

$100-150: Rooms at the **Seaside Colony Motel** (65 Hiering Ave., 732/830-2113, www.seasidecolonymotel.com,) are wood paneled and spacious, with air-conditioning, fridge, and microwave. There's also a pool.

$150-200: In a commendable effort to keep complaints to a minimum, the 23-room **Luna Mar Motel** (1201 N. Ocean Ave., 732/793-8991, 877/LUNAMAR, or 877/586-2627, www.lunamarmotel.com) observes a 21-and-over policy. You must show ID to get a room, and the motel's focus is on couples and families. The motel offers both rooms and efficiencies, and amenities include a mini-fridge in every unit and a swimming pool.

Food and Nightlife

Seaside Heights is the place to come for New Jersey nightlife the way most people from out-of-state imagine it: gold chains, skimpy tees, teased hair, and fake IDs dancing butt cheek–to–butt cheek until all hours of the morning. However, bars do exist in Seaside that stand on their own with no help from the Jersey image, and are good places to stop for a drink and even a bite to eat. Like other Shore towns, many of Seaside Heights' establishments taper off business hours until they are locked and bolted in January.

The **Bamboo Bar** (201 Blvd., 732/830-3660, www.bamboobar.com) is the ultimate in Seaside nightlife and gets crazy packed in summer when it stays open until 4 A.M. Friday and Saturday nights. Those 18 and older pile onto the huge outdoor deck grooving to DJ spins at this bar that's quite an attraction among the single crowd.

Another Seaside scene is **Temptations** (612 Blvd., 732/830-3410, www.temptationsseaside.com, 10 P.M.–3 A.M. Fri., until 4 A.M. Sat.), a full-out techno dance party that takes place in a warehouse-style space. For those seeking a more subdued experience, the club features a VIP champagne lounge.

A long-running boardwalk institution in the **Saw Mill Restaurant & Tavern** (1807 Boardwalk, 732/793-1990). Known for its enormous pizza slices, the Saw Mill also features a varied menu of eats, including jalapeno poppers ($5) and Cuban sandwiches ($5.50). Above the restaurant, the **Green Room** is the B-spot (that's "boardwalk spot") for dancing and live music. Theme nights include Tijuana Tuesdays, and Wave Wednesdays, when surf movies run all night long.

Seaside's most respectable space is the long-standing **Klee's Bar and Grill** (101 Blvd., 732/830-1996, www.kleesbarandgrill.com), an Irish pub serving casual eats such as pizza, burgers, and house-made entrees like Klee's Pot Pie ($10.95) and Klee's Meatloaf Platter ($10.95). The bar features live music on weekends.

Getting There

Seaside Heights is located off exit 82 of the Garden State Parkway.

ISLAND BEACH STATE PARK

One of the most pristine stretches of beach along the entire New Jersey coastline, the 3,000-acre Island Beach State Park (Seaside Park, 732/793-0506, www.njparksandforests.org/parks/island.html) is 10 miles of white-sand beach, wildlife preserve, nature trails, fresh water bogs, and coastal maritime plant life.

Situated between the Atlantic Ocean and Barnegat Bay, this narrow barrier strip is a major route along the migratory Atlantic Flyway and a great spot for bird-watching. Peregrine falcons, waterfowl, and warblers all make their way through, and the park is home to New Jersey's largest nesting osprey colony. Also in residence are red foxes and turtles, and seasonal visitors include butterflies, and in the nearby waters, bluefish and striped bass. It's also a good spot to catch a glimpse of bottle-nosed dolphins during summer months, and the occasional harbor or gray seal from December to March.

The park consists of three sections: a northern natural area, a central recreational zone, and a southern natural area, which contains the park's primary wildlife habitat. Access to the northern zone is somewhat limited, as it's been set aside to protect coastal habitat.

Sports and Recreation

There are eight nature trails, each less than a mile long, scattered throughout the park, including one that begins from the Aeolium Interpretive Center in the northern natural area, another from the center's A-7 year-round comfort station, and a third leaving from the bird blind in the southern zone's Area 20. The park features a five-mile-long bike path that begins in the northern natural area near the main entry, and from here you can access each of the remaining two zones.

In the center's aptly named recreation zone there's a mile-long beach designated for swimming, with a lifeguard, concession stand, first-aid station, and bathhouses in service Memorial Day–Labor Day. Horseback riding is allowed on designated trails in the central and southern regions October–April.

Diving is permitted for 2.5 miles in waters off the southern zone, beginning from Barnegat Inlet and heading north. Divers are required to first register with the park service. The southern tip of Ocean Bathing Area #3 in the central area is designated for surfing and windsurfing.

Island Beach offers some of the Shore's best saltwater sportfishing—especially for striped bass and bluefish—and the southern tail of the park, overlooking the nearby Barnegat Bay Lighthouse (about an hour by car as access is restricted to mainland routes) on the north tip of Long Beach Island, is strictly for fishing. There's no camping allowed, and parking along the beach is only for those who have permits,

and, preferably, four-wheel drive. Sportfishing is also allowed at the central zone's Bathing Area #2 during the off-season.

The southern natural area also offers the park's best bird-watching ops (waterfowl are best sighted May–Oct.) as well as a boat launch for canoes and kayaks at Area 21. In summer, guided canoe and kayak excursions take place along Barnegat Bay, exploring the nearby Sedge Islands.

Information and Services

Park admission fees are $6 weekdays, $10 weekends per vehicle Memorial Day–Labor Day, $5 daily in the off-season.

The park hosts two interpretive centers—the northern zone's Aeolium Interpretive Center, and the Forked River Coast Guard Station No. 112 Interpretive Center in the southern natural area. Island Beach offers select tours and programs daily during July and August, beginning from the central zone's First Pavilion at Ocean Bathing Area #1.

You'll find public restrooms throughout the park, including at the park entryway, in the middle and southern portions of the central recreation zone, and in numerous spots along the southern natural area. A year-round facility is located at lot A-7 in the central recreation zone, which also hosts a wooden walkway to the sea suitable for visitors with disabilities. Big wheel rolling chairs are available at the central zone's Ocean Bathing Area #1 and #2 pavilions during summer, and from the park service (offices are located between the two beaches) in the off-season.

Picnicking with the use of grills is allowed in the central zone on the beach south of the designated swimming area.

THE JERSEY SHORE

Long Beach Island and Vicinity

Long Beach Island, or L.B.I., is a thin 18-mile barrier island made up of numerous boroughs and one large township scattered among them. There's only one bridge leading onto and off of the island, accommodating everyone from Barnegat Light on the island's northern tip south through to Holgate. L.B.I. was once notorious for the shipwrecks that occurred off its coast. Today it's laid-back and family-friendly—a lackadaisical island where north meets south, or New York meets Philly—filled with surfing enclaves, cedar shacks, modern mansions, and one long boulevard.

As L.B.I. is one long narrow stretch you'll easily pass from one town to the next without realizing it. Because of its length, and the fact that there's only one main road, it wouldn't be feasible to stay in Barnegat Light on a visit to Beach Haven, but overnight accommodations in nearby Long Beach Township would be fine. The towns mentioned below run from north to south along the island.

Getting There and Around

L.B.I. is easily reached from exit 63 of the Garden State Parkway. There's only one bridge on and off the island.

BARNEGAT LIGHT

Along the north tip of L.B.I., Barnegat Light is home to the island's most deserted beach. Not to be confused with the mainland's Barnegat Township, the Light has a population less than 800 and a size smaller than a square mile. It's home to one of the most photographed lighthouses in the state.

◖ Barnegat Lighthouse State Park

At the point where the Atlantic Ocean and Barnegat Bay meet is 32-acre Barnegat Lighthouse State Park (Barnegat Light, 609/494-2016, www.state.nj.us/dep/parksandforests/parks/barnlig.html, dawn–dusk), a picturesque place filled with sandy expanses, maritime forest, an interpretive center, nature trail, and plenty of waterfront property. Along the inlet separating Barnegat from Island Beach State Park (although it's only a few hundred yards distance by sea, it takes an hour to reach by car) is a 1,033-foot concrete walkway ideal for strollers and often used by fishers, who cast their lines for bluefish, weakfish, and flounder. The park is a popular spot for wildlife viewing and birds are regular visitors, with waterfowl making an appearance during summer shoulder seasons, shorebirds throughout the high season, and warblers in the fall. It's possible to sight gray and harbor seals along Barnegat's beaches December–March, and the forest hosts thousands of monarch butterflies migrating through the region in late summer and early autumn.

Barnegat is home to one of the state's most beloved lighthouses, affectionately known as **Old Barney.** Said to be the most photographed

the Barnegat Lighthouse, Long Beach Island

lighthouse in New Jersey, this 172-foot, 217-step red-and-white structure was built in the 1850s after sailors complained that the then-present lighthouse could be mistaken for a passing ship. Today visitors can climb to the top of Barney's deactivated light tower for a wonderful view of the surrounding region; not to worry, a number of rooms featuring small exhibits serve as makeshift rest areas on the way up the spiral stairs. The lighthouse is open 9 A.M.–4:30 P.M. daily Memorial Day–Labor Day and 9 A.M.–3:30 P.M. the rest of the year, and the fee is $1.

Viking Village

With all the signs pointing to Viking Village (19th St. and Bayview Ave., 609/494-0113) you'd think you were in for something special. Guess again. Along the bay you'll find little more than a small row of stores and a few scattered buildings. The shops sell some cute items and the shanty setting is *slightly* romantic, but arrival at this destination is disappointing at best. If you're already here, have a look at the antiques in **The Sea Wife** (609/361-8039), and maybe a quick browse around **Viking Outfitters** (609/361-9111), a clothing store for sea captains. That being said, Viking Village is one of the largest suppliers of fresh fish on the east coast and the Village restaurant selling daily catches is a definite winner.

Beaches

The best beach access in Barnegat Light is below 20th Street. Daily beach tags are $3, one of the least expensive spots along the Shore. Beach wheelchairs are available at Borough Hall (10 W. 10th St., 609/494-9196). Public restrooms are available at Barnegat Lighthouse State Park.

Accommodations

$250-300: The romantic **Sand Castle** (710 Bayview Ave., 609/494-6555 or 800/253-0353, www.sandcastlelbi.com) is a luxury B&B, located on a side road near Barnegat Lighthouse State Park. Modern on the outside, beachy Victorian on the inside, it features five rooms and two suites, all with private bath and daily

gourmet breakfast, and a heated outdoor peanut-shaped pool. Rooms have their own outdoor entrances, and there's a rooftop deck for watching the sunset. Additional amenities include fireplaces, TVs with VCR/DVD player, and bicycles for guest use.

Food and Nightlife

If you're looking for a bite to eat close to the lighthouse try **Kelly's Old Barney Restaurant** (3rd St. and Broadway, 609/494-5115, $4–9)—you can walk over from the park's parking lot. Kelly's is basically an enclosed side porch doused in a nautical theme with plenty of lighthouse paraphernalia. The menu is simple: burgers, fries, and grilled cheese on white bread—and reasonably priced. There's outdoor seating in the back, and counter service and tables indoors. Kelly's is cash-only and open seasonally.

For a year-round option and a cocktail with your meal, there's **Rick's American Cafe** (4th St. and Broadway, 609/494-8482, $5–15), just across the street from Kelly's. Inside this weathered tavern you'll find standard steaks and seafood, as well as a pool table and a large center bar.

Located along the boats at the lackluster Viking Village, **Viking Fresh Off the Hook LLC** (1905 Bayview Ave., 609/361-8900, www.viking offthehook.com, $6.95–24.95) is a definite diamond in the rough. This fish market sells straight-off-the-boat seafood accompanied by fries, slaw, or smashed potatoes, as well as salads, soups, sandwiches, and fried appetizers to go. Hours vary throughout the year, so call ahead.

HARVEY CEDARS AND LOVELADIES

Once a whaling station, Harvey Cedars is now a residential bayside and oceanfront community, and to its south is Loveladies, part of the larger Long Beach Township but separated from its siblings further down the island. Loveladies was a major casualty of the 1962 three-day storm that wreaked havoc on L.B.I., and many of the community's homes were completely destroyed. They've since been rebuilt as exclusive roadside enclaves of grand,

THE JERSEY SHORE

modern homes, most raised high on pilings. You'll still see the occasional single story here and there, but very rarely. It's one of the thinnest portions of the island, and public beach access is quite limited. Loveladies is completely without restaurants, though a couple of excellent dining options exist in Harvey Cedars. Options for overnight stays in Harvey Cedars and Loveladies are limited—try the bed-and-breakfast in Barnegat Light to the north, or if you're up for the drive, make your way down to Beach Haven along L.B.I.'s southern stretch, about a 13-mile drive. This is where you'll find the island's best accommodation choices, although weekend traffic can make the distance extremely daunting.

Beaches

Harvey Cedars daily beach badges run $6, free for children under 12. Harvey Cedars features a children's beach at 77th Street, but beaches can be accessed from any street. Harvey Cedars' **Sunset Park** (W. Salem Ave.) has showers and restrooms for use.

Loveladies beach is $5 daily, free for those under 12 and over 65. Much of Loveladies' shoreline is considered private, and public beach access points are located in only a handful of spots, including Coast Avenue, Loveladies Lane, and Seashell Lane. Public restrooms in Loveladies are located at Harbor South.

Events

The **Long Beach Island Foundation of the Arts and Sciences** (609/494-1241, www.lbi foundation.org) hosts an annual August **Seashore Open House Tour** ($30) of some of Loveladies' finest.

Harvey Cedars hosts a summer concert series at 7 P.M. Wednesdays throughout summer at **Sunset Park** (W. Salem Ave.) on the bay.

Food

Plantation (7908 Long Beach Blvd., Harvey Cedars, 609/494-8191, www.plantation restaurant.com, $10–25) is a year-round restaurant specializing in rum-induced drinks and contemporary fusion cuisine. Inside is a large center bar lined with tables, and a more intimate dining room to the side. The refined island decor is much more Bogart and Bacall than Monchichi. Plantation is open for lunch 11:30 A.M.–2:30 P.M. daily, and for dinner 4:30–9:30 P.M. Sunday–Thursday, until 10:30 P.M. Friday and Saturday.

Next door is the casual **Harvey Cedars Shellfish Company** (7904 Long Beach Blvd., 609/494-7112), a BYO seafood market that has been in business since 1976. Get comfortable at one of the indoor picnic tables and chow down with the lively crowds. The eatery opens at 4:30 P.M. nightly during the summer; off-season hours are limited.

SURF CITY

The less-than-one-square-mile borough of Surf City is filled with residential shacks, casual eateries, and plenty of bare feet. It's a lax surfing community.

Beaches

Beach tags cost $6 daily (under 12 and over 65 free). Surf City features a designated surfing beach between First and Third Streets, and a bayside beach at 15th and Barnegat Avenue. Public access is not restricted and beaches can be accessed from any side street. Public restrooms are located at **Borough Hall** (813 Long Beach Blvd., 609/494-3064).

Sports and Recreation

If you want to take a ride on a surrey, check out **Surf Buggy Center** (1414 Long Beach Blvd., 609/361-3611, www.surfbuggycenters.com). If family four-wheeling isn't your thing, they also rent bicycles. Surf City has a **surf-only beach** between First and Second Streets—just look for the flags.

Local bait and tackle shop **Bruce & Pat's** (317 Long Beach Blvd., 609/494-2333) is one of many shops along the island where you can pick up a clamming license.

Accommodations

$150-200: The **Surf City Hotel** (8th St. and Long Beach Island Blvd., 609/494-7281, www

.surfcityhotel.com) is one of the island's oldest hotels—a large white clapboard that practically spells salty air. Rooms have air-conditioning, TV, and fridge, and there's a cottage for rent that's equipped for guests with disabilities.

Food and Nightlife

At the Surf City Hotel is a bar, adjacent liquor store, restaurant, and clam bar. Live entertainment is featured on summer evenings and Sunday afternoons. The hotel's happy hour draws a random assortment of clientele that includes tourists, locals, and commuters from New York.

For breakfast eats, including chocolate chip pancakes, try **Scojo's** (307 N. Long Beach Blvd., 609/494-8661), a year-round establishment that also serves lunch and dinner.

SHIP BOTTOM AND LONG BEACH TOWNSHIP

Long Beach Township comprises a number of smaller areas, including Brant Beach (south of Ship Bottom), Spray Beach, Brighton Beach, and Beach Haven North. Ship Bottom is the island's centermost borough, the place where Route 72 drops you onto L.B.I. For this reason, Ship Bottom is more commercial than the rest of the island, and seems to lack the small-community feel that the other boroughs possess. Businesses have grown sporadically along the wide main street and traffic can get quite congested as weekenders make their way along Long Beach Boulevard.

Beaches

Long Beach Township's daily beach tags cost $5, and Ship Bottom's are $6 (children under 12 free and seniors over 65 $2). Restrooms are located within Ship Bottom's Borough Hall (1621 Long Beach Blvd., 609/494-2171), and at Branch Beach's Bayview Park (68th Street). Many of Ship Bottom's beaches are wheelchair-accessible.

Sports and Recreation

Brant Beach hosts one of the largest windsurfing shops along the Mid-Atlantic coast, and les-

sons are available at **Island Surf & Sail** (3304 Long Beach Blvd., Brant Beach, 609/494-5553, www.islandsurf-sail.com).

LBI Scuba (342 W. 9th St., 609/494-5599, www.lbiscuba.com) offers wreck diving for all levels and basic scuba classes throughout the year.

What started off as a little surfing shack has grown into a mega-retail business. **Ron Jon Surf Shop** (201 W. 9th St., Ship Bottom, 609/494-8844, www.ronjons.com) in Ship Bottom is the original, but the company runs a handful of revered locations in both California and Florida. Old-timers who haven't visited the island in a while won't even recognize this place—standing like Oz at the island's causeway entry. You'll still find surfboards and gear, as well as the hippest in fashion for surfer dudes and ladies and skateboard fanatics, but if history is what you're after, it's buried beneath the jams and tees.

Food and Nightlife

La Spiaggia (357 W. 8th St., 609/494-4343, www.laspiaggialbi.com, $25–36) is an upscale Italian BYO located at the base of the causeway. The entrées are excellent and the service superb, and while they're understanding of casual Shore fashion, you should forgo the tanks and flip-flops. The restaurant is open for dinner only, beginning at 5 P.M. Tuesday–Sunday during summer, Wednesday–Sunday spring and fall.

For L.B.I. nightlife try **Joe Pop's Shore Bar** (2002 Long Beach Blvd., 609/494-0558), featuring live bands and DJs throughout the summer. Joe's has been in the community for almost 50 years and with its bright yellow and green-awning exterior, it's easy to spot. The bar serves a menu of simple American eats and offers weekly drink specials. They're open lunch, dinner, and late-night Wednesday–Sunday throughout summer and into the shoulder seasons. Call ahead for exact hours.

Cross over the causeway bridge onto L.B.I. from the mainland and **The Quarter Deck** (351 W. 9th St., 609/494-9055) is the first thing you see. This large octagon-shaped, two-story bar has its own restaurant and hotel.

There's food on deck, karaoke on weekends, and live music acts—ranging from the rockin' B Street cover band to Vanilla Ice—featured throughout the week.

BEACH HAVEN

Toward the south of L.B.I. is Beach Haven, a predominantly residential area that hosts the island's only amusement park. The Haven has a small historic district with a museum as its centerpiece, surrounded by weathered cedar Victorians donning American flags. To keep with its family image, the borough has an 11 P.M. strictly enforced curfew for minors.

Sights

For over 20 years, **Fantasy Island Amusement Park** (320 W. 7th St., 609/492-4000, www.fantasyislandpark.com) has been entertaining families at Beach Haven. Most of the rides are kid- and teen-oriented, like a miniature "Giant" Ferris wheel and the swinging Sea Dragon. There's plenty of Shore cuisine on hand, including funnel cake and an ice cream parlor with hand-scooped and soft-serve cones. There's an old-school shooting gallery ($1) and a casino arcade with hundreds of ticket-producing slot machines, skeeball, and giant cranes. Cash in your wins for some of the best prizes along the Shore, including miniature flat-screen TVs and a ceramic ensemble of Rudolph the Red Nose Reindeer collectibles. For $15 you'll get a roll of 20 ride tokens; most rides require 3–5 tokens. The park opens at 5 P.M. daily throughout the summer, and the arcade opens at noon.

Run by the LBI Historical Society (Engleside and Beach Aves., 609/492-0700, www.lbi.net/nonprof/lbimusm.html, $3 donation) the **Long Beach Island Museum** features an informative display on the three-day 1962 storm that destroyed many of the island's homes and forever changed its geography. You'll also find information on its beginnings as a whaling community. The museum is located along the square in the historic district and provides self-guided walking-tour brochures of the area. Hours are 2–4 P.M. weekends throughout May–June

Beach Haven's historic district

© LAURA KINIRY

and mid-September, and 10 A.M.–4 P.M. daily throughout the summer. It's also open to visitors on Tuesdays throughout the year; just knock on the back door.

On the southern tip of L.B.I., just below Beach Haven, is the **Edwin B. Forsythe National Wildlife Refuge's Holgate Unit** (www.fws.gov/northeast/forsythe/), nesting site for the endangered piping plover and numerous other bird species. This unit of the wildlife refuge (there's a larger, more accessible unit in Brigantine to the south) is open to pubic visits during non-nesting season, September–March. It's a wonderful place for a quiet beach stroll.

Beaches

Beach Haven's daily beach fee is $5; over 65 and under 12 are free. Beaches can be accessed from anywhere, but Centre Street Beach has a wheelchair ramp. Restrooms are available at Centre and Dock Streets, bayside, and in the Bay Village shopping area.

Entertainment

Located within the borough's historic district, the 450-seat community **Surflight Theatre** (Engleside and Beach Aves., 609/492-9477 or 609/492-4469, www.surflight.org, $25) has been entertaining islanders for decades. It's Ocean County's only professional theater, hosting musicals and plays—including children's theater—throughout the summer and fall and during the holiday season.

So much more than an ice cream parlor, the **Show Place Ice Cream Parlor** (200 Centre St., 609/492-0018) is an evening event. Inside you'll find a decor of checkered black and white floors and candy-striped walls, red-backed chairs and bright-red table settings. The singing teenage staff, or "cast" as they're called, don outfits like a barbershop quartet. And a warning to the folks—it's almost required that you join in the fun. This cash-only place has stroller parking and is located right next to the borough's theater—what could be a better night out? Show Place opens at 6 P.M. daily throughout summer.

Shopping

Beach Haven's shopping village, **Bay Village and Schooner's Wharf** (9th St. between Ocean and Bay Aves., on the bay, 609/492-2800, www.lbinet.com/pthandbay) is an array of multi-level shops housed in dark-wood-shingled buildings and an old sea schooner. Shop for pajamas aboardship, or try the other shops for kites, ocean art, environmental gifts, and candy. Most stores are individually accessed from the wide brick outdoor walkways.

Sports and Recreation

The double-decker Southern-style **Crystal Queen** riverboat (Centre St. and Bayfront, 609/822-8849 or 609/492-0333 in-season, www.blackwhalecruises.com, May–October) offers sightseeing cruises and day-trips to Atlantic City. One-hour evening bay cruises take place daily July–September, at 7 and 8:30 P.M.

The seasonal **Thundering Surf Waterpark** (Taylor and Bay Ave., 609/492-0869, www.thunderingsurfwaterpark.com, 9 A.M.–7:30 P.M. daily, $18.75 for two hours) features eight water slides, a large kid's play area with a dancing fountain, and a lazy river. Adjacent to the park is **Settler's Mill Adventure Golf** (9 A.M.–11:30 P.M. daily), featuring two maritime-themed 18-hole mini-golf courses, both with freshly laid Astroturf.

Beach Haven's list of water sports includes personal watercraft riding or parasailing with **Beach Haven Parasailing** (2702 Long Beach Blvd., 609/492-0375, www.bhparasail.com); and sportfishing with **Fish Trap** (525 2nd St., on the bay, 609/492-0819, www.fishtrapinfo.com), **June Bug Charters** (Beach Haven Yacht Club, Engleside Ave. at the bay, 609/685-2829), or **LBI Fishing Charters** (Morrison's Beach Haven Marina, Second St. and the Bay, 609/492-2591, www.lbifishingcharters.com). Just south of Beach Haven in Long Beach Township's Holgate section, you can rent kayaks from **Rick's Kayak Shack** (83 Tebco Terrace, 609/548-1797). A single-kayak rental runs $25 for two hours. Tandem kayaks are also available.

Formed to encourage the understanding and protection of Long Beach Island's changing ocean and bay ecosystem, the **Alliance for a Living Ocean** was formed (2007 Long Beach Blvd., 609/492-0222, www.livingocean.org). The Alliance hosts three-hour barrier island eco-tours select days during July and August ($10 adults, $5 kids), and a variety of educational trips to area bays throughout the summer. Contact the center for more info.

Accommodations

Beach Haven features numerous B&Bs in its downtown historic district, as well as a few beachfront motels.

$200-250: One of Beach Haven's finest, the **Amber Street Inn** (118 Amber St., 609/492-1611, www.amberstreetinn.com) is an 1885 Victorian with five individually decorated guestrooms and one suite, each with private bath, air-conditioning and fans, TV, and phone. Afternoon refreshments are served on the outdoor veranda, and during the day

THE JERSEY SHORE

you can take advantage of the inn's bicycles and beach tags. A full breakfast is included. The inn is mostly closed through the winter months, but reopens for weekends beginning in February.

Julia's of Savannah (209 Centre St., 609/492-5004) features a wraparound porch decked with wicker furniture, ideal for enjoying the ocean breeze. Don't let the modern exterior of this Victorian fool you—Julia's is plentiful with antiques. Air-conditioned rooms are small but lovingly decorated, with the kinds of beds you want to jump into, and there's a room with private porch accessible to guests with disabilities. Private baths and full breakfast are included.

$250-300: The beachfront **Engleside Inn** (Engleside Ave. and oceanfront, 609/492-1251 or 800/762-2214, www.engleside.com) offers both motel room and efficiency-style accommodations. Rooms are spacious if not a bit worn, and all have TV, VCR, fridge, and high-speed Internet connection. Larger units feature kitchenettes and some have oceanfront views. The motel features an outdoor beach bar kept secluded by dunes where casual eats are served, a sushi bar, and the highly rated Leeward Room, an American fine-dining restaurant. Pets are welcome for a $10 charge in the off-season (Sept.–May).

Food

For pizza, **Slice of Heaven** (610 North Bay Ave., 609/492-7437, $3–20) is a must. Grab a cheesesteak-topped slice or go for the baked-ziti pizza—it's sooo worth it. The shop stays open until 4 A.M. on Friday and Saturday evenings in the summer.

Uncle Will's Pancake House (3 South Bay Ave., 609/492-2514) serves the finest breakfast in town, as well as a Caribbean-inspired dinner menu that includes mahimahi with citrus sauce and plantain grits ($25), and spinach and portobello ravioli alongside summer veggies ($19). It's a casual and roomy space situated in a small shopping strip along the main street. Summer hours are 7 A.M.–1 P.M. daily, 5–9 P.M. Thursday–Sunday for dinner.

Reservations are recommended at **Sweet Vidalia** (122 N. Bay Ave., 609/207-1200, $16–35), an 85-seat BYO serving innovative American entrées in a contemporary fine-dining setting. Vidalia's in-season hours are 5–11 P.M. Thursdays and weekends; the restaurant is closed November–March except for Valentine's Day and Easter weekend.

The Chicken or the Egg (207 N. Bay Ave., 609/492-FOWL or 609/492-3695, $6–10) is a seasonal 24-hour American diner that plays heavily on the poultry decor. Plentiful wood booths act as little havens for late summer nights.

Long a statewide favorite, the Green Gables Inn & Restaurant came under new ownership in 2005 and is set to reopen in 2006 as **The Gables** (212 Centre St., 609/492-3553). This renovated restaurant plans to combine a menu of Asian-inspired New American entrées with the fixed-price multicourse dinners the establishment is reputed for.

MAINLAND
Tuckerton Seaport Village

Separated from Long Beach Island by Little Egg Harbor is the 40-acre village of Tuckerton Seaport (120 W. Main St., 609/296-8868, www.tuckertonseaport.org). It may be one of New Jersey's numerous living-history displays, but it stands out as the only one to highlight maritime culture. Opened in 2000, it has all the makings of an authentic seaport village: Visitors can walk along waterfront docks and witness craftspeople carving decoys, boat builders engaged in carpentry, and fishers cleaning their catch. A highlight of the village is the Tucker's Island Light, standing along Route 9 just north of the entrance to **Great Bay Boulevard.** This lighthouse is a re-creation of one that originally stood on Tucker's Island, off the southern tip of Long Beach Island, but was washed out to Shore during a 1927 storm. The village is also home to the **Jacques Cousteau National Estuarine Research Center,** which features a visitors center and exhibit open to the public.

Tuckerton Seaport Village is open 10 A.M.–5 P.M. daily during summer, 11 A.M.–4 P.M.

Friday–Sunday in the off-season. Admission is $8 adult, $6 senior, and $3 child (5–12), five and under admitted free.

Camping

While there are no camping resorts on L.B.I., the following are close enough to the island to be considered for an overnight stay.

The large **Baker's Acres Campground** (230 Willets Ave., Parkertown, 609/296-2664 or 800/648-2227) is open May–November and features more than 300 sites and two in-ground pools. Situated on the eastern edge of the Pinelands and close to L.B.I., amenities include hot showers, and many sites are shaded. There are volleyball nets for play, and organized events scheduled throughout the season. Tent sites

cost $24/night for a family of four; call ahead for RV site fees and availability.

Located eight miles from Long Beach Island on the mainland, **Sea Pirate Family Campground** (Rte. 9, West Creek, 609/296-7400, www.sea pirate.com, May–Oct.) has an indoor/outdoor sports complex with a baseball diamond and basketball court and invites kids to camp free. Crabbing opportunities are available on-site, and there's a game room with arcade games and ping-pong table. Motorboats are available for rental ($20/hour plus tax). Basic tent sites are $34/night, and sites with water and electric run $40. Cabins are also available for rental, $59/night with air-conditioning, $99/night with air-conditioning and heat, and $129/night with air-conditioning, heat, and one or two bedrooms.

Atlantic City

Grown from America's Playground into the city that's "Always Turned On," Atlantic City is one for the books. This oceanfront town has seen it all—the Rat Pack to the worst pack, the Donald to the women of the Miss America Pageant—and its history is filled with oddities like diving horses and million-dollar beaches, the first boardwalk and an eternal place on the Monopoly board. Finally, the glam is returning to this long down-and-out Shore town, and while some complain AC is pulling a Vegas with its swanky shops, open-air bars, and attempts to become a foodie destination, why shouldn't it? No one said, "Let there be light—but only in Vegas." Since the opening of the Borgata Casino in 2003 Atlantic City has taken off, and the city that for years drew almost exclusively senior citizens is again becoming young—luring singles with tightly clothed cocktail staffs, tasty martini bars, pulsating dance clubs, and shopping galore.

There's so much to do in the Atlantic City region you could spend days without leaving—when the clank of the casino coins becomes unbearable there's the Boardwalk, the beach, and the shops to explore, not to mention the nearby golf courses, wineries, nature preserves, and Shore towns. Both accommodations and eateries are plentiful in the area, but for the best in dining venture outside the casinos, where food tends to be overpriced and underwhelming. An exception is Tropicana's The Quarter—not quite a casino but affiliated enough to be mistaken for one. As for cocktails, they are easy to find any hour of the day or night.

History

When the first trainload of passengers arrived from Camden to Atlantic City on July 1, 1854, "America's Playground" was born, and it spent no time messing around. The city grew quickly, adding taverns, boarding houses, grand hotels, and a quickly growing population, as many African Americans arrived from the South looking for work. Atlantic City was the place to be during the late 19th and early 20th centuries—the world's first boardwalk came into existence, as well as the first amusement piers. There was the Steeplechase Pier and the Heinz Pier, where every day for 46 years H. J. Heinz (yes, of

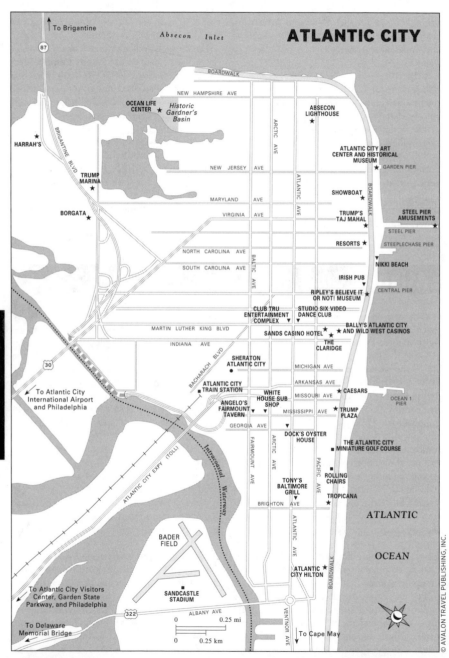

THE JERSEY SHORE

ATLANTIC CITY

To Brigantine

87

Absecon Inlet

BOARDWALK

NEW HAMPSHIRE AVE

OCEAN LIFE CENTER ★ Historic Gardner's Basin

ABSECON LIGHTHOUSE ★

★ HARRAH'S

BRIGANTINE BLVD

TRUMP MARINA ★

ARCTIC AVE

ATLANTIC CITY ART CENTER AND HISTORICAL MUSEUM ★ GARDEN PIER

NEW JERSEY AVE

ATLANTIC AVE

SHOWBOAT ★

BOARDWALK

BORGATA ★

MARYLAND AVE

VIRGINIA AVE

TRUMP'S TAJ MAHAL ★

STEEL PIER AMUSEMENTS ★

STEEL PIER

RESORTS ★

STEEPLECHASE PIER

NORTH CAROLINA AVE

BALTIC AVE

SOUTH CAROLINA AVE

NIKKI BEACH ▼

IRISH PUB ▼

RIPLEY'S BELIEVE IT OR NOT! MUSEUM ★

CENTRAL PIER

CLUB TRU ENTERTAINMENT COMPLEX ▼

STUDIO SIX VIDEO DANCE CLUB ▼

30

MARTIN LUTHER KING BLVD

SANDS CASINO HOTEL ★

BALLY'S ATLANTIC CITY AND WILD WEST CASINOS ★

INDIANA AVE

THE CLARIDGE

BACHARACH BLVD

SHERATON ATLANTIC CITY ●

MICHIGAN AVE

To Atlantic City International Airport and Philadelphia

ATLANTIC CITY TRAIN STATION ▲

ARKANSAS AVE

MISSOURI AVE

★ CAESARS

WHITE HOUSE SUB SHOP

OCEAN 1 PIER

ANGELO'S FAIRMOUNT TAVERN ▼

MISSISSIPPI AVE

★ TRUMP PLAZA

GEORGIA AVE

DOCK'S OYSTER HOUSE

FAIRMOUNT AVE

ARCTIC AVE

THE ATLANTIC CITY MINIATURE GOLF COURSE ■

ATLANTIC CITY EXPY (TOLL)

Intracoastal Waterway

PACIFIC AVE

ROLLING CHAIRS ■

TONY'S BALTIMORE GRILL ■

TROPICANA ★

BRIGHTON AVE

ATLANTIC

To Atlantic City Visitors Center, Garden State Parkway, and Philadelphia

BADER FIELD

ATLANTIC AVE

OCEAN

322

SANDCASTLE STADIUM

ATLANTIC CITY HILTON ★

To Delaware Memorial Bridge

ALBANY AVE

VENTNOR AVE

0   0.25 mi

0   0.25 km

BOARDWALK

To Cape May

the ketchup) gave away free pickles and pickle lapel pins. At the Million Dollar Pier you could catch a performance by the legendary magician Harry Houdini or the Jersey-boy comedy act of Abbott and Costello, or at the Steel Pier line up to view kangaroo boxing and the famous High Diving Horse Act, where a horse with a woman on its back dove off a 40-foot platform into a pool.

By the middle of the 20th century, Atlantic City had been abandoned for more prosperous destinations. The grand hotels were no longer stately. The people stopped coming. City officials looked for a way to improve their situation and in 1976 gambling was approved, making Atlantic City the first U.S. location outside Las Vegas where a person could place a legal bet. As part of the deal, all casinos agreed to be part of a hotel complex with at least 50 guestrooms. Revenue starting pouring in, but what was happening behind the windowless walls of the casinos amid the happy coin jingles didn't reflect what was happening on the streets. The city looked just as punched in the face as it had looked for years. Under the Boardwalk, a community of drug and gambling addicts set up makeshift homes, while busloads of senior citizens descended into their worlds of plastic buckets, diamond-print carpets, and all-you-can eat buffets. To get an idea of how the casinos have changed Atlantic City, consider that the number of people employed by the casinos is higher than the city's total population.

Atlantic City earned a reputation as a day-tripper destination for old folk and those celebrating their 21st birthdays, and seemed content on steering this path until the opening of the Borgata in 2003. Soon after, new doors opened and investors came. While the city has a long way to go toward cleaning up its streets and improving its image, it's on an upward path. Plans call for new construction to be built in the old seafront style, opening outward onto the Boardwalk rather than caving inward into the dark recesses of the slot machines.

For a picture of Atlantic City just before and after the casino boom, rent *The King of Marvin Gardens,* starring Jack Nicholson and Bruce Dean, and *Atlantic City,* with Susan Sarandon and Burt Lancaster. Both films expose the city in all of its urban-grit glory, and Atlantic City plays a leading role in each.

THE BOARDWALK

The six-mile, 60-foot-wide Boardwalk (that's Boardwalk with a capital "B") is the largest of New Jersey's beachfront walkways. Like the rest of the city, it's getting into the reconstruction spirit with a $100-million renovation planned over the next couple of years. For now, it's a seemingly endless array of psychic-palm-reading shacks, hourly massage houses, casino arcades, greasy food stands, T-shirt shops, and a couple of amusement piers. The city's "world famous" **Rolling Chairs** are all over the place. They're large wicker seats on wheels pushed by chatty men and women who'll cart you wherever you want to go. Have one of them take you to the 88 Cent Store to visit the iguana named Jimmy—he's not for sale, but you can say hello, and while you're there you can spend time with the shop's scurrying hermit crabs. Rolling Chairs cost $5 for the first five Boardwalk blocks, $10 for 6–12 blocks, $15 for 13–21 blocks, $20 for 22 blocks or more, $25 for a half-hour tour, and $40 for a one-hour tour. Each chair seats two; they run 8 A.M.–1 A.M. Sunday–Thursday, until 4 A.M. Friday and Saturday.

No one's quite sure where saltwater taffy was born, but it's rumored to be Atlantic City, and here on the boards there's no better place than **James' Salt Water Taffy** (1519 Boardwalk, 609/344-1519, www.jamescandy.com), an age-old institution. If it's fudge you're after, **Steel's Fudge, Inc.** (1633 Boardwalk, 609/345-4051, www.steelsfudge.com) claims to be the oldest continuously family-owned and -operated fudge company in the world. Since Mr. Peanut is one of the city's many unofficial spokespersons, it seems only fitting that the numerous branches of **Boardwalk Peanut Shoppe** (609/272-1511,

ATLANTIC CITY'S RUNAWAY QUEEN

So long, Miss America! The woman with the crown and sash has pivoted her hand to the crowds for the last time in Atlantic City. In August 2005, after 84 years, the pageant announced it was leaving the only home it has ever known, citing the high costs of operating the event at Boardwalk Hall as a deciding factor.

This infamous beauty, brains, and talent scholarship competition, which began as part of a "Fall Frolic" festival formed to help extend AC's summer season beyond Labor Day, had dropped out of national favor, pulling in well-below-average TV ratings and being released by a number of networks, most recently ABC. In 2005, the pageant had even considered adding elements of reality TV to revive interest in the seaside show.

The first Miss America – then known as the "Most Beautiful Bathing Girl in America" – was crowned in 1921. The pageant started out featuring eight contestants from nearby cities and towns, but things soon escalated as beauties from other states entered the competition. In 1940, the contest adopted the name of Miss America, and in 1954, the ladies walked the catwalk straight onto the small screen and secured an annual place in the livings rooms of millions of families for decades. Little girls nationwide dreamed of wearing the crown, and

those who lived close enough to the Boardwalk would flock down the Shore to catch a glimpse of the contestants as they dined in the restaurants and paraded down the boards in the city's famous rolling chairs, showing off their decorative shoes as they glided past crowds. For two weeks every year, the city gave its attention, publicity, and hotel rooms over to the show, which was as synonymous with Atlantic City as the diving horse and Heinz pickle pins.

Like any good event, scandal rocked the pageant. Miss America 1984 Vanessa Williams, now a successful entertainer, was de-crowned when previously published *Penthouse* images surfaced, and for years, women's rights groups fought to get the contest's bathing suit segment thrown out. But in the end, Miss America stood her ground and remained at the heart of American modesty and goodness, even in her bikini.

Although Miss America has chosen Las Vegas as her new temporary home, Atlantic City shows traces of her past throughout the city. The Sheraton Hotel, part of the Atlantic City Convention Center, features one of the country's largest collection of pageant memorabilia, including dresses and shoes, and photos of former contestants continue to adorn the walls of such places as the Quarter's Carmine's restaurant and Arctic Avenue's White House Sub Shop.

www.boardwalkpeanuts.com) should be a mainstay for visitors. You can find this favorite in more than a handful of the casinos, including Resorts, Trump Plaza, and Sands.

Considered a popular Boardwalk attraction, the much-hyped **Ripley's Believe It or Not! Museum** (New York Ave. and Boardwalk, 609/347-2001, www.ripleys.com, $10.95 adult, $6.95 child) is little more than a tourist trap. The museum has locations throughout the country, and though it may be better than losing your quarters to slots, it's not by much. The museum is open 10 A.M.–10 P.M. daily during summer months, 11 A.M.–5 P.M. Monday–Friday, 10 A.M.–8 P.M. weekends the remainder of the year.

Atlantic City Art Center and Historical Museum

On Garden Pier at the north end of the Boardwalk's commercial strip is the joint Atlantic City Art Center and Historical Museum (New Jersey Ave. at Boardwalk, 609/347-5837, www.acmuseum.org, 10 A.M.–4 P.M. daily, free). Both museums are free to the public, and the Historical Museum features a permanent exhibit titled "Atlantic City: Playground of the Nation." The city has one of the kitschiest pasts in history and the museum highlights this (be sure and watch the *Boardwalk Ballyhoo* video). You'll receive your own Heinz pickle pin and get to visit with Mr. Peanut, who used to haunt the Boardwalk in earlier days. There's a good collection of Miss America memorabilia and sand art, and the art center has three exhibition galleries and a shop selling local works such as Wheaton Village glass.

Boardwalk Hall

The landmark Atlantic City Boardwalk Hall (2301 Boardwalk, 609/348-7000, www.board walkhall.com) opened in 1929 to become the longest-running home of the city's Miss American Pageant, which gave its final hand-turn wave to Atlantic City in 2005. Although Miss America has found some new digs, Boardwalk Hall remains a primary showcase, home to the Boardwalk Bullies (www.allsports.com/echl/bullies) minor league ice hockey team and a host of concerts and conferences. This is still the place to come to catch exclusive big-name acts, and while you're here, sneak a peek at the world's largest pipe organ.

Boardwalk Recreation

Across from Boardwalk Hall is AC's only mini-golf course, **The Atlantic City Miniature Golf Course** (1 Kennedy Plaza, 609/347-1661, www.acminigolf.com). It's an easy 18 holes, but new Astroturf and sand traps give the course a professional feel and draw in the crowds on summer weekday afternoons.

Stocked with go-karts, a covered arcade with a ton of mechanical-claw games, and a Shoot the Geek paintball game with live targets, the seasonal **Central Pier** (St. James Pl. and Tennessee Ave., 609/345-5219) is the place to stop for a quick bit of entertainment.

Since 1898 the **Steel Pier** (Virginia Ave. and 1000 Boardwalk, 866/386-6659, www .steelpier.com) has been drawing crowds to Atlantic City. Though it's changed a lot in the last century—it's still *mucho* fun. At this large open-air amusement palace you'll find games of chance, a log flume, helicopter rides, and, harkening back to the old days, a couple who perform stunts while riding a motorcycle along a 60-foot-high tightrope. The pier is open daily throughout the summer, 3 P.M.–midnight, Monday–Friday, noon–1 A.M. weekends.

OTHER SIGHTS
Absecon Lighthouse

The Absecon Lighthouse (31 S. Rhode Island Ave., 609/449-1360, www.abseconlighthouse .org, $5 adults, $2 child) is New Jersey's tallest lighthouse and the third-tallest in the country. If you want a feel for AC before the days of gambling, and even preceding the city's reputation as America's Playground, then come here. Built in 1857, it's an attractive 228-step yellow and black partitioned structure with the lightkeeper's house located next door, and it still has its first-order fresnel lens. The lighthouse is open 11 A.M.–4 P.M. Thursday–Monday, September–June, and 10 A.M.–5 P.M. daily July–August.

Atlantic City Convention Center

Since opening in May 1997, the Atlantic City Convention Center (1 Miss America Way, 609/449-2000, www.accenter.com) has hosted many of the city's largest events, including the bi-annual antique fair, Alantique City, and the Atlantic City Classic Car Show. The center features five second-floor showrooms and more than 500,000 square feet of contiguous exhibit space, as well as its own Sheraton Hotel. It's conveniently located just off the Atlantic City Expressway next to the city's train and bus station.

BEACHES

Atlantic City's beaches are free.

◖ CASINOS

Atlantic City is home to more than a dozen casinos, most lined up along the Boardwalk, though a few are situated along the bay. These are 24-hour all-inclusive establishments where you'll find hotel rooms, restaurants, bars, shops, entertainment venues, often arcades, and all the blackjack tables, roulette wheels, and *Wheel of Fortune* slot machines you could wish for. Anyone under 21 is prohibited from entering the casino floor and this rule is strictly enforced, but underage visitors are permitted in all accessible non-gambling areas (except nightclubs, etc.).

Parking garages are located at all casinos and charge a few dollars, but most casinos will give you two receipts upon entry—one to use as

© LAURA KINIRY

Atlantic City casinos

proof of payment and the other to use for complimentary parking at any second casino.

Most casinos offer some sort of VIP card that offers substantial discounts the more time and money you spend there. If you're planning a trip to a particular casino, inquire about obtaining a card at the customer service desk.

Atlantic City's jitney bus service offers round-the-clock transport between all the casinos. This is a great way to get around, although the bulk of the casinos can be reached by walking along the Boardwalk or taking a ride in a Rolling Chair. A walkway connects the bayside casinos to one another, and it's not heavily trafficked.

Borgata

The bayside Borgata (One Borgata Way, 609/317-1000, www.theborgata.com) is the latest introduction to Atlantic City's casinos. This is the city's own fountain of youth, and water seems to be flowing out of every hand-blown Dale Chihuly chandelier found swirling above the entryways like wild sea creatures, in translucent shades of orange, yellow, red, and blue. The Borgata is not just about dollar slots, it is

also, as one *Washington Post* writer describes it, a "purple tower of cool."

Inside you'll find Borgata Babes delivering drinks on the casino floor, and surrounding the slots and game tables are numerous shops, restaurants, bars, and entertainment venues. The 1,100-seat **Music Box** (800/736-1420) is the Borgata's intimate showcase for live stage acts, and **Ombra** ($17.50–59, 5–10 P.M. Tues.–Thurs., until 11 P.M. Fri. and Sat., closed Sun. and Mon.) is its answer to fine dining, serving rustic Italian cuisine in a wine-cellar setting. Long curtains are all that separate the round 24-hour **B Bar** from the action on the casino floor, and the casual **Metropolitan** ($11) features American eats all hours of the day and evening.

One of the Borgata's most notable offerings is **Club Mixx**, a weekend nightclub and Latin/Asian fusion restaurant. Situated on the far side of the casino floor, this dimly lit space features balcony seating, world beats, and a sushi bar. Dinner and sushi are served 5–10 P.M. Sunday and Monday, and until 10:30 P.M. Friday and Saturday, and the club's nightlife transformation begins at 10 P.M. Thursday–Saturday. The restaurant is closed Tuesday–Thursday.

If you're visiting in the evening and you've parked in the garage, be sure and take note of the awesome view of the Boardwalk casinos lit up in the night sky.

Harrah's

On the border between Atlantic City and Brigantine is Harrah's (777 Harrah's Blvd., 609/441-5000, www.harrahs.com), a longstanding casino removed from the bustle of the downtown gambling scene. I grew up at Harrah's—playing Pac Man in the kid's arcade while my grandmother hit the slots. Now that we're both older, Grandmom's moved on to the Showboat, while Harrah's still appeals to me. Maybe it's nostalgia, or maybe it's the trendy spots they've added to keep this gem up and running, like the 24-hour **Xhibition Bar,** a stylish circular lounge located within the casino floor, or the restaurant **'Cesca** (5–10 P.M. nightly, $21–27), serving up contemporary Southern Italian cuisine.

Showboat

Since the late 1980s, the Boardwalk's northernmost casino, Showboat (801 Boardwalk, 609/343-4000, www.harrahs.com/our_casinos/sac), has been a steady slot-filled favorite with the 65-and-older crowd, but this image is hoping for a facelift with the 2005 opening of the **House of Blues** (609/236-BLUE or 609/236-2583), a national music venue showcasing big-name acts and hosting a signature Southern-style Sunday gospel brunch buffet ($33, seatings at 10 A.M. and 1 P.M.). An entire section of the casino has been devoted to the two-story nightclub and restaurant, which also includes a souvenir store and its own slew of nearby slot machines. The casino has hit two high notes with the long-running stage version of *The Price is Right* and a newly built 544-room hotel, **Orlean Tower.**

Taj Mahal

One of Donald Trump's three contributions to the Atlantic City skyline, the Taj (1000 Boardwalk at Virginia Ave., 609/449-1000, www.trumptaj.com) opened in 1990 with great fanfare, and with onion-shaped domes and Aladdin-like lettering, its exterior is easily recognizable. This is probably the most ornate of the city's casinos, featuring a deep red and purple color scheme, hundreds of yards of gold trimming, massive chandeliers, and a wide-open gambling floor. Restaurants and nightclubs are theme-named, like the fashionable **Casbah** (10:30 P.M.–5 A.M. Friday, until 6 A.M. Saturday), a happening dance club with a strictly enforced dress code, and **Dynasty** (opens at 6 P.M. nightly, $12–45), serving Asian-inspired entrées, sushi rolls, and sake martinis. Gambling rooms bear names like The Dragon Palace and Sinbad's.

Trump's Taj Mahal is also home to the **Mark G. Estes Arena** (609/449-5150), often used for big-draw boxing matches. Other places of interest include the Atlantic City locale of the **Hard Rock Cafe** (1000 Boardwalk, 609/441-0007, 11 A.M.–midnight Sun.–Thurs., until 1 A.M. Fri. and Sat.), the affordable all-you-can-eat **Sultan's Feast** buffet ($18.95), and for kids, the **Ali Baba Video Arcade** with basketball toss and skeeball.

Resorts

Resorts (1133 Boardwalk, 800/336-6378, www.resortsac.com) debuted in 1976 as Atlantic City's first casino, and after somewhat of a dry spell is back on top with the 2005 addition of its fabulously fine beach bar **Nikki Beach,** an oceanfront, open-air lounge and nightclub dressed in strewn white lights and natural wood, and dubbed "the sexiest place on earth" by its marketers, with locations already in such places as Miami Beach, Florida, and Puerto Vallarta, Mexico. Situated adjacent is **Penrod's Elbo Room,** which adds a summer concert venue to the beachfront mix.

Back indoors, Resorts has taken off with a plethora of new gaming space and a 399-room, 27-story hotel unit called **Rendezvous Tower.** With all this new construction it may appear Resorts has forgotten its roots, but to be easily swayed otherwise stop by the exterior of the casino's Boardwalk entrance, where you'll find Atlantic City's own Walk of Fame. Handprints and signatures that seemingly haven't been added to in years include Steve Martin, Lou Rawls, Donna Summer, and Barry Manilow. You can still catch Tom Jones at the casino's **Super Star Theatre,** or a local funnyman at the **Catch a Rising Star Comedy Club** (www.catcharisingstar.com), and down on the gambling floor recent AARP inductees continue their hand at the slots.

Bally's

Bally's is a three-casino complex made up of **Bally's Atlantic City** (Park Place and Boardwalk, 609/340-2000, www.caesars.com), the **Claridge,** and the themed **Wild West Casino.** It's somewhat unsettling how vastly different each of these are, probably the reason the complex tends to draw a mixed-age crowd.

Wild West Casino has a faux-Western, extremely colorful Boardwalk facade, and inside you'll find steam-train murals and Wells Fargo wagons, cartoonish cowboys and a gold-digger's wishing well, and the 24-hour **Mountain Bar,** a lounge decorated with fake cacti, leather maroon seats, and a two-foot-tall train that circles the space's perimeter. Accessible only through the casino floor is the upstairs **Virginia City Buffet**

(11 A.M.–9 P.M. Sun.–Thurs., until 10 P.M. Fri. and 11 P.M. Sat.), popular with older crowds.

Across the Boardwalk is the **Bikini Beach Bar** (11:30 A.M.–10 P.M. Sun.–Thurs., until 2 A.M. Fri. and Sat., June–August), an extension of Bally's Atlantic City. Wrought iron tables with shading umbrellas, palm trees, and private gazebos are all part of the decor, and cocktail waitresses dress in yellow bikini tops and matching skirt bottoms, delivering drinks while Britney Spears sings over the sound system and a Philadelphia crowd ogles at the bar.

The Claridge is my favorite of the three-casino complex, as my uncle "hit the jackpot" here in the early 1980s and gave me his winning T-shirt. My love for the Claridge has since only grown. This 1930s structure was the last of AC's grand hotels to be built, as well as the last one left standing, and Sinatra spent a lot of time here in the 1940s. Today it's home to the **Blue Martini Bar,** featuring a plethora of vodkas and more than a hundred martini concoctions, in addition to one of the best shows in the city, **Legends in Concert** ($17.50–25), a superstar-impersonation extravaganza.

Sands Casino Hotel

Set back from the Boardwalk behind the Claridge is the Sands Casino Hotel (Indiana Ave. and Brighton Park, 609/441-4000 or 800/227-2637, www.sandsac.com), a casino with an established reputation and many years in Atlantic City. Its latest addition is **Swingers** (1 P.M.–1 A.M. Mon.–Thurs., 1 P.M.–4 A.M. Fri., noon–4 A.M. Sat., and noon–1 A.M. Sun.), a glowing lounge and bar located right on the casino floor, shaped like the center portion of a horseshoe and dressed with hanging flat-screen TVs, plush leather chairs, and a giant screen that serves as backdrop for the *Cocktail*-like bartender sporting a fedora. The "Geator with the Heator" or Mr. Oldie himself, Jerry Blavat, entertains patrons 5–7 P.M. every Thursday, and live music is featured throughout summer Thursday–Sunday evenings. On the upper level is the piano bar **Copa Lounge** (4 P.M.–2 A.M. Fri., 2 P.M.–3 A.M. Sat., noon–10 P.M. Sun.), and for eats, there's the **Brighton Steakhouse** (5:30–10 P.M. Mon., Thurs., and Fri., until 11 P.M.

weekends, $22–47), a dark wood place with a maroon and orange motif, where you'll find a changing menu with steak and seafood highlights, and an expansive wine selection. For something more casual, Sands features **The Boardwalk Buffet** ($10.99 breakfast, $13 lunch). Set to resemble the Atlantic City of old, there are black and white photos of the city decorating the walls and a diving horse replica above one of the buffet stations.

Caesars

Massive renovations are underway at Caesars (2100 Pacific Ave., 800/443-0104, www.caesars .com), one of the city's best-known casinos. In addition to the construction of a new shopping plaza across the boards on Million Dollar Pier, the casino has torn down its entire Boardwalk facade and is undergoing a facelift. The Roman theme remains throughout the casino, with a section of slot machines bearing the name Cleopatra's Garden, and the **Centurian Tower** providing lodging for the night. Cover bands jam at **Toga** (11 A.M.–6 A.M. daily), and dining options include the Italian **Primavera** ($26–48) and the fixed-price six-course American menu of **The Bacchanal** ($60). Both restaurants require advanced reservations, and are open for dinner only, 6–11 P.M. Friday–Sunday during the off-season, with expanded hours during summer months. Across the Boardwalk is Caesar's **Sandbox,** an outdoor beach bar plentiful with Romanesque statues and kept private from foot traffic by sand dunes. It features live music and drink specials nightly during summer months.

Trump Plaza

Trump Plaza (Mississippi Ave. and Boardwalk, 609/441-0608, www.trumpplaza.com) has some major work ahead of it. Its Boardwalk entrance screams "desperate for a makeover," and inside are a couple of overpriced mediocre restaurants and the smell of fast food mingled with cigar smoke. Even on a Friday the scene on the large casino floor dominated by slots is decidedly geriatric. Most of the plaza's restaurants are found down a long escalator from the casino floor, and the kid-friendly, semi-chain

Rainforest Café (609/345-5757, $8.99–16.99) can be entered from the boards. **Evo** (609/441-0400, $17–22, 10 A.M.–11 P.M. daily) is a casual Italian restaurant with white linen and outdoor seating, recommended by a casino employee as the Plaza's best eatery.

The Plaza's "trump card" does exist however—it lies across the boards and down a long wooden walkway. Called **Beach Bar,** this seasonal outdoor venue features a huge platform decked with blue and white decor, umbrella tables, and a number of open-air bars.

Tropicana

Located just north of the Hilton along the AC boards, the Tropicana (S. Brighton Ave. and the Boardwalk, 609/340-4000, 800/THE-TROP or 800/843-8767, www.tropicana.net) has really kept up with the times. A non-gambling, upscale shopping and dining addition called **The Quarter** and constant renovations have scored this casino a younger crowd. It's also one of the best-ventilated casinos, void of the stagnant, smoky air that seems to fill many of the others. Tropicana has been around since the early 1980s, and continued improvements include a 502-room accommodation tower, making the Trop one of the state's largest hotels.

Along with the shopping plaza (which includes an IMAX theater), you'll find the casual casino-floor **Tiffany Lounge** (11:30 A.M.–3 A.M. daily) featuring entertainment nightly, and in the **Tropicana Marketplace,** the beer-drinker-friendly **Firewaters,** a sports bar featuring a massive beer selection, as well as some tasty martinis. Here you can sit beneath neon Budweiser signs and watch a game on the tube, or grab a partner for cutthroat competition on the Ms. Pac Man table game.

Karaoke lovers can venture to The Quarter's 24-hour **Planet Rose** (The Quarter, 609/344-6565), where zebra-print armless chairs and neon lighting offer a decidedly *Lost in Translation* look, and lights are dim enough that you can sing to your heart's desire without a hint of self-consciousness (well… maybe). There's also a sushi bar. Nearby, the **Comedy Stop** has a non-alcoholic café that opens onto the square

and features a full espresso bar. For information on comedy shows, including prices and showtimes (the average ticket price is $22), call 877/FUN-NYAC (877/386-6922).

Also in The Quarter is **Red Square** (609/344-9100), a vodka bar and restaurant awash in red tint, with curtain-draped tables and a gorgeous chandelier that resembles the top of the Kremlin. A statue of Lenin greets patrons on their way in. Food is served noon–11 P.M. Sunday–Thursday, until midnight Friday and Saturday.

There's no doubt about it—the Trop is one of the city's best.

Atlantic City Hilton

The Boardwalk Hilton (Boston Ave. and Boardwalk, 609/347-7111, www.hiltonac.com) is Atlantic City's southernmost casino, a Resorts' property that's often bypassed for flashier spaces. But the Hilton, as the name implies, offers some of AC's best overnight accommodation and is a good place to begin your casino exploration, especially if arriving from one of the southern Shore towns. Inside you'll find the Boardwalk-level **Dizzy Dolphin** (609/347-7111, 10 P.M.–2 A.M. Sun.–Thurs., 24 hours Fri. and Sat.), a casual lounge draped in fun colors and featuring a bar that is actually made from a sailboat. Cover bands groove here occasionally throughout the week. The bar is open year-round.

A more upscale locale is the restaurant **Peregrine's** (609/236-7870), an elegant place with high-back red velvet chairs and white tablecloths, serving halibut ($38) and milk-fed veal ($46). It's open for dinner Thursday–Sunday. Above the casino is an 804-room hotel.

ENTERTAINMENT

Minor league baseball's **Atlantic City Surf** play home games at The Sandcastle (545 N. Albany Ave., 609/344-8873, www.acsurf.com, $6–12), a 1998 5,900-seat ballpark situated just off Routes 322/40 on the city's southwest side.

The **IMAX Theater** (888/505-1435, www.imaxtheaterattropicana.com, $9.95) has a 3,500-square-foot screen and a 12,000-watt digital sound system, and is AC's only movie theater. It's located within The Quarter at the Tropicana.

THE JERSEY SHORE

Atlantic City Cruises (800 N. New Hampshire Ave., 609/347-7600, www.atlanticcitycruises.com, $17 adults, $8.50 child) offers 1–2 hour harbor cruises during summer months, including a dolphin cruise and a moonlight dance party. Bay and ocean cruises are also available.

NIGHTLIFE

Atlantic City is one of New Jersey's few, if not only, 24-hour destinations, and no visit to the city would be complete without a little evening entertainment. You'll always find something happening in the casinos (for a list of options, see the *Casinos* section), and some of the city's best nightlife options are found in Tropicana's **The Quarter** (for more information, see the *Shopping* section). During the summer, the stretch of beach along the Boardwalk comes alive with white lights, thumping beats, and exclusive venues that seemingly sink back into the sand at the first sign of winter. Those who'd like to experience the real Atlantic City with their Maker's Mark will have to venture out of the casinos and away from the crashing waves.

Downtown

For the ultimate in Atlantic City clubbing there's no better place than **Club Tru Entertainment Complex** (9 S. Martin Luther King Jr. Blvd., 609/344-2222, www.clubtru.com), a multiple-bar, three-level space with plenty of dance floor. Grab a beer at Joe's Sports Bar or go for a Red Bull pick-me-up at the Tru Energy Bar—you'll need it if you're going to continue grooving to the tunes of house DJs through the early morning hours. The club's third floor is the ultimate in VIP, including an upscale champagne lounge with a balcony overlooking the dance floor. **Studio Six Video Dance Club** (12 S. Mt. Vernon Ave., 609/348-3310, www.studiosix.com/about.htm) is also part of the complex. The club features a karaoke lounge and hosts occasional drag shows. The complex is open 10 P.M.–dawn, nightly throughout summer, Thursday–Saturday only during the off-season. Cover charge for both clubs usually runs $10–15.

If you're looking for a Boardwalk bar (minus the casino) try **Flames** (2641 Boardwalk, 609/344-7774), just north of the Tropicana. This long, narrow space is dimly lit and decorated with flat-screen TVs and neon tube lighting, its ambiance set by thumping dance music that pours from the speakers. The bar doubles as a restaurant, serving average Mediterranean and American eats like gyros ($5.75) and mushroom cheeseburgers ($4.25). Flames offers some interesting people-watching, especially during warmer months when its tables spill out onto the boards.

Set back from the Boardwalk is the **Irish Pub** (164 St. James Pl. at Boardwalk, 609/344-9063, www.theirishpub.com), a good, old-fashioned, down-and-dirty sort of place, with 24-hour service and very little sunlight. You can't beat this place for cheap eats—a bacon burger runs $3.95 and daily dinner specials $4.95—and the pub even rents out rooms above the bar ($30 basic, $55 private shower, twin beds) so you never have to leave. The kitchen closes 7–11 A.M. daily.

EVENTS

The two-day **New Jersey Fresh Seafood Festival** (2915-17 Atlantic Ave., 609/FISH-FUN or 609/347-4386, www.njfreshseafoodfest.com) takes place at Historic Gardner's Basin annually in June. The event features music, crafts, rides and exhibits for the kids, and plenty of fresh seafood.

Held for four days annually in February, the **Antique and Classic Car Auction & Flea Market** (Atlantic City Convention Center, 800/227-3868, www.acclassiccars.com/events.html) is the ultimate auto extravaganza, featuring tons of classic vehicles ranging from vintage Fords to classic Volvos, a custom streetcar display, and a swap meet of hard-to-find parts and accessories. This top event also hosts an antique show of furniture, jewelry, and miscellaneous collectibles for those of us just along for the ride.

August's annual **Around the Island Marathon Swim** (www.acswim.org) is a 22.5-mile race through the ocean and backbay waters surrounding Absecon Island. The event takes 7–9 hours on average to complete, but there are numerous places to cheer on swimmers (including Harrah's Casino at the foot of the Brigantine Bridge) if you'd rather participate from the sidelines.

The twice annual **Atlantique City** (www.atlantiquecity.com) is held at the city's Convention Center on weekends in March and October. Billed as "the largest indoor art, antique, and collectibles fair in the world," this event—celebrating its 20th year in 2006—is one of the country's best, hosting everything from books, bottle openers, clocks, and cereal boxes to coin-operated fortune teller machines.

SHOPPING

Worthwhile shopping is a recent addition to the city's portfolio, but Atlantic City is wasting no time earning itself a reputation as a retail destination. Though most casinos have designated commercial space, the shops—most notably in the older casinos—are often pricey and lack selection. While things are beginning to change, AC's best retail is found away from its slots, even if only separated by a hallway.

The Quarter

The Quarter (Brighton and Boardwalk, 800/THE-TROP or 800/843-8767, www.tropicana.net/thequarter) is a shopping, dining, and entertainment plaza that's been described as a Cuban paradise. There's no need to step inside a casino to visit—this emporium, while part of the Tropicana complex, is self-contained. Restaurants and bars center around Fiesta Plaza, the integral fountain and square, and in the evenings they overflow onto the upper circular balconies, beckoning passersby inside. Above the square, lights hang low across the painted-sky ceiling, and down below planted palm trees and rounded street lamps add to the Havana theme.

Just off the square is an IMAX movie theater, and heading toward the casino entrance is a long mall-like hall filled with national retail shops, like Chico's and Brooks Brothers, as well as upscale boutiques. One of the most interesting is **Houdini's Magic Shop** (609/572-1010), a small store packed with 007-type gadgets and high-tech toys. You'll find telephone scramblers, x-ray-vision cameras, envelope x-ray sprays, and trick coins. My favorite Quarter shop is **Zephyr Contemporary American Craft Art Gallery** (609/340-0170, www.zephyrgallery.com), which sells an outstanding array of eye-catching, and sometimes functional, art pieces. Look for hand-blown glass, metal bugs twisted with friendship beads, super-cool handbags made from recycled license plates, and 3-D posters of famed local cities.

The Walk

The Walk (609/343-0081, www.acoutlets.com, 10 A.M.–9 P.M. Mon.–Sat., 11 A.M.–6 P.M. Sun.) is an outlet-shopper's paradise. Located downtown along Michigan Avenue between Baltic and Artic Avenues and just off the Atlantic City Expressway, it features two blocks of stores on either side of the street, with well-known names like Harley Davidson, American Eagle Outfitters, and Izod; chain eateries like Stewart's Root Beer and Subway; and rapper Jay-Z's **New York 40/40 Club** (2120 Atlantic Ave., 609/449-4040, www.the4040club.com), which opened in October 2005. This modern retail area is right near the Convention Center, Sheraton Hotel, and Atlantic City train station, and just a few blocks' walk from the Boardwalk.

The Pier

Replacing the Million Dollar Pier's ship-shaped Ocean One Mall, Caesar's The Pier (www.thepieratcaesars.com) will feature upscale restaurants and luxury stores such as Gucci, Louis Vuitton, Armani Exchange, and Burberry. This four-story center is set to open in 2006, directly across from Caesar's Casino on the Boardwalk (the two are to be connected by a glass walkway).

ACCOMMODATIONS

There's no shortage of overnight accommodations in Atlantic City, with its more than 15,000 rooms, but some are far better than others. The city is a casino resort first and foremost, and while things are indeed changing, accommodations are not a reason to book a trip here. That said, there are some fine places to stay, and many offer discounts to frequent casino trippers and AAA members. It's best to inquire ahead of time about these deals.

You'll notice numerous motels lining the roadways in and out of town, but many of these are intended for those who'd rather spend their hours and money at the craps table and stop in for a quick power nap before continuing on.

Casino Hotels

All of Atlantic City's casinos are required by law to include hotels, but since rooms aren't a casino's main focus, check-in tends to be slow and rooms standard. Exceptions are the newer towers that many casinos are building as part of the city's revival and effort to attract a younger crowd. Remember that many casinos have older towers as well, and you must specify where you would like to stay before checking in. Otherwise, a room you expected to be roomy and modern may turn out to be cramped and worn.

It's important to note that while rates of Shore accommodations almost always fluctuate, those of Atlantic City's casinos can range anywhere from $99 to $500 a night, depending on your relationship to the casino (meaning if you gamble here a lot), the time you call (rates change daily), and whether or not you book the room as part of a package deal. For this reason, the prices listed below are a calculated average of mid-week high season rates without any of the fru-fra, which gives the best indication of what weekend prices will be like if you simply plan ahead.

$150-200: Built in 2003, the Showboat's **Orleans Tower** (801 Boardwalk, 800/621-0200, www.harrahs.com/our_casinos/sac) is the best overnight lodging choice for visits to attractions along the Boardwalk's north end, including the House of Blues, Atlantic City's Historical Museum, and Steel Pier. Many rooms offer ocean and bay views.

Conveniently perched above the Tropicana's Quarter on the southern end of the Boardwalk is **Havana Tower** (S. Brighton Ave. and the Boardwalk, 800/345-8767, www.tropicana.net/thequarter) a recent addition to the AC

skyline. This is good accommodation choice for those in town for shopping.

Resorts may be the city's first casino, but the 27-story **Rendezvous** (Resorts, 1113 Boardwalk, 800/336-6378, www.resortsac.com) is still in its early years. Art deco is the theme, and rooms come equipped with marble-accented bathrooms and "his and her" sinks—perfect for a little pampering.

$200-250: As Atlantic City's newest casino, it's hard to go wrong at the bayside **Borgata** (One Borgata Way, 609/317-1000), where you'll have an excellent view of the Boardwalk skyline and some of the most modern rooms in town. The hotel features a pool with side bar, and downstairs you'll find plenty of shops, restaurants, an intimate music venue, and a nightclub. All Borgata rooms are double occupancy, and although the cost of an overnight stay may skyrocket over summer weekends ($349–459), keep in mind that the price refers to the room and not the amount of people in it.

One of the Boardwalk's best is the **Atlantic City Hilton Casino Resort** (Boston Ave. & Boardwalk, 609/347-7111)—the name says its all. The Hilton features an indoor pool, and a 5 P.M. check-in time on weekends.

Non-Casino Hotels

While there are many non-casino hotels in the AC area, only a couple stand out. Ocean City, to the south, offers a number of bed-and-breakfast options for those who don't mind the half-hour drive.

$100-150: A few miles west of Atlantic City is the **Hampton Inn Atlantic City Bayside** (7079 Black Horse Pk. and Rte. 40, West Atlantic City, 609/484-1900), a clean and affordable option with its own bayside beach. The hotel offers complimentary breakfast daily, and wireless Internet throughout.

$150-200: Connected to Atlantic City's Convention Center is the 15-story **Sheraton Atlantic City** (2 Miss America Way., 609/344-3535, www.sheraton.com/atlanticcity), conveniently located near the train station and the city's outlet shopping. Beds are comfy and rooms large, and many offer views of the Boardwalk's neon skyline. The hotel lobby hosts a large collection of Miss America memorabilia, and a framed picture of a former contestant decorates every room. Pets are welcome.

FOOD
Downtown

Atlantic City's most cherished dining establishments are found outside of the casinos and away from the boards, in the heart of the downtown district.

Located in the center of AC's Ducktown, **Angelo's Fairmount Tavern** (2300 Fairmount Ave., 609/344-2439, www.angelosfairmount tavern.com, $9.75–23.75) is a classic Italian, family-owned eatery, as far as you can get from the bright lights and big city of the nearby casinos. Walk into a cozy bar and behind a side door you'll find the restaurant, a loud, bustling place decorated with framed baseball photos and an autographed Sinatra shot. Huge entrées are accompanied by bread and large house salads. Angelo's is open for lunch 11:30 A.M.–2:30 P.M. Mon.–Fri., and dinner 5–11 P.M. nightly.

The 24-hour **Tony's Baltimore Grill** (2800 Atlantic Ave., 609/345-5766, $6–25) is a spaghetti and pizza joint just west of the Tropicana. It's an old white stucco structure with red shutters and a bar inside. If you're longing for pizza, this is the place to come.

The best sandwich shop by (many, many) miles is **White House Sub Shop** (2301 Arctic Ave., 609/345-1564, 10 A.M.–9:30 P.M. Mon.–Thurs., until 10:30 A.M. Fri. and Sat., 11 A.M.–9 P.M. Sun., $5–10), in business since 1946. There's a rumor that Sinatra was such a fan of their sandwiches he would have them flown out to him while performing in Vegas. The tiny space is always packed and while there are a few tables for dining in, you'd do best to grab one to go and dash to the boards for an oceanview picnic. It's easy to get to from the AC Expressway, and the inside is wallpapered with framed celebrity mugs. Try a half of a hot Italian sausage sub for $5.45 (a full runs $10.90).

Another full-on favorite old-school eatery is the renovated **Dock's Oyster House** (2405 Atlantic Ave., 609/345-0092, www.docksoyster house.com, 5–10 P.M. Sun.–Thurs., until 11 P.M. Fri. and Sat., $23–50), a family-owned place serving traditional American cuisine with a heavy seafood hand, often accompanied by live piano tunes.

The Quarter

The Quarter at the Tropicana features many of the city's best new eateries, like **Cuba Libre** (The Quarter, 609/348-6700, www.cuba librerestaurant.com, $11–23), a restaurant and rum bar serving classic Cuban eats in an ultra-suave setting. Dimmed lights, a balcony terrace, and palm trees decorate this multi-level space, which spills out into the square in the later hours. A stone floor and blue-and-white checkered wicker furniture add to the decor, and the grand staircase and classic car parked curbside are enough to transform the scenery into an ideal Havana setting. In the evening, the restaurant turns into a salsa club. Lunch is served 11:30 A.M.–3 P.M. Monday–Friday, and dinner 4–11 P.M. daily. A tropical brunch is available 10:30 A.M.–2:30 P.M. weekends, and there's a late-night menu 11 P.M.–1:30 A.M. every Friday and Saturday.

The classic **Carmines** (The Quarter, 609/572-9300, www.carminesnyc.com, 11:30 A.M.–midnight Sun.–Thurs., until 1 A.M. Fri. and Sat., $19–40) is a Southern Italian eatery that features photos of celebrities and former Miss America beauties adorning its walls—a sharp, no-nonsense sort-of-place.

At **The Sound of Philadelphia** (The Quarter, 609/887-2200, www.tsoplive.com, $18.95–29.95), enjoy a "soul-infused" menu and a dress code that forbids sneakers and Timberlands. This swanky supper club features a large stage for jazz and Latin performers, with a red velvet curtain as backdrop. Dinner is served 5:30 P.M.–2 A.M. Sunday–Thursday, until 5 A.M. Friday and Saturday, and weekends include a champagne brunch 10 A.M.–2 P.M.

Rí~Rá (The Quarter, 609/348-8600, www.rira.com, $9.95–24.95, 11 A.M.–2 P.M.) is a semi-chain that's as Irish as they come, decorated with salvaged Irish goods and serving

Beef and Guinness Stew, potato pancakes, and a traditional Irish breakfast. A dark interior adds refinement, but the flat-screen TVs behind the bar lend the place a sporty feel. Lunch can get quite crowded.

Brûlée (The Quarter, 609/344-4900, 7–11 P.M. Mon.–Fri., Sun., 6–11 P.M. Sat.) is a dessert-only bar with a selection of after-dinner and espresso drinks. It transforms into the chichi **32 Degrees Luxe Lounge** (609/572-0032, www.32lounge.com) in the wee hours.

GETTING THERE AND AROUND

The **Atlantic City Expressway** is the most direct and quickest route (sans weekend traffic) to the city from South Jersey and Philadelphia. From Philly, take I-295 to Route 42—this leads to the Expressway, about a 50-minute ride from its beginning, with a couple of tolls. An alternative is to take Route 322 (from the Commodore Barry Bridge), which turns into the Black Horse Pike, east until joining with Albany Boulevard, and leading directly into the heart of AC.

From the **Garden State Parkway,** take exits 40/38 southbound or 36/38 northbound.

NJ Transit trains run from the Philadelphia Amtrak station, 90 minutes one-way. A round-trip ticket costs $13.20. There is no train service from New York City.

It's easy to find all-inclusive bus packages to AC from both Philadelphia and New York, as well as numerous places throughout New Jersey. Churches, Elks lodges, synagogues—everyone seems to be running them, and you often get cash back in the form of slot credits or a meal.

Spirit Airlines has daily flights into **Atlantic City International Airport** (609/645-7895, www.acairport.com) from such destinations as Las Vegas and Fort Lauderdale.

Once in town, **Jitneys** (609/344-8642, www.jitneys.net, $2) are the way to get around. These 13-passenger buses operate along various number- and color-coded routes throughout the city: The no. 1 Pink travels back and forth down Pacific Avenue, the no. 2 Blue and no. 3 Green both travel to and from the Marina (where you'll find the bayside casinos), and the no. 4 Orange carries passengers traveling to and from the Convention Center, train station, and bus terminal—and they're available 24/7 (however, the no. 4 Orange runs 7 A.M.–7 P.M. daily). All buses can be accessed from various points along Pacific Avenue (look for the color-coded signs located on street corners a block west of Boardwalk casinos).

Greater Atlantic City Region

The Shore towns and suburbs around Atlantic City offer quiet reprieve from their big city neighbor. You'll find excellent golfing, standard hotel alternatives, brighter beaches, and some of the Shore's best dining in Margate. Between the mainland and Absecon Island are marshlands, bays, and creeks, where a fishers' world is waiting to be discovered.

BRIGANTINE

Just north of Atlantic City is Brigantine, a suburban city with a great deal of natural land. In fact, the entire north end of its nearly 10 square miles remains undeveloped, protected for wildlife. The name Brigantine means "two-masted vessel," perhaps a fitting memorial to the hundreds of shipwrecks that occurred off the city's coast over the centuries.

E. B. Forsythe National Wildlife Refuge

The Brigantine division of the E. B. Forsythe National Wildlife Refuge (Great Creek Rd., 609/652-1665, http://forsythe.fws.gov, $4 vehicle, $2 walk-in or bicycle, daily dawn–dusk) is a premier birding locale. With salt meadows and marshlands, tall grass and scrub, and numerous waterways, it's one of the best places in the state to spot great and snowy egrets, Canada geese, snow geese, mallards, glossy ibis, and blue herons. The refuge is open to autos, cyclists, and those on foot, although ticks, mosquitoes, and green flies are definite problems during summer months. The best times to visit are in May and October, when the Atlantic Flyway (a migratory bird route) is in full swing and the bugs are at a minimum. The refuge includes a one-way, eight-mile dirt trail intended for cars and bicycles (upon entry you'll see the Atlantic City casinos looming in the distance), with numerous pullouts (a speed limit of 15 mph encourages tailgating) and a series of numbered points of interest. You can pick up a print-out describing each point at the information kiosk. If it's not open, the park headquarters (just south of the driving loop's entrance, 8 A.M.–4 P.M. weekdays) has a number of informative pamphlets related to the sights. Be sure to pack your binoculars and make use of the restrooms located by the parking lot before embarking on the route.

Other Sights

The **Marine Mammal Stranding Center** (P.O. Box 773, 3625 Brigantine Blvd., 609/266-0538, www.marinemammalstrandingcenter.org, $1) cares for injured sea life, including dolphins, turtles, seals, and whales, in hopes of re-releasing them to the water. Guests can visit the **Sea Life Education Center** (10 A.M.–4 P.M. daily Memorial Day–Labor Day, winter hours vary), where there's an underwater tank for viewing regional sea life, and locally found shells and marine mammal bones on display.

Just down the road from Brigantine's branch of the Wildlife Refuge is the **Noyes Museum of Art** (733 Lily Lake Rd., Oceanville, 609/652-8848, www.noyesmuseum.org, 10:30 A.M.–4:30 P.M. Tues.–Sat., noon–5 P.M. Sun., $3 adult, under 12 free). Established in 1983 by the Noyes family, it displays folk and fine-art pieces, including a display of vintage bird decoys that belonged to Fred Noyes, a serious decoy collector; changing exhibits are often featured. This is one of the southern Shore's largest and most well-respected museums.

Beaches

Daily beach tags cost $7.

ABSECON

A large percentage of Absecon's population works nearby in Atlantic City. This 5.72-square-mile city is not found on Absecon Island, but two miles west of Absecon Bay. Close enough to both Atlantic City and the few Shores south, this bedroom community offers overnight alternatives to the pricier beach hotels with a number of chain hotels and motels. There are also campgrounds here.

Storybook Land

Along the Black Horse Pike in the town of Cardiff is Storybook Land (6415 Black Horse Pike, Cardiff, 609/641-7847 or 609/646-0103, ext. 5, www.storybookland.com, $16.95, under 12 free), a world of fairytales and amusements. Every kid whose parents take them past the white roadside castle longs to get a glimpse behind its walls. Having celebrated its 50-year anniversary in 2005, Storybook Land has grown exponentially over the years but remains as oddball and exciting as when I was five. You can visit the home of the Three Bears, take a ride down Jack and Jill's slide, or tour through the Day-Glo cave of Alice in Wonderland only to emerge into a life-size maze of cards. And if you think this make-shift wonderland sounds fun in the summer, you should see it during the holidays, when hundreds of thousands of Christmas lights are turned on display, and the big man in red makes a nightly appearance. This winter light show is just as popular with couples as it is with families, a new generation of which will hopefully keep the Land up and running another half a century.

Storybook Land hours vary depending on the season, but normally run 11:30 A.M.–5:30 P.M. weekends in late March and April and daily throughout the summer, and 2–9 P.M. during winter.

WINERIES

The Shore offers a desirable grape-growing climate because of long growing seasons and nutrient-rich sandy soil.

Renault Winery

Renault Winery (72 N. Bremen Ave., Egg Harbor

City, 609/965-2111, www.renaultwinery.com) has grown from a small establishment into an expansive resort. Founded in 1864 by Frenchman Louis Nicholas Renault, it is today one of the oldest continuously operating wineries in the United States, and in addition to its vineyards features the Gourmet Restaurant, golf course, and a hotel/restaurant called Tuscany House. Renault's blueberry champagne is excellent, as is the Sunday brunch, where you feast on a decadent buffet in a dimly lit castle-like space strewn with white lights. Tours of the winery are given 11 A.M.–4 P.M. Monday–Friday, 11 A.M.–8 P.M. Saturday (a free tour is included with dinner), and noon–4 P.M. Sunday. The Gourmet Restaurant ($20–41.50) is open 5–8:30 P.M. Friday, 5–9 P.M. Saturday, 4:30–7:30 P.M. Sunday, and brunch ($18.95) is served 10 A.M.–2 P.M. Sunday.

Tomasello Winery

Tomasello Winery (225 White Horse Pike, Hammonton, 888/MMM-WINE or 888/666-9463, www.tomasellowinery.com, 9 A.M.–8 P.M. Mon.–Sat., 11 A.M.–6 P.M. Sun.) is New Jersey's largest winery (out of the state's 22), and features award-wining red raspberry and blackberry wines, as well as others. It's run by third-generation Tomasellos and has been around for more than 70 years. The winery has a free tasting room and a Vintner's Room where annual galas are held (check website for schedule).

Balic Winery

Since the 1960s, Chateau Balic (6623 Rte. 40, May's Landing, 609/625-2166, www.balicwinery.com) has been serving the southern Jersey Shore. Vineyard specialties include pomegranate, blackberry, and cranberry wines. A tasting room is open to the public 9 A.M.–8 P.M. Monday–Saturday, and 11 A.M.–7 P.M. Sunday.

GOLF

The area around Atlantic City is a popular golfing destination with numerous courses open for play. The following are the region's best.

Harbor Pines Golf Club (500 St. Andrews Dr., 609/927-0006, Egg Harbor Township, www.harborpines.com) is a daily fee course known for its wide fairways and wooded seclusion. The club also hosts on-site classes for those who'd like to improve their game (609/927-0006, ext. 10). Daily weekday afternoon rates are $50–60, $55–70 weekend afternoons during the off-season, with prices increasing during high season. Tee times can be booked up to 14 days in advance without restrictions.

The 36-hole **Blue Heron Pines Golf Club** (W. Country Club Dr., Cologne, 609/965-1800, www.blueheronpines.com) features two 18-hole daily fee courses, each with its own clubhouse. The West Course is the older of the two, opening in 1993 and since achieving a 4.5-star rating from *Golf Digest* magazine. The East Course opened in 2000 and features native bentgrass and rolling terrain incorporated into the landscape, making for a number of challenging holes. Morning rates range $56–126 depending on the time of year; twilight (afternoon) prices are less expensive.

The **Seaview Marriott Golf Club** (410 S. New York Rd., Galloway, 609/652-1800, www.seaviewgolf.com) is situated on an exquisite 670-acre resort easily reachable from Route 9. These 36 holes divided between two courses have been in play since the early half of the 20th century. The annual Shop Rite LPGA Classic takes place on the renowned Bay Course, and a gorgeous 297-room luxury hotel adorns the property. Weekday rates are $49–99 depending on time of year, and weekend rates range $59–129. Twilight rates run $29–69.

VENTNOR, MARGATE, AND LONGPORT

Heading south from Atlantic City you'll encounter the lovely Shore towns of Ventnor, Margate, and Longport. The towns hark back to an earlier era, when AC remained the favored playground but today you'll notice a notable difference from the hoopla of its nearby neighbor. Ventnor's boardwalk stands adjacent to Atlantic City's and extends the famous "B" 1.8 miles, though it is without commercial establishments. The city features a long, pleasant fishing pier, and there are a number of historic homes close to the beach.

Margate is a stately city with large white and brick houses, many with barn-pitched roofs. The city's main thoroughfare, Ventnor Avenue, features central islands where trees bloom in flowers of pink and green, and there's a stark white steeple pointing above the spacious estate-like homes that line this grand old street. It's a great little city—home to one of the state's much-beloved pop culture icons (Lucy the Elephant) as well as some of the most fabulous fine-dining eateries along the Jersey Shore.

To the south, Longport is a mostly residential area, a mid-way point between Atlantic City and Ocean City. The towns get more noticeably residential as you continue south.

Many of the streets in Ventnor and Margate are narrow one-way streets, and there is a little-known island between Longport and Ocean City called Seaview Harbor.

(Lucy the Elephant

Built in 1881 as a way to lure prospective buyers to Margate, Lucy (9200 Atlantic Ave., Margate, 609/823-6473, www.lucytheelephant.org, $4 adult, $2 child) is now a National Historic Landmark that has withstood ocean winds, encroaching development, and time. Things have not been easy for this 65-foot wooden elephant, who's been used as a hotel, tavern, and private residence during her days. She (Lucy's tusks actually make her a "he") is the last of three such elephant structures still standing—one in the Cape May vicinity caught fire in 1896 and the other, located on New York's Coney Island, was torn down in 1900—and high-rise apartments are now blocking her ocean view. Lucy has had some major work done and is looking better than ever, with brightly painted toenails.

Standing within a small fenced-in park near the beach and now serving the public as a museum, Lucy is open to visitors 10 A.M.–5 P.M. weekends September–December and April–mid-June, 10 A.M.–8 P.M. Monday–Saturday, 10 A.M.–5 P.M. Sunday, mid-June–Labor Day, and tours are given every half hour. The last tour begins 30 minutes before close.

Beaches

Ventnor, Margate, and Longport each sell weekly beach tags that cost $10 adult, free for those 12 and under. (Tags must be individually purchased for use of each town's beach.) Margate has a public restroom at Huntington Avenue and the beach.

Sports and Recreation

Go old-school mini-style at the seasonal **Margate Mini Golf** (211 N. Jefferson Ave., 609/822-0660). Bike rentals (clunky cruisers and tandem riders) are available in Ventnor at **AAAA Bike Shop** (5300 Ventnor Ave., 609/487-0808).

Accommodations

$200-250: The **Carisbrooke Inn** (105 S. Little Rock Ave., Ventnor, 609/822-6392, www.carisbrookeinn.com) features seven guestrooms and one suite, each with private bath and complimentary evening refreshments. Amenities include TV with DVD player, air-conditioning, ceiling fans, and wireless Internet. The inn stands on the original spot of Ventnor's first hotel.

Food

For breakfast try **Ma France Creperie** (5213 Ventnor Ave., Ventnor, 609/822-3067, 8:30 A.M.–3:30 P.M. Mon., until 9:30 P.M. Tues.–Sat., 9:30 A.M.–2:30 P.M. Sun.), where you'll find delicious crepes both sweet and savory.

Trendy **Mojo** (223 N. Washington Ave., Margate, 609/487-0300, www.mojonj.com, $20–26) serves an eclectic menu of California-style cuisine amid the soothing sounds of live jazz. A modern minimalist decor in white and orange, with light wood floors rounds out the package. Dinner begins at 5:30 P.M. nightly, though hours are limited during the off-season. Call ahead.

(**Tomatoes** (9300 Amherst Ave., Margate, 609/822-7535, www.tomatoesmargate.com, 5–10 P.M. Sun.–Thurs., until 11 P.M. Fri. and Sat., $31–49) is a top establishment serving upscale Asian-infused eats in sharp, sleekly inspired decor. This spacious BYO features towering bayside windows, a sushi bar, and a glass-enclosed, climate-controlled wine cellar that houses hundreds upon hundreds of vintages.

Steve & Cookie's By the Bay (9700 Amherst Ave., Margate, 609/823-1163, www.steveandcookies.com, 5–10 P.M. Mon.–Thurs., until 11 P.M. Fri. and Sat., $16–39) is a New American waterside restaurant with large wall-like windows that offer stupendous sunset views over the inlet. The menu is strongly seafood-focused and the restaurant includes an oyster bar. Save room for a heavenly slice of chocolate peanut butter pie.

Getting There and Around

You can reach Ventnor from Garden State Parkway exits 38/36 southbound, 29/36 northbound; use exit 36 for both Margate and Longport. There is a $1 toll to reach Margate from the mainland. No toll exists while driving between Atlantic City and Longport.

SMITHVILLE

Smithville is a restored historic village of brick pathways and charming shops selling antiques, collectibles, and specialty wares. At its center stands Lake Meone, lined on one side by a short boardwalk with an arcade shooting gallery and a place to rent paddle boats (609/748-6160). The village hosts a lovely B&B and a number of dining options that range from casual to fancy. It's a wonderful place to bring the family for an afternoon stroll or a bit of shopping—kids will especially love the geese and ducks that meander across the nearby roadways, often causing entertaining traffic backups. Smithville also hosts a number of events throughout the year.

Shopping

Smithville has more than 60 shops and restaurants, including **Made in Italy** (609/748-0709), an Italy-centric gift store; **Ireland and Old Lace** (609/404-0477, www.irelandandoldlace.com), where you'll find imported cable-knit sweaters and gold Claddagh rings; and **The British Connection** (609/404-4444), a U.K. novelty shop. **Rose of Sharon Antiques** (609/652-6300) and **Country Folk** (609/652-6161) are

© LAURA KINIRY

Smithville, along Route 9

some of the handful of antique stores, and additional specialty shops include **Little Egg Harbor Soap** (609/652-9300, www.LittleEgg HarborSoap.com), which features a unique selection of locally created bath products made from vegetable oils, and **Celebrity Collectibles** (609/652-8110), where you can pick up that framed Elvis photo you've always wanted. Candy, clothing, collectible, and pet stores are also represented.

Village shops are open 10 A.M.–6 P.M. Monday–Friday, 10 A.M.–7 P.M. Saturday, 11 A.M.–6 P.M. Sunday.

Accommodations

$150-200: If you're not ready to leave, stay at the **Colonial Inn Bed & Breakfast** (615 E. Moss Rd., 609/748-8999, www.colonialinn smithville.com) located next to the main parking lot on the edge of the village. The inn offers eight traditional period guest rooms, each with private bath and modern amenities such as televisions and DVD players, and continental breakfast is served. **The Colonial Coffee Café** is on-site and open year-round.

Food

For fine dining, a village highlight is the **Smithville Inn** (Rte. 9 and Moss Mill Rd., 609/652-7777, www.smithvillenj.com/ smithvilleinn, $15–24) overlooking Lake Meone. This historic restaurant—the structure dates back to 1787—serves traditional American fare in a cozy setting, with numerous indoor fireplaces. The restaurant is open 11:30 A.M.–3:30 P.M. for lunch, 4:30–8 P.M. for dinner Monday–Saturday and 10:30 A.M.–8 P.M. Sunday. For something more casual, try the village's **Fred & Ethel's Lantern Light Tavern** (609/652-0544), a family-friendly place with a popular happy hour and a standard American menu.

The Cape

At the southernmost point of the Jersey Shore, the Cape is made up of seasonal towns and wealthy enclaves. Towns like Ocean City and Wildwood have two of the best boardwalks in New Jersey, while Avalon and Stone Harbor are two of the most expensive Shore towns. Numerous barrier islands give way to a narrow point upon which sits the Victorian Cape May City, so different from the Doo Wop–wacky Wildwood to its north. The beaches in the north are constantly being pumped with sand, which washes away to the half-mile long beach of Wildwood with every small storm. One can drive from Atlantic County straight through to Cape May along Ocean Drive and most islands have a one-way $1 toll between them. There is a town for everyone, from families to college kids to honeymooners to retirees, along this southern stretch, a wonderful way to round out the magnificent, magical, most-excellent Jersey Shore.

◖ OCEAN CITY

Originally founded by Methodist ministers as a 19th-century Methodist summer retreat, Ocean City continues to shine as an all-around favorite. Though alcohol distribution is not allowed within its borders, the blue laws of the past—preventing business on Sundays—are gone. It's where families congregate, teens find summer love, and writers go (or dream of going) to retire. And at it's heart is a 2.5-mile boardwalk, home to a giant Ferris wheel, the city's tallest structure.

The boardwalk is built up on the west side in Spanish-style architecture; to the east the sea crashes only a couple hundred yards away. Beach erosion is a problem here—with every storm the sands condense, most of them washing away toward Wildwood to the south. There was a time when the beach was so small that during high tide the waves would crash up under the boards, tickling your feet.

Ocean City's downtown main street is Asbury Avenue, lined with colorful two-story buildings and airy department stores. On the city's north end is the Garden District, which more closely resembles those towns to its north, such as Longport and Ventnor. On the city's southern tip is Corsen's Inlet, a natural habitat of marshlands and sandy expanse and a great place for fishing and to take a break from the typical Shore action.

Trust me. Bring you family—all of them: grandparents, kids, cousins, aunts, and uncles. You'll never want to leave.

Boardwalk

Here in the OC the boardwalk reigns supreme. It's not your all-out type of walkway that you'd find in Wildwood or Seaside (no casino arcades or games of chance in this religious town), but a subtler, family-style place with interesting shops, decent rides, and plenty of boardwalk eats. Catch Southside Johnny or the Pitman Hobo Band at the Music Pier or hang on one of the benches with a slice of pizza and a plastic bin of caramel corn. But conserve your energy—there are numerous mini-golf courses to play and a carousel to be ridden. Why not browse the awesome kite selection at **Air Circus** (1114 Boardwalk, 609/399-9343) or consider a longboard at the **7th Street Surf Shop** (654 Boardwalk, 609/391-1700)? If it's morning, rent a bike and join the swarms pedaling away, stopping for an easy beach read at **Atlantic Books** (609/398-3343) or for a pancake breakfast at one of the many morning eateries.

Other Sights

The **Discovery Seashell Museum** (2717 Asbury Ave., 609/398-2316, www.shellmuseum.com) is a great place to browse, especially on a rainy day. There are literally hundreds of thousands of shells here from the world over, as well as coral and shark teeth. Buy yourself a seashell change purse or a white shell necklace—they make great souvenirs. Hours are 10 A.M.– 8 P.M. Monday–Saturday, noon–6 P.M. Sunday, April–October. The museum is free.

Located within the city's large Cultural Arts Center, the **Ocean City Historical Museum** (1735 Simpson Ave., 609/399-1801, www.ocnjmuseum.org, $4 adult, under 15 free) gives insight into local history, and provides a 45-minute self-guided walking tour of historic sites. Be sure and check out the *Sindia* display, highlighting the British ship that crashed just off the 16th Street beach in the early 1900s. The ship could still be seen about 15 years ago, but today is completely submerged in sand. It was rumored to be carrying over $1 million in valuables. Hmmm… The museum is open 10 A.M.–4 P.M. Monday–Friday and 11 A.M.– 2 P.M. Saturday May–November, 1–4 P.M. Monday–Friday and 11 A.M.–2 P.M. Saturday the remainder of the year.

Beaches

Ocean City's daily beach fee is $5 adult, free for 12 and under.

Events

There are tons of activities that take place in Ocean City during summer months, and additional events are scattered throughout the year. For more information on any of them you can call 609/525-9300.

The Cape's fine sand beaches make for superb castle-making, and Ocean City offers two chances to give your artistic hand a go. The first event takes place in July, but my recommendation is to wait for the second, the **Sand Sculpting Contest** in August. Beginning at 9 A.M. on the 6th Street beach, it's part of a day-long celebration that culminates with the crowning of the year's most fetching hermit crab at the **Miss Crustacean Pageant.** No worries if your crab ain't a looker, there's also a hermit race.

The **Doo Dah Parade** is an annual city event, taking place in late April. You'll see plenty of Elvis impersonators and bagpipe blowers, but the highlights are the over 300 basset hounds that wiggle their way down the street and up to the boardwalk's Music Pier. The parade is based on a similar Pasadena, California, event, and the day continues with comedy and impersonators on the boards. Ocean City celebrates the Jersey Shore version of Groundhog Day with **Martin Z. Mollusk Day,** an annual May event.

Find out who will be the Garden State's Miss America representative at the **Miss New Jersey Pageant,** which takes place annually in June at the Music Pier. The annual July **Weekend in Venice** (609/525-9300) begins with the **Merchants in Venice Seafood Festival,** an evening smorgasbord along downtown's Asbury Avenue. The following evening an elaborate display of decorated and lighted vessels take to the bay in what is said to be one of the world's longest boat parades, the **Night in Venice,** sailing from the Longport Bridge to Tennessee Avenue.

Events described as "Wacky but not Tacky" take place during **Weird Week,** an annual August occurrence.

The **Second Friday Art Walk** is an art and music festival that takes place along downtown's Asbury Avenue, 6–9 P.M. every second Friday of the month April–September.

Candlelit **Ghost Tours of Ocean City** (609/814-0199, www.ghosttour.com, $13 adult, $7 child) take place every evening during the summer, starting 8 P.M. at Central Emporium (9th St. and Central Ave.). Tickets go on sale at 7 P.M. and tours last a little over an hour.

Sports and Recreation

Gillian's Wonderland Pier (6th St. and Boardwalk, 609/399-7082, www.gillians.com) is the boardwalk's northernmost amusement park, an indoor/outdoor place that's been in business over 40 years. Most rides are geared toward kids and teens, with a few that are adult-friendly, including the bumper boats, log flume, and a giant Ferris wheel with enclosed seating. For me, Wonderland's highlight is the carousel, especially during evenings when those who score a seat on the outer horses get to compete for a gold ring (not yours to keep) and a free ride. Individual tickets for rides run $0.75 each, a book of 30 is $20.

Playland's Castaway Cove (1020 Boardwalk, 609/399-4751, www.boardwalkfun.com) is a land of kiddie rides and arcade games, including the best old-school, slightly beat-up

skeeball in town. It's still only a quarter, and 270 points wins a free game. Hours vary during the shoulder season (check the website) but the Cove opens at 1 P.M. daily from late June to Labor Day. Individual tickets are $0.85, or a book of 35 is $25. At **Gillian's Island Water Theme Park** (6th St. and Boardwalk, 609/399-7082, www.gillians.com, $18/two hours), thrilling waterslides offer prime ocean views. Take a ride down the Lazy River, or go for a quick soaking on Shotgun Falls. $22 scores an all-day pass. The park is open weekends through June and daily during July and August.

It's easy to find a new, well-manicured miniature golf course these days, but for teenage turtles, wacky lions, and funky frogs head to **Goofy Golf** (920 Boardwalk, 609/398-9662). It may not be the hardest, but it's oh so fun. Another favorite is **Tee Time Golf** (7th St. and Boardwalk, 609/398-6763), where holes are blocked by spinning dice and other creaky paraphernalia. Be sure and call last on the final hole—you'll want to savor that chance at a free game.

Midway down the boardwalk jutting out into the sea is the **Music Pier** (825 Boardwalk, 609/525-9245), Ocean City's prime entertainment venue. The pier hosts annual events and both regional and national music, and is home to the **Ocean City Pops Orchestra** (www.oceancitypops.org), which performs throughout the summer and into September.

Moorlyn Theater (820 Boardwalk, 609/399-0006) is back in business. The theater encountered a string of unlucky incidents including a fire, but now the fourplex is up and running. Films run in the evening during summer months, with additional "rain shows" put on during overcast skies or showers. **Frank's Strand Theatre** (9th St. and Boardwalk, 609/398-6565) is a five-screen multiplex, and features evening shows and additional screenings during the afternoon on "bad beach days."

There are plenty of places to rent a bicycle during the summer. They're permitted on the boards before 11 A.M., but flat terrain makes the whole city great for riding—just use extreme care at the intersections. **Surf Buggy**

Center has numerous rental locations, including Eighth Street at the Boardwalk, and 55th and West Avenue. Cost is $6/hour for multispeed cruisers. Others to try are **Ocean City Bike Center** (740 Atlantic Ave., 609/399-5550) and **Oves Bike Rental** (4th St. and Boardwalk, 609/398-3712).

Bay Cats Kayaks and Catamarans (316 Bay Ave., 609/391-7960) gives kayaking tours of the back bays. Excursions leave twice a day during the summer, at 9 A.M. and 4 P.M., and run two hours. **Wet & Wild** (3rd St. and Bay Ave., 609/399-6527) offers full- and half-hour personal watercraft rentals on the bay.

The city's best spot for surfing is the **7th Street Beach.**

Fishers toss their lines from the toll bridge over **Corson's Inlet** (609/861-2404), a 341-acre park accessible from the southern end of Ocean City at the northern foot of the Ocean Drive toll bridge. It's a great place to enjoy nature walks, sailing, fishing, and kayaking.

Accommodations
HOTELS

Ocean City is well-equipped to handle overnight stays, with dozens of motor lodges, hotels, guesthouses, and inns, and only one nationwide chain. A cluster of accommodation is at 9th Street, where a bridge leads off the island into Somers Point.

Along the boardwalk is the towering pink **Port-O-Call** (15th St. and Beach, 609/399-8812, www.portocallhotel.com), featuring spacious shell-colored rooms, each with private balcony. Many offer ocean views, and all include TV, air-conditioning, phone, and coffee maker, and use of the in-ground pool. "Shower rooms" are available after checkout for those who aren't quite ready to leave the beach. A three-night stay is required during July and August, with rates at $280–375 a night.

The Spanish-style **Flanders Hotel** (719 11th St., 609/399-1000, www.theflandershotel.com) is centrally located along the boards, and features an outdoor heated pool and rooms with separate bedroom, cable TV, individual climate control, and complimentary beach tags. This

grand 1923 hotel is rumored to be haunted. Rooms and suites run $179–239, $309–429 in the summer months.

The three-floor **Watson's Regency Suites** (Ocean and 9th St., 609/398-4300, www.watsonsregency.com) features condo-like accommodations decked out in typical Shore decor: pinks, greens, and beach wood. Each unit includes a kitchen, dining area, pull-out couch, bedroom, two television sets, and a spacious two-door balcony. With inside entry, plenty of closet space, and enough room to fit up to six comfortably, Watson's is a good choice for extended stays. Rates for July and August are $279–299. The remainder of the year varies from $100 to $200.

B&BS AND GUESTHOUSES

Ocean City has never been known as a bed-and-breakfast city, but these days you'll find a couple that are definitely worth a stop. Guesthouses around town range from comfortable to inconvenient—stick with those listed and you'll be fine.

The **[** **Atlantis Inn Luxury Bed & Breakfast** (601 Atlantic Ave., 609/399-9871, www.atlantisinn.com) is a wonderful place featuring 10 suites with private bath, goose-down duvets, air-conditioning, TV/DVD, and access to an on-site spa facility that offers hot-stone, deep-tissue, and Swedish massage. Each room is handsomely decorated in subtle colors with Victorian accents, and a rooftop deck is the ideal place for watching the day wind down. Rates are $170–385 in the high season, $130–215 low season.

The three-floor **Scarborough Inn** (720 Ocean Ave., 800/258-1558, www.scarborough inn.com) is a larger space with 24 individually decorated rooms. Amenities include private bath, air-conditioning, TV, and telephone, and a full breakfast daily. Rates are $135–225 high season, $95–150 low season.

The family-owned **Osborne's Fairview Inn** (601 E. 15th St., 609/398-4319, www.osbornes inn.com) offers a handful of small, well-kept guestrooms and a few apartments, all with TV, fan, air-conditioning, and private bath. It's a beachy sort of place, just around the corner from the boards. Rates are $95–110 for guest-rooms throughout the summer.

Ocean City has an abundance of weekly and seasonal rentals. Agencies to try include **Grace Realty** (34th and Central, 800/296-HOME or 800/296-4663) and **Monihan Realty Inc.** (3201 Central Ave., 609/339-0998 or 800/255-0998, www.monihan.com).

Camping

The year-round **Yogi Bear's Jellystone Park Camp-Resort** (1079 12th Ave., Mays Landing, 800/355-0264, www.atlanticcity jellystone.com) is the perfect place for families, with a miniature golf course, playground, and plenty of planned activities for adults and kids to enjoy together. The campground is located on the mainland, close to both Ocean City and Atlantic City. Full hook-up tent and RV sites are $37/night for two people Sunday–Thursday, $40/night for two people Friday and Saturday.

Only three miles from Ocean City, **Whippoorwill Campground** (810 S. Shore Rd., Marmora, 609/390-3458 or 800/424-8275, www.campwhippoorwill.com, Apr.–Oct.) features large wooded campsites and hosts various themed events throughout the season. Sites run $43/night for two.

Ten minutes from Ocean City is **Frontier Campground** (84 Tyler Rd., Ocean View, 609/390-3649, www.frontiercampground .com, mid-Apr.–mid-Oct.), a low-key place with shaded tent and RV sites. You'll find no bustling activities here—this is for the family that just wants to relax. The resort also rents fully furnished "tree houses"—cabins on stilts—that sleep five and include a kitchen ($89/night for two, $10/night each additional person). Basic sites are $25/night, $29/night with water and electric.

Food

For a thin-crusted slice of pepperoni pizza hit up one of the three **Mack and Manco's** (609/399-2548) located at 8th, 9th, and 12th Streets along the boardwalk. No lie—it's the best EVER! The 9th and Boardwalk location stays open throughout the year.

My father never makes a trip to Ocean City without picking up a bucket of **Johnson's Popcorn** (1360 Boardwalk, 609/398-5404, www.johnsonspopcorn.com), the most delicious caramel corn around. Buckets are large enough to last a week, but most likely you'll devour it in a day.

For a true Ocean City breakfast, park your bike at **Oves** (5th and Boardwalk, 609/398-3712), on the northern end of the boardwalk well past Wonderland Pier. Grab an outdoor table on the upper deck, but keep all eyes on your food—the seagulls think they own the place! Oves also serves a menu of casual lunch eats and is known for its dinner seafood selection ($11–40).

The popular **Periwinkles** (822 9th St., 609/814-9500, $17.95–26) serves beef, chicken, and seafood in a fine dining setting.

For standard American eats away from the boards, try **The Chatterbox** (500 9th St., 609/399-0013), a year-round, 24-hour OC institution. Bring the family, and save room for the ice cream. **Luigi's Restaurant** (300 9th St., 609/399-4937) has been serving up traditional Italian dishes in a cozy corner locale for decades.

The **4th Street Café** (400 Atlantic Ave., 609/399-0764, $15–25) is a casual coffee house by day and a fine dining restaurant serving New American cuisine by night. Situated along Ocean City's downtown main street stretch, the café features the work of local artists on its walls. A chalkboard menu changes daily. Summer hours are 6 A.M.–9 P.M. daily, with dinner served 5–9 P.M.

Information and Services

The city's **Information Center** (800/BEACH-NJ or 800/232-2465) is located along Route 52 on the Stainton Memorial Causeway, just over the 9th Street Bridge from the island.

Ocean City is a dry town, but you are allowed to bring your own alcohol into the city. To make this easier, there are more than a handful of liquor stores that are ideally located literally just outside the city boundaries. Two to try are **Circle Liquor** (Somers Point,

THE JERSEY SHORE

609/927-2921), on the west side of the 9th Street Bridge, and **Boulevard Super Liquors** (501 Roosevelt Blvd., 609/390-1300), across the 34th Street Bridge.

Getting There and Around

Ocean City is 20 minutes south of Atlantic City, easily reachable by Garden State Parkway exits 30/25 southbound or 25/29 northbound.

SEA ISLE CITY AND STRATHMERE

Although Sea Isle has long been a haven for college students and weekend renters who believe the Miller Lite bottle to be the epitome of Jersey Shore life, the city is seeing some drastic changes. The number of families setting up year-round residence is increasing dramatically, and the summer-shack bungalows once prevalent throughout the island are coming down, replaced by million-dollar homes. This shift has been in the works since the new millennium when Fun City—Sea Isle's only amusement park—was torn down, and quiet zones were established to keep summer noise levels to a minimum. Sea Isle may be headed in a calmer direction—it's true—but that's not to say the party scene isn't still going strong.

Just north of Sea Isle's city limits, across the bridge from Ocean City, is Strathmere, a thin stretch of land with a few restaurants, a bar, and numerous homes—it's often mistaken as a Sea Isle extension. Landis Avenue connects the two and acts as a main thoroughfare: This is where you'll find many of the island's clubs and eateries.

Promenade

Sea Isle's oceanfront paved Promenade (also called a boardwalk) plays host to a couple of casino arcades and a number of sweatshirt and trinket shops, as well as casual eateries where you'll find burgers, pizza, and ice cream. The bulk of the businesses are located on the bottom floor of the Spinnakers condo towers at the north end of the walkway. A bit south is the **Boardwalk Casino Arcade** (42nd and Boardwalk, 609/263-1377) and

Sea Isle City's Promenade

© LAURA KINIRY

Gunslingers Old Time Photos (43rd and Boardwalk, 609/263-4771), where you can dress up in Western attire for a framed 8x10, but you won't find much else.

Sand dunes and shrubbery separate the 1.5-long Promenade from the beach. Bicycles, inline skates, and skateboards are welcome 6 A.M.–3 P.M. Monday–Friday, until noon on the weekends.

Beaches
Sea Isle City's daily beach fee is $4, free for those 11 and under. Strathmere's beaches are free.

Entertainment and Nightlife
Cover bands, dancing, and drink specials are the norm throughout Sea Isle. While most of the city's bars and clubs are open nightly throughout summer, hours are severely limited or nil during the off-season. The **Ocean Drive** (40th and Landis Ave., Sea Isle, 609/263-1000) is an all-out summer party that gets packed on the weekends, with wall-to-wall drunken college buddies looking for a sweet singles scene. It's a seasonal place open 10 A.M.–2 A.M. daily through the summer, with bar foods available for munching, though it does host occasional holiday events throughout the year.

A slightly older crowd frequents the spacious **Springfield Inn** (43rd and Pleasure Ave., Sea Isle, 609/263-4951, opens at 8 P.M. nightly throughout the summer). If you're craving an afternoon cocktail, go to the inn's backyard Carousel Bar next to the Promenade. **La Costa** (4000 Landis Ave., Sea Isle, 609/263-3611) features a causal happy hour, but for something a bit more refined there's the **Dead Dog Saloon** (3809 Landis Ave., Sea Isle, 609/263-7600). Slip out of your flip-flops and, guys, make sure your shirt has a collar if you want to enter after 6 P.M.

A Strathmere classic is the **Deauville Inn** (201 Willard St., Strathmere, 609/263-2080, www.deauvilleinn.com, $22–30). Dock your boat and enjoy bayside seating, or down some brews around the fire pit at the inn's beach bar. The Deauville doubles as a restaurant serving traditional American fare and $0.35 wings on Tuesday afternoons. The bar/restaurant opens at 11 A.M. Monday–Saturday throughout the year, noon on Sunday.

Once a prohibition speakeasy, **Twisties Tavern** (232 S. Bayview Dr., Strathmere, 609/263-2200) is a hidden bayside establishment favored by locals, and is known for its wood-paneled walls, mounted fish, and chiseled coconut collection. Food is available—from mozzarella sticks ($6.95) and onion rings ($5.95) to homemade linguini and crab cakes ($19.95). Hours are noon–2 A.M. daily, closed Tuesday throughout the year.

Sports and Recreation
Two- and four-wheel cycles can be rented at **Surf Buggy Center** (JFK and Pleasure Blvd., Sea Isle, 609/628-0101 or 800/976-5679, www.surfbuggycenter.com). For over a decade **Sea Isle City Parasail** (86th St. and the Bay, Sea Isle, 609/263-5555) has been sending riders 500 feet over the ocean to enjoy spectacular views. On a clear day you can see all the way to Atlantic City. Boats depart hourly throughout the summer beginning at 8 A.M. from the southern Sunset Pier.

Accommodations
Sea Isle doesn't offer many overnight stays. I suggest driving north into Ocean City, or setting up your tent at one of the camping resorts across the bridge along Route 9.

$100-150: The **Sea Isle Inn** (6400 Landis Ave., 609/263-4371, www.seaisleinn.com,) motel offers standard rooms with TV, air-conditioning, private balcony, and a large outdoor swimming pool. It's located at a busy intersection along the city's main strip and is better suited for those preferring late nights to early mornings. Prices are a bit higher for stays of less than four nights.

$150-200: The **Colonnade Inn** (4600 Landis Ave., 609/263-0460) features 11 guestrooms with either private or shared bathrooms. It's an inviting antique-filled place where you can feast on a full complimentary breakfast.

Camping
By far the state's largest private campground,

Ocean View Resort Campground (2555 Rte. 9, 609/624-1675, www.ovresort.com, mid-Apr.–mid-Oct.) is an enormous place with 1,173 tent and RV sites. Events are scheduled throughout the summer, including live music and dances, a Sunday flea market, and a Christmas in July celebration. The resort is located just across the causeway bridge from Sea Isle. Campsites are $39–48/night, lakeside sites run a bit more ($46–58). Cabins are available for rental, $65–105/night. All rates are for a family of four.

West of the barrier islands closest to Sea Isle is **Hidden Acres** (1142 Rte. 83, Cape May Court House, 609/624-9015 or 800/874-7576, www.hiddenacrescampground.com, mid-Apr.–mid-Oct.), a 200-site campground with wooded lots for tents and RVs, and a freshwater lake for swimming. Sites run $31/night for family of four, with water, electric, and cable.

Food

Bayside at Park Road are a number of good seafood restaurants, including **Carmen's Seafood Restaurant** (343 43rd Pl., Sea Isle, 609/263-3471 or 609/263-1634), where you can order 100 steamed clams for $30.50, and **Marie's Seafood Restaurant & Take-Out** (4304 Park Rd., Sea Isle, 609/263-2526), a family-owned BYO serving traditional dishes on a deck overlooking the bay. Hours are 8 A.M.–10 P.M. daily seasonally.

Though **Mildred's Strathmere Restaurant** (Ocean Dr. and Prescott Rd., Strathmere, 609/263-8209) has changed ownership, this cozy Italian and seafood BYO continues to conjure up crowds. Open 4–10 P.M. daily.

The upscale **Busch's Seafood** (8700 Anna Phillips Ln., Sea Isle, 609/263-8626, www.buschsseafood.com) has been serving Sea Isle since 1882. The restaurant's signature is its crab dishes, including the crabmeat au gratin ($25.25) and Busch's famous she-crab soup, offered on Tuesdays and Sundays only ($7/bowl). They're open for dinner 4 P.M. Tuesday–Sunday late June–late September, closed Monday, and on Wednesdays kids eat free. The restaurant is open limited weekend hours the remainder of the year.

For breakfast eats there's the '50s-themed **Shoobies Restaurant** (3915 Landis Ave., Sea Isle, 609/263-2000), also good for ice cream; and **Brennan's Bayside Cafe** (50th and Landis Ave., Sea Isle, 609/263-8881, 8 A.M.–noon, 4:30–10 P.M. seasonal), the perfect stop for a cozy morning meal or a more sophisticated Italian dinner.

For a late-night slice or a decadent pizza turnover there's **Amici's** (38th and Landis Ave., Sea Isle, 609/263-2320, 11 A.M.–11 P.M., $5.95–22.95). The take-out window stays open until 3 A.M. summer weekends. **McGowan's Food Market & Deli** (3900 Landis Ave., Sea Isle, 609/263-5500) makes hoagies and sandwiches perfect for eating on the beach.

Services

The **Acme** at 63rd and Landis Avenue is the only large supermarket on the island.

Getting There and Around

To reach Sea Isle from the Garden State Parkway take exit 17 southbound or 13 northbound.

AVALON AND STONE HARBOR

The towns of Avalon and Stone Harbor are together known as Seven Mile Island, a barrier island approximately four city blocks wide. Both are wealthy enclaves mixed with classic bungalows, two-story beach houses, and massive beachfront homes, kept private behind dense tree stands. Avalon has some of the tallest sand dunes in the state, adding to the privacy of the beach. The dunes also act as important habitat for plant life. Stone Harbor is well known for its commitment to preserving bird habitat—along the beach, within the borough, and throughout the surrounding wetlands.

Together the two towns offer a relaxed beach atmosphere with casual shopping, a number of fine restaurants, and a few longstanding bars.

Stone Harbor's downtown centers around 96th Street and Third Avenue, where you'll find a variety of specialty shops including a surf shop, a bookstore, a home accessory place, a few bars, and a couple of restaurants. Avalon's downtown district is between the circle and 33rd Street along Dune Drive.

Wetlands Institute

Located on the mainland just over the bridge from Seven Mile Beach is Stone Harbor's Wetlands Institute (1075 Stone Harbor Blvd., 609/368-1211, www.wetlandsinstitute.org, $7 adults, $4 child), an environmental education center with 6,000 acres of salt marshes, a salt-water aquarium, an observation tower, and the wonderful **Tidewater Museum Store.** Visitors can take a self-guided tour along an outdoor walkway, which is a mixture of mud flat and boardwalk offering some excellent bird-watching opportunities. Indoors, guests will find a small aquarium filled with a series of wall-mounted tanks, home to delicate seahorses and big-lipped fish. There are also a few exhibits on local creatures, including horseshoe crabs, fiddler crabs, and moon snails, and a touch tank that kids can enjoy.

The Wetlands Institute works extensively with the local population of diamondback terrapins by rescuing the eggs of injured females and raising them onsite before releasing them back into the wild. A number of pamphlets and displays make visitors aware of these turtles that can live up to 40 years if they manage to avoid predators and cars.

The center is open 9:30 A.M.–4:30 P.M. Monday, Friday, and Saturday, 10 A.M.–4 P.M. Sunday, mid-May–mid-October, and 9:30 A.M.–4:30 P.M. Tuesday–Saturday, mid-October–mid-May.

Stone Harbor Bird Sanctuary

In the center of Stone Harbor is the 21-acre Stone Harbor Bird Sanctuary (114th St. and 3rd Ave., 609/368-5102), one of the largest heronries on the Atlantic coast. At this registered landmark you may spot blue and green herons and yellow-crowned night egrets. From the road it looks like nothing more than a long sectioned-off stretch filled with shrubs and forest in an otherwise built-up town. There's a viewing platform from the roadside where you can watch the birds returning home in the evenings.

Beaches

From 43rd Street to 58th Street beach access is limited, as this is where the multi-million-dollar homes (of Ed McMahon, Oprah Winfrey, and others) are located. They are not easily (if at all) seen from the streets, blocked by a growth of towering trees. You can reach the beach from numerous intervals by following the marked trails between stands. Avalon's beaches are accessible to visitors with disabilities, and rolling chairs are available for the sand. For more on Stone Harbor's wheelchair access call 609/368-5102.

Both Avalon and Stone Harbor beach fees run $5/day, $10/week.

Entertainment and Nightlife

Between Stone Harbor and Avalon are a few of the most popular nightlife spots on the Cape. Both intimate watering hole and lively club, **Fred's Tavern** (314 96th St., Stone Harbor, 609/368-5591, 10 A.M.–2 A.M. Mon.–Sat., noon–2 A.M. Sun.) is the ultimate summer hangout for live music and drink specials.

Jack's Place (3601 Ocean Dr., Avalon, 609/967-5001, www.jacksavalon.com, May–Labor Day) is a seasonal party spot and the place to catch established cover bands like Love Seed Mama Jump.

The seasonal **Princeton Bar & Grill** (2008 Dune Dr., Avalon, 609/967-3457, www.princetonbar.com) features live bands and cheap eats ($4.50–6) like burgers and wraps.

Frank Theatre-Stone Harbor 5 (271 96th St., 609/368-7731) is the only movie theater on Seven Mile Beach.

Sports and Recreation

Pirate Island Golf (2378 Dune Dr., 609/368-8344) is an 18-hole miniature golf course, with additional locations in Sea Isle and the Ocean City boardwalk.

TI Kayaks (354 96th St., 609/368-5501, www.tikayaks.com) runs two-hour eco-tours of nearby wetlands during summer. A half-day single-kayak rental for self-guided ocean or bay trips is $35, $45 double.

Rent a bike at the **Harbor Bike and Beach**

Shop (9828 3rd Ave., 609/368-3691) between 98th and 99th Streets along Third Avenue in Stone Harbor, or at **Hollywood Bicycles** (2528 Dune Dr., 609/967-5846) in Avalon. All these places are only open in summer.

Accommodations

Avalon and Stone Harbor meet up at 80th Street, and this is where you'll find a bulk of the island's overnight accommodations.

$150-200: The 44-room **Avalon Inn Resort** (7929 Dune Dr., Avalon, 609/368-1543, www .avaloninn.org) is a remodeled inn with amenities that include air-conditioning, TV, and fridge, and an outdoor pool. Off-season rates run as low as $49, and for those who'd like a bit of the beach but can't get to the Shore, the hotel will send you a gift jar of Avalon sand for $10.

Concord Suites (7800 Dune Dr., Avalon, 609/368-7800) is open early May–late September, and weekends in early October. Every room has a bedroom and a separate living space with a sofa bed. Two swimming pools are available to enjoy.

$300-350: The **Golden Inn** (Oceanfront at 78th St., Avalon, 609/368-5155, www.golden inn.com) offers great ocean views, an Italian restaurant, and a poolside sandbar. Big Band Gateway weekends are scheduled throughout the year. If you can do without a view, the cost of a room is about $50 less.

The newly renovated **Windrift Resort Hotel** (80th St. and the Beach, Avalon, 609/368-5175, www.windrifthotel.com) features a restaurant serving three meals daily and a lounge with nightly specials, including $1 draft and $0.33 wings on Tuesday nights. Four-night stays during the week will drastically reduce the price.

Camping

Just outside of Avalon is **Avalon Campground** (1917 Rte. 9 N., Clermont, 609/624-0075 or 800/814-2267, www.avaloncampground.com, mid-Apr.–Sept.), a pleasant place with shaded sites and log cabins available for rental ($50–80/night). Basic tent sites run $32, RV sites are $39–48, depending on amenities.

Food

At Avalon's **Sea Grill** (225 21st St., Avalon, 609/967-5511, $16–24), orders are placed directly with the chef. Steak and seafood are the specialty and a wonderful wine selection is available. The restaurant opens at 5 P.M. daily, year-round.

The tiny **Café Loren** (23rd St. and Dune Dr., Avalon, 609/967-8228, 5:30–9 P.M. nightly, $27–30.50) serves an upscale menu of continental cuisine seasonally amid sophisticated-country decor.

Maggie's (2619 Dune Dr., Avalon, 609/368-7422) serves homemade breakfast and lunch beginning at 6:30 A.M. daily throughout the summer.

The family-owned **Henny's Restaurant** (9628 Third Ave., Stone Harbor, 609/368-2929, www.hennys.com, $20–26) is known for its steak, seafood, and early-bird specials (4–5 P.M. nightly). Breakfast is served on weekends seasonally and daily throughout the summer. Hours are 8:30 A.M.–10 P.M. daily in-season, and 11:30 A.M.–9 P.M. weekdays, 8–10 P.M. Saturday, until 9 P.M. Sunday during the off-season.

Green Cuisine (302 96th St., Stone Harbor, 609/368-1616, 10 A.M.–8 P.M. Mon.–Thurs., until 8:30 P.M. Fri.–Sun., $7–10) serves healthy salads and sandwiches that offer an excellent alternative to typical Shore eats.

Kuishimbo (330 96th St., Stone Harbor, 609/967-7007, $16–22) is a popular BYO serving Japanese cuisine. It's open for dinner 5:30–9:30 P.M. daily during summer; off-season hours vary, so call ahead.

Getting There and Around

The Garden State Parkway exit for Avalon is 13; Stone Harbor is reached by taking exit 10A southbound or 10B northbound.

THE WILDWOODS

Though collectively known as "Wildwood-By-The-Sea" or simply "Wildwood," the Wildwoods actually consist of North Wildwood, the central Wildwood City, and to the south, Wildwood Crest, as well as a couple smaller towns that make up the landscape of Five Mile Island. In the 1950s the Wildwoods earned the nickname "Little Vegas." Already established as a vacation resort, it was becoming a full-on music venue, with Bobby Rydell singing about his "Wildwood Days," Chubby Checker performing his first twist, Bill Haley and the Comets publicly debuting "Rock Around the Clock," and Dick Clark carting his *American Bandstand* entourage to dance at the boardwalk's former Starlight Ballroom, destroyed by fire in 1981. Hundreds of mom-and-pop motels sprung up around the island, most notably in Wildwood Crest, each trying to outdo the other with a more elaborate sign, higher voltage lights, even plastic palm trees.

Today the Wildwoods are finally beginning to recover from years of neglect, the towns left to sulk while airplanes carry tourists farther and faster. Thankfully, this is what saved—at least for a time—the affectionately dubbed "Doo Wop" motels that give the Wildwoods the kitschy character they're known for. Couple these with the island's half-mile-wide beach, two-mile boardwalk, and numerous amusement piers, water parks, and games of chance, and you've got one quirky place.

Though the Wildwoods' newfound "rediscovery" is evident in the excessive construction of upscale townhouses and condos, and the demolition of Doo Wop throughout the island, the place still retains all the resemblance of its working-class roots and remains the resort of choice for plenty of South Jerseyans and Philadelphians.

Cheap eats, nightlife, and airbrushed, fringe-lined T-shirts are around every corner, and the island—most notably Wildwood City—feels more like a night at the fun house than a walk in the park. For now, the Wildwoods remain mostly seasonal, practically turning into a ghost town by late October and not starting back up until May. Most restaurants and some hotels completely shut down for the winter, though when the crowds return by June you'll be hard-pressed to find a parking space anywhere.

◖ Boardwalk

There is nothing quite like the two-mile-long Wildwood boardwalk, a smorgasbord of color and kitsch built up on both sides with T-shirt shacks, gyro shops, arcades, and the largest stuffed Looney Tunes you can find. This is New Jersey's ultimate people-watching place, and well worth a trip if only for the sights, sounds ("watch the tram car, please"), and smells of garlic fries and funnel cake wafting through the air. As tacky goes, there's little you won't find on these boards—air-brushed tees and tattoos, painted hermit crabs, and shorts reading "Save a horse, ride a cowboy," are just the beginning. To be sure, there's no elitism here, and black, white, Latino, grandparents, teens, and families will all fit in nicely.

One of the best attractions along the boards are the infamous **tram cars,** which run the two-mile length in a continuous loop and are often full, carrying weary feet finishing a day on the beach, and attempting to run down whoever gets in their paths. Heed those warnings and "wa-wa-watch the tram car" or you may find yourself just another boardwalk attraction. The transport stops wherever you like, and costs $2 each way.

Another great staple is the multi-level **Boardwalk Mall** (3800 Boardwalk, 609/522-4260), a shopping palace (as boardwalks go) filled with flimsy gold rings, Hawaiian-print totes, and that Johnny Depp poster you've been searching for.

The **Seaport Aquarium** (3400 Boardwalk, 609/522-2700, $5.50 adult, $4.50 child) offers visits with numerous shark species, including lemon, sand tiger, nurse, and black-tipped, in addition to alligators, crocs, pythons, and piranhas. If such famed predators don't pique your interest, maybe the employee beckoning unsuspecting mothers with a live boa wrapped around his neck will. The serpent is available for photo ops.

Amusement Piers

Wildwood's piers rate right up there with traditional amusement parks—they aren't kiddie lands—this is serious stuff! The Morey family (www.moreyspiers.com), developers of the first Wildwood amusement pier, currently own all three in operation, and passes bought for one can be used at any. Games of chance and boardwalk eats are easy to come by.

Situated at Spencer Avenue and Boardwalk, the **Spencer Avenue Amusement Pier** features one of New Jersey's best roller coasters, the **Great White,** a hybrid of wood and steel that runs 50 mph and reaches heights of over 100 feet. Other rides include the Tilt-A-Whirl, Wacky Whip, and Mini-Scrambler, their combined efforts enough to keep you from seeing straight for days.

Morey's 25th Avenue Amusement Pier is home to 2005's **AtmosFEAR,** a free-fall tower that keeps riders in the dark, literally. The Great Nor 'Easter Roller Coaster, a carousel, and a giant slide are a few of the other attractions.

The former Mariner's Landing is now known as **Schellenger Avenue Amusement Pier,** the most central and popular of the piers, and home to both the log flume and the **Giant Wheel,** an open-car Ferris wheel that's one of the tallest in the state. From here you'll get an excellent bird's-eye view of the expansive beach and boardwalk, and the power-punch of amusements packed multi-layer onto the relatively small pier below, including flying swings, twirling scallop shells, and the cars of the Sea Serpent roller coaster set loose in their tracks. If you're not into heights or open spaces, then this ride is not for you.

The Moreys also own two **Raging Water** water parks located along the boards at 25th Street and Schellenger Avenue, on the piers behind the rides. Both water parks features numerous slides, a lazy river, and an area for kids. A three-hour water park pass is $25.75 adult, $20 child.

Access to all Morey Piers is free, and rides can be paid for individually (at ticket booths) or by purchasing an admission pass—good for rides at all three piers—which runs $41 weekends, $39 weekdays for those over 54 inches tall, $39 weekends, $37 weekdays for anyone 48–54 inches tall, and $29 weekends, $27 weekdays for those 48 inches and under. Combo passes for the amusement piers and water parks are available for $46 weekends, $44 weekdays for anyone over 54 inches tall, $44 weekends, $42 weekdays for those 48–54 inches tall, and $34 weekends, $32 weekdays for those 48 inches and under. All go-kart rides cost extra.

Another water park visible from the street is the colorful **Splash Zone** (Schellenger Ave. and Boardwalk, 609/729-5600, www.splashzonewaterpark.com). It's a kid-friendly place with 16 water-themed rides. A three-hour ticket costs $23 adult, $19 child.

Other Sights

Just across the bridge from Stone Harbor in North Wildwood is the active **Hereford Inlet Lighthouse** (1st and Central Ave., 609/522-4520, $4 adult, $1 child). This 1874 Victorian structure hardly resembles a lighthouse, with five indoor fireplaces and English gardens that attract hundreds of butterflies during an early summer bloom. An inside museum houses the original whale-oil lamp. Visitors are welcome to tour the lighthouse 9 A.M.–5 P.M. daily, mid-May–mid-October, and 10 A.M.–4 P.M. Wednesday–Sunday, mid-October–mid-May.

Beaches

Wildwood's beaches may be free, but at a half-mile in width, it takes work to enjoy them! Really, it's not so bad: Benches are scattered along the beaches at about the midway point to the ocean, offering a brief respite for weary feet before continuing on. Playgrounds, volleyball nets, and shuffleboard courts are also found along the sand, closer inland and most notably in the boardwalk vicinity. North Wildwood's Moore's Inlet is the only beach in the Wildwoods allowing dogs and barbecues.

Festivals and Events

Since opening in 2002, the Doo Wop–inspired **Wildwood Convention Center** (4501 Boardwalk, 609/846-2631, 800/WW-BY-SEA or 800/992-9732) has brought new life to the city by hosting close to 500 events each year, including the annual June **Polka Spree by the Sea** (www.polkaspree.com), and the annual October **Fabulous '50s Weekend** (www.gwcoc.com/fifties), a weekend festival highlighting the Wildwoods' place in music history. Past weekends have included a screening of the documentary *Wildwood Days,* a street fair, and an evening dance hosted by the infamous Philadelphia DJ and "Geator with the Heator," Jerry Blavat.

Wildwood's **National Marbles Tournament** (301/724-1297) takes place on a permanent beach location along the boardwalk, complete with a number of marble playing boards. You can visit the **Marbles Hall of Fame** at Wildwood's **George F. Boyer Historical Museum** (3907 Pacific Ave., 609/523-0277).

Held annually during Memorial Day weekend, the **Wildwood International Kite Fest** (Cresse to Burk Aves. on the beach, 609/729-4000, www.gwcoc.com) includes world-renowned kite-builders, kite-making workshops and exhibits, and an illuminated Night Kite Fly. Kite Ballet, the kite version of figure skating, is one of the most serious events, as fliers come prepared for any and all weather conditions.

Recreation and Entertainment

The oceanfront **Promenade** in Wildwood Crest is a welcome reprieve from its northern boardwalk neighbor, and a great place for a jog or a bike ride. You can rent a cruiser at **Bradley's Bikes** (Rambler Rd., 609/729-1444) across the street from the Admiral's Quarters restaurant. Bicycles are allowed on the boards from 5 A.M. to 11 A.M. daily.

The borough's **New Jersey Surf Camps** (Ocean Outfitters, 6101 New Jersey Ave., 609/729-7400, www.newjerseysurfcamps.com) hold private and group surfing lessons throughout the year, and camps June–August at two locations: off of Rambler Road or on nearby Stone Harbor at 81st Street.

For parasailing 500 feet above the ocean, try **Atlantic Parasail Inc.** (1025 Ocean Dr., 609/522-1869, www.atlanticparasail.com).

The Mississippi-style **Delta Lady** (609/552-1919) gives riverboat cruises of the bay. Choose from the Captain Kidd Cruise (departs 10:30 A.M. daily, $15.95 adult, $6.95 child under 12), the Wildlife & Nature Cruise (2 P.M. daily, $15.95 adult, $6.95 child under 12), or the Sunset Buffet Dinner Cruise (6:45 P.M. daily, $33 adult, $6.95 child under 6). There's also a sing-along banjo cruise on the weekends. Docked adjacent is the 70-foot-long, 147-passenger **Silver Bullet** (609/522-6060, www.silverbullettours.com), billed as the world's fastest speedboat. Rides take off from Schooner Landing at the foot of the George Reading Wildwood Bridge, last 90 minutes, and include dolphin-spotting and a water soak.

North Wildwood's **Moore's Inlet** is a great spot for fishing and personal watercraft riding. There's a surfing beach between 8th and 10th Avenues in North Wildwood, and at Rambler Road in Wildwood Crest.

Accommodations

Many of the Wildwoods' motels are so old-school that they have to advertise whether or not they have cable TV (forget about blow dryers). Motels are the norm in the Wildwoods, and there are plenty of them, but they're going fast—replaced by luxury condo units and sterile rental spaces. Many of those that remain continue to be family-owned, with the same clientele returning year after year. It's not hard to find a bad motel in Wildwood—they're all over the place—and even if the exterior is something out of this world, chances are the interior leaves a lot to be desired. But find one that's good (try those listed below) and you're in for one of the most unique experiences along the Jersey Shore. In these parts Doo Wop is endangered, so it's best to check them out before they're no more. Can ya dig?

$100-150: With its plastic palms, angular rooftop, and kidney-shaped pool, the **Caribbean** (5600 Ocean Ave., Wildwood Crest, 609/522-8292, www.caribbeanmotel.com) is the epitome of Doo Wop design. This classic 1950s motel has been revamped while keeping with the authentic style: The lounge features leopard-print couches and a plasma-screen TV. All rooms feature air-conditioning, fridge, microwave, and TVs with HBO, and are decorated in simple furnishings and light tropical colors. Shuffleboard and an upper sundeck are added pluses.

THE WILDWOODS' DESIGNS ON DOO WOP

The Wildwoods' motel boom happened in the 1950s when the automobile ran rampant but air travel wasn't as ubiquitous as it is today. Americans were catching glimpses of far-away places on TV, but didn't have the time or means necessary to reach them. In stepped North Wildwood, Wildwood, and Wildwood Crest, where families could stay in beachside motels that evoked far-off places like Hawaii and Singapore without leaving the Delaware Valley tri-state area. Most of these establishments were mom and pop-owned, ordinary cement buildings with smallish rooms and efficiencies. So in order to differentiate themselves from one another, they added oversize flashy neon signs, angular roofs, kidney-shaped pools, exotic themes (evident in larger than life names like Pink Champagne, Monaco, and Caribbean Breeze), "perks" like air-conditioning and television, and parking spots only a few feet away from their doors. The kitschy decor ranged from pirates to Tiki to futuristic motifs.

While it's true that such places were popular throughout the United States, many are long since gone, either rebuilt as condos or replaced by homes. However, during much of the '80s and '90s, the Wildwoods were all but forgotten, and this lack of commercial attention left these tacky jewels as diamonds in the rough, just waiting to be uncovered.

In 1997, the late architect Steve Izenhour did just that. A proponent of Vegas-style kitsch (the Wildwoods were often referred to as "Little Vegas" during the 1950s), Izenhour was enamored with the Wildwoods' wacky motels and first coined the term "Doo Wop" in talking about the Wildwoods' architectural offerings. (This style is also known as "Populuxe," "California Google," and "Jetsonian" in other parts of the country.) Together with one of the great founding sons of the Wildwoods, Jack Morey, Izenhour developed the **Doo Wop Preservation League** (www.doowopusa.org), a non-profit aimed at highlighting and protecting the Wildwoods' unique architectural contribution.

Unfortunately, the league was formed just as the Wildwoods were being rediscovered as a beach resort, but not for their pop culture attractions. As Preservation members were attempting to inspire businesses to promote the Doo Wop spirit, dozens of motels were meeting the wrecking ball, and what was once the largest collection of "mid-century commercial" architecture found in one place quickly began disappearing. Today the trend continues. Doo Wop is out of style, man, lacking many of the modern amenities that other Shore towns have to offer. Money is talking, and many motel owners are taking the more lucrative road when faced with the choice between selling or investing millions in a property that needs a complete overhaul.

In 2005, more than half of the Wildwoods' Doo Wop properties had already been demolished; at the same time, local chain and independent businesses garnished themselves with Doo Wop accessories, including the Harley Davidson shop, the Wawa convenience

---

The seasonal **Fleur de Lis Resort Motel** (6105 Ocean Ave., Wildwood Crest, 609/552-0123, May–mid-Oct.) is a three-story beachfront motel featuring clean rooms equipped with fridge, microwave, and air-conditioning, a heated pool, and a spacious sundeck overlooking the beach.

While the boardwalk is not at its doorstep, the **Le Voyageur Motel** (232 Andrews Ave., Wildwood, 609/522-6407) is within walking distance. This is a quiet and cozy place with well-kept rooms that feature air-conditioning

and TV with HBO, and there's a heated outdoor pool.

$150-200: I love North Wildwood's **Lollipop Motel** (23rd and Atlantic Aves., North Wildwood, 609/729-2800, www.lollipop motel.com), if only for its roadside cherubic-faced taffy sign and candy-colored doors. Renovated rooms are each equipped with TV with HBO, air-conditioning, and microwave, and outside there's a barbecue for guest use and an in-ground pool with diving board.

With its palm trees, private balconies,

store along Rio Grande Avenue, and the Blue Olive Restaurant (formerly Maureen's), whose exterior is graced with a massive martini glass. The entire Doo Wop motel district is listed as one of **Preservation New Jersey's** (www.preservationnj.org) "Ten Most Endangered Sites for 2005" and has been nominated for listing on the New Jersey State Register of Historic Places. The Caribbean became the first of the motels to gain an official historic listing in July 2005.

For those interested in Doo Wop, there are a number of outlets. Cape May's Mid-Atlantic Center for the Arts (MAC) runs a Doo Wop architectural trolley tour through the Wildwoods' streets on evenings during July and August. Tickets may be purchased at the **Greater Wildwood Chamber of Commerce** (3306 Pacific Ave.) or in Cape May, at the **Washington Street Mall Information Booth.** Tours begin at 7 P.M. from Cape May, 7:45 P.M. from Wildwood, $10/8 adults, $5/4 child. For further information and times, call 609/884-5404 or 800/275-4278. Doo Wop fans may also want to check out the 2003 documentary *Wildwood Days* by filmmaker Carolyn Travis, who spent her childhood summers vacationing in Wildwood. The movie is a nostalgic look into Wildwood's past and is heavy on the Doo Wop shots. The **Wildwood Crest Historical Society** (116 E. Heather Rd., 609/729-4515, www.cresthistory.org) offers some excellent information on the borough's Doo Wop history, and visitors can pick up a map of current and former

© LAURA KINIRY

Cherubic faces welcome visitors to the Lollipop Motel in North Wildwood.

Doo Wop properties at the **Greater Wildwood Chamber of Commerce** (3306 Pacific Ave., 609/729-0639).

A Doo Wop Museum is expected to open in Wildwood near the Wildwood Convention Center by summer 2006 and will feature an outdoor garden of discarded signs from now-perished Doo Wop properties.

THE JERSEY SHORE

heated round pool, and beachfront locale, **The Pan American Hotel** (5901 Ocean Ave., Wildwood Crest, 609/522-6936, www.panamericanhotel.com) is so Miami beach. While not ultra-swanky indoors, rooms are clean and comfortable, and equipped with fridge and TV/VCR. An elevator, game room, and in-season activities for the kids make this a family-friendly choice.

$200-250: The **Armada By-The-Sea** (6503 Ocean Ave., Wildwood Crest, 609/729-3000, www.armadamotel.com) is a three-story

motel in a quiet part of town. Amenities include an elevator, heated outdoor pool, and air-conditioning, fridge, and microwave in all guestrooms. This is a good place for families.

The **◖ Starlux Motel** (305 E. Rio Grande Ave., Wildwood, 609/522-7412, www.thestarlux.com) is what every Doo Wop establishment strives to be—hip, modern, and always full. The motel is a renovated property—the Morey family (of boardwalk amusement pier fame) took the former Wingate and transformed it into a space congruent with Wildwood's motels of old, while adding updated amenities such as Internet access, an elevator, a whirlpool, and heated pool. Designers used recycled goods salvaged from the throwaways of demolished Doo Wop properties to create the most stylish and desirable place in town. Rooms are small and simple—wood furnishings, stainless steel doors—but include personal touches like lava lamps, and downstairs guests are treated to the all-glass Astro lounge. Behind the motel, renovated Airstream trailers offer a unique overnight experience.

Camping

About a 10-minute drive from Wildwood is **Acorn Campground** (Rte. 47, Green Creek, 609/886-7119, www.acorncampground.com, late May–early Sept.), a wooded resort with 330 sites for tents and RVs. Perks include free hot showers and two swimming pools. Sites run $35–40/night for a family of four.

Nearby is the family-friendly **King Nummy Trail Campground** (205 Rte. 47 S., Cape May Court House, 609/465-4242, www.kingnummytrail.com, late Apr.–Oct.). Tent and RV sites cost $28–30/night depending on amenities, and on-site cabins run $45–80/night.

Food and Nightlife

The Wildwoods are not a culinary hotspot, though you will find a number of places that are worthwhile. Schellenger Avenue, near the center of Wildwood, hosts a couple restaurants, including the campy **Schellenger's Restaurant** (3516 Atlantic Ave., 609/522-0533, $9.95–28.95, lunch and dinner in-season). This seasonal "Lobster City" serves up American entrées in a nautically themed setting, with early-bird specials and a children's menu. You can't miss it—just look for the waving lobster and yellow-clad fishermen on the roof. **Neil's Steak and Chowder House** (222 E. Schellenger Ave., 609/522-5226, $14–25) is a popular surf-and-turf where customers can chow down in dark wood booths under Tiffany-style lampshades. Free parking and an early-bird special are big draws. Neil's is open 4:30–10 P.M. daily

throughout summer, Friday and Saturday evenings until 9:30 P.M. in the shoulder seasons.

The **Blue Olive** (3601 Atlantic Ave., 609/522-7747, 5–10 P.M. Tues.–Sun., $23.50–39.50) is the swankiest joint in Wildwood and easily recognizable by the giant highball glass that decorates its exterior. The bar's high-back stools are the perfect place to relax while enjoying one of the Olive's specialty martinis. Or take a seat in the restaurant to sample the eclectic cuisine and excellent service.

In Wildwood Crest, locals recommend **Admiral's Quarters** (7200 Ocean Ave., 609/729-1133, 7 A.M.–2 P.M. daily throughout summer), on the bottom floor of the Admiral Resort Motel, for a good morning meal. Nearby, the upscale **Marie Nicole's** (9510 Pacific Ave., 609/522-5425, www.marienicoles.com, 5–10 P.M. daily, closed Tuesday, $21–32) serves eclectic American cuisine in an intimate setting.

If you're looking for a boardwalk snack, a stop by **Curley's Fries** (822 Boardwalk, 609/398-4040, $3.95) is a must. For something a bit more substantial, **Mack's Pizza** (4200 Boardwalk, 609/729-0244) serves the best slices in town.

If you're looking for a drink to go with your meal, stick to Wildwood and North Wildwood, where the food is good and the liquor is plenty. You can begin your night in true Irish fashion at the **Anglesea Pub** (116 W. 1st Ave., North Wildwood, 609/729-1133, 9 A.M.–3 A.M.), an authentic Irish pub housed in an 1885 building, and with all the features of its European homeland: Smithwicks draft, shepherd's pie, and Irish bands. The food receives high ratings and the crowd is decidedly more refined than Wildwood's typical twentysomething scene.

The massive **Moore's Inlet** (Spruce St. and Old New Jersey Ave., North Wildwood, 609/522-1016, www.mooresinlet.com) has been entertaining the Wildwoods for more than half a century, with five bars, including an outdoor patio. Enjoy a pitcher while watching the antics of local persona Cozy Morley or the Mummers' Avalon String Band as they strut their stuff. Moore's is open noon–3 A.M. daily throughout the summer, weekends April–mid-June.

The **Boathouse** (Rio Grande Ave., Wildwood, 609/729-5301, www.boathousewildwood.com) is a food and drink stop found at the foot of the Rio Grande Bridge. Go for the casual happy hour (4–6 P.M.) on the waterside deck, with discount drinks and apps, and stay for the broiled flounder ($17.95) and a martini as the sun slowly creeps away.

Information and Services

Wildwood's **Downtown Visitor Center** (609/729-4000) is located at 3306 Pacific Avenue, between Oak and Wildwood Avenues. It's open 9 A.M.–4:30 P.M. weekdays throughout the year. Be sure and pick up a map for the Doo Wop self-guided walking tour—though somewhat out of date (some of the motels have been torn down), it's still informative and makes for a great souvenir. Many of Wildwood's downtown streets are have metered parking—quarters only.

Along Route 47 on the mainland just before the bridge into Wildwood is the **Greater Wildwood Hotel Motel Association** (609/522-4546, www.wildwoods.org, 9 A.M.–5 P.M. Mon.–Fri., 10 A.M.–2 P.M. weekends), an information center stocked with maps and brochures pertaining to the Wildwoods, the majority in reference to overnight accommodations and area dining choices.

Getting There and Around

Wildwood is accessible from exit 4B southbound and 4 northbound off the Garden State Parkway, from Stone Harbor along scenic Ocean Drive, or heading east along the picturesque Route 47.

Cape May and Vicinity

With gas-lit streets, horse-drawn carriages, and over 600 gingerbread Victorians, Cape May feels like a step back in time. What began as a prosperous whaling town in the 17th century became by the 1850s the nation's "most famous seaside resort" and a choice presidential retreat, even hosting Abraham Lincoln. But by the 1970s the city had lost much of its charm, and its outdated architecture was bypassed for more modern towns like Beach Haven and Ocean City. Step in the Mid-Atlantic Center for the Arts, an organization that decided to use the Victorian overload to their advantage. There's no question as to whether it worked. Today the city is home to over 80 bed-and-breakfasts, as well as a plethora of tours, festivals, and events that center around the Victorian theme. Add to this the most moderate temperatures in New Jersey, and you've got yourself a 10-month tourist destination—a beachside resort that's just as popular in December as it is in July. Cape May takes a break after the first of the year, and many establishments close their doors for the month of January, trickling to a start in mid-February and slowing adding hours until reaching a full schedule by July. Some of the best months to visit Cape May are April–May and September–October, when crowds are fewer, prices are lower, and most of the city's seasonal establishments still hold limited business hours. Many of the city's finest festivals take place in fall, and butterfly and bird migration in the extended region is at its peak as well. The winter holidays are also a wonderful time to experience Cape May, with all the candlelight house tours, heated trolley rides, and horse-drawn carriage excursions, and with festive lights decorating much of the city's historic district and adding new life to already picturesque Victorian homes.

SIGHTS
The Emlen Physick Estate

In 1970, on the verge of demolition and about to be replaced with modern homes, the four-acre Physick Estate (1048 Washington St., 609/884-5404 or 800/275-4278, www.capemaymac.org)

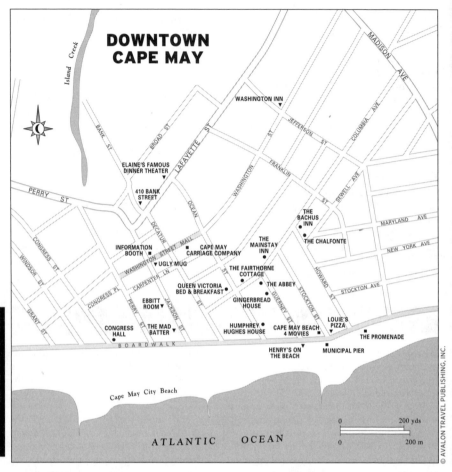

was saved by a group of preservationists, today known as the Mid-Atlantic Center for the Arts (MAC). The estate is now one of the city's jewels, a highlight on trolley rides and Christmas tours and a centerpiece to the community, and to the MAC organization. The estate includes a late-18th-century, 18-room Victorian mansion that was once the home of Dr. Emlen Physick, a descendant of the "father of American surgery." Its exterior is adorned with such exaggerations as gigantic inverted chimneys, while indoors you'll find finely furnished Victorian rooms and exhibits on 18th-century life that change throughout

the year. The estate's Carriage House displays a changing gallery of art and collector's exhibits ($2 adult, $1 child) and is home to the **Twinings Tea Room** (609/884-5404, ext. 138), serving a selection of finger sandwiches, snacks, and teas.

Tours of the estate are available 10:30 A.M.–3 P.M. daily May–October, 11 A.M.–3 P.M. daily November–December, 11 A.M.–2 P.M. weekends in January and March, call ahead for February hours, $8 adult, $4 child.

The Promenade

Lining the beachfront along Ocean Avenue is

Cape May's Congress Hall

Cape May's Promenade, a semi-commercial walkway that's perfect for a morning bike ride or a stroll, taking in the ocean view. This is where you'll find the city's arcades, as well as a couple of breakfast eateries and snack shops. Stop by **Morrow's Nut House** (609/884-4966) for beach essentials, as well as chocolates and candies (including red fish), and a bag of mixed nuts served warm and fresh.

BEACHES
Daily beach fees are $4/day, $9 for three days.

FESTIVALS AND EVENTS
As with Cape May's tours, many of the city's events are sponsored by MAC (609/884-5404 or 800/275-4278, www.capemaymac.org).

The **Cape May Food and Wine Festival** is an annual four-day September event that includes wine, beer, and gourmet meal-tasting around town. It resembles a conference, and a few classes are offered. Some events are free to attend—others cost varying amounts.

The **Cape May New Jersey State Film Festival** (609/884-6700, www.njstatefilm festival.com) takes place in late November.

For a true Victorian experience, attend one of two **Sherlock Holmes Weekends** held in March and November. These sleuthing adventures feature an entire cast of characters, including local Victorian-era businessman John Wanamaker, as well as Holmes himself and his partner Watson. Prizes are awarded for the best Victorian costumes if you're so inclined, and part of the clue-sniffing includes a tour through the city's famous B&Bs. If a weekend isn't enough for a step back in time, a 10-day **Victorian Week** takes place in October, chock-full of murder mysteries, antique shows, house tours, music, and a Victorian fashion show.

SHOPPING
Most of Cape May's shopping ops are found along **Washington Street Mall** (609/884-2133, www.washingtonstreetmall.com), a pedestrian-only stretch lined with stores and restaurants. Here and along the nearby side

streets are shops selling antiques, lighthouse collectibles, Cape May logo sweatshirts, clothing and footwear, and bookstores stocking local folklore and legend. Many items are unique to Cape May, though this is not the place to come for extensive retail shopping. On the first floor of nearby **Congress Hall** (251 Beach Ave.) is a hallway of shops, again catering to antiques and historic souvenirs. Across from the city's beachfront Promenade (Beach Ave.) you'll find additional stores selling clothing and specialty items, worth a look if you're in the area.

RECREATION AND TOURS

For bicycles, try **Shield's Bike Rentals** (11 Guerney St., 609/898-1818, 7 A.M.–7 P.M.), where you can rent both two-seat ($15/hour) and four-seat ($30/hour) surreys or individual cruisers ($9) for the day.

Aqua Trails (956 Ocean Dr., 609/884-5600, www.aquatrails.com) offers guided, sunset, and full-moon kayak nature tours ($40 single, $75 double), and rents kayaks for use on the bay or the Atlantic. They're located along the road leading south from Wildwood Crest. Rental rates are $20/$30 for one hour with a single/double kayak, $75/$85 for full-day or overnight use. A surf kayak, intended for ocean use, runs $75 for a full day.

The **Cape May Whale Watcher** (609/884-5445 or 800/786-5445, www.capemaywhalewatcher.com) runs two- and three-hour whale-and dolphin-watching tours on a 110-foot boat March–December. Trips leave from the Miss Chris Marina along the Cape May Canal, and cost $23/$30 adult, $12/$18 child. **Salt Marsh Safari** (609/884-3100, www.skimmer.com, $22 adult, $12 child) offers two-hour coastal tours through the Cape's back bays aboard *The Skimmer,* a 41-passenger covered pontoon boat. Trips depart daily at 10 A.M., 1:30 P.M., or 6 P.M. March–December from Cape May's Miss Chris Marina near the causeway into Wildwood Crest. However, every Wednesday and Thursday mid-June–Labor Day, they depart from Stone Harbor's Wetlands Institute (the 6 P.M. Thursday excursion continues to depart from Miss Chris Marina throughout summer).

The Mid-Atlantic Center for the Arts (www.capemaymac.org) runs most of the city's tours, selling tickets at the **Washington Street Mall Information Booth** (429 Washington St., 609/884-2368). Stop by the booth or check MAC's website for an updated schedule. Popular tours include day and evening **Trolley Tours, Historic Walking Tours,** and the annual **Christmas Candlelight House Tours** (these are a favorite so book ahead).

Across the street from the information booth is the carriage stop for the **Cape May Carriage Company** (641 Sunset Blvd., 609/884-4466, www.capemaycarriage.com), which offers daily horse-drawn-carriage historic tours throughout the summer, continuing on weekends during spring and fall. Private tours are available December to New Year's. An eight-person group tour costs $10 adult, $4 child; private tours are up to $50 for up to four people.

ENTERTAINMENT AND NIGHTLIFE

The city's not a nightlife hotspot per se, but there are a few establishments that are good choices for a night out.

Locals tend to hit up the seasonal Marques De Lafayette's **Fin Bar** (510 Beach Ave., 609/884-3500) in the late afternoon on their way home from the beach. Those in the know still refer to it as the "Barefoot Bar," the former incarnation of this poolside place. Next it's on to the nearby **Rusty Nail** (Coachman's Motor Inn, 205 Beach Ave., 609/884-0220, mid-May–mid-October) for a second round of drinks. Located just across the street from the beach, the Nail also serves breakfast, lunch, and dinner daily throughout summer, with the bar usually closing around 2 A.M. Live music rocks the weekends at this casual space. The third stop is Congress Hall's **Brown Room** (251 Beach Ave., 609/884-8421, open nightly year-round), not your typical beach establishment. With a chocolate-mahogany interior resembling a library and a faded zebra-print rug welcoming sandaled feet, this place is styling, and worth an inland effort to prep for the evening. A fireplace makes it the perfect martini hangout during cold winter months. In the hotel's basement is the trendy **Boiler Room** (609/884-6507). Built into Congress Hall's original foundation, this nightclub is the place to come for dancing, jazz, and blues.

The **Ugly Mug** (426 Washington St., 609/884-3459, 10:30 A.M.–midnight Mon.–Fri., 10:30 A.M.–1 A.M. weekends) is the best place to chill with a draft anytime of the year. Grab a stool at the center bar after pumping the jukebox with quarters (but no more Jimmy Buffet, please), and linger through the evening.

The fourplex **Cape May Beach 4 Movies** (711 Beach Ave.) is a first-run movie theater located across the street from the Promenade.

For something different try **Elaine's Famous Dinner Theater** (513 Lafayette St., 609/884-4358, www.elainesdinnertheater.com, $39.95 adult, $27.95 teen, $16.95 child). Located within Elaine's Victorian Inn, this fun place specializes in entertainment both frightening and fun, and all shows are accompanied by a three-course meal. Elaine's also features a "haunted" restaurant open mid-May–late October, and hosts hour-long Ghost Tours of Cape May ($10 adult, $5 child) nightly during summer.

ACCOMMODATIONS
Hotels

While bed-and-breakfasts make up the bulk of Cape May's accommodations, there are a handful of stately hotels that are definitely worth a stay.

$250-300: Over a century and a quarter old, the **Chalfonte** (301 Howard St., 609/884-8409 or 888/411-1998, www.chalfonte.com,) is a 70-room hotel featuring gorgeous wraparound covered porches, a solarium, a Southern-style restaurant, bar, and three additional cottages for overnight stays. You won't find heating, air-conditioning, or the usual modern amenities here, and many of the rooms have shared bath, though they do include sinks with separate hot and cold faucets. Rates may be a bit steep for your average getaway, but the price is worth it for this step back in time. For those who are intrigued but would rather not part with the cash, the Chalfonte offers spring and

fall work weekends—for $25 and 10 hours of work split between two days (with afternoons off), you get meals (Fri. evening–Sun. lunch) and a two-night stay.

Once serving as a summer White House for President Benjamin Harrison and host to numerous other U.S. presidents, the restored **Congress Hall** (251 W. Beach Ave., 609/884-8421 or 888/944-1816, www.congress hall.com) is a Cape May treasure. The first floor of this 1816 L-shaped hotel is filled with gift shops, a favored American restaurant, a zebra-accented lounge, and a day spa—all are open to the public. Upstairs, 107 guestrooms have been gloriously remade in subdued modern colors that blend perfectly with their historic surroundings. All feature DVD players and wireless Internet. One of Cape May's only nightclubs is tucked below within the hotel's basement, and outside an in-ground pool and adjacent bar stand just across the road from the beach. Book well ahead—plenty of advance notice is needed to score a room during high season.

Bed-and-Breakfasts

Cape May has one of the largest and best selection of B&Bs on the planet. While many of these places offer modern amenities, others are as Victorian as their exterior, without phones, TVs, or air-conditioning, and some with shared bath only. Unfortunately, the city's B&Bs are no longer allowed to provide complimentary beach tags to guests, though some places will allow you to "borrow" their personal stock. Many of the city's overnight establishments require a minimum stay during the high season, and parking is not always provided—it's best to check ahead.

$150-200: The Abbey (34 Guerney St., 609/884-4506, www.abbeybedand breakfast.com) is an 1869 Gothic Victorian elegantly decorated in traditional period furniture, like puckered chaise lounge chairs and dark walnut beds. Guestrooms, which include those in a nearby cottage, come with full breakfast, private bath, fan, and an in-room refrigerator. Some air-conditioned units are available and parking is provided with main house stays, though the cottage tends to be more economical.

The Bacchus Inn (710 Columbia Ave., 609/884-2129, www.bacchusinn.com) is a simple B&B offering four rooms and one suite, each with private bath, TV, and air-conditioning, and some with fireplace. A full breakfast and afternoon wine and cheese are offered daily, but the highlight here is the billiards table.

$200-250: The year-round **Queen Victoria Bed & Breakfast** (102 Ocean St., 609/884-8702, www.queenvictoria.com) is centrally located within the city's historic district. Handmade quilts adorn many of the beds of this spacious Victorian inn, and amenities include private bath, air-conditioning, TV, wireless Internet, and fridge, as well as a buffet breakfast, rooftop deck, and complimentary use of bicycles.

Also within the historic district is the two-story **Gingerbread House** (28 Guerney St., 609/884-0211, www.gingerbreadinn.com), a lovely 1869 Carpenter Gothic–style B&B with six antique-filled guestrooms, some with private bath, and all with air-conditioning and flat-screen TV. A buffet breakfast and afternoon refreshments are served daily, and board games are available for rainy days. Wireless Internet is available.

Built in 1892 by a whaling captain, **The Fairthorne Cottage** (111 Ocean St., 609/884-8791 or 800/438-8742, www.fairthorne.com) is a pretty B&B, its wraparound porch lined with rocking chairs. Four guestrooms and two suites are each elegantly decorated in Victorian design, and include private bath, TV/VCR, and fridge.

$250-300: One of Cape May's largest B&Bs, the **Humphrey Hughes House** (29 Ocean St., 609/884-4428, www.humphreyhugheshouse.com) features a sweeping veranda and generously sized Victorian-inspired guestrooms. Full breakfast is served daily, and amenities include TV, air-conditioning, private bath, and toiletries.

$300-350: The Mainstay Inn (635 Columbia Ave., 609/884-8690, www.mainstayinn.com) is made up of three buildings, the most

prominent of which is a 19th-century Italian villa that once served as a gambling club. The inn has nine guestrooms and seven suites, all with private bath, air-conditioning, flat-screen TV, and wireless Internet. Parking is provided with some of the rooms, and a family-style breakfast is served.

FOOD

Cape May has some of the best restaurants in the state, let alone the Jersey Shore. While the selection is not ethnically diverse, its style is quite impressive, and restaurants run the gamut from beachside breakfast eateries to casual grills to fine dining amid grand Victorian settings. You'll find something to fit every level of comfort, morning, noon, and night—so eat up; it's worth it.

Casual Eateries

The **Ugly Mug** (426 Washington St., 609/884-3459, 10:30 A.M.–midnight Mon.–Fri., 10:30–1 A.M. weekends, $9–17) is one of my favorite spots. Sure, it's somewhat touristy, but this just adds to the plethora of people-watching opportunities both inside and along the Washington Street Mall, where you can snag an outdoor table during warmer months. The food is good, with simple American eats—pair a crab cake sandwich with a Yuengling draft and you can't go wrong. If you're headed indoors, be sure to request a seat in the original section under the ceiling of mugs (those of deceased Mug members face seaward)—the authentic atmosphere is worth it.

For weekend brunch there's no place better than **The Mad Batter** (19 Jackson St., 609/884-5970, www.madbatter.com, $19.50–32), located within the Carroll Villa Bed-and-Breakfast in the heart of the downtown historic district. Menu items include oatmeal pancakes with real maple syrup ($8.50) and orange and almond French toast ($6.50). I recommend choosing a table on the outdoor porch if it's open—these are some of the best seats in town.

On the first floor of Congress Hall is the **Blue Pig Tavern** (Congress Hall, 251 W. Beach Ave., 609/884-8421, 7 A.M.–3 P.M. and

5–10 P.M. daily), an American eatery serving three meals daily in two eye-catching dining rooms of pink, white, and dark wood decor. During summer tables spill outdoors under umbrellas and onto covered porch seating. Fish-and-chips ($15) is a favorite.

Though a bit of a tourist trap, **The Lobster House** (Fisherman's Wharf, Schellenger Landing, 609/884-8296, $18.50–39.95) remains a popular place for its family atmosphere, well-rounded meals, and dockside location. This spacious, seafaring restaurant serves fresh lobsters, and also has a casual raw bar and market where you can sit back with a shrimp melt ($7) or a burger with fries ($6). Hours are 11:30 A.M.– 3 P.M. and 5–10 P.M. Monday–Saturday, 2– 9 P.M. Sunday, mid-June–late November, and vary the rest of the year—call ahead.

For pies and slices there's **Louie's Pizza** (711 Beach Ave., 609/884-0305, 10 A.M.–10 P.M.), located at the end of a side street across from the Promenade.

My sister-in-law grew up in Cape May and swears by **McGlades** (722 Beach Ave., 609/884-2614, $6–17) as the best breakfast in town. Known for their selection of omelets, this beachfront property also offers an unbeatable view of the Atlantic and an endless ocean breeze. Open daily throughout the summer.

Fine Dining

Cape May offers some of the best fine-dining options in the state. Most restaurants are open throughout the year, though hours are gradually cut back after Labor Day, sometimes even closing through January before beginning back up again on weekends only, and operating a nearly full schedule (5–7 nights a week) by Memorial Day.

Godmother's Restaurant (413 S. Broadway, 609/884-4543, $20–28) is another local favorite that's been in business for over two decades. The BYO has changed chefs, but its high-caliber Italian cuisine hasn't suffered. Steak and seafood are both well-represented, but one of Godmother's best features is its mix-and-match pastas and sauces ($9.95–11.95). The restaurant is open 5–9 P.M. daily through-

out summer, tapering off to weekends only as the year progresses.

Located on the lower floor of the Virginia Hotel is the **Ebbitt Room** (25 Jackson St., 609/884-5700, www.virginiahotel.com, 5–9 P.M. nightly, $25–34), an elegant New American dining room that's been renovated and restored to its posh Victorian splendor. A pianist provides a musical backdrop for meals weekends throughout winter, expanding to a nightly performance by July and August. Fresh baked desserts, homemade ice cream, and a full bar are reasons to return—as if you need any.

The Louisiana-style **410 Bank Street** (410 Bank St., 609/884-2127 $29.95–36.95) is a Cape May staple, serving up French-inspired Cajun and Creole cuisine in a clapboard cottage flanked by an entryway that curves through dense vegetation and overhang. Numerous dining areas include a glass porch and outdoor patio, and overhead fans keep indoor patrons cool during steamy summer months. A well-versed staff adds to the experience.

Revered for its outstanding wine selection, the **Washington Inn** (801 Washington St., 609/884-5697, www.washingtoninn.com, $19–40) also features a seasonally changing menu of American entrées served in a fine Victorian setting. Specials include a three-course early dinner menu served 5–6 P.M. Wednesday–Sunday evenings ($19), and a 25 percent discount on wines/no corkage fee for BYO on Sundays. The restaurant opens at 5 P.M. daily during summer months, trickling off to weekends only by November. Closing hours vary.

The **Black Duck on Sunset** (1 Sunset Blvd., West Cape May, 609/898-0100, 5–10 P.M. daily June–Sept., $22–29) serves New American cuisine in a comfortable space that includes black and white photos of old Cape May adorning the walls, and a porch for warm summer evenings. Call for off-season hours.

Away from the bustle of downtown, **Peter Shields Restaurant** (1304 W. Beach Ave., 609/884-9090, $22–34) serves a rotating menu of New American entrées in a spacious and romantic setting with lovely ocean views. Although a selection of Cape May Vineyard wines is available for purchase, the restaurant is also a BYO. Dinner is served starting at 5:30 P.M. daily throughout the year, and the restaurant is closed on Mondays in the off-season.

SERVICES

The **Cape May Spa at Congress Hall** (609/898-2429, www.capemaydayspa.com) offers an array of massages, treatments, and baths, as well as manicures and pedicures.

GETTING THERE AND AROUND

Cape May and Cape May Point are located at the beginning of the Garden State Parkway. From Wildwood Crest, travel south along Ocean Drive (Route 621) over the causeway bridge, turning east onto Lafayette Street (Route 109) to reach the city. To get to Cape May Point from downtown Cape May follow Sunset Boulevard west. Both Cape May and Cape May Point can be reached from the mainland by traveling Route 47 (from Philadelphia take Route 42 to Route 55, which runs into Route 47) to Route 9 South and following the signs to Cape May.

CAPE MAY POINT

Ten minutes west of Cape May City is Cape May Point, a less-than-square-mile borough where you'll find quiet beaches, a state park and a lighthouse, and the meeting of the Atlantic Ocean and Delaware Bay. Unlike its big sister to the east, the Point has only one general store and no bed-and-breakfasts, and strict zoning laws keep homes mostly single-family. There's good opportunity for kayaking and sailing around the point, and this is one of the best spots in the state, if not the country, for birdwatching. Possible sightings include hawks, falcons, eagles, ducks, geese, and herons.

Cape May Point State Park

Sand dunes, woods, and coastal freshwater marshes and ponds make up the 235-acre Cape May Point State Park (Lighthouse Ave., Cape May Point, 609/884-2159, free), a key spot on the New Jersey Coastal Heritage Trail. In

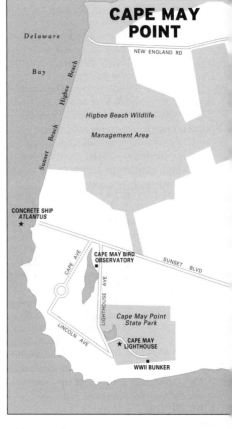

addition to hosting numerous walkways and boardwalks, the park is a great place to spot birds—watch for waterfowl, songbirds, raptors, shorebirds and sea birds from the raptor viewing platform. Upon the grounds is the romantic **Cape May Lighthouse,** an active 199-step whitewashed lighthouse, 157 feet tall and nearly 150 years old. It's a popular spot for couples to get engaged, and tours are given at varying times throughout the year ($5 adult, $1 child). Nearby there's an old WWII defense bunker being devoured by the sea.

In 2004–2005 the Army Corps of Engineers pumped millions of yards of sand onto the beach in efforts to save the migratory wildlife. In the process the beaches were rescued for

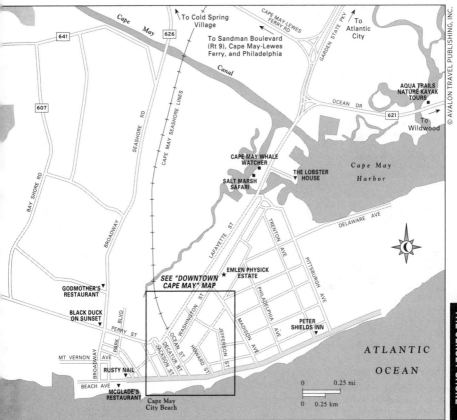

the public—a good thing, because long Shore drifts were causing the coastline to disappear.

Sunset Beach

Sunset Beach (800/757-6468, www.sunsetbeach nj.com) is a gorgeous little beach with a cluster of shops and a flag-lowering ceremony held every evening at dusk. This is the only beach in the state where the sun both rises and sets over water, and the only place to find Cape May Diamonds—bits of crystal quartz churned into creation by the sea. These sparkling gems are all over the sands, plentiful and free. Fifty yards out to sea are the still-visible remains of the *Atlantus,* a WWI concrete ship that continues to be slowly swallowed by the ocean.

The **Sunset Beach Gift Shop** (502 Sunset Blvd., 609/884-7079) sells candles, lighthouse collectibles, calendars, and a small stock of local literature and Jersey Shore tunes, including the Al Albert classic "On the Way to Cape May." Local jewelers will polish your diamond finds, or you can purchase them pre-polished here for $1 a package. The shop also sells Cape May Diamonds as part of a necklace, ring, or earrings. Additional beachfront stores include **Sunset Apparel,** a fossil shop, and a grill.

Higbee Beach

Just around the western bend from Sunset Beach is Higbee Beach, a 1.5-mile crescent-shaped sliver of white sand scattered with wood

© LAURA KINIRY

sunset over the concrete remains of the *Atlantus*, Sunset Beach, Cape May Point

shoots and bordered by smooth blue waters. In the early summer the armor of horseshoe crabs lies along the beach, casualties to the hungry shorebirds, and throughout the year you can watch the ferry take route from the nearby Cape May Canal. This is truly a peaceful place.

Separating the beach from the parking areas is a coastal dune forest of holly, cedar, beach plum, and brush fields, and you'll find marked nature trails within. Both the beach and the forest are part of the **Higbee Beach Wildlife Management Area** (609/628-2103), open daily 5 A.M.–9 P.M.

The beach is dog-friendly and was "clothing-optional" until 2000, but these days covering up is strictly enforced.

Cape May–Lewes Ferry

The Cape May–Lewes Ferry (Sandman Blvd. and Lincoln Dr., North Cape May, 800/64-FERRY or 800/643-3779, www.capemaylewesferry.com) is a car and passenger ferry linking Cape May to Lewes, Delaware, seven miles north of the resort town of Rehoboth Beach.

Ferries run round-trip throughout the year (70 minutes one-way) but schedules vary according to season. One-way fares are $13 for foot passengers with shuttle, $20/$25 for car and driver, and $6/$8 for each additional passenger.

Cape May Bird Observatory

The Cape May Bird Observatory has two locations, each run by the New Jersey Audubon Society. The **Northwood Center** (701 East Lake Dr., 609/884-2736, 9 A.M.–4:30 P.M. Thurs.–Mon.) is located just up the road from the Cape May Lighthouse and is a central spot for bird enthusiasts. If you're a gardener, the **Center for Research and Education** (609/861-0700, 1–4:30 P.M. daily) along Route 47 North in Cape May Court House features a Model Backyard Habitat, which shows how to manifest your own backyard wilderness, replete with hummingbirds. The observatory hosts public programs year-round that include nature walks, butterfly and bird sightings, and the popular seasonal Back Bay Birding by Boat ($30). For more information on where to meet and how to register, check the Audubon Observatory website at www.njaudubon.org/Centers/CMBO, or call the Cape May Natural History and Events Hotline at 609/861-0466. For updates regarding recent bird sightings in the region, call 609/898-BIRD (609/898-2473).

The **Nature Center of Cape May** (1600 Delaware Ave., 609/898-8848, www.njaudubon .org/Centers/NCCM) is the official home of Cape May's Audubon Society and hosts a variety of volunteer and educational programs throughout the year. The center is open 9 A.M.–4 P.M. daily June–September, 10 A.M.–3 P.M. Tuesday–Saturday October–December and April–May, 10 A.M.–1 P.M. Tuesday–Saturday January–March.

World Series of Birding

In 2005 over 1,000 people participated in the **World Series of Birding** (609/884-2736, www.njaudubon.org/WSB), an annual Audubon Society event that takes place over a 24-hour period in May. Teams consist of 4–6 players, and bird-spotting can be done in one of two ways—either on a regulated platform or by travel within a specified region. Everyone in a group must spot the bird for it to count, and teams must check in at Cape May Point State Park before the allotted time is over. The competition is open to all.

Camping

Cape Island Campground (709 Rte. 9, Cape May, 609/884-5777 or 800/437-7443, www.capeisland.com, May–Nov.) hosts themed activities like a Hawaiian pig roast, Mexican fiesta night, and a country Western night. The campground is located right across from Cold Spring Village, minutes from downtown Cape May. Tent and RV sites run $27–41/night with water and electric, $32–47/night with the addition of sewer and cable.

A bit further north is the enormous **Seashore Campground** (720 Seashore Rd., Cape May, 609/884-4010, mid-Apr.–Oct.), a 600-site resort with amenities that include a heated swimming pool, billiards tables, a camp store, and a lake. Basic tent sites run $20–35,

tent and RV sites with water, electric, and cable cost $20–42.

ROUTE 9: SOMERS POINT-CAPE MAY COURT HOUSE

Route 9 is an alternative route to the Garden State Parkway and Ocean Drive. The road averages about 50 miles an hour and has plenty of stops—you can spend an entire day just exploring the shops and sights. Along the way you'll see plenty of campgrounds, miniature golf courses, and seasonal ice cream stands. Numerous antique stores that give this stretch the nickname "antique alley" remain open throughout the winter. Route 9 continues north into Atlantic County, past Smithville and the Brigantine Wildlife Refuge, and on through Forked River and Tuckerton on the way toward Toms River.

Cold Spring Village

Cold Spring Village is a seasonal 19th-century outdoor living-history museum (720 Rte. 9, 609/898-2300, www.hcsv.org, $8 adult, $5 child) with 25 restored buildings and costumed interpreters displaying forgotten crafts like bookbinding, weaving, and basket-making. In addition to farm animals, a restaurant, and an ice cream parlor, a highlight is the **Seashore Lines Train** (www.seashorelines.com, 609/884-2675, $5 adult, $4 child round-trip) that runs a loop into downtown Cape May and the nearby Cape May Zoo during summer months. Cold Spring Village is open 10:30 A.M.–4:30 P.M. weekends Memorial Day–mid-June and Labor Day–mid-September, and Tuesday–Sunday mid-June–Labor Day.

Nearby, take note of the striking **Cold Spring Cemetery,** a Presbyterian cemetery open to all denominations.

Cape May National Wildlife Refuge

Bird-watching enthusiasts will love the Cape May National Wildlife Refuge (24 Kimbles Beach Rd., Cape May Court House, 609/463-0994, www.fws.gov/northeast/capemay), where you may see migratory birds such as flycatchers, orioles, and tanagers, and endangered species

THE JERSEY SHORE

like the piping plover. The habitat is one of the state's newer wildlife refuges, founded in 1989, and caters to hundreds of bird species and dozens of reptiles, mammals, and amphibians, as well as sea life and invertebrates. In the fall, over 15 species of raptors can be spotted from here.

A handful of nature trails are ideal for spotting wildlife and for nature photography. Headquarters are open 8 A.M.–4:30 P.M. Monday–Friday. The trails are open to the public daily.

Cape May Zoo

My parents love bringing my nephews to the free Cape May Country Park and Zoo (Rte. 9 and Pine Ln., 609/465-5271, www.capemaytimes.com/cape-may-county/zoo). Some kids may find the reptile house a little frightening, but they'll love seeing the monkeys and giraffes. Lions, tigers, and bears are all accounted for on the park's 178 wooded acres. It's open 10 A.M.–4:45 P.M. daily.

Cape May Court House

Not to be confused with an actual courthouse, the town of Cape May Court House is centrally located along Route 9 and has a charming stretch of stores and small cafés. Grab a cup of coffee before heading back on the road, or take time to explore the **Cape May County Historical Museum** (504 Rte. 9 N., 609/465-3535).

Leaming's Run Gardens

The largest annual gardens in the United States are Leaming's Run Gardens (1845 Rte. 9 N., Swainton, 609/465-5871, www.leamings rungardens.com, $7 adult, $4 child), 30 acres of individual landscapes that draw swarms of hummingbirds in the late summer. Stroll through 25 themed sections and the **Old Hickory Arboretum & Display Gardens,** past a brook, and along a mile-long walking path that meanders through the property. Hours are 9:30 A.M.–5 P.M. daily, mid-May–mid-October.

CENTRAL JERSEY AND THE PINELANDS

Central Jersey is often overlooked when it comes to the Garden State. Travelers pass through en route from Philadelphia to New York aboard interstate systems and Amtrak trains, and New Jersey's own residents opt for city lights and the Shore. To many, the central portion of the Garden State is little more than a crossroads. And that's what it always has been. From the time of the American Revolution, central New Jersey was where men met and battles were fought. Armies traversed the land from Mercer to Monmouth and back again, and their legacy is evident throughout the region today. Historic villages and parks are plentiful in this center portion, as are bustling cultural centers and intellectual towns.

While not an area of sharp geological contrast, Central Jersey does span a uniquely diverse geographical region. Cities along the Delaware River give way to undulating hills and plentiful horse farms. "Pick-your-own" orchards line the path between tiny hamlets and new development, and traffic-congested highways carve a route from one town to the next. Toward the east the land gives way to affluent suburbs and funky river towns.

Central Jersey's towns and cities are as distinct as its attractions. You could spend a day touring old battlefields and state museums, or instead drive through an African safari and later picnic at the fictitious landing ground of martians. You might spend an evening dining in Trenton's Italian neighborhood or an afternoon people-watching along Red Bank's main drag.

Both Princeton and Rutgers University are found in Central Jersey, and Albert Einstein

© LAURA KINIRY

HIGHLIGHTS

LOOK FOR ◖ TO FIND RECOMMENDED SIGHTS, ACTIVITIES, DINING, AND LODGING.

◖ **Grounds for Sculpture:** Jump into the Impressionist surrounds of this unique outdoor museum and delight in a world of mythical creatures, never-ending dinner parties, and sculptured parasols (page 221).

◖ **Following Washington's Footsteps:** General George was all over Central Jersey – this is where America got its groove back during the Revolution, and there's no better place to be walking in the leader's shoes. **Washington Crossing State Park** is where he landed after his famous trip across the Delaware, and **Monmouth Battlefield State Park** commemorates the longest battle of the war (page 224 and 253).

◖ **Princeton University:** One of America's oldest universities, this gorgeously Gothic campus features a world-class art museum, an administrative building once bombarded by cannons, and all the greenery you can get. Add to this a faculty that includes author Joyce Carol Oates and mathematician John Nash, as well as an alumni list for the books, and you've got yourself a must-see (page 226).

◖ **Jane Voorhees Zimmerli Art Museum:** The largest collection of non-conformist ex-Soviet art in the West is in New Brunswick? You betcha – and what a display (page 237).

◖ **Food in Red Bank:** If it's summer, choose from the plethora of sidewalk tables along Broad Street, or in the winter take it indoors to one of the borough's numerous cafés, restaurants, and bars. Not only are the choices eclectic, but the people-watching is fab (page 243).

◖ **Six Flags:** Where else can you drive through an African safari, see Batman take on Catwoman, tackle more than a dozen roller coasters, and follow it up with a float down the river, all in one afternoon (page 256)?

◖ **Canoeing and Kayaking in the Pinelands:** The largest track of forest from Maine to Virginia, and all the tea-colored water you can ask for. Grab a paddle and go (page 264)!

and Thomas Edison each spent great portions of their lives here. The area has remained throughout the years an intellectual hub, and a cultural one as well.

For those interested in the outdoors, Central Jersey offers sloping hills and hiking trails at Monmouth Battlefield State Park, golf and horseback riding around Colts Neck, and kayaking along the Manasquan and Toms Rivers. Of course, some of the best outdoor opportunities are found within the New Jersey Pinelands, a heavily forested, sandy-soiled acreage beginning in Central Jersey and pulling downward into the state's southern region. Remnants of abandoned iron towns can still be seen, but don't venture too far or you may come face to face with the Jersey Devil himself. Bat-like wings, cloven hoofs, and a horse-like face are possible ways to identity him, the 13th child of a Mrs. Leeds.

PLANNING YOUR TIME

Like much of the state, the possibilities for weekend trips in Central Jersey are endless. If you're heading south from New York City, consider making Red Bank your base and explore the shops and restaurants around town. The next day, take a drive over to Rumson Road for a tour of all the fancy houses that aren't hiding behind walls and trees. Afterward, you can either head north to explore the Bayshore region, or drive west for golfing in Colts Neck or a picnic in one of Holmdel's parks.

If history is your thing, there's plenty to see, and Trenton is an ideal base for exploring. At the Old Barrack's Museum, you can brush up on your knowledge of the French and Indian War. Take a stroll down State Street and maybe stop in the Department of State, driving north along Route 29 to Washington Crossing State Park. From here you can travel the backroads east to Princeton, where's there's plenty of history to explore and restaurants to eat at. Depending on the time, take a detour through Cranbury's historic village—and be sure to stop at the War of the Worlds monument in Van Nest Park. The following morning, head south to Bordentown for a self-guided history tour. If you've traveled from New York, detour through Monmouth Battlefield State Park before heading home.

Other possible excursions include combining an afternoon shopping in Princeton with an evening of fine dining and theater in New Brunswick, followed up with a day at the Freehold horse races or a fossil excursion in Holmdel Park. Do the pop culture thing by hitting up Springsteen's hometown of Freehold, Kevin Smith's adopted town of Red Bank, and making a pit stop at the Hindenburg Crash Site. Explore the great minds of New Jersey in Princeton and Edison by taking a tour of Einstein's town and visiting the extremely interesting Edison museum.

INFORMATION

The **Molly Pitcher Travel Plaza and Information Center** (609/655-4330) is located along the New Jersey Turnpike at mile marker 71.9 South in Cranbury.

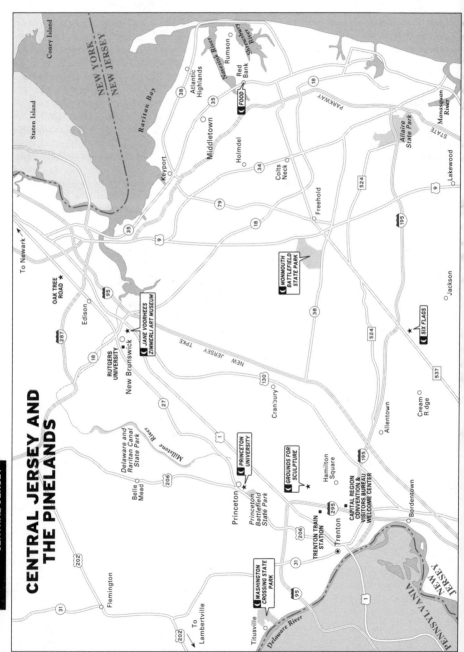

CENTRAL JERSEY

CENTRAL JERSEY AND THE PINELANDS

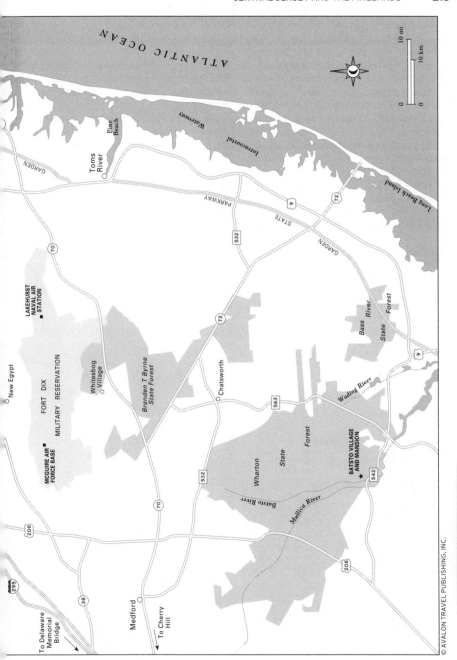

ATLANTIC OCEAN

10 mi
10 km

Intracoastal Waterway

Pine Beach

Toms River

GARDEN

Long Beach Island

PARKWAY

STATE

9

72

GARDEN

532

70

LAKEHURST NAVAL AIR STATION ■

Bass River State Forest

72

9

New Egypt

FORT DIX MILITARY RESERVATION

Whitesbog Village

Brenden T Byrne State Forest

Chatsworth

Wading River

MCGUIRE AIR FORCE BASE ■

563

Wharton State Forest

BATSTO VILLAGE AND MANSION ★

542

532

70

Batsto River

Mullica River

206

206

295

38

Medford

To Cherry Hill

To Delaware Memorial Bridge

CENTRAL JERSEY

Trenton and the Capital Region

What began as a small river settlement was re-established in 1721 as the industrial township of "Trent's Town." William Trent, a wealthy Philadelphia merchant and Trent's Town founder, chose his location in part because of its central proximity to Philadelphia and New York City. Today Trenton, New Jersey's state capital, remains an essential crossroads of the Northeast Corridor and centerpiece to the state's history. Though the city has seen better days, both aesthetically and financially, Trenton's downtown district is surprisingly inviting and has much to offer visitors, including numerous museums and a handful of eateries—there's even a minor league baseball club and stadium. Nearby is Trenton's revitalized **Mill Hill** section, home to an excellent theater company, and a bit further from downtown the largely residential **Chambersburg District.** Sometimes called "Little Italy" and known locally—and to fans of Janet Evanovich's best-selling Stephanie Plum series—as "the Burg," it's a haven of long-established and reputable restaurants serving as Trenton's own historic dining region.

Just outside the city, the Capital region is one of New Jersey's most prolific hubs. Route 295 and I-195 form a crossroads of congested traffic, carrying drivers east and south across the state. Route 29 heads north into the Skylands, hugging the Delaware River, and Route 1 travels diagonally northward, crossing through university towns straight through to the Hudson River. Historic towns and sprawling suburbs share this surrounding space, offering numerous afternoon excursions from Trenton.

History

Trenton has a history as varied as its inhabitants, with some of the most important events occurring between the 17th and 20th centuries. Colonists in Trenton, along with those

State Street, downtown Trenton

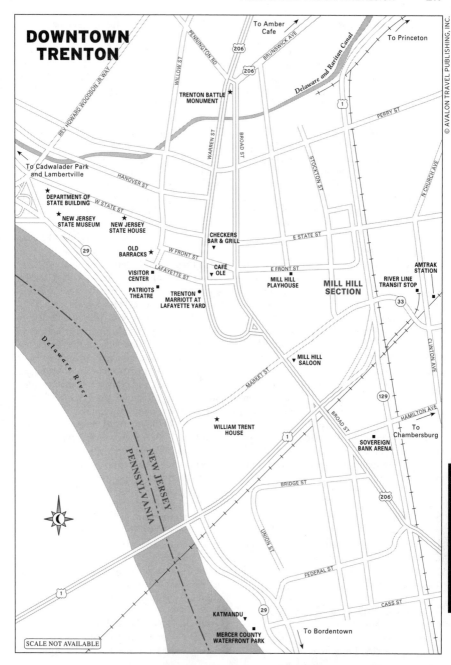

DOWNTOWN TRENTON

To Amber Cafe

To Princeton

PENNINGTON RD

BRUNSWICK AVE

206

206

Delaware and Raritan Canal

1

PERRY ST

WILLOW ST

★ TRENTON BATTLE MONUMENT

WARREN ST

BROAD ST

STOCKTON ST

N CHURCH AVE

REV. HOWARD WOODSON JR WAY

To Cadwalader Park and Lambertville

HANOVER ST

★ DEPARTMENT OF STATE BUILDING

W STATE ST

E STATE ST

★ NEW JERSEY STATE MUSEUM

★ NEW JERSEY STATE HOUSE

29

★ OLD BARRACKS

W FRONT ST

CHECKERS BAR & GRILL ▼

E FRONT ST

AMTRAK STATION

LAFAYETTE ST

CAFÉ OLE ▼

RIVER LINE TRANSIT STOP

VISITOR CENTER ■

MILL HILL PLAYHOUSE ■

MILL HILL SECTION

33

PATRIOTS THEATRE ■

TRENTON MARRIOTT AT LAFAYETTE YARD ●

CLINTON AVE

MILL HILL SALOON ▼

Delaware River

MARKET ST

129

HAMILTON AVE

To Chambersburg

NEW JERSEY

PENNSYLVANIA

★ WILLIAM TRENT HOUSE

1

BROAD ST

SOVEREIGN BANK ARENA ■

BRIDGE ST

206

UNION ST

FEDERAL ST

1

CASS ST

KATMANDU ▼

29

To Bordentown

MERCER COUNTY WATERFRONT PARK ●

SCALE NOT AVAILABLE

© AVALON TRAVEL PUBLISHING, INC.

CENTRAL JERSEY

living at Philadelphia and Easton, Pennsylvania, heard their newly penned Declaration of Independence read aloud—surely a time of tremendous amazement, fear, anxiety, and anticipation for those in attendance. Trenton also saw one of the most famous events in American history just six months later, in the early morning hours of a bitterly cold and windy December 26, 1776. A stately Virginian General George Washington led 2,400 troops across an icy Delaware River, and after nearly four hours of transporting men and weaponry, Washington, Sullivan, Greene and their regulars surprised Hessian Colonel Johann Rall and his 1,400 soldiers with a brilliant attack at dawn, mortally wounding Rall and capturing close to 900 before retreating back to Pennsylvania.

Less than 100 years later, Trenton had become less revolutionary and more commercial, and what is now New Jersey's capital began manufacturing rifles, ammunition, and Trenton Oyster Crackers as provisions for the Union soldiers. This shift to manufacture continued for the next century. Today's visitor can still see the famous motto emblazoned upon the Delaware River Bridge: "Trenton Makes, the World Takes." Coined by S. Roy Heath in 1910, this slogan speaks to the continued colorful history of Trenton as a major industrial center—producing an array of goods from pottery to porcelain to rubber to wire rope.

But Trenton took a decidedly bad turn for the worse beginning in 1958 with riots that destroyed a significant portion of the downtown business district, and the soon-after closing of John Roebling's mill.

SIGHTS

Historical significance combined with its status as state capital add up to numerous sights of interest in Trenton. Its selection of historic and civil points of interest makes the capital a favorite class-trip destination.

City Museums and Monuments

Trenton's downtown district, centering around **State Street,** is a good jumping-off point for exploring the city. From here you'll be able to walk to a few of the sights and maybe gain an appreciation for Trenton's revitalizing efforts.

Trenton's **Old Barracks** (Barrack St., 609/396-1776 or 609/777-3599 weekends, www.barracks.org, 10 A.M.–5 P.M. daily, $6) was one of five U.S. barracks used to house prisoners during the French and Indian War, and the only freestanding structure to have survived. Also used as a hospital during the Revolution, the Barracks is now a museum favored by class trips and historians. Inside is a unique display of period furniture and artifacts from the 18th century, including a working baker's oven. Baking demonstrations are usually held Thursdays and Saturdays, while various events, including Revolutionary reenactments, are scheduled throughout the year. A one-hour walking tour is available during all hours the museum is open.

The **Trenton City Museum at Ellarslie Mansion** (Parkside and Stuyvesant Aves., 609/989-3632, www.ellarslie.org, 11 A.M.–3 P.M. Tues.–Sat., 1–4 P.M. Sun., free), established in 1978 as the city's first museum, is housed in a 19th-century Italian villa on the grounds of **Cadwalader Park,** north of downtown's State Street. Showcasing permanent and changing exhibits of fine art and craft, it includes an interesting display of Trenton pottery and a history of its contribution to the capital city.

The 1719 **William Trent House** (15 Market St., 609/989-3027, www.williamtrenthouse.org) was home to Trent's Town's founder. The oldest remaining house in Trenton, this period-restored mansion is open for tours.

At the coming together of North Broad and North Warren Streets stands the **Trenton Battle Monument** (609/737-0623, 9 A.M.–4 P.M. Sat., 1–4 P.M. Sun., free), a 148-foot granite beaux-arts structure commemorating the site where Washington placed his artillery for the First Battle of Trenton. An elevator carries visitors upward to an outdoor pedestal and a bird's-eye view of the city.

New Jersey State Museum

Four floors of exhibits include locally excavated fluorescent minerals, Native American beads and textiles, an African American art collection and a cultural history exhibit featuring the work of New Jersey artisans and craftspeople. The State Museum (205 W. State St., 609/292-6464, www.state.nj.us/state/museum, free) is also home to a 150-seat **planetarium** and a couple of auditorium galleries.

Currently closed for renovations, the museum's main building is scheduled to reopen in spring 2007. Changing exhibits hosted in the nearby Department of State building will remain open during repairs.

New Jersey State House

Built in 1792, the New Jersey State House (State St., 609/633-2709, www.njleg.state.nj.us, 10 A.M.–3 P.M. Mon.–Fri., noon–3 P.M. Sat.) is the United States' second-oldest operating state house (the first is in Annapolis), though much of the original structure was destroyed by fire in 1885. Today the elegantly designed and updated building is open to the public. Tours last about an hour and usually include the assembly and the senate chamber and the state house annex, among others, but can vary depending on government schedules. To ensure the proper tour, call ahead.

An on-premise cafeteria is open for breakfast and lunch weekdays.

Department of State Building

The New Jersey Department of State is home to the **New Jersey State Archives** (225 W. State St., 609/292-6260, www.njarchives.org, 8:30 A.M.–4:30 P.M. weekdays). On the building's first floor are a number of exhibit halls used by the State Museum to house rotating displays. It's also where you'll find the **Capital Bookstore** (609/943-4444, www.booksnj.com, 10 A.M.–3 P.M. Mon.–Fri.), a thorough collection of books, videos, magazines, and puzzles pertaining to the Garden State.

SPORTS AND ENTERTAINMENT

There are a number of entertainment venues in downtown Trenton, ranging from neighborhood theaters to stadium-size arenas and fea-

turing everything from drama to minor league baseball.

The recently restored 1,807-seat **Patriots Theatre at War Memorial** (Memorial Dr., 609/984-8400, www.thewarmemorial.com) specializes in music, dance, and comedy performance. Located along Lafayette Street in downtown Stacy Park (just across from the visitors center—you can't miss it!), this 1932 Italian Renaissance structure has hosted the inauguration of every New Jersey governor since its opening. Outdoor concerts take place seasonally at the **War Memorial Landing.**

Sovereign Bank Arena (81 Hamilton Ave., 609/656-3200, www.sovereignbank-arena .com) is stomping ground for the **Trenton Titans** (609/599-9500, www.trentontitans.com), a minor league ice hockey team and AA affiliate of the Philadelphia Flyers and New York Islanders. Opened in 1999, the arena has hosted large-scale musical acts, ice shows, and the Ringling Bros. and Barnum & Bailey Circus.

The 6,440-seat **Mercer County Waterfront Park** is home to minor league baseball's **Trenton Thunder** (609/394-3300, www.trentonthunder.com), a Yankees AA farm club. Club seats run $9 and terrace seats $6.

The cozy 120-seat **Mill Hill Playhouse** (Montgomery and Front Sts., 609/392-0766) is stage to the **Passion Theatre Company,** Trenton's oldest professional theater group. This is the place to catch locally produced and directed drama, musicals, and comedy.

ACCOMMODATIONS

Oddly enough, there's only one hotel of interest in downtown Trenton (could be the reason there are so many signs pointing the way), and most visitors to the capital city opt to spend the night in nearby Princeton, easily reachable by NJ Transit and only about 20 minutes (depending on traffic) by car.

$150-200

Don't worry about finding it—there are signs pointing the way to the ◖ **Trenton Marriott at Lafayette Yard** (1 W. Lafayette St., 609/421-4002, fax 609/421-4002) all over downtown. This seven-story premier hotel features rooms with free HBO and high-speed Internet (the lobby is wireless) and extremely comfortable beds. The hotel offers a special package to visitors during the Ten Crucial Days reenactment (www.10crucialdays.org), held annually the week between Christmas and New Year's (offer excludes New Year's Eve).

FOOD

Some of the best Italian eateries in the state are gathered together in Trenton's Chambersburg district (the Burg), southeast of the downtown center. Around the capital you find a few worthwhile places serving American fare, and in the nearby Polish neighborhood, a restaurant offering substantial portions of ethnic cuisine.

Downtown

There are a few good eats within walking distance of the downtown sites.

For an easy egg sandwich to go with your cappuccino, try **Café Olé** (126 S. Warren St., 609/396-CAFE or 609/396-2233, www.cafeolecoffee.com, $3–6), a coffeehouse and eatery that's as casual as it is cute. Olé features rotating artwork and a delectable soup of the day, but catering to the downtown crowd keeps it closed on Sunday. Hours are 7 A.M.–4 P.M. Monday–Thursday (until 6 P.M. every other Thursday), until 9:30 P.M. Friday, 8 A.M.–noon Saturday, closed Sunday.

A good place to detour for a no-nonsense lunch is **Checkers Bar & Grill** (14 S. Warren St., 609/394-3895, 11 A.M.–2 P.M. Mon.–Fri., $5). Go for one of New Jersey's famous pork roll sandwiches, or a larger-than-life burger topped with American, cheddar, or blue cheese ($4.50).

Located within the Mill Hill neighborhood, the **Mill Hill Saloon** (300 S. Broad St., 609/394-7222, www.millhillsaloon.com, 11:30–2 A.M. Mon.–Fri., 5 P.M.–2 A.M. Sat., closed Sun.) serves American fare and microbrews in a building dating back to the 1850s. The Saloon is known as a live jazz venue and houses a brew cellar for the late-night crowd.

The following restaurants require a short drive from State Street.

The tropically inspired **KatManDu** (Mercer Waterfront Park, 50 Riverview Dr., 609/393-7300, www.katmandurestaurant.com, $8–18), conveniently located next to Waterfront Park, is as much nightclub as it is restaurant, though its frozen drinks seem to be favored over its American-Caribbean cuisine. The fun atmosphere keeps crowds coming—as does a dance floor, live bands, and a seasonal outdoor deck overlooking the Delaware. KatManDu is open from 11:30 A.M. Monday–Saturday, 10 A.M. Sunday. The bar stays open until 2 A.M. Thursday–Saturday, but closing hours vary the remainder of the week.

Hungry diners come to tackle the lunch buffet at the **Amber Cafe** (901-905 Brunswick Ave., 609/695-7333, 8:30 A.M.–11 P.M. daily), located two miles northeast of State Street in Trenton's Polish district. For dinner try the assorted pierogies ($11) and a cup of borscht ($5), or have a blintze for breakfast. But don't let the mahogany bar fool you—you'll get only sodas and shakes at this BYO.

The Burg

Perhaps the best-known Italian district in New Jersey, Chambersburg can be described as Nana's kitchen, a heap of pasta, and a carafe of Chianti. To an outsider it may feel like dense row housing and narrow streets. That's because the Burg is primarily a residential neighborhood with a dozen or so much-loved restaurants scattered throughout. Even with the many signs adorned with knife, fork, and plate posted within the district, it's best to have an idea where you're headed. Parking can be hard to come by, but a number of establishments offer valet and limited spaces.

It's hard to get more Burg than **Marsilio's** (541 Roebling Ave., 609/695-1916, $18–33). A favorite among local residents and political powerhouses, this Southern Italian eatery serves regulars their wine in personalized Italian carafes. The restaurant is open 11:30 A.M.–2 P.M. and 5–9 P.M. Monday–Friday, and 5–10 P.M. Saturday; closed Sunday.

In this neighborhood, the only name in pizza is DeLorenzo's. But which to choose? Hudson Street's **DeLorenzo's Tomato Pies** (530 Hudson St., 609/695-9534, 3:30–10 P.M. Tues.–Sun., closed Mon.) serves crisp-crusted pies to a bevy of regulars in a pizza-house setting, while its Hamilton Avenue cousin, **DeLorenzo's Pizza** (1007 Hamilton Ave., 609/393-2952, www.delorenzospizza.com, 11 A.M.–1:30 P.M. and 4–8:45 P.M. Tues.– Thurs., 11 A.M.–8:45 P.M. Fri. and Sat., $8– 17, closed Sun. and Mon.) features a spacious dining area where a loyal following enjoys traditional pizza with an extra topping of cheese. Both places are BYO, but only Hamilton Avenue has a restroom.

For casual eats head to **Rossi's** (501 Morris Ave., 609/394-9089, 11 A.M.–10 P.M. daily). A full bar with over 30 tap beers, and the infamous Rossiburger ($4.95)—the juiciest, fattest burger around—make this place a regional favorite.

John Henry's (2 Miffin St., 609/396-3083, www.johnhenrysseafood.com, $16–27) is the place for classic and Italian seafood dishes. The decor is nothing spectacular, but the ingredients are fresh and the portions large. The restaurant is open for lunch 11:30 A.M.– 2:30 P.M. Tuesday–Friday. Dinner hours are 4:30–10 P.M. Tuesday–Thursday, until 11 P.M. Friday and Saturday, and 3–9 P.M. Sunday.

Amici Milano (Chestnut and Roebling Aves., 609/396-6300, www.amicimilano.com, $11– 23) serves Italian fare in a *familia* setting (you'll find both a children's menu and an early-bird special). Three dining rooms, an extensive wine list, and a piano player (Wed., Fri.–Sun.) are reason enough to come here. Lunch is served 11:30 A.M.–2:30 P.M. Monday–Friday, dinner 4–10 P.M. Monday–Thursday, until 11 P.M. Friday and Saturday, 1–10 P.M. Sunday.

INFORMATION AND SERVICES

Housed in a 1793 lodge on the corner of Lafayette and Broad Streets, the **Capital Region Convention & Visitors Bureau Welcome Center** (Lafayette at Barrack St., 609/777-1770, www.trentonnj.com, 10 A.M.–4 P.M. daily) is the mother of all visitors centers. Ask for a bag at the information desk and hit the kiosks. The center has brochures covering the entire state, from Cape May to High Point, as well as some great local stuff.

While in the city, pick up a copy of the free *Downtowner* (you can find them everywhere) to get word on the monthly happenings.

GETTING THERE AND AROUND

Both the **River LINE** (www.riverline.com) and Amtrak's **Northeast Corridor Line** (72 S. Clinton Ave., 215/580-7800, www.amtrak.com) run directly to Trenton, a central hub for most of New Jersey, as well as the Philadelphia to New York City route. The stations are located across the street from each other.

The **Capital Connection** shuttle stops at all major points around the city, most notably the River LINE/Amtrak stations and the State House Complex.

HAMILTON

Hamilton, a nearly 40-square-mile township bordering Trenton, is one of New Jersey's fastest-growing suburbs. It has a population slightly larger than its Capital City neighbor, and while there's no downtown center to speak of, there are a few attractions that make a trip here well worth your time.

◖ Grounds for Sculpture

Grounds for Sculpture (18 Fairgrounds Rd., 609/586-0616, www.groundsforsculpture.org, 10 A.M.–6 P.M. Tues.–Sun., Nov.–March; 10 A.M.–8 P.M. Tues.–Sun. Apr.–Oct., closed Mon. year-round) is an imaginative display of three-dimensional artwork set upon 35 acres of hills and hideaways. The works range from tacky to terrific, though you'd be hard-pressed not to find something you like. Created in 1992 by art collector, sculptor, and Johnson & Johnson heir J. Steward Johnson Jr., the park is truly unique and holds over 200 art pieces. It's nearly impossible to spot them all your first go around, but a few you may encounter are an

© LAURA KINIRY

a sculpture of a woman and man sitting in front of a lake at Grounds for Sculpture

Impressionist-inspired life-size garden party, a woman behind a curtain of steam, and a rosy-cheeked shepherd tending his cartoonish flock of sheep.

Two spacious halls house a rotating display of indoor exhibits, a museum shop, and a café selling salads and sandwiches. There's also an outdoor amphitheater and snack gazebo—both come to life during the summer months. Across the grounds **Toad Hall Shop and Gallery** sells items designed by local and international artists and features a changing exhibit of saleable art.

Although walking paths lead to many of the ground's sculptures, navigating them may be difficult for wheelchair users due to the rocky terrain.

Admission fees are $5 adults, $4 seniors and students, and $1 children under 12 Tuesday–Thursday, $8 adult, $7 seniors and students, and $4 children under 12 Friday and Saturday, and $12 general admission Sunday.

Sayen Gardens

The 30-acre Sayen Gardens (155 Hughes Dr., 609/587-7356, www.sayengardens.org, dawn–dusk daily, free) was created in 1912 by gardening and travel enthusiast Frederick Sayen. Today the gardens feature hundreds of azaleas and rhododendrons, many of which are strands Sayen gathered on his journeys. The original arts and crafts–style bungalow he built with his wife remains on the property, surrounded by nature trails, ponds, and pinewoods, and is open to the public annually on Mother's Day.

Kuser Farm Mansion and Park

Kuser Mansion (2090 Greenwood Ave., 609/890-3630, 11 A.M.–3 P.M. Thurs.–Sun. May–Nov., weekends Feb.–Apr., free, donations accepted) was built as a country home for the Kusers, a prominent New Jersey family responsible for the creation of Fox Film Industry (now known as 20th Century Fox). The 17-room 1892 Queen Anne Victorian is now open to the public and a tour includes a look at the mansion's private projection room. The surrounding 22-acre estate, known as "the farm," is open to the public during tour hours.

Food

As magical as the adjacent Grounds for Sculpture is the whimsical **Rat's** (16 Fairgrounds Rd., 609/584-7800, www.ratsrestaurant.org, $25–37), a French restaurant whose seasonal cuisine and ambience are both top-notch. You'll enter through a bright red gypsy wagon (unless you enter through the grounds from the rear, amidst a waterfall and rising steam), and arrive in a world of decadence. Such luxury can be heavy on your wallet and since proper attire is required, your best bet for an impromptu afternoon is to try the restaurant's more casual **Kafe Kabul** (11:30 A.M.–9 P.M. Wed.–Fri., and 11:30 A.M.–2:30 P.M., 5–9 P.M. Sat.). Try the diced beet salad ($8), the organic burger served with fries ($13), or the cheese plate with accompanying nuts and figs ($7). The ambience—deep reds and oranges, cloth-covered high-back chairs, beaded curtains, and afternoon sun-lit tables—is reason enough to come. But stay for the food—it's excellent.

Both Rat's and the Kafe have seasonal outdoor seating. Rat's dinner hours are 5:30–8:30 P.M. Tuesday–Thursday, until 8:45 P.M. Friday, 5:15–9:30 P.M. Saturday, and 5:15–8 P.M. Sunday. Sunday brunch is fixed-price, fixed-seating in two-hour intervals, beginning at 11–11:30 A.M. and once again at 1–1:30 P.M. Rat's is open for lunch seasonally. The bar is open 11:30 A.M.–10 P.M. Tuesday–Thursday, until midnight Friday and Saturday, and 11 A.M.–10 P.M. Sunday. Free park entry comes with a Rat's meal.

BORDENTOWN

This handsome riverside city was once described as a "hotbed of fervor" during America's War for Independence and provided residence to such Revolutionary figures as Francis Hopkinson, signer of the Declaration of Independence and designer of New Jersey's State Seal, and Thomas Paine, author of 1776's "Common Sense," the first publication challenging the British government's authority over America. Today Bordentown is a bustling and friendly community with a disproportionately large number of bookstores, as well as some interesting art galleries and popular eateries.

Clara Barton School

Clara Barton established New Jersey's first free public school in downtown Bordentown in 1852, before she went on to found the American Red Cross. The building still stands, restored with money raised by school children in 1921, and is now owned by the **Bordentown Historical Society** (609/298-1740). It's located at 142 Crosswicks Street. Walking tours given by the society include a stop at the small brick building. Call for hours.

Art Galleries

Bordentown is a popular residence for artisans and a number of galleries can be found along Farnsworth Avenue and its side streets.

The **Artful Deposit** (201 Farnsworth Ave., 609/298-6970, www.theartfuldeposit.com) showcases local, national, and international fine art. At **The Bordentown Gallery** (204 Farnsworth Ave., 609/298-5556, www.bordentowngallery.com) you'll find fine art and crafted wares, including etched glass and Raku pottery. The **Pavs Gallery** (148 Farnsworth Ave., 609/298-PAVS or 609/298-7287) displays exquisite pieces of wearable textile art.

Along a shaded side street down a short path is the **Firehouse Gallery** (8 Walnut St., 609/298-3742), exhibiting contemporary artwork including a notable number of portraits. Art classes for both adults and children are scheduled throughout the year.

Entertainment and Events

For over 15 years Bordentown has celebrated the annual weekend **Cranberry Festival** (www.downtownbordentown.com/cranberry.htm) in early October. Events include the Miss Cranberry Fest Pageant and live music.

The Thomas Paine Society (609/324-9909) hosts a free **Thomas Paine Walking Tour** following in the footsteps of the Revolutionary author at 4 P.M. the first Saturday of each month, June–November. Tours leave from the Paine Historical Site sign at Farnsworth Avenue and West Church Street.

Shopping

Walk along between the brick buildings lining Farnsworth Avenue and you'll be amazed at the large number of bookstores you see on such a relatively small stretch. Most of these shops specialize in used and antiquarian books.

By the Book @ U & I Gift Shop (150 Farnsworth Ave., 609/298-3334) features used and hard-to-find books and is a member of the Antiquated Booksellers of New Jersey. Much of the store's selection is available at www.abebooks.com. For mystery novels and historic accounts try **Q.M. Dabney & Co. Booksellers** (300 Farnsworth Ave., 609/298-1003). You'll find a stash of modern and antiquarian books at **The Bohemian Bookworm** (102 Farnsworth Ave., 609/291-7170), including literature, cookbooks, and travel.

CENTRAL JERSEY

© LAURA KINIRY

Bordentown homes

The **Old Book Shop of Bordentown** (200 Farnsworth Ave., 609/324-9909) specializes in 19th- and 20th-century baseball and literary greats like Hemingway and Thomas Wolfe.

Food

There are a couple of good restaurants along Farnsworth Avenue, or you can venture out to the ill-scenic Route 130 for a great diner experience.

The **Jesters Cafe** (233 Farnsworth Ave., 609/298-9963, 11 A.M.–10:30 P.M. Mon.–Thurs., until 11:30 P.M. Fri. and Sat., $10.95–17.95) serves Italian/American fare in a casual setting, and features a full bar and live jazz throughout the week.

Housed in a corner three-story brick building, the **Farnsworth House** (135 Farnsworth Ave., 609/291-9232, $10.95–28.95) is a popular fine dining eatery featuring Italian cuisine and a varied selection of red wines. Lunch is served 11 A.M.–3 P.M. daily, and dinner 3 P.M.–midnight Monday–Saturday, until 10 P.M. Sunday.

It may be a diner, but **Mastoris** (Rtes. 130 and 206, 609/298-4650, 4 A.M.–2 A.M. week-

days, until 3 A.M. weekends, $4.50–17.95) is one of the best eats in town. Family-owned and -operated, this multi-room establishment's interior may resemble a gaudy wedding hall, but full-on diner dishes and complimentary cinnamon bread have created a loyal clientele.

For your morning brew head to **Katie's Coffeehouse and Cafe** (1½ Crosswicks St., 609/324-7800), also showcasing live music in the evenings.

◖ WASHINGTON CROSSING STATE PARK

After four hours spent crossing the Delaware River in the early morning of December 26, 1776, General George Washington and 2,400 Continental soldiers came ashore on what is now Washington Crossing State Park (355 Washington Crossing–Pennington Rd., Titusville, 609/737-0623). You'll find over 700 Revolutionary War artifacts interpreting this event and what became known as the Ten Crucial Days on display at the park's visitors center, and tall trees, open fields, and seasonal wildflowers make this 2,009-acre park as scenic as it is historic.

CENTRAL JERSEY

KING OF THE BLUFF

On the outskirts of Central Jersey's Bordentown once stood the estate of a king. Joseph Bonaparte, ex-king of Naples and Spain and older brother of Napoleon, arrived in the United States in 1816 after the fall of Waterloo led to his family's exile from France and tense relations with other European countries kept him from settling elsewhere on the continent. The "Count de Survilliers," as he preferred to be known (though local residents referred to him simply as Mr. Bonaparte), acquired more than 1,000 acres just outside Bordentown upon a bluff overlooking Crosswicks Creek. He built a grand estate that he called Point Breeze (which came to be known as Bonaparte Park) and landscaped his grounds with gardens, even damming a portion of the creek to create a lake for his property. Underneath it all, Bonaparte ran long tunnels connecting his home to various nearby points. Some speculated that Napoleon himself lived out his days in these tunnels, having secretly escaped St. Helena where he was held as a political prisoner.

From all accounts, Bonaparte was both kind and personable, and during his time in Bordentown, he opened his home to numerous notable figures that included John Quincy Adams, local resident Joseph Hopkinson, and the Marquis de Lafayette. He was an avid art lover and his Point Breeze collection consisted of pieces by Da Vinci, Van Dyck, and Raphael. Although Bonaparte never became a U.S. citizen, he was granted the right to own land.

Bonaparte remained in Bordentown until 1832, eventually returning to Europe to reunite with his wife who had remained behind and to retrieve a treasure that he'd left as well. He would re-visit the United States a couple of times, in 1835-1836 and again in 1837-1839, before dying in Europe in 1844.

Bonaparte bequeathed Point Breeze to his oldest grandson Joseph Lucien Bonaparte, who immediately sold it. Purchaser Henry Beckett demolished the estate (and earned the nickname "the Destroyer" as a result) and built a new, less attractive home in its place. The ex-king's art collection was auctioned off, and soon nothing remained of Bonaparte Park save the remnants of underground tunnels leading nowhere.

Today the Divine Word Seminary for the Instruction of Roman Catholic Priests stands on the grounds of former Point Breeze.

Recreational opportunities include 15 miles of multiuse trails suitable for nature walks, hiking, mountain biking, cross-country skiing, and horseback riding. Group camping facilities are available throughout summer months, $1 per person for up to 115 people. The park is also a good place to spot birds and wildlife, including fox, deer, hawks, and owl. Washington Crossing State Park is open dawn–dusk daily year-round and is free to enter the majority of the time, although a $5 admission fee is charged weekends Memorial Day–Labor Day.

Washington Crossing Visitors Center Museum

Two galleries within the **Washington Crossing Visitors Center** (609/737-9303, 9 A.M.–4:30 P.M. Wed.–Sun.) highlight both the Ten Crucial Days and New Jersey's larger role within the Revolution. Ninety-nine percent of what's exhibited is part of the **Swan Historical Foundation Collection,** and includes a historic gun display and a rare 18th-century soldier's uniform.

Johnson Ferry House

Owned by Garret Johnson, who operated a ferry across the Delaware in the 1700s, this farm home was standing on the morning of Washington's crossing, and possibly used by the General and his troops before they headed south to Trenton. The Johnson Ferry House (609/737-1826) has been restored as an 18th-century tavern and furnished with period pieces. It's open to the public periodically throughout summer (usually weekends) and often holds living-history demonstrations during this time. Call for exact hours.

Events
An **annual Delaware River crossing re-enactment** takes place on Christmas morning. Costumed performers steer authentically reconstructed vessels across the river, leaving from Pennsylvania's Washington Crossing Historic Park. Unfortunately, inclement weather often causes the canceling of this event. To find out more information, including whether the crossing will actually be taking place, contact Pennsylvania's Washington Crossing Historical Society at 215/493-4076.

In the summer months, the **Washington Crossing Open Air Theatre** (609/737-1826) comes alive with entertainment such as the musical performances *Oklahoma!* and *Annie Get Your Gun.* Tickets are sold only on-site and run $8 adult, $7.50 senior, $4 child for Wednesday–Friday performances, and $10 adult, $9.50 senior, and $5 child for Saturday performances. Tickets go on sale at 7:30 P.M., and all shows begin at 8 P.M.

Information and Services
The **Visitors Center** (609/737-2515) is open 9 A.M.–4:30 P.M. Wednesday–Sunday through-out the year. There's staff on hand to answer questions, and public restrooms are available.

HOWELL LIVING HISTORY FARM
One of New Jersey's numerous living-history farms, the 130-acre Howell Living History Farm (101 Hunter Rd., Titusville, 609/737-3299, www.howellfarm.org) is also one of its better ones. Striving to depict 19th-century farm life in an authentic manner, costumed workers take to the fields and tend to the animals. A few buildings are original to the site, including the large Philips Barn and the farmhouse, both listed on the State and National Registers of Historic Places. A variety of demonstrations take place on Saturdays throughout the year, catering to both kids and adults, and include dairying, sheep shearing, and bee-keeping. Chickens, horses, cows, and oxen all live on the property. The farm features an enormous corn maze in the fall.

Parking and admission are free, though there's a fee for any additional activity. The farm is open 10 A.M.–4 P.M. Tuesday–Friday February–November, and 10 A.M.–4 P.M. Saturdays throughout the year. It's also open for self-guided tours noon–4 P.M. Sundays, April–November.

Princeton and Vicinity

Once a stagecoach stop between Philadelphia and New York City, Princeton borough and the adjoining Princeton Township played a prominent role in America's fight for independence. Today these two separate entities also share a library and health department, as well as grounds to the illustrious university. Brimming with shops, restaurants, historic sites, dense greenery, and plenty of stately colonial and Federal estate–style homes, the two Princetons are a must-see.

Nassau Street is the borough's main thoroughfare, where you'll find everything from take-out Indian cuisine to Princeton U. sweat-shirts, to a makeshift memorial to former Princeton resident Albert Einstein. Across the street lies the extraordinary Gothic architecture of the infamous Ivy League university.

◖ PRINCETON UNIVERSITY
Founded in Elizabeth, New Jersey, in 1746 and moved briefly to Newark before ending up in Princeton, Princeton University is one of America's top institutions and one of the country's oldest, not to mention having one of the most exquisite campuses around. A walk around the grounds will reveal sharpened steeples, pointed arch windows, stained glass windows

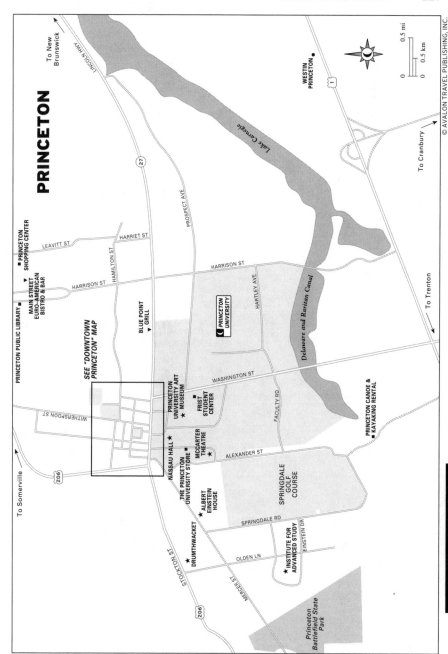

PRINCETON

To New Brunswick

LINCOLN HWY

Lake Carnegie

WESTIN PRINCETON

To Cranbury

0   0.5 mi
0   0.5 km

© AVALON TRAVEL PUBLISHING, INC.

PRINCETON SHOPPING CENTER

LEAVITT ST

HARRIET ST

HAMILTON ST

MAIN STREET EURO-AMERICAN BISTRO & BAR

PRINCETON PUBLIC LIBRARY

HARRISON ST

(27)

PROSPECT AVE

HARRISON ST

HARTLEY AVE

PRINCETON UNIVERSITY

Delaware and Raritan Canal

To Trenton

BLUE POINT GRILL

SEE "DOWNTOWN PRINCETON" MAP

WITHERSPOON ST

WASHINGTON ST

PRINCETON UNIVERSITY ART MUSEUM

FRIST STUDENT CENTER

FACULTY RD

PRINCETON CANOE & KAYAKING RENTAL

NASSAU HALL

McCARTER THEATRE

THE PRINCETON UNIVERSITY STORE

ALBERT EINSTEIN HOUSE

ALEXANDER ST

SPRINGDALE GOLF COURSE

To Somerville

(206)

DRUMTHWACKET

STOCKTON ST

MERCER ST

SPRINGDALE RD

EINSTEIN DR

OLDEN LN

INSTITUTE FOR ADVANCED STUDY

(206)

Princeton Battlefield State Park

CENTRAL JERSEY

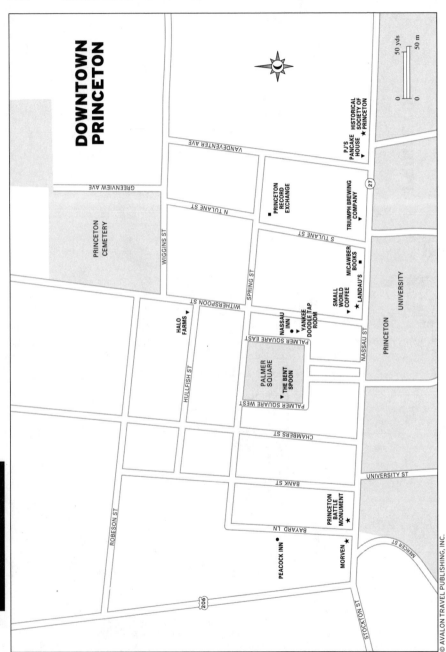

DOWNTOWN PRINCETON

GREENVIEW AVE

VANDEVENTER AVE

PRINCETON CEMETERY

WIGGINS ST

N TULANE ST

PRINCETON RECORD EXCHANGE

S TULANE ST

TRIUMPH BREWING COMPANY

PJ'S PANCAKE HOUSE

HISTORICAL SOCIETY OF PRINCETON

27

SPRING ST

WITHERSPOON ST

MICAWBER BOOKS

LANDAU'S

SMALL WORLD COFFEE

HALO FARMS

NASSAU INN

YANKEE DOODLE TAP ROOM

PALMER SQUARE EAST

PALMER SQUARE

THE BENT SPOON

PALMER SQUARE WEST

HULFISH ST

NASSAU ST

PRINCETON UNIVERSITY

CHAMBERS ST

BANK ST

UNIVERSITY ST

ROBESON ST

BAYARD LN

PRINCETON BATTLE MONUMENT

PEACOCK INN

MORVEN

206

STOCKTON ST

MERCER ST

0   50 yds
0   50 m

and unique gargoyles accenting the many ivy-covered buildings.

Princeton began as a struggling college—known as The College of New Jersey until 1856—and didn't quite take off until alumnus Woodrow Wilson took over the reigns of University President in 1902, implementing changes that would carry the institution successfully into the 21st century. These changes, coupled with ever-faithful and generous alum, helped catapult Princeton to a top position both academically and financially.

The University is one of the United States' eight Ivy League institutions, and its alumni roster features such notables as James Madison, Aaron Burr Jr., Ralph Nader, Donald Rumsfeld, Brooke Shields, Jimmy Stewart, and F. Scott Fitzgerald (who did not graduate). Professors include mathematician John Nash Jr. (portrayed in the film *A Beautiful Mind*), and authors John McPhee, Joyce Carol Oates, and Toni Morrison.

Nassau Hall

Princeton University's most famous structure is Nassau Hall—set back from Nassau Street across from the borough's downtown shops, it's been a campus mainstay since the university's Princeton beginnings. The hall was built in 1756 and acted as the school's entire campus—housing students, holding seminars—for almost 50 years. Today it serves as an administrative building, though more interesting uses were as a barracks and hospital during the Revolutionary War, and as the U.S. Capital June–November 1783. According to *The Daily Princetonian,* one of the numerous legends associated with the ivy-covered hall tells of students who used cannonballs that had been hidden by Revolutionary troops to do a bit of bowling in the passageways.

The building itself is a grand stone structure, a combination of architectural styles ranging from colonial to Federal to Italianate, this mix-match resulting from a series of fires inciting the hall's constant reconstruction. Though no large letters hang outside proclaiming its name, you'll easily recognize the hall by

© LAURA KINIRY

gravesite of Grover Cleveland, Princeton University and U.S. President, Princeton Cemetery

the two bronze tigers gracing either side of its main entry. Lions once stood in their places, but once Princeton adopted its school colors of orange and black in the late 19th century, it only made sense to make the change.

Ivy that covers the front and a portion of the back of Nassau Hall is a gift from the university's graduating classes.

Princeton University Art Museum

Founded in 1882, the Princeton University Art Museum (McCormick Hall, 609/258-3788, www.princetonartmuseum.org, 10 A.M.–5 P.M. Tues.–Sat., 1–5 P.M. Sun., free) features artwork from a wide range of mediums, cultures, and time periods. A highlight of the museum's collection is a version of Monet's *Water Lilies and Japanese Bridge* (1899), one of the best among twenty originals. Andy Warhol's *Blue Marilyn* is also on display here, as are a number of Roman mosaics from Antioch.

The museum offers its own Highlight Tour at 2 P.M. Saturdays and Sundays, beginning at the front of the museum near the museum store and lasting about an hour.

McCarter Theatre

The much-loved McCarter Theatre (91 University Pl., 609/258-2787, 888/ARTSWEB or 888/278-7932, www.mccarter.org) showcases theater, dance, and music, including many original productions. Built as a home for a Princeton Triangle Club, the university's madcap comedy and musical troupe whose previous members include Jimmy Stewart and Brooke Shields, the 1929 theater is also the residence of the American Repertory Ballet.

The property added a second theater, the Roger S. Berlind Theatre, in 2003.

Information and Services

Orange Key Tours are one-hour tours of campus given by students and intended to offer an overview of campus life. Though geared toward prospective undergrads and their families, you will find out a bit about the university's history and folklore. To arrange a tour, which begins and ends in front of campus's **Frist Campus Center,** call 609/258-1766 or go to www.princeton.edu/~okkey.

The Princeton University Store (36 University Pl., 609/921-8500, ext. 238, www.pustore.com) sells university sweatshirts, stuffed tiger mascots, and all the black and orange you could ask for. Hours are 9 A.M.–9 P.M. Monday–Saturday, 11 A.M.–6 P.M. Sunday.

OTHER SIGHTS

Princeton's many sights are both historically and culturally significant, and a few hours are worth spent exploring them.

Historic Sites

A good place to begin your exploration of Princeton is at the **Historical Society of Princeton** (158 Nassau St., 609/921-6748), located within the 1766 **Bainbridge House** on the corner of Nassau Street and Greenview Avenue. The Society gives a two-hour tour of Princeton's historic sites beginning at 2 P.M. Sundays ($7 adult, $3 child) in front of the Bainbridge House. If you'd rather explore on your own they give directions for a self-guided two-mile walking tour. The Historical Society features a library

and photo archive open 1–4 P.M. Tuesday and Saturday ($5), and a free museum that's open noon–4 P.M. Tuesday–Sunday.

The **Princeton Cemetery** (29 Greenview Ave., 609/924-1369) hosts many of Princeton's illustrious alumni at their final resting place, including Grover Cleveland, Aaron Burr Jr., Paul Tulane (Tulane University), and Donald Lambert, an African-American jazz musician born in Princeton and who spent many an evening playing piano in a Newark nightclub. Be sure and have a look at the Princeton University President's Plot, where all but four of the Ivy League's distinguished deceased lay in rest. You can pick up a map of the 1757 cemetery upon entry, though the groundskeepers seem happy to assist you in finding the best-known plots.

After serving as New Jersey's governor's mansion for 27 years from 1953 to 1981, the handsome 1759 colonial known as **Morven** (55 Stockton St., 609/683-3740, www.historicmorven.org, 11 A.M.–3 P.M. Wed.–Fri., $5 adults, $4 seniors and students) opened to the public in 2004 as a museum showcasing New Jersey's cultural heritage. Two floors of exhibits feature artwork on loan from private collections and public institutions like Trenton's State Museum and the New Jersey Historical Society in Newark. Morven's own history is also displayed. Visitors can also tour Morven's gardens, which include 18th- and 19th-century annuals and a rotation of seasonal blooms.

Since 1982 **Drumthwacket** (354 Stockton St., 608/683-0057, www.drumthwacket.org) has been New Jersey's official governor's mansion. Built in 1835 by Charles Smith Olden, who became the first state governor to live here, the estate has only housed two governors since: Jim Florio, during the 1970s and '80s, and most recently James McGreevey. The lengthy and narrow Greek Revival mansion seems more suitable for entertaining, perhaps the reason most of New Jersey's governors have chosen to reside elsewhere. Tours of Drumthwacket's first floor, including the library, governor's study, and solarium, and the estate's gardens, are given every Wednesday (tours for individuals begin at noon) and run approximately 45 minutes. Admission is free, though a $5 donation is suggested.

On the corner of Stockton Road (Route 206) and Bayard Street is the **Princeton Battle Monument.** This 1922 sculpture depicting the battle, often described as one of the Revolution's fiercest, stands next to the eastern border of Morven estate. A number of benches make it a nice spot for a picnic lunch.

Princeton Battlefield State Park

After engaging in the Second Battle of Trenton, General Washington and his army moved on to Princeton, where they met with Lord Cornwallis and his troops on January 3, 1777. Princeton Battlefield State Park (500 Mercer Rd., 609/921-0074, www.state.nj.us/dep/parksandforests/parks/princeton.html) commemorates this battle, part of the Ten Crucial Days that proved a turning point for the Revolutionary War. Comprised of 681 acres of mostly open field, this is an ideal locale for a midday break from downtown Princeton. Historic sights include the **Thomas Clark House** (609/921-0074, 10 A.M.–noon and 1–4 P.M. Sat., 1–4 P.M. Sun.), which was used as a hospital for both American and British troops after the battle, and the **Mercer Oak,** said to have sheltered General Hugh Mercer after being impaled by a Brit's bayonet. Actually, the current Oak is a smallish acorn-grown offspring of the original, which crashed to the ground during a 2000 storm.

Einstein's Footsteps

Located at 112 Mercer Street, the **Albert Einstein House** was this scientist's home for the 22 years that he resided in Princeton, December 1932–1955. The house is today a private residence, but it's a good place to begin a walk in Einstein's footsteps. During the time that he lived in Princeton, Einstein worked nearby at the **Institute for Advanced Study** (Einstein Dr., 609/734-8000). Though the center is also off-limits to public viewing, visitors can get their brain fix at the institute's 588-acre **Institute Woods,** a community space located adjacent to Princeton Battlefield State Park.

An Einstein **mini-museum** can be found against the back wall inside Landau's (102 Nassau St., 609/924-3494, www.landauprinceton.com, 9:30 A.M.–5:30 P.M. Mon.–Fri., 11:30 A.M.–4:30 P.M. Sun.), a wool shop and Princeton University apparel store on Nassau Street. It's an odd place for a museum, but it's here, and it happens to be Princeton's only museum dedicated to Einstein's life. You'll find photographs, newspapers articles, photocopied letters, and personal items once belonging to the wild-haired man with the goofy smile. In addition, a 300-pound bronze bust at Princeton's Borough's Hall was dedicated in April 2005.

In 2003 the Historical Society of Princeton acquired 65 pieces of Einstein's furniture that, as of 2005, are still awaiting display. To find out more, go to www.princetonhistory.org/thinkeinstein.shtml.

SPORTS AND RECREATION

The 300-acre **Charles H. Rodgers Wildlife Refuge,** located within the Institute Woods on the grounds of the Institute for Advanced Study, hosts a number of public nature trails. For bicycle rentals try **Jay's Cycles** (249 Nassau St., 609/924-7233), part of the community since 1977. Bikes go for $8/hour with a two-hour minimum, or $32 for a full day. To rent canoes or kayaks head to **Princeton Canoe & Kayaking Rental** (483 Alexander St., Turning Basin Park, 609/452-2403, www.canoenj.com). Boats are available for use on the Delaware and Raritan Canal, which runs through town, or nearby Lake Carnegie, used as training grounds for both Princeton University and the U.S. Olympic rowing teams—paying heed to the rowers comes with the territory. The cost of renting canoes/kayaks is $12/$9 for the first hour, $6/$5 for any additional hour, or $35/$25 for an all-day pass.

SHOPPING

As with most university towns, Princeton offers a good selection of shops to meet the needs of its younger transient population, such as fashionable retail, numerous boutiques and specialty shops, and a superb bookstore.

Downtown

You can spend hours browsing the great selection of shops in downtown Princeton, many of which are found along the streets of Palmer Square.

The independently owned **Micawber Books** (110-114 Nassau St., 609/921-0282) is really two stores. Enter on the left for used and out-of-print books, as well as travel narratives and local info. On the right you'll find a good blend of literature and academics, including a superb classic studies collection. Be sure and pick up a map of Princeton's Literary Legacy ($10).

Princeton Record Exchange (20 S. Tulane St., 609/921-0881, www.prex.com) is where to shop for vinyl. This shop has a reputation that supercedes its smallish storefront, selling new and used CDs, DVDs, records, and more.

The center of borough shopping is most definitely **Palmer Square** (800/644-3489, www.palmersquare.com). Easily intercepted en route down Nassau Street, the Square is brought together by four main streets—Nassau, Palmer Square East and West, and Hulfish Street—and includes more than 40 shops, ranging from local boutiques to national chains. Look for J.Crew and Ann Taylor alongside shops such as **Zoe** (11 Hulfish St., 609/497-0704), a fantastically funky women's clothing and shoe store, and **Jazams** (15 Hulfish St., 609/924-8697), stocking plush Ugly Dolls, hieroglyphic writing sets, pinhole photography kits, and rockin' *Sesame Street* CDs.

Princeton Shopping Center

The best shopping in Princeton Township is found at the **Princeton Shopping Center** (609/921-6234, www.shoppingprinceton.com), where you'll find over 50 stores, including many independent boutiques and businesses, nearly a dozen eateries, and a gourmet grocery store. The center has been in business for half a century, and includes highlights like **The Winged Pig** (609/924-1212), a home furnishing and gift store; **Princeton Video** (609/497-9333), offering free popcorn with movie rentals; and **GlenmarieWoolworks** (609/921-3022), selling handmade knits, felted bags, and portable projects for "knitters on the go," and featuring kitting workshops throughout the year.

ACCOMMODATIONS

Princeton has a number of fine accommodations to choose from—but good luck booking them during May graduation.

$150-200

Built in 1756, the **Nassau Inn** (Palmer Square, 609/921-7500, www.nassauinn.com) is one of Princeton's most prominent accommodation choices. Located at the heart of Palmer Square and just across Nassau Street from Princeton University, it features 203 rooms and suites, and 14 banquet rooms with names like Paul Robeson and Albert Einstein. The inn features high-speed Internet throughout and an ATM in the lobby.

Within walking distance to the borough's shops is the 17-room **Peacock Inn** (20 Bayard Ln., 609/924-1707, www.peacockinn.com), a bed-and-breakfast housed in a 1775 colonial mansion. A number of distinguished guests have stayed here throughout the years, including author F. Scott Fitzgerald, a Princeton undergrad. The inn features its own French restaurant, open for dinner Monday–Saturday.

Along Route 1 is the **Hampton Inn Princeton** (4385 Rte. 1, 609/951-0066, www.hamptoninn.com), a pleasant hotel offering complimentary hot breakfast each morning, and breakfast-to-go on weekdays. Rooms come equipped with high-speed Internet.

$250-300

The **Westin Princeton** (201 Village Blvd., 609/452-7900, www.westin.com/princeton) features 249 modern rooms and four luxury suites. Its highlights include tennis courts, a sushi bar, and an indoor/outdoor pool with sauna. Also on premises are a cocktail lounge and a restaurant serving American fare.

Situated in the Carnegie office complex just off Route 1, about a mile from Princeton Borough, is the **Hyatt Regency Princeton** (102 Carnegie Center, 609/987-1234, http://princeton.hyatt.com/hyatt/hotels/index.jsp). The hotel features an on-site bar, restaurant, and comedy club, and room service is available throughout the day and evening. Both high-speed and wireless Internet access is available. Rates run considerably less on weekends.

FOOD

Princeton's dining options run the gamut from casual breakfast joints to brewpubs to fine-dining establishments. While it may not be considered a foodie destination, you should not have trouble finding something that suits your needs.

Pj's Pancake House (154 Nassau St., 609/924-1353, www.pancakes.com, 7 A.M.–10 P.M. Sun.–Thurs., 7 A.M.–midnight Fri.–Sat., $7) serves every kind of pancake imaginable: raspberry, raisin, banana pecan… And the best part? They're available all day. This fun place also serves an expanded breakfast menu, as well as sandwiches and burgers after 11 A.M.

The popular pastime of coffee consumption occurs at **Small World Coffee** (14 Witherspoon St., 609/924-4377, www.smallworldcoffee.com, $3.95–8.95), where you'll also find breakfast eats like nutty granola and an interesting selection of sandwiches, soups, and salads. The shop has two counters—one for food and the other for beverages—better to accommodate the hordes of students, locals, and lovable eccentrics that frequent this neighborhood institution. The café is open 6:30 A.M.–10 P.M. Monday–Thursday, until 11 P.M. Friday and Saturday, and 7:30 A.M.–10 P.M. Sunday.

Walk down a long hallway off Nassau Street to get to the **Triumph Brewing Company** (138 Nassau St., 609/924-7855, www.triumphbrew.com, 11:30 A.M.–1 A.M. Mon.–Thurs., until 2 A.M. Fri. and Sat., noon–midnight Sun.), a laid-back brewpub with live music and daily beers on tap. Come for the open-faced sandwiches, or try a dinner entrée like the Nassau St. pork chop ($16.95) or Chicken and Sausage ($17.95). In the underbelly of the Nassau Inn is the **Yankee Doodle Tap Room** (10 Palmer Square, $13–23), a dark mahogany favorite with a massive stone fireplace and wood booths, and a mural painted by Norman Rockwell adorning the wall behind the bar. Check out the framed photos of famous Princeton alums or the initials of university graduates carved into tabletops while enjoying

traditional American fare. The Tap Room is open for breakfast, lunch, and dinner 7 A.M.–11 P.M. daily.

The **Blue Point Grill** (258 Nassau St., 609/921-1211, www.bluepointgrill.com, 5–9:30 P.M. Mon., until 10 P.M. Tues.–Fri., 4:30–9:30 P.M. weekends, $19–24) is a wonderful seafood establishment. Daily chalkboard specials and a bright interior are reason to come to this BYO, which also provides seasonal sidewalk seating.

Located within the Princeton Shopping Center is the casual **Main Street Euro-American Bistro and Bar** (301 N. Harrison St., 609/921-2779, www.mainstreetprinceton.com, 11:30 A.M.–9:30 P.M. Mon.–Thurs., until 10 P.M. Fri. and Sat., 5–8:30 P.M. Sun., $9.95–18.95). The internationally inspired menu changes monthly, and the restaurant features its own baked goods and sidewalk seating.

Princeton has two superb ice cream shops, both located within Palmer Square. For delicious organic ice cream and freshly made sorbet head to **The Bent Spoon** (35 Palmer Square West, 609/924-BENT or 609/924-2368). Must-try homemade scoops at **Halo Pub** (9 Hulfish St., 609/921-1710, 10 A.M.–6 P.M. Mon.–Thurs., until 8:30 P.M. Fri. and Sat., noon–5 P.M. Sun.) include chocolate-chocolate almond and peanut butter ($1.50 for a heaping scoop). Both shops are open year-round.

INFORMATION AND SERVICES

The **Princeton Public Library** (301 N. Harrison St., 609/924-9529, www.princetonlibrary.org, 9 A.M.–9 P.M. Mon.–Thurs., until 6 P.M. Fri. and Sat., 1–6 P.M. Sun.) offers wireless Internet access throughout—including the library's third floor, which has been turned into a rec room for teens and collegiates to congregate. Internet access is set to extend to the library's newly constructed plaza upon completion. For additional Wi-Fi service, try the chain eatery **Panera Bread** (136 Nassau St., 609/683-5222) on Nassau Street.

Princeton's downtown parking garage, between Spring and Wiggins Streets, provides free parking for up to 30 minutes. For longer stays, pay on foot **Quick Pay Stations** are featured at all main garage entrances.

You can purchase **Smart Cards** at parking garages and Princeton Borough Hall. Use them on any of Princeton's parking meters, and whatever time you don't use will be credited to you. On-street parking is usually limited to two hours, 8 A.M.–7 P.M. Parking throughout the borough is free on Sundays.

GETTING THERE AND AROUND

Bicycle routes run along many roads in both the borough and the township and are the choice mode of transport for students, as traffic is often horrendous.

Princeton's train station is located at University Place (one block north of Alexander Rd.), alongside campus and within walking distance to the borough's downtown shops. This unmanned station includes bike racks and vending machines for ticket purchases.

CRANBURY

The history of this 300-year-old village, all of which is listed on the State and National Registers of Historic Places, is oozing from the whitewash and faded pastels of the colonial clapboard structures lining its Main Street. Within these buildings are small shops and businesses, a couple of restaurants (one a historic inn), and a local museum. Situated on **Brainerd Lake** in downtown Cranbury is **Village Park,** a neighborhood park featuring basketball and tennis courts, baseball fields, and a playground.

West of the village, along Cranbury Road, is **Grover's Mill.** Part of the larger West Windsor Township, this hamlet played alien crash pad for Orson Welles' famous 1938 *War of the Worlds* radio broadcast.

Cranbury Museum

Run by the **Cranbury Historical & Preservation Society** (609/860-1889), the circa-1834 **Cranbury Museum** (4 Park Pl., 609/655-2611, 1–4 P.M. Sun., $3 suggested donation) displays historic village artifacts like farming tools and

© LAURA KINIRY

War of the Worlds monument, Van Nest Park

various items recovered from a downtown archaeological dig. A twelve-panel quilt describing Cranbury's long history hangs on the museum's first floor.

You can pick up a copy of Cranbury's self-guided walking tour brochure at the Society's History Center (6 South Main St.).

War of the Worlds

For a little bit of pop culture history, head to the nearby town of **Grover's Mill.** There's not a lot to do here, but the beauty of this hamlet lies in its status as fictitious landing site for the aliens of Orsen Welles' October 30, 1938 radio broadcast. The now-known "Panic Broadcast" was based on the 1889 science fiction novel *War of the Worlds* by H. G. Wells, and scared the shirts off of locals and listeners everywhere.

An old wooden water tower that bore bullet holes from that evening (the tower was supposedly mistaken for an approaching UFO) was taken down, but you'll find **Van Nest Park** (Cranbury Rd., 609/799-6141), a tiny neighborhood park featuring a six-foot marker commemorating the event, erected in 1988 to honor the broadcast's 50th anniversary. If you can get past the Canada geese that like to graze in front of the statue you'll see a plaque depicting Welles, a spaceship, and a very frightened family hovering together around their radio. The park has little to offer in addition, but for pop culture fans it's definitely worth the trip.

Food

Dining choices in Cranbury are limited to the following favorable options.

The **Cranbury Inn** (21 S. Main St., 609/655-5595, $17–23) began as a mid-18th-century tavern and stagecoach stop, and later became the United States Hotel before its present in-carnation. This traditional American eatery houses both a lounge and a liquor store, and features an early-bird dining menu. Lunch hours are 11 A.M.–4 P.M. Monday–Saturday. Dinner is served throughout the week, 5–9 P.M. Monday–Thursday, until 10 P.M. Friday and Saturday, and 2–9 P.M. Sunday, with brunch 11 A.M.–2 P.M.

The 60-seat BYO **Hannah & Mason's** (30 N. Main St., Cranbury, 609/655-3220, $23–28) opened at its present location in 2004. The restaurant features contemporary American cuisine served in a converted home with wood floors, dim lights, and three dining areas. Lunch is served 11 A.M.–2:30 P.M. Monday–Friday. Dinner hours are 5–10 P.M. Friday and Saturday. Closed Sunday.

New Brunswick and Vicinity

Home to Rutgers University, Johnson & Johnson World Headquarters, and Robert Wood Johnson University Hospital, this Middlesex County seat is both a commuter town and cultural hub. A small but lively theater district has brought a number of excellent restaurants to the area, though there are few shopping opportunities along **George Street,** the city's brick-laid (driving it can be hell) main avenue.

New Brunswick features numerous small-scale high-rises, rolling hills, narrow streets, and plenty of traffic. The city stands along the southern bank of the Raritan River and has a couple of neighborhood parks, one that hosts festivals throughout the year. Route 27 cuts through New Brunswick's center, separating Rutgers' main campus from the downtown district. Known here as **French Street,** it's the city's Hispanic district.

RUTGERS UNIVERSITY

Rutgers (542 George St., 732/932-1766, www.rutgers.edu) was founded in 1766 as Queen's College. Today it is New Jersey's official state university and includes additional campuses in Camden and Newark, as well as Cook College—the agricultural school located along the New Brunswick/Piscataway border. The Old Queens/Voorhees Mall campus in downtown New Brunswick dates back to the university's origins, as is made evident by its large percentage of colonial architecture.

Historic tours of the downtown campus are held 11:30 A.M. Friday and Saturday by appointment throughout the fall and spring semesters. These tours are free (as long as you arrange it by 10 A.M. the Thursday before), last about an hour, and begin at Riverstede (542 George St., 732/932-9342), the Rutgers New Brunswick center for campus information services. Ghost tours, beginning at the same point, are held in October. For more info, check http://campusinfo.rutgers.edu/ghosttour.

Rutgers Geology Museum

On the second floor of Geology Hall in the Old Queens section of Rutgers campus, this more-than-a-century-old museum (Geology Hall, 732/932-7243, http://geology.rutgers.edu/museum.html, 1–4 P.M. Mon., 9 A.M.–noon Tues.–Fri., closed weekends during summer, call for weekend hours during the academic year, free) houses such treasures as an Egyptian

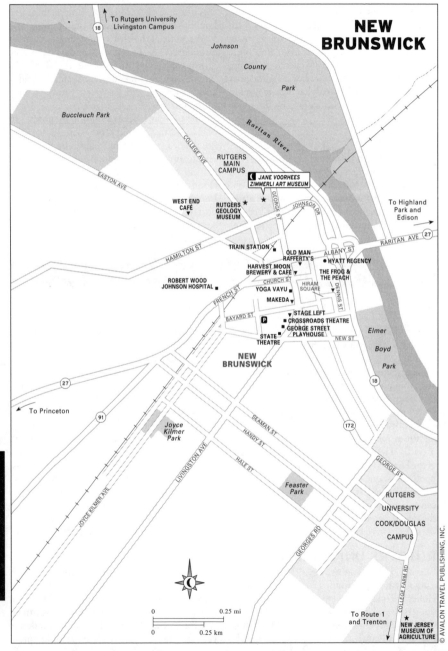

NEW BRUNSWICK

To Rutgers University
Livingston Campus

18

Johnson

County

Park

Buccleuch Park

Raritan River

COLLEGE AVE

EASTON AVE

RUTGERS MAIN CAMPUS

JANE VOORHEES
ZIMMERLI ART MUSEUM

WEST END CAFÉ

RUTGERS GEOLOGY MUSEUM

GEORGE ST

JOHNSON DR

To Highland Park and Edison

ALBANY ST

RARITAN AVE 27

HAMILTON ST

TRAIN STATION

OLD MAN RAFFERTY'S

HYATT REGENCY

HARVEST MOON BREWERY & CAFÉ

THE FROG & THE PEACH

CHURCH ST

ROBERT WOOD JOHNSON HOSPITAL

FRENCH ST

YOGA VAYU

HIRAM SQUARE

DENNIS ST

MAKEDA

BAYARD ST

P

STAGE LEFT

CROSSROADS THEATRE

STATE THEATRE

GEORGE STREET PLAYHOUSE

NEW ST

Elmer

Boyd

Park

NEW BRUNSWICK

27

18

To Princeton

91

SEAMAN ST

172

Joyce Kilmer Park

LIVINGSTON AVE

HANDY ST

GEORGE ST

HALE ST

JOYCE KILMER AVE

Feaster Park

RUTGERS

UNIVERSITY

COOK/DOUGLAS

CAMPUS

GEORGES RD

COLLEGE FARM RD

0   0.25 mi

0   0.25 km

To Route 1 and Trenton

NEW JERSEY MUSEUM OF AGRICULTURE

CENTRAL JERSEY

mummy, locally found dinosaur prints, and a nine-foot-tall mastodon skeleton discovered in South Jersey's Salem County in 1869. Ask around campus and you'll realize many students don't know the museum exists. Good for you—you'll have this treasure all to yourself.

New Jersey Museum of Agriculture

Located south of town on the Rutgers Cook Campus off Route 1 in North Brunswick, Rutgers' New Jersey Museum of Agriculture (103 College Farm Rd., N. Brunswick, 732/249-2077, www.agriculturemuseum.org, 10 A.M.–5 P.M. Tues.–Sat., $4 adult, $2 child) tells the story of New Jersey's farming history. Here you'll find agricultural tools, photographs depicting farm life over the decades, butter churns and tractors, and a fully stocked general store. The two-story space also features a number of changing exhibits and a gift shop. Educational events, mostly geared toward kids, are held on weekends throughout the year.

(Jane Voorhees Zimmerli Art Museum

Zimmerli Art Museum (71 Hamilton St., 732/932-7237, www.zimmerlimuseum.rutgers .edu, $3 adult, under 18 free), the fourth-largest university museum in the United States, is also home to the largest collection of nonconformist former Soviet artwork outside of Russia. It seems like a strange place to find such a display, but it's here, and much of it was created underground during the Soviet regime. The museum's exhibit of Soviet Union theater posters is truly outstanding, as is its collection of European printmaking, including a notable number of Belgian art nouveau posters.

The museum's many other highlights include an interesting display of locally designed stained glass windows, and Japonisme—a collection of Japanese and European paper art and ceramics showing Japan's influence on the West in the late 19th century.

A small gift shop and adjacent café are located on the first floor. Museum and shop hours are 10 A.M.–4:30 P.M. Tuesday–Friday,

noon–5 P.M. weekends; closed Mondays throughout the year, Tuesdays in July, and daily throughout August. The first Sunday of the month is free.

ENTERTAINMENT AND EVENTS

New Brunswick hosts the state's largest concentration of theaters, as well as a couple of festivals that are worth your time if you're in the area. Dinner and a show is a great way to enjoy New Brunswick's offerings.

Theaters

Just off George Street on a one-block stretch of Livingston Avenue is New Brunswick's own theater row. Public parking lots exist nearby on Banyard, Kirkpatrick, and Neilson Streets.

New Brunswick's first professional theater, the **George Street Playhouse** (9 Livingston Ave., 732/246-7717) has produced numerous plays and musicals since its inception in 1974. Today the theater continues to showcase original productions and established plays in a cozy 375-seat setting. Next door is the famed **State Theatre** (15 Livingston Ave., 732/246-SHOW or 732/246-7469, www.statetheatrenj.org), which has undergone massive renovations to restore the interior to its 1921 vaudeville splendor. This 1,800-seat venue hosts big-name acts and dance, operas, and orchestras, among others.

The 264-seat **Crossroads Theatre** (7 Livingston Ave., 732/545-8100) was built in 1991 to house the Crossroads Theatre Company, which specializes in "literary works that examine the African American experience." The company was awarded a Tony for best U.S. regional theater in 1999, but the theater has since experienced financial difficulties and remains open on a limited basis.

Festivals

Held at the city's Boyd Park annually in September, the **Raritan River Festival** (www.raritanriverfest.com) has been a New Brunswick tradition since 1980. The daylong event features food, music, kiddie rides, and a cardboard canoe race down the Raritan River.

COURTESY OF THE STATE THEATRE

State Theatre, New Brunswick

The **New Jersey Film Festival** (www.nj filmfest.com), hosted by the Rutgers Film Co-op/New Jersey Media Arts Center, showcases a variety of new and established films at various city locations throughout the months of June and July. You can view documentaries, international, and experimental works Friday–Sunday evening, and filmmakers are sometimes on hand to discuss their work. Thursday evenings are reserved for classic features.

SPORTS AND RECREATION

New Brunswick is home to a number of parks, including the 78-acre **Buccleuch Park.** Located between the Raritan River and Easton Avenue just above the main Rutgers campus, it's a neighborhood recreation area with a 1.5-mile fitness trail, a couple of tennis courts, and a baseball field. The 20-acre **Boyd Park,** on the edge of the Raritan River, features a nearly mile-long multiuse towpath. Signs posted throughout the grounds offer insight into the city's history and that of the Raritan River, including information on the D&R

Canal. The park also hosts festivals throughout the year.

Washington Riding Stables (1707 S. Washington Ave., 732/249-2471, www.washington stables.com) in nearby Piscataway offers guided horseback riding on 30 miles of trails, suitable for riders beginner–advanced ($30 for one hour).

ACCOMMODATIONS
$200-250

New Brunswick's top hotel is the **Hyatt Regency** (2 Albany St., 732/873-1234, http://newbrunswick.hyatt.com), conveniently located close to Rutgers University and the train station, as well as George Street and the Livingston Street theaters. Stylish rooms come equipped with high-speed Internet access and individual climate control. A restaurant serving American fare is located downstairs.

FOOD AND NIGHTLIFE

New Brunswick has a great selection of bars and restaurants, ranging from college pub to suit-and-tie attire. The dining is top notch and, as this is a university town, there's no shortage of drinks at the bar.

One of New Jersey's consistently top-rated restaurants, **Stage Left** (5 Livingston Ave. at George St., 732/828-4444, www.stageleft.com, $23–35) serves New American cuisine using fresh ingredients to create ultimate flavor. The restaurant is conveniently located along theater row and features a wine library and fireplace, and seasonal sidewalk seating. Cell phones are not welcome. Lunch is served noon–2:30 P.M. Friday only. Dinner hours are 5:30–9:30 P.M. Monday, until 11 P.M. Tuesday–Saturday, 4:30–9 P.M. Sunday.

The Frog and the Peach (29 Dennis St. at Hiram Sq., 732/846-3216, www.frogand peach.com, $22–37) serves internationally inspired modern American cuisine within an industrial building in the residential Hiram Square. The restaurant's sleek decor and glass-covered all-season garden are as favored as the food. The restaurant is open 11:30 A.M.–2:30 P.M. and 5:30–10:30 P.M. Monday–Friday, 5:30–10:30 P.M. Saturday, and 4:30–9:30 P.M. Sunday.

The casual **Harvest Moon Brewery and Cafe** (392 George St., 732/249-6666, www.harvest moonbrewery.com, 11:30 A.M.–2 A.M. daily, $14–25) features American eats and home-brewed beers, supplemented by a choice selection of Belgian ales. A late-night menu (before midnight) and live entertainment nightly make this place a standout.

Old Man Rafferty's (106 Albany St., 732/846-6153, www.oldmanraffertys.com, 11:30 A.M.–11 P.M. Mon.–Thurs., until midnight Fri. and Sat., noon–midnight Sun., $8–18) is an American eatery and full bar, popular with the university crowd.

Named for the Queen of Sheba, the stylish **Makeda** (338 George St., 732/545-5115, www.makedas.com, $11.50–24) is New Jersey's first, perhaps only, Ethiopian restaurant. An exciting menu features a nice selection of vegetarian dishes, and all meals are served with *injera,* a flatbread that doubles as silverware. Live reggae and calypso music play on the weekends. Next door is a shop/gallery selling African and African-inspired wares. Lunch is served 11:30 A.M.–4 P.M. Monday–Friday, and noon–4 P.M. Saturday. Dinner hours are 4–10:30 P.M. Monday–Friday, until midnight Saturday, noon–10:30 P.M. Sunday.

West End Café (125 Easton Ave., #1, 732/249-5282) is where Rutgers students go for their daily dose of caffeine, with comfy couches and late-night hours.

INFORMATION AND SERVICES

Between Paterson and Banyard Streets is **Yoga Vayu** (354 George St., 732/249-8245, www.yogavayu.com), a yoga and dance studio offering discounted student and senior rates.

GETTING THERE AND AROUND

New Brunswick's train station (French and Albany Sts., 5:30 A.M.–9 P.M. Mon.–Fri., 6:40 A.M.–8 P.M. weekends) is west of George Street. There are bike racks at the station, and vending machines for times when a ticket seller is not available. Both Amtrak and NJ Transit

run lines through the city (though you're much better off taking NJ Transit if traveling a short distance), and New Brunswick is 50 minutes by train from New York City. To reach New Brunswick from South Jersey, take the River LINE from Camden to Trenton, and cross the street to hop a local train north to this university city.

If you're driving, validated parking is available with a number of businesses—be sure to check—when parking in a lot run by the **New Brunswick Parking Authority** (NBPA, 732/545-3118, www.njnbpa.org).

EDISON

Edison Township is the birthplace of recorded sound and, combined with nearby Iselin, home to New Jersey's largest Indian and Chinese population. Once known as Raritan, the township was renamed in 1954 after Thomas Alva Edison who, in the late 19th century, built what is now known as the world's "first organized research facility" in the area's Menlo Park section. Edison grew quickly in the 1950s as a manufacturing hub, developing like a donut around the borough of Metuchen and never forming its own town center. Plans are currently in the works to create a lifestyle center—a modern-day Main Street—to serve this purpose. In the meantime, the Edison Memorial Complex and Oak Tree Road, a six-block Little India located west of Route 27, are must-visits on your way through town.

Thomas Alva Edison Memorial Museum and Tower

Although Edison's original research laboratory is long gone, the Edison Memorial Museum, Tower, and Information Trail (37 Christie St., 732/549-3299, www.edisonnj.org/menlopark/museum.asp, 10 A.M.–4 P.M. Tues.–Sat., free) are fine reminders of what once stood in their place. Named for the section of Edison Township where the inventor lived and worked, the Menlo Park Museum is a tiny two-room building bursting with Edison memorabilia, including numerous phonographs and photographs. The space is so tightly packed, in fact, that there are plans for a new, larger museum to be constructed beginning in spring 2006. To the left stands the 131-foot Tower, a popular roadside attraction topped with a 13.5-foot working light bulb.

The museum and surrounding grounds offer plenty to see if you look closely, but the best feature of this place is the people who work here. They're so well versed in Edison trivia and speak about his life with such enthusiasm it's contagious. Who knew that the life of Edison and his cronies would be so interesting?

Oak Tree Road

Turn west onto Oak Tree Road from Route 27 to discover a throng of sari shops, Bollywood video stores, and Indian snack shops. Although locals refer to it simply as Oak Tree, this six-block stretch of roadway running through Iselin Township is New Jersey's own Little India, where the food selection is phenomenal, and you can find some great buys through a little old-fashioned bargaining.

Food

You'll be able to find fast-food joints and chain restaurants in Edison easily, but one of the best reasons to come here is the ethnic cuisine. Most of the restaurants are found along Oak Tree Road, and a few along Route 27.

Chowpatty (1349 Oak Tree Rd., 732/283-9020, www.chowpattyfoods.com, 11:30 A.M.–10 P.M. Tues.–Sun.) serves south Indian vegetarian dishes and is one of the United States' first *chaat* houses. Try your hand at one of these authentic Indian treats or go for a combination platter (Chowpatty Thali, $11.99).

Reservations are recommended at **Ming** (ShopRite Plaza, 1655-185 Oak Tree Road, 732/549-5051, www.mingrestaurants.com, noon–2:45 P.M., 5:30–10 P.M. Tues.–Thurs. and Sun., until 10:30 P.M. Fri. and Sat., $13–23), a 90-seat BYO with a Far Eastern decor and a superb selection of Pan-Asian fare. Next door is **Moghul** (ShopRite Plaza, 1655-195 Oak Tree Rd., 732/549-5050, noon–2:45 P.M., 5:30–10 P.M. Tues.–Thurs. and Sun., until 10:30 P.M. Fri. and Sat., $10–17), Ming's sister restaurant serving Indian cuisine in an authentic

Edison Memorial Tower, Menlo Park

© LAURA KINIRY

setting. This BYO features an outstanding lunch buffet ($12.95) and Sunday brunch. Moghul also runs a fast-food eatery across the road called **Moghul Express** (1670A Oak Tree Rd., 732/549-6222, $7.50). The menu includes Indian, Chinese, and Thai selections, and a number of vegetarian dishes.

For traditional Cantonese dim sum served on the weekends (11 A.M.–3 P.M.), go to **Wonder Seafood Restaurant** (1984 Rte. 27, 732/287-6328, $15–25) on Route 27. Friendly and professional service keeps the crowds coming.

Meemah (19-F Rte. 27, 732/906-2223, 11:30 A.M.–10 P.M. Mon.–Thurs., until 11 P.M. Fri. and Sat., noon–9:30 P.M. Sun., $9–17) serves Chinese-Malaysian cuisine in a strip-mall setting. Despite the bland atmosphere, the food at this BYO receives good ratings.

Information and Services

The free publication *Little India,* found in newspaper dispensers along Oak Tree Road, offers ideas on where to shop in the area.

Red Bank and Vicinity

Sitting upon the clay-lined Navesink River, Red Bank is a destination unto itself. The "Dead Bank" nickname applied to the borough in the 1970s no longer fits. While Red Bank is now a swanky urban area filled with nouveau restaurants, eclectic specialty shops, and great people-watching opportunity, the borough hasn't gone overboard. Despite the exterior spotlights and spanking-new paint jobs on many of Broad Street's two- and three-story brick buildings, you'll still find such funky treasures as a 24-hour diner, a gritty pub, and an open-mic space with rec-room decor. Smaller than two square miles, Red Bank does feature a few distinct enclaves, including an antique district and a Hispanic community along the borough's west side.

The surrounding vicinity, easily described as the Bay and River region, stretches north to the edge of the Raritan and Sandy Hook Bays, west to encompass all of Middletown Township, and east to take in the borough of Rumson and hug the western coast of the Jersey Shore. Keyport and the Atlantic Highlands, both small bayside communities, are easy ferry rides from Manhattan, and it's probably this traffic-saver that has created the area's more affluent communities further out, as city dwellers head south for a nearby escape. Route 36 cuts horizontally across the region's northern portion, and Route 35 travels south, dividing Middletown Township and continuing on to Red Bank, and acting as a traffic-light alternative to the Parkway that runs parallel.

While the bulk of your time exploring this region will probably be spent in Red Bank, the outlying areas are worth exploring for their recreational potential and, in some cases, outstanding architecture.

ENTERTAINMENT AND EVENTS

The 1926 **Count Basie Theatre** (99 Monmouth St., 732/842-9000, www.countbasietheatre .org), named for the great jazz musician and Red

Broad Street in downtown Red Bank

Bank's most famous native son, is a 1,575-seat venue that has undergone major renovations and now includes a high-powered sound system and a brand-new marquee. The theater is once again equipped to show films, but it's primarily a venue for musical acts, dance, and comedy.

The **Two River Theatre** (21 Bridge Ave., 732/345-1455, www.trtc.org) enjoyed its inaugural season during 2005–2006 as the new home of the Two River Theater Co. It's located across from the Galleria (see Shopping below) and an easy walk from the train station. Inside you'll find a 350-seat main theater and a 99-seat experimental theater specializing in regional adaptations of established shows.

Clearview Cinema (36 White St., 732/777-FILM or 732/777-3456, $8.75) shows art house and foreign flicks. For live local music, head to the **Dublin House** (30 Monmouth St., 732/747-6699), a brightly lit neighborhood dive bar set inside a mansard-roof Victorian.

Festivals and Events

Vulgarthon is Kevin Smith's festival homage to the movie world. It's an occasional Red Bank event (in 2005 Vulgarthon was held in Smith's new hometown of Los Angeles) showcasing Smith's regional-centric films and the work of other independent filmmakers.

For a wider movie selection there's October's **Red Bank International Film Festival** (www.rbiff.org).

The **Red Bank Jazz & Blues Festival** (www.redbankfestival.com) is a two-day annual event taking place the first weekend in June, featuring lots of music, food, and crafts. Three stages share the performances within **Marina Park,** along Wharf Avenue and the Navesink River.

SHOPPING

Some of the most unique shops in New Jersey are found in downtown Red Bank, most notably along Broad Street—the borough's main thoroughfare—and Monmouth Street, which runs perpendicular. Take the time to browse around even if shopping's not really your thing—there's sure to be something that catches your eye.

Antique Shops and Art Galleries

West Front Street, known as Antique Alley, is home to a number of large spaces collectively housing over 150 antique dealers. Art galleries can be found throughout the borough.

The **Antique Center of Red Bank** (Nos. 226, 195, and 195B, W. Front St., 973/741-5331, 732/842-4336, or 732/842-3393), features over 150 dealers spaced among three old factories. What began in 1964 has been described as the country's "longest running antique co-op," and everything from china to furniture to jewelry boxes and fossils can be found. The nearby **Monmouth Antique Shoppes** (217 W. Front St., 732/842-7377) provide room for over 50 antique dealers, and stock includes tableware and vintage clothes and accessories.

When it opened in 1978, the **Art Alliance of Monmouth County** (33 Monmouth St., 732/842-9403) was located within the Count Basie Theatre. It has since moved to 33 Monmouth Street, where it displays a broad range of visual art. The popular **Laurel Tracey Gallery** (10 White St., 732/224-0760) features many nationally recognized painters and sculptors. **Art Forms** (16 Monmouth St., 732/530-4330) is a contemporary gallery showcasing a unique and colorful selection of fine art and ceramics. For vintage posters of the 19th and 20th century, including travel and art deco design, go to **Inheritance Gallery** (30 Monmouth St., 732/530-5417). **Lloyd's Gallery** (25 Broad St., 2nd Fl., 732/224-3993, www.lloydgarrison.com) features the 19th-century-inspired fine art of local painter Lloyd Garrison, as well as related toys and sculptures.

Specialty Shops and Boutiques

Red Bank has some great shops to explore along Monmouth and Broad Streets.

Fameabilia (42 Monmouth St., 732/450-8411) stocks an awesome collection of framed and autographed items, from photos to sports jerseys, that take up every last inch of wall space. You can literally spend hours browsing the wares—from George and Barbara Bush to *The Sopranos'* Johnny Sach—in this pseudo-museum space. And not to worry—the friendly staff is helpful but far from overbearing.

At **Jay and Silent Bob's Secret Stash** (35 Broad St., 732/758-0020, www.viewaskew.com), look for lots of Smith film paraphernalia alongside Star Wars figures and Jersey Girl goods. The name says it all at **Funk and Standard Variety Store** (40 Broad St., 732/219-5885, www.funkandstandard.com). Tacky shower curtains, mini Voodoo kits, and Mexicali design wear—it's all here.

Rumor has it that the Boss shops at **Jack's Music Shoppe** (30 Broad St., 732/842-0731) for hard-to-find albums. Jack's offers cash for used CDs and musical instruments.

Bees Knees (24 Broad St., 732/758-1900, www.thebeeskneesboutique.com) is a self-described "chic boutique" stocking Queen Beads bracelets and the bright spring colors of Lilly Pulitzer. The first-floor shop shares its space with the **Jersey Shore Apparel Co.** (732/530-1048, www.jerseyshoreapparel.com), a subsidiary of the **Firehouse Specialty Shop,** which can be found in the upstairs loft. A monogram station stands to the rear of the store. The **Wooly Monmouth** (9 Monmouth St., 732/224-YARN, www.woolymonmouth.com) stocks styling hand-knit and crocheted fashions and a full-on selection of yarns. The shop holds workshops throughout the year. The fashionable **Wisteria** (17 Broad St., 732/747-7425) carries My Flat in London handbags by designer Jan Haedrich.

The Galleria

The Galleria (2 Bridge Ave., 732/842-9000) is 80,000 square feet of modern retail and dining housed within an old uniform factory, situated near the train station in the northwest part of the borough.

ACCOMMODATIONS
$150-200

The **Molly Pitcher Inn** (88 Riverside Dr., 732/747-2500, www.mollypitcher-oyster-point.com) is a 1928 boutique hotel overlooking the Navesink River. It features 106 rooms of varying size, a swimming pool, a top-notch

bar and restaurant, and a marina for guests arriving by sea. Wireless Internet is available throughout.

Next door is the inn's sister property, the 58-room **Oyster Point Hotel** (146 Bodman Pl., 732/530-8200). This smaller space offers the same fantastic river view from many of its rooms. Individual amenities include a basket of toiletries (including shoe polish) and two home-baked chocolate chip cookies upon your nightstand. What you don't get is coffee, though you can have a pot delivered to your room for $6. The hotel often hosts conferences and the parking lot can get crowded.

It's about a 10-minute walk from both hotels to Broad Street, where you'll find the bulk of Red Bank's shops and eateries.

【 FOOD

As well as its great mix of shops, Red Bank also offers a superb mix of eateries, everything from low-key taquerias to trendy sushi clubs. With such a great selection, it's hard to go wrong.

American Eateries

No Ordinary Joe Café (51 Broad St., 732/530-4040, 6:30 A.M.–5 P.M. Mon.–Thurs., until 10 P.M. Fri., 7 A.M.–11 P.M. Sat., 8 A.M.–4 P.M. Sun.) is an A.M. coffee house that turns eatery in the afternoon. Order a Soup Sampler—your choice of any three soups for $6.95—or try the "create your own pressed panini" ($6.95). Breakfast options include bagels and berry-filled oatmeal.

For a sit-down morning meal, there's the **River Edge Café** (35 Broad St., 732/741-7198, $6.95–25). This country-style restaurant serves homemade American eats for breakfast (go for the cheese omelet, $6.95) and lunch—dinner is available later in the week. Morning and afternoon hours are 8:30 A.M.–3 P.M. Monday–Thursday, until 4 P.M. Friday, 8 A.M.–4 P.M. Saturday and Sunday. Dinner is served 5–9 P.M. Thursday, until 10 P.M. Friday, 4–10 P.M. Saturday, and 4–8 P.M. Sunday.

Visitors and locals alike insist the **Molly Pitcher Inn** (88 Riverside Dr., 732/747-2500, www.mollypitcher-oysterpoint.com) is the place to go for fine American cuisine in Red Bank.

The inn offers superb views from its dining room above the Navesink River, and an equally favored Sunday brunch. Jackets are required after 5 P.M.

The **Broadway Diner** (45 Monmouth St., 732/224-1234, $7) is Red Bank's only 24-hour eats. The comfy booths that line the kitchen in this attractive space get excellent service—the wait staff hardly has to move a muscle. The world's best pancakes may be an exaggeration—liven things up by adding pecans ($5.25), and then finish off your meal with a vanilla shake.

Eclectic Cuisine

From sushi to Russian to Mexican fare, the choices are endless…

Teak (64 Monmouth St., 732/747-5775, www.teakrestaurant.com, $18–25) is a 170-seat restaurant and lounge serving sushi with an edge amongst sleek decor. Choose from the Jersey Girl roll and the Bruce Spring roll, and follow up your order with a Sake-tini ($9)—that's sake, vodka, and blackberry puree—from the unique martini menu. Merengue dancing takes place the second Friday of each month. Lunch is served noon–3 P.M. Monday–Saturday. Dinner hours are 5–10 P.M. Monday–Thursday, until midnight Friday and Saturday.

(Down to Earth (7 Broad St., 732/747-4542, www.downtoearthnj.com, $9–15) is an organic vegan eatery housed in a stylish basement space, serving tasty soy shakes, a menu of raw eats, and a wonderful selection of entrées made with tempeh, tofu, rice, beans, and veggies. The cuisine is internationally inspired, unique, and definitely worth the experience. Lunch hours are 11 A.M.–3 P.M. Monday and Wednesday–Saturday. Dinner is served 5–9 P.M. Wednesday, Thursday, Sunday, and Monday, until 10 P.M. Friday and Saturday. Closed Tuesday.

The Bistro (14 Broad St., 732/530-5553 or 732/530-5553, $8.95–41.95), a BYO featuring a long dining room with two rows of tables and a warm red brick wall, serves a diverse menu ranging from sushi to pizza. The restaurant is open for lunch noon–2:30 P.M. Monday–Friday. Dinner hours are 5–9:30 P.M. Monday–Thursday, until 11 P.M. Friday and Saturday, and 5–9 P.M. Sunday.

You can't get any swankier than **Red** (3 Broad St., 732/741-3232, www.rednj.com, $16–26), an eclectic eatery and sushi bar with a dining mezzanine, upstairs lounge, and live Sunday jazz. Specialty drinks and dessert are a must! **Café Everest** (30 Monmouth St., 732/747-6699, 10 A.M.–11 P.M. Mon.–Thurs., until midnight Fri., 1 A.M. Sat., 10 P.M. Sun., $12–20) serves Russian cuisine in a mediocre fine-dining setting. Appetizers include Russian-style crepes ($6.95) and classic dumplings ($7.95).

Carlos O'Connor's (31 Monmouth St., 732/530-6663, 5–9 P.M. Tues.–Thurs., until 9:30 P.M. Fri. and Sat., 5–9 P.M. Sun.) is a BYO Irish-Mexican eatery with an over-the-top decor. Stuffed parrots, plastic peppers, and fruit baskets hang from the ceiling of this colorful joint, and wicker chairs washed in reds, yellows, and greens provide seating. Go for a quesadilla ($7.95) or a taco platter ($11.95).

For truly authentic Mexican fare try **Juanito's** (159 Monmouth St., 732/747-9062, noon–10 P.M., $4.95–16.95), a popular eatery near the train station.

INFORMATION AND SERVICES

Red Bank's **Visitors Center** (732/741-9211, www.visit.redbank.com) is located in the train station at Monmouth Street and Bridge Avenue. It's only open 1–5 P.M. Thursday and Friday, and 1:30–3:30 weekends.

For Internet access try the **Internet Café** (1 West Front St., 732/842-4503, www.icafenj.com, 11 A.M.–11 P.M. Mon.–Tues. and Thurs., until 1 A.M. Fri, 2 P.M.–1 A.M. Sat., 2–11 P.M. Sun., closed Wed.), a rec room–style set-up with coffee, snacks, and the occasional open mic. Walk-in yoga classes are held at **Synapse Studios** (10 Broad St., 3rd floor, 732/219-6662). Cost is $18.

GETTING THERE AND AROUND

Red Bank lies along Route 35 on the tail of the Navesink River and is 48 miles south of New York City, 8 miles from the Jersey Shore, and 85 miles northeast of Philly. You can reach it from exit 109 of the Garden State Parkway, or by taking NJ Transit's **North Jersey Coast line** (800/772-2222, njtransit.com). The borough is easy to navigate on foot from the train station, which is located at Bridge Avenue between Monmouth and Oakland Streets.

RUMSON

It's hard to keep from staring at the magnificent mansions lining **Rumson Road** en route to Sea Bright, especially when you're convinced one of them belongs to the Boss himself. Regardless of whether you're a Springsteen fanatic, the homes here (what's not hidden behind stone walls and dense greenery) are truly spectacular, and offer a rewarding Sunday drive.

Fromagerie

Jackets and reservations are required at this excellent French restaurant (26 Ridge Rd., 732/842-8088, www.fromagerierestaurant.com, $25–38) located within an old Victorian on a residential street. The restaurant is open for lunch 11:30 A.M.–2:30 P.M. Monday–Friday throughout the months of December and January, and for dinner 5–10 P.M. Monday–Saturday, beginning at 4 P.M. Sunday.

KEYPORT-ATLANTIC HIGHLANDS

Situated on the bank of the Raritan Bay, the small borough of Keyport was once an oyster-harvesting and shipbuilding capital. These days the "Pearl of the Bayshore" is striving to get its weathered downtown up and running. Despite good efforts, there's little offered in the way of shops and restaurants. There are, however, a couple of reasons to stop here for fishers and those interested in Bayshore history.

Continuing east on Route 36 will bring you to the borough of **Keansburg,** where you'll find a boardwalk-style amusement park and water park, and on to the Atlantic Highlands, boasting the highest point on the entire eastern seaboard.

Steamboat Dock Museum

The **Keyport Historical Society** runs the Steamboat Dock Museum (Broad St., Keyport, 732/739-6390), a seasonal museum dedicated to the town's rich maritime history, including steamboat building and the oyster industry. Well-thought-out exhibits and special events such as a vintage swimsuit fashion show are reason enough to visit. Hours are typically 1–4 P.M. Sunday and 10 A.M.–noon Monday, mid-May–mid-September.

Keansburg Amusement Park

Occupying a few blocks of prime bayfront property, this carnival-style amusement park (275 Beachway, Keansburg, 732/495-1400, www.keansburgamusementpark.com) has been entertaining crowds for over a century. Its most recent addition is **Runaway Rapids Amusement Park,** a suit-soaking extravaganza of tube shoots and waterslides. The park's amusements include the DoubleShot drop tower, the dizzying Chaos, speedway racecars, and lots of stuff for the kids. Admission to the amusement park is free, and a book of 100 ride tickets costs $39.95. A three-hour admission to the water park is $20.95. Combination tickets are available. The park is open daily from 10 A.M. throughout July, August, and most of June, and on a limited schedule (including most weekends) from late March–mid-June, and September. Closing times vary.

Mount Mitchell Scenic Overlook

Topping the Atlantic Highlands at 266 feet above sea level, Mount Mitchell (Ocean Blvd., 732/842-4000, 8 A.M.–dusk daily) is the highest point on the eastern seaboard. Hard to believe—but true. The site provides a great view of Sandy Hook and the Raritan and Sandy Hook Bays, and on a clear day you're able to get a glimpse of the New York City skyline. A recent addition to the overlook is a 9/11 memorial honoring Monmouth County residents who died in the terrorist attacks.

Sports and Recreation

Both Keyport and Keansburg maintain **fishing piers** on the Raritan Bay, which has a large striped bass population. Bait and tackle shops in the area include **Crabby's Bait and Tackle**

CENTRAL JERSEY

(229 W. Front St., Keyport, 732/335-9311), **Skipper's Shop** (35 1st Ave., Atlantic Highlands, 732/872-0367), and **Little Fish** (17 Avenue D, Atlantic Highlands, 732/872-2601).

The **Henry Hudson Bike Trail** is a paved 10-mile multiuse trail that travels from Aberdeen, just east of the Garden State Parkway, continuing through the Raritan Bay towns along Route 36 until reaching the Atlantic Highlands. Plans are in the works to connect the trail south to Freehold; a portion of this stretch is already open.

Food

For hearty German cuisine in authentic beer-hall surrounds, try **Hofbrauhaus** (301 Ocean Blvd., Atlantic Highlands, 732/291-0224, www.hofbrauhausnj.com, $20–26). Live bands play traditional tunes on the weekends. Hours are 4–10 P.M. Monday–Thursday, until 11 P.M. Friday, noon–11 P.M. Saturday, and noon–10 P.M. Sunday.

Getting There and Around

Seastreak ($35 round-trip peak, $29 round-trip off-peak) runs a weekday commuter ferry from the Atlantic Highlands to New York City. The boat leaves from the bottom of First Avenue at the Atlantic Highlands Municipal Marina and the trip takes approximately 35 minutes.

MIDDLETOWN

The 41 square miles of Middletown Township makes up the largest portion of the Bay and River region, stretching up toward Keyport, east along the Navesink River, and south past Red Bank. Like many of the surrounding areas, Middletown was heavily impacted by the events of September 11, 2001, suffering one of the nation's highest death tolls. It's an affluent suburb, home to both rocker Jon Bon Jovi and the Quick Stop Grocery Store immortalized in Kevin Smith's film *Clerks* (the store's found in the township's Lincroft section). Despite its recent recognition, Middletown has a long history. A plaque upon entering the township's village historic district reads "Middletown Village is the oldest settlement in New Jersey (1613)… and (once) a haven for Captain Kidd's pirates."

A drive through Middletown, down the bicycle-friendly **Oak Hill Road** and past the jaw-dropping estates lining **Navesink River Road** is highly recommended, as well as a stop at the one or two sights that stand firmly on their own.

Monmouth Museum

Monmouth Museum (Brookdale Community College, Newman Springs Rd., 732/747-226, www.monmouthmuseum.org, 10 A.M.–4:30 P.M. Tues.–Sat., 1–5 P.M. Sun., $5) is an educational and cultural museum located on the campus of Brookdale Community College (which looks like a cross between an upscale senior center and a ski lodge). The museum hosts changing exhibits in a variety of disciplines and media, and kids are well-represented with two children's wings: the Becker's Children's Wing and the Wonder Wing, a *Goonies*-type playground with a slide-through whale, a rope bridge, and a pirate ship.

Monmouth Museum is also home to one of North America's largest collections of 18th- and 19th-century sewing clamps. Also known as "bird clamps," these ornately designed pieces were made to assist sewers in holding material in place before the advent of the machine. Adornment options were later expanded to include snakes, dolphins, and cherubs, among other designs.

Recreation

The scenic **Oak Hill Road** is an ideal stretch for cyclists. There's no set shoulder, but the road is wide enough to handle both automobile and bicycle traffic. Instead of continuing on to Navesink Road to explore the area, it's best to stick to the back streets where there's much less traffic and the roads are safer for bicycling. To get a glimpse of the area's estates, cyclists may want to begin from nearby Red Bank and travel east along **River Road** or **Rumson Road.**

Situated along Oak Hill is the 250-acre **Poricy Park Conservancy** (345 Oak Hill Rd., 732/842-5966, www.monmouth.com/~

poricypark/), a wildly scenic reserve with nature trails, marshland, even a fossil bed. Educational programs take place at the property's 18th-century **Murray Farmhouse,** which still contains its original beehive oven. Events like star searches, trail runs, and ghost hunts are held throughout the year. A nature center within the park is open 9 A.M.–4 P.M. Monday–Friday, 12:30–3:30 P.M. Sunday, closed Saturday, but trails remain accessible year-round dawn–dusk. The Murray Farmhouse is open to the public 1–2:30 P.M. the last Sunday of the month, excluding February, May, and October.

Quick Stop & RST Video

This is a must-stop for any Kevin Smith fan—the filming location for the Jersey boy's directorial debut, *Clerks.* Smith worked days at the Quick Stop (58–60 Leonardo Ave., Lincroft) and spent his midnight hours filming. It's not much to see, but it's the significance, right?

Food

Middletown is a large township with no shortage of dining options. Those listed below offer a nice overview.

For an order of cheese fries and more Kevin Smith trivia, stop at the **Marina Diner** (Route 36 and Seeley Ave., Belford, 732/495-9749,

$5–16), featured in the film *Chasing Amy.* The diner is open until midnight Sunday–Thursday and 24 hours Friday and Saturday.

The **Lincroft Inn** (700 Newman Springs Rd., Lincroft, 732/747-0890, 11:30 A.M.–10 P.M. Mon.–Thurs., noon–11 P.M. Fri. and Sat., noon–9 P.M. Sun., $14.95–28.95) serves continental cuisine in a historic setting. The restaurant includes a dining room separate from its popular sports bar.

A widely revered establishment, **Restaurant Nicholas** (160 Rte. 35 S., Red Bank, 732/345-9977, www.restaurantnicholas.com, 5:30–10 P.M. Sun.–Thurs., until 11 P.M. Fri. and Sat., $38–75) specializes in New American cuisine and features an excellent wine list comprised of lesser known vintages and vintners. The changing fixed-price menu includes two- and three-course options, as well as a vegetarian selection.

If you're in the township's Bayshore region, stop by the family-owned **Navesink Fishery** (A&P Shopping Center, 1004 Rte. 36 S., 732/291-8017, $28) for fresh seafood. The restaurant is located in the rear of this strip-mall location, behind the market. It's open year-round for lunch noon–2:30 P.M. Tuesday–Friday, and dinner 5–9 P.M. Tuesday–Thursday, until 10 P.M. Friday and Saturday.

The Central Plains

Rolling hills and horse farms occupy a large portion of the plains that stretch horizontally across the lower and middle portion of Monmouth County. From Allaire west to Allentown, I-195 takes a direct route, but unless you're in a hurry (and it's not rush hour), skip the highway and take the back roads—Route 524 to Route 537 is a good place to start—and meander past the county parks and golf courses, numerous orchards and more horses than you can count. You'll find the area's best restaurants in Freehold, as well as a fine B&B. For additional accommodation options, try New Egypt and the camping resorts of Jackson.

HOLMDEL

Holmdel is an attractive rural suburb that was once the home of Mattel Toys, and continues to serve as a major hub for Lucent Technologies Bell Labs Innovations. Its location along the Shark River and proximity to the Shore make it an ideal spot for fossil-hunting, where you can find anything from arrowheads to shark teeth. A number of parks, including a reconstructed living-history farm, and the township's outdoor amphitheater draw visitors to the area. Holmdel is home to the United States' first museum entirely devoted to the Vietnam War.

CENTRAL JERSEY

© LAURA KINIRY

hogging it up at Longstreet Farm, Holmdel

CENTRAL JERSEY

Sights

Located in Telegraph Hill Park at exit 116 off the New Jersey Turnpike, the **New Jersey Vietnam Veteran's Memorial and Vietnam Era Education Center** (732/335-0033 or 800/648-8387, www.njvvmf.org, 10 A.M.–4 P.M. Tues.–Sat., $4 adults, $2 seniors and students, under 10 free) was created to help visitors understand the Vietnam War. Exhibits include photographs and letters centering around rotating themes relating to the war, and a resource gallery of books, videos, and other reference materials is open to the public. An on-site outdoor memorial pays tribute to the Americans, New Jerseyans especially, who died in Vietnam.

A nice place to bring the kids is **Longstreet Farm** (Holmdel Park, 732/946-3758, www.monmouthcountyparks.com), an 1890s restored farming village found within Holmdel Park. The village is free to enter (though donations are accepted) and features hogs, cows, horses, and sheep; costumed interpreters; and a number of reconstructed and authentic structures, including a 1770s 14-room farmhouse and the oldest Dutch barn in Monmouth County. Demonstrations in such crafts as needlepoint and lace-making take place throughout the year. The farm is open daily 9 A.M.–5 P.M. Memorial Day–Labor Day, and 10 A.M.–4 P.M. the remainder of the year.

PNC Bank Art Center

This 17,500-seat outdoor amphitheater (732/203-2500, www.artscenter.com/main.html) is a popular summer music venue, showcasing big-name performers and smaller acts and staging a couple of festivals throughout the season. It's strategically located at the Garden State Parkway's exit 116, adjacent to the Vietnam Education Center, and attracts crowds from up and down the Jersey Shore, as well as New York City. Reserved tickets and general lawn seats are available.

Sports and Recreation

The 572-acre **Holmdel Park** (44 Longstreet Rd., 732/946-9562) offers numerous short nature trails that are easy to walk and can be combined for longer hikes. They vary in length from the easy 0.4-mile Pond Walk Trail to the more moderately strenuous 3.1-mile Cross Country Trail. While here, stop by the **Holmdel Arboretum** for a picnic lunch under a crab apple tree. In the winter, the park's hilly terrain is perfect for sledding. Ice-skating is allowed on Lower Pond, and cross-country skiing can be enjoyed on the hiking trails.

For a good workout, try the **Ramanessin Greenway Trail** (www.holmdelenviro.org/ramtrail.htm), a seven-mile trail crossing Holmdel Township from **Phillips Park** to **Thompson Park**. The Greenway is an ongoing project of the Holmdel Environmental Commission (732/946-8897), which schedules guided walks—such as an Earth Day Walk and a Fall Foliage Tour—throughout the year.

One of the most interesting things to do in Holmdel is to search for fossils, and the best place to get started is at the **Ramanessin Brook** (www.holmdelenviro.org, www.njfossils.net), where even beginners can dig up shark teeth and arrowheads. Your own equipment is needed, such as rubber boots, shovel, and sieve. Naturalist Jim Peck also hosts guided fossil hunts in the region throughout the late spring/early summer. Cost is $35 adults, $15 kids, and tools are included. For more information, call 800/665-1004, or go to www.natureaudiowalks.com.

COLTS NECK

Horses have held a prominent place in Colts Neck for centuries. In fact, the township's name changed from Atlantic to its current equestrian-inspired title in 1962, and names such as "Hunt" and "Walling" can be seen on neighborhood street signs. Strict zoning laws and scarcity of water have helped keep Colts Neck exclusive, and what isn't used for housing is given back to the township to create parks and golf courses. What acts as a makeshift town center is really the meeting of Routes 537 and 34, though there's little more than a general store, steakhouse, hotel, and a couple of produce and garden centers.

Polo Field

Polo matches are held at Bucks Mill Park and Polo Field (105 Bucks Mill Rd., 732/946-4243, www.coltsneckpolo.com) on Sunday afternoon throughout the summer (call or check the website for exact dates and times). Dress ranges from casual to formal, and you should bring your own lawn chair and snacks. Admission is $25 adults, free for 12 and under. It costs $50 to reserve sideline parking for the afternoon, or $5 for guest parking.

Produce and Garden Centers

Delicious Orchards (Rte. 34 S., 732/462-1989, www.deliciousorchardsnj.com, 10 A.M.–6 P.M. Tues.–Sun.) has been serving the community for nearly a century. This delightful center features fresh in-season produce; a bakery with homemade pies, cakes, cookies, and apple cider doughnuts; an international cheese selection; and a deli. You'll also find a wide selection of coffee and teas, and organic fruits and vegetables.

All of your gardening questions can be answered at **Brock Farms** (Rte. 34 S., 732/462-0900, www.brockfarms.com). In addition to a great variety of plants, flowers, and produce the center hosts lawn and gardening classes. Brock's is best known for its fabulous Christmas display.

Recreation

Colts Neck Township is a popular golfing locale. Public courses include **Hominy Hill Golf Course** (92 Mercer Rd., Colts Neck, 732/462-922), an 18-hole, 72-par course that's been rated in the top 25 of *Golf Digest*'s "America's top 75 golf courses." The 7,059-yard course is known for its challenging layout and has hosted two USGA championship events. At the 18-hole **Pebble Creek Golf Club** (40 Rte. 537 E., 732/303-9090) you can reserve tee times up to seven days in advance. With tall trees and sand traps, the par-5 eighth hole is the course's most difficult.

For horseback riding try **Jockey Hollow Farm** (64 Hominy Hill Rd., 732/761-0391).

ALLAIRE STATE PARK

Located within Wall Township, the 3,086-acre Allaire State Park (Route 524, 732/938-2371, www.state.nj.us/dep/parksandforests/parks/allaire.html, dawn–dusk daily,) is a favorite

NEW JERSEY SPEEDWAYS

What would New Jersey be without motorsports? The majority of the state's speedways are located within Central Jersey and the Pinelands, and most are seasonal venues (Apr.–Nov.) that allow overnight camping without supervision or liability. The following speedways are currently open, but keep your eyes peeled for the **New Jersey Motorsports Park** (www.njmotorsportspark.com), to be constructed in the South Jersey city of Millville in 2006.

On the western outskirts of the Pinelands is **Atco Raceway** (1000 Jackson Rd., Atco, 856/768-0900, www.atcorace.com), a quarter-mile drag racing strip and motorcross park with bleacher stands and plenty of parking. The venue is also home to **Jim Harrington's Drag Racing School** (732/690-3716, www.thedragraceschool.com). For information on weather and currently scheduled events call the raceway's Weather and Info Hotline at 856/768-2167.

On Route 34 across from Allaire State Park is **Wall Township Speedway** (1803 Hwy. 34 S., Wall, 732/681-6400, www.wallspeedway.com), which features stock car racing along an oval track – purportedly the state's last asphalt speedway. Go-karts compete on the track's 0.2-mile inner oval Friday nights.

Resurrected in 1997, the **New Egypt Speedway** (720 Rte. 539, New Egypt, 609/758-1900, www.newegyptspeedway.net) hosts a half-mile clay oval racing track. The speedway has plenty to offer in addition to racing, including kid-centric features like a monitored playground and weekly pit tours. Events take place Saturday evenings and occasionally during the week.

Old Bridge Township's long running **Raceway Park** (230 Pension Rd., Englishtown, 732/446-7800, www.etownraceway.com) includes two drag racing strips – a quarter-mile National Hot Rod Association (NHRA) track and a one-eighth-mile junior that hosts the weekly NHRA Junior Drag Racing League Competition. There are also off-road facilities for motorcross and paved go-kart courses. A road course is set to open in the near future. The park also hosts the annual spring and fall Sport Compact Nationals, and the Summer Sport Compact Slam.

At the foot of the Commodore Barry Bridge is South Jersey's **Bridgeport Speedway** (Floodgate Rd., Swedesboro, 856/467-4407, www.bridgeportspeedway.net), a five-eighths-mile oval dirt stockcar tract.

The Skylands' **Island Dragway** (20 Island Rd., Great Meadows, 908/637-6060 during the week, 908/637-6536 during races, www.islanddragway.com) features a quarter-mile drag racing strip and weekly "street legal racing," open to any and all automobiles for competition, every Friday and the first Wednesday of the month.

stop for outdoor enthusiasts, nature lovers, cultural historians, and families. Features include an antique steam train, a nature center and nature trails, and a restored bog-iron village. The park offers numerous recreational opportunities, including horseback riding, bicycling, kayaking, bird-watching, hiking, and camping, as well as nearby golf and skydiving. A $5 fee to enter the park is charged weekends only, Memorial Day–Labor Day.

Historic Allaire Village

Created in 1822 as a bog mining village to "insure a good source of iron for [James Peter Allaire's] New York City steam engine works," and formerly known as Howell Works Company, Allaire Village (www.allairevillage.org) today features a gristmill bakery, blacksmith and carpenter shops, a blast furnace, and many other historic oddities of interest. When cheaper and more efficient coal was discovered in Pennsylvania's Allegheny Mountains, Howell Works became known as the "Deserted Village," since there was no longer any use for its pitch pine charcoal furnaces. The Historic Allaire Village showcases an interpretive center, a visitors center and museum in an old row home, a working bakery with a beehive oven, plenty of period-dressed workers employed on daily demonstrations in the summer months, and walking trails through both the working area and the natural surrounds.

Allaire Village is open 11 A.M.–5 P.M. Tuesday–Sunday throughout the summer, and 10 A.M.–4 P.M. weekends in May, and September–November. On weekends May–October, admission is $5 adults, $2 children; otherwise the village is free to enter. A visitors center located on the grounds is open 10 A.M.–5 P.M. daily Memorial Day–Labor Day, 10 A.M.–4 P.M. Wednesday–Sunday the remainder of the year.

Pine Creek Railroad

The New Jersey Museum of Transportation, Inc. runs an antique steam train along a 0.75-mile loop within the park weekends only March–December (every half hour noon–4:30 P.M., $3). Known as the Pine Creek Railroad (732/938-5524), it's been operating for over 50 years. Volunteers stage various productions aboard the locomotive throughout the year, including The Great Train Robbery of Old Creek ($5/person) and Halloween's Haunted Night Express ($7.50/person). One of the most popular excursions is the afternoon Christmas Express ($5/person), running every half hour 11 A.M.–4 P.M. weekends Thanksgiving–Christmas.

Sports and Recreation

There are four hiking trails within the park, ranging 0.5–16.5 miles in length. Color codes mark these trails and rate their difficulty—red, yellow, and green being shorter and pedestrian-only. Orange designates the 16.5-mile multiuse trail.

The Manasquan River flows through the park and is a good place for canoeing and kayaking. **Mohawk Canoe & Kayak Livery** (Squankum-Yellowbrook Rd., 732/938-7755, $25 two-hour solo, $35 two-hour tandem) runs trips along the river both within the park and through the Manasquan River Estuary, ranging 1–3.5 hours.

The **Edgar Felix Bike Path** is a 5.5-mile relatively smooth surface that runs from the park east to Manasquan Inlet. Two wood bridges carry cyclists over the Garden State Parkway.

Circle A Riding Academy (116 Herbertsville Rd., Howell, 732/938-2004, $30/hour)

gives guided horseback riding tours through Allaire State Park, 9 A.M.–6 P.M. daily throughout summer and 9 A.M.–4 P.M. the remainder of the year.

Skydive Jersey Shore Inc. (Rte. 34, Monmouth Executive Airport, 732/938-9002, www.skydivenjshore.com) offers tandem and solo jumps over Central Jersey, with a possible view of the New York City skyline. Tandem jumps cost $215 weekends and $195 weekdays; solo jumps run $190 per jump.

Nearby golf courses include **Howell Park** (Preventorium Rd., 732/938-4771), a 6,964-yard perfectly manicured public course open mid-March–late December, and the **Bel-Aire Golf Course** (3108 Allaire Rd., 732/449-6024), 27 holes separated into two courses, an 18-hole executive course and a 9-hole par 3. Tee times for this course are first-come, first-served.

Camping

Allaire State Park features 45 sites ($20) suited for tent camping or trailers, available mid-April–late October. The park also hosts a handful of group sites that accommodate up to 300 persons ($1 each), as well as four lockable yurts ($30) and six shelters, each with four beds and stove ($10 per bed).

FREEHOLD

This Monmouth County seat is also the childhood home of Bruce Springsteen, a small-town borough with a large Hispanic population and a recently revamped downtown area that mixes the best of mom-and-pop establishments and fancy eateries. Freehold has caught on to the sidewalk dining craze, and on a warm summer weekday tables along Main Street's brick-lined walkways are packed with patrons, including lawyers, clerks, and potential jurors.

Just outside the borough is Freehold Township, where you'll find numerous orchards and a sprawling park, site of the longest battle in Revolutionary history. The two Freeholds are closely related: While the borough is home to the country's oldest daytime harness racetrack, the township is where you'll find the mall named after it.

Much of Freehold's history can be heard in

the lyrics of Springsteen's songs, including the closing of the A&M Karagheusian Rug Mill. The textile mill, featured in "My Hometown," was once the region's largest employer.

Sights

There is no doubt that Springsteen is the chosen son of this hometown. Occasional tours given by Jean Mikle and Stan Goldstein (authors of *Rock & Roll Tour of the Jersey Shore*) include a drive past the Boss's childhood homes, including one on **Institute Street,** and a stop at the tree where he posed for a "Born in the USA" tour book. You can find the self-guided **Monmouth County Music Heritage Map,** which includes some of these sites, at www.freeholdcenter.com.

For die-hard bicycle historians there's **Metz Bicycle Museum** (54 W. Main St., 732/462-7363, www.metzbicyclemuseum.com), which features a large collection of antique bicycles dating back to the mid-19th century, including high-wheels, tandems, and wood-frame cycles. The museum features a variety of other antiques including children's toys, bike accessories, and a really cool collection of antique bottle openers. You have to call and make an appointment if you want to get inside.

The **Freehold Raceway** (Rtes. 9 and 33, www.freeholdraceway.com, free) is the nation's oldest daytime harness racetrack. Live harness racing around its half-mile track takes place August–May.

Pick-Your-Own Orchards

Despite recent build-up you can still find a number of pick-your-own farms in Freehold Township.

At **Battleview Orchards** (91 Wemrock Rd., 732/462-0756, 9 A.M.–6 P.M. daily) you can pick your own strawberries, sour cherries, nectarines, and pumpkins, among other produce. Hayrides take place in the fall, and a country store sells produce and baked goods year-round. You can obtain a complete picking schedule online at www.battlevieworchards.com/pickurown.htm.

Wemrock Orchards (300 Rte. 33 W., 732/431-2668, 9 A.M.–6 P.M. daily) grows raspberries, blackberries, and strawberries for picking. Autumn brings pick-your-own pumpkins, a haunted hayride, and a corn maze. Tomasello Winery operates a tasting center on the premises, and you'll also find a country store stocking fresh fruit pies and artisan breads.

Shopping

Built in 1990, the **Freehold Raceway Mall** (3710 Rte. 9, 732/577-1144, www.freehold racewaymall.com, 10 A.M.–9:30 P.M. Mon.–Sat., 11 A.M.–7 P.M. Sun.) is one of New Jersey's largest indoor malls and includes such shops as Old Navy, Guess, and Spencer Gifts. A large food court and five anchor stores make this a popular area attraction.

In nearby Englishtown is the famous weekend **Englishtown Auction** (90 Wilson Ave., 732/446-9644, www.englishtownauction.com, 7 A.M.–4 P.M. Sat., 9 A.M.–4 P.M. Sun.). Established in 1929, this humongous flea market has five indoor buildings and 40 acres of outdoor space. The show goes on, rain or shine.

Food

Freehold is home to a good number of established eateries, as well as a few newer haunts. During the warmer months East Main Street comes to life with an abundance of sidewalk seating.

◖ **Tony's Freehold Grill** (59 E. Main St., 732/431-8607) has been a local institution for over 60 years. It's a shoebox of a place, all booths, stools, mauve and chrome steel. The food is delicious, though nothing fancy—just typical diner fare. Sandwiches—like the Alpine Chicken ($7.95)—come with a side of coleslaw and a pickle. On the wall there's a framed photo of Springsteen with the chefs who are cooking your meal, and tableside jukeboxes list his songs in handwritten script. Tony's hours are 6 A.M.–3 P.M. Monday–Friday, 6:30 A.M.–3 P.M. Saturday, and 6:30 A.M.–2 P.M. Sunday.

The **Olde Court Jester** (16 E. Main St., 732/462-1312, 11:30 A.M.–2 A.M. Mon.–Sat., noon–2 A.M. Sun., $12–20) is a casual place serving American eats and seasoned fries. It can get quite crowded during lunch, when County workers descend on the sidewalk tables.

Federici's (14 E. Main St., 732/462-1312, 11:30 A.M.–10:30 P.M. Mon.–Thurs., until 11 P.M. Fri. and Sat., 9:30 P.M. Sun., $4.95–28.95) is "home of the spicy pizza," a unanimous favorite among locals.

Sweet Lew's Hometown Café (6 E. Main St., 732/308-1887) is the community stalwart, open for breakfast and lunch. Blueberry pancakes are a morning specialty. Hours are 7:30 A.M.–2:30 P.M. Tuesday–Friday, 7 A.M.–2 P.M. Saturday, 8 A.M.–1 P.M. Sunday, closed Monday.

The **Cornerstone Caffe and Restaurant** (2 E. Main St., 732/845-5300, http://thecorner stonecaffe.com, $5.50–16.95) serves espresso drinks alongside sandwiches, steaks, stir-fries, and eight-ounce beef burgers. Sweets are another specialty, and the large open space plays host to live music throughout the week.

For Asian fusion cuisine and stylish decor try the BYO **Citrus** (32 West Main St., 732/294-0202, 5:30–10 P.M. Tues.–Thurs., until 11 P.M. Fri. and Sat., 8:30 P.M. Sun., $18–32).

Accommodations
$100-150: An 1885 Victorian bed-and-breakfast, **The Hepburn House** (15 Monument St., 732/462-7696) features five guestrooms and a shaded outdoor porch. All rooms include television, phone, and private bath, and guests can enjoy complimentary refreshments and sherry throughout their stay.

◖ MONMOUTH BATTLEFIELD STATE PARK
On June 28, 1778, General George Washington and his troops took on the British under the command of Sir Henry Clinton in what would become the longest battle of the Revolutionary War. The 2,764-acre Monmouth Battlefield State Park (347 Freehold Rd., 732/780-5782, dawn–dusk daily, free) commemorates this battle, which produced such historic legends as Molly Pitcher, the woman who carried pitchers of water to troops who were fighting in the sweltering heat, and who took the place of her husband when he was wounded in battle. The park is a large stretch of open land with a number of multiuse trails

suitable for hiking, horseback riding, and cross-country skiing.

Visitors Center
The Monmouth Battlefield visitors center (732/780-5782 or 732/462-9616, 9 A.M.–4 P.M. daily) features numerous displays and interpretive stations, including rare coins and arrowheads found within the park's boundaries and an archaeologist's analysis of cannonballs, used to determine the length of the battle. An interesting display on "the many faces of George Washington" shows over 30 artist portrayals of this man that "nobody could quite agree on." Faces include the infamous "pig-eyed" portrait and a blue-eyed painting, though Washington's eyes were gray.

Historic Craig House
This 18th-century farmhouse was the home of farmer John Craig and his family during the time of the 1778 battle. The building has since been restored and refurnished. Tours are occasionally offered. For more information, inquire at the visitors center.

Battle of Monmouth Bike Route
The Battle of Monmouth Bike Route is a 28.5-mile loop linking Monmouth Battlefield and Holmdel Park, planned by the New Jersey Department of Transportation. Most of the cycling takes place along roadways. To obtain a free map of the route go to www.state.nj.us/transportation/commuter/bike/freeinfo.shtm.

The Battle of Monmouth Reenactment
Hundreds of costumed actors and spectators come out to take part in the reenactment of the Battle of Monmouth, held annually the last weekend of June.

ALLENTOWN AND CREAM RIDGE
In the early 18th century Nathan Allen built three mills on land he'd acquired from proprietor Rob R. Burns and thus began "Allens Town." Today Allentown is a picturesque borough, its Main Street lined by spaciously set colonial,

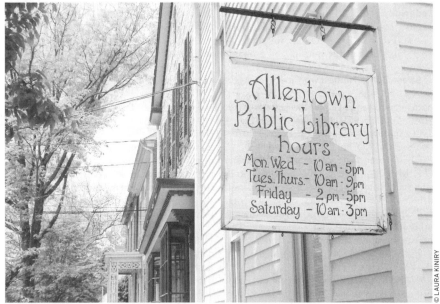

historic Allentown

© LAURA KINIRY

Federal, and Victorian structures, many of which house specialty shops selling handcrafted wares. Two small parks are located within town, and an old mill stands as the borough's most prominent feature. Built on the site of one of Allen's original mills, it houses numerous shops and an excellent Bavarian restaurant.

Just east of Allentown is the village of Cream Ridge, part of the largely rural Upper Freehold Township. Wide stretches of hillside, a bevy of horse farms, and miles of open sky make it easy to forget you're so close to a major hub of highway system.

Sights

Walnford (609/259-6285, 8 A.M.–4 P.M. daily, free) is a 36-acre reconstructed mill village centered around a restored and operating gristmill. It's located on the grounds of 1,046-acre **Crosswicks Creek Park** (Walnford Rd., 609/259-5794), just off Route 539, and is meant to provide the public with an understanding of the village's more than 200-year

history that began in the 1730s and during which time it was adapted for farming. A former sawmill, carriage house, cow barn, and the 1773 **Waln House,** a bright-blue colonial mansion, are included on the property. You can pick up a map for a self-guided walking tour at the information center, located at the end of Walnford Road next to the parking lot.

The 147-acre **Horse Park of New Jersey at Stone Tavern** (Rte. 524, Cream Ridge, 609/259-0170, www.horseparkofnewjersey.com) holds equine shows on most weekends and many weekdays March–November. Food stalls are set up during most performances. The park does not offer horseback riding.

You can taste over a dozen wines daily at **Cream Ridge Winery** (145 Rte. 539, Cream Ridge, 609/259-9797, www.creamridgewinery .com, 11 A.M.–6 P.M. Mon.–Sat., until 5 P.M. Sun.), whose specialties include fruit wines made from locally grown cranberries and blueberries. In September the winery hosts a free annual **Fruit Crush and Pig Roast Festival.**

Specialty Shops

Allentown's Main Street is an easily walkable downtown strip where you'll find the area's best shopping. Most stores and restaurants are closed on Monday, and often Sunday. All of the shopping listed below is found on Allentown's Main Street.

The **Quilter's Barn** (34 S. Main St., 609/259-2504) sells patterns, fabrics, and instructional books for the beginning to advanced quilter, and hosts a variety of quilting classes throughout the year. At **Necessities for the Heart at Wisteria** (28 S. Main St., 609/208-1349) you'll find a gorgeous selection of handbags, totes, jewelry, and watches from such famed design names as Vera Bradley and Brighton. **Weaves** (35 S. Main St., 609/208-9990) offers hand-embroidered items and rare linens for sale.

The **Allentown Feeding Co.** (42 S. Main St., 609/208-2050), known also as the Old Mill, features second-floor stores and a number of adjacent shops including **Mill Stream Pottery** (609/208-0054), where you'll find handcrafted pottery created at a working on-site studio, as well as paintings and photography. Pottery and fine-art workshops are held here throughout the year. **Off the Wall Craft Gallery** (609/259-0725) sells beautiful glass art, including blown-glass and stained glass pieces. Additional items include handcrafted kaleidoscopes and wood-carved jewelry boxes.

Accommodations

$50-100: Located on an organic farm, the recently remodeled **Earth Friendly Bed & Breakfast** (17 Olde Noah Hunt Rd., 609/259-9744,) features three guestrooms and a couple of greenhouses. Visitors can pick their own blueberries and blackberries and explore nature trails. Free-range chickens provide fresh eggs daily.

$150-200: Only minutes from downtown Main Street, the **Peace Fields Inn** (84 Walnford Rd., 609/259-3774, www.peacefields inn.com,) is an 1850 colonial home featuring five rooms, each with private bath and TV/VCR, and the use of an in-ground swimming pool mid-June–mid-September. This lovely B&B offers packed lunches for you to bring while exploring the region.

Food

You'll have no problem finding a restaurant or deli along Allentown's Main Street, though only a couple are true standouts.

Located on the first floor of the Old Mill is one of New Jersey's best Bavarian eateries, the **Black Forest Restaurant** (2 S. Main St., 609/259-3197, $13–24), serving up hearty helpings of potato dumplings and Wiener schnitzel in a German-inn setting. Lunch is served 11:30 a.m.–4 p.m. Tuesday–Saturday, dinner 4–9 p.m. Friday and Saturday, closed Sunday and Monday.

Allentown's cozy **Garden Tea Room** (4 S. Main St., 609/208-1880, www.innerharmony center.com/tearoom.html, 11 a.m.–4 p.m. Tues.–Sat.) is an ideal setting for a break from window-shopping. Choose between the Teddy Bear Tea ($7.50), which includes your choice of drink along with a sampling of sweets and a peanut butter and jelly, or fluff, sandwich, and the Afternoon Tea ($13.95), complete with beverage, an assortment of finger sandwiches, and raspberry jam. A variety of individual teas, sandwiches, and snacks are also available.

Outer Ocean County

On the upper reaches of the Pinelands, the land begins to turn from sandy soil to suitable agricultural land, and you'll find a large number of pick-your-own farms. While blueberries and blackberries, which are plentiful further south, continue to grow here, additional fruits such as strawberries and nectarines flourish. Migrant workers find the bulk of their employment in this region.

Route 9 travels down the Pinelands' eastern border and straddles the land just west of the Shore, carrying vehicles south from Freehold through Lakewood and down to the village of Toms River, once a seafaring town between Barren and beach. In these outer Pinelands narrow two-lane roads and sprawling shopping centers are the norm, and new development continues to sprout around countrified suburbs.

€ SIX FLAGS

Here's one thing that New Yorkers and Philadelphians definitely have in common: New Jersey's extremely popular Six Flags theme park (1 Six Flags Blvd., 732/928-1821, www.sixflags.com), one of 37 of the company's parks around the globe. Opened in 1974, the Garden State version features three distinct parks and includes over a dozen roller coasters (one of them being, in 2005, the world's tallest and fastest), a 350-acre drive-through safari, and one of the largest water parks in the country. With at least a weekend's worth of attractions, Six Flags is easily its own destination.

Great Adventure

According to an article in *New Jersey Monthly,* "In 2001 Guinness World Records listed Great Adventure as having the highest concentration of rides anywhere in the world." And with 14 roller coasters, a freefall tower, drenching rapids, and a 150-foot Ferris wheel among many other attractions, it seems an honor difficult to dispute. The park is constantly updating and adding, and new additions include Superman Ultimate Flight, where riders fly horizontally around heart-stopping twists, turns, and loops, and the Golden Kingdom, which includes a tiger show, kiddie park, and the ultimate roller coaster ride.

In the summer of 2005 the world's largest, fastest roller coaster debuted at Great Adventure's Golden Kingdom. Reaching a speed of 128 miles per hour in 3.5 seconds (ouch!), Kingda Ka takes about 50.6 seconds to complete. The 456-foot-tall coaster is twice the size of the park's other hip highlight, the 230-foot Nitro, which opened in 2001. If you want to catch a glimpse of Kingda Ka but don't have time for a day at the park, you can view it from the main rest area at the entrance to Wild Animal Safari.

Set to debut in summer 2006 is El Toro, a hybrid wooden roller coaster that's already being touted as one of the world's "tallest and fastest." The ride will be the focal point for a new theme area called Plaza del Carnaval. Kids can look forward to the Bugs Bunny National Park, which will include a train ride and racing cars.

Concerts and shows are a Great Adventure specialty, and include big-name acts in addition to a varied line-up that includes Batman vs. Catwoman and Temple of the Tiger, a Bengal tiger production. Saturday-night fireworks take place throughout the summer.

Wild Animal Safari

At 350 acres, Wild Animal Safari is home to over 1,200 animals and is known as "the largest drive-through safari park outside of Africa." Almost every visitor has experienced a monkey climbing onto their car or a giraffe holding up traffic. Of course, not every animal is given free rein. Lions, tigers, and bears are all secure from tromping on your vehicle. Wildlife runs the gamut from flamingos to elephants with lots of variation in between.

If you'd rather not ruin your car (soft-top vehicles are not allowed) you can board the Safari tour bus for an additional fee. Buses leave numerous times daily from the park entrance—they're air-conditioned and include a tour guide. For your own in-vehicle guide, tune into 530 AM, where you'll receive information pertaining to the wildlife you encounter. The safari takes about 45 minutes to go around.

Hurricane Harbor and Splashwater Park

Hurricane Harbor and Splashwater Park (www.sixflags.com/parks/hurricaneharbornj) features a half-mile lazy river for floating, nearly 20 waterslides ranging from 50-foot-tall super speed slides to winding tube slides, a giant wavepool, and a kiddie waterland. It's the perfect place for cooling off in the humid midsummer air before heading over to the amusement park for a bit of roller coaster riding as the sun goes down. A water park–only pass runs $29.99 adult, and $22.99 junior (under 54 inches) and senior (55 and over).

Information and Services

A combination ticket to Great Adventure and Wild Safari is $48.99 adult, $29.99 junior (under 54 inches) and senior (55 and over). Tickets are $10 cheaper if you purchase them online, or you can pick up a Six Flags coupon (many libraries carry them, as does Burger King) for a $20 savings. A regular price three-park combo is $62.99.

All parks are open daily throughout the summer months and typically on weekends during the shoulder season (Apr.–May, Sept.–Oct.). Great Adventure hosts the ghoulish FrightFest on weekend evenings in October, transforming the park into an all-out Monster Mash.

Getting There

Six Flags is located at exit 7A of the New Jersey Turnpike (to I-195 exit 16A), and exit 98 of the Garden State Parkway.

JACKSON

At more than 100 square miles, Jackson is Ocean County's largest township—an expanse of horse fields and produce farms, cranberry bogs, recently constructed estate-style homes developed around existing towns, and according to writer Susan Orlean, "the highest concentration of tigers per square mile of anywhere in the world." Tra-

versing upper Jackson, I-195 connects with major roadways that transport hundreds of thousands of visitors to the township each year. What's the big draw? Could be the tigers, or even the outlet shopping, but my bet Jackson's biggest draw is the massive Six Flags theme park (home to a large number of those tigers). Unfortunately, the area has a limited number of accommodations to host its weary travelers, and you may spend numerous hours in traffic on a hot summer day only to find there's nowhere to stay in New Jersey's heartland. Book ahead.

Cassville

The Russian section of Jackson Township, known as Cassville, clusters around the intersection of Routes 571 and 528. Here you'll find a tavern and a couple of small eateries that double as country stores. Cassville is a sleepy, countrified village where the heritage is evident in local names like Pushkin Park. It's also embodied in its most notable structure, **St. Vladimir's Church** (132 Perrineville Rd. off Rte. 571, 732/928-1337), one of two Russian Orthodox churches located at Rova Farm's Resort, a historic Cassville site that has long been a gathering spot for local residents. The church is adorned with massive wood doors and an onion-shaped dome and occupies a prominent piece of property atop a small hill. It's worth a look if you're in the area, especially on Tuesday mornings when the **Rova Farms Flea Market** (732/928-0928)—although not worthwhile in its own right—takes place at the foot below, and a neighboring Russian eatery opens its doors to the public (additional hours Sat. and Sun.).

Jackson Outlet Village

Jackson Outlet Village (537 Monmouth Rd., 732/833-0503, 10 A.M.–9 P.M. Mon.–Sat., 11 A.M.–7 P.M. Sun.) is one of New Jersey's nicest outlet centers—it's clean and modern and offers plenty of selection. Over 70 factory outlet stores include J.Crew, Vans sneakers, and Fossil.

Sports and Recreation

Jackson Roller Skating Center (Rte. 526, 732/363-2222) is an up-to-date roller rink where you can rent both skates and blades. The center features a snack bar and arcade, and offers a variety of public skate times and themes, including an Adult Organ Music Skate (10 A.M.–12:30 P.M. Tues. and Thurs.) and a Saturday Family Fun Night (7:30–10:30 P.M., $6 adult, $5 child). Cost for skate rentals is $2, inline skates $4.

Accommodations

One of Jackson's greatest obstacles keeping it from becoming a mega-resort is its lack of accommodation choices. Other then camping facilities, the township offers nothing in the way overnight options, and visitors to Great Adventure will have to make the drive elsewhere if they want to enjoy the park for numerous days. The Central Plains' New Egypt, Freehold, and Cream Ridge all offer recommendable lodging, as does Mount Laurel (40 miles, exit 4), conveniently located off the New Jersey Turnpike.

Camping

There are a few resort campgrounds within Jackson Township, and they all offer Six Flags discount packages. The campgrounds are centrally located, an easy drive to the theme park and a half hour from the Jersey Shore.

Butterfly Camping Resort (360 Butterfly Rd., 732/928-2107, early Apr.–late Oct., $38 water, electric, and cable) has 135 sites usable by RV and tent campers. The resort is fairly quiet and amenities include shaded sites, a mini-golf course (geared toward kids), a camp store, and updated restrooms (though the "hot" showers tend to run more lukewarm). The camp is located adjacent to Butterfly Bogs State Wildlife Refuge, which allows fishing and the use of non-motor boats.

Tip Tam (301 Brewers Bridge Rd., 877/TIP-TAM1 or 877/847-8261, www.tiptam.com, mid-Apr.–late Sept., $30 water, electric, and cable) has 202 RV and tent sites. Activities include horseshoes and volleyball, and the resort has a game room, tiki bar, and in-ground swimming pool.

Toby's Hide-Away Campground (856 Green Valley Rd., 732/363-3662, early May–late Oct., $25 water and electric) has 50 full-service campsites. Many sites are wooded, and the restrooms include hot showers.

Food

Finding good food in the Jackson area can be somewhat of a chore. One place to try is **Java Moon Cafe** (1022 Anderson Rd. and Rte. 537, 732/928-3633, 8 A.M.–10 P.M. Mon.–Sat., until 8 P.M. Sun., $8–18), a local chain establishment that's located just south of the outlets along Route 537, and just a few miles' drive from Six Flags. This is a nice place to enjoy a sandwich and dessert before returning to the shops or park.

NEW EGYPT

The bull's-eye of New Jersey's geographical center is the village of New Egypt, part of the larger Plumstead Township. Its downtown center is filled with weathered saltbox structures housing little more than a few service industries and locally geared eateries, but on the outskirts of town you'll find a number of pick-your-own farms, a large antique barn, and a drag racing speedway.

Pick-Your-Own Farms

There are plenty of pick-your-own farms in the New Egypt area, including **Hallocks U-Pick Farms and Greenhouse** (38 Fischer Rd., 609/758-8847, www.hallocksupick.com, 7 A.M.–7:30 P.M. weekdays, 7 A.M.–5:30 P.M. weekends and holidays), specializing in strawberries and an array of vegetables. The on-site greenhouse features 30,000 square feet of display space for marigolds, geraniums, and candy corn plants, among others plants and flowers.

The more-than-200-acre **De Wolf's U-Pick Farm** (10 W. Colliers Mills Rd., http://dewolfsupickfarm.com, 609/758-2424) grows strawberries, blackberries, and raspberries for picking and is home to **Kim's Country Store** (609/758-6288), where you'll find home-baked pies, fresh picked veggies, and an assortment of jams and jellies. Farm and business hours are 9 A.M.–4 P.M. daily April and November, and 7 A.M.–7 P.M. daily May–October. Call ahead for holiday hours.

Emery's Berry Farm (346 Long Swamp

Rd., 609/758-2424, 9 A.M.–5 P.M. daily, late Mar.–late Dec.) is a certified organic farm specializing in blueberries and raspberries. There's a market and bakery (with fresh-made pies), and a number of farm animals for feeding.

Accommodations

$250-300: (**Dancer Farm Bed & Breakfast** (19 Archertown Rd., 609/752-0303, www.dancerfarm.com) is housed on a 250-acre working farm that includes seasonal wildflowers, nature trails, and a vineyard. The farm was once the property of prominent horse trainers and remains a boarding facility and training ground for Standard-bred horses. The 10 themed guestrooms of this gorgeous 19th-century farmhouse include private bath, television, cable, and telephone. Many also feature a fireplace or fire-stove, and a balcony.

LAKEWOOD

What was once a retreat for high-profile New Yorkers such as J. D. Rockefeller, boasting close to 100 hotels, is now a township of worn storefronts and 1970s shopping centers, though a few highlights make it worth a trip. Lakewood's downtown center exists along **Clifton Street,** most notably between 3rd and 4th Streets. It's an ethnically diverse area where you'll find plenty of Mexican groceries and a kosher deli. Clifton Street's grand dame is a recently restored vaudeville theater.

Sights

Once the estate of railroad mogul George J. Gould, **Georgian Court University** (900 Lakewood Ave., 732/987-2263 or 800/458-8422, www.georgian.edu) is now an institute of higher learning. The public grounds include a free arboretum where you'll find an Italian Garden, Formal Garden, and a Japanese Garden complete with blossoming cherry trees, a waterfall and brook, and a teahouse. You can take a 1.5-hour guided tour of the former Gould mansion, along with the gardens and other campus highlights such as **Raymond Hall,** home to the university's School of Education, on select Tuesday mornings throughout the academic year. Tours begin at the Gould mansion and a reservation is required. Cost is $10.

The 1,100-seat **Historic Strand Theatre** (400 Clifton Ave., 732/367-7789, www.strandlakewood.com) began in 1922 as a vaudeville and silent movie venue. After years of disrepair—and a brief foray into porn—the theater has been completely restored to its original glamour and now serves as a stage for live comedy, dance, music, and plays. It is said to be one of the best acoustical theaters in the country.

Sports and Recreation

FirstEnergy Park (2 Stadium Way), home to the minor league Lakewood Blueclaws (732/901-7000, www.lakewoodblueclaws.com, $6–9) is one of New Jersey's best minor league ballparks. What makes it so great? General admission lawn seats, numerous food courts, and kid-friendly promotions, including fireworks.

Eagle Ridge Golf Course (2 Augusta Blvd., 732/901-4900, www.eagleridgegolf.com) is an 18-hole "championship" golf course open to the public.

Festival

A two-day **Renaissance Faire** takes place annually each September in Pine Park (Country Club Lane, behind the Lakewood Country Club), situated in the township's northwest corner. Hosted by the Lakewood Lions, the fair features shiny knights, distressed damsels, and plenty of crafts and food stands. Visitors are encouraged to dress in costume and take part in the festivities, but if you don't have a costume to wear there are plenty on hand to purchase.

TOMS RIVER

It may be called Toms River (www.downtowntomsriver.com), but the official name of this sprawling township is Dover (the village of Toms River is only a small portion). The county seat, Toms River lies on the eastern Pinelands border along a river that bears its name. The town's nautical history is preserved in the village center along Washington and Main Streets, among the civic buildings and commercial shops. But it's a couple of wetland and river-based activities, a planetarium, and a newly established ice cream festival that make the township worth a trip.

Sights

The **Robert J. Novins Planetarium** (Ocean County College, College Dr., 732/255-0342, www.ocean.edu/campus/planetarium/index.htm, $6 adult, $4.50 child) is a 188-seat 40-foot dome theater featuring programs that range from the local sky to intergalactic star shows. All the shows run about an hour and there's typically a student astronomer on hand to answer questions afterward. The planetarium's main office (732/255-0343) is open weekdays 9 A.M.–4 P.M., but most shows take place Friday and Saturday evenings and weekend afternoons.

The **Cooper Environmental Center** (1170 Cattus Island Blvd., 732/270-6960, 877/OC-PARKS or 877/627-2757, 10 A.M.–4 P.M. daily) at Cattus Island Park features numerous displays aimed at the budding naturalist. Inside you'll find snakes and reptiles, and outdoors a butterfly garden. The center runs scheduled nature walks that offer background on the area's bogs, swamps, and marshes. For children a popular event is the center's free Sunday turtle feedings.

Entertainment and Events

Take a cruise down Toms River on the **River Lady Cruise and Dinner Boat** (1 Robbins Parkway, 732/349-8664, www.riverlady.com, May–Oct.). This Mississippi-style riverboat runs 2–3-hour cruises three or four times daily. All trips include a sit-down meal (except the historic sightseeing tour) on a covered deck with seating at long communal dining tables.

Held annually in July, the **New Jersey Ice Cream Festival** (www.downtowntomsriver.com/icecream/festival.htm) features unique ice cream flavors created by both local and national retailers. For $5 you can purchase a sampling kit and taste-test the year's contestants.

The **Ocean County Canoe and Kayak Race** takes place on Toms River in October along an 8.5-mile course. Anyone can enter ($12 solo entry, $22 double) and prizes are awarded in a variety of categories ranging from beginner to old pro. For more information call the Ocean County Department of Parks and Recreation at 877/OC-PARKS (877/627-2757), or log onto www.co.ocean.nj.us/parks/infopage.htm.

Sports and Recreation

Seaside Sailing Rides (3430 Rte. 37 E., Pier 1 Marina, 732/830-9285, www.seasidesailing.com) offers 2.5-hour trips on a sailboat holding up to six people. The boat departs twice in the afternoon and once in the evening throughout the summer, and cost is $40. **Underwater Discovery** (2722 Rte. 37 E., 732/270-9100, www.underwaterdiscoveryinc.com) is a retail shop that rents dive equipment and offers underwater diving instruction.

The upper portion of Toms River offers excellent canoeing and kayaking. You can bring your own boat, or arrange a rental at **Pineland Canoes** (26 Whitesville Rd., 732/364-0389). The shop is located nearby in Jackson, but you can arrange a pick-up in Toms River if you call beforehand. The Ocean County park system runs seasonal canoe trips on local lakes and rivers, include Toms River and the nearby Mullica River. Cost is $10, $5 if you supply your own boat. For dates and times, go to www.co.ocean.nj.us/parks or call 877/OC-PARKS (877/627-2757).

In addition to numerous nature trails and bird-watching opportunities at **Cattus Island Park** (1170 Cattus Island Blvd., 732/270-6960), between Silver and Barnegat Bays, there are also fishing and crabbing **Pontoon Boat Tours** (www.co.ocean.nj.us/parks/boat%20tours.htm) occasionally offered in the summer. Cost is $7, and you must bring your own equipment.

Accommodations

$100-150: With only three guestrooms, it's best to make reservations at **Victoria on Main** (600 Main St., 732/818-7580, www.victoriaonmain.com) early. This century-old Victorian's features include numerous indoor common areas, a wraparound porch, and plenty of antique furniture. Each guestroom has a writing desk, TV, telephone, and private bath.

The Pinelands

Beginning in Central Jersey's Ocean Township and extending south along the western edge of the Jersey Shore are the Pinelands, or the **New Jersey Pinelands National Reserve** (www .nps.gov/pine), 1.4 million acres that make up the largest tract of forest existing along the United States' East Coast from Boston to Richmond, Virginia. In 1983 most of this land gained protection from development by being declared the Pinelands International Biosphere Reserve. A truly remarkable stretch of space, the Pinelands are home to endangered tree frogs and forgotten towns, stunted pygmy pitch trees and a horse-headed creature known as the Jersey Devil.

The vast abandon of the Pinelands is quite an unusual sight in the middle of the country's most densely populated state, especially when you realize that underneath it all runs a naturally pure and seemingly endless water supply. You can drive for long stretches without seeing another soul, but a gun club comes into view every few miles. Cranberry bogs lay like marshy fields between dense forest stands, and people who call themselves "Pineys" busy themselves in the small towns that are encountered few and far between. Ironworks and glass factories that once prevailed in the region are now little more than the remains of a furnace.

The Pinelands, or Pine Barrens, are home to over 100 rare flora and fauna species. It really is an outdoor paradise, both for its natural features and its recreational opportunities. Three rivers run through the region: the Batsto, the Mullica, and the Wading, and canoeing the cedar-stained back streams of these waters is the highlight of a visit. There is plenty of opportunity for hiking and camping within the numerous state forests that are found here, and the flat, long mileage of empty roadways is ideal for cyclists. Horseback riding, swimming, fishing, and of course hunting, are all possibilities.

© LAURA KINIRY

Batsto Mansion, the Pinelands

CENTRAL JERSEY

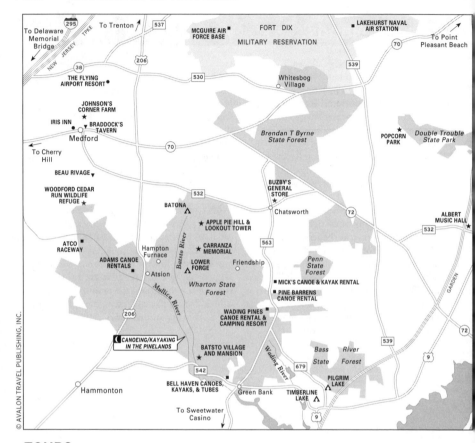

CENTRAL JERSEY

TOURS

There are a few tours that run within the Pinelands, each with a different specialty. I highly recommend taking one if you'd like to get better-acquainted with the region, or just for fun.

The nonprofit **Pinelands Preservation Alliance** (609/859-8860, www.pinelandsalliance.org) hosts numerous excursions throughout the year, ranging from day-long cougar hunts to ghost-town tours, canoe trips, and campouts. Some of the most popular are the **Jersey Devil Hunts** ($10), which take place in the evenings twice monthly. Led by Pineland naturalist Russ Juleg, these "hunts" are really more of a guise to stir interest in the region. They include an easy hike and some well-spent time

around the campfire (bring your own marshmallows). The Preservation Alliance's website provides an up-to-date listing of events.

White Star Farms (888/272-6264, www.whitestarcs.com, $19 adult, $14 youth (7–12), $5 child (3–6), under 3 free) is a working cranberry farm that hosts harvest tours in the fall, and blueberry tours in the summer. Brenda and Joe, both fifth-generation cranberry farmers who run the farm, also run the tours, and can offer valuable Piney insight into local culture.

Naturalist Jim Peck takes visitors on all-day bus tours of the Pinelands, providing an overview of the region's flora and fauna and a glimpse into the region's history. Lunch is included in the price, and tours (8:30 A.M.–4:30 P.M., $75

THE
PINELANDS

Toms
River

Pine
Beach

STATE

PKY

9

Forked
River

Waretown

Waterway

Intracoastal

Long Beach Island

ATLANTIC OCEAN

0   10 mi
0   10 km

Forest (Rtes. 70 and 72, New Lisbon, 609/726-1191) now bears the name of the New Jersey Governor instrumental in establishing the Pinelands as a national reserve. The Civilian Conservation Corp planted much of today's forest in the early 20th century to replace trees depleted by logging, and the area now thrives with a mixture of oak trees, low-lying pitch pines, and Atlantic white cedar, most notable in the 735-acre **Cedar Swamp Natural Area,** situated just north of Route 72. An easy way to access the natural area is by way of the Batona Trail, a portion of which makes up part of the forest's 25 miles of marked trails. These trails also include easy nature trails, the **Mount Misery Trail,** which doubles as a mountain bike trail, and the wheelchair-accessible **Cranberry Trail.** Cross-country skiing, snowshoeing, and horseback riding are also popular forest activities.

Whitesbog Village, a semi-active 19th-century agricultural town that's home to the cultivated blueberry, is situated within the forest, as are the remnants of some of the Pinelands' many forgotten towns.

Brendan T. Byrne State Forest is open dawn–dusk daily, and entrance is free. For additional information, stop by the park office located off Route 72 just east of the Four Mile Circle (the intersection of Routes 70 and 72).

Bass River State Forest

Selected as New Jersey's first state forest in 1905, Bass River State Forest (762 Stage Rd., New Gretna, 609/296-1114) has since grown from a humble 597 acres to more than 25,000. The forest is situated along the Pinelands eastern edge and visitors will find plenty of opportunities for fishing, boating, horseback riding, hunting, and easy hiking.

Another of the forest's recreational highlights is swimming, allowed along the eastern Shore of 67-acre **Lake Absegami** throughout summer; lifeguards are on duty daily. The lake also features a public boat launch and a seasonal concession stand that rents rowboats. Just east of the lake is the 128-acre **Absegami Natural Area,** used as U.S. military barracks during World War II. A one-mile nature trail

in van, $40 with own vehicle) take place year-round. For exact dates, call 800/665-1004 or visit www.natureaudiowalks.com.

FORESTS

The majority of the Pinelands are part of protected state forests, the three largest being Wharton, Brendan T. Byrne, and Bass River. Many of the region's sights and attractions fall within the boundaries of these forests, which all offer their own unique opportunities.

Brendan T. Byrne State Forest

Originally named for the Lebanon Glass Works that operated here in the mid-19th century, the massive 34,725-acre Brendan T. Byrne State

CENTRAL JERSEY

circles through this wetland forest, offering an up-close and personal look at the pine, oak, red maple, Atlantic white cedar, and magnolia trees that grow here. A second natural area is the 3,830-acre **West Pine Plains Natural Area,** also known as the Pygmy Forest. Home to the freakishly short stunted-growth trees often associated with New Jersey's Pinelands, this maturely developed four-foot-high pine and oak forest is a definite must-see.

Bass River State Park can be reached easily by taking exit 50 (N) or 52 (S) from the Garden State Parkway. A parking fee of $5 weekday, $10 weekend is charged Memorial Day–Labor Day.

Wharton State Forest

Wharton (4110 Nesco Rd., Hammonton) is New Jersey's largest forest, a 114,793-acre tract of land stretching from Burlington County south through Atlantic County, and west to include portions of Camden County. It's definitely one of the Pinelands' great highlights, home to Atsion Recreation Area and the bog-iron village of Batsto, as well as two natural areas—the 9,949-acre **Batsto Natural Area** and the 1,927-acre **Oswego River Natural Area,** prime habitat for the endangered Pineland tree frog. There are plenty of hiking opportunities to be found here, including a major stretch of the Batona Trail linking Wharton to nearby Bass River and Brendan T. Byrne State Forests, as well as miles of unpaved trails ideal for mountain biking and horseback riding. The Mullica, Batsto, Oswego, and Wading Rivers all wind their way within forest boundaries and offer an excellent chance to take advantage of the many canoeing and kayaking liveries that operate in the region. Swimming is allowed at **Atsion Lake** (744 Rte. 206, Shamong, Memorial Day–Labor Day, $5 weekdays, $10 weekends, $2 walk-in or bicycle), where lifeguards are on duty daily. The lake also hosts a concession stand, bathhouse, and canoe and kayak rentals.

Wildlife is easily spotted throughout Wharton and possible sightings include great horned owls, bluebirds, bald eagles, beaver, fox, and river otter. The forest hosts numerous additional attractions that take a bit of sleuthing to find

but are fun to uncover, such as the remnants of forgotten Piney towns, a memorial dedicated to Captain Emilio Carranza Rodriguez (the Charles Lindbergh of Mexico), and an old fire lookout tower. Wharton celebrated its 50th anniversary in 2005.

The forest has two park offices—one at the Atsion Recreation Area (744 Rte. 206, 609/268-0444) and the other at Batsto Village (Rte. 542, 609/561-0024).

◨ CANOEING AND KAYAKING

The Pinelands offer some of the best canoeing and kayaking opportunities in the state, and many visitors come to the region specifically for this purpose. The Wading, Batsto, Mullica, and Oswego Rivers all wind through the Pines, and local canoe liveries (rental agencies) run excursions along at least one of them, providing transport both to and from the river. If you're planning a canoeing or kayaking excursion, you'll benefit from an early start—most trips (excluding overnight trips) must be completed by 5 P.M. As for how to choose a livery, all of the following rental agencies are dependable, so it really just depends on convenience and personal preference. This is truly an ideal way to explore the Pinelands.

Wading Pines Canoe Rental (85 Godfrey Bridge Rd., Chatsworth, 888/726-1313, www.wadingpines.com) rents canoes and kayaks for use along the Wading River. Trips leave from the Wading Pines Camping Resort and vary in length and price, from a one-hour excursion ($35 canoe, $25 kayak) to five hours ($50 canoe, $40 kayak). The two-hour trip ($40 canoe, $30 kayak) will get carry you back to the resort by way of the river, without the need for motor transport.

Trips run by **Mick's Canoe and Kayak Rental** (3107 Rte. 563, Chatsworth, 609/726-1380, 800/281-1380, www.mickscanoerental.com) include day or overnight excursions down either the Wading or Oswego River ($40 canoe, $30 kayak), with drop-off and pick-up transport. Canoes can also be rented for use on the Bass River or Lake Absegami for an additional $5. Mick's has an on-site general store where you can pick up essentials like bug spray and snacks. The livery opens at

8 A.M. weekends, 8:30 A.M. Monday–Friday, and offers discounts throughout October.

Pine Barrens Canoe Rental (3260 Rte. 563, Chatsworth, 609/726-1515, 800/732-0793) offers one-day canoe trips along the Wading and Oswego Rivers for $40, the Batsto River for $48, or you can add an overnight stay along either river for an additional $27. One-day double kayak rentals are the same price, single kayaks go for $30 (Wading and Oswego Rivers) or $35 (Batsto River), with overnight an additional $20/30. The livery offers October discounts.

Just east of Batsto, **Bell Haven Canoes, Kayaks, & Tubes** (1227 Rte. 542, Green Bank, 609/965-2205, 800/445-0953, www.bellhaven canoe.com) runs a variety of canoe, kayak, and tubing excursions. Trips along the Wading and Oswego Rivers cost $40 canoe and $30 kayak; those along the Batsto and Mullica Rivers run $48 canoe, $35 kayak. They also offer a two-hour float in a tube along the Mullica for $15 (three-person minimum). Kayaks can also be rented for day trips ($40 Wading and Oswego Rivers, $48 Batsto and Mullica Rivers) or overnight ($20 extra per single kayak, $30 extra per double kayak), and sea kayaks ($45) are available for use along the lower Mullica River. If you're in the market for a ride of your own, Bell Haven features an on-site indoor showroom (9 A.M.–5 P.M. Tues.–Sun., until 7 P.M. Thurs., closed Mon.) of canoes, kayaks, paddles, and accessories for sale. Bell Haven is my top pick among the liveries.

Most easily reached by way of the Atlantic City Expressway and located north of Hammonton, **Adams Canoe Rentals** (1005 Atsion Rd., Shamong, 609/268-0189) rents canoes ($60) and kayaks ($40) for 5–8 hour trips along Mullica and Batsto Rivers, with overnight excursions available ($75 Mullica River, $80 Batsto). The livery also rents canoes for use on nearby Atsion Lake ($40).

OTHER RECREATION
Batona Trail
The Pinelands' best-known hike is the Batona Trail, which winds easily from Brendan T. Byrne State Forest through Wharton State Forest and the heart of the Pinelands, and

ends at the Bass River State Forest. Although nearly 50 miles in its entirety, the trail can be shortened by access from a number of intersecting roads, and is easy enough for everyone from young to old, as the only challenges are a few hills and wetlands. Along this clearly marked trail, the rambler may encounter huckleberries, orchids, deer, waterfowl on land and birds of prey flying overhead.

There are also numerous opportunities for camping, including a few backcountry sites.

Bike Route
The **Pine Barrens River Ramble** is a 42.6-mile bicycling loop through the Pinelands, routed by the New Jersey Department of Transportation. To obtain a free map, go to www.state.nj.us/transportation/commuter/bike/freeinfo.shtm.

FESTIVALS
Cranberry Festival
Chatsworth's annual two-day Cranberry Festival (609/726-9237, www.cranfest.org/festival.html) takes place in October, and features over 100 artists and craftspeople, live music, antique dealers, and all things cranberry, including pies, jams, jellies, cakes, and ice cream. Two-hour cranberry bog tours ($7) leave from the festival grounds.

Admission to the festival is free, though a $5 donation is requested if you decide to park at the highly recommended lot at the Second Street School.

Blueberry Festival
Held annually at Whitesbog Village—home of the cultivated blueberry—this June festival (www.whitesbog.org) features country crafts, Piney music, and of course, blueberry picking.

SIGHTS
Naval Air Engineering Station at Lakehurst
On May 6, 1937, the dirigible Hindenburg crashed, killing 36 of 97 passengers at one of the world's foremost "lighter-than-air"-vessel airbases. Reporters and cameramen stood to watch the hulking aircraft, 804 feet long, 147 feet tall, and 135 feet in diameter, land at the Lakehurst

CENTRAL JERSEY

Naval air station (Rte. 547, 732/818-7520, www
.lakehurst.navy.mil/nlweb/). Instead they witnessed one of the most famous airship disasters
in world history when a cast spark set the alu-
minum paint ablaze, consuming the Hindenburg in a mere 34 seconds. Although the site
is a bit stark, tours include access to the crash
site, a visit to the impressively massive Hangar
#1, and a re-creation of the cabin from Rob-
ert Wise's 1975 film *The Hindenburg,* starring
George C. Scott and Anne Bancroft. A two-
week advance reservation is required for tours
(individual and group), which are given on the
second and fourth Saturday of each month (call
for specifics). Walk-ins are not accepted.

Forgotten Towns

The Pine Barrens' sandy soil is notorious for
"swallowing" villages abandoned at the end of
the bog-iron and glassmaking eras. If you're
out searching on your own for lost towns, the
best way to recognize where they once stood
is to identify ebony spleenwort. This smooth
and shiny red-brown stem is non-native to
Pinelands soil because of its high acidity, but
it grows rampant in areas where lime was used
for building.

Easily recognizable forgotten towns include
Martha's Furnace, named for the wife of the
"town" founder (all that remains is the furnace
ruins); **Hampton Furnace**; and **Atsion,** the
remains of a bog-ore mining village. The company store now acts as a ranger station, and
there's still the old iron-maker's mansion standing and a number of houses. All three towns
are located within Wharton State Forest.

Albert Music Hall

Every Saturday night the music of the Pines
comes alive at Albert Music Hall (125 Rte. 532,
609/971-1593, www.alberthall.org, $5 adult,
$1 child under 12) in Waretown, located just
west of Route 9 along the Pinelands eastern
border. Here you'll find your foot a' tapping to
bluegrass, country, and folk performances by
native Piney musicians. To keep things moving, performers change stage every half hour,
and a typical evening includes about seven acts.

Ask about the improv **Pickin Shed,** where you
may witness a jam session unlike any other—
fiddles, washtubs, dulcimers, banjos are all a
possibility. Doors open at 6:30 P.M. and music
begins at 7:30.

Carranza Memorial

On July 12, 1928, 23-year-old Captain
Emilio Carranza Rodriguez, known as "the
Charles Lindbergh of Mexico," died in a plane
crash while attempting to navigate through a
storm that struck on the final leg of a good-
will flight to the United States that included
stops in Washington, DC and New York
City. Today a stone memorial, erected two
years after his death, stands on a sandy roadside clearing in the middle of the Pinelands
Reserve, commemorating the spot where his
plane went down. Every year since the trag-
edy, the Mount Holly American Legion and
the Mexican consulate in New York have held
a small ceremony at the site to honor his sac-
rifice (second Sunday in July, 1 P.M.). The
memorial is located in Wharton State Forest
along Carranza Road, a few miles south of
Tabernacle and just past the turn-off for the
juvenile correctional facility.

Apple Pie Hill and Lookout Tower

The highest point in the Pinelands and in all
of New Jersey's southern portion is Apple Pie
Hill, which stands 205 feet above sea level. Located three miles outside Chatsworth within
Wharton State Forest, the hill is topped by a
60-foot lookout tower once used for spotting
fires. From the top of the tower, you'll have
an excellent view of the surrounding forests.
Apple Pie Hill and tower are easily reachable
by way of the Batona Trail, north of the Carranza Memorial.

Batsto

The former bog-iron mining and glassmaking
village of Batsto (4110 Nesco Rd., 609/561-
0024, www.batstovillage.org, $5 Memorial
Day–Labor Day) is today one of the Pinelands'
top attractions. Located on the southern edge
of Wharton State Forest along Route 542, this

restored 19th-century village is made up of 33 structures, including a general store, gristmill, sawmill, and a number of former workers' quarters, as well as a picturesque lake, but the centerpiece of the property is an Italianate-style 32-room **mansion,** originally the home of ironmaster William Richards, his son, and grandson. It was later purchased and renovated to resemble its current exterior by Joseph Wharton. Three floors of the mansion—including 14 rooms—are open for tours daily.

A **nature center** (9 A.M.–4 P.M. Wed.–Sun., daily Memorial Day–Labor Day) provides canoes for guided trips on the lake during summer months, and on the third weekend in October the village hosts an annual **Country Living Fair,** featuring handmade quilts, pony rides, and numerous demonstrations, including (my favorite) chain-saw art.

A visitors center is open 9 A.M.–4 P.M. daily, and includes a small gift shop where you can stock up on Piney history and culture, including numerous books and a rolled-up map of forgotten towns ($0.27 plus tax). Restrooms are available.

Chatsworth

Once an iron-mining and glassmaking village, this self-proclaimed "capital of the pines" is today strictly agricultural, dominated by the region's two largest cranberry producers, A. R. DeMarco and Sons and Ocean Spray. The town has a big reputation for such a little place, and when you do eventually reach it (driving along Route 536 you'll pass nothing but gun clubs for what seems like forever), you'll hardly know you're there.

Chatsworth stands at the crossroads of Routes 563 and 532, where you'll also find the 1860 **White Horse Inn,** a somewhat dilapidated two-story colonial clapboard originally built as a stagecoach stop. The building was later used as an annex to the **Chatsworth Club,** a popular country club established by Italian Prince Mario Ruspoli, who was introduced to the Pinelands by his in-laws and built a home here soon after. Members of this onceprosperous elitist center included DuPonts, As-

tors, and Vanderbilts. Today the club is long deceased and the inn is slowly undergoing renovations to turn it into a community center.

Down the road is **Buzby's General Store** (First St. and Rte. 563), perhaps the best-known shop in the Pinelands as it was featured in John McPhee's 1973 *Pine Barrens.* Things have changed a lot in 30-plus years—no longer does the store sell supplies like cigarettes, animal feed, and kerosene, but instead acts like a makeshift information center for the region. If you have a question about Piney culture, this is the place to come. Inside you'll also find the **Cheshire Cat Gift Shop** (609/894-4415), hosting the largest selection of books relating to Piney fact, fiction, and legend around, as well as numerous country goods.

Whitesbog Village

Whitesbog (Mile Marker 13, Rte. 530) is home of the commercial high-bush blueberry. Founded in 1870 by Joseph J. White, the village grew into a successful agricultural town in the late 19th century and filled quickly with workers' cottages, a packing and storing facility, and a company store. Cranberry bogs and blueberry bushels occupied the land surrounding the village. It was White's daughter Elizabeth who successfully cultivated the first blueberry here in 1916. Unlike many other Pineland towns, much of Whitesbog Village remains intact, and some of its homes continue to be inhabited. A working cranberry bog still stands nearby. Whitesbog is owned by the state of New Jersey and is currently leased to the **Whitesbog Preservation Trust** (12103 Whitesbog Rd., Browns Mills, www.whitesbog.org), a non-profit group that organizes tours, events, and volunteer workdays to help raise money to restore the village. Most events cost $5, and a current schedule can be found on the Preservation's website.

CAMPING
Resorts

Just south of Chatsworth, **Wading Pines Camping Resort** (85 Godfrey Bridge Rd., 609/726-1313, www.wadingpines.com) is the premier Piney campground. Situated along the

Wading River, this 50-acre resort has 300 sites, ranging from waterside to open field, to accommodate tents and RVs. There are 26 cabins available for rental, and a general store, snack bar, and laundry on the premises. Sites with water, electric, and cable run $33/night for two people. The campground is open March–mid-December. Wading Pines also runs a canoe and kayaking company.

Pilgrim Lake Campground (New Gretna, 609/296-4725 or 800/218-2267, early Apr.– late Oct., $22) has 116 sites situated in the middle of Bass River State Forest. Many of the campsites are wooded, and amenities include hot showers, general store, and a lake for swimming with a lifeguard on duty.

Timberline Lake Camping Resort (609/296-7900, early May–mid-Oct., $31) features 158 wooded and lakefront sites, a swimming pool, table tennis, and a lake for fishing and swimming. The resort hosts numerous activities throughout the season, including bingo nights and a Hawaiian luau.

Car Camping

All of the Pineland forests offer overnight camping facilities that are accessible by road. At **Brendan T. Byrne Sate Forest** (609/726-1191) you'll find sites for more than 80 tents and trailers, with nearby restrooms facilities, which are available year-round ($20/night). Visitors can also rent one of three furnished cabins ($45/night, Apr.–Oct.) situated along the bank of **Pakim Pond** and sleep up to six or rent one of three circular yurts ($30/night) that can accommodate four.

Bass Forest (609/296-1114) has a variety of overnight facilities, including 176 family-style campsites ($1/person, based on site capacity, Mar.–Nov.) and six group campsites ($20/night, year-round). There are no electrical hook-ups, but flush toilets and showers are located nearby. The forest also features nine fully enclosed lean-tos ($30/night, year-round) that can house up to six people; six simple shelters ($10/bunk, Apr.–Oct.), each with two bunkrooms, a living room, and a small stove, that can accommodate four; and six cabins ($65/night,

Apr.–Oct.) situated along Lake Absegami, each with screened-in porch, bathroom, living rooms, fireplace, water, and electricity, that can house up to six.

Wharton State Forest (609/268-0444, 609/561-0024) has 50 tent and trailer sites available around Atsion Lake ($20/night, Apr.–Dec.) with nearby showers and toilets and 49 primitive campsites at Godfrey Bridge ($20/night), with water, picnic tables, and pit toilets, open year-round. A number of other campsites are scattered throughout the forest, each equipped with only a hand pump for water and a nearby pit toilet. These sites are only $1/night per person and are able to accommodate 50–250 persons. Wharton State Forest also hosts nine furnished cabins (Apr.–Oct.) along Atsion Lake, two accessible to those with disabilities. The cabins can sleep 4–8 and range in price $45–85/night, depending on the number of occupants.

To make a reservation for any of the above campsites you can log onto www.state.nj.us/dep/parksandforests/parks/campreserv.html, or contact the specific park office.

Backcountry

Wharton State Forest hosts a couple of backcountry sites, accessible only by foot, canoe or kayak, or on horseback. The **Lower Forge Wilderness Site** is situated just off the Batona Trail along the Batsto River, about 10 miles north of Batsto. The site can accommodate up to 50 people ($1/night per person) and is without running water. The **Mullica River Wilderness Site** is located along the Mullica River, 3.5 miles north of Batsto and 5.3 miles south of Atsion. It has a 100-person capacity ($1/night per person) and is equipped with running water. Permits for either site can be picked up at the **Batsto Visitor Center** (Wharton State Forest, 4110 Nesco Rd., Hammonton, 609/561-0024) or the **Atsion Office** (Wharton State Forest, 744 Rte. 206, 609/268-0444).

FOOD

Your best bet for Pinelands dining is in sticking to the region's outskirts, Medford and Mount Holly (covered in the *South Jersey* chapter) to the west, and Route 9—separating the region from the Jersey Shore—running along its eastern border. When you're in the heart of the Pinelands a good meal can be hard to come by. Thankfully there's the **Sweetwater Casino** (2780 7th Ave., 609/965-3285, $12–19), an American restaurant, bar, and entertainment venue located in Sweetwater along the Mullica River, just a few miles south of Batsto Village. With gold-rimmed chairs, a faded leaf-print rug, and worn green and pink decor, it's somewhat outdated, but the fishing nets that hang from the vaulted ceiling and the ship's wheel on the wall give it an edge of fun. On days when there's no entertainment, muzak plays over the speakers, but somehow you can tell that when this place is hopping there's no stopping it. "Casino cheese," a house-made concoction served with a basket of sesame pretzels and individual packets of crackers, is their specialty, and is served before every meal. Portions are large, sundaes are huge, and during summer you can pull your boat up to the dock. Black and white photos provided by the Atlantic City Historical Society (it's not that far away) are displayed upon the walls, as are a couple of signed photos of local actress Kelly Ripa, who writes, "To Sweetwater Casino: My favorite South Jersey restaurant." With such adornments, as well as a classic cigarette machine still occupying restroom space, how can you go wrong?

The bar hosts live music on weekends, and the restaurant often sponsors murder mysteries. Call ahead.

MEDFORD

The 40.29-square-mile township of Medford skirts the western edge of the Pinelands and travels south, where it meets up with Camden County's retail hub. It's a largely residential area, once home to numerous glass factories and mills. Today only one mill remains and it's a major focal piece of Medford Village, which itself serves as a community center. The Village's Main Street is as American as they come—lined with attractive Victorian build-

ings housing small specialty shops and eateries. Surrounded by scenic woodlands and featuring a few sites of historic interest, it's a great place to walk around. The township is home to a couple of sights that are worth the short drive, but otherwise stick close to the village center. It's where all the action is in this otherwise sleepy town.

Historic Medford Village

Downtown Medford Village is still dotted with historic sites left over from its days as a milling and glassworks town. At **Cranberry Hall** (17 N. Main St., 609/654-2512), which serves as the township's park and recreation department, you can pick up a free self-guided walking tour brochure to the areas historical and architecturally significant structures, as well as information on the Pinelands. One of the townships most famous attractions is **Kirby's Mill** (275 Church Rd., 609/654-7767), a 225-year-old working mill that closed for use in 1969, and is today owned by the Medford Historical Society. There's also a waterwheel, blacksmith shop, and small museum on the premises.

Trimble Street, on the east side of Main Street, was once home to a number of Star Glasswork's factory workers. Many of the clapboard structures have since been restored.

Other Sights

A staple in the Medford community since 1953, **Johnson's Corner Farm** (133 Church Rd., 609/654-8603, www.johnsonsfarm.com) is a family-owned establishment where you'll find berry-picking, barnyard animals, hayrides, and homemade pies, cobblers, and quiches. In the fall Johnson's offers popcorn-, peanut-, and cotton-picking hayride excursions, and events such as "Strawberry Jam Weekends" are held seasonally.

For over 50 years the **Woodford Cedar Run Wildlife Refuge** (4 Sawmill Rd., 856/983-3329, www.cedarrun.org, 10 A.M.–4 P.M. Mon.–Sat., 1–4 P.M. Sun., $5 adult, $3 child) has rescued and cared for injured native wildlife. Begun by James and Betty Woodford, the center is now run by their daughter, Jeanne, and features the **Woodford Education Center,** where you'll find a variety of amphibians and reptiles, and a host of interactive educational materials geared at children. The refuge includes a wooded nature walk and an area for those animals with insurmountable injuries that must remain on the property, such as a bald eagle and a groundhog. Weekend "critter-fests" highlight a different native species monthly.

Festivals and Events

The **Festival of Art and Music,** held annually the first Sunday in June, features jugglers, magicians, Victorian trolley rides, and four music stages. Strolling musicians saunter down Main Street, which is closed off to all automobile traffic. The Medford Historical Society hosts an annual **Quilt Show** the same weekend (Sat. and Sun.) at Kirby's Mill.

For a step back in time I recommend the **Dickens Festival** (www.hmva.org). The village annually transforms into a Victorian Christmas town on the first Friday in December as costumed carolers stroll the sidewalks and holiday music pours from open storefronts. Events include a tree-lighting ceremony and the welcomed arrival of the big man in red.

Shopping

Medford Village offers the township's best shopping, with an easily walkable Main Street that hosts an array of antique stores and specialty shops and a couple of interspersed eateries.

Creative Genius (32 N. Main St., 609/714-1131) highlights arts and crafts created by local artists, including photographs, masks, jewelry, and mosaics. Classes ranging from pottery to painting are held for both kids and adults. **Scherzer Antiques** (134 S. Main St., 609/953-2950) is an artfully restored antique store occupying the former company store of Star Glass Works, one of the region's original glass manufacturers. The shop's abundantly full front porch beckons onlookers inside. **The Knitting Room** (26 S. Main St., 609/654-9003) is a great place to check out

the latest knits and fibers. **Catch the Wind** (23 S. Main St., 609/654-9393) features an interesting collection of wind chimes and wind socks. For antique and estate jewelry, including engagement rings, vintage compacts, and pocket watches, head to **The Way We Were** (10 N. Main St., 609/654-0343).

Accommodations

$100-150: The **Iris Inn** (45 S. Main St., 609/654-7528, fax 609/714-0277, $100–150) is a nine-room bed and breakfast housed in a 1904 Queen Anne Victorian. It features a front porch and communal fireplace, and is conveniently located on Main Street in Medford Village. Each room has private bath, TV, and telephone.

The **Flying W Airport Resort** (60 Fostertown Rd., 609/267-8787, www.flyingw airport.com) includes a 1960s 38-room motel, restaurant, lounge, landing strip, and an inground swimming pool shaped like a Cessna. If this weren't enough, flying camps operate from the grounds during the summer. The motel has recently been updated and amenities include TV with HBO, microwave, and refrigerator. The resort is quite popular with day guests, who come for the restaurant's Sunday brunch, the summer Doo-Wop concerts, and take off.

Food

Medford has a handful of choice restaurants, found both within the village and scattered throughout the township.

Located in the heart of Medford Village, **Braddock's Tavern** (39 S. Main St., 609/654-1604, www.braddocks.com) offers casual and fine dining in an 1823 historic setting. Not for the light of appetite, the restaurant includes such heavy-handed entrées as Colonial Game Pie ($20.95) and Tavern Chicken Supreme ($20.95). A second-story porch overlooking Main Street is a favored dining locale. Braddock's is open for lunch 11:30 A.M.–2:30 P.M. and dinner 5:30–10 P.M. Monday–Friday, and brunch 11 A.M.–2:30 P.M. Sunday.

For romance try **Beau Rivage** (Taunton Blvd.,

856/983-1999, www.beaurivage-restaurant .com) a top-notch dining experience. In the last few years this lakeside establishment has updated its traditional French menu, added bistro options, and foregone its dress code. New owners are responsible for the transformation, which includes an interior addition called La Cave—a dining space converted from an old wine cellar. The restaurant is open 11:30 A.M.–2:30 P.M. and 5:30–9:30 P.M. Tuesday–Friday, 5:30–9:30 P.M. Saturday, and 4–8 P.M. Sunday.

Café Noelle (20 S. Main St., 609/953-1155, $21–30) is a BYO dishing out eclectic cuisine for lunch and dinner, and receiving consistently high ratings from loyal patrons.

Getting There and Around
Historic Medford Village is located along Route 541 north of Wharton State Forest. To reach the village and the township from Chatsworth, take Route 532 west about 15.5 miles to Route 541 (where you'll find Medford Lakes), and head north for three miles. If traveling from Brendan T. Byrne State Forest, take Route 70 west for about 13 miles and turn south onto Route 541/ Main Street.

SOUTH JERSEY

Far from New Jersey's exit ramp—and—rest stop reputation lies a quaint and countrified southern section that lives up to the Garden State motto. Often overlooked, South Jersey—as it's referred to by local residents—is a quiet reprieve filled with charming towns and back-road beauty, a treasure chest of environmental and cultural wealth only recently being discovered.

Stretching from the banks of the lower Delaware River eastward toward the shore, and upward to include Camden and southwest Burlington Counties, South Jersey encompasses roughly one-third of the state's landmass while housing only about one-quarter of its residents. For many years the greater metropolitan region of South Jersey was little more than shopping centers and traffic jams, but revitalization efforts have sparked new life into downtown centers from Mount Holly to Haddonfield. Still, there's great diversity among South Jersey's regions. The industrial cities of Gloucester and Pennsauken sit right down the road from the white-collar, suburban stretch of Cherry Hill and Marlton, and the Delaware Bayshore—with vast wetlands that are a nature lover's paradise—is dotted with seafarers' settlements, strong with the scent of salty air. Seventeenth-century towns such as Woodbury share county space with Washington Township, an area that's been developed for less than 50 years, and in the counties of Gloucester, Salem, and Cumberland, agriculture and farmlands are abundant and the true Garden State can be found.

Many visitors to New Jersey's southern half

© LAURA KINIRY

HIGHLIGHTS

◖ Aunt Charlotte's Candies: The downstairs candy store is a gorgeous sight, but it's what's happening upstairs that makes Aunt Charlotte's cocoa beans above the rest (page 284).

◖ Camden Waterfront: Roam the decks of a floating museum over three football fields in length, swim with sharks, and chill out to minor league ball with the Philadelphia skyline as your backdrop (page 290).

◖ Haddonfield: You will find everything from snowboards to string lights to glass art pieces while shopping in one of South Jersey's most picturesque downtown centers (page 298).

◖ Clementon Amusement Park and Splash World Water Park: This century-old amusement park continues to pack 'em in with a new roller coaster thrill-ride and plenty of old-time favorites (page 303).

◖ Mullica Hill: South Jersey may be plentiful with shopping, but no place embodies antiquing better than the village of Mullica Hill. From the Yellow Garage to the Old Red Barn, it's a wonderful place to spend an afternoon (page 312).

◖ Cowtown Rodeo and Flea Market: Cowboy up and mosey on down to the East Coast's longest continuously running rodeo, and don't let the winter's inaction deter your spirits – there's always the flea market to wrangle you in (page 318).

LOOK FOR ◖ TO FIND RECOMMENDED SIGHTS, ACTIVITIES, DINING, AND LODGING.

◖ Wheaton Village: For a glimpse into South Jersey's glass history a trip here is a must. Take a tour of the Museum of American Glass, watch fellowship artists create their wares, or make a paperweight of your own (page 328).

are surprised to find it so green, and so well-suited for outdoor recreation. Rivers and lakes are numerous in South Jersey's counties, and the scenic country roads of Gloucester and Cumberland Counties are perfect for two-wheeling. As the weather warms, stalls selling sweet Jersey corn, mouth-watering blueberries, and the plumpest and reddest of the famous Jersey tomatoes appear by the roadside.

The southern half of New Jersey was originally settled by Lenape Indians and later Swedes, Finns, and Quakers, and retains a history much different than the state's northern half. You won't drive far without seeing a Friends meeting house, or pass a patch of land that doesn't have a tale to tell. In fact, there's such a distinction between South Jerseyans and their northern counterparts that you might think you've crossed into a different state. Down here the accents are softer, the pace a bit slower, and the tri-state area includes Delaware and Pennsylvania rather than Connecticut and New York.

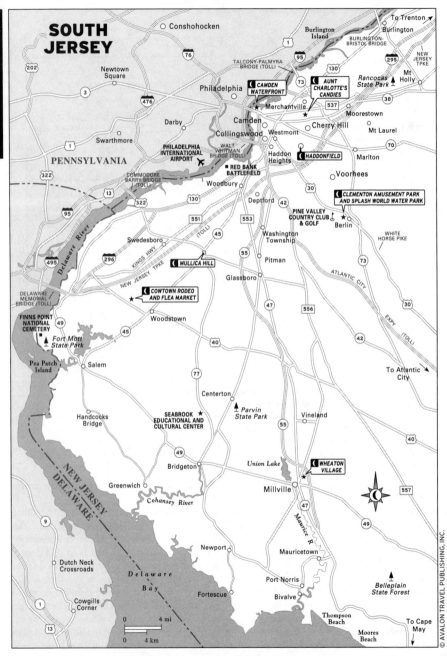

© AVALON TRAVEL PUBLISHING, INC.

The state's industry planners believe that any new growth in New Jersey will take place in the south, though big name businesses such as Subaru of America (Cherry Hill), NFL Films (Mount Laurel), and Sony Music (Sewell) have been based here for years. Houses are being built faster than they can be filled, and mega-stores are making their way onto some of the last remaining farmland—a potentially dangerous combination. Today South Jersey is still part farmland, part suburbia, and it's often easy to feel you're in the middle of nowhere, or, to put it another way, in a quiet refuge between a bustling urban center and weekend resorts.

PLANNING YOUR TIME

South Jersey offers up a number of quick day- or weekend-trip possibilities, though those who would like to explore all of the region in one trip should allow at least five days. Consider giving a day to Burlington County, visiting the many historic sights in Burlington City and Mount Holly. Travel south into Camden County for an essential stop at Merchantville's Aunt Charlotte's Candies. Shoppers will want to head to Marlton.

The numerous attractions at Camden's waterfront are often paired with an overnight stay in Cherry Hill. On a second day in Camden County, stroll around Cooper River and make an early visit to Haddonfield's Indian King Tavern. During the afternoon, browse the borough's specialty shops, as well as those in nearby Collingswood. Spend the evening at the Haddonfield Inn. If you find yourself with an extra afternoon during the summer, spend it at Clementon Amusement Park and Splash World Park, along White Horse Pike.

Gloucester, Salem, and Cumberland Counties' sights are many and make an easy weekend trip. Begin on a Saturday morning at the Cowtown Flea Market before driving west to Fort Mott State Park. Then drive north on Kings Highway to Woodbury, and from there drive south for some antiquing in Mullica Hill. Continue east, making a stop at Heritage Station and

Winery for a free wine tasting. Turn north to get to Pitman, where you can shop the main street or catch a movie at the Broadway Theatre.

A good place to spend the night is in nearby Deptford, and in the morning, go south into Cumberland County to spend a few hours at Wheaton Village. Then take a drive through the back roads of Cumberland County, stopping at Mauricetown and the East Point Lighthouse before traveling back through Bridgeton (if you have time, visit the white tigers at the Bridgeton City Zoo). Make a detour into Greenwich to see the tea-burning monument, and continue on to Salem to head home.

GETTING THERE AND AROUND

South Jersey is easily reachable from a number of points. From Delaware take I-95 North across the Delaware Memorial Bridge and continue north onto I-295, and from nearby Philadelphia International Airport you can either travel south on I-95 to the Commodore Barry Bridge, bringing you to Route 322, or head north and look for signs to the Ben Franklin Bridge, which will drop you into the heart of Camden County.

From North Jersey, it's possible to take either I-295 South, or the New Jersey Turnpike to exit 4 (Mt. Laurel) or exit 5 (Hwy. 541 Westampton, midway between Burlington City and Mount Holly). You can also travel Route 130 from Trenton all the way through to Gloucester County and Route 45. Unless it's rush hour, I-295 will get you where you need to be the quickest; otherwise be prepared for quite a backup. I don't recommend Route 130 unless you're looking for a bite to eat—the road can get bumpy and is ridden with abandoned shopping centers.

Scenic back roads include Route 47 from Deptford through to the shore (you can also take Route 55 for a quick, no-hassle drive) and the southern portion of King's Highway, running parallel to I-295 from the Delaware Memorial Bridge to Woodbury. Route 49, running west–east, and the southern portion of

Route 45 from Salem to Mullica Hill are also pleasant.

NJ Transit (www.njtransit.com) provides extensive bus service throughout South Jersey, connecting most of its major and smaller cities and towns as well as providing service into Philadelphia. **PATCO**—a high-speed line of the Delaware River Port Authority (www.drpa.org/patco)—links towns along the White Horse Pike and Haddon Avenue to Philadelphia. PATCO connects with NJ Transit's **Atlantic City line** in Lindenwold to provide access to southern shore communities. The new **River LINE** travels north along the Delaware River, connecting Camden to Burlington City and continuing further north into Trenton, and stopping at various points in between.

Southwest Burlington County

Bordering the Delaware River to the northeast of Philadelphia, southwest Burlington County is plentiful with revitalized historic towns as well as modern commercial spreads. Route 130 lines the western border of the county, easily accessible from Central Jersey's Capital region and Gloucester and Salem Counties to the south, but for something more scenic travel Route 537 west from Mount Holly past open fields, attractive Victorians, and through tiny downtown centers. The road intersects with Route 73, stretching south from the Talcony-Palmyra Bridge and making its way toward the lower Pinelands, and passing through townships well known for their convenient locations, shopping, and restaurants.

Getting There

Burlington County can be reached from Philadelphia via I-95 and crossing at Talcony-Palmyra Bridge (Rte. 73) or the Burlington-Bristol Bridge, putting you just south of the Burlington Historic District.

BURLINGTON

Burlington was the capital of West Jersey and for a brief time, the county seat. Today it is a city often overlooked by people en route from Trenton to Cherry Hill. But if you're a history buff or a fan of colonial architecture—the kind found in Williamsburg, Virginia or Philadelphia's Society Hill—then Burlington is not to be missed. The city boasts a one-square-mile historic district that has been carefully main-

tained and preserved and lists over 40 historic sights. Many of its buildings are of red brick, trimmed in colonial shades of green, red, and blue, and date back over 200 years. A convenient riverfront location made it a bustling port town in the early 1800s, but Burlington was soon bypassed for Philadelphia, further down the river but closer to the shore. Still, the city continued to see many well-known faces pass through its streets, assuring itself a settled place in history.

New Jersey Firsts

Founded in 1677 by English Quakers who arrived aboard the *Kent,* Burlington touts a large number of New Jersey firsts. Among them is the first recorded English settlement in New Jersey (1624) and the first recorded murder, both taking place on **Burlington Island,** a large island easily viewed from the city's one-mile riverfront walkway. At various times the island housed a school and an amusement park; today it sits vacant. **The Revell House** (1685) at 213 Wood Street is the oldest building in Burlington, and thought to be among the county's oldest residences. At 301 High Street is New Jersey's oldest continuously operating pharmacy, **The Burlington Pharmacy.** Now known as **Wheatley's,** it is believed to have been a stop on the Underground Railroad. And less than a block west on High Street is **Temple B'nai Israel,** one of the oldest synagogues in South Jersey.

Neighborhoods

Burlington holds the distinction of being one of

© LAURA KINIRY

along High Street in downtown Burlington City

America's first planned towns. Richard Noble, an original colonist, mapped out the city in a well-laid grid stemming from High Street. Settlers were separated into neighborhoods according to their religious sects. To the south of High Street went the **London** sect, and to the right the **Yorkshires.** These neighborhoods are still in use today, and signs identifying them can be seen on Pearl Street near the Delaware River.

Historic Sites

Burlington's historic downtown centers around High Street, where you'll find a number of sites dating back to the 18th century. Though some establishments no longer exist, their history is worth noting, and walking through this district is like taking a step back in time—something I truly recommend.

While strolling through the downtown district, take note of **206 High Street,** the former site of Isaac Collins Print Shop. It was here that Benjamin Franklin printed New Jersey's first colonial currency. Though no longer a print shop, a plaque marks the

spot. On the southeast corner of High and Broad Streets is the former site of the **Blue Anchor Inn,** established 1750. It is now a senior housing complex. Rumor tells of an arm-wrestling match that took place here between then–presidential candidate Abraham Lincoln and Ulysses S. Grant. The **Ulysses S. Grant House** (1856) at 309 Wood Street was home to General Grant and his family during the Civil War. Grant was at this residence when he learned that President Lincoln had been shot at Ford's Theatre. Upon hearing the news, he rushed to the Blue Anchor Inn to catch a train to Washington, D.C. Two blocks north of Grant's house, at 114 East Union Street, is the **Oliver Cromwell House** (1798). This is the final residence of Cromwell, a black Revolutionary War soldier who crossed the Delaware with General George Washington on December 25, 1776.

The birth homes of two of Burlington's most famous historical sons stand side by side along High Street between Broad and Federal Streets. At 457 High Street is the **James Fenimore**

Cooper House (1782). Cooper, author of *The Leatherstocking Tales,* was born on September 15, 1789. His family moved to what would become Cooperstown, New York, a year later. Next door at 457 High Street is the **Captain James Lawrence House** (1742). Captain Lawrence, a naval war hero whose dying words, "Tell the men to fire faster and not to give up the ship," were paraphrased "Don't Give Up the Ship" and adopted as the motto for the U.S. Navy, was born here on October 1, 1781. Both houses, along with the **Bard-Howe House** (c. 1743) at 453 High Street, are part of the **Burlington County Historical Society** complex (451 High St., 609/386-4773, fax 609/386-4828, 1–5 P.M. Tues.–Sat., $3 adult, $1.50 12 and under). Tours of the three homes are given every 50 minutes during the hours the Society is open.

Riverfront Park

Situated along the waterfront in downtown Burlington City is the mile-long Riverfront Park, a perfect place for picnicking or attending one of the many events held here throughout the year, including a farmers market and a summer evening concert series. The park hosts a launch for permitted boats on its north end, an amphitheater, and views of both Burlington Island and Burlington-Bristol Bridge to its south. Riverfront Park serves as a central point for the **Delaware River Heritage Trail,** a 50-mile long "work in progress" multiuse trail that when finished will form a loop between New Jersey and Pennsylvania.

Boat permits are available at the park on weekends (8 A.M.–4 P.M.), or at **City Hall** (525 High St., 9 A.M.–4 P.M.) during the week, April–October. Cost is $15/day New Jersey residents, $25/day out-of-state.

Entertainment and Events

For a historic overview of the city given by guides in colonial garb, stop by the **Tour & Guide Office at the Carriage House** (c. 1876) (12 Smith Ln., 609/386-3993). These tours are only offered at 11:30 A.M. and 2 P.M. on Friday, Saturday, and Sunday during the summer months ($5 adult, $3 senior, $3 child under 12),

or by appointment throughout the year. To obtain a walking-tour brochure to be followed at your own pace, go to www.tourburlington.org/Us.html or call the number listed.

The **Riverfront Summer Concert Series** (Promenade Park, 609/386-0200, ext. 135) takes place Thursday nights in July and August on Burlington's one-mile riverfront promenade. The concerts are free, and bands playing everything from jazz to big band to rock perform. Call for performances, and don't forget your blanket.

The Festival of Lights & Illuminated Boat Parade takes place in mid–late August with an illuminated parade of watercraft and a fireworks display, and is an excellent choice for an evening on the river with the family. Free parking and admission. For additional information visit www.tourburlington.org/DoEvents.html. It's a day-long event also featuring a 5K run, music throughout the afternoon, and plenty of kid things to do.

Want to get the inside scoop on Burlington's historical homes? Take the annual December **Holiday House Tour** (609/366-7125), during which you'll visit over a dozen private houses and historical sites.

Shopping

Shopping opportunities in Burlington are limited, though what effect the River LINE will have on Burlington's downtown district remains to be seen. For now, antique stores are the city's main offerings.

ANTIQUE AND SPECIALTY STORES

Philip's Furniture and Antiques (307 High St., 609/386-7125, www.burlington-nj.net/bus/philips.html) is three stories of furniture and collectibles ranging from antiques to present-day items, including typewriters, bedroom sets, and sofas. The shop's a community staple, having been located in Burlington for over 20 years. Farther east on High Street is the **Burlington Antiques Emporium** (424 High St., 609/747-8333, www.antiquesnj.com), home to more than 80 antique dealers. The selection here is superb: Grandfather clocks, antiquarian books, country items, and Depression glass are among the items you can find. High ceilings and 14,000 square feet of space add to your shopping comfort.

If you're looking for a unique souvenir, check out **The Willing Mind** (348 High St., 609/386-8786, www.thewillingmind.com), an art gallery and shop that creates large-sized graphic prints based on unique photos, postcards, and advertisements. Much of the production takes place in the back room, and many pieces are New Jersey–themed, including historic trolley and devil imagery.

THE BURLINGTON COAT FACTORY OUTLET STORE

Begun in 1972 as a single outlet, the Burlington Coat Factory (1250 Rte. 130 N., 609/386-3314, www.coat.com, 10 A.M.–9 P.M. Mon–Fri., until 6 P.M. Sat, 11 A.M.–6 P.M. Sun.) has grown into a national enterprise with over 300 stores in 42 states. This is the original factory, a large, white, nondescript building still in operation, and selling everything from baby products to home furnishings (and of course coats). The Coat Factory is one of the top 10 employers of Burlington County residents.

Food

Burlington has a couple of lovely downtown restaurants. For more casual fare, head to Route 130, a congested road heavy with traffic lights and diners.

On the corner of High and Pearl Streets in Burlington's historic district is **Café Gallery** (219 High St. at Pearl St., 609/386-6150, www.cafegalleryburlington.com), a fine-dining establishment that has been in the community for over 25 years. Ask for a table upstairs to enjoy a sweeping view of the Delaware River or, during warmer months, request a seat near the fountain on the outdoor patio. This two-story restaurant serving French-American doubles as an art gallery and is known for its Sunday brunch. Lunch hours are 11:30 A.M.–4 P.M. Monday–Saturday, and for Sunday brunch 11:30 A.M.–3 P.M. Dinner begins at 5 P.M. daily, but closing hours vary according to crowds.

Following High Street east you'll come to **Thommy G's** (345 High St., 609/239-8133). On the southwest corner of High and Broad Streets, it occupies the former site of Merchant National Bank. Thommy G's has been serving up Italian cuisine with a decidedly New Orleans touch in this location since 1999, but evidence of former banking days are everywhere. The vault still stands at the rear of the massive restaurant (with seating available inside), and to the right is a wall of teller posts now used to separate the bar from a more formal dining area and offer added seclusion for a row of booths. Friday nights tend to be more informal, with music provided by piano or jazz ensemble. The restaurant is open for lunch 11:30 A.M.–3 P.M. Tuesday–Friday. Dinner hours are 4–9:30 P.M. Tuesday–Thursday and until 10 P.M. on Fridays, closed Sunday and Monday.

For more casual dining head out to Route 130 South and look for **Big Ed's Barbeque** (259 Rte. 130, 609/387-3611, www.bigedsbbq.com), a small brick building to your right. Big Ed's is a local chain offering some of the best all-you-can-eat ribs in New Jersey, and it's kid-friendly. Grab some napkins—they're a must! There are plenty of diners along Route 130. Try the **Prince Inn Diner** (4520 Rte. 130, 609/386-5522) or further south, the **Harvest Diner-Restaurant** (2602 Rte. 130, 856/829-4499).

Tri-state residents rave about **Fuji** (404 Rte. 130 N., Cinnaminson, 856/829-5211, www.fujirestaurant.com), a BYO Japanese and sushi restaurant located in a tiny unremarkable space along Route 130 in nearby Cinnaminson. Prices are reasonable—two pieces of hamachi sushi go for $5—and you're not going to find meals this wonderful on every corner. Lunch hours are 11:30 A.M.–2 P.M. Tuesday–Friday; dinner is served 5–9:30 P.M. Tuesday–Thursday, 5–10 P.M. Friday and Saturday, 4–8:30 P.M. Sunday, closed Monday.

MOUNT HOLLY

Mount Holly is a blend of cottage-style storefronts, historic sites, darkened pubs, and homes hovering at sidewalk's edge. Somehow it all comes together to produce a township definitely worth a visit, both for its historic downtown district and nearby attractions.

High Street

High Street is Mount Holly's main boulevard and home to a few notable 18th-century structures including **The Friend's Meeting House** (High and Garden Sts.), where in 1779 assemblies of the New Jersey State Legislature took place when Mount Holly was deemed the state's temporary capital. A year earlier the Meeting House was also used as a commissary by British troops, and you can still see the butcher's cleaver marks on some of the benches.

Mount Holly is the seat of Burlington County, and the original **Historic Burlington County Courthouse** stands at 120 High Street. Designed by Samuel Lewis, whose work includes Philadelphia's Congress Hall, the courthouse is a well-known Mount Holly landmark and a striking colonial structure.

The Historic Burlington County Prison Museum

The Historic Burlington County Prison Museum (128 High St., 609/265-5476 or 609/265-5858, 10 A.M.–4 P.M. Thurs.–Sat., noon–4 P.M. Sun., $4 adult, $2 child) is a massive structure designed by famed architect Robert Mill, whose additional accomplishments include the Washington Monument in Washington, D.C. Today a National Historic Landmark, the prison operated for 155 years (1811–1965) and at the time of closing was the oldest operating prison in the United States. Featuring stone and brick walls and a vaulted ceiling of poured cement, the building is both fireproof and virtually maintenance-free. It has changed little over the years, and the massive front door—with its large hinges—is original.

Smithville Mansion

Situated within Smithville Park on the northern outskirts of town is the Greek Revival Smithville Mansion (49 Rancocas Rd., 609/265-5068), once home to Hezekiah B. Smith—a woodworking machinist and developer of the Bicycle Railroad—and his wife, Agnes, who acquired the property in 1865. Adding to original structures put in place by former owners Samuel and Jonathan L. Shreve, the Smiths created a "model industrial town" on their estate, growing from a small mill operation into a major industrial plant. Smithville included a factory complex, dormitory for unmarried workers, opera house, schoolhouse, and a public park where employees could picnic on their days off, and is considered by many to be a pioneer of sustainable employment. The town continued to thrive after Smith's death in 1877 and until the Great Depression, and today many of the buildings remain standing.

Tours of the mansion, now listed on both the New Jersey and National Registers of Historic Places, are conducted 1–3 P.M. Wednesday and Sunday, May–October ($5 adult, $4 senior, $3 student), and a popular evening candlelight tour is offered in December ($8 adult, $6 senior). The mansion grounds are open for unguided visits, 8 A.M.–5 P.M. weekdays.

Smithville Park

Centered around Smithville Mansion is 280-acre **Smithville Park** (Smithville Rd., 609/265-5068, dawn–dusk), a county park with 4.4 miles of easy multiuse and hiking trails, and 22-acre **Smithville Lake,** a perfect place for canoeing, kayaking, and fishing. The park has recently expanded to include 170 acres of woodlands across Smithville Jackson Road from the original property, and the new section—aptly named **Smithville Woods**—features nature trails, a bird-watching vista, picnic tables, and a rest stop for canoeists along Rancocas Creek. The park's short, easy hikes include a 600-foot floating walkway along the lake and the 0.5-mile interpretive **Ravine Nature Trail,** which can be picked up at the main park entrance (for a bit longer walk), or further down the drive past the mansion. This is a hikers-only trail, forming a loop through the wetland forest near Rancocas Creek, and like the rest of the park, is frequented by deer, rabbits, and wild turkey. Horses are allowed on the yellow trail only, accessible along West Rail

Avenue or within Smithville Woods. Boats are not available for rental, though you can bring your own to launch on Smithville Lake or along the creek, and in the winter a number of the trails accommodate snowshoeing and cross-country skiing.

Smithville Park is the centerpiece to Burlington County's **Kinkora Trail**, a proposed 13-mile rails-to-trail that when finished will link the Delaware River and the Pinelands.

Woolman House

The Woolman House (99 Branch St., www.woolmancentral.com) stands as a memorial and information center on the life of John Woolman, a Mount Holly resident, devout Quaker minister, and abolitionist who's well-known for his journals condemning slavery. A small brick structure built in the late 18th century and located in one of Woolman's former apple orchards, the home is owned by the John Woolman Memorial Association and is open to tours. Hours vary but you call 609/267-3226 for more information.

Events

A fairly new downtown event is winter's annual **Fire & Ice Festival** (www.mainstreetmountholly .com), where amateur ice carvers compete for prizes while creating sculptures from 300 pound "vlocks" of ice, and those who prefer warmth gather in the Mount Holly fire station for a chili-eating contest of scorching proportions.

Originally held at nearby Rancocas Woods, the **Rancocas Craft Shows** (609/265-1553, www .rancocascraftshows.com) moved to Mount Holly after growing too big for their britches and are held whatever the weather on the last Saturday of the month, March–November. Over 150 vendors set up shop in the Park Drive municipal parking lot.

Shopping

Most of Mount Holly's downtown shops are situated within a small specialty village on the east end of High Street. The town is also home to a wonderful antique store, and the entire district has three percent sales tax.

Behind the Robin's Nest restaurant is the colorful **Mill Race Village** (www.millrace shops.com, www.millracevillage.com, 11 A.M.–6 P.M. Wed.–Thurs., until 7 P.M. Fri., 10 A.M.–6 P.M. Sat., 11 A.M.–4 P.M. Sun., closed Mon. and Tues.), a conglomeration of nearly a dozen small specialty shops housed within a lovingly restored colonial mill village, including **Teddies of Mount Holly** (609/702-9386), selling an array of teddy *bears* (not lingerie) and holding workshops in bear-making, and **Pineland's Folk Music** (609/518-7600), a relatively new village addition stocked with acoustic individually crafted dulcimers and offering private instrument lessons. Other shops include **The Spirit of Christmas** (609/518-1700), and **The Village Quilter** (609/265-0011).

On the corner of Rancocas Road and King Street is **Center Stage Antiques** (609/261-0602, www.centerstageantiques.com), an 18,000-square-foot facility with a fine selection of Persian rugs, a large number of dining room sets, and top-notch Victorian love seats.

Along High Street is the **Book Shelf of Mount Holly** (72 High St., www.mhbooks.com), a new, antiquarian, and out-of-print bookstore that has a small, makeshift coffee stand and a side annex with a large reading table. Free Internet access is available for those who bring notebook computers.

Accommodations

$100-150: The **Hampton Inn Mount Holly** (2024 Rte. 541, Westampton, 609/702-9888, fax 609/261-9370, www.hamptoninnmount holly.com,) is a fairly new hotel conveniently located between Burlington and Mount Holly, offering clean quarters with free in-room movies, as well as a business center on premises with Internet access, printing, and fax machines. A breakfast bar is included with your room price.

Food and Nightlife

Expect a few delicious options in Mount Holly, where dining and nightlife tend to mix. Atmosphere can range from casual to classy in the same space—it really depends on what you're in the mood for.

Housed in a corner two-story cottage is **The Robin's Nest** (2 Washington St., 609/261-6149, www.mountholly.com/robinsnest, $17–21), a French-American restaurant and bakery nestled at the entry to downtown's Mill Race Village. If the comfy ambience isn't enough to draw you in, the dessert display case will: Homemade apple Bavarian cheesecake is just one of the samples, and if you'd rather be outside, there's a creekside patio to be enjoyed during warmer months. Hours are 11 A.M.–2:30 P.M. Monday–Tuesday, 11 A.M.–9 P.M. on Wednesday and Thursday, and until 9:30 P.M. on Friday and Saturday. Brunch is served 10 A.M.–4 P.M. Sunday.

My friend Becky says you can tell a lot about a place by its fries—at Robin Winzinger's **Bridgetown Pub** (42 High St., 609/261-6900, www.bridgetownpub.com, 11:30 A.M.–11 P.M. Mon.–Thurs., until 1 A.M. Fri., 3 P.M.–1 A.M. Sat., $7–14), they are of medium thickness, brown, and crisp—some of the best that I've tried in awhile. There's no doubt this place is something special, with its casual atmosphere and unique motif of New Colonial decor. It's easy to while away your hours sampling the cheese fondue ($6.95) under a darkened guise. If you have somewhere to be, request one of the two brightly lit window tables—and be sure to visit the restrooms before leaving (they're something to see). A separate bar stands next to the dining room, and live music plays on weekends.

The High Street Grill (68 High St., 609/265-9199, www.highstreetgrill.net, $19–$24) is a cozy, dimly lit piano bar serving New American cuisine and an all-day tavern menu on weekends. Downstairs it's a long and narrow place with both dinner and cocktail tables, while on the second floor you'll find a more formal dining setting. Jazz, classical music, and blues are featured on varying nights, and repeat customers rave that the beer is not only good, it's cold! Lunch is served 11:30 A.M.–2:30 P.M., and dinner 5:30–10 P.M. Tuesday–Saturday. Sunday hours are 10 A.M.–2 P.M. brunch and 4–8 P.M. dinner.

RANCOCAS STATE PARK

Rancocas State Park is one of New Jersey's less-discovered state parks—1,252 wooded acres ideal for bird-watching and trail walking. Douglas firs, oak, and conifers line the pathways, and the Rancocas Creek makes its way along the park's southern portion, adding to a serene, often deserted environment. White-tailed deer, beaver, and rabbit are sometimes spotted, especially within the park's 58-acre natural area, and both a nature center and an Indian reservation and museum are accessible from Rancocas Road, running down the park's western border.

Rancocas Nature Center

Housed within an old whitewashed farmhouse is the **Rancocas Nature Center** (794 Rancocas Rd., Mt. Holly, 609/261-2495, rancocas@njaudubon.org, 9 A.M.–5 P.M. Tues.–Sat., noon–5 P.M. Sun., until 4 P.M. daily Nov. 15–Mar. 15, closed Mon.), run by the local Audubon Chapter. The center provides pamphlets and handouts on the area's hikes and wildlife, includes a small classroom, nature store, and a few live reptiles, and schedules beginners' bird-watching trips throughout the year—you'll also find a couple of trailheads just outside. And don't be shy about asking questions—the volunteers who run this place are extremely helpful.

Rankokus Indian Reservation

Down Rancocas Road from the nature center is a turnoff for Rankokus Indian Reservation (609/261-4747, www.powhatan.org), a 350-acre parcel of land leased by the Powhatan Renape Nation, whose longtime leader Chief Roy Crazy Horse passed away in 2004. It's here that you'll find the **American Indian Heritage Museum,** a collection of exhibits showcasing the culture and art of American Indians. Sculptures, woodcarvings, and sketches by modern-day artists are all on display, as well as large dioramas depicting village life of various tribes. Combined tours of the reservation and museum are given 10 A.M.–3 P.M. on Saturdays, and Tuesdays and Thursdays by appointment ($5 adult, $3 child).

Powhatan Renape Indian Arts Festival

The three-day Indian Arts Festival ($10 adult, $5 child, free under five) takes place on Rankokus Indian Reservation annually during spring and fall. Storytelling, traditional and modern arts and crafts, music, dancing, and a kickboxing demonstration are some of the highlights. The festival features over 150 arts and crafts booths and a plethora of Native American cuisine. For more information, including exact dates, visit the Powhatan Renape Nation website at www.powhatan.org.

MOORESTOWN

Moorestown is an established community awarded top honors in *Money* magazine's "Best Places to Live 2005" national survey. Though there's not a lot to do, it's worth a drive through town to have a look at some of the architecture—grand Victorian and Federal homes on large plots of land, set back from the street and accompanied by tree-lined walkways. Many former residences in old Moorestown (the town features a more modern section to the

east) have been converted into businesses, and along Main Street (Rte. 537), you'll find brick buildings interspersed with Victorians.

Philly Soft Pretzel Factory

If you're experiencing hunger pangs on your Sunday drive, a good place to stop for a to-go snack is Main Street's Philly Soft Pretzel Factory (131 W. Main St., 856/642-1135, 6 A.M.–6 P.M. Mon.–Sat., 8 A.M.–3 P.M. Sun.). There's nothing like a Philly soft pretzel—long, dense, doughy, and perfectly salted—and these guys will save you a trip over the Delaware. Three pretzels sell for $1, mustard for $0.25, and melted cheese for $0.50.

MERCHANTVILLE

Continuing south of Moorestown along Route 537 you'll reach Merchantville. Like Moorestown, this borough is filled with attractive architecture, though it's composed primarily of Victorians, many with mansard roofs and intricate trimmings. Centre Street and Maple Avenue is Merchantville's main intersection, a small downtown strip with an Italian restaurant

© LAURA KINIRY

candy heaven at Aunt Charlotte's, Merchantville

worth a visit, but consider saving your appetite, as the town's main attraction, Aunt Charlotte's Candies, lies west along Maple.

The Collins House

Located within a late 19th-century three-story brick building just north of the borough's downtown stretch is The Collins House Restaurant (2 S. Centre St., 856/661-8008, $11–29), a spacious place featuring an internationally inspired Italian menu and an extensive wine list. This sister spot to Bordentown's Farnsworth House cooks up a popular weekend brunch that includes frittatas, omelets, and sweet potato and apple pancakes ($7.95), and live jazz plays Friday and Saturday evenings. The restaurant is open for lunch and dinner 11 A.M.–11 P.M. weekdays, and for brunch 11 A.M.–3 P.M. Saturday, 10 A.M.–3 P.M. Sunday.

💶 Aunt Charlotte's Candies

Can chocolate really be that special? There's something about Aunt Charlotte's Candies (5 West Maple Ave., 856/662-0058) that makes me believe so. It could be the rows of boxed chocolates, the glass counter of sweets, or the giant bowls of brightly colored hard candies twist-wrapped and teasing with names like Ice Blue Mints and Cinnamon Buttons, but I think it's the second-floor chocolate factory that does it. Don't expect an Oompa Loompa to escort you up the stairs; you have to ask to visit the factory. They might tell you that there's nothing going on and there wouldn't be much to see, but don't be fooled. Drizzling, gooey chocolate and tray upon tray of nonpareils were reason enough for me. (The aisles are a tight squeeze. Be careful with your scarf.)

Aunt Charlotte's came about in 1920 when Charles Brooks Oakford Sr. began making candy at his home and selling it from the back of his truck, soon purchasing a small storefront. When Oakford died in 1945 his son Brooks Oakford Jr. took over the business and moved it to its current location, which was at the time a one-story grain shop. He and his wife Bunny added a second floor in 1984, where the chocolate has since been made. A third generation of

Oakfords is now running the business, though you're still likely to bump into Oakford Jr. on your way up the stairs.

Don't get me wrong—this is no Willy Wonka. But whether your name is Charlie or Augustus, you can't help but leave here happy.

MOUNT LAUREL

Route 73 carries you into the center of Mount Laurel, where I-295 and exit 4 of the New Jersey Turnpike meet. Here you'll find a cluster of hotels and fast-food chains but little else. The township is a mix of residential property and industrial parks and is easily reachable from most locations throughout New Jersey and Philadelphia.

The Falls

If you're looking for a fun place to bring the family, try The Falls (3320-24 Rte. 38, 856/273-9666, www.thefallsnj.com). Here you'll find a miniature golf course, driving range, batting cage, even laser tag. The Falls is an indoor/outdoor center and has numerous rides that kids will enjoy—like child-sized go-karts and a mini-Ferris wheel—as well as an arcade with both air hockey *and* skeeball. The center stays open throughout the year, noon–8 P.M. Monday–Thursday, 4–9 P.M. Friday, and 10 A.M.–8 P.M. Sunday. Indoor and outdoor hours vary so it's a good idea to call before you go.

PAWS Farm Nature Center

Most kids don't make it out the back door at the PAWS Farm Nature Center (1105 Hainesport–Mt. Laurel Rd., 856/778-8795, www.pawsfarm.com, 10 A.M.–4 P.M. Wed.–Sun., $5 adult, $3 child). They're too busy playing with the trains, games, and toys that are available inside, but it's through the back room and past the corn snakes Albert and Samantha that the real fun begins. PAWS is home to over 80 birds and animals, including Benjamin the miniature cow and a sheep named Hershey Kiss, as well as a butterfly garden, nature trail, hay jump, playground, a dairy barn where kids can do some pretend grocery shopping, and a farmhouse with a play veterinary clinic.

PAWS is geared toward children eight and under, and offers numerous educational programs throughout the year. Barbara Holmes, who's been with the center for more than a decade, will make certain your kids are enjoying themselves and learning in the process.

Rancocas Woods

Though suspiciously close to Rancocas State Park, Rancocas Woods (123 Creek Rd., 856/222-0346, www.rancocaswoods.net, 10 A.M.–5 P.M. daily) is a log cabin shopping village actually located in Mount Laurel. The stretch of shops hosts numerous specialty stores, a couple of art galleries, a **Toy Train Emporium** (856/273-0606), and **William Spencer, Inc.** (118 Creek Rd., 856/235-1830, www.williamspencerinc.com), a highly respected lighting and furniture center. Stop by the **Corner Pretzel Shoppe** (856/234-7442) for a snack to go, to be enjoyed while meandering the woodsy pathways.

Accommodations

Mount Laurel has nearly a dozen accommodation options clustered around exit 4 of the New Jersey Turnpike.

$50-100: A reasonable place to stay is the **Super 8 Mount Laurel** (554 Fellowship Rd., 856/802-2800). The motel's rooms are small but extremely clean, and have standard features such as a table and chair, TV, and alarm clock. Pets are welcome for a small deposit.

$100-150: I highly recommend the **Radisson Hotel Mount Laurel** (915 Rte. 73 N., 856/234-7194). This 10-floor hotel is undergoing extensive renovation, and from the moment I entered I felt at home. An elegant lobby, a friendly staff, and well-kept and spacious rooms all work together to make this a great place to stay. The outdoor pool is soon to be enclosed, and there's a restaurant and sports bar with pool table on the premises. The hotel features high-speed Internet throughout, and pets are welcome for a $50 non-refundable fee.

$150-200: The **Courtyard by Marriott** (1000 Century Pkwy., 856/273-4400) has a newer feel, with moderately sized rooms that contain a couch, desk, and big-screen TV. The Courtyard offers high-speed Internet access, an outdoor pool, a courtyard, and a small restaurant where breakfast is served daily. The rooms' long entryways keep hallway noise to a minimum.

MARLTON

Though the Olde Village of Marlton is only a small portion of Evesham Township, the two names are interchangeable. On the surface, Marlton—a name derived from the marl pits once located in the area—bears a resemblance to nearby Cherry Hill, most notably in its location along Route 70, but the former has managed to retain an affinity with its natural surroundings while promoting some of the best retail shopping around.

Shopping

There is a lot of good shopping to be done in Marlton, especially along Route 73, but the best by far is at **The Promenade at Sagemore** (Rte. 73, Sagemore Dr., 856/810-0085, www.thepromenadenj.com), a fashionable open-air shopping center hosting such favorites as Lilly Pulitzer (856/489-6751), J. Crew (856/988-9046), Sur La Table (856/797-0098), and L. L. Bean. (856/810-5560). The Promenade is itself magnificent, lit up in the evening like Caesar's Palace, its entryway flanked by a large outdoor fountain and spotlights. Just north of the Promenade is the smaller, slightly older **Marlton Square** (300 Rte. 73), where you'll find a Pottery Barn (856/489-7110) and Trader Joe's grocery store (856/998-3323). Across the highway in the space once occupied by Zagara's gourmet grocery is South Jersey's only REI outdoors store (856/810-1938).

Food

You'll have your pick of casual eateries as well as a few fine-dining options in Marlton.

In the Greentree Square Shopping Center is **Whole Foods Market** (Rte. 70 and Greentree Rd., 856/797-1115, www.whole foodsmarket.com). Though a chain, it's one of the only large specialty markets in South Jersey and a favorite place to shop for natural, organic, and international foods.

Olga's Diner (Rtes. 70 and 73, 609/596-1700, $15, closes 12:30 A.M. daily) stands central on the Marlton traffic circle like a queen guarding her throne, and serves as a casual, somewhat grimy, old-school haunt and an easily reached meeting point between north and south. Along Route 70 is the **Marlton Diner** (781 W. Rte. 70, 856/797-8858), with a gorgeous sea-green and silver facade calling to mind a mermaid's castle. It's open 24 hours and dishes out standard American fare that receives rave reviews from locals.

Nestled within the Marlton Crossing Shopping Center is **Food for Thought** (129 Rte. 70, 856/797-1126), an upscale BYO boasting three lavishly decorated dining areas and preparing much of its New American menu using organic ingredients. Try the sesame tuna served with Asian black rice ($28). Dinner hours are 5:30–9:30 P.M. Tuesday–Saturday, and 4:30–8 P.M. Sunday. Lunch is served 11:30 A.M.–2:30 P.M. Tuesday–Saturday. The restaurant is closed Monday.

In Marlton's brief downtown center is the **Marlton Tavern** (65 E. Main St., 856/985-2424, 11 A.M.–2 A.M. daily, $15.95–23.95). Housed within a Queen Anne Victorian, you'll find an extensive menu of continental cuisine, a downstairs pub, and two second-floor dining rooms.

Perkfection

Ideally situated within the Promenade shopping complex is Perkfection Coffee House (856/810-7375, 7 A.M.–10 P.M. Mon–Sat., 9 A.M.–9 P.M. Sun.). Order yourself a "perkuccino" and take a seat on one of the expansive couches by the gas fireplace, savoring a decor that blends Pottery Barn, a day spa, and a doctor's waiting room into a concoction of muted brown and camel colors and bright lights, with a massive TV and a Nuevo sound system. The cafe offers free wireless Internet, and features live music on Friday and Saturday evenings.

Camden County

Though part of the greater Philadelphia metropolitan area, Camden County is easily its own destination, with plenty of shopping and dining choices. South Jersey's most cosmopolitan region, the area is known for its attractive small towns, sprawling commercial suburb, and waterfront sights. Haddon Avenue is one of the county's main thoroughfares. Once a Native American trail, it later became a toll road between Haddonfield and Camden, and today is an eclectic mix of shops, restaurants, cafés, and businesses, ideal for an afternoon of browsing and/or people-watching, and of enjoying some of the best in culture that South Jersey has to offer. The White Horse Pike, running parallel to the south, is an alternative route to Atlantic City passing old railway towns, numerous diners, and a number of entertaining sights. The two roads join together in Berlin and continue through the Pinelands before growing heavy once again with restaurants, as well as motels and a few wineries.

CHERRY HILL

It's a given that you're going to hit some traffic on your way through Cherry Hill. And when you do you may find yourself thinking it's hard to believe this was all once farmland, especially when you encounter the next traffic light, shopping center, or turn-off for a housing development. But not only was Cherry Hill once covered with open space, before it was a traffic nightmare it was a considered an entertainment mecca. Today it is by and large a residential and commercial suburb, home to a number of corporate centers, plenty of chain retail stores, and stretched from east to west along Route 70 with nearly nowhere left to build. Long without a cohesive town center, the city is constructing one where the

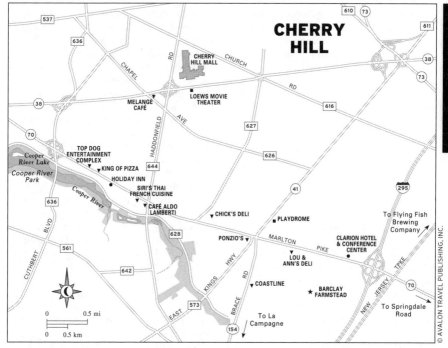

Garden State Racetrack once stood. In the meantime, Cherry Hill residents flock to their churches, synagogues, and the mall. But the township does offer a wonderful array of dining choices, as well as a few entertainment and lodging options. It also runs parallel to **Cooper River Park,** a 345-acre park that's the best in Camden County.

Sights

The only working farm left in Cherry Hill, **Springdale Farms** (1638 S. Springdale Rd., 856/424-8674, www.springdalefarms.com, 8 A.M.–6 P.M. daily) has been in operation for over 50 years. Flowers and herbs are available for purchase, and an on-site conservatory holds special events like Music and Wine Under the Stars. During the fall the farm hosts hayrides and a corn maze, and annual events scheduled throughout the year include the Strawberry Social and Fall Harvest Weekend. As sort of

a top-off bonus Springdale serves up freshly baked pies of the month, using the best in farm ingredients.

At the **Holocaust Education Center** (Jewish Community Center, 1301 Springdale Rd., 856/751-9500, ext. 224, www.holocaust educationcenter.com) you'll find a permanent display of Holocaust memorabilia consisting of donated objects, letters, and photographs from survivors and relatives. The center is more of a community exhibit than a fully fleshed-out museum, but it offers valuable insight into the Holocaust from a local and personal level, and there's a lending library on hand for individual research. Hours are 10 A.M.–5 P.M. Sunday–Thursday, and 10 A.M.–5 P.M. Friday, closed on Saturdays and Jewish holidays.

Built in 1816 by a Quaker farmer named Joseph Thorn, **Barclay Farmstead** (209 Barclay Ln., 856/795-6225, www.barclayfarmstead.org, noon–4 P.M. Tues.–Fri., $2 adult, $1 child) is today listed on the National and New Jersey Registers of Historic Places and has been operated by Cherry Hill Township since 1974. The property contains scenic nature trails, a picnic area, and a Federal-style brick farmhouse open for tours, and occasional events include a Living History Day, where visitors can churn butter and try their hand at the spinning wheel. Don't be surprised if you see more than one "Barclay" on your way to the farm, the surrounding development and a nearby shopping center share the name. In addition to its regular hours, the farmstead is open 1–4 P.M. on the first Sunday of each month.

Cooper River Park

I have a soft spot for Cooper River (856/795-PARK or 856/795-7275, www.ccparks.com). Maybe it's because my dad and I used to walk together along the park's pathways when he worked nearby, or because this is where I stood for Hands Across America, or maybe because it's where I spent the afternoon rather than attend the 1985 Live Aid concert across the Delaware, but I think the real reason Cooper River appeals to me is that it's just a great park. With nearly 350 acres spread among Cherry Hill, Collingswood, and Haddon Township, Cooper River features a 3.8-mile multiuse loop path, picnic areas, baseball diamonds, volleyball courts, even a miniature golf course (856/665-0505). The river itself is an excellent place for sailing, and hosts major crew events on its "Olympic caliber 2,000-meter straightaway," including the century-old **IRA National Collegiate Rowing Championships** (www.ecac.org). In the summer free concerts are held at the park's **Jack Curtis Stadium,** and a Movies in the Park series takes place in the evening a couple of times a month.

Cherry Hill Mall

A description of Cherry Hill would not be complete without mention of the Cherry Hill Mall (2000 Rte. 38, 856/662-7440, www.cherryhillmall.com), the first indoor temperature-controlled mall on the East Coast.

Since its opening in 1961, the mall has served as sort of a community center, and as malls go, it's none too shabby. Stores include Banana Republic, M.A.C., Coach, French Connection, and Abercrombie & Fitch, with Strawbridge's, Macy's, and J.C. Penney operating as its anchors. Inside you'll find a food court, and some really cool miniature escalators to use when you're just not feeling the manual footwork.

Entertainment and Nightlife

Top Dog Entertainment Complex (2310 Rte. 70 W., 856/486-1001) is the best-known nightclub in South Jersey. If you're undecided, come to Top Dog—there's a little something for everyone. Upstairs is a dance club; downstairs is a restaurant/bar that often has cover bands, and in the summer Top Dog opens an outdoor deck and dance floor—on any given night there'll be a line out the door.

The **Coastline** (1240 Brace Rd., 856/795-1773, www.coastlinerestaurantbar.com, 11 A.M.–3 A.M. daily) is a favorite hangout among college students and seniors (strange, but true). Monday night is the Oldies Dance Party, while DJs spin a more eclectic mix Thursday–Saturday. The Coastline fell into the national limelight in 2004 when it was sued for offering Ladies' Night drink specials. Though the court ruled in favor of the prosecution, a new take on Ladies' Night has returned on Wednesday evenings.

To catch the latest blockbuster, head to the multiplex **Loews Movie Theater** (2121 Rte. 38, 856/486-1722), located across the road from the Cherry Hill Mall. South Jersey's first microbrewery is the **Flying Fish Brewing Company** (1940 Olney Ave., 856/489-0061, www.flyingfish.com). Originally founded in 1995 as a "virtual brewery," a web-only site allowed visitors to assist in the brew-building process by naming beers and designing tees. Today Flying Fish is one of the largest craft breweries in the state, and free tours and tasting are given every Saturday 1–4 P.M., usually lasting about 40 minutes. If you're only in town on a weekday, give them a call and they may be able to accommodate you.

The **Playdrome** (1536 Kings Hwy., 856/429-0672) is so much more than a bowling alley; it's like a house party where everyone's wearing funny shoes. There's a pool hall and a bar and grill, but the best thing about this place is Future Bowl. With black lights, fog machines, and a DJ spinning tunes from the 1970s, '80s, and '90s, Future Bowl has got the night spot covered.

Accommodations

$100-150: The **Holiday Inn-Cherry Hill** (Rte. 70 and Sayer Ave., 856/663-5300) offers sizable, reasonably priced rooms, and features room service, and both an outdoor and small indoor pool. The popular restaurant chain **Red, Hot, and Blue** (856/665-RIBS or 856/665-7427) is adjacent to the hotel, and often features live blues acts.

$150-200: The rooms at the **⟨⟨ Clarion Hotel & Conference Center** (1450 Rte. 70 E., 856/428-2300) are quite spacious and equipped with a microwave, refrigerator, and two telephones. On-site recreational facilities include tennis courts and an outdoor pool, and next to the main entrance is a British-style restaurant/pub. But the best thing about the Clarion are the Utopia Exotic Suites ($229), eight luxurious suites with themes ranging from Arctic to Amazon (my favorite is the Far East Suite). They're each equipped with a fireplace, whirlpool, board games, and a wet bar.

Food

CASUAL EATERIES

Corned beef sandwiches of heaping proportions are the reason to come to **Kibitz Room** (100 Springdale Rd., 856/428-7878, www.kibitzroom.net, $4–13), a Jewish deli located south from Route 70 on Springdale Road. **Lou and Ann's Deli** (257 Rte. 70, 856/795-2307, 8 A.M.–6 P.M. Tues.–Sat.) has been a family-run institution for almost 50 years. A favorite is the Italian hoagie, loaded with Italian meats and provolone cheese. Hidden along a nondescript side street is **Chick's Deli** (906 Township Ln., 856/429-2022, 7 A.M.–5 P.M. Mon.–Sat., closed Sun.), a tiny place with only six tables and home

to what's called "the best cheesesteak in South Jersey." To get here from Route 70, cross the former Ellisburg Circle (where Route 70, Brace Rd., and King's Highway intersect) heading east and make a right at Virginia Avenue, then a quick left onto Township Lane.

Ponzio's (7 Rte. 70 W., 856/428-4808, www.ponzios.com, 7 A.M.–1 A.M. daily, $7–12) tops the list of South Jersey's most revered diners. Desserts made on the premises are exceptional (try the pumpkin pie if you're visiting in the fall), and though the brown and stone facade may not call to mind your typical diner, late hours and nice prices do.

Located in the parking lot next to Top Dog, **King of Pizza** (2300 Rte. 70, 856/665-4824, $6–14) is a Cherry Hill staple. Back in the 1970s when the township's restaurants and nightclubs were rivaling those in Philly, the famous King appeared, and one of its original owners was singer Frankie Avalon, who actually worked in the restaurant. In March 2004 King of Pizza closed due to fire, but has since reopened grander then ever, serving outstanding thin-crust pies rich with marinara.

FINE DINING

Caffe Aldo Lamberti (2011 Rte. 70 W., 856/663-1747, www.lambertis.com, 11 A.M.–10 P.M. Mon.–Thurs., until 11 P.M. Fri. and Sat., 1–9 P.M. Sun., $14.95–29.95) is the original, and best, of the Lamberti family's numerous eateries throughout the tri-state area. The restaurant offers traditional Italian fare and an extensive wine list.

Just up the road, **Siri's Thai French Cuisine** (2117-19 Rte. 70 W., 856/663-6781 or 856/663-6128, www.siris-nj.com, $16–23) is known both for its desserts and eclectic style. Chef Sirinant Yothchavit opened her namesake BYO restaurant in 1994 in an effort to introduce South Jersey to Thai food. She succeeded, and while prices range higher than a traditional Thai meal, it's worth the added cost. Siri's is located in a shopping center and has a no-cell-phone policy. Lunch is served 11:30 A.M.–3 P.M. Monday–Saturday, and dinner 3–10 P.M. Sunday–Thursday, until 11 P.M. Friday and Saturday.

SOUTH JERSEY

One of the most romantic restaurants in town has to be **La Campagne** (312 Kresson Rd., 856/429-7647, www.lacampagne.com, $27–36). Housed in a rustic old farmhouse with hardwood floors and numerous fireplaces, this BYO serves only the freshest in French cuisine. Though the entrées change seasonally, recent menus have included spiced crab cakes over roast-tomato fondue, and seared filet mignon with red-wine glaze. There's an outdoor garden and terrace to be enjoyed in the summer months, and La Campagne offers culinary classes in the restaurant's upstairs. This is a white-tablecloth sort of place. The restaurant is open for lunch 11:30 A.M.–2 P.M. weekdays, and dinner 5–9 P.M. Monday–Saturday, 4–7 P.M. Sunday. Brunch is served 11 A.M.–2 P.M. Sunday.

Southern-style cooking and a smaller-portioned "grazing menu" are reasons to make the trip to **Melange Café** (1601 Chapel Ave., 856/663-7339 or 856/663-9493, 11 A.M.–10 P.M. Tues.–Thurs., until 11 P.M. Fri., 4–11 P.M. Sat., 2–10 P.M. Sun., $22–27), where chef Joe Brown cooks up dishes that are a blend of Italian and New Orleans fare. There's often a craw-fish entrée on special at this BYO, and though the decor is somewhat drab, the meals are unique enough for you not to notice.

◖ CAMDEN WATERFRONT

Camden has a bad rep. I'm not saying it's undeserved, but regardless of the corruption, crime, and ultimately shabby living conditions, this county seat's waterfront is one of South Jersey's best entertainment venues. Though it offers little indication of what the city is really like, its stretch of river property hosts quality attractions that should not be passed up, and at the center stands **Wiggins Park,** an attractively rounded marina that's a good starting point for exploring the area.

Signs leading to the neighborhood are clearly marked and easy to follow from the highway, and by doing so you'll avoid some of the less than desirable parts of the city, which I highly recommend steering clear of. Definitely use caution in Camden, especially when venturing away from the waterfront area. Those sections close by, such as Rutgers University campus and the area around the Walt Whitman house, are relatively

© LAURA KINIRY

Battleship *New Jersey*, Camden waterfront

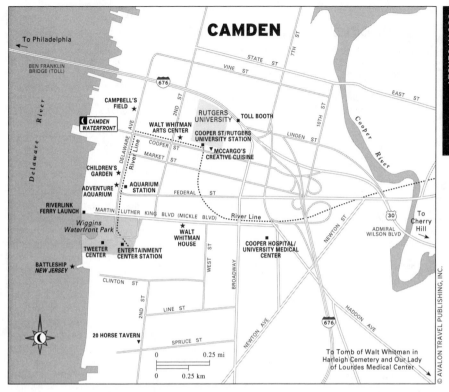

CAMDEN

To Philadelphia

BEN FRANKLIN BRIDGE (TOLL)

STATE ST
VINE ST
7TH ST
EAST ST

676

CAMPBELL'S FIELD ★

2ND ST

RUTGERS UNIVERSITY
TOLL BOOTH
10TH ST
Cooper River

CAMDEN WATERFRONT
WALT WHITMAN ARTS CENTER ★
COOPER ST/RUTGERS UNIVERSITY STATION
LINDEN ST

DELAWARE AVE
River Line
COOPER ST
MARKET ST
MCCARGO'S CREATIVE CUISINE ▼

Delaware River

CHILDREN'S GARDEN ★
AQUARIUM STATION
FEDERAL ST

ADVENTURE AQUARIUM ★

RIVERLINK FERRY LAUNCH ★
MARTIN LUTHER KING BLVD (MICKLE BLVD)
River Line
30
To Cherry Hill

Wiggins Waterfront Park
WALT WHITMAN HOUSE ★
WEST ST
COOPER HOSPITAL/ UNIVERSITY MEDICAL CENTER
NEWTON ST
ADMIRAL WILSON BLVD

TWEETER CENTER ■
ENTERTAINMENT CENTER STATION

BATTLESHIP NEW JERSEY ★

CLINTON ST

BROADWAY

2ND ST
LINE ST

HADDON AVE

676

20 HORSE TAVERN ▼
SPRUCE ST
NEWTON AVE

0   0.25 mi

0   0.25 km

To Tomb of Walt Whitman in Harleigh Cemetery and Our Lady of Lourdes Medical Center

safe—just know where you're going before you get there.

Camden was the original home to Campbell Soup and the RCA-Victor Talking Machine Company, and was one of America's first musical recording centers. Today, after years of deterioration, the city is starting to regain its footing with a couple of eateries and art centers, its waterfront venues, and a new regional tourism center scheduled to open in 2006.

Battleship *New Jersey*

When the Battleship *New Jersey* (62 Battleship Pl., 866/877-6262, www.battleshipnewjersey.org) made its final journey from the Philadelphia shipyard to the Camden waterfront hundreds stood along the banks of the Delaware to watch. Nicknamed "Big J," it's the third-largest battleship ever built in the world, and is the United States' most decorated. Nearly three football fields long (877 ft., 7 in.) and eleven stories high, it's built of steel and teakwood and could travel at a speed of 33-plus knots—approximately 38 miles an hour.

The USS *New Jersey* is one of four Iowa-class battleships constructed during World War II, the others being the *Iowa, Wisconsin,* and *Missouri.* Though it was allotted 5–6 years to build, U.S. involvement with World War II called for quicker construction, and within a year and a half the battleship was ready to be commissioned. It was launched into action on December 7, 1942, fighting in World War II, the Korean and Vietnam Wars, Beirut, and the Middle East before it was called out of service permanently in 1991.

CAMPBELL'S CONDENSED HISTORY

Ever wonder who made cookin' up soup so easy? A few cans thrown into your backpack, only to be opened and mixed with some water above the campfire and voila! You're enjoying that homemade taste just as if Mom were sitting there next to you.

Condensed soup was the invention of Dr. John T. Dorrance, a European-trained chemist whose uncle was the general manager of a small business called the Joseph A. Campbell Preserve Company, operated out of Camden in South Jersey. Joseph Campbell, a fresh fruit salesman, started the business in 1869 along with Abraham Anderson, a local ice-tray manufacturer. Canned tomatoes and vegetables, preserved fruits, condiments, and minced meats were its specialties – until Dorrance invented a way to take the water out of soup, lowering processing and shipping costs by one-third of those previous,

and a new Campbell star was born. Campbell's condensed soup became so popular, in fact, that "soup" was added to the business name, thus beginning what we know as the Campbell Soup Company.

Quickly becoming a U.S. favorite, Campbell's soup was touted on radio and television by such celebrities as Jimmy Stewart, Donna Reed, and George Burns and Gracie Allen. Two faces synonymous with Campbell Soup are the Campbell Soup Kids, whose advertising appeal and cherubic mugs preceded the way for such marketing mascots as Snap, Crackle, and Pop; the Pillsbury Doughboy; and Punchy, the Hawaiian Punch boy. As famous to the Campbell Soup Company as chicken noodle and tomato soups, these kids were a welcome addition in 1904.

Another image that comes hand-in-hand with Campbell Soup is the familiar red-and-

---

Today the battleship stands massive and majestic along the waterfront to the south of Wiggins Park, having been completely restored by volunteers and now operating as a museum and an overnight "encampment" program for kids who have the opportunity to sleep in the bunks, stow their gear in the lockers, and eat in the mess hall. Tours of the ship are offered daily, take about two hours, and include the ship's upper and lower decks, combat engagement and communications centers, bridge, machine shop, and cabins once belonging to the admiral and captain. There's a videotaped tour available for those physically unable to walk the ship. Costs range from $13.50 adult, $9 child and senior for a self-guided tour to $15/$10 for a guided tour. A Firepower Tour, which includes the regular tour along with the BB 62's weapon's systems, is also offered, $17 adult, $11 child. Encampments take place on Friday and Saturday evening throughout the year ($45 per camper). The Battleship *New Jersey* is open 9 A.M.–3 P.M. October–March, until 5 P.M. April–September.

Adventure Aquarium and Children's Garden

The New Jersey State Aquarium opened with much hoopla in 1992 and immediately earned criticism—what was supposed to be at the forefront of Camden's revitalization was little more then a few local fish species. But after extensive renovations the **Adventure Aquarium** (1 Riverside Dr., 856/365-3300, www.njaquarium.org, 9:30 A.M.–5 P.M. daily, $16.95 adult, $13.95 child) reopened in May 2005 with a complete makeover and a new name. Innovative features include a West African River Exhibit complete with hungry crocodiles and one of the only underwater hippopotamus exhibits on the planet (the two female hippos are eight-year-old Button and five-year-old Genny), and a 40-foot walk-through shark tunnel with over 20 *JAWS*-like creatures. There's also a hands-on science lab, daily animal feedings, and an opportunity to swim with the sharks for those 12 and older—much more exciting then a tank filled with bluefish.

Located adjacent to the Adventure Aquar-

white-striped label on its cans. This color combo got its start when a company executive named Herbert Williams witnessed the new red and white uniforms being won by the Cornell University football team. Williams was so taken by the uniforms that he was able to persuade his employer into taking on the colors as their own.

Campbell Soup soon gained success not only as a substantial meal but also as an individual ingredient in the easy-to-prepare dishes of the baby-boom era. A staple of American culture, Campbell Soup found its way past consumers' taste buds and into their hearts by sponsoring such programs as *Lassie* and the *Campbell Playhouse Radio* series, previously known as *The Mercury Theater on the Air* and featuring well-known radio persona Orson Welles.

Of the four world-class corporations that enjoyed great prestige in Camden (others were RCA, the NY Shipbuilding Corporation, and R.M. Hollingshead), Campbell Soup Company is the only to remain. Although its main factory closed its doors and was demolished in the early 1990s, its headquarters still operate along the waterfront, providing jobs to more than 1,200 employees.

The image of Campbell Soup cans became immortalized to the world in the pop artwork of Andy Warhol, but for former factory employees, Campbell Soup holds deeper meaning. Many of them shared stories with local public broadcasting WHYY's Ed Cunningham, telling of a time in which "the streets in Camden literally ran red with tomato juice and the air of all north Camden smelled sweet with soup."

Today, the Campbell Soup conglomeration includes Pepperidge Farms, V8 Vegetable Juices, and Godiva Chocolates.

---

ium is the **Camden Children's Garden** (3 Riverside Dr., 856/365-TREE or 856/365-8733, www.camdenchildrensgarden.org, $5 adult, $3 child), a four-acre interactive play and learning center where kids can run rampant at an outdoor dinosaur garden, picnic garden, and storybook garden featuring Alice in Wonderland and Frog Prince Grotto. Indoors is an educational center where 200 butterflies soar, bask, and lay eggs in a tropically heated environment. Train and carousel rides are available for an additional cost.

Walt Whitman Sites

One of Camden's most beloved residents was the grey poet, Walt Whitman, who spent his final 18 years living in a home on Mickle Boulevard. Though he wrote extensively about New York City, Whitman's most revered piece of work is the epic poem *Leaves of Grass,* versions of which were written in his still-intact two-story Camden home. Visitors to Whitman's abode included the playwright Oscar Wilde and Bram Stoker of *Dracula* fame, and today the **Walt Whitman House** (328 Mickle Blvd., 856/964-

5383, 10 A.M.–noon and 1–4 P.M. Wed.–Sat., 1–4 P.M. Sun., reservations required) is a museum displaying many of his personal belongings, including books, papers, and the bed where he died on March 26, 1892.

Whitman and his family are buried in a self-designed tomb at **Harleigh Cemetery,** just east of Our Lady of Lourdes Hospital and west of Route 130 along Haddon Avenue. The cemetery is actually quite lovely, with decorative headstones and numerous family mausoleums, some built into the hillsides. Signs to Whitman's grave are well-marked—as long as you go in the main entrance—and the tomb is set in the hospital's shadow, its stone door opened and replaced with an iron gate for visitors to peek inside. I definitely recommend a visit.

Sports and Entertainment

Baseball and non–sports fans alike will love **Campbell Field** (856/963-2600, www .riversharks.com), a 6,425-seat venue home to the minor league **Camden Riversharks.** This old-style ballpark opened in 2001, and

The Campbell Soup Kids welcome fans to Camden's Campbell Field, home of the minor-league Riversharks.

its main entrance is guarded by the statuesque figures of the Campbell Soup kids—their cherubic smiling faces almost guaranteeing a good time. And how could it not be? You've got a fantastic view of Center City Philly and the Ben Franklin Bridge, packed with traffic you're not stuck in.

In 1995 the opening of the **Tweeter Center** (1 Harbour Blvd., 856/365-1300, www.tweetercenter.com) brought live music to the Jersey side. This 25,000-seat outdoor amphitheater showcases big-name acts during summer months, when you can bring your blanket and lay out under the stars, and like everything else along the waterfront, your view of Philly is unbeatable. The center converts into a smaller climate-controlled theater seating anywhere from 1,600 to 7,000 to host smaller events, including local acts and graduations.

The Tweeter Center is home to **The South Jersey Performing Arts Center** (856/342-6633, www.sjpac.com), a theater coalition that hosts numerous events throughout the area.

Food

Camden is not a place you'd visit just for the food, but if you're here and you're hungry there are a couple of options.

Close to both the courthouse and Rutgers University's campus is **McCargo's Creative Cuisine** (415 Cooper St., 856/964-7900), where you'll find traditional American eats and a mixed clientele of students and City employees. The restaurant is open for both breakfast and lunch, 8 A.M.–3 P.M. Monday–Friday during summer and until 5 P.M. throughout the school year.

The **20 Horse Tavern** (835 S. 2nd St., 856/365-9211, www.20horsetavern.com, 11 A.M.–10 P.M. Mon.–Fri., 4–10 P.M. Sat., closed Sun., $12–24) is the city's only fine-dining eatery, serving American cuisine in a historic setting that was once used as stables for a lumberyard. Inside is decorated with old black and white photos depicting the city's industrial days. To get here follow Clinton Street east from the riverfront, passing the Tweeter Center on your left, and make a right onto South Second Street—the tavern is on the northwest corner of Second and Spruce.

Information and Services

The **Parking Authority of Camden City** (856/757-9300, www.camdenparking.com/ parking.html) runs a few garages in Camden's most-touristed areas, including a waterfront garage and one located across from the Tweeter Center (used for shows and visits to the Battleship *New Jersey*).

Getting There and Around

One of the newest additions to the Camden Waterfront is the **River LINE** (www.river line.com) transit, which opened in 2004 and travels from Camden to Trenton with numerous stopping points in between. The River LINE costs $1.25 for a one-way trip between any two points, and the rail cars are clean, compact, and run approximately every 30 minutes (every 15 during peak weekday hours) from 6 A.M. to 10 P.M. on weekdays, Sundays, and major holidays, and until midnight on Saturday. Intercity stops include Cooper at Second Street (Rutgers University) and two stations along the waterfront, and most transit stations offer free parking.

The **Riverlink Ferry** (215/925-5465) offers service across the Delaware to Pennsylvania's Penn's Landing, running every 40 minutes from 9:20 A.M. to 5:40 P.M. Monday–Thursday, until 6:20 P.M. Friday–Sunday. Round-trip fares are $6 adult, $5 child and senior, and parking is available on both sides of the river.

COLLINGSWOOD

When it comes to downtown revitalization, Collingswood is queen. Only a decade ago its main shopping district of Haddon Avenue was hardly there then a few occupied storefronts, but those with a keen eye could see its potential. Businesses steadily began moving in, attracted by a localized shopping district ideal for foot traffic, and at the same time a gay community was establishing itself, drawn by the town's proximity to Philadelphia (10 minutes

from Center City by PATCO) and affordable housing. Today Collingswood's main business thoroughfare is looked upon as the ultimate success by nearby towns struggling to revamp their downtown districts. The neighborhood's cafés are top-notch, and you'd be hard-pressed not to find an Italian dish that suits your tastes (just follow the scent of puttanesca wafting through the air). Specialty shops, boutiques, and antique stores offer an array of shopping ops, and in 2005 the borough broke ground on a "transit village" around the PATCO line, directly south of Haddon Avenue.

Entertainment

Collingswood has a couple of cafés with two distinct personalities, and a wonderful theater venue that's been recently resurrected.

The Treehouse Coffee Shop (690 Haddon Ave., 856/833-0060, www.treehousecoffee .com) is a corner space haphazardly strewn with chairs wearing tennis ball footsies. There's a small stage near the entryway, a comfy fireside couch, and a *Starry Night* motif painted on the ceiling. Friendly baristas and tasty hot apple cider make this place ideal during a light winter snow, but if you stop in the remainder of the year try a pizza bagel with your morning brew—it's sooo South Jersey. The Treehouse is open 7 A.M.–9 P.M. Monday and Tuesday, until 11 P.M. Wednesday–Friday, 8 A.M.–11 P.M. Saturday, and 9 A.M.–11 P.M. Sunday.

Trendy **grooveground** (647 Haddon Ave., 856/869-9800, www.grooveground.com) is much more than a coffee house, and multiple personalities include a music store with CD listening station, art gallery, T-shirt shop, and newsstand. The café offers a free wireless Internet connection, and mixes non-alcoholic drinks with "room on top" for those who request it (wink, wink).

On the White Horse Pike is the **Collingswood Theater** (315 White Horse Pike, 856/858-1000), a large 1932 classic structure set back from the street, with Greek columns adorning its entry. The theater seats 1,050 and showcases musical and theatrical performances and individual performers, and has a working pipe organ in its main auditorium.

Specialty Shops

Collingswood has a fun selection of independent shops interspersed between its many restaurants, including specialty stores and a couple of antique shops. Many of the retailers offer extended hours Friday and Saturday evenings.

On the south side of Haddon Avenue is the **Funky Frog** (806 Haddon Ave., 856/854-0012), an inviting shop with a nice selection of handmade gifts and jewelry, as well as glass art, stuffed animals, and trickling fountains. **Vintage Rose** (720 Haddon Ave., 856/833-0900) stocks a "little bit of everything," including furniture, picture frames, and gifts for newborns.

Across the street is **Green Heart Environmental Shoppe** (661 Haddon Ave., 856/833-1144, www.greenheartstore.com), Collingswood's alternative store. Stop here for all that's environmentally friendly, including organic pet supplies and vegan-based bath products, recycled wares, Fair Trade coffee mugs, and natural yarns. **Jubili Beads & Yarns** (713 Haddon Ave., 856/858-7844, www.jubilibeadsandyarns.com) is a two-story retail store and workshop area, offering classes in such arts and crafts as crocheting, knitting, beading, flameworking, and weaving. The first-floor shop features a multitude of beads up front and a back section devoted to yarn.

For your music needs try **Abbie Road New & Used CDs** (723 Haddon Ave., 856/833-0145) or the **grooveground café,** where you'll also find locally designed tees plastered with such Garden State–centric slogans as "Don't Mess With Jersey" and "London, Paris, Tokyo… Collingswood!"

For antiques, try **Heirlooms** (542 Haddon Ave., 856/854-8551, www.heirloomsshop.com), a bright space specializing in shabby chic. The shop stocks dressers, mirrors, linens, lamps, chairs, and hard-to-find parts, and offers custom furniture restorations.

Food
CASUAL EATERIES
Weber's Drive-In (Rte. 130 N., 856/456-4138, 11 A.M.–10 P.M. Sun.–Thurs., until 10:30 P.M. Fri. and Sat.) is actually located a bit south of Collingswood on Route 130, 10 minutes by car, but for a true South Jersey experience, it's worth the detour. Weber's is a hassle-free drive-in (first opened in 1954 and operating for approximately six months out of the year mid-April–mid-September) where the burgers are cheap ($3) and good. It's easy to spot—a small, boxy place painted orange and white, right next to the double miniature golf course. (If you're going to play, go for the course on the right. It's old-school.) Weber's has no indoor dining and only a few picnic tables outside. The beauty is in having your food delivered to your car window, à la 1957.

The best place for full, unadulterated, lump crab cakes without a pinch of filling is unquestionably **🄲 Bobby Chez** (33 W. Collings Ave., 856/869-8000, www.bobbychezcrabcakes.com, 11 A.M.–7 P.M. Tues.–Sat., $3.50–14), but make one false move toward the counter before your number has been called and hordes of salivating patrons will stare you down—it's just *that* good. Bobby Chez is take-out only, and most items require heating—directions are provided with your purchase.

Villa Barone (753 Haddon Ave., 856/858-2999, 11:30 A.M.–10 P.M. Mon.–Thurs., until 11 P.M. Fri. and Sat., until 10 P.M. Sun., $8–18) is the matriarch of the Collingswood dining scene. With a wood-burning brick oven and latticed ceiling, this is one of the coziest restaurants in town. Twelve-inch pizzas go for $8–11, depending on the topping, and choices include roasted peppers, lump crabmeat, and provolone. It's a great place to bring the family.

Collingswood hosts South Jersey's largest **Farmers Market** (Irvin and Collings Ave., 856/854-6724), where you'll find everything from fresh in-season fruits and veggies to breads, seafood, and body products. The market takes place Saturday mornings, 8 A.M.–noon May–Thanksgiving.

FINE DINING
For superb sushi try **Sagami** (37 Crescent Blvd., 856/854-9773, $10–15), just off of Route 130 on your way into Collingswood. This BYO restaurant has been a South Jersey favorite for

years. Lunch hours are noon–2 P.M. weekdays, and dinner 5:30–9:30 P.M. Tuesday–Thursday, until 9:30 P.M. Friday, and 5–10 P.M. Saturday and Sunday.

Drive east on Haddon Avenue and you'll come to the borough's bustling downtown, where you'll have your pick of the litter. **Nunzio's** (706 Haddon Ave., 856/858-9840, $15–19) is one of the neighborhood's newer Italian restaurants, with an interior painted to look like an Italian seaport, complete with cloudy skies. Order the homemade gnocchi and if you're with a large party, head for the chef's table, which seats up to 12. Cooking classes and take-out are available. Lunch is served 11:30 A.M.–2:30 P.M. weekdays, dinner 4:30–10 P.M. Monday–Thursday, until 10:30 P.M. Friday and Saturday, and 3:30–9:30 P.M. Sunday.

For something a bit more casual try **Brianna's** (712 Haddon Ave., 856/854-0660, 7:30 A.M.–9 P.M. Tues.–Thurs., until 10 P.M. Fri. and Sat., 8 A.M.–8 P.M. Sun., $12–18), which also serves breakfast. The restaurant moved from the north side of the street and is now located down a long hallway in a large, open space. Try one of their specialty sandwiches (my favorite is the Brianna) and be sure to get it on the South Philly Sarcone bread.

If decadent is what you're after, **Word of Mouth** (729 Haddon Ave., 856/858-2228, lunch $10–14, dinner $17–27) is the place. Occupying the former site of the Gordon Phillips Beauty School, the restaurant—younger sister to Marlton's Food for Thought—serves only the freshest ingredients. Appetizers include lobster dumplings ($9.50) and duck quesadilla with pineapple salsa ($9.50), and applewood-smoked bacon-wrapped shrimp ($11). Word of Mouth is open for lunch 11:30 A.M.–2:30 P.M. and dinner 5–9:30 P.M. Tuesday–Saturday, and 4–8:30 P.M. Sunday.

For gourmet Mexican there's no better place than **The Tortilla Press** (703 Haddon Ave., 856/869-3345, 11 A.M.–9 P.M. Mon.–Thurs., until 10 P.M. Fri. and Sat., 11 A.M.–8 P.M. Sun., $11–17), where servers start you off with homemade chips and salsa and keep them coming throughout the meal. Bring your own tequila

and they'll concoct a tasty margarita treat—there's even a take-out burrito bar. With such an upbeat atmosphere, no wonder there's a line out to the corner on most nights.

WESTMONT

Continue south on Haddon Avenue, crossing over Cuthbert Boulevard, to reach Westmont, part of the larger Haddon Township. Westmont is easily considered the middle child, sandwiched between Collingswood and Haddonfield and lacking a cohesive town center, easily forgotten. But what it lacks in shopping and storefronts it makes up for in alcohol sales—Westmont is the only one of the three regions to allow liquor distribution. As far as foot traffic goes, community members are working to redevelop its downtown district into a working center. For the moment, however, it's a stretch of scattered shops far from walkable and not quite scenic, but a great place to stop for a mid-afternoon martini, a beer and some potato skins, or a frozen margarita in the summer heat on one of the outdoor patios. Westmont's also home to a couple of favorite establishments faithfully serving the community for years, as well as an outstanding restaurant.

Driving along Haddon Avenue keep your eye out for the **Westmont Theater** (49 Haddon Ave.). Originally opened in 1927, the theater went through numerous incarnations before closing for good in 1986. The marquee still spells out Westmont in capital letters, and the community has plans to turn it into a performing arts space, as well as housing a café and restaurant in the upcoming years. Steven Spielberg, who spent his childhood years in Haddon Township, is reported to have seen his first movie, *The Greatest Show on Earth,* here, and famed actor Michael Landon once worked here as a doorman.

Food and Nightlife

I've never seen anything like the cream donuts served at **McMillan's** (15 Haddon Ave., 856/854-3094)—with filling oozing out in every direction it's hard to keep a lid on them. According to South Jersey's *Courier Post,* the "cream donuts are so popular they're shipped across country." And man, are they good.

Franco's Pizza (235 Haddon Ave., 856/854-0771, $5–10) makes the best panzarottis around. These plain or stuffed deep-fried pizza turnovers are so popular be prepared to wait in a line—Franco's has a dining room, but many prefer to take these masterpieces to go.

Giumarello's (329 Haddon Ave., 856/858-9400, www.giumarellos.com, $18–24) is a cozy trattoria serving Northern Italian cuisine in a crisp and modern setting. The martinis come highly recommended, and can be enjoyed at one of the elegantly rounded booths that line the lounge, or in the warmer months in the outdoor courtyard. This is the perfect date place. Lunch hours are 11:30 A.M.–2:30 P.M. Tuesday–Friday, dinner 5–10 P.M. Tuesday–Thursday, and until 10 P.M. Friday and Saturday, closed Sunday and Monday.

P. J. Whelihan's Pub (700 Haddon Ave., 856/427-7888, www.pjwhelihanspub.com) is a mix between a sophisticated sports bar and a family eatery, with a plethora of TVs, tables, and cozy booths. They serve the best potato skins—loaded with cheddar, bacon, and sour cream ($5.79)—and jalapeno poppers.

West on Crystal Lake Avenue you'll find **R.Mac's Pub** (427 W. Crystal Lake Ave., Haddon Township, 856/854-4255, $5.95–23.95), a recently remodeled and spacious bar/restaurant with one of the largest outdoor decks in the area, open as weather permits. In the summer this wooden patio hosts a raw oyster bar, and showcases weekend cover bands that play good, old fashioned rock and roll. The restaurant serves a fine mix of pub food, entrées, and daily specials. R.Mac's is open 11:30–2 A.M. Monday–Saturday, and until midnight on Sunday.

Additional nightlife options include **Pat's Pub** (239 Haddon Ave., 856/854-5545), a local neighborhood hangout, and **Tom Fischer's Tavern** (18 W. Cuthbert Blvd., 856/854-6650, 10 A.M.–2 A.M. Mon.–Sat., 11 A.M.–2 A.M. Sun.), where you'll find a fully stocked bar and award-winning buffalo wings.

◖ HADDONFIELD

Easily recognizable by its exquisite colonial, Federal, and Victorian architecture, attractive downtown, and tall trees standing curbside, Haddonfield is a must-see. Elizabeth Haddon, whose courtship of Quaker Minister John Estaugh is described in Henry Wadsworth Longfellow's poem *Tales of a Wayside Inn,* founded the town in 1701 on land belonging to her father, and the borough has long since been considered one of South Jersey's darlings. Surrounding the intersection of Haddon Avenue and Kings Highway you'll find a plethora of antique stores, art galleries, consignment shops, women's boutiques, specialty wares, and a large number of businesses catering to kids and teens—many families reside in Haddonfield, and students often congregate along the downtown's brick sidewalks after school. Driving south down Kings Highway will bring you past individually designed mansions in a variety of architectural styles, with perfectly manicured lawns and winding drives.

Architecture

Haddonfield's a beautiful town, and I suggest you take the time to drive around and have a look at the architecture. The grandest homes are along West Kings Highway and **Chews Landing Road.** From Haddon Avenue make a right onto Kings Highway and veer left onto Chews Landing, taking the road approximately a mile and a half to the White Horse Pike, or turning right onto one of the numbered avenues crossing back over to West Kings Highway, where you'll make another right to complete a triangular loop. Chews Landing's largest homes will be toward the beginning of the street, and in the spring and summer the large buttonwood trees lining the sidewalks bloom full. If you've got no traffic behind you, this makes for the perfect afternoon drive.

While returning on Kings Highway keep an eye out for the legendary **Purple House,** on the street's western side. The home was painted its present-day lavender in the early 1990s, and while there were no color restrictions in Haddonfield at the time, this bold choice of shade was unprecedented. The purple house received more than its share of attention for its odd hue in a borough of browns and whites, but in the end it outlasted the press. Today it remains a landmark, albeit a faded one.

Indian King Tavern Museum

On the east side of Kings Highway are many of the town's colonial structures, including the Indian King Tavern Museum (223 E. Kings Hwy., 856/429-6792, www.levins.com/tavern.html, 10 A.M.–noon Wed.–Sat., 1 –4 P.M. Sun., free). Built in 1750 and designated New Jersey's first historic site in 1903, the Indian King Tavern witnessed first-hand New Jersey's birth as a state, and the adoption of the state seal in 1777. Its name honors a friendship between local Quakers and Lenape Indians, and although the furniture used is not original, the interior has been completely restored to its 18th-century appearance, and the museum is considered one of the best examples of a traditional 18th-century tavern surviving today.

Hour-long tours include the tavern's first two floors; unfortunately, underground cellars said to have housed British prisoners during the Revolution, and once thought to be an underground tunnel, are not open to the public. Regardless, the Indian King has a fascinating history and is well worth a visit.

Dinosaur Site

From East Kings Highway, turn west onto Grove Street and right onto Maple Avenue to reach **Hadrosaurus Park.** It is here that William Parker Foulke discovered the world's first nearly complete dinosaur skeleton, unearthing the bones in 1858 at the bottom of a marl pit. The species was given the name *Hadrosaurus foulkii,* and the skeleton went on to become the first dinosaur bones ever to be displayed in a museum, and can still be viewed across the Delaware at the **Philadelphia Academy of Natural Sciences.** The park is only a small bit of manicured land that's easy to overlook, but two markers designate the site: one is a stone mounted marker placed

in 1984 by a local boy scout, the second is a mounted plaque erected in 1994 when the site was named a National Landmark.

In honor of Haddonfield's dinosaur history a human-sized dinosaur sculpture has been given life on Lantern Lane in the borough's shopping district, just off West Kings Highway. Though numerous events seem to center around this dinosaur known as "Haddy," he's nothing to go out of your way for.

Events and Festivals

One of the best times of year to visit Haddonfield is during the holiday season. Lights adorn many of the homes, and **Candlelight Shopping** is offered the entire month of December. Carolers dress in period costumes, horse-drawn carriages ride down the streets, Santa makes his appearance, and shops hold extended hours on Thursday and Friday evenings and Sunday afternoons. To top off year's end and ring in the new, **First Night Haddonfield** (www.firstnighthaddonfield.org) is an alcohol-free block party held every New Year's Eve.

A **Holiday House Tour** (856/216-7253) of some of the borough's finest homes is held annually in December.

Haddonfield's **Craft and Fine Arts Festival** (856/216-7253) takes place annually the second weekend in July. Over 200 kiosks featuring everything from handmade jewelry to oil paintings, knitted baby wear to fiber-art crowd Kings Highway, and music is performed daily.

Entertainment

Both a wonderful locally owned coffee house and a nonprofit theater are reasons to come to town during evening hours.

The organically grown **Three Beans Coffee Co.** (140 N. Haddon Ave., 856/354-2220) is a big place with couches, mismatched tables, and plenty of books lying around—there's even a pool table. A combo of young souls and intellects keeps things rolling. Three Beans is open 6:30 A.M.–10 P.M. Monday to Thursday, until 11 P.M. Friday, 7:30 A.M.–11 P.M. Saturday, and 8 A.M.–8 P.M. Sunday.

Since 1935, **Haddonfield Play and Players**

(957 S. Atlantic Ave., 856/429-8139, www .haddonfieldplayers.com, $16) has been entertaining the community with a variety of theater, including comedies, mysteries, and musicals. This is an excellent local venue and shows performed in the 150-seat main theatre are top-notch.

Shopping

Haddonfield offers excellent shopping opportunities, with a mix of small boutiques, individually owned specialty shops, and a couple of upscale chains. There are a number of consignment shops in the area, and quite a few stores that cater to kids and teens.

Woolplay (22 N. Haddon Ave., 856/428-0110, www.woolplay.com) stocks a large selection of yarns, including Artyarns, Dancing Fibers, and Blue Sky Alpacas. The shop is closed Sunday and Monday.

The result of a joint venture between an Internet book shop and a seller based in nearby Merchantville is **Haddonfield Books Rare and Used** (210 E. Kings Hwy., 856/795-9011), a wonderful store with a unique collection of hard-to-find books.

Jamaican Me Crazy (139 E. Kings Hwy., 856/616-1291, www.jmcrazy.com) is an eye candy of interesting wares, including stickers, tie-dyes, pink-flamingo string lights, UGG boots, and Birkenstocks. If you're looking to find a good selection of comfort and style for those weary feet try **Benjamin Lovell Shoes** (212 E. Kings Hwy., 856/429-7801), an upscale regional chain.

Velvet Paws (107 E. Kings Hwy., 856/428-8889, www.velvetpaws.com) has all you need to pamper your pet, including freshly baked treats, outerwear, and sweaters. There's a little something for owners too—how about a life-size animal sculpture?

114 Her Sport (114 E. Kings Hwy., 856/795 7514, www.hersport.com) caters to women athletes with a wide selection of clothing, shoes, and equipment for sports ranging from field hockey to cheerleading. For one of a kind women's wear try **Secrets** (10 Mechanic St., 856/354-9111), a vintage consignment shop.

Nearby is **Six** (6 Mechanic St., 856/216-0666), stocking a wide variety of women's retail such as jeans, sweaters, jackets, dresses, and purses.

Snow bunnies and surf betties love **The Powder Room** (112 E. Kings Hwy., 856/216-1670), stocking female boards and accessories for all seasons.

You'll find baseball cards and sports memorabilia at **Post Game Memories** (138 E. Kings Hwy., 856/216-9881).

On the corner of Haddon Avenue and Kings Highway is **Happy Hippo** (201 E. Kings Hwy., 856/429-2308), a toy store for both kids and adults packed with Thomas the Train tanks, Monopoly board games, colorful kites, Madame Alexander dolls, and a Radio Flyer wagon or two.

ANTIQUES AND ART GALLERIES

The **Haddonfield Antique Center** (9 E. Kings Hwy., 856/429-1929) is a co-op where you'll find vintage maps, old books, glass vases, and furniture. **N. K. Thaine Gallery** (150 E. Kings Hwy., 856/428-6961, www.nkthaine.com) is an art gallery and shop showcasing unique items such as lamps made from recycled instruments, animal-faced wall clocks, and footstools that wear shoes. **Accent Studio** (207 E. Kings Hwy., 856/795-8800, www.accent-studio.com) features contemporary glass art, both functional and fun, and fine art paintings. The gallery displays the work of numerous artists, and also offers custom framing and art restoration.

Accommodations

$150-200: Housed in a Queen Anne Victorian within walking distance to the borough's shops and transit line, the ◖ **Haddonfield Inn** (44 West End Ave., 856/428-2195 or 800/269-0014, fax 856/354-1273, www.haddonfieldinn .com) is a convenient and romantic getaway. Eight guestrooms and one suite are decorated in individual themes like the Tokyo Room, which features Asian art and a small fountain, and gourmet breakfast is served daily. Each of the rooms have private bath, Internet access, TV, telephone, and fireplace, and the inn has a spacious wraparound porch and an elevator.

Food

Haddonfield is much better-known for its retail than for its food selection, though you'll have no problem finding a snack to revive your shopping momentum. If you are looking for a close-by sit-down meal, there are a couple of places to choose from. Otherwise, head west on Haddon Avenue (or take a quick jaunt on the PATCO line) to either Westmont or Collingswood for a ton of dining choices.

In 2005 **The Little Tuna** (141 E. Kings Hwy., 856/795-0888) relocated to its present, larger space in the center of the main shopping spread. Entrées at this trendy BYO include seafood, steak, and pasta dishes, with burgers, wraps, salads, and sandwiches rounding out lunch. Seasonal outdoor tables take some of the strain off the still-noticeably close dining room seating. The restaurant is open 11 A.M.–3 P.M. and 5–9 P.M. Tuesday–Thursday, 11 A.M.–3 P.M. and 5–10 P.M. Friday, 5–10 P.M. Saturday, and 5–8:30 P.M. Sunday.

Tucked along Kings Court between the downtown shops is **Gracie's Water Ice & Ice Cream** (9 Kings Ct., 856/427-9239, 12:30–10 P.M. Sun.–Thurs., until 10:30 P.M. Fri. and Sat.), an old-fashioned parlor whose specialties include chocolate-covered pretzels and bananas, milkshakes, and banana splits. Bring the kids and enjoy your scoops in the court's outdoor gazebo.

Information and Services

Located at 12 Kings Court in the middle of the downtown district is the **Haddonfield Visitors Center** (856/216-7253), open noon–6 P.M. Monday–Friday, until 4 P.M. Saturday. There's a restroom here.

Drop-ins to the hour-long classes at **Yoga Center of Haddonfield** (20 Haddon Ave., 856/428-9955, www.haddonfieldyoga center.com) run $14, an extra half hour is $16, and meditation only $10. Check the website for a complete schedule.

Getting There

Downtown Haddonfield is located at the intersection of Haddon Avenue (Rte. 561) and Kings Highway (Hwy. 551), just east of Westmont (about a five minute drive) along Haddon Avenue.

It takes about 20 minutes to reach Haddonfield from Center City Philadelphia on the PATCO speedway, which drops you off right downtown at Washington Avenue and Kings Highway.

VOORHEES

A 10-minute drive east along Haddon Avenue—which turns into Haddonfield-Berlin Road—will bring you to Voorhees, a suburban commercial township with a number of good restaurants and a significant Asian population.

Ritz Sixteen

Voorhees is home to one of the only movie theaters in South Jersey showing independently produced and foreign films. The modern 16-screen Ritz Sixteen (900 Haddonfield-Berlin Rd., Voorhees, 856/770-9065) offers stadium seating and popcorn served with real butter. A "no children under 12" rule is a big hit with locals, and the fact that those 12–18 must be accompanied by an adult keeps lobby-lingering (a popular teenage activity in South Jersey) to a minimum.

Food

Voorhees has a few good restaurants and a casual coffee shop.

Before seeing a show at the Ritz stop by **Coffee Works Roastery & Café** (910 Berlin Rd., 856/784-5282, www.coffee-works.com), a high-speed Internet café and coffeehouse hosting a variety of events, including book readings and coffee tastings. The café is stocked with numerous games and reading materials, and there's a dessert display featuring homemade muffins, cookies, and chocolate-covered pretzels. Hungry? Try a salad made to order.

At **Bangkok City** (700 Berlin Rd., 856/309-0459), you'll find authentic Thai cuisine, including the ever-popular pad thai. This BYO is located in the Eagle Plaza Shopping Center and is open for lunch 11 A.M.–3 P.M. Monday–Saturday, and dinner 4:30–10 P.M. Monday–Thursday and Sunday, until 11 P.M. Friday and Saturday.

Tucked away in a shopping plaza is **A Little Café** (Plaza Shoppes, 118 White Horse Rd. E., 856/784-3344, $19–25), a tiny, popular BYO serving Asian-influenced cuisine. Lunch hours are 11:30 A.M.–3 P.M. Monday–Saturday, and dinner 4:30–10 P.M. Monday–Thursday and Sunday, until 11 P.M. Friday and Saturday.

Across the street from the Echelon Mall is **Fieni's Ristorante** (800 S. Burnt Mill Rd., 856/428-2700, 11 A.M.–3 P.M. Mon.–Fri., 3–10:30 P.M. Mon–Thurs., until 11 P.M. Fri. and Sat., until 9:30 P.M. Sun., $16–21), a warm and casual BYO serving up Italian cuisine like mom used to make. Almost everything here is homemade—bread, sauces, desserts—and the award-winning scarpel soup, a light chicken broth filled with spiraled crepes, is a must-try.

WHITE HORSE PIKE

Originally known as Lonaconing Trail, the White Horse Pike (Rte. 30) began as an Indian travel route that stretched between the Delaware River and the Atlantic Ocean. *Lonaconing,* meaning "where waters meet," later became a main shore route before the opening of the Atlantic City Expressway. Today it acts as a built-up alternative, the length of its western portion packed by a variety of mom-and-pop and chain stores, chrome diners, and neighborhood pubs. This hodgepodge of commercialism and roadside oddities, while not quite aesthetically pleasing, is far more interesting than a toll road, and there are a number of small towns and short detours worth a stop along the way.

You can take the Pike east from Route 130, continuing through South Jersey and lower stretches of the Pinelands until coming to shore territory and eventually Atlantic City. The entire journey is about 60 miles and takes a little over an hour to complete if you drive straight through. Stopping for a bite to eat, cup of coffee, and a visit to the Peter Mott Museum will add a couple of hours to your time.

Oaklyn

From Route 130 the White Horse Pike will carry you east through Collingswood, past the massive Sutton Towers, and into the borough of Oaklyn, established in 1903. Oaklyn has a couple of places of interest, including the **Ritz Theatre Co.** (915 Whitehorse Pk., 856/858-5230, www.ritztheatreco.org), easily recognizable by a scarlet red marquee spelling Ritz in white letters and contrasting the building's simple brown brick facade. This historic theater has been running musicals and theater for over 20 years, and was once a vaudeville venue. It stood abandoned for many years until the current director purchased it in 1985—he continues to act in the theater's productions.

For dining in Oaklyn try **Aunt Berta's Kitchen** (639 White Horse Pk., 856/858-7009, www.auntbertaskitchen.com, $5–10), a tiny place with counter space, a few front tables, and a small side area, where you can get the best home-style meals around. Aunt Berta's sells breakfast items like fish and grits, but regulars really come for the macaroni and cheese, cornbread, Cajun wings, and for dessert, sweet potato pie. Hours are 11 A.M.–9 P.M. Wednesday and Thursday, until 10 P.M. Friday and Saturday, and 11:30 A.M.–7:30 P.M. Sunday.

Haddon Heights

There's plenty to like about the once-railway town of Haddon Heights, about a mile and a half east of Oaklyn, including its community feel, familiar storefronts, refurbished train station, and small cafés. Station Avenue is the main thoroughfare, where you'll find a short stretch of shops leading toward an entrance to **Camden County Park,** a 74-acre neighborhood park centered around a large lake. While in town, stop by the **Cool Beans Coffee Shop** (615 Station Ave., 856/310-9000, 9 A.M.–10 P.M. Mon.–Thurs., 7 A.M.–11 P.M. Fri., 8 A.M.–11 P.M. Sat., 9 A.M.–2 P.M. Sun.) for a cappuccino and a rest on one of the red plush couches, or purchase a picnic-to-go across the street at **John's Friendly Market** (856/547-6132), the town's unofficial meeting place.

If you're looking for some breakfast eats **Twisters Coffee House** (601B Station Ave., 856/573-9707) sells a bagel with cream cheese combo, or you can try the cozy atmosphere

Haddon Heights train station

and home cooking of the **Station House Restaurant** (600 Station Ave., 856/547-5517, 7 A.M.–3 P.M. Mon.–Sat., until 2 P.M. Sun. $4.99–9.99). **Elements Café** (517 Station Ave., 856/546-8840, $5–9) is an excellent place to stop for lunch or dinner—it's an inviting space featuring New American tapas-style dishes. Lunch hours are 11 A.M.–3 P.M. Monday–Saturday, and dinner is served 4–9 P.M. Tuesday–Friday and 5–10 P.M. Saturday, closed Sunday.

Lawnside

Once known as Snow Hill, the borough of Lawnside is the only historically African American–incorporated municipality in the United States and played a significant role in the Underground Railroad. Today visitors can tour the **Peter Mott House** (26 Kings Ct., 856/546-8850, www.petermotthouse.org, noon–3 P.M. Sat., appointment only weekdays, $2 donation), a stop on the Underground Railroad and the former home of Peter Mott, a free black 19th-century farmer and minister. It's the borough's oldest home and houses a collection of Lawnside memorabilia.

Stratford

Stratford is not really a place you'd come to hang out, but the town does have a couple of notable features. Continuing down the White Horse Pike from Lawnside you'll pass the **Stratford Diner** (19 S. White Horse Pk., 856/435-4300) on your left, and right after will be the turnoff for the **PATCO Park and Ride.** This is where the Delaware Port Authority's Philadelphia transit line meets the **NJ Transit Atlantic City line,** with both lines offering convenient access to the outlying areas. A bit further and you'll come to the 80-lane **La Martinique Bowling Alley** (501 S. White Horse Pk., Stratford, 856/783-0558), voted by South Jersey's *Courier Post* as one of the top bowling alleys in the region.

◖ Clementon Amusement Park and Splash World Water Park

Since 1907 Clementon Amusement Park (144 Berlin Rd., 856/783-0263, www.clementon park.com) has been welcoming visitors through its gates, though things have changed quite a bit in the last century—even in the last few years. Splash World Water Park—with family fun slides and a lazy river—is a fairly recent

PINE VALLEY

A small community exists just beyond Clementon Lake, hidden from view by a dense stand of trees and protected from the street by a large iron gate and a stoic security guard. Don't even think about trying to sneak inside because this borough, population 20, has its own police force. Welcome to Pine Valley, home to the United States' most consistently rated number one private golf course and one of the top 10 courses in the world. What makes it so special? Amateur architect George Crump developed the course in such a way that no one hole sits parallel to the next. Add to this the sandy soil of New Jersey's coastal plains, plenty of wooded land, and a hole known as "Hell's Half Acre," and you've got yourself a course that's hosted presidents, celebrities, and the best golfers in the world. But rarely does this ultra-exclusive establishment see an ordinary Joe. Mondays are reserved for staff members and their guests, and women are limited to Sunday afternoons.

addition, and the J2—or Jackrabbit Two—a hybrid wood and steel roller coaster said to have "the steepest vertical drop of any wooden roller coaster in North America," opened in fall 2004. (The Jack Rabbit, the park's original roller coaster, which was once the longest continuously operating ride in the same location in the world, finally shut down in 2002.) New Jersey's second-oldest amusement park is looking better than ever, grown from a class-trip and office-party locale into a full-blown fun land, though still family-oriented. The older rides are still my favorites: A giant Ferris wheel, the classic carousel, and a log flume built entirely over Clementon Lake, but newer rides like the Inverter, an upside-down not-for-the-faint-hearted, are just as popular. The park is open for long weekends in June, and daily throughout July and August, but call ahead—occasionally groups still rent out the park for company picnics. Weekend evenings in October are also a great time to visit, as the park transforms into a haunted fun house and attractions include a haunted trail, railway, and mansion.

For an after-the-park sit-down meal try **Cotardo's Ristorante Italiano** (Blackwood-Clementon Rd., Clementon, 609/627-2755), a popular Italian eatery with a steady clientele, situated within a nearby shopping strip. Regulars can't get enough of the seafood pescatore ($27/50), a mound of pasta served on a double-sized plate, covered in red or white sauce with mussels, clams, scallops, shrimp, lobster tail, and crab legs. On weekend evenings couples line out the door of this BYO with their bottles of wine, so get here early to reserve a spot. The restaurant is open for lunch 11 A.M.–3 P.M. Monday–Saturday, and dinner 3 P.M.–10 P.M. Monday–Thursday, until 11 P.M. Friday and Saturday.

Berlin Farmer's Market

From Clementon Park take Berlin-Clementon Road south about 2.5 miles to reach the Berlin Farmer's Market (41 Clementon Rd., Berlin, 856/767-1284, www.berlinfarmers market.com). This is one of those places that you'll either really like, or never want to return to, but it's an experience unlike any other. The market was established in 1940 and consists of a large indoor mart and a weekend outdoor bazaar that packs in over 700 stalls (If you're prone to claustrophobia, this isn't the place for you). Much of the stock is easily considered junk, but one man's trash is another's treasure, and this is the place you'll find that off-the-wall item impossible to come by elsewhere.

Nothing like a mall, the indoor mart consists of two long aisles lined by tightly packed stores, each with numerous entryways. One that's worth a visit is **Sam's Fabric Center** (store #120, 856/767-2552), which sells all types of dress fabric, drapery, vinyl, even foam rubber, and has been voted "the best fabric center in South Jersey." The indoor market is open 11 A.M.–9:30 P.M. Thursday and Friday, 10 A.M.–9 P.M. Saturday, and 10 A.M.–6 P.M. Sunday. Hours for the outdoor market are 8 A.M.–4 P.M. on weekends, weather permitting.

Gloucester County

Somewhere between farmland and suburb is Gloucester County, a region filled with attractive small towns, large old homes, rampant new development, and '50s-style split-levels. A mix of shopping centers, retail conglomerates, and mom-and-pop stores lines the roads, just down the way from produce stands and county parks, and the region hosts a number of historic sites, including a handful of 18th-century inns. Route 45 carries visitors south from Camden County's Route 130 past shopping strips and through some of the county's most picturesque towns before heading into Salem County, and Route 47 runs through Deptford's retail center into Pitman and Glassboro before continuing on to Cumberland County, but for something a bit more straightforward, hop onto Highway 55, an easy route with plenty of exits and little scenery. From **Commodore Barry Bridge** Route 322 stretches east from Pennsylvania through Mullica Hill and Glassboro as it makes its way to the Jersey Shore.

DEPTFORD

Deptford Township is known for two things: a balloon landing and the Deptford Mall. While the landing of Jean Pierre Blanchard's hot air balloon, which took off from Philadelphia and traveled 15 miles to become the first manned aerial flight in America, is the one that's featured on the township's seal, it is the mall that has most defined this community. The **Deptford Mall** (1750 Deptford Center Rd., 856/848-6400) opened in 1975 in the middle of this country-suburban township. Separating wooded neighborhoods from the shopping center were dozens of pig farms scattered over Deptford's almost 18 square miles. More than two centuries before, the area had been ground for fox hunting. But in the last quarter century Deptford has acquired a plethora of shopping centers, restaurant chains, and mega-stores. And while it continues to build, existing structures are growing worn. Its movie theaters are multi-screen, though they seem ancient compared to theaters in Cherry Hill or Washington Township. Its homes are suburban, but they're ranch houses and split-levels from the early 1960s. Deptford is a commercial town there's no doubt, and although the town has managed to retain its woodlands and a fair number of pigs, it's difficult to know how much longer it might be until they all disappear.

Deptford's most famous resident is perhaps Jonas Cattell (though rock singer Patti Smith spent her pre-teen and teen years in Deptford and graduated from Deptford High). Cattell was a well-known hunter and woodsmen, and spotter for the Gloucester County Fox Hunting Club. On October 22, 1777, Cattell ran the distance from Haddonfield to Fort Mercer in the present-day borough of National Park to inform the American Army that Hessians were on their way. Cattell Road now runs through one of Deptford's few remaining wooded areas. He and his family are buried in a small private cemetery in Deptford's Gardenville neighborhood.

Accommodations

Both of Deptford's hotels have been built within the past decade to accommodate the growing number of business workers and visitors to the Philadelphia Metropolitan Area. Each is clean and spacious, and offers the best options for exploring Gloucester County.

$100-150: Right behind the Deptford Mall near the off-ramp for Route 42 is **Residence Inn by Marriott** (1154 Hurffville Rd., 856/686-9188, http://marriott.com), which features a heated indoor pool and whirlpool, an exercise room, and a number of efficiency units. Pets are welcome for an additional $75. In the adjacent lot is the **Fairfield Inn** (1160 Hurffville Rd., 856/686-9050, http://marriott.com/fairfield-inn), a more basic, small-scale hotel with an indoor heated pool and whirlpool.

Food and Entertainment

Deptford has a ton of fast food and chain restaurants in the area, but for something more unique try **Filomena Lakeview** (1738 Cooper St., 856/228-4235, www.filomenalakeview .com, $17–25), a picturesque two-story restaurant serving Italian and continental cuisine. The main dining areas have hardwood floors and ceiling beams, and the bar has live music on the weekends.

For late-night dining there's no better place than the 24-hour ☕ **Phily Diner** (31 S. Black Horse Pk., Runnemede, 856/939-4322, $5–15). Decked in rich colors and neon and with a classic car parked in it foyer, this place is the epitome of fab and serves some of the best burgers around. To get here take Clements Bridge Road west to the Black Horse Pike and turn right.

Adelphia (1750 Clements Bridge Rd., 856/ 667-2220, www.adelphiarestaurant.com) is a huge nightclub, restaurant, and banquet facility that a friend once described as "the place where women go when they want to get away from their husbands." This compound hosts giant plasma TVs, karaoke nights, dancing, beach parties with drink specials, and all the "cheese" you could wish for. The restaurant serves an extensive menu of American dishes and is open for lunch 11 A.M.–1 P.M. daily, with brunch served 9 A.M.–2 P.M. Sunday. The bar and nightclub are open 11 P.M.–2 A.M. Sunday–Thursday, until 3 A.M. Friday and Saturday.

WASHINGTON TOWNSHIP

For 40 years an exodus of South Philadelphians in search of manicured lawns, better schools, and parking spaces have settled on the once-farmlands of Washington Township. "South Philly South" or "Township" as it's often called is now 21 square acres of residential and commercial development interspersed with the occasional country road. Township, which is made up from numerous smaller communities, the oldest being Grenloch, rests on former Indian sites and burial grounds. To get a feel for what it was before all the SUVs and soccer moms, there are a few remaining farms that continue to do a good business. Township's oldest remaining structure, **The Old Stone House** (856/227-9681) and the small village that surrounds it are open for tours on the weekends.

Duffield's Farm

Duffield's Farm (280 Chapel Heights Rd., Sewell, 856/589-7090, www.duffieldsfarm.com) is one of a handful of farms still operating in Washington Township. It's a family-run business selling fruits, vegetables, high-quality meats and cheeses, hot soups, and fresh baked goods at its on-site market, a popular stop for locals. Much of their bread and a variety of pies are baked on the premises, as are the delicious apple-cider doughnuts that Duffield's is known for.

The farm offers numerous activities, including hay rides and spring egg hunts geared toward kids, and strawberries, peas, and pumpkins available for seasonal picking. An annual festival with over 100 crafters takes place in the fall, and don't worry about Duffield's going anywhere—they're enrolled in Farmland Preservation, so regardless of nearby development, they'll continue to remain a farm.

Commerce Bank Arts Centre

Located on the grounds of Washington Township High School, the Commerce Bank Arts Centre (529 Hurffville-Crosskeys Rd., 856/218-8902, www.sjlivearts.com) was originally designed as a 2,500-seat auditorium for the school's overload of students. It is now a public venue, hosting such acts as Wayne Brady and Clay Aiken, and serving as an intimate and convenient suburban showcase for South Jerseyans.

Skydive Cross Keys

Skydiving in South Jersey? You bet! If you're ready to try tandem, Skydive Cross Keys (300 Dahlia Ave., 856/629-7553, www.skydive crosskeys.com) has got your back. Planes take off from Cross Keys Airport in nearby Williamstown and reach 14,000 feet before relinquishing you to the skies. Cost is $153 for your first assisted jump, plus $30 gear rental. The center is open 10 A.M.–sunset Monday, 9 A.M.–sunset Tuesday–Friday, and 8 A.M.–sunset Saturday and Sunday throughout the year, weather permitting.

Hospitality Creek Campground

Hospitality Creek Campground (117 Coles Mill

Rd., 856/629-5140, www.hospitalitycreek.com, mid-Apr.–Sept.) features more than 200 tent and RV sites, an Olympic-size swimming pool, and a 30-acre lake with swimming, fishing, and boat rentals. The resort is conveniently located en route to the shore. Sites run $38/ night, $5 extra with electricity.

Food

Washington Township has a mix of chain restaurants, mostly along the Black Horse Pike, and family-owned Italian eateries. Lately the region has also been working to establish a name as a fine-dining venue.

Why should Hoboken get all the Frank? At the Rat Pack–inspired **Blue Eyes** (130 Egg Harbor Rd., 856/227-5656, www.blueeyes restaurant.com, $18–42) order a martini, score a high-backed booth, and relax to the Friday night sounds of a wannabe Sinatra crooner. Dine on steak and potatoes in this supper club soiree and don your Sunday best—though there are rumors flying that the dress code isn't as strict as some swingers would like. The restaurant and adjacent lounge are open 11:30 A.M.–11 P.M. Monday–Wednesday, until midnight Thursday and 1 A.M. Friday. Weekend hours are 4 P.M.–1 A.M. Saturday and 3–9 P.M. Sunday.

Sal's Pizza (404 Egg Harbor Rd., 856/468-2226) has been baking superb pepperoni pies in this non-descript location for more than two decades. If you're looking for something easy, this is the place.

PITMAN

The charming borough of Pitman is an organically grown community filled with porch-adorned soft-colored cottages surrounding narrow streets that radiate from a center square like sunbeams. Its main thoroughfare, Broadway, is a pleasant mix of commercial and locally owned businesses, and walking along it is like being transported to a small 1950s town. In 2005 Pitman celebrated its 100th anniversary as an incorporated community and as per tradition, the famous **Pitman Hobo Band,** a 40-piece marching band dressed in tattered costumes and hole-punched hats, headed the centennial Fourth of July parade.

Pitman takes its name from the famous preacher Reverend Charles Pitman, and was begun as a Methodist summer camp in the late 1800s. Residences started only as seasonal homes, but many families soon decided to live in them year-round, and eventually land was sold to those outside the congregation. While it's no longer a Methodist camp, the religious influence is still apparent in town life, most noticeably in laws restricting liquor sales.

Broadway

Most of Pitman's shops and sights are located along the few-block stretch of Broadway, as close to Main Street, USA, as you can get. Many of the borough's stores and eateries are closed Monday.

The best place to begin exploring is on the corner of Pitman Avenue and Broadway, in the center of town, where you'll find **Bob's Hobbies and Crafts** (67 S. Broadway, 856/589-1777). Bob's sells everything from country crafts to toy trains, coin-collecting gear to wooden racecar parts, and the shelves are packed. If you're thinking about acquiring a hobby, this is the place to come.

North of Bob's you'll see the marquee for **The Broadway Theatre** (43 S. Broadway, box office 856/589-7519, hotline 856/589-4616, www.pitmansbroadway.com). This restored 1920s theater closed its doors in 2005 after a long spell of financial difficulty. Money is currently being raised to reopen its doors, and here's hoping that as you're reading this they're screening campy horror flicks and silent movie matinees once again.

On the street's western side a bit past the main row of shops is **Penelope's Antique Gallery and Tea Parlour** (106 N. Broadway, 856/218-8455). Penelope's is housed in a large old Victorian with a front porch cluttered by furniture and knick-knacks, and an Amish buggy parked on the lawn. The shop occupies the converted home's upper floors, displaying a mix of paintings, glass, crystal, and jewelry scattered around like grandma's attic.

Inhabiting a small Victorian down the street is **My Fair Lady Consignment Shoppe** (20 S. Broadway, 856/256-0111, www.myfair ladynj.com), where you'll find a number of tiny rooms each displaying a different clothing genre. Eveningwear is located in an upstairs bedroom, and in the bathroom lingerie hangs above a claw foot tub. This store sells only women's clothing and offers a wide selection of internationally and locally made new jewelry. According to Kathy, a longtime employee, over 2,700 women from across the Mid-Atlantic consign with them. What's the best thing about My Fair Lady? You're free to browse on your own.

Pitman Grove

Where Pitman Avenue and Broadway intersect stands a raised plaque in a park-like plot between buildings. This is the entryway to Pitman Grove, the borough's original neighborhood, established in 1871. The Grove is listed on both the New Jersey and the National Registers of Historic Places, and if you walk through the entry you'll come upon tiny porch-front cottages, each with intricate latticework and all facing inward toward a pathway from either side. Though a few of the homes have been torn down and replaced, most are original, and they seem so small it's hard to believe people actually live in them. At the far end of the sidewalk is the preaching auditorium, around which Pitman was formed. From here you'll have a good view of the borough's twelve radiating streets (one that you just walked down), each representing an apostle.

Food

Pitman's eateries are mostly small establishments catering to locals. You're not going to find any culinary treasures here, but you can get a decent breakfast or sandwich to hold you over.

The **Broadway Café** (13 S. Broadway, 856/589-2669) is a little country diner dressed in blue and yellow gingham decor, where you can get a short stack of pancakes, eggs, side of bacon, and a cup of coffee for under $10. The café is open 8 A.M.–2 P.M. Tuesday–Friday,

8 A.M.–noon Saturday, 8:30 A.M.–12:30 P.M. Sunday, closed Monday.

For a superb hoagie stop by **Pal Joey's Deli** (58 S. Broadway, 856/256-1333), or if you're looking for a quick snack, try a sticky bun from **Pitman Bakery** (130 S. Broadway, 856/589-4276).

On the bottom floor of Penelope's Antique Gallery is **Penelope's Tea Parlour,** a country nook serving tea and snacks, and American entrées for lunch and dinner. The Parlour is open 11:30 A.M.–4 P.M. Tuesday–Saturday, with dinner hours 5:30–9 P.M., closed Sunday and Monday.

GLASSBORO

Continuing south along Broadway from Pitman will lead you to Glassboro, where the road becomes Main Street. Once known as Glass Town, Glassboro began as the glass factory of German immigrant Solomon Stanger, who had worked for Wistar Glassworks in Salem. Today it's primarily a university town, but for a number of decades Glassboro was the largest glass producer in South Jersey. Downtown hovers around Main and 11th Streets, although there is really no cohesive center. Residents are looking to change this and in 2004 the borough was accepted into Main Street New Jersey, a revitalization program aimed to improve downtown districts. In the meantime, there are a few places worth a stop on your way through town.

Rowan University

The centerpiece to Glassboro Township, Rowan University (201 Mullica Hill Rd., 856/256-4000) was founded in 1923 as a training school for teachers, expanded in the 1950s to become Glassboro State College, and was granted an additional name change and university status in the late 20th century. The school occupies much of the land once belonging to Glassboro's original founder, Solomon Stanger, and later home to Whitney Glassworks. On the campus still stands the 1840s Italian villa–style **Hollybush Mansion,** built by the Whitney family when they took over the property. The home has been used as a dormitory, administrative building, and museum, and is currently a reception space, though its claim to fame occurred in July 1967, when the mansion played host to a last-minute Cold War summit between President Lyndon B. Johnson and Soviet Premier Aleksey Kosygin.

Sights

Unless you're a glass fanatic, I wouldn't recommend a trip out of your way to the **Heritage Glass Museum** (High and Center Sts., 856/881-7468, 11 A.M.–2 P.M. Sat., 1–4 P.M. last Sun. of every month), but if you happen to be passing through Glassboro on a Saturday afternoon it does offer a nice peek into South Jersey's glass heritage. No larger than a one-bedroom apartment (but with better ceilings), its local collection includes amber bottles and jars blown at the Whitney Glassworks.

Heritage Station and Winery (480 Rte. 322, Richwood, 856/589-4474, www.heritagestationfruit.com) is one of the few New Jersey wineries in the Philadelphia region. This farm and winery has 115 planted acres of fruit trees and grapevines, and some of their specialty wines include peach, blueberry, and sugar plum. The main shop is housed in a large barn and stays open even in winter, selling gift baskets and fresh baked goods, and offering free wine-tasting. Events such as apple picking, pumpkin picking, hay rides, and a corn maze take place throughout the year.

Recreation

When the summer heat gets unbearable take Route 553 south from Glassboro to **Lake Garrison** (Monroeville, 856/881-2972, $5 Mon.–Fri., $6 Sat., Sun., and holidays), a favorite day-trip watering hole. There are plenty of picnic tables, and canoes ($5/hr), rowboats ($5/hr), and paddleboats ($5.50/hr) can be rented to explore this large cedar lake, but swimming is contained to a small section toward the front. The lake is open Memorial Day–Labor Day.

In nearby Franklinville is **Scotland Run Park** (980 Academy St., Rte. 610, Franklinville, 856/881-0845), a 940-acre county park filled with meadowlands, marshes, nature trails, and an 80-acre lake ideal for fishing and boating.

Food and Entertainment

Glassboro has a couple of casual eateries that cater to college students and a local crowd. There are a few university hangouts in the area, though only one true option fit for a more diverse crowd.

Since 1946 **Angelo's Glassboro Diner** (26 N. Main St., 856/881-9854, 5 A.M.–9 P.M. Mon.–Sat., until 8 P.M. Sun., $4–15) has been hashing out an authentic South Jersey diner experience—very small, and worn around the edges, it's home to a bevy of regulars who like their eggs how they like 'em. Angelo's is not open the week between Christmas and New Year's.

If you'd rather be sipping a mocha among university students, try the **Eleven East Café** (11 E. High St., 856/307-1107, www.eleveneastcafe.com), which doubles as a used bookstore and somewhat furniture store, with a few "for sale" chairs occupying an unfinished basement. All coffee and teas are organic and fair trade, and everything on the menu uses whole grains. Book readings are held on the weekends. The café is open 7 A.M.–11 P.M. Monday–Friday, 9 A.M.–11 P.M. Saturday, and 9 A.M.–5 P.M. Sunday.

Landmark Tap and Grill (1 East/West St., 856/863-6600, www.landmarkamericana.com, 11 A.M.–2 A.M. Mon.–Sat., noon–midnight Sun., $10–17) is the hottest spot in Glassboro, with good food, a dance club, a massive bar, and a liquor store, and it stands on the longest continuously running tavern spot in town, dating back to 1781. College students tend to congregate around the center bar, while a mix of families, seniors, and twentysomethings enjoy burgers and fries in the quieter outskirts of the main dining area. Landmark is best known for its beer towers, which run about three feet high, have numerous taps, and are served with individual pitchers. Cold rods run through the tower's middle to keep the beer chilled, and the price is reasonable for the ridiculous amount of beer you get. The adjoining **Spot Dance Club** (www.thespotmusicclub.com) has a DJ spin on the weekends and attracts mostly a college crowd.

WOODBURY

It's hard not to notice the history in a place like Woodbury, with the many colonial-brick and century-old structures that line Broad Street, its main thoroughfare, and the spacious yards and grand homes seen as you drive west on Delaware Avenue, or east along Cooper Street. You can almost envision Hessian soldiers marching through town on their way to fight the American Army at Fort Mercer in nearby National Park. But these days Woodbury's position as the county's political seat takes precedence over history, and power lunches are the norm at area restaurants and cafés. In the last decade the town has sprung back to life. Long-empty storefronts are finally beginning to fill, spurred by another Main Street program (a government project aimed to improve downtown districts), and many of Broad Street's structures are receiving much-needed makeovers. The city has numerous sights of historical interest, both downtown and nearby, as well as a few cafés and shops that make it worth a trip.

Heading east onto Cooper Street or west onto Delaware from Broad Street, the main thorough-fare, will give you a good feel for the city's history. Many of the homes found here are colonial with Victorian additions, and each is unique.

Sights

Woodbury is filled with historic architecture. Take a drive around the city, or walk along Broad and Delaware Streets downtown to take in some of the sights.

Situated atop a hill on the east side of Broad Street is the **Friend's Meeting House** (120 N. Broad St.). Built in 1715, its western portion is considered one of the oldest meeting houses in South Jersey, and the eastern side was added in 1785. During the nearby Battle of Red Bank the building was used as a hospital for Hessian soldiers, and at one point as a barracks for British soldiers. A bit south is an attractive brick colonial building known as the **Hunter-Lawrence-Jessup House** (58 N. Broad St., 856/848-8531, $2 adult, free 12 and under), which has seen numerous additions since being built in 1765, including a mansard roof. The house was once owned by Reverend Andrew Hunter, a chaplain in the Revolutionary Army,

Ann Whitall House on the site of Red Bank Battlefield, National Park

© LAURA KINIRY

and was the boyhood home of Captain James Lawrence, who was born in Burlington. In the 1800s it became the home of John S. Jessup, a judge and civic leader, and now operates as an 18-room museum run by the **Gloucester County Historical Society,** open to the public 1–4 P.M. Monday, Wednesday, and Friday, and 2–5 P.M. the last Saturday and Sunday of the month. The Historical Society's library (856/845-4771) is located in a smaller building at 17 Hunter Street, and is open 1–4 P.M. Monday–Friday, and 6–9:30 P.M. Tuesday and Friday. Additional hours are 10 A.M.–4 P.M. the first Saturday of the month, and 2–5 P.M. the last Sunday.

Stretching from Woodbury Creek south to Kings Highway is the city's Historic District. At the corner of Broad and Delaware Streets stands the **Gloucester County Courthouse** (1 N. Broad St.), a Romanesque-style brownstone built in 1885. Its clock tower has long stood as one of Woodbury's most recognizable sights. Next door on Delaware Street is the 1925 **Courthouse Annex.** Though different in style from the main courthouse, this limestone and granite structure is as architecturally pleasing. Across the street is Woodbury's **City Hall,** a colonial revival structure whose eastern lower portion was the first permanent school for the Woodbury Society of Friends. The **Friendship Fire Co. #1** (29 Delaware St.), originally founded as the Woodbury Fire Company in 1799, is next door. The present structure wasn't built until the 1920s, but the company has a long history within the city. A museum of photos, helmets, badges, hoses, and other such items is located behind the fire hall, and is open 7 A.M.–9 P.M. on weekdays. You can arrange a tour of the museum and the firehouse by calling 856/845-0066.

Further south on Broad on the western corner of Centre Street is the **G. G. Green Building,** a large barn-red structure with faded white trim. It's currently unoccupied but plans are underway for a major renovation, including turning this former opera house into a performing arts theater, and providing retail and office space. Green, a prominent figure in local history, brought pharmaceutical manufacturing to Woodbury and is most responsible for the city's growth between 1880 and 1900. Production of his patent medicines ended after World War II, but many homes and buildings built around the company remain.

Red Bank Battlefield

On October 22, 1777, more than 1,000 Hessian soldiers were defeated at Red Bank Battlefield (100 Hessian Ave., National Park, 856/853-5120) by 600 American troops. Marching through Haddonfield on their way to Fort Mercer, a fort protecting Philadelphia that once stood here, the Hessians hoped to surprise the Americans with a land attack but instead suffered nearly 500 casualties. Today the battlefield is a federally owned park with riverfront access, two playgrounds, a number of historic monuments, and the **Ann Whitall House** (856/853-5120, 9 A.M.–4 P.M. Wed.–Fri., 1–4 P.M. Sat. and Sun.), a colonial farmhouse built in 1748 and now operating as a museum. Tradition states that Mrs. Whitall stayed inside her home as the battle proceeded outdoors, and afterward tended to the wounded soldiers. Tours of the home are free.

Red Bank Battlefield is a great place to come in the evenings to watch the sun set over the Delaware, or anytime in the afternoon to watch the airplanes land at Philadelphia International Airport across the river (they're flying so low you can practically see the passengers). The park hosts numerous events throughout the year, including a costumed reenactment of the famous battle, held the third Saturday in October, and the Jonas Cattell Run, a 10K race based on Cattell's famous journey (see *Deptford* in this chapter) from Haddonfield to Fort Mercer.

Food and Entertainment

Woodbury's eateries are the kind that invite you to sit for a while, and you'll find a few good restaurants in both Woodbury proper and neighboring **Woodbury Heights.** Fast food is rampant in the outlying areas, but the local selection is such that you don't need to go down that road.

It doesn't look like much from the outside, but the 24-hour **Colonial Diner Restaurant** (924 N. Broad St., 609/848-6732, $4–15) serves a great breakfast, complete with a table hotpot for self-service coffee. The front room, with its counter seating and long rows of booths, is the best. The spacious back dining area resembles a gaudy reception hall.

On the corner of Broad Street and Delaware is **CHC Coffee Shop** (856/845-0607), one of the latest additions in Woodbury's revitalization efforts. Inside are cozy couches, tables and chairs, gourmet coffee dispensers, and a mix of professionals and students from the nearby public high school. Snacks are available, and the shop is open 7 A.M.– 5 P.M. Monday–Friday, 9 A.M.–5 P.M. Saturday, closed Sunday.

Cafe Neena (20 S. Broad St., 856/845-3110, $16.95–21.95) is an established Italian eatery frequented by lawyers and court employees. The restaurant features an oft-crowded bar, and sidewalk seating when weather permits. There's parking in the rear. Neena's is open 2–9:30 P.M. Monday and Tuesday, 11:30 A.M.–10 P.M. Wednesday and Thursday, until 11:30 P.M. Friday and Saturday, 3–9 P.M. Sunday.

At Woodbury's Saturday morning **Farmers Market** (Cooper St. and Railway Ave., 856/845-1300, ext. 123, May–mid-November), you'll find a good selection of baked treats, produce, and freshly cut flora.

Drive south on Route 45 through Woodbury to nearby Woodbury Heights to reach the **Hollywood Cafe Diner** (940 Rte. 45, 856/251-0011). You can't miss its bright red exterior with yellow trim and silver and blue accents. It's an eye-catching place that many people claim only *looks* like a diner, due to its enormous size and attached bar (and it's definitely not movable). Regardless, the bacon in my dad's BLT was *perfecto*—and the bathrooms are spotless. What's more to say?

The recently relocated **Café Italia** (777 Rt. 45, 856/384-8684) is a delicious Italian restaurant serving huge portions of ravioli, gnocchi, and eggplant parmesan. This is the kind of place to bring the folks to. Hours are 11 A.M.–

9 P.M. Tuesday–Thursday, until 10 P.M. Friday, and 3–10 P.M. Saturday and Sunday, closed Monday.

MULLICA HILL

South along Route 45 en route toward Salem County is the village of Mullica Hill, a colorful array of colonial, Federal, and Victorian homes used for both residence and business. I highly recommend a stop here. You can easily spend hours browsing the specialty shops, where you'll find a great selection of antiques, crafts, furniture, books, dolls, collectibles, and individual wares. In the late 1700s a Finn named Eric Molica purchased much of the surrounding land for farming, and he and his brothers are regarded as Mullica Hill's founders. The area remains largely rural today.

There is no parking along Main Street (Rte. 45), but many of the shops provide spaces in back. I don't advise walking the whole village as traffic on Main Street can be heavy and the stores are fairly spread out. Instead, park in one of the lots and explore the range of shops in that area.

Antiques and Specialty Shops

Many of Mullica Hill's stores are closed at the beginning of the week, so it's best to visit Wednesday–Saturday, but be warned—during the summer months, traffic on Route 322, which snakes through the village center, can be a nightmare with folks heading to and from the shore. If you are planning a Saturday visit, get here early.

On the south end of the village atop the hill is **Yellow Garage Antiques** (66 S. Main St., 856/478-0300, 11 A.M.–5 P.M. Wed.–Sun.), a former bus terminal now home to 35 antique dealers. The shop has provided props and furniture for all of director M. Night Shyamalan's movies. Down the eastern side of the road you'll find **The Treen Studio Pottery Shoppe** (43 S. Main St., 856/223-2626, 10 A.M.–4 P.M. Wed.–Sun.), selling handmade pottery and fine art and next door, **The Mews at Mullica Hill** (43–45 S. Main St., 856/478-6773), an antique gallery specializing in 18th- and 19th-century furniture. Hours are noon–5 P.M. Wednesday–Saturday and Sunday "by chance."

On Main Street's western side is **De Ja Vu Antiques Gift Gallery** (38 S. Main St., 856/478-9994, 11 A.M.–5 P.M. Tues.–Sun., closed Mon.), where you'll find Christmas decorations, candles, and Ty collectibles. The **Old and New Collectible Shop** (36 Main St., 856/223-0900, 11:30 A.M.–5 P.M. Wed.–Sat., noon–5 P.M. Sun.) is an adorable dark-wood-paneled shop featuring teddy bears and sports figurines.

North of the eastern turn-off for Route 322 is **The Old Mill Antique Mall** (1 S. Main St., 856/478-9810, 11 A.M.–5 P.M. daily), a large maroon barn housing 50 dealers, selling everything from Barbie dolls to 1950s furniture to glass bottles. **The Antiques Corner at Mullica Hill** (45 N. Main St., 856/478-4754, 11 A.M.–5 P.M. Wed.–Sun., Mon. and Tues. by appointment) specializes in wood furniture and fine antique crafts.

Occupying one of the village's oldest structures is **Debra's Dolls** (20 N. Main St., 856/478-9778, www.debrasdolls.com, noon–4 P.M. Thurs.–Sat., other days by appointment), where you'll find paper dolls, doll clothing and accessories, and designer dolls by Madame Alexander and Effanbee.

One of my favorite shops is **Murphy's Loft** (53 N. Main St., 856/478-4928, 11 A.M.–5 P.M. Wed.–Sun.). Set back from the street in a two-story farm building, it's packed with used books, magazines, maps, and postcards. The selection seems less varied since the advent of EBay, but it's still a wonderful place to spend an afternoon. Murphy's specializes in out-of-print and collectible books, and will buy from your personal stash.

Mood's Farm Market

If you take Route 77 a few miles east past groves of apple and peach trees (this is farm country), you'll come to Mood's Farm Market (901 Rte. 77, 856/478-2500, www.moodsfarmmarket.com). Like many farms in the area, Mood's offers hayrides and pick-your-own fruit, but has a wider selection to choose from, including blackberries, sweet plums, raspberries, and pears. There's also farm-made apple cider and roasted peanuts for sale. Mood's is open seasonally beginning at 8 A.M. June–Thanksgiving, closed Sundays.

Food

Take a break from your afternoon shopping and stop by the ◖ **Hilltop Restaurant** (47 S. Main St., 856/478-2112, 6 A.M.–9 P.M. Mon.–Sat., 7 A.M.–9 P.M. Sun., $6–9) for heaping portions at an excellent price. The atmosphere is that of a cozy country diner—there's counter service and plenty of tables, both in the entry room and a "breakfast room" up front. Sandwiches (I highly recommend the crab cake) come with a choice of French fries, waffle fries, or chips, but make sure and save room for dessert, because the homemade apple pie is outstanding. Order it à la mode and you receive a slice served warm with two gigantic scoops of vanilla ice cream. The freshly brewed coffee is just as good, and the wait staff keeps it coming. All this for less then $20—Grand!

Standing at the northern junction of Routes 322 and 45 is the **Harrison House** (Rtes. 45 and 322, 856/478-6077, www.harrisonhousediner.com, 6 A.M.–11 P.M. daily, $5–16.95), a favorite stop among travelers en route to the shore. Its red brick exterior and spacious dining room make it hard to tell the Harrison House was once a movable diner, arriving to its present location in 1985 and receiving a makeover to fit the surroundings. The diner serves breakfast throughout the day, as well as a large selection of sandwiches, pastas, meats, and fish. Mini-meals are available throughout the work week beginning at 11:30 A.M., and include soup or salad, potato or veggie, rolls and coffee for $8.95.

Outside the village center within the Mullica Hill Plaza is **Crescent Moon Coffee & Tea** (141 Rte. 77, Store D, 856/223-1237, 6:30 A.M.–6 P.M. Mon.–Fri., 7:30 A.M.–6 P.M. Sat., 8:30 A.M.–2 P.M. Sun.), a clean café attracting a mixed crowd with organic and artisan coffees, as well as salads, sweets, and specialty sandwiches like a turkey panini ($6.95). Wireless Internet is available.

HISTORIC INNS OF SOUTH JERSEY

Inns were traditionally built at major cross-roads to act as rest stops, meeting houses, dining halls, and taverns for travelers making arduous, multiday journeys from one destination to the next, such as from Philadelphia to the Jersey Shore. Many of those established in South Jersey during the 18th and 19th centuries still stand and today serve as dining establishments that ooze history out of every wall painting, window, and ceiling tile. Most serve traditional American fare, and while some have been updated with modern amenities and decor, their significance remains easily recognizable. For a romantic glimpse into South Jersey's past and a walk in America's footsteps, stop by one of the following haunts.

Formerly known as the Spread Eagle, the 1720 **Barnsboro Inn** (699 Main St., Sewell, 856/468-3557, www.barnsboroinn.com, $22-27) originated as a hotel but obtained its first tavern license in 1776. Situated at a five-way intersection west of Pitman in Gloucester County, the inn's original portion acts as a bar — dark and narrow with a low beam ceiling, plenty of stools, a dartboard, and a CD jukebox. The adjoining restaurant is more formal — a favorite among couples who come to dine on crocks of French onion soup ($4.25) and veal puttanesca ($24.95). Lunch is served 11 A.M.-2:30 P.M. Tuesday-Saturday, and dinner 4:30-9:30 P.M. Tuesday-Thursday, until 10 P.M. Friday and Saturday, 3-8 P.M. Sunday. The bar remains open until 1 A.M. Monday-Thursday, until 2 A.M. Friday and Saturday, and midnight Sunday.

Now known as **Swedes Cafe Bar and Restaurant** (301 Kings Hwy., Swedesboro, 856/467-2032, www.swedesinn.com), the once-named Old Swedes Inn was built and licensed as a tavern in 1771 and occupies a prominent piece of real estate along downtown Swedesboro's main strip. The exterior of this pine green colonial has been touched with Victorian fixtures including a front porch and mansard roof, but indoors is a decidedly modern

Getting There

Mullica Hill is easily reached by taking Route 322 West from Glassboro, or East from Swedesboro and the Commodore Barry Bridge (PA). From Salem and Woodstown, take Route 45 North, or Route 45 South from Woodbury.

KINGS HIGHWAY SOUTH

Kings Highway (Hwy. 551) can be picked up from Broad Street in Woodbury or by taking Ogden Road west from Route 45 in Mantua, traveling south through farmland, past homes converted into businesses, small residential enclaves, and a handful of historic sites. The road is a pleasant drive and a wonderful alternative to both the New Jersey Turnpike and I-295, each running parallel en route to Salem County's Delaware Memorial Bridge.

Roadside Sights

While driving along Kings Highway, keep your eyes peeled for these roadside attractions.

Approximately 2.5 miles from downtown Woodbury along the western side of the street in Mount Royal, in East Greenwich Township, is the **Death of the Fox Inn** (217 Kings Hwy.), a colonial stone structure built in the early 1700s and named for the Gloucester County Fox Hunting Club who gathered at the inn after fox chases. This was one of America's first fox-hunting clubs, and is now a private residence threatened by encroaching development. Notable members of the club included Deptford's Jonas Cattell and Dr. Bodo Otto Jr., whose former residence is located further south along the road.

Continue south for exactly two miles into the Mickleton section of East Greenwich, and you'll see a sign pointing the way to **Haines Pork Shop** (521 Kings Hwy., 856/423-1192), a butcher and smokehouse hidden behind a street-side Victorian home. Locals rave about this place, which sells only the freshest cuts of ribs and tenderloin,

setting – especially the café, with its large plate glass windows, muraled walls, art deco bar, and set-up for live music on weekends. The inn stood vacant for 35 years until owner Mark Beltz purchased it in 1979 – sufficient time for Edith, the resident ghost of a 12-year-old girl, to get comfortable living on her own. Hours are 4 P.M.-midnight Monday–Thursday, 11:30 A.M.-2 A.M. Friday, 4 P.M.-2 A.M. Saturday, and 3-10 P.M. Sunday.

As old inns go, the **The Franklinville Inn** (Delsea Dr./Rte. 47 and County Rd. 538, Franklinville, 856/694-1577, www.franklinvilleinn.com, 4-9 P.M. Tues.-Thurs., 4-10 P.M. Fri. and Sat.) seems quite modern at first glance, perhaps because of its large size and resemblance to many of South Jersey's suburban homes. But step inside and its an entirely other story. Wood paneled walls, historic paintings, mounted rifles, and a low ceiling set the ambience for this traditional inn, which once acted as a stagecoach stop between Cape May and Philadelphia. Although the exact date is unclear, the inn, originally known as Cake's Tavern, dates back to the beginning of the 19th century and operated as a hotel and restaurant, until the middle of the 20th century.

At the intersection of Routes 553 and 540, just northwest of Parvin State Park, is **Ye Olde Centerton Inn** (1136 Almond Rd., Pittsgrove, 856/358-3201, www.centertoninn.com, 5-10 P.M. Tues.-Thurs., until 11 P.M. Fri. and Sat., 2-9 P.M. Sun., $14.95-24.95), a former stagecoach stop and freight shop between Cumberland County's Greenwich and Philadelphia. This is South Jersey's oldest surviving inn, dating back to 1706. Its exterior looks a little worse for wear – with peeling paint and chipping clapboard – but its interior is authentically colonial and quite spacious, with eight dining rooms on two floors and an extensive wine cellar. Beneath the inn are the graves of three Revolutionary War soldiers, who share haunting privileges with a female ghost that goes by Margaret.

and people travel from all around to buy their pork here. Across the street is the **Bodo Otto House,** formerly home to Dr. Bodo Otto Jr., the well-known surgeon who accompanied General George Washington during the Battle of Valley Forge. The house is privately occupied and rumored to be haunted. A blue marker standing in front of the property makes it easily identifiable and offers additional background info.

Swedesboro

About five miles from the Bodo Otto House, Swedesboro is a tiny incorporated borough at the heart of Woolwich Township, settled by Swedes in 1638. As you enter town keep an eye open for **"Old Swedes" Trinity Episcopal Church** (208 Kings Hwy., 856/467-1227, Mon.–Sat. by appointment) on the street's western side. The church was built in 1784 to replace an old and damaged log cabin church, and now stands on the oldest deeded church property in South Jersey. Take a walk around toward the back and visit the graveyard now called home by many of the area's original Swede settlers, as well as Dr. Bodo Otto Jr. and Eric Molica, the founder of nearby Mullica Hill. Swedesboro has a small downtown with a couple of commercial storefronts, dominated by an eye-catching Swedes Café Bar and Restaurant, a historic inn that features a New American menu and a modernized bar.

For a nice side trip, take Swedesboro Road east from downtown Swedesboro about eight miles to reach the **C. A. Nothnagle Log House** (406 Swedesboro Rd., Gibbstown, 856/423-0916). Built in 1638 by recently arrived Swedish and Finnish settlers, it's the country's oldest surviving log cabin, and though it doesn't look like much from the outside, it's a truly unique piece of America's early settlement history. Free admission is available by advance appointment.

Salem County

New Jersey's least-populated county, Salem remains a mostly rural setting with deep historic routes. The region (its name derived from the Hebrew word for peace, shalom) was once a part of New Sweden, established by Finns and Swedes in the early 17th century, and grew to become a primary Quaker colony and port arrival. Located in New Jersey's southwestern-most corner, Salem was originally connected with Burlington by way of Kings Highway but has since managed to retain relative isolation, as areas to its north grow heavy with development. Filled with silos, fruit orchards, farmhouses, and a large number of patterned brick homes built during the 18th century, the county connects most readily with its neighbors across the river, in Delaware and Pennsylvania's Brandywine Valley, and retains an agricultural charm unlike anywhere else in the state, though that's not to say industry hasn't touched here. Glassmaking and ice cream production were once big businesses, and **DuPont,** a chemical developing company located along the Delaware River in **Carney's Point,** is one of the county's major manufacturers. Salem is also home to the nation's second-largest nuclear complex, the **Salem/Hope Creek Nuclear Power Plant,** standing in juxtaposition to its large number of wildlife reserves.

SIGHTS

Salem County's historical significance is evident in its sights and architecture, especially in and around the city with which it shares a name. The region is also one of the state's most agricultural, and is home to the one of the best-known rodeos on the East Coast.

Salem

Salem was established in 1675 by English Quaker John Fenwick and remains one of South Jersey's oldest cities. Today it stands somewhere between manufacturing community and agricultural town, with large rectangular brick buildings clustered around its downtown center and spaciously set colonial farmhouses lining the streets beyond. There's no denying the city's history. In fact, Salem's downtown streets of Market and Broadway are those originally laid out by Fenwick, and are now listed on the National Register of Historic Places. The city is slowly starting to emerge as an antique-shopping center, but the main draw remains its historic significance. Traditional and cultural history buffs will find plenty of interesting sites within the city center and just beyond.

Founded in 1884, the **Salem County Historical Society** (79–83 Market St., 856/935-5004, schs@verizon.net, noon–4 P.M. Tues.–Sat.) contains a superb collection of archival materials such as photographs, diaries, and oral histories, and a museum featuring changing and permanent exhibits, including a wonderful display on Wistarburgh Glass. It's made up of four buildings—the **Alexander Grant House** (1721), the **John Jones Law Office** (1721), the **Stone Barn Museum,** and the **Log Cabin Educational Center.** The Society also sponsors a tour of many of Salem County's historic homes and gardens the first Saturday in May.

The **Friend's Burial Ground** stands due west of where Market and Broadway meet, and on the property's edge is the **Salem Oak,** a hauntingly beautiful White Oak tree under which John Fenwick acquired the property that was to become Salem from the local Lenape Indians. The tree remains one of the city's most revered features.

Salem's claim to fame is as the birthplace of the "edible tomato," though the story is most likely legend. It's said that in 1820 Colonel Robert Gibbon Johnson, a graduate of the College of New Jersey (present-day Princeton), declared he would eat an entire bushel of tomatoes on the steps of the **Salem County Courthouse** (92 Market St.). Tomatoes were widely thought to be poisonous and a large crowd gathered to watch Johnson die. When he didn't, tomatoes became a part of the American diet.

The country's first successful glass factory was established in Salem, and though **Wistarburgh** is long gone the city retains its connection with the glass industry. West of the region in nearby **Carney's Point** you'll find **Salem Community College** (460 Hollywood Ave., 856/299-2100, www.salemcc.org), which offers America's only associate degree in scientific glassblowing. Facilities include the **Paul J. Stankard Gallery,** a showcase of glass art and scientific glass pieces named for internationally acclaimed local alum Paul Stankard, best known for his intricate paperweights.

Just east of Salem in the village of Hancock's Bridge is the **Hancock House** (Hancock's Bridge Rd. off Rte. 27, 856/935-4373, www.fohh.20fr.com), known for both its role in Revolutionary War history and its architectural significance. In 1778 it was the site of a brutal massacre in which British troops, lead by local loyalists, entered and bayoneted to death nearly 30 colonial militia who were sleeping in the upstairs attic. Among those killed was the home's owner, Judge William Hancock, himself a British faithful. The house was built in 1738 by Judge Hancock's parents and is an excellent example of British Quaker patterned brickwork associated with the region. Features include the initials of William and Sarah Hancock and the year of the home's construction adorning the western exterior wall, and a herringbone design (achieved by interspersing regulated bricks with blue-hued ones) decorating the outer side walls. Tours are given 10 A.M.– noon and 1–4 P.M. Wednesday–Saturday, and 1–4 P.M. Sunday. Admission is free, but donations are welcome.

Fort Mott State Park

Located on the banks of the lower Delaware River, Fort Mott State Park (856/935-3218, dawn–dusk daily, free) was once a self-contained military community, built in the late 1800s as part of a three-fort coastal defense system. Today it is a 104-acre state park that includes a visitors center, picnic areas, a small playground, nature trails, and remnants of the original fort. In the summer a ferry runs round-trip to nearby Fort Delaware on Pea Patch Island, and throughout the year the park hosts numerous interpretive programs including a Fort Mott all-access tour. Maps for self-guided tours are available at the visitors center, which also serves as a **Regional Welcome Center** for the **New Jersey Coastal Heritage Trail Route** (NJCHTR).

Drive down Cemetery Road—a striking, tree-lined street hardly larger than a walking path—or stroll along the **Finns Point Interpretive Trail** through the **Killcohook Wildlife Refuge** to reach **Finns Point National Cemetery.** This small cemetery, secluded by tall reeds and marshes, is the resting place for nearly 2,500 Confederate soldiers, many of whom died as Civil War prisoners on Pea Patch Island and are buried together in a mass grave on the cemetery's western side. Union soldiers are also buried here, as are veterans from other wars.

The **Three Forts Ferry** runs from Fort Mott to Fort Delaware, the second of the three defense forts, beginning in April and throughout the summer months until Labor Day. Ferries depart every two hours 10:30 A.M.–4:30 P.M. weekends only until mid-June, and Wednesday– Sunday July and August.

Finns Point Rear Range Lighthouse

Outside Fort Mott Park at the nearby intersection of Fort Mott and Lighthouse Roads is Finns Point Rear Range Lighthouse (Pennsville, 856/935-1487), part of Supawna Meadows Wildlife Refuge. No longer a working lighthouse, this 115-foot-tall, thin, darkly painted tower features an external support structure and was built as part of a two-light system, operating in conjunction with a front range light. Ship captains lined up the two lights to guarantee their path, but dredging of the Delaware River in the 1950s rendered them useless; the lights were decommissioned and the front light taken down. Although the lighthouse is not much to look at on the outside, free tours of the interior are given noon–4 P.M. every third Sunday, April–September.

New Jersey Coastal Heritage Trail

The New Jersey Coastal Heritage Trail (856/447-0103, www.nps.gov/neje) is an auto and bicycle route highlighting significant cultural and natural sights of coastal New Jersey from Fort Mott east to Cape May, and upward to Central New Jersey's Perth Amboy. This "work in progress" has a couple of regional offices currently open, including the Delsea Regional Office located at Fort Mott State Park. Stop in for brochures, maps, and an informative video highlighting the many sights featured along the trail.

Woodstown

Approximately 10 miles north of Salem along Route 45 is Woodstown, an attractive settlement with a small downtown and a community of varying-sized Federal and Victorian–era homes. In December, the **Pilesgrove-Woodstown Historical Society** (42 N. Main St., 856/769-4588) hosts a candlelight tour of many of these historic structures.

The borough's outlying region consists of farmland and plenty of open country where you'll find **Cowtown Cowboy Outfitters** (Rte. 40 W., 856/769-1761, www.cowtowncowboy.com). Stop in for a felt hat and a Wrangler fittin' before heading across the street to New Jersey's most famous rodeo and flea market.

◀ Cowtown Rodeo and Flea Market

For over 50 years Cowtown Rodeo (780 Rte. 40, Pilesgrove, 856/769-3200, www.cowtownrodeo.com) has been wrangling in crowds to its 4,000-seat stadium to witness the longest continuously running rodeo on the East Coast. Every Saturday night from Memorial Day to mid-September you may see bull riding, team roping, steer wrestling, and women's barrel racing. The grounds aren't hard to find—just look for the giant cowboy smiling down onto Route 40.

On Tuesdays and Saturdays (8 A.M.–4 P.M.) throughout the year, Cowtown hosts a flea market with over 500 vendors. Wander the dirt paths and you'll find everything from frilly shirts to giant beach towels, styling belt buckles to E.T. barrettes. Graze on fish-and-chips or down some funnel cake while you check out the wares—this indoor/outdoor market is by *no* means fancy, just good fun. Cowtown also hosts a livestock auction every Tuesday at noon.

RECREATION

Because of its proximity to the Delaware Bay and River in New Jersey's lower western corner, Salem County is a natural for swamplands and marshes. There are a handful of natural areas ideal for fishing and wildlife-viewing.

Natural Areas

Supawna Meadows (197 Lighthouse Rd., Pennsville, 856/935-1487, dawn–dusk) is 2,800 acres of protected wetland intended for the feeding, nesting, and resting of migratory birds, including waterfowl, ospreys, and bald eagles. The refuge is part of the Cape May National Wildlife Refuge Complex and offers nature trails, as well as opportunities for fishing, crabbing, hunting, and wildlife observation. Eighty percent of the Meadows is marshland, accessible only by boat (and you must provide your own).

The county's additional wetland areas include **Stow Creek Viewing Area** (609/628-2103, dawn–dusk daily), a nesting place and educational facility for bald eagles that features a boardwalk and interpretive exhibits (located off of 623 between the Hancock House and Greenwich), and the **Alloway Creek Watershed** (888/MARSHES or 888/627-7437, dawn–dusk daily), which has observation platforms and a nature trail.

Parvin State Park

Just beyond the Cumberland County border near the city of Vineland is Parvin State Park (791 Almond Rd., Pittsgrove, 856/358-8616, www.state.nj.us/dep/parksandforests/parks/parvin.html, open all year), a 1,135-acre park with 400 forested acres of designated natural area, two lakes, and opportunities for hiking, biking, canoeing, swimming, bird-watching, and camping. Parvin has 15 miles of hiking trails, many of them suitable for mountain bikes and horses, and is home to over 50 types of trees. During summer months you can rent one of 16 cabins ($45/night for four-bunk cabin, $65/night for six-bunk cabin, Apr.–Oct.) situated along the western bank of the smaller **Thundergust Lake,** or go swimming and canoeing at Parvin Grove in the larger **Parvin Lake,** which also offers a snack bar, boat ramp, and licensed fishing. One of the best ways to spend an afternoon is to rent a canoe (or bring your own) and paddle along **Muddy Run,** a tributary of Parvin Lake, to the town of **Canterton.** Campsites ($20/night year-round) for tents and trailers are located on the lake's south side, and are available throughout the year. The park charges a $2 walk-in/bicycle fee charged Memorial Day–Labor Day. The remainder of the year the park is free.

The park has an interesting history, including being used as a day camp for the children of displaced Japanese Americans during the 1940s and, during the same decade, as a camp for German war prisoners who'd been sent from Fort Dix to work at area farms and factories. The remains of numerous Indian encampments have been found within park boundaries over the years.

ENTERTAINMENT AND EVENTS
Appel Farm

Appel Farm Arts and Music Center (457 Shirley Rd., Elmer, 856/358-6513 or 800/394-1211, www.appelfarm.org) is a nonprofit organization that holds visual and performing arts workshops for children, teens, and adults. This 176-acre farm has also earned its reputation as a live music venue, showcasing a variety of acts including folk singers, country stars, and classical violinists, open to the public throughout the year. An annual **Arts and Music Festival** is held each June.

To reach Appel Farm, drive east along Route 40 from Cowtown about 12.5 miles, making a right onto Route 77 and a left onto Route 611 (Shirley Rd.) toward Elmer. The ride should take about 20 minutes.

Festivals

Along Route 40 in Pilesgrove Township is the **Salem County Fairgrounds,** host to Labor Day weekend's annual **Delaware Valley Bluegrass Festival** (www.brandywinefriends.org/index .php), featuring three days of bluegrass performances, improv jams, and on-site camping. Cost is $60 adult for advance weekend tickets, and $30 for students. The annual **Harvest Sheep & Fiber Festival** (856/467-2889, www.sheepandfiber.org) takes place here in late September, with highlights that include sheep shearing, felting, spinning, dance demos, and a silent auction.

ACCOMMODATIONS

$100-150: At the foot of the Delaware Memorial Bridge you'll find the **Hampton Inn** (429 N. Broadway, Pennsville, 856/351-1700, fax 856/351-9554, www.hampton innpennsville.com), which shares its parking lot with the popular chain restaurant Cracker Barrel. The hotel provides free wireless Internet access and has an outdoor pool, and offers complimentary cookies upon check-in. The **Comfort Inn & Suites** (634 Sodder's Rd., Carney's Point, 856/299-8282) is a newly built comfortable hotel located across from a horse farm on a quiet end street. Room amenities include microwave, refrigerator, and Internet connection, and price includes a deluxe breakfast with pancakes, eggs, waffles, and three choices of toast. The **Holiday Inn Express Hotel and Suites** (506 Pennsville-Auburn Rd., Carney's Point, 856/351-9222) is located just east of I-295. Rooms are standard size with large bathrooms, and the lobby is cozy with both a fireplace and chessboard.

Camping

Recommended for families is the **Yogi Bear's Jellystone Park at Tall Pines** (49 Beal Rd., Elmer, 856/451-7479 or 800/252-2890, fax 856/455-3378, www.tallpines.com). Open late

March–the end of October, this kid favorite has campsites and cabins for rental and offers an extensive variety of recreational activities for both children and adults throughout the season.

FOOD

There are not a lot of dining options to choose from in Salem County, but the few listed below do offer good American food and pleasant surrounds. For a larger variety try nearby Gloucester County, or a bit further north, Camden County.

To get to the heart of Salem County, head straight to the **Salem Oak Diner** (113 W. Broadway, Salem, 856/935-1305, 5 A.M.–9 P.M. Mon.–Fri., 6 A.M.–9 P.M. Sat. and Sun., $4–14), a local hangout and regional favorite that's been serving up breakfast, lunch, and dinner in good ol' diner fashion since 1955.

For fancier American fare try **JG Cook's Riverview Inn** (60 Main St., Pennsville, 856/678-3700, lunch $7–16, dinner $19–27), located on the waterfront next to Riverview Beach Park. The restaurant's lobby displays classic photos of the Riverview Amusement Park, which once occupied the nearby space but closed in the 1960s. Have a seat by the fire during cold winter months and stay for the live music and comedy events that take place on various evenings throughout the week, or come for the dancing on Friday and Saturday evenings. The inn is open for lunch 11:30 A.M.–4 P.M. Tuesday–Saturday, and dinner 4–10 P.M. Tuesday–Thursday, until 11 P.M. Friday and Saturday, and 2–9 P.M. Sunday.

Best known for its ice cream, **Richman's Restaurant** (849 Rte. 40, 856/769-0356, $5–8) is also a great place to come for an inexpensive sit-down meal. Bring the family, and make sure to order a shake to go with your fries. Counter service, well-worn booths, and an ice cream take-out window (during summer months) make it easy to think you've stepped back into the 1940s. The plastic cow hanging above the exterior entryway is a personal favorite. Richman's is open 6 A.M.–9 P.M. daily.

Cumberland County

Wetlands, fishing villages, and charming river towns are plentiful in Cumberland County, often referred to as the Bayshore region, an area also home to numerous historic districts, a budding arts scene, and New Jersey's largest city in landmass, Vineland. Once one of the world's leading oyster harvesters, the county has held tight to its maritime heritage and remains a prime locale for boating, crabbing, and fishing. Cumberland's scenic rivers, estuaries, salt marshes, and coastal meadows provide excellent opportunities for spotting egrets, red-tailed hawks, blue jays, and American bald eagles, and the county's open fields are often visited by Eastern coyotes and white-tailed deer. During the summer months the region comes alive with dozens of produce stands, and fresh seafood markets can be found in most of the community towns. Like much of South Jersey, Cumberland has deep routes in the glass industry and the tradition is evident in the county's shops and galleries.

Often overlooked by visitors to South Jersey, this surprisingly diverse region is one not to be missed—for its culture and beauty, as well as its people.

Information and Services

The **Bridgeton-Cumberland Tourist Association** (50 E. Broad St., 856/451-4802) is a self-service center located in downtown Bridgeton at the intersection of Routes 77 and 49. If you'd like to speak with someone in person, the staff at the nearby **Cumberland County Library** (800 E. Commerce St., 856/453-2210, www.clueslibs.org) is extremely helpful.

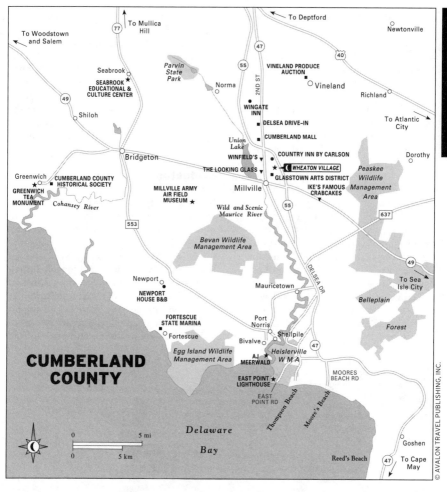

© AVALON TRAVEL PUBLISHING, INC.

The **New Jersey Department of Agriculture**'s website (www.state.nj.us/jerseyfresh/) offers updated information on roadside markets, community farmers markets, and pick-your-own farms within the county and throughout New Jersey. For a full list of Cumberland County's marinas, charter boat companies, and favorite fishing spots check out www.co.cumberland.nj.us, where you can also download a copy of the "Fisherman's Paradise" brochure.

Getting There and Around

Route 55 is a direct route from Gloucester County into Cumberland, and has exits for Millville and Vineland. The road eventually leads into Route 47, where you'll find a turnoff for Mauricetown, the Bayshore beaches, and the East Point Lighthouse.

An alternative route to 55 is to travel Route 47, also known as **Delsea Drive,** straight from Deptford. This commercial stretch received its name when a newspaper reporter quipped the road ran "from the 'Del'aware River to the Atlantic 'Sea.'"

BRIDGETON AND VICINITY

The seat of Cumberland County, Bridgeton boasts New Jersey's largest continuous historic district: over 2,000 homes and building of colonial, Federal, and Victorian design that are listed on the National Register of Historic Places. Unfortunately, many of them look as though they've been used as crash pads, and the city has the feel of a forgotten town once swelling with life. Bridgeton lays claim to a number of New Jersey firsts: The state's first zoo is still in operation, and New Jersey's first newspaper *The Plain Dealer,* which ran from 1775 to 1776, was written at **Potter's Tavern** (W. Broad St., 856/451-4802, noon–4 P.M. Sat., Apr.–Oct., $1), today a restored museum.

Like so many South Jersey communities Bridgeton is making strides to revitalize its downtown streets, but progress is slow. Many of its storefronts remain empty and foot traffic is minimal. Bridgeton is not a place you'd want to spend the night, but it maintains numerous attractions that are worth an afternoon visit. The **Cohansey River** runs through the city center and during summer months the **Bridgeton Riverfront** comes alive with a variety of events, most notably a Friday **farmers market** (10 A.M.–2 P.M.). Apple and peach orchards, spacious farms, quaint maritime towns, and a unique shopping village are part of the surrounding vicinity and offer scenic drives, but take it slow—many of the roads are curved and narrow.

Bridgeton City Park

West of the Cohansey River in downtown Bridgeton is 1,100-acre Bridgeton City Park (Mayor Aitken Dr., 856/455-3230), home to some walking trails and **Sunset Lake,** an attractive river-fed lake that offers opportunity for swimming and canoeing, with seasonal boat rentals available at **Bridgeton Canoe House** (Washington and Mayor Aitken Dr., 856/451-8687). A few of the city's museums are located within the park, as well as an amphitheater hosting occasional summer events.

Bridgeton seems like an odd place to find

grinning llamas at the Cohanzick Zoo

© LAURA KINIRY

white tigers, but they're here, along with pumas, lemurs, monkeys and birds at the park's **Cohanzick Zoo** (856/455-3230). Opened in 1934, the zoo is New Jersey's first municipal zoo and remains free to enter. It's a small place, but definitely worth a walk through (keep an eye on those peacocks!). Hours are 10 A.M.–6 P.M. spring/summer, and 9 A.M.–4 P.M. fall/winter.

Museums

Bridgeton City Park is home to numerous attractions, including the **Nail Mill Museum** (856/455-4100, 10:30 A.M.–3:30 P.M. Tues.–Sat., free), an unassuming building that was once the office of the Cumberland Nail and Iron Works during the 19th century. Today it's a museum displaying items from Cumberland County's industrial past, including examples of Bridgeton glass. Nearby is the **New Sweden Farmstead Museum** (Bridgeton City Park, Mayor Aitken Dr., 856/455-9785). A replica of a 17th-century Swedish farmstead, it's a circular log village that includes a stable, blacksmith shop, bathhouse, smokehouse, and a main residence. Sweden's King and Queen officially opened the farmstead in 1988 to honor the 350th anniversary of Swedish settlement in America. Hours are 11 A.M.–5 P.M. Saturday and noon–5 P.M. Sunday, mid-May–Labor Day, and it's open to reserved tours throughout the year.

Just past the baseball diamonds off of Babe Ruth Drive, skirting the outer border of the park, is a small white building resembling an American Legion. This is the **Bridgeton Hall of Fame Sports Museum** (Bridgeton Recreation Center, Burt St., 856/451-7300), an exhibit of memorabilia from regional and national amateur and professional sports teams. Notable features include a Cincinnati Reds bat collection, Willie Mays' 1960 Golden Glove, and items relating to the 1980 Philadelphia Phillies, World Series Champs. The museum is open 10 A.M.–2 P.M. in the spring/summer, 10 A.M.–3 P.M. fall/winter, with an hour lunch break between noon and 1 P.M. Entry is free.

Downtown on the lower level of the **Bridgeton Public Library** (150 E. Commerce St.) is the **George Woodruff Indian Museum** (856/451-2620, 1 P.M.–4 P.M. Mon.–Sat., except during summer), displaying an extensive collection of items relating to the area's original inhabitants, the Lenni-Lenape Indians. For additional books on the Lenape tribe, visit the Cumberland County Library.

Dutch Neck Village

Dutch Neck Village (97 Trench Rd., Bridgeton, 856/451-2188, www.dutchneckvillage.com) is a planned country village located south of Bridgeton. Built in 1976, it's made up of a handful of shops selling crafts, knick-knacks, and Red Hat Society wares; a café; a restaurant specializing in home-style cooking and baked breads; and a **Country Living Museum,** which features such items as old sewing machines, typewriters, clothing, and books that "reflect the country living styles of the area in the past century." The village also hosts a number of festivals throughout the year, including an annual **Strawberry Festival** in June, a **Peach Festival** in August, and a **Walk of Lights** during the first three weekends in December.

Walking among the shops is an easy stroll, and there's an arboretum on the premises where you can relax and picnic in the warmer months. The shops are open 10 A.M.–5 P.M. Monday–Saturday, and the café and restaurant are open daily.

To get here from Bridgeton, take Route 49 to Fayette Street and turn left, driving approximately one mile to a fork and bearing right onto Cubby Holly Road. Make a right at the first crossroad you come to, Trench Road.

Seabrook Educational and Cultural Center

Seabrook Educational and Cultural Center (1325 State Hwy. 77, Seabrook, 856/451-8393, 9 A.M.–2 P.M. Mon.–Thurs.) is a nonprofit museum showcasing the history of Seabrook, a unique farming village that came into fruition when Charles F. Seabrook turned his father's 57-acre farm into a facility for growing, processing, and freezing vegetables. In search of employees,

Seabrook visited Japanese internment camps and offered room, board, and children's education for those who agreed to a six-month commitment. Over the course of the farm's history numerous cultures were brought together including Caribbean migrant workers, African Americans, Italians, and Eastern Europeans.

The center was founded by Japanese Americans, Seabrook's largest ethnic group, and includes photos, memorabilia, and a model display of Seabrook Farms as it looked during the 1950s, and provides educational materials such as published works relating to the community.

Greenwich

Southwest of Bridgeton is the boat-building town of Greenwich. Pronounced GREEN-which, the town boasts extremely well-preserved colonial architecture, and it's worth a side-trip to stop here. Greenwich is one of America's handful of tea-burning towns, and a **Greenwich Tea Burning Monument** (Ye Greate St.) stands in commemoration of the 23 tea burners who broke into a cellar on the night of December 22, 1774, and carried the tea stored there to a nearby field, burning it in protest of British taxes imposed on the American colonists.

The town is also home to the **Cumberland County Historical Society** (981 Ye Greate St., 856/455-4055, lummis2@juno.com). Established in 1908, it consists of a library (10 A.M.–4 P.M. Wed., 1–4 P.M. Fri.–Sun.) and numerous museums, including the **1730 Gibbon House** (noon–4 P.M. Tues.–Sat., 2–5 P.M. Sun., Apr.–mid-Dec.), a brick-patterned mansion with 18th- and 19th-century furnishings; and the **John DuBois Maritime Museum** (1–4 P.M. Sun., Apr.–Nov.), showcasing 19th- and 20th-century maritime artifacts.

Festivals and Events

Sunset Lake's **Donald Rainear Amphitheater** (800/319-3379) in Bridgeton City Park hosts the annual summertime **Bridgeton Folk Festival,** a day's worth of live music, arts and crafts, and picnicking. A number of other productions, including children's plays, are held here throughout the summer.

Food and Entertainment

Family-owned and -operated since 1888, **Weber's Candy** (16 S. Laurel St., 856/451-7811) is a Bridgeton favorite and is easily recognized by its red and white awning. Try the famous cream peanut clusters, or go for the peanut brittle. Nearby **Bridgewater Pub & Restaurant** (22 Laurel St., 856/455-9551) is *the* place to dine in Bridgeton. The menu is extensive and includes "bar munchies," sandwiches, burgers, and entrées such as chicken cordon bleu ($12.99) and steak and shrimp ($17.99). For a bit of old school try **Angie's Bridgeton Grill** (1½ E. Broad St., 856/451-0220), a local institution since 1940. The barn red exterior of this Silk City diner may be peeling its layers, but the customers continue to flock here. And why not? It's a South Jersey diner at its best.

El Tequilitas (125 E. Commerce St., 856/453-0943) is a popular place serving traditional and vegetarian Mexican fare. A small breakfast menu features huevos rancheros ($3.75)—eggs, cheese, and salsa served atop a tortilla with a side of beans.

DELAWARE BAYSHORE

Villages, wetlands, and bayside beaches make up the Delaware Bayshore, a region home to plenty of wildlife and the mouth of the **Wild and Scenic Maurice River,** a waterway ideal for boating and fishing. One publication called the Mullica River–Great Bay Estuary "one of the least disturbed ecosystems" in the Northeast Corridor. Situated along the western bank of the river is Commercial Township, once one of the world's leading oyster harvesters. Though disease has wiped out much of the region's oyster population, the township has turned to other seafaring endeavors to fuel its economy, including crabbing, fishing, and maritime tourism, and its livelihood is evident in tiny fishing communities and small port towns.

With the exception of Mauricetown, this region has little to offer in the way of architecture or downtowns. Rather, the Bayshore provides some of the state's best bird-watching opportunities, as well as excellent cycling, gorgeous natural scenery, and plenty of maritime history.

Sights

South off Route 47 is the highlight of Commercial Township, **Mauricetown,** a charming seafaring village situated along the Maurice River and filled with brightly painted saltbox structures, many with gingerbread add-ons, that were once the homes of oystermen and sea captains. The names of these men are carved into plaques still gracing the homes' exteriors ("1862—Captain David P. Haley," "1860—Captain Seth Bowen," "circa 1865—Captain Issac Peterson") and at the village center stands the **Mauricetown M. E. Church** (9574 Noble St.), a large 19th-century United Methodist church with a tall, white steeple and lovely stained glass windows.

On the water's edge is **Maurice Waterfront Park,** one of the best spots for taking in the Maurice River. The park is a small, open space with a couple of picnic tables and a parking lot, and a posted sign warns "no swimming or diving."

When you arrive to the villages of **Bivalve, Port Norris,** and **Shellpile** you won't think you've arrived at much. Shacks once operating as oyster stations line the docks, fishing vessels stand in port, one-story houses nestled in tall grass and wetlands line the roads, and a salty sea stench lingers in the air. But it's here that you'll find New Jersey's official tall ship, the **A.J. Meerwald** (2800 High St., Bivalve, 856/785-2060 or 800/485-3072, www.ajmeerwald.org), a 1928 oyster schooner. It's 155 feet long and can hold up to 45 passengers, and is used as a sailing classroom by the nonprofit **Bayshore Discovery Project,** dedicated to the education and preservation of the region's maritime tradition. Both adults and children can set sail on the *A. J. Meerwald* and learn about local culture while taking on the skills of operating an oyster vessel. The schooner can also be chartered for private events. Public sails take place both in the morning (9 A.M.) and afternoon (1 P.M.), and last for three hours. The cost is $30 adults, $15 children. Evening sails run $35 for all passengers. Check the website for a current sailing schedule.

Be sure and plan ahead before arriving in Bivalve. The ship is often out of port for overnight stays (secondary ports include Burlington, Camden, and Cape May) and though the Discovery Project does maintain a small maritime museum (1–4 P.M. Sat. and Sun., Apr.–Oct.) at the dock, there's little to do around the area, save for a few nature trails and bicycling routes.

Situated within the **Heislerville Wildlife Management Area** by the east foot of the Maurice River is the **East Point Lighthouse** (East Point Rd. off Rte. 47, Heislerville, 856/327-3714). Built in 1849 it is New Jersey's second-oldest lighthouse, and its Cape Cod style is both unique and picturesque. The lighthouse stood vacant for almost 40 years when, at the public's request, the U.S. Coast Guard restored it to use in 1980. Now it remains the state's last operating lighthouse on the Delaware Bay, and is open to the public the third Sunday of each month.

Sports and Recreation

Many of the Bayshore roads are graced with "Bike Route" and "Share the Road" signs, and with light traffic, wide-open marshes, and relatively flat terrain, the entire area is ideal for **bicycling.** Be sure to bring along bug spray, and pay heed to the "Muskrat Crossing" signs that stand roadside. Also, carry a map. Signage isn't so hot around here and it's easy to get lost. Though often burdened with shore traffic, Route 47 remains a popular cycling road due to its wide shoulder, heavy greenery, and direct route from Gloucester County through to Cumberland and on to the Jersey Shore. Across from the *A. J. Meerwald* docking port in Bivalve is a bike route/nature trail.

Dubbed the "Weakfish Capital of the World," **Fortescue** is a bayside village with a state-owned marina and numerous bait and tackle shops. It's a great little spot for surf-fishing, night fishing, and bird-watching, and a large number of charter boats are available for half- and full-day rentals, though unless your interests fall within these categories, there's little to do.

One of the Bayshore's most unique annual events occurs late May/early June when thousands of horseshoe crabs descend upon the beaches of the Delaware Bay to lay their eggs, and shorebirds enjoy a "feast" of enormous proportions. In 2005 many of the beaches were closed to public access during this time but they sometimes remain open, and the best places to catch a glimpse of this natural phenomenon are the **Heislerville Wildlife Management Area** east of the Maurice River, **Thompsons Beach,** and **Reed's Beach,** both easily reachable by way of Route 47, east of Mauricetown.

Filled with tidal marsh, tall reeds, and mud flats, the Heislerville Wildlife Management Area is a great place to search for wildlife. Travel Thompson Road en route to Thompson's Beach and you'll pass strange, thin, bent trees of varying half-length sizes all resembling spilt ends—a unique foliage that's definitely something to see. Along the road—which is billed as a "wildlife viewing driving tour"—is a popular bird-watching platform. Look for osprey nesting in the trees.

Reed's Beach lies along the Bayshore on the far side of a long stretch of marshland. A single-lane road lined with shorefront bungalows, shacks, and trailers—many that are built directly above Bayshore waters—leads to a parking area ($1) for shorebird viewing. A short walk is required to reach the platform.

Throughout the Bayshore region keep your eyes open for turtles and monarch butterflies in late summer and early fall, especially in the **Egg Island Wildlife Management Area** and around East Point Lighthouse. Songbirds travel through the region in spring and autumn, and raptors frequent the area in autumn and winter.

Thompson's Beach and East Point are both good locations for spotting shorebirds migrating in May. Bald eagles can be spotted on the **Wild and Scenic Maurice River** (http://mauriceriver.igc.org) in the winter, which acts as a migratory path for shorebirds, raptors, waterfowl, and fish.

Events
Mauricetown is home base for the region's annual **Winter Raptor Festival** (Mauricetown Fire Hall, 856/453-2180), a day-long bird-spotting festival that takes place in February.

Delaware Bay Days (www.ajmeerwald.org, 856/785-2060) is a free two-day festival celebrating the Delaware Bay region's rich maritime history. Events such as land and boat parades, river tours, and wetland walks take place within and between Port Norris, Bivalve, Shellpile, and Maurice Township's East Point Lighthouse. Live music, fresh seafood, arts and crafts stalls, and kids' face painting are some of the perks. The festival is held in early June and is sponsored by the Bayshore Discovery Project.

Accommodations and Food
The best out-of-the-way dining experience in the region has to be the **Newport House** (52 Husted Ln., Newport, 856/447-3597, www.newporthouse.net, $14.50–33.95), located on the edge of a farm down a quiet road off Route 553. This BYO restaurant features three fireplaces and an enclosed patio with large glass windows perfect for spotting roaming deer at dusk, and entrées include selections of meat, fish, and seafood. Reservations are encouraged, as the restaurant is only open for dinner beginning at 5 P.M. Friday–Sunday throughout the year.

Making the most of an idyllic setting, the owners have opened a four-room bed-and-breakfast (856/447-5297) in a nearby farmhouse. Each room has a private bath, and there's an indoor heated pool on the premises. Room rates range $100–150.

Getting There and Around
From Mauricetown to Port Norris is about five miles. The roads within the Delaware Bay region can be difficult to navigate and some backtracking is often involved. To reach Greenwich, take County Road 607 south from Bridgeton approximately seven miles, or from Salem follow the Coastal Heritage Trail east along County Road 658 to 623, about 10 miles.

Fortescue can be reached by taking Route 49 east from Bridgeton to Route 553, where you'll turn right and travel south to County Road 732. Another right will bring you to the town of Newport. Drive approximately 10 more minutes south along County Road 637 to arrive at Fortescue. Continuing south on Route 553 will take you to the town of Dividing Creek. From here it's about five miles to Bivalve, and an extra mile to Port Norris. To reach Mauricetown, take a left onto North Avenue from Port Norris, and after two miles it will turn into Mauricetown Road. Bear right onto Noble Street and you'll enter the downtown center.

Located at the mouth of the Maurice River, the East Point Lighthouse is even more remote. From Mauricetown, take the Mauricetown Bypass East until you reach Route 47 (Delsea Drive), where you'll make a right and continue south onto County Road 616. Travel about 15 minutes to the town of Heislerville, turning right onto East Point Road. This will take you through the Heislerville Wildlife Management Area to the lighthouse.

MILLVILLE

Nicknamed the "Holly City" for its extensive cultivation of holly trees, the industrial city of Millville has been busy establishing itself as a major arts center. At the heart of its downtown is High Street, a revitalized stretch where you'll find the work of local and internationally renowned glass artists available for sale in many of the brick and painted three-story structures, alongside sketches, sculptures, and jewelry. Yoga studios have set up shop next to organic cafés and a gorgeous old vaudeville theater stands in hopes of restoration (www.levoy.org). In Millville, even the candy is considered art.

Despite its downtown renaissance, the areas of Millville surrounding the arts district are still in need of recovery, and it's best to stick to the city center or the attractions located nearby.

Glasstown Arts District

In efforts to revamp a dilapidated downtown district and a floundering economy, Millville created the **Glasstown Arts District** in 2001 as a way of attracting artists and new business to the area. The work has paid off, and now what had been a long expanse of half-empty storefronts along High Street from Main to Broad Streets is filled with galleries, gift shops, artists' studios, and educational facilities, including a **Clay College** (106 N. High St., 856/765-0988) and the **Riverfront Center for the Arts** (856/327-4500), a regional hub hosting exhibits, lectures, and classes, and offering studio time to artists.

The idea to turn Millville into an arts community wasn't far-fetched. The glass industry has been rooted in the city for over two centuries, and **The Barn Studio of Art** (814 Whitaker Ave., 856/825-5025), an "anything goes" fine arts center run by well-loved resident "wet-lands" painter Pat Witt, has been a part of Millville's infrastructure for over 40 years.

There's plenty of parking available in the arts district, both in lots and on the nearby streets.

Air Force History

The **Millville Army Air Field Museum** (Bldg. 1, Millville Municipal Airport, 856/327-2347, www.p47millville.org) is dedicated to the history of local and national aviation. Located at the Millville Airport, known as "America's first defense airport" and operated as an army airfield for three years during World War II, it showcases a large collection of aviation memorabilia including uniforms and photographs, and offers tours focusing on Millville's role in aviation history, often led by WWII veterans. Each May the airport plays host to the **Millville Wings and Wheels Show,** a two-day festival with performance planes, fighter demonstrations, and a classic car display.

To reach the airport, take Route 49 west from Millville's downtown center and turn left onto Dividing Creek Road (County Road 555). The airport's access road is approximately three miles from the turn.

On the side of City Hall at the corner of High and Main Streets in downtown Millville is the **Wall of Remembrance,** a mural dedicated to Millville's 14 fallen WWII pilots.

Recreation

Millville is a riverfront community, and just west of High and Broad Streets down a small hill you'll find the **Millville Riverwalk,** a 700-foot walkway along the water that leads to a public boat ramp and the **Millville Marina.** To the north is **Union Lake,** New Jersey's largest manmade lake and a good spot for swimming and boating.

Events

One of the city's most popular events is **Third Fridays** (800/887-4957, www.3rdfriday.org), when the arts district's galleries, shops, and restaurants extend regular hours, and artist residences open their doors to the public. A variety of live music entertains crowds who stroll the streets sampling free wine and hors d'oeuvres. The event takes place in the evening of the third Friday of every month, with most businesses staying open until 9 P.M.

Food and Entertainment

Millville has the best selection of eateries in Cumberland County and a number of much-loved restaurants.

Locals rave about the sushi at **Peking Tokyo** (101 E. Main St., 856/765-1818, $7–14), a restaurant serving both Chinese and Japanese cuisine. Hours are 11 A.M.–10:30 P.M. Monday–Thursday, until 11 P.M. Friday and Saturday, and noon–10 P.M. Sunday. Next door is **Jim's Lunch** (105 E. Main St., 856/327-1299, 7 A.M.–7 P.M. Mon.–Sat.), a simple steak-and-eggs sort of place with counter service and orange booths that's been serving the neighborhood for nearly a century. Jim's closes during summer months and is packed the remainder of the year.

Head to **The Looking Glass** (16 N. High St., 856/327-1666, $5–9) for a coffee and a seat on one of the comfy couches in back, or some tasty California cuisine at a window side table. It's hard to feel out of place at this BYO. Hours are 8 A.M.–3 P.M. Monday, Tuesday, and Saturday, and until 8 P.M. Wednesday–Friday, closed Sunday.

For fine dining try **Winfield's Restaurant** (106 N. High St., 856/327-0909, www.winfields restaurant.com, $13.50–26.95), serving continental cuisine in a chic decor. Winfield's is open for lunch 11:30 A.M.–3:30 P.M. Monday–Friday, and dinner 5–10 P.M. Monday–Saturday.

For a night out try the **Old Oar House Brewery** (123 N. High St., 856/293-1200, www .oldoarhousebrewery.com, 11 A.M.–1 A.M.

Mon.–Sat., $3.95–10.95), an upscale, Irish-style pub serving tasty appetizers, sandwiches, and a full dinner menu. There's live music on the weekends and an outdoor garden to enjoy during summer months. Cigar smoking is welcome.

A great place to satisfy your sweet tooth is **Edible Art and Sweet Shoppe** (135 N. High St., 856/825-2882). With its black and white checkered floor and tall stools, you'll feel like you're in a 1920s candy store.

East of the city center along Route 49 is **Ike's Famous Crabcakes** (888/302-CRAB or 888/302-2722, www.ikescrabcakes.com), a seafaring eatery featuring better-than-average homemade crab and lobster cakes.

◖ WHEATON VILLAGE

Built in 1968, Wheaton Village (1501 Glasstown Rd., 800/998-4552, www.wheatonvillage.org) is a remarkable glass and craft village located two miles northeast of Millville's Glasstown Arts District. With spacious street-style walkways leading to shops, museums, and demonstrations devoted to South Jersey's varied craft history, there's plenty to see and do here.

Sights

Wheaton Village's **Glass Studio** is a working re-creation of Millville's 1888 T. C. Wheaton Glass Factory. Here you can sit front row and center as resident artists gather glass from the massive furnace, working together to create exquisite glass sculptures, goblets, and vases. Want to get involved? Visitors have the opportunity to make their own paperweight with the aid of an instructor (advance booking is required: 856/825-6800, ext. 2744).

At the village center the **Museum of American Glass** offers insight into the history of American glass, from the 18th century through Tiffany, Carnival, and the Studio Glass Art Movement. I recommend one of the docent-led tours offered throughout the day.

Established in 1994, the **Down-Jersey Folklife Center** celebrates South Jersey's somewhat covert cultural diversity with changing exhibits that highlight the arts, crafts, and lifestyles of the state's eight southernmost counties. The center hosts occasional dance and music demonstrations and has a large audio and visual archive focused on South Jersey traditions.

Wheaton Village also features an old-time **General Store** with a penny-candy counter, wheel-throwing and flame-working displays, a playground, and a miniature train ride (additional cost).

Glass Weekend

One of the best times to visit Wheaton Village is during the bi-annual **Glass Weekend** held in July during odd years. World famous glass artists are on hand to demonstrate their crafts, and some of the world's most celebrated glass artwork is on display. Though it can get crowded, for those who appreciate glass this is an event not to be missed. Exhibits at the village rotate throughout the year, and there are a couple of shops that sell books, jewelry, souvenirs, and the work of resident artists.

Accommodations

$50-100: Adjacent to Wheaton Village is the pleasant **Country Inn by Carlson** (1125 Village Dr., Millville, 856/825-3100). This quiet, country-style two-story hotel (no elevator) has a front porch and a lending library, and a family-style restaurant and lounge next door.

Information

Wheaton Village is open 10 A.M.–5 P.M. Friday–Sunday in January, February, and March, and 10 A.M.–5 P.M. Tuesday–Sunday April–December. The village is also open Memorial Day, Labor Day, and Columbus Day, and its stores are open daily Thanksgiving–Christmas. Admission is $10 adults, $7 students for access to the museum, glass studio, folklife center, and daily demonstrations, though there is no charge to walk about the grounds and browse the shops. The village is closed most major holidays.

VINELAND

Charles K. Landis founded Vineland as a planned agricultural settlement in 1861, and today it is a mix of urban and country-suburban sprawl.

Landis Avenue is the city's main thoroughfare, a wide road lined by nondescript storefronts that give way to Southern-style homes, though most of the area's retail shopping takes place at the nearby **Cumberland Mall** (3849 S. Delsea Dr., 856/825-9507). Over the years Vineland has gone through numerous incarnations: Named for the vines once plentiful in the area, which were the beginnings for Welch's grape juice, the city later became known as a leading producer of poultry and was often referred to as the "egg basket of America." These days Vineland is reputed as the "Dandelion Capital" and hosts an annual April dinner (856/691-7400) featuring the plant as a main culinary ingredient. The city continues as an agricultural center and is residence to the Vineland Produce Auction (1088 N. Main Rd., 856/691-0721, www.vinelandproduce.com, 10 A.M. Mon.–Sat., Apr.–Nov.), a co-op with hundreds of members that sells to area farmers, including **Arbittier Farms** (344 N. Main Rd., 856/697-3200).

Since its beginnings Vineland has been a mainstay of cultural diversity, reflected in the area's shops, markets, and restaurants, and remains home to large Italian and Hispanic populations, hosting events that celebrate the heritage of these and other communities each year.

Recreation

In the state where the drive-in theater was invented, the **Delsea Drive In** (2203 S. Delsea Dr., 856/696-0011) is now New Jersey's one and only, reopening in 2004 after 13 years and sporting a 120- by 85-foot screen showing double features and a concession stand stocked with nutrition bars and peanut butter and jelly sandwiches in addition to popcorn and candy. The theater is closed on Mondays and Tuesdays and tickets are $6 adults, $3 children under 12.

One of the best golf centers around is the **Lincoln Falls Golf Learning & Family Fun Center** (1987 S. Lincoln Ave., 856/696-PLAY or 856/696-7529, www.lincolnfalls.com), home to a 19-hole mini-golf course, driving range, pro shop, and on-site golf clinic. An indoor snack and ice cream shop keep energy levels up, and for rainy days there's a small arcade. The center stays open throughout the year.

Entertainment
The annual **Jersey Fresh Festival** takes place at the city's **Giampietro Park** (Lincoln and Landis Aves., 856/794-4077) the first Sunday in August, and features music, crafts, and plenty of Jersey produce.

Accommodations
Though there are numerous hotels in the area, only a couple are worthy of an overnight stay.

$50-100 The **Wingate Inn** (2196 W. Landis Ave., 856/690-9900) is one of Vineland's newest hotels, and the best of the bunch. It's conveniently located between exits 32A and 32B off of Route 55. Next door, the **Ramada Inn** (2216 W. Landis Ave., 856/696-2371) is a decent place with its own lounge, restaurant, and coffee shop.

BELLEPLAIN STATE FOREST
Filled with oak trees, pitch pine, and Atlantic white cedar, Belleplain State Forest (Rte. 550, Woodbine, 609/861-2404) is over 20,000 acres located on the southern outskirts of the Pinelands, occupying a portion of both Cape May and Cumberland Counties. Tall trees line the roadway into the forest, where you'll find a visitors center, trailheads, and vehicle pathways leading toward Belleplain's numerous recreational features, including two lakes, hundreds of campsites, a wildlife-viewing area, and over 40 miles of marked and unmarked trails. Fishing, hunting, trapping,

mountain biking, horseback riding, and winter sports such as snowmobiling, cross-country skiing, and ice-fishing are all enjoyed here, and swimming and boat rentals are available in the summer. Belleplain is popular with scout troops, company picnics, and those looking for a natural escape close to the shore and the Philadelphia metropolitan region. The forest is free to enter during the off-season and $5 weekdays, $10 weekends Memorial Day–Labor Day.

Recreation
Belleplain has a ton of hiking paths and multiuse trails, but the **East Creek Trail** is a favorite. At an average speed this easy seven-mile loop takes a few hours to complete, and surrounds East Creek Pond, the forest's largest body of water. Ticks can be a problem, so dress accordingly. The trail begins on Champion Road next to Lake Nummy.

Lake Nummy, a former cranberry bog, features a seasonal swimming area with lifeguards, a concession stand, and canoe rentals. The lake is surrounded by campsites, and is definitely one of Belleplain's highlights.

A boat ramp is also situated on the western shore of East Creek Pond.

Camping
There are nearly 200 campsites ($15/night, March–Nov.) at Belleplain, including l4 lean-tos ($25/night, year-round) and five yurts ($25/night)—domed, lockable structures—for rent, all with picnic table and close to restrooms with shower. A group cabin accommodating 30 people ($150/night) is also available.

BACKGROUND

The Land

Situated about midway along the United States' Eastern Seaboard below New York State, east of Pennsylvania, and north of Delaware sits New Jersey, a peninsula-like landmass with a larger-than-life reputation and a geographic make-up that varies both physically and culturally. In the north you'll find mountainous terrain, hard rock, and valleys, all formed by glaciers thousands of years before, while in the south you'll see mostly flat land that never rises more than a few hundred feet above sea level— a fertile landscape radiating south and east to become sandy and barren soil. New Jersey is heavily urban but also exceedingly natural, with unique flora and fauna, abundant sealife and birds, and a higher density of black bear than you would expect.

GEOGRAPHY

At 7,417 square land miles, New Jersey is the United States' fourth-smallest state. Although the state is best known for its intricate system of highways and a heavily industrialized northeastern section, only one-third of New Jersey is developed land, and the rest is filled with salt marshes, protected estuaries, swamps, undisturbed forests, mountain and river valleys, white sand beaches, and fruitful agriculture land. The state itself is separated into four main land regions: the Appalachian Ridge and

Valley Region, the Highlands, the Piedmont, and the Atlantic Coastal Plain.

Ridge and Valley

Nestled in the state's northwestern corner, this region is part of the large Appalachian range and covers only about eight percent of New Jersey's landmass. Mountains—most notably the Kittatinny Mountain Ridge—slope down into low-lying valleys, the largest being the Kittatinny Valley. New Jersey's highest point, the aptly named High Point (1,803 feet), is in this region. Along the western edge, the Delaware River carves a route between New Jersey and Pennsylvania.

Highlands

The Highlands region surrounds the Ridge and Valley to its east and south and is part of the larger Reading Prong, an extension of the Blue Ridge Mountains that stretches from New England to Pennsylvania. This is where you'll find most of New Jersey's glacier-formed lakes, as well as flat-top rock ridges, crystal formations, and the remnants of old mining towns. Although the area was heavily deforested to provide fuel for the prospering mining industry, much of the woodlands have since grown back.

The Highlands stretch from the mountainous New York border—where the Ramapo Mountains stand along the region's eastern edge, spreading west into the Vernon Valley—and south into the central lake region, continuing west to encompass Warren County. The average elevation here is about 1,000 feet above sea level, and the area provides water for about 15 percent of the Northeast Corridor.

Piedmont

The Piedmont, or "foothill," is considered the lowlands of the state's Appalachian region, which makes up 40 percent of New Jersey's landmass and its entire northern portion. Stretching southwest from the New York state line through the urban northeast toward Trenton, the Piedmont is also known as the Newark Basin, and a system of faults line the region's western edge. The Raritan, Passaic, and Hackensack Rivers run through the area, emptying along the state's eastern coast.

Atlantic Coastal Plain

New Jersey's final land region, known collectively as the Atlantic Coastal Plain, makes up a whopping 60 percent of the state's landmass. It expands south from Central Jersey to encompass all of South Jersey, the Pinelands, and the Jersey Shore. The land here is flat, with low-lying hills, and more than half of the region stands less than 100 feet above sea level. Barrier islands line much of the eastern coastline and are separated from the mainland by wetlands, back bays, and canals.

The Atlantic Coastal Plain can be separated into two sections: the Outer and Inner Coastal Plains. In the Outer Coastal Plains, barren sands give way to reeds and marshlands. This section is highly developed with a couple of pristine wildlife habitats and relatively untouched lands, including Sandy Hook, Island Beach State Park, and both E. B. Forsythe Wildlife Refuges. The Inner Coastal Plains offer some of the state's most fertile farming soil.

Geology

Three glaciers have entered New Jersey territory over the past two million years, and North Jersey has been shaped by these glaciers. Limestone remains are found in Sussex, Passaic, Hudson, Essex, Somerset, Hunterdon, and Mercer Counties; ancient glacial deposits mark Jenny Jump State Forest's terrain; and natural lakes fill the landscape.

Metals ores are plentiful within the state, and the Highlands contain minerals found nowhere else in the world, as well as iron, zinc, and marble. Copper is abundant in the spread of land north of Trenton. The silica sand ideal for glassmaking is reaped in South and Central Jersey, and Cape May Diamonds—a unique type of quartz pebble—are isolated to Sunset Beach along New Jersey's southern coast.

Bodies of Water

Water plays a leading role in New Jersey's geographic and cultural make-up, from the surrounding ocean and bays to the inland rivers, lakes, and wetlands. The Raritan (1,105 square miles), Passaic (949 square miles), and Maurice (570 square miles) Rivers are the state's three largest, and others include the Delaware, Hudson, Mullica, Maurice, and Musconetcong. Lake Hopatcong is New Jersey's largest natural lake; notable man-made lakes include South Jersey's Union Lake in Millville, and Sparta's Lake Mohawk, in the Skylands.

New Jersey has abundant wetlands that play an essential role in the state's ecosystem. They prevent soil erosion and floods, improve water quality, and provide important habitat for migratory birds, fish, and other wildlife. Atlantic, Ocean, and Cape May Counties host the state's highest concentration of wetlands, and the most noteworthy wetland areas to visit include the E. B. Forsythe National Wildlife Refuge Brigantine Division, the Meadowlands, and the Great Swamp of Morris County.

Lying along the Atlantic coastline from Boston, Massachusetts, south to Key West, Florida, the Intracoastal Waterway is a series of bays and inlets that provide a protective passageway for fishing and leisure boats. New Jersey's portion of this throughway flows between its barrier islands and the mainland, extending from Manasquan Inlet south along Barnegat Peninsula and onto Cape May and the Delaware Bay.

CLIMATE

New Jersey enjoys a temperate climate and is a relatively easy state to negotiate during all seasons. The state has four distinct seasons, with temperatures ranging from the high 90s in the summer to below freezing in the winter, with January being the coldest month and August the warmest. Fall and spring offer moderate weather. The northwestern Highlands tend to see colder temperatures and the heaviest precipitation, while the Jersey Shore gets the least amount of snowfall and has the state's most judicious climate. Rain is common throughout the year, turning to snow in the colder months and often accompanied by thunder and lightning in the

summer, when humidity levels are high. The state's average rainfall is 45 inches.

Hurricanes are possible in New Jersey, although most weaken before making it to land. The Shore regions have been evacuated numerous times over the last 20 years, and a heavy storm can do thousands of dollars in damage to the coastline. Hurricanes occur June–November, Nor'easters—counter-clockwise storms that can result in blizzard-like conditions—arrive September–April. In years past, severe weather conditions have caused serious flooding, most recently in Medford in July 2004 and in early April 2005 in Hunterdon County.

ENVIRONMENTAL ISSUES

As a main throughway and essential contributor to the Great Northeast Corridor, not to mention being a major pharmaceutical manufacturer and having an over-the-top population density, New Jersey—not surprisingly—has issues with pollution. For years its Meadowlands region—a marshy landmass that once seemed uninhabitable—served as a dumping ground for trash, toxic waste, and the occasional body, earning its nickname "The Armpit of America." Today New Jersey hosts over 100 Superfund sites, more than anywhere else in the country (for a complete list, go to www.epa.gov/superfund/sites). While efforts to restore some sites have met with great success—such as Pitman's Lipari Landfill—others continue to have problems, most notably a section of Ringwood that, despite earlier cleanup efforts, remains contaminated with paint sludge left behind by Ford Motor Company.

Mercury within New Jersey's northeast corner's rivers and streams has also been a major concern over the last couple of decades. This toxic chemical is the offshoot of industrial smokestacks located in the area, and it threatens the region's fish supply and those who eat them. Contamination also occurs throughout state from the leachate runoff of landfills, farms, and waste sites that seep into water supplies.

New Jersey's Atlantic coastline has its fair share of environmental concerns. In 1988 a number of the state's beaches were indefinitely closed when hypodermic needles dumped in the sea began washing up along their shores. Measures have since been taken to prevent future such incidents. Beach erosion is another serious issue. Storms cause many of the state's beaches to reduce in size and their sands to relocate out to sea or to towns farther south. The Army Corps of Engineers is constantly pumping the shore with sand and creating dunes to act as barriers between ocean waters and beachfront homes.

Sprawl is prevalent throughout New Jersey. Shopping centers are abandoned and homes and mega-stores are built faster than occupants are found. South Jersey is currently receiving the brunt of new development, and new construction is swallowing many of the region's remaining farmlands.

The Pinelands and the Highlands

John McPhee's 1973 book *The Pine Barrens* changed the way many people looked at New Jersey, including Brendan T. Byrne, the state's then-governor (1974–1982), who enacted legislation to designate over one million acres in the central and southern stretches of New Jersey as "America's first National Reserve." Today the New Jersey Pinelands Commission cares for this region, which remains relatively unchanged, although outlying areas have suffered because of the preservation effort. Pinelands' legislation states that development must be "highly regulated" in the reserve's central region and, to a lesser extent, in the outlying Protection Area (the perimeter). This means that any new construction—and taxes—are relocated to the boroughs, towns, and cities surrounding the Pinelands.

A similar situation is occurring in the Highlands, a section of New Jersey's Skylands that supplies water to a large percentage of the Northeast Corridor. In efforts to preserve this area's delicate ecosystem, the government introduced the Highlands Water Protection and Planning Act in 2004, a law shielding much of the Highlands region from future development. Unfortunately, this preservation effort interferes with local building rights and zoning laws, and those living on the Highlands' outskirts fear they'll be faced with an onslaught of construction and an increase in taxes.

Flora and Fauna

New Jersey boasts more than 2,600 species of plants, both introduced and native. Forests cover about 40 percent of the state, and flowers are abundant, with 50 species of orchids, 30 species of violet, and the swamp pink (an endangered perennial wildflower native to the Pinelands) living in New Jersey. The state tree is the red oak and the state flower the purple violet.

New Jersey is also an ideal habitat for supporting a varied array of fauna, including 325 bird species, 90 mammal species, 79 reptile and amphibian species, and over 400 fish species. The state hosts a number of rare and endangered species such as the blue-spotted salamander, piping plover, and the Pine Barrens tree frog.

TREES AND SHRUBS

On average, the state's forests are dominated by oak trees, but in the Skylands, where the soil is wetter and more nutrient rich, sugar maple, white ash, and black birch are also prominent. The ridges and the Pinelands feature pitch pine and scrub oak. Pygmy pines, dwarf pine trees topping off at 4–6 feet tall, are something you'll see elsewhere, but they're a major attraction of the Pinelands.

Wetland forests vary throughout the state but include red maple and Atlantic white cedar. Lowland blueberry, black huckleberry, and mountain laurel grow alongside tree growth stands throughout the state. Sandy Hook, at the northern tip of the Jersey Shore,

flora of the Delaware Bayshore

has the largest American holly forest on the East Coast.

FERNS AND GRASSES

New Jersey has over 70 types of grasses, including beach grass, used to ward off storms, and the considerably invasive phragmites, tall reed grass once used by Native Americans for thatching and seeds for flour, prominent in the Meadowlands and along the coast in areas like Cape May and Sea Isle. The state has used restoration ecology to ward off phragmites' aggressive growth while replenishing the land, stopping erosion, restoring groundwater, and providing wildlife habitat.

Pinelands grasses include switchgrass, Indian grass, wild rice, sweet vernal grass (a scented grass), and Pine Barrens reed-grass. One way to recognize sites where communities once existed in the Pinelands is to identify ebony spleenwort, a green, semi-glossy fern with a dark brown stem that is not native to Pineland soil. It is plentiful, but only found where lime was once used to build structures.

SALT MARSHES AND LIMESTONE SINKS

New Jersey has 245,000 acres of salt marshes, and salt hay is harvested as cattle feed, packing material, and insulation. In the Kittatinny Mountain region of the Skylands are limestone sinks, formed when the acidic groundwater eats at the ground and creates cavities into which the topsoil collapses. These sinkholes often contain ponds that dot the landscape and whose water levels fluctuate according to season, creating a hotbed for unique vegetation.

MAMMALS

New Jersey houses a surprising mix of mammals, many that you wouldn't expect in a place with such an urban reputation. Part of the reason is that the state lies at both the southern and northern borders of wildlife terrain, but also because the state's varied landscape and large swaths of connected land give these mammals plenty of roaming room. Many of the state's mammal populations are increasing, such as those of beaver, eastern coyote, and black bear (the last causing the first bear hunt in 33 years to be reinstated, amid massive protest, in 2003).

The waters off the New Jersey coast host a large array of seals, dolphins, and whales, and notable species include the harbor seal, beluga whale, Atlantic killer whale, and the endangered blue and humpback whales. Smaller mammals plentiful within the state include hairy-tailed moles; gray, red, and flying squirrels; striped skunk; and the southern bog lemming.

While not native to New Jersey, eastern coyotes were introduced to the state in the early 1900s and today number about 3,000. They're found in every one of New Jersey's 21 counties, their howls known to keep campers in Cape May Point up at night, and their scraggly figures "haunting" graveyards in Gloucester County.

New Jersey is home to over 1,000 black bear, with numbers currently increasing. Once prominent throughout the state, Europeans reduced the population to the state's upper northwest, though in recent years they've made their way east into the Urban Outskirts, and as far south as Cumberland and Cape May Counties. Black bear are known to inhabit forested regions, but are found in the suburbs foraging inside improperly sealed garbage cans or disturbing camping resorts where food has not been suitably contained.

Bobcats are rare in New Jersey but have been spotted, increasingly so over the past few years.

New Jersey has about 200,000 white-tailed deer, many of which can be viewed in backyards, in natural areas such as state and county parks, and scampering along roadsides, especially around dusk. Their numbers are decreasing, partially because of the large number of traffic accidents in which they are involved. Extreme caution is required while driving, especially in the Skylands region, where you're sure to spot a recent casualty every few miles.

There are nine species of bats in New Jersey, including six that are year-round residents. They reside in attics, barns, under bridges, and in deep, dark caves found within the Skylands.

MARINELIFE

Lined on three sides by water, there's no doubt that New Jersey has some interesting sealife. The state fish is the brook trout. Oysters and shellfish were once prominent in the Delaware Bayshore (as well as the Raritan Bay), but disease and overharvesting have wiped out much of the population. Shad—long-disappeared from a polluted Delaware—have returned to swim upstream every April. Trout is plentiful in the state's lakes, streams, and rivers, both stocked and natural, and New Jersey is a great place for freshwater and saltwater species. You'll often spot dolphin off the coast, as well as whales and the occasional shark. Seal, porpoises, sea turtles, and seaweed are all prominent in the waters off the coast. July and August are jellyfish season, and beaches are sometimes closed because of them.

Blue crabs are delicacies prominent in the Atlantic waters, and can be found in both the ocean and the bays. They must molt in order to grow, and become highly prized soft-shell crabs in the day or two it takes to do so. Horseshoe crabs are hard-shelled invertebrates, and sometimes called the "king crab," they feature long tail spines and oversized black shells that resemble suits of armor. One of the earth's largest horseshoe crab populations can be found along the Delaware Bayshore. In May and June, thousands of horseshoe crabs make their way onto the beaches to lay eggs.

New Jersey waters have three clam species. Hard shell clams, including littleneck, chowder, cherrystone, and top-neck, exist in the bays and are harvested in small amounts with hand utensils. Surf clams and ocean quahogs are native to the Atlantic Ocean and are dredged from the ocean floor to be used in cuisine.

BIRDS

A major stop along the Atlantic Flyway, New Jersey offers some of the best bird-watching in the country. The number of species that nest, breed, or migrate through the state stretches well into the hundreds, and along with sealife, accounts for the bulk of the state's fauna. The state bird is the eastern goldfinch, a tiny songbird

© LAURA KINIRY

waddling geese along the Delaware River

that transforms from a dull-brown color into a yellow-coated, black-wing beauty during summer. Songbirds, shorebirds, and raptors all make their home here or migrate through the state, and New Jersey's bird population includes sparrows, cardinals, mourning doves, seagulls, warblers, and turkey vultures.

Canada goose, once only a migratory species within the state, is now a year-round resident. They're identifiable by a long, black neck and a distinctive squawk, and tend to wreak havoc in county parks, soiling grass and chasing away anyone who comes within a short distance.

Raptors

A raptor is a predatory bird with keen eyesight, sharp talons, and a hooked beak. Species seen within New Jersey include red-tailed hawks, which are the state's most commonly sighted year-round raptor, osprey, peregrine falcons, American kestrels (falcons), bald and golden eagles, merlin, and broad-winged and sharp-shinned hawks. The state's annual hawk migration takes place from northwest New Jersey and carries downward to Cape May and the Delaware Bayshore during fall.

Peregrine falcons are listed on the state's endangered list, and nest on tall cliffs, as well as artificially constructed platforms like buildings and bridges. These attractive birds may be gray, slate blue, or white with yellow features, and they eat small birds.

Shorebirds

Three gull species—herring, laughing, and black-backed—are found in New Jersey along the shore, around inland water bodies, and dining on heaps of trash. Along the state's shoreline, these birds have gotten a rep for being aggressive, often swarming innocent boardwalkers or helping themselves to entrées already being enjoyed at an outdoor table. Before 1900, laughing gulls were the only gull species prevalent in the state.

Shorebirds are a common sight along the Atlantic coast, and at least 20 species migrate through New Jersey regularly in the spring and fall. Five species breed along the coasts, including the piping plover. One of the shorebirds' primary stops on the way toward arctic breeding grounds is Cape May and the Delaware Bay for three weeks in May to feast on the eggs of horseshoe crabs. Spotted sandpipers nest near ponds, and killdeers—ring-necked plovers—in short-grass fields, as well as in front lawns and driveways. The piping plover, pale brown with a white underbelly and black features, is a federally endangered species that nests along the shore and within the Pinelands.

Herons and Egrets

The best place for spotting herons and egrets is along the coast's marshlands and estuaries and the Delaware Bayshore. These birds fly south for the winter and return around April, nesting in colonies that are often large and noisy. The most eye-catching is the great blue heron, which exists inland in New Jersey as well as along the coast, though other species found in-state include the snowy egret, great egret, and glossy ibis. Herons and egrets eat fish, as well as small delicacies such as frogs, mice, and eggs.

© LAURA KINIRY

an egret hanging out at E. B. Forsythe National Wildlife Refuge, Brigantine Division

REPTILES

New Jersey's reptiles consist almost entirely of turtles and snakes, with a few lizard species, including the northern fence lizard and the ground skink. Most of the snakes are non-poisonous, though northern copperheads (in the Skylands) and timber rattlesnakes (in South Jersey, the Pinelands, and the Skylands) are New Jersey's two venomous species. Loss of habitat and illegal killing has endangered the state's population of timber rattlesnake, and numbers are dwindling.

New Jersey has 15 native turtle species, including the common snapping turtle, stinkpot, eastern mud turtle, and the bog turtle. Endangered species include the Atlantic loggerhead and the Atlantic leatherback. The endangered northern diamondback terrapin is the only marine turtle species to favor both saltwater and freshwater environments. Unfortunately, female diamondbacks crawling ashore from marshland habitat to bury their eggs (late May–July) are often killed while crossing the busy coastal roads.

INSECTS

With all of the state's marshlands, woodlands, and orchards, it's easy to see why insects are alive and well in New Jersey. In years past the state earned the nickname "The Mosquito State," as its namesake insect infested much of the land, including the coastal inlets and estuaries, the Gateway's Meadowlands, and the Great Swamp of Morris County. Thankfully, air-conditioned automobiles, bug spray, and various other technologies have helped ease the pain, although mosquitoes are still very much at home in the Garden State. The green-headed fly, nasty little biting creatures with bulbous transparently green heads, also breed in wetlands and prosper during July and August. New Jersey also hosts the infamous deer tick, known for spreading Lyme disease along the East Coast like it was 1999. With these three species, you've got yourself one wild feeding frenzy.

That's not to say all of New Jersey's insects are vile. In fact there are more than 100 butterfly species common to the state, found especially throughout the Pinelands and Cape May County during warmer months. Monarch butterflies make their way through the state in fall, on their way south to Mexico, and are easily spotted in the Cape May region.

While not native to the state, the honeybee is New Jersey's state insect. One of the state's most prolific insect species only appears during summer months: The firefly, also known as a "lightning bug," is a beetle that flashes a yellow light on and off through the nighttime sky.

AMPHIBIANS

New Jersey hosts 32 species of amphibians, 16 of which are salamanders, including the endangered blue-spotted salamander. The mountain dusky and the northern red salamander are only found in the state's northern counties. Frogs and toads exist throughout the state, notably within the Pinelands, which is home to the endangered Pine Barrens tree frog, a tiny plum and green species with bright yellow on its underside and suction cups on its toes. It's found around the Pinelands acidic water, preferring fish-free waters and bogs, and it makes a very distinct calling sound, often heard throughout the summer and consisting of a series of rapid nasal honks.

History

EARLY HISTORY

The area that became New Jersey was originally home to the Lenni-Lenape Indians, also called Delaware Indians. Many roads later built by European settlers were based on paths traversed by these native inhabitants, who often traveled throughout the region hunting, foraging, and even making excursions to the coastal shore.

The Dutch were the first Europeans to arrive in present-day New Jersey, establishing a trading post in 1618 in what is now Bergen County as part of the larger New Netherland settlement, encompassing the nearby island of Manhattan. In 1638 Swedes and Finns founded the state's first settlement along the banks of the Delaware Bay. Together with waterfront portions of Delaware and Pennsylvania, it was known as New Sweden, created to aid in the trading of tobacco and furs. In 1654 the Dutch, under rule of the Peter Stuyvesant, easily overtook New Jersey's southern half and incorporated it into New Netherland, holding together for 10 years before the British claimed the entire region as their own.

Under the British, the land that would become New Jersey was separated into two colonies and was known as East and West Jersey by 1676, named after the British Isle of Jersey. The two provinces were joined under a royal governor in 1703, and the colony of New Jersey shared its governor with New York for the next 35 years.

REVOLUTIONARY YEARS

With no large cities brimming with revolutionary fervor like Boston and Philadelphia, New Jersey was not a key player in the fight for independence from British rule (although South Jersey's Greenwich did host one of the 13 colonies' infamous tea-burning parties), and a large percentage of the population remained loyal to the crown. As the war grew closer, however, William Franklin, the colony's royal governor (and illegitimate son of Benjamin Franklin), grew increasingly remote and was finally arrested in June 1776, marking New Jersey's tentative acceptance of the Revolution.

While New Jersey did not play a large part in pre-revolution events, it made up the lack once the war began. Its central location between New York and Philadelphia guaranteed its place as a major crossroads for both British and American soldiers during the early battle years, and

© LAURA KINIRY

Aaron Burr gravesite, Princeton Cemetery

early hours, General Washington and an army of 2,400 crossed the Delaware River north of Trenton and arrived at present-day Washington Crossing State Park, in Titusville, before turning south toward Trenton. They separated into two groups and attacked a Hessian brigade at Trenton at 8 A.M. The Americans won this battle with only a few injuries and no casualties.

Washington and his men retreated back to Pennsylvania, but finding Trenton deserted, returned to New Jersey later that week. In the interim, General Cornwallis and his army were drawn from nearby Princeton and on January 2, 1777, the Second Battle of Trenton ensued. Later that evening Washington and his men escaped over back roads and continued on to Princeton, where under the leadership of General Hugh Mercer, they fought British troops at a local orchard. Mercer was killed, but Washington rallied the troops to continue on and defeat the British. Collectively known as the Ten Crucial Days, this became the turning point of the war. Bruised and battered, the British retreated through the state, leaving New Jersey almost entirely by the year's end.

Other Revolutionary Events

The British later tried to return to New Jersey through Philly, leading to the Battle of Fort Mercer in present-day Gloucester County (Red Bank Battlefield park now occupies this site). This attempt was unsuccessful, but British troops did eventually make their way back into the colony by the southern route. General Washington and his army followed closely behind and engaged them at the Battle of Monmouth, the longest battle of the American Revolution. The outcome was non-decisive, but the battle was the last major battle of the northern colonies. One last assault on New Jersey would take place in June 1780 at the site of Elizabeth (south of Newark) today. Americans resisted a take-over by British and Hessian troops but fire was set to nearby towns.

In addition to the major Revolutionary battles in New Jersey, many other areas of New Jersey played a part in the war. South Jersey

George Washington spent more time in New Jersey than in any other colony during the Revolution. Still, much of the population shied away from involvement. Many Quakers, who occupied much of New Jersey's western side, opposed the war and remained pacifist, while the New Jersey militia proved less than adequate.

On November 20, 1776, the British attacked New Jersey. As General Howe and his troops captured Fort Lee along the Hudson River, General Cornwallis and a British army of 6,000 scaled the Palisades cliffs and headed west, sending Washington and his men on a retreat across the colony and into Pennsylvania, where they spent a long and discouraging month at Valley Forge. The morale of the Continental Army had reached an all-time low, and in New Jersey, fearful rebels signed oath to the crown under the watchful eyes of British soldiers. The fight for the cause was looking defeated.

Ten Crucial Days

Things began to change on the morning of December 26, 1776, on New Jersey land. In the

© LAURA KINIRY

Burlington County Prison Museum, Mount Holly

saw a number of skirmishes, and Salem County's Hancock House was the site of a massacre of supposed rebels by British soldiers. Bergen County, in New Jersey's upper northeast corner, saw plenty of bloodshed, as fights between Tories and loyalists ensued. Washington is known to have stayed overnight in present-day Lambertville and Somerville, among numerous other towns, and spent two long winters in Morristown—one of them at the Ford Mansion.

The war ended in 1783, and New Jersey entered into statehood on December 18, 1787, America's third state. On November 20, 1789, it was the first state to ratify the Bill of Rights.

NEW JERSEY'S INDUSTRIAL REVOLUTION

With its strategic position along the Northeast Corridor and a large number of immigrants looking for employment, New Jersey couldn't help but become a significant contributor to the nation's Industrial Revolution. In the 18th century, southern areas, like Gloucester and Cumberland Counties, were alive with glass factories prospering from the region's sandy silica terrain and heavily wooded areas that provided fuel for furnaces. During the same period iron was mined throughout the state, and it was a Newark inventor, Seth Boyden, who changed the world's iron industry by developing a way to produce malleable cast iron in 1826.

But the state's industrial revolution really has its roots in the 1791, when Alexander Hamilton established Paterson. He wanted to build a planned industrial town, and decided that the Great Falls of the Passaic was the place to do it. (Paterson later earned the nickname "Silk City" from the textile industry that grew up there.) Thereafter, New Jersey blossomed with a wealth of manufacturing, invention, and industry, and today New Jersey is one of the most industrialized states in the nation.

Newark in particular prospered as a manufacturing center. Breweries were big in the city through the 1800s and into the 20th century and were the city's fourth-largest industry by the time of Prohibition. Leather was another of the city's major manufactured items. Tanneries were plentiful and patent leather was a Newark specialty, invented by Seth Boyden in 1818. Outside the manufacturing sector, insurance providers, most notably Prudential, made Newark their home as well.

Trenton, with its prime location along the Delaware River, also flourished. It was a significant contributor to the rubber industry and was also the center of the state's ceramics industry, fueled by northeastern New Jersey's clay resources. Trenton was the nation's headquarters for Sanitary Ware in the late 1800s and early 1900s, manufacturing porcelain toilets, sinks, bathtubs, and kitchen appliances.

Canals

During the early half of the 19th century, canals were a main mode of industrial transport in New Jersey. Completed in 1834, the Delaware & Raritan Canal carried goods, mainly coal from Pennsylvania, from Bordentown along the Delaware River up to Trenton, turning east to New Brunswick where it would connect with the Raritan River. A feeder canal entered at Trenton down from the river town of Stockton. It mainly served as a cargo carrier, and in 1866 the canal is said to have carried more cargo than New York's Erie Canal ever carried in a year. After the 1890s, though, the canal faced increasing competition from railroad carriers, and the D&R finally closed for transport in 1932—but its expanse now makes up a popular state park.

Completed one year earlier, the Morris Canal carried goods from Phillipsburg to Newark across the northern part of the state. It was later expanded to reach Jersey City and the nearby Hudson River. The canal featured a 760-foot incline from the west and a 914-foot decline to the east, reaching a total elevation change of 1,674 feet—more than any other canal in the world. Like the D&R, the canal's main cargo was coal from Pennsylvania, and also like its neighbor to the south, the canal thrived during the 1860s and 1870s, but eventually succumbed to the success of the railroads by 1924. Today portions of the canal remain in the Skylands and Gateway Region. (In Newark, the subway rides through its portion of the former canal.)

CIVIL WAR YEARS

New Jersey gets mixed reviews on its Civil War efforts. Some claim it was sympathetic with the south, and the state was, in fact, slow to grant rights to blacks and slaves. By 1860, New Jersey still had nearly 20 slaves, making it the last northern state to abolish slavery. By the time of the Civil War, New Jersey was evenly divided down the middle. Still, when the Union Army needed people to fight, the state responded, and the Civil War ensued from 1861 to 1865.

After the war, black males were granted the right to vote in 1870 with the passing of the 15th Amendment, and Thomas Mundy Peterson of Perth Amboy became the country's first African American to cast a ballot under the new law.

The Underground Railroad

Whatever its legislature's stance on slavery, New Jersey played an important role on the eastern line of the Underground Railroad, which traveled up the Atlantic coast from as far south as Florida. Along this route slaves would enter New Jersey from the south through Delaware or east from Pennsylvania and travel north to New York. Stops can be traced to a number of New Jersey towns and cities, including Lawnside and Burlington, among many others.

New Jersey has claims to two famous Underground Railroad figures, Harriet Ross Tubman and William Sill. Tubman worked as a cook at numerous Cape May hotels during the period 1849–1852, and she used the money she earned to assist as a Railroad conductor. (She earned the nickname "Black Moses" for her part in helping more than 300 slaves to freedom.) William Sill, who grew up in New Jersey, moved to Philadelphia where he became the head of the General Vigilance Committee, an organization that aided runaway slaves.

THE GROWTH OF THE SHORE

While steamboats were responsible for the first development along the Jersey Shore in Cape May and Long Branch, it was the railroad that really spurred its growth. New Jersey's first train line, the Camden and Amboy Railroad, opened in the early 1830s, but it wasn't until after the Civil War that the state's railroads really began to take off, especially in bringing people to the shore.

Before the railroad, the shore region was thought to be inaccessible: It took a long, open carriage ride in the sweltering heat through swarms of mosquitoes and green flies to even get there. But with the train, people could go down the shore for the day and come home later that evening, in time for work the following day. The first train arrived in Atlantic City in 1851, sparking the birth of "America's Playground." Lines were built across South and Central Jersey and down the coast from New York City, turning an empty stretch of barren sand into New Jersey's most prolific tourist industry, full of hotel resorts and boardwalks. New towns were springing to being up and down the state's coastline and continued to do so until the turn of the 20th century. Trains prospered until after World War II, when competition from automobiles and bus lines led to consolidation to keep lines running.

THE EARLY 20TH CENTURY
Woodrow Wilson

The major movements and events of the early 20th century affected New Jersey in a myriad of ways, beginning with the Progressive Era (1890–1920), which grew as a reaction to the country's swift industrial growth. The state was singled out for being plagued by political corruption, corporate bullying, and violence resulting from labor movements seeking fair wages and work conditions. This all changed when Woodrow Wilson was elected New Jersey's governor. The former President of Princeton University (where he completely revised the curriculum to its current form) won the governorship with the support of Democratic bosses, but quickly abandoned them after his election and put forth progressive ideals—establishing a corrupt practices act, Public Utilities Commission, workers compensation, and laws to assist schools and labor. Although Wilson went into the governorship top-strong and failed to produce toward the end of his term,

he left the position with a substantial Progressive following that eventually scored him the U.S. presidency.

World War I

With the banning of all German products during World War I, including textiles that the United States so heavily relied on, New Jersey's industries were called on to produce. Salem County's DuPont became the country's number one dye maker, pharmaceutical companies began expanding their research, and blacks immigrated from the South to take advantage of the state's growing number of factory jobs. Women found employment with ships and railways, and numerous soldiers traveled overseas to fight after training in New Jersey. Through it all the state's cities were experiencing huge demographic changes, with the influx of immigrants and the persecution of the state's German population. Germans were blamed for an explosion at Black Tom in Jersey City, and businesses and towns dropped German names.

Prohibition and Women's Suffrage

The state was not much deterred by the country's decree of Prohibition. In fact, New Jersey was one of three states that refused to ratify the 18th Amendment. Both sides of the Hudson River earned a reputation for rum smuggling and speakeasies, and the mob took control of the region's liquor trade. (Prohibition was repealed in 1933 with the passage of the 21st Amendment.)

The state accorded voting rights to women—granted, unintentionally—before the rest of the nation granted them with the 20th Amendment in 1920. The state constitution, hastily written at the onset of the American Revolution, gave "adult residents worth 50 pounds" the right to vote, and women were known to cast ballots until the loophole was sealed in 1807. The battle for women's suffrage, however, continued on with Alice Paul, a Mount Laurel native, leading the National Woman's Party in a right for female suffrage at the federal level.

The Great Depression

The Great Stock Market Crash of October 29, 1929, sent the nation reeling in a downward spiral, and New Jersey was no exception. The state suffered severely, especially African Americans who moved to New Jersey from the South during World War I in search of employment. New Jersey would not bounce back until World War II.

WORLD WAR II

Like the First World War, the Second World War created heavy industrial demands on New Jersey. The NY Shipbuilding Yard provided more than 100 ships for the second war effort. Blacks poured into the state's cities in even greater numbers to take advantage of job opportunities, and they propelled Jersey legislation in terms of anti-discrimination laws.

German U-boats were positioned off the Jersey Coast during each of the wars, posing a threat to merchant ships, especially during 1942. Many American vessels sank, torn by torpedoes or accidentally crashing into another ship in an effort to avoid enemy fire by running a zigzag (and often miscalculated) course. U-boats were able to identify American vessels by the backlights that shone from the coast, illuminating them in the night sky, and until they were ordered to do so, towns refused to extinguish the lights for fear of losing tourists. The U.S. Navy eventually employed information obtained by the British, who'd captured a U-boat in 1940, to prevent future surprise attacks.

After World War II, GI Bills brought an influx of soldiers to study at Rutgers, leading to its designation as New Jersey's "state university," and home-loan provisions further altered the state's physical and cultural geographic makeup. Though suburbanization had been occurring since the railway, the shift from urban getaways like Lakewood to year-round homes located far from train routes was substantial.

CONTEMPORARY TIMES
The Automobile

Although trolley cars were responsible for the state's first suburbs, nothing changed the face of New Jersey like the automobile. With the popularity of cars, suburbia took on a whole new form, especially in this state that already served as a main transport route. The onslaught of the auto saw the end of expansive railway transport. With cars, people began moving farther from city centers and abandoned older suburbs (contributing to "white flight"), and this distance required a new dependency on the state's roads.

This led to the construction of bridges, tunnels, and interstate highway systems to further link the state to New York and Philadelphia, as well as to link the state's barrier islands to the mainland. Much of New Jersey's bridge building took place during the early–mid-20th century.

The New Jersey Turnpike, one of the busiest highways in the world, was proposed by state governor Alfred E. Driscoll in 1947. The first 118 miles of the now 148-mile turnpike were opened by 1952. This infamous toll-road (New Jersey's first) now stretches like nylon across the state from the Delaware Memorial Bridge up to New York, decorated with over two dozen exits, rest stops with names like "Vince Lombardi," "Clara Barton," and "Molly Pitcher" (all famous New Jerseyans at some point in their lives), and boasting anywhere from four to 12 lanes across.

The state's system of highways and interstates grew to one of the country's most intense, with traffic that is notoriously bumper-to-bumper (to bumper) and thoroughfares in constant need of expansion to meet growing demands.

Civil Rights

For a state slow to abolish slavery, New Jersey was quite progressive, though this did not prevent the Newark Riots of 1967 or riots that broke out in Camden later in the century. Incidents of racial discrimination continued to occur throughout the state, including the controversial arrest of Rubin Hurricane Carter.

Late 20th Century

The final few decades of the 20th century saw a few major changes for the state's economy, including the opening of the Meadowlands Sports Arena in 1976, the legalization of gambling

New Jersey's state capital, Trenton

in Atlantic City in 1978, and the rise of pharmaceutical manufacturing companies. The state's century-old organized crime organizations prospered in metropolitan regions like Newark, Camden, and AC, with the tri-state area's most arguably famous mobster, Little Nicky Scarfo, being banished to New Jersey before receiving a life sentence.

GOVERNMENT

Like the federal government, New Jersey has executive, legislative, and judicial branches. Its governor is one of the few in the nation to be elected on odd-numbered years. New Jersey's best-known governors include Woodrow Wilson (1911–1913), who went on to become president of the United States; Alfred E. Driscoll (1947–1954), responsible for the New Jersey Turnpike; Brendan T. Byrne (1974–1982), "Savior of the Pinelands"; Christine Todd Whitman (1994–2001), New Jersey's first female governor, and James E. McGreevey, who announced himself a "gay American" before resigning from office (because of "out-of-tune" governmental appointments) in fall 2004.

New Jersey is sometimes considered a swing state, but it leans Democrat. The more urban areas around New York, Philly, and Trenton have the largest Democratic demographics, and rural counties such as Warren, Sussex, and Ocean (along the coast) are considerably Republican.

Economy

In 2004, New Jersey's per capita personal income was $41,332, third-highest in the country behind Connecticut and Massachusetts, with 8.5 percent of New Jerseyans living below the poverty level, the fifth-lowest percentage in the country. The reason for these impressive statistics is the state's prime location between Philadelphia and New York City. As a double-edged sword, New Jersey also has some of the highest property taxes in the country. The state's economy has shifted over the years from focusing on agriculture to manufacturing to service, although pharmaceuticals are currently the state's number one industry.

AGRICULTURE

About 17 percent of New Jersey's land is currently used for agriculture, which makes up 0.2 percent of the state's economy. The bulk of the production comes from South Jersey's Cumberland, Salem, and Gloucester Counties, the bogs and bushels of Atlantic and Burlington Counties, and Central Jersey's Monmouth County.

The state's central region raises large percentage of standardbred horses for race and recreation, so it's not surprising that its official animal is the horse. New Jersey is said to have more horses per square mile than anywhere else in the country.

During the 1800s, the state saw the world's first mason jar, invented by Vineland native John Mason as a way of preserving perishables. Soon canned fruits and vegetables became a large part of New Jersey's economy, especially with the founding of the Campbell Soup Company in Camden. The state's focus on produce paved way for Welch's grape juice, begun in Vineland, and Ocean Spray, which had its start as a cranberry co-op in the Pinelands.

Produce

New Jersey is home to the cultivated blueberry, "invented" by Elizabeth White of Whitesbog in 1916, and today ranks second in the nation in blueberry production. In 2003 the blueberry was deemed New Jersey's official state fruit. The peach has replaced the apple as New Jersey's number one fruit (though you'll see orchards of both fruits throughout South Jersey).

New Jersey ranks second in the nation in potato production and third, behind Massachusetts and Wisconsin, in the production of cranberries, harvested throughout Burlington, Ocean, and Atlantic Counties.

It's botanically a fruit, but the tomato was designated a vegetable in the 1800s for reasons of taxation, and for all intents and purposes remains a veggie throughout the Garden State, a place that even raised legislation to make it the state vegetable. Today most every roadside stand advertises "Jersey tomatoes" that are locally, if not nationally, famous.

Corn is another item with a large in-state following, and most locals have a favorite produce stand where they head for sweet, white, Jersey corn. Most heavily produced in South Jersey, the Skylands, and Monmouth County, corn is increasing in cultivation with the popularity of maize mazes in summer and fall.

MANUFACTURING AND INDUSTRY

New Jersey was at the forefront of the country's industrial revolution, and early manufacturing included iron, glass, textiles, and paper. Today the state's number one manufacturing industry is pharmaceuticals—their research, development, and production. Most of the industry is centered in New Jersey's urban northeast. Johnson & Johnson, one of America's leading suppliers of health care products, was founded and remains in New Brunswick.

Oil refineries make up one of the state's most visible industries, and there are currently six—three in the Gateway and three in South Jersey (two in Paulsboro and one in Westville on the way to Gloucester)—in the state.

Notable businesses that help define New Jersey's economy include Subaru of America, which is headquartered in Cherry Hill and began as the U.S. distributor of Fuji autos, and NFL Films, which films every game for the National Football League and has been a major employer in Mount Laurel since 1979. Atlantic City's casinos are also leading contributors to the state, creating jobs and supporting businesses.

TOURISM

The state's second-largest industry, tourism in New Jersey dates back to the late 1800s when steamboats leaving from New York and Philly would carry visitors along the coast to Long Branch and Cape May. With the coming of railways, the Shore was developed, and inland resorts like Lake Hopatcong and Lake Mohawk prospered. Air travel carried some of the industry out-of-state, but coastal towns have bounced back, especially with the recent trend of travelers to stay closer to home. Although most of the tourism capital comes from shore resorts—Atlantic City is the state's number one destination—the Skylands places second in bringing in the crowds.

The People

In 2004, New Jersey had an estimated population of 8.5 million, ranking 10th among the 50 states. At 1,172 people per square mile (372 per sq. km), it's the United States' most densely populated state and exceeds the density of both China (139 per sq. km) and India (358 per sq. km). Still, a drive through New Jersey doesn't make it seem densely populated, with about two people per square mile in some parts of the Pinelands.

Immigration plays a large role in the state's population. Even before Ellis Island welcomed inhabitants to the New World, New Jersey, with its prime locale along the Eastern Seaboard and Northeast Corridor, was an ideal stop for the country's new arrivals and for those searching for employment.

After New Jersey's initial settlement of Dutch, Swedes, and the British, the state's first wave of immigration was mostly Irish and German. Germans arrived in the late 19th century and earlier, as craftsmen such as glassmakers and ironworkers who settled in South Jersey and the upper Highlands. The Irish came to New Jersey in massive numbers during their country's Great Potato Famine (1845–1851), continuing through the 19th and well into the 20th century, though they have been arriving in the state since its beginning. Irish immigrants gained positions as political powerhouses throughout state, setting up neighborhoods in Newark's Ironbound, Jersey City,

Trenton, and what are known as the "Dublin sections" of Morristown and Paterson.

Italians, today New Jersey's largest ancestry group, didn't really begin arriving until the late 19th century, mostly from southern Italy. Originally working on farms in South Jersey, they eventually sought work in the state's northeast. Populations of Italians settled in Newark's First Ward, Trenton's Chambersburg, Camden, Morristown, and Paterson. Large numbers of immigrants from West and North Europe came to New Jersey around this time, as did Eastern Europeans. As in other places across the country, restrictions were placed on this latter group, as well as Chinese and other Asians—a discrimination that was eventually challenged and lifted.

The state's population of African Americans increased dramatically during the two World Wars, as blacks immigrated from southern states drawn by industrial opportunities. Many settled into impoverished regions in Camden and Trenton, and in Newark's Third Ward, then home to a large Jewish population.

New Jersey saw a great number of Cuban immigrants after Castro gained control of the regime and today has the nation's second-largest Cuban population after Florida. The state has also seen an influx of Indian, Bangladeshi, Colombian, Dominican, Asian, Latin American, and Middle Eastern populations in the latter half of the 20th century.

Arts and Culture

Where you are in the state will define the culture you're in: Step foot in South Jersey's Deptford, say, and you're in Philadelphia territory—where Philly sports teams get prime air time; cheesesteaks, soft pretzels, and hoagies are common food staples; water-ice is sold at seasonal stands, and ice cream comes topped with jimmies. Refer to the tri-state region and you're talking about New Jersey, Pennsylvania, and Delaware. But take a ride up to Bergen County in the state's northern half and a change takes place—the Yankees become your major league team, your favored ice is now called Italian ice, subs are sold at convenience stores, and ice cream's condiment of choice are now called sprinkles. This tri-state region encompasses New York and Connecticut.

It may seem the state is divided across the middle, but its similarities transcend its differences. You're a girl from New Jersey, and you're a "Jersey Girl" across the state, hands down; going "down the Shore" is a right belonging to all New Jerseyans; and Jersey jokes generalize to encompass the entire state, no matter where you're from. It's okay to call it "Jersey"; in fact, many locals do. This is a place where its reputation precedes it, and residents can't help but be proud.

ARTS, CRAFTS, AND FOLK TRADITIONS

Living-history farms are plentiful throughout the state and demonstrate a way of life now uncommon, displaying skills like butter churning and beekeeping. Such farms include Howell Living History Farm, Longstreet Farm, and Historic Allaire Village in Central Jersey, Cold Spring Village in Cape May County, and Fosterfield's Living History Farm in Morristown. For a look into the folk traditions of the state's eight southernmost counties stop by the Down Jersey Folklife Center in Wheaton Village. The Tuckerton Seaport is a good place to learn about the maritime history of the Jersey

The Tomb of the Good Gray Poet, Walt Whitman, Camden

JERSEY DEVIL

In a state that prides itself on being weird, what could be more strange than a flying creature with the wings of a bat, the head of a horse, and cloven hooves on its hind legs that it uses to stand upright? How about this same creature being spotted over the centuries by dozens of people in the Pinelands and South Jersey regions? The Jersey Devil, as it came to be known, is shrouded in myth, but the story goes that he was the 13th child of a Mrs. Leeds, who lived along the outer eastern Pinelands along the Atlantic Coast. At news of a 13th child, Mrs. Leeds is said to have proclaimed, "Let this one be the devil!" and the rest is Jersey history. Today the devil is to the state as the monster is to Loch Ness – a legend that only adds to the region's mystique. Is there such as creature? Some believe so, and there's really no harm in it (so far...).

Shore, and more specifically, the Delaware Bayshore Project runs educational outings on the state's official tall ship—the *A. J. Meerwald*—teaching visitors about the local culture and history.

South Jersey's prosperous glassmaking history lives on at Wheaton Village, where artisans are invited for resident visits and their work is later placed on display in the village's glass museum. For a complete overview of New Jersey arts, an indisputable resource is **Discover Jersey Arts** (800/THE-ARTS or 800/843-2787, www.jerseyarts.com), a guide to all the theater, dance, galleries, and entertainment venues throughout the state, as well as information on local craft fairs and events.

LITERATURE

The state's ties with literature are varied, as New Jersey has played host to a large number of writers and acts as a muse for numerous authors as well. Poets such as William Carlos Williams and Allen Ginsberg have found inspiration in the manufactured city of Paterson, where one once lived and the other was born, while poet Amiri Baraka sets his heart in Newark. Former Poet Laureate Robert Pinsky is a Long Branch native, and though Walt Whitman was a definite New Yorker he and spent his last years here in New Jersey. Stephen Crane (*The Red Bad of Courage*), another writer heavily associated with New York, was born and raised in Asbury Park in the late 19th century and began his career writing commentary for a local paper.

Modern-day literary authors inspired by New Jersey include Philip Roth, who grew up in Newark's Third Ward when it was primarily a Jewish neighborhood. Roth's experiences breathe life into such works as "Goodbye, Columbus," and his Pulitzer Prize–winning *American Pastoral*. It's easy to find evidence of the Garden State in works by Joyce Carol Oates, an adopted New Jerseyan, most notably in a mystery titled *The Barrens* and written under her pseudonym Rosamond Smith.

Though she lives in New Hampshire, Janet Evanovich's most famous bail-bond enforcer Stephanie Plum is a Jersey Girl through and through, and this highly successful series follows her through love interests, car explosions, and countless dinners at the family homestead in Trenton's Chambersburg district. Jersey author Joshua Braff is one of the latest in a series of writers that continue to be inspired by New Jersey. His fictional *The Unthinkable Thoughts of Jacob Green* is set in the state.

Other literary greats who've left their mark on the Garden State include F. Scott Fitzgerald, who placed *This Side of Paradise*'s main character as an undergrad at Princeton University, where Fitzgerald himself was once a student; Toni Morrison, who wrote *Beloved* while living in New Jersey; and Dorothy Parker, who employed a table at the Stockton Inn along the Delaware River as a "country" Algonquin Round Table.

MUSIC

New Jersey has one of the most prolific music histories in the country, producing such greats as Frank Sinatra, Frankie Valli, Sandra Dee, Connie Francis, Pete Yorn, Whitney Houston, Sarah Vaughan, Count Basie, Queen Latifah,

Redman, Kool & the Gang, and Lauryn Hill. The state has inspired huge hip-hop and jazz movements, as well as an entire genre known as "Jersey Shore Music," out of which came such musicians as Jon Bon Jovi, Little Steven Van Zandt, Southside Johnny, Patty Scialfa, Gary U.S. Bonds, and the one and only Bruce Springsteen. Rocker Patti Smith, though not a native, spent her formative years in Deptford, an experience she continues to recall today. Like those of Nashville, Tennessee, and New Orleans, Louisiana, New Jersey musicians take such pride in their environment and are heavily influenced by it, creating a sound that's like no other.

Asbury Park and Wildwood stand as two centers to the state's musical testament. Asbury Park remains an inspirational venue, and a New Jersey Music Hall of Fame is scheduled to open in the city in summer 2006. During the 1950s Wildwood altered the course of music history: The city was the first to witness a live performance of Bill Haley and his Comets' rock-and-roll classic "Rock Around the Clock," and hosted the first-ever "Twist" by Chubby Checker. It was also the summertime home of Dick Clark's *American Bandstand*.

New Jersey—its cities, people, and culture—has inspired countless songs, including Springsteen's "Atlantic City," "Jersey Girl," written by Tom Waits, Bobby Rydell's catchy "Wildwood Days," and the shore standard "On the Way to Cape May," best performed by Philadelphia TV personality Al Albertson. The entire soundtrack to *Eddie & the Cruisers,* a movie about a Jersey Shore band, can be considered a local anthem.

Not to be overlooked, the Pinelands is infused with its own unique sound known as Piney music, which includes the use of stringed instruments and washtubs and is a blend of country and bluegrass beats. Albert Music Hall in Waretown is the place to hear these lively sounds, every Saturday night.

IN TV AND FILM

No overview of New Jersey would be complete without mention of its role in motion pictures and television. The state is home to the world's first film studio. Known as "The Black Maria," it was built by Thomas Edison on the grounds of his West Orange Laboratory. For a brief time in the early 20th century New Jersey was the center of the silent picture industry, and the term "cliffhanger" was coined in reference to a series of films shot on location at the Palisades cliffs. The necessity for year-round production is what eventually led to the industry's move to Los Angeles, but not before New Jersey, most specifically Fort Lee where many of the studios were located, earned a spot in the history books. Less than two decades later New Jersey became the birthplace of the drive-in movie theater, and in 1933 the first movie to air was *Wife Beware* on a screen along Admiral Wilson Boulevard between Camden and Pennsauken.

The state has produced numerous big- and small-screen actors, among them Paul Robeson (Princeton), Jack Nicholson (Neptune), Danny DeVito (Asbury Park), Meryl Streep (Summit), Bud Abbott (Asbury Park) and Lou Costello (Paterson), Bette Midler (Paterson), Bruce Willis (Penns Grove), James Gandolfini (Westwood), and Kelly Ripa (Stratford). In addition, the shore was the summer haunt of Grace Kelly (Ocean City), Kevin Bacon (Ocean City), and Will Smith (Wildwood). Michael Landon attended Collingswood High, Jimmy Stewart and Brooke Shields attended Princeton, and Steven Spielberg is said to have seen the first movie that made him want to direct motion pictures in Haddon Township.

Films in which New Jersey or one of its cities have played a starring role include *On the Waterfront* (Hoboken), *The King of Marvin Gardens* (Atlantic City), *Atlantic City* (Atlantic City), *Eddie and the Cruisers* (South Jersey), *Friday the 13th* (Blairstown), *The Station Agent* (Skylands), and most recently, *Garden State* (Gateway region). Director Kevin Smith's New Jersey Trilogy—including *Clerks, Mallrats,* and *Chasing Amy*—casts the state's distinct culture as a leading character, but New Jersey's most arguably award-worthy performance goes to its role in the HBO television series *The Sopranos*.

ESSENTIALS

Getting There

Its relatively small size and location between two of the country's most prosperous cities on the Eastern Seaboard make New Jersey one of the most convenient places to travel to in the United States.

BY AIR

Both **Newark Liberty International Airport** (888/EWR-INFO or 888/397-4636, www.panynj.com) and New York's JFK, or **John F. Kennedy International Airport** (718/244-4080 or 800/AIR-RIDE, www.kennedyairport.com), serve the northern half of the state, while those exploring South Jersey or the southern shore will either fly into **Philadelphia International Airport** (215/580-7800 or 215/937-6800, www.philadelphia-phl.com) or the smaller **Atlantic City International Airport** (609/645-7895, www.acairport.com), served by Spirit Airlines (www.spiritair.com). I dare say it's fun trying to configure the cheapest flight from your starting point to New Jersey, but with so many points to choose from it's almost always easy to find an inexpensive flight. Southwest (www.southwest.com) flies to Philly, while Jet Blue (www.jetblue.com) offers flights into JFK and Newark. If you're traveling from many places in Europe, a direct flight into JFK will most likely be the cheapest and most direct route, though flights into Philly from

© LAURA KINIRY

London's Heathrow can run as low as $159 round-trip during the off-season. Cross-country flights into the three major airports often offer rock-bottom deals, running about $250 (with taxes) round-trip. Pennsylvania's **Lehigh Valley International Airport** (3311 Airport Rd., Allentown, PA, www.lvia.org) is the closest airport to the Skylands, only a 40-minute drive to Clinton and an hour to Flemington. Continental (www.continental.com) and Northwest (www.nwa.com) both fly here. New Jersey has dozens of smaller airports, including ones in Princeton, Medford, and Sussex, and a handful of airports throughout the Skylands are equipped for hot air balloons.

BY CAR

If arriving by motor vehicle, I-95 is a direct toll-route along the East Coast from Maine south to Florida, turning into New Jersey's famed Turnpike on its leg through the state. In an east–west direction, I-80 can be taken from the Gateway region's Fort Lee across the country to Oakland, California, if so desired. Cars are allowed on the **Cape May-Lewes Ferry** (609/889-7200, www.capemay-lewes ferry.com), which connects Delaware and Cape May.

BY TRAIN

Amtrak (800/USA-RAIL or 800/872-7245, www.amtrak.com) offers service to both Philadelphia and New York City, with transfer stops in numerous places throughout the state, including Trenton, Princeton, New Brunswick, Cherry Hill, Atlantic City, and Newark. If you have the time, I highly recommend taking the train, which offers discounts for students, seniors, veterans, children, and international travelers. Check their website for more info.

Philadelphia's **30th Street Station** can be reached from the city's airport by **SEPTA** (215/580-7800, www.septa.org). Amtrak has a station at Newark Liberty International Airport, and offers bus connections from JFK.

NJ Transit (800/772-2222 North Jersey, 800/582-5946 South Jersey, 973/762-5100 out-of-state, www.njtransit.state.nj.us) runs trains out of New York City and into the Garden State with stops in the eastern Skylands, throughout the Gateway Region, and along the Jersey Shore's northern coast.

BY BUS

America's ultimate hippie bus, the **Green Tortoise** (www.greentortoise.com), offers cross-country 10-day and two-week trips that arrive in New York City, just a hop, skip, and jump from New Jersey's Gateway Region. **Greyhound** (800/231-2222, www.greyhound .com) is an inexpensive, albeit boring (and often scary) bus alternative for in-state arrivals, and has stations in Atlantic City, Mount Laurel, Newark, and Trenton, among others.

From New York City, **Transbridge Lines** (www.transbridgebus.com) operates daily bus service to Newark Airport, as well as the Skylands' Clinton, Flemington, Phillipsburg, and Frenchtown.

BY BOAT

For those looking to arrive by boat, **Cunard Cruises** (www.cunard.com/transatlantic.asp) offers trans-Atlantic cruises that end in New York City, an excellent starting point for exploring New Jersey. If you have a water vessel of your own, the state is part of the Intracoastal Waterway that runs along the Atlantic seaboard from Boston down to the Gulf of Mexico, and offers protective passageway for sea travelers.

Getting Around

BY CAR

To really delve into New Jersey, it's essential to have a car, and rental agencies are found at each of the airports, though its often cheaper to rent in-state away from the urban areas. Some to try are **Alamo** (800/327-9633, www.alamo.com), **Hertz** (800/654-3131, www.hertz.com), **Avis** (800/831-2847, www.avis.com), and **Budget** (800/527-0700, www.drivebudget.com). Anyone renting a car in New Jersey, and any additional drivers, must be 25 or older.

Taxis are available in most of the state's larger cities. Atlantic City has its own 24-hour **jitneys** (609/344-8642 or 877/92-TRAIN, http://jitney.bigstep.com)—transport buses that run approximately every 15 minutes and stop at all the major locations—and many of the Shore towns operate trolleys during summer months.

Roadways

New Jersey's major roadways have the well-deserved reputation of being nothing but traffic and construction and everything that nightmares are made of. It's best to avoid these interstates and highways—which include Interstates 295, 195, 282, 80, Route 1, and the infamous New Jersey Turnpike—if at all possible during rush hours. The Atlantic City Expressway and Garden State Parkway should be added to the list, with the further suggestion to steer clear of them in the direction of the Shore at all costs on Friday evenings and Saturday mornings during summer. The introduction of E-Z Passes, allowing drivers to slowly drive through, instead of stopping at, tolls, and electronically deducting the fare from a pre-paid account, has speeded things up a bit but not by much.

Shore traffic occurs elsewhere as well, including Route 72 en route to Long Beach Island (and the island's only existing entry), Route 322 from the Commodore Barry Bridge on the Delaware River across the state to Atlantic City, and Route 55, a highway connecting Route 47 to the southern Shore towns. If you're planning a weekend down the Shore, heading out early

© LAURA KINIRY

the River LINE heading south from Trenton to Camden

BARRIERS AND CIRCLES

New Jersey roads are responsible for one well-known invention and known for one frightening feature: the Jersey barrier and the traffic circle. The Jersey barrier is that short, movable wall that stands between lanes of oncoming traffic on a major roadway – a few feet tall and tapered as it rises to prevent vehicle rollover. It was developed as a way to prevent trucks from jumping lanes, resulting in head-on collisions.

The traffic circle, while not developed here, has long been a feature of the state's roadways, beginning with Pennsauken's Airport Circle in the early 1900s. Similar to the British roundabout, drivers enter the circle from a feeder road and either skirt the outer lane only to be poured out onto another joining roadway, or they merge into the inner circle (from which there often seems no escape) to avoid other "merging" traffic (and out-of-state drivers) until ready to make their way back out into the world of straight lanes once again. Although many circles have been replaced with traffic lights and corner edges (sometimes just as dangerous), you'll still find quite a number of them throughout New Jersey, three in the Flemington area alone. As if circles weren't enough, the state also features a large amount of "left turns from right lane only" jug-handles.

on a Friday afternoon or at the crack of dawn on Saturday should help alleviate some of the bumper-to-bumper pain. From South Jersey, a nice alternative from the Garden State Parkway for reaching the Northern Shore towns is to take Route 70 through the Pinelands from Marlton. It's a long and straight, though somewhat mundane, route that will eventually lead you to Point Pleasant Beach and the surrounding Shore towns. Still, as toll roads go (sans traffic) the 173-mile Garden State Parkway, extending from the New York border south to Cape May, is actually quite nice, with snake-like curves,

plenty of greenery, and enough natural bumps to give your car a rhythmic *Dukes of Hazzard* feel. Again, disregarding traffic, Route 55 is one of the nicest roads for reaching the shores of Cape May County. It connects with Route 47 and travels alongside the Delaware Bayshore region through heavy woods and passing farms and wetlands, eventually carrying traffic right to Wildwood and Cape May. Drivers can disembark early from Route 55 onto Route 49 east to reach Ocean City, but be aware that such back routes to the Shore are often two-lane roads that can get pretty dark at night.

Some of the state's older roads like Route 17 (the Gateway Region), Route 130 (from Camden County to Bordentown), and Route 1 (Trenton to South Brunswick) all experience unworldly traffic, and are heavy with stop lights and abandoned shopping centers, but along these routes you'll also find plenty of diners. Other such roads include Route 30 and 46.

Roads that are pleasant and easily navigable include Route 29 north of Lambertville, Route 537 from Merchantville northeast to Freehold (a good back route for reaching Jackson Township's Six Flags), and I-22. Route 9 north from Cape May is a nice alternative to the Garden State Parkway, and is lined with campgrounds, shopping centers, miniature golf courses, and individual antique shops—the road starts to get a bit congested as it enters Ocean County. I-287 is a modern, easy route traveling south from New York State through the center of North Jersey (bypassing the Gateway congestion) and connecting with the Turnpike and the Garden State Parkway near Perth Amboy, along Raritan Bay. It's an easy way to get to many Skylands and Gateway locations, and a good connection to the rest of the state.

Tolls exist along the **Garden State Parkway** (732/442-8600), **New Jersey Turnpike** (732/247-0900, www.state.nj.us/turnpike), **Atlantic City Expressway** (609/965-6060, www.acexpressway.com), and many of the bridges connecting the coastal barrier islands in the southern half of the state. New Jersey is connected to Delaware, Philadelphia, and New York City by bridges, most of which require a one-way toll paid when exiting the state. Many of the bridges connecting the Skylands to Pennsylvania's Lehigh Valley are free.

Helpful Hints

The **New Jersey Department of Transportation** website offers real-time traffic updates throughout the state at www.state .nj.us/transportation/commuter/trafficinfo as well as significant road construction updates in the New York metropolitan region at www.state.nj.us/transportation/commuter/ roads/. For information on road closures and traffic throughout the Philadelphia metropolitan area, including much of South Jersey, try AM radio news station **KYW 1060.** On the FM dial, New Jersey 101.5 broadcasts traffic through Central Jersey and the outlying regions. In the Gateway Region, tune to AM **1010 WINS** (www.1010wins.com).

New Jersey allows the use of E-Z Pass on all major toll roads and participating bridges, which include all those in the New York and Philly regions, and all along the upper Delaware River traveling west into Pennsylvania's Lehigh Valley. E-Z Passes can also be used in New York, Massachusetts, Pennsylvania, Delaware, Maryland, and West Virginia.

Don't even attempt to pump your own gas in New Jersey—it's a practice that's been illegal since 1949. New Jersey shares this honor of mandatory full-service with one other state—Oregon. Just pull up, specify the amount and type of gas you require, and allow yourself the freedom to be pampered. You'll need the extra energy for navigating the nearly 100 traffic circles that New Jersey roads are known for.

PUBLIC TRANSPORTATION

NJ Transit (800/772-2222 North Jersey, 800/582-5946 South Jersey, 973/762-5100 out-of-state, www.njtransit.state.nj.us) operates buses throughout the state, serving even the hard-to-reach Skylands region, as well as rail service in the New York metropolitan region, and a transit line between Philadelphia and Atlantic City (connecting with PATCO). Additional services provided by NJ Transit include

the **Hudson-Bergen Light Rail** along the Gateway's Gold Coast, the Newark Subway, and the **River LINE** (800/626-7433, www.river line.com), which operates along the Delaware River between Camden and Trenton.

PATCO (856/772-6900, www.drpa.org/ patco), a division of the Delaware River Port Authority, is an easy way to get from Philly to numerous Camden County locations, including Camden, Collingswood, and Haddonfield, or if you'd rather travel by boat the **Riverlink Ferry** (215/925-5465, www.river link.org) connects Philly's Penn's Landing to the Camden Waterfront (March–Dec.), where you can easily connect with the River LINE to Trenton's Amtrak Station. In North Jersey, the Port Authority Trans-Hudson, or **PATH** (800/234-7284, www.panynj.gov/path/) operates between New York City and Hoboken, Jersey City, and Newark. The **New York Waterway** (800/53-FERRY, www.nywaterway.com) runs ferries from New York to points all along New Jersey's Gold Coast, including Weehawkin, Hoboken, Jersey City, and Belford, along Raritan Bay, and **Seastreak** serves the Atlantic Highlands.

TOURS

Tours that explore all of New Jersey are not yet offered, but specialized tours—best-known are those to Atlantic City—are available. Trips to the casinos are often senior-centric excursions aboard charter buses run by schools, churches, and other organizations, though quite a few are regularly scheduled trips geared toward a more eclectic crowd leaving from Philly or New York City. Bus trips to AC often include vouchers for food and drink, or cash back in the form of casino coins and chips. One to try is **Academy** (www.academybus.com), offering daily bus service from Philly, New York, and numerous places throughout Central and North Jersey, with packages that include cash-back bonuses.

Other popular New Jersey tours include *The Sopranos* filming locales and visits to the Pinelands cranberry bogs, as well as walking tours of Princeton and Rutgers Universities (see destination chapters for more information).

Transbridge Lines (908/859-1125, www.transbirdgebus.com) runs scheduled one-day tours throughout Central and South Jersey and along the Jersey Shore, including trips to Atlantic City, Wildwood, Camden's Adventure Aquarium, Cape May (multiday tour), and Ocean City. All trips leave from Phillipsburg in the state's Skylands region.

Bicycle Touring

Bike touring is a wonderful way to experience New Jersey's back routes and undiscovered towns, and is becoming increasingly popular, as with cycling itself. Relatively low elevation, wide shoulders, and winding roads that are light on traffic make for some great riding statewide. For those planning to explore New Jersey by bicycle, a wonderful resource is the **Adventure Cycling Association** (www.adventurecycling.com). Bicycles are allowed on most NJ Transit lines during off-peak hours, and on the company's buses that are "bike friendly"—about half, including all those that run within South Jersey. Bikes are also permitted on all PATCO lines that run from Philly through South Jersey, connecting with NJ Transit en route to Atlantic City. A limited number of bicycles are allowed on PATH trains during off-peak hours.

Sports and Recreation

With 39 state parks, 11 forests, and three recreation areas, not to mention miles and miles of coastline, New Jersey is a haven for outdoor enthusiasts. There is sometimes a fee to enjoy the state's offerings, most notably between Memorial Day and Labor Day. Prices tend to be hiked up on weekends throughout the season, though there are plenty of county parks that don't cost a penny. All cyclists, in-line skaters, and skateboarders 12 and under are required by law to wear helmets.

GENERAL RESOURCES

A good place to get an overview of the recreational activities that the state offers is on the **Department of Environmental Protection**'s website at www.state.nj.us/dep/. The link for the Department of Parks and Forestry provides information on many of the state's natural resources, which you can search by location or activity. The website also offers insight into local environmental concerns, and supplies up-to-date information on fishing and hunting licenses and seasons. The **National Park Service** (www.nps.gov, then search for a park) provides an overview of the state's national recreation areas, historic sites, parks, routes, and scenic trails, including links to the **Delaware Water Gap National Recreation Area** and the **New Jersey Pinelands National Reserve.**

The **New Jersey Sierra Club** (139 W. Hanover St., Trenton, 609/656-7612, www.new jersey.sierraclub.org) is a local chapter of the San Francisco–based organization that sets out to "explore, enjoy, and protect the planet." They plan local events and activities that include coastal clean-ups, hikes, canoe trips, and river tubing, all open to both the club's members and non-members. More localized Sierra groups exist throughout the state, each representing a number of counties, and often host their own meetings and events. Many excursions are free, though sometimes a nominal fee, such as a park entrance fee, is charged.

The **Outdoor Club of South Jersey** (856/427-7777, www.ocsj.org) is an excellent organization that runs trips in everything from cycling, mountain biking, and hiking, to overnight wilderness and survival outings. One-year membership is $13 and will allow you access to the lists and participation in all events offered throughout the year. It's open to anyone, regardless of your place of residence. Most of the activities take place in the South Jersey region, though a number of North Jersey and out-of-state trips are also organized.

The **Appalachian Mountain Club: New**

York/North Jersey Chapter (www.amc-ny .org) hosts hiking events, as well as other excursions, in the New York tri-state area, while the **Appalachian Mountain Club: Delaware Valley Chapter** is better-suited for those in the Philadelphia and Trenton metropolitan areas. Membership is not required in either group to participate in many of the activities.

For outdoor leadership skills, one of the top schools in the country is **Tom Brown Jr.'s Tracker School** (www.trackerschool.com) in the Pinelands.

AGRITOURISM AND ECOTOURISM

The **New Jersey Department of Agriculture** (www.state.nj.us/jerseyfresh/) provides information on in-season produce, locations of pick-your-own farms and roadside stands, horseback riding facilities, wineries, and gardens within the state. Another website with a list of pick-your-own farms is www.pickyour own.org/NJ.htm. The non-profit **Surfrider Foundation** (www.surfrider.org), dedicated to protecting the country's coastal waters and beaches, has two New Jersey chapters—the Jersey Shore chapter in Belmar (www.surf rider.org/jerseyshore/) and the South Jersey chapter (www.surfrider.org/southjersey/), which centers around the Cape. Both websites list numerous area activities open to the public. Two of New Jersey's last remaining relatively untouched stretches along the Eastern Seaboard are Sandy Hook (732/872-5970, www.nps.gov/ gate) and Island Beach State Park (732/793-0506, www.state.nj.us/dep/forestry/parks).

FISHING

Fishing opportunities abound throughout the state and include rivers and streams, state park waters, wildlife management areas, coastal shores, back bays, and deep-sea charter boats. The state sponsors two free fishing days (609/292-9450, www.statenj.us/dep/fgw) in June, though anglers remain accountable for catch size and limits regularly implemented within the state. During the remainder of the year anyone between the ages of 16 and 69 must have a valid freshwater fishing license, including for the use of privately owned water bodies, and trout fishing requires an additional stamp. Both licenses and stamps can be obtained online, by post, or at area municipal offices and some sporting goods stores.

Resident fishing licenses are $22.50 ($34/ non-resident) and additional trout stamps are $10.50 ($20/non-resident). Non-residents can also purchase a seven-day ($19.50) or two-day ($9) fishing license. All fishers must abide by the size and catch requirements set forth by the New Jersey Department of Fish and Wildlife. There are no license requirements for saltwater fishing, though they are needed for crabbing ($3), clamming ($11/resident, $21/non-resident), and the collection of oysters ($11).

The Department of Environmental Protection stocks freshwater annually, and some places ideal for trout fishing include the trophy lakes of Round Valley Recreation Area and Lake Aeroflex in Kittatinny State Park, and the streams of Big Flatbrook, Toms River, Manasqaun River, Pequest River, and the lower Musconetcong. New Jersey waters are popular among fly-fishers, and Big Flatbrook has four miles of "fly-fishing only" waters beginning just above the park office of Stokes State Forest along Route 206. Wild trout streams include Van Campens Brook, which runs within the Delaware Water Gap National Recreation Area. **Delaware River Outfitters** (www.droltd.com) offers classes in fly-fishing.

Saltwater fishing can be enjoyed from piers, docks, jetties, private and commercial boats, beaches, and in the bays, ocean, and other coastal waterways. Fishing for blue crabs is most popular in the bay regions, namely Barnegat, Delaware, and Little Egg Harbor, and can be done from a boat, dock, or on land. Towns to head to for commercial fleets include Keyport, Point Pleasant Beach, Cape May, and Fortescue. Fishing piers exist at coastal towns such as Margate, Ocean City, Beach Haven, Keyport, Keansburg, and Seaside Heights.

New Jersey operates four public marinas: the Leonardo State Marina along the Raritan Bay, Forked River State Marina near Point Pleasant,

Senator Frank S. Farley State Marina outside of Atlantic City, and the Fortescue State Marina along the Delaware Bayshore.

HUNTING

Hunting opportunities in New Jersey include deer, wild turkey, waterfowl and migratory birds, small game, and black bear. Resident licenses require six months residency, or proof of current serving status in the armed forces. Under standard requirements, one-day licenses may be purchased at licensed commercial shooting preserves. License costs are as follows: A firearm hunting license is $27.50/resident, $135.50/non-resident; bow and arrow hunting—$31.50/resident, $135.50/non-resident; trapping—$32.50/resident, $200.50/non-resident. Additional stamps are required for waterfowl, pheasant, quail, turkey, and permits for rifles, bows, shotguns, and muzzleloaders. Those between the ages of 10 and 16 must register for a free youth license, and seniors over 65 can apply for discounted licenses.

HIKING

Hiking in New Jersey runs the gamut from easy, flat-terrain loop trails to rugged, high-elevation throughways designed for only the most experienced in the field. **Rails to Trails** (www.railtrails.org) has for a long time been involved in converting the state's old railway beds (there are plenty) into multi-use tracks that connect towns and often counties, ranging in length 1–87 miles. The **New York/ New Jersey Trail Conference** (www.nynjtc .org) maintains the regular hiking trails in the North Jersey vicinity, including the **Highland Trail,** a work in progress that is set to extend 150 miles upon completion, from New York's Storm King Mountain along the Hudson River southwest to Phillipsburg, along the Delaware. The trail connects with some already in existence, including a portion of the Appalachian, with newly established stretches. Other New Jersey trails cared for by the conference, which is a conglomeration of numerous hiking clubs, environmental groups, and individuals, include

those in Palisades Interstate Park, High Point State Park, and the Delaware Water Gap National Recreation Area.

Seventy-four miles of the **Appalachian Trail,** one of the country's best-known through-hikes spanning a length from Georgia north to Maine, lie within New Jersey, cutting northeast from Pennsylvania through the Kittatinny Mountain Range and along the state's northern border before heading into New York.

CAMPING

Camping is available in many of New Jersey's state parks, as well as in private resorts that are often open seasonally and clustered along Route 9 in Cape May County and within the state's upper northwest corner. A few back-country camping facilities are available in the Pinelands, as well as at Round Valley Recreation Area in the Skylands. State park camping facilities are relatively inexpensive, and are often located near restrooms and showers. The resorts offer more of a home away from home, usually with laundry, electricity, and (somewhat) hot showers. Most of the state's private and public campgrounds are listed in the annual **New Jersey Campground & RV Guide** (www.newjerseycampgrounds.com), which includes a list of amenities and current prices.

RV campers will find plenty of resorts that welcome them, even a few RV-only parks, including one in the Gateway Region. Some of these resorts require seasonal stays, so check ahead.

CYCLING

The **New Jersey Department of Transportation** offers some excellent free maps for road cycling routes that can be obtained by logging onto www.state.nj.us/transportation/ commuter/bike and clicking "free information." If you're interested in cycle touring, a nationwide organization to try is **Adventure Cycling** (www.adventurecycling.org). **Morris County Trails Conservancy** (http://morris trails.org) lists a handful of mountain biking trails in the area.

SPECTATOR SPORTS

When it comes to professional sports, most New Jerseyans are fans of either New York teams—such as pro-football's Giants or Jets, and baseball's Yankees—or teams from Philadelphia, like the Flyers (hockey), Eagles (football), Sixers (basketball), and Phillies (baseball). Although for now both the Giants and the Jets play their home games in New Jersey's Meadowlands, the state has only a handful of pro teams it can truly call its own: hockey's **NJ Devils** (www.newjerseydevils .com), basketball's **NJ Nets** (www.nba.com/ nets/), soccer's **NY/NJ MetroStars** (http:// metrostars.mlsnet.com/MLS/met/), and lacrosse's **NJ Pride** (newjerseypride.com), who play at Kean University Alumni Stadium in the Gateway's Union.

New Jersey has eight minor league baseball teams and stadiums, including those in Atlantic City, Newark, Montclair, and Camden. The state also has two minor league hockey teams—the **Atlantic City Boardwalk Bullies** (www.allsports.com/echl/bullies/) and the **Trenton Titans** (www.trentontitans.com).

FESTIVALS AND EVENTS

At any time during the year, you'll find festivals and events occurring somewhere in New Jersey. The state celebrates its four seasons with a variety of happenings ranging from afternoon outings to weeklong activities, and new festivals are being created annually. Each city and town seems to hosts some sort of local event, whether it be a neighborhood street fair, an arts and crafts festival, or a holiday house tour, but the following is a list of New Jersey's largest and most notable happenings. For more detailed information on local events, check out the regional chapters of this book.

Spring

New Jersey hosts numerous events that highlight the spring season, beginning with Newark's annual **Cherry Blossom Festival** (973/268-3500, www.branchbrookpark.org), held in the city's Branch Brook Park in April. This three-week event features thousands of cherry trees and demonstrations of traditional Japanese crafts. Also in April is Lambertville's annual two-day **Shad Festival** (609/397-0055, www.lambertville.org), a celebration honoring the restoration of the Delaware River. Food, crafts, and live music are included in the festivities. The **New Jersey Marathon** (732/578-1771, www.njmarathon.org) takes place from Long Branch, along the Jersey Shore, in April.

In May the N. J. Audubon Society sponsors the **World Series of Birding** (609/884-2736, www.njaudubon.org/wsb) in Cape May County. Group participants have 24 hours to spot and record as many birds as possible while competing for the title of "World Series" champs. On Memorial Day weekend the Skylands' Somerville hosts the annual four-day **Tour of Somerville** (www.tourofsomerville.org), the United State's oldest bike race.

Summer

There's no doubt that New Jersey comes alive Memorial Day–Labor Day, as obvious by the number of festivals and events that take place statewide. Held in South Jersey's Cumberland County during early June, **Delaware Bay Days** (856/785-2060, www.ajmeerwald .org) is a free two-day festival celebrating the Delaware Bay region's maritime history with parades, walks, and river tours.

The first weekend in June is an extremely popular time for festivities, beginning with the **Red Bank Jazz & Blues Festival** (www.redbank festival.com), an annual two-day event highlighting the region's musical heritage. The state's two major seafood festivals are also held this weekend: Belmar's **New Jersey Seafood Festival** (800/523-2587, www.belmar.com), featuring local catch and cuisine, and Atlantic City's **New Jersey Fresh Seafood Festival** (2915-17 Atlantic Ave., 609/FISH-FUN or 609/347-4386, www.njfreshseafoodfest.com), also highlighting crafts, music, and educational exhibits. **Michael Arnone's Crawfish Festival** is a three-day annual June event held at the Skylands' Sussex County Fairgrounds. Music, camping, and Big Easy eats are just a few of the helpings that you'll find here.

New Jersey is the birthplace of the motion picture, and to celebrate this the state hosts a number of film-related events, including the Rutgers Film Co-op/New Jersey Media Arts Center **N.J. Film Festival** (www.njfilm fest.com), occurring throughout the months of June and July. The Pinelands' village of Whitesbog holds its annual **Blueberry Festival** (www.whitesbog.org), which celebrates the home of the cultivated blueberry, for one day in late June.

July is just as eventful with one of the state's most popular arts and crafts fairs, Haddonfield's **Craft and Fine Arts Festival** (856/216-7253, www.haddonfieldnj.org/ eventscrafts.php), occurring the second weekend in July. The shore's Ocean City celebrates a **Weekend in Venice** in late July, beginning with a Friday night seafood block party and following the second night with a spectacular lighted boat parade along the barrier island's backbay waters. At the end of the month the Skylands puts on a three-day **Quick Chek Festival of Ballooning** (800/HOT-AIR-9 or 800/468-2479, quickchk.balloonfestival.com) in honor of the hot air balloon, a frequent visitor to area skies. The event takes place at Solberg Airport in Readington, outside of Somerville.

One of the state's most unique events is held in August in the waters surrounding Atlantic City—it's the **Around the Island Marathon Swim** (www.acswim.org) a 22.5-mile race around Absecon Island. Known for many years as the Sussex County Horse and Farm Show, the annual August **New Jersey State Fair** (Sussex County Fairgrounds, 973/948-5500, www.newjerseystatefair.org) is a week's worth of rides, crafts, cuisine, and agricultural competitions.

Fall

Although summer's winding down, New Jersey sees no shortage of festivals in the fall. In addition to hay rides, pumpkin picking, corn mazes, and Halloween fright nights, the state hosts a number of weekend and weeklong events, beginning with South Jersey's annual **Delaware Valley Bluegrass Festival** (www.brandywine friends.org/index.php), a music and camping extravaganza held at the Salem County Fairgrounds over Labor Day weekend. The following weekend in North Jersey is the **Hoboken Italian Festival** (www.hobokenitalianfestival .com), a celebration of dining, desserts, tradition, and music, capped off with evening fireworks. Central Jersey's New Brunswick hosts the **Raritan River Festival** (www.raritanriv-erfest.com) annually in September, a one-day event complete with a cardboard canoe race. The shore's Cape May extends its summer season with a number of events and festivals, including the four-day **Cape May Food & Wine Festival** (www.capemaymac.org), highlighting the city's reputation as a foodie destination. In October Cape May hosts a 10-day **Victorian Week** (www.capemaymac.org), featuring everything from haunted house tours to a vintage ball, where proper Victorian dress is encouraged.

The **New Jersey Lighthouse Challenge** (856/546-0514, http://njlhs.burlco.org) takes place in mid-October. Partakers have two days to visit and climb the state's 11 participating lighthouses, after which they receive a commemorative souvenir. Around this time Chatsworth—the self-proclaimed "capital of the Pinelands"—hosts the region's annual two-day **Cranberry Festival** (609/726-9237, www.cranfest.org/festival.html), featuring arts, crafts, and cranberry-made treats. South Jersey's Rankokus Indian Reservation, located within Rancocas State Park, is host to October's three-day **Indian Arts Festival** (www.powhatan.org), highlighting traditional and modern Native American culture, including storytelling, music, and dance. A second annual festival takes place in the spring.

Winter

Most of the state's winter festivities tend to take place in South and Central Jersey and along the Jersey Shore, where temperatures are more moderate than in northern sections. During the month of December, Cape May transforms into a full-fledged holiday town, with carriage rides, candlelight house tours, and a spectacular light display. For additional holiday lights, check out Atlantic City and Vicinity's **Storybook Land** (www.hmva.org). This fairytale village also hosts Santa and his reindeer throughout December. The Pineland's Medford Village holds its annual **Dickens Festival** (www.hmva.org) the first Friday in December, complete with costumed carolers, late-night shopping, and a tree-lighting ceremony.

On December 31 South Jersey's Haddonfield starts the New Year off with **First Night Haddonfield** (www.firstnighthaddonfield.org), a block party intended for the entire family. Mount Holly holds a **Fire & Ice Festival** (www.mainstreetmountholly.com), with ice-carving and chili eating in late January, and by February the state's winter temperatures have taken their toll, inciting hundreds of disillusioned frolickers to take to freezing ocean waters for Point Pleasant Beach's annual **Polar Bear Plunge** (732/213-5387, www.njpolar plunge.org), in the name of charity, of course. Cumberland County's Delaware Bayshore hosts the **Winter Raptor Festival** (856/453-2180), a day-long birding event, in early February.

March's big event is Belmar's **St. Patrick's Day Parade** (732/280-2648, www.belmar parade.com), the beginning of a day-long celebration complete with a beauty-pageant, bagpipes, and all the corned beef you can stomach.

Accommodations

New Jersey has a plethora of overnight choices ranging from wonderfully elegant to downright seedy. In general, many of the older motels that exist along once-frequented roadways now home to roadside attractions and prevalent potholes are not the kind of place you want to be checking into. I found that it's best to stick to chain hotels, small-town establishments, and B&Bs, and to steer clear of independently owned motels *unless* you're at the Shore—that's a whole other ballgame.

RATES

Rates listed in this book are for double occupancy, high-season rooms (and are subject to change). Visitors to much of New Jersey, most notably the Shore, can save a ton of money by booking ahead or by planning their vacation during the shoulder season. Some Shore accommodations slash prices in half—sometimes three-fold—after the summer rush, though not all remain open throughout the year. In-season, simply by crossing the bridge onto the mainland from the barrier islands you can save plenty of cash by staying at a chain hotel or even one of the many camping resorts located close by (though they also fill up quickly during summer). If you're looking to break your bank account, book a last-minute room on a weekend evening (a two-night minimum is often required) during July or August in any of the Shore towns.

ALTERNATIVE ACCOMMODATION OPTIONS

Home exchanges are one economical way to find accommodations. **Home Exchange** (www.home exchange.com), a membership-based organization that acts as a middle-man, introducing potential home swappers to one another early on with the intention of establishing mutual trust. All swappers must be members, and a one-year membership costs $49.95. If you're presently without a home to trade (but will soon have one to offer) and you don't mind living in someone else's while they're still living there too, two websites that can help are www.globalfreeloaders.com and www.couch surfing.com. Both sites are online communities of people willing to offer a night of couch surfing on their IKEA sleeper for one on yours—or someone like you—in the future. Global Freeloaders requires anyone crashing in someone else's crib to have one of their own to offer within six months time (it's all about karma), but Couch Surfing can be just that.

© LAURA KINIRY

the Royal Hawaiian Resort Motel, Wildwood Doo Wop

Renting a home at the Shore is another alternative to hotels and motels. Most Shore rental units are actually bought as second properties for the purpose of renting them out during the summer season, and are decorated in a distinct Jersey Shore decor: pastel pinks and greens, seashell paintings and ocean scenes, lighthouses, ship wheels, and a thickly matted light-colored rug that works especially well at hiding sand. Menus of local seafood delivery and pizza places are fanned out on the dining table upon your arrival, and behind the house is an enclosed outdoor shower and a low-lying faucet where guests can wash off their gritty feet. Renting a house for a week at the Shore is considerably pricey, but many people get around this by going in on a seasonal rental with a dozen or more people, some of whom will only be down on weekends and others who schedule one week for themselves and their families when no one else is around—a situation similar to a time-share.

Food and Drink

New Jersey is not a place traditionally known for its cuisine, but it's grown into a place where you can find most anything if you look hard enough. The state's unique foods include diner fare and boardwalk eats. Depending on where you are in the state, you can get yourself a hearty sub or a stuffed hoagie, and if you're anywhere near Philly, say Cherry Hill, you can delve into one of the best cheesesteaks around. Philadelphia soft pretzels are a common staple in a South Jersey diet, and Tastykakes—cakes, cupcakes, and pies—have made their way throughout the state.

BOARDWALK EATS

What you'll find to eat on the boardwalk is a makeshift menu of all the so-bad-it's-good food you can think of. Pizza slices, funnel cake, gyros, grilled sandwiches, soft-serve ice cream, cotton candy, saltwater taffy, and fudge are traditional board favorites. One of the latest additions is deep-fried Oreo cookies.

DINERS

For a true New Jersey experience, eating at a diner is a must. The state is said to have more than 600 of them, the highest concentration in the country, and they range from shiny chrome and neon rail-like cars to stationary stone-walled brown tops. The definition of a diner includes cheap eats, an extensive menu, and often 24-hour service. Diners usually have long front counters, and many of the older ones feature comfy worn booths with table-top jukeboxes now just for show. Glass rotating dessert displays often greet patrons upon entry, and cashier stands hold bowls of powdered mints that act as after-dinner treats. Diners serve as after-church excursions, power-lunch spots, writers' havens, conversational hangouts, and late-night joints. It's not uncommon to walk into a diner at 2:20 in the morning and find the place packed, with all the bars having just let out. This is when coffee hotpots, crocks of French onion soup, Greek salads, and the lemon meringue pie have their glory run.

Diner specialties include cheese fries with gravy, Taylor pork roll sandwiches, and all-day breakfast meals with pancakes, eggs, and scrapple.

ETHNIC FOOD

With Italians claiming the state's largest ethnic heritage, it's no wonder that Italian cuisine is intertwined with New Jersey culture. Many who move out of state claim a good Italian meal is hard to come by elsewhere, as is a good slice of thin-crust pizza. Trenton's Chambersburg district is perhaps the state's best-known neighborhood for Italian eats, but family-owned restaurants are found statewide.

The state's diverse population hosts a large number of ethnic enclaves that specialize in particular cuisines. Cherry Hill and Lakewood are good places to find kosher food, and authentic Mexican eats are prevalent in Lakewood and Red Bank. For Indian cuisine you can't go wrong along Edison's Oak Tree Road or Jersey City's western portion of Newark Avenue. Fort Lee is known for its Korean cuisine, while the state's finest Spanish, Brazilian, and Portuguese cuisine, and soul food, is found in Newark. Cuban eats are found throughout Union City, and Middle Eastern markets are common in Paterson. Throughout much of the state, most notably in South Jersey and the Skylands, you'll find historic taverns serving traditional American fare. Seafood, most notably crab cakes, flounder, and shellfish, is the cuisine of choice along the Atlantic seaboard.

FOR FOODIES

New Jersey's foodie towns include Hoboken, Red Bank, Cape May, Morristown, Collingswood, and lately Atlantic City. Two excellent online message boards for food lovers are the **eGullet Society for Culinary Arts & Letters,** or "eG Forums" (http://forums.egullet .com/index.php?showforum=5), and **Chowhound's** Mid-Atlantic message board (www.chowhound.com/midatlantic/boards/ midatlantic/midatlantic.html). Vegetarians may want to check out the online **New Jersey Vegetarian Travel Guide** (www.vegetarian usa.com/city/NewJersey.html), a short list of vegetarian-friendly restaurants, farmers markets, farms, and co-ops. I found a few of the links to be outdated, but it's a good overall source. For written resources look for *Ed Hitzel's Restaurant Magazine* (www .edhitzel.com), a free publication focusing on Central and South Jersey and the Shore and found at area restaurants, and *New Jersey Tables* (www.njtables.com), a bi-annual publication featuring select menus of North and Central Jersey restaurants, available for purchase in bookstores or free at area restaurants.

CONVENIENCE STORES

New Jerseyans love their convenience stores, which are heavily frequented for their sandwiches, snacks, and coffee. In the state's southern half you can't go more than a few blocks its seems without seeing a **Wawa** (www.wawa.com). These omnipresent stores were a gift from Pennsylvania and have recently begun converting into megasized convenience centers complete with gas stations. Wawa is the place to go for a quick cup of coffee, an inexpensive hoagie, or a Philly soft pretzel, which many stores have delivered fresh each morning. Also in South Jersey, more localized to the Philadelphia metropolitan area, are **Heritage's Dairy Stores** (www.heritages.com), another great place to grab a sandwich to go. The Skylands convenience equivalent is **Quick Chek** (www.qchek.com), easily recognized by its forest-green sign.

For convenient ice cream there's nothing better than the seasonal **Mister Softee** (www.mistersoftee.com), a must if he happens to be in your vicinity. Though this soft-serve ice cream truck exists in other states, its home base is in South Jersey. When you hear his song (don't worry—you'll recognize it) go running toward the tune.

DRINK

New Jersey has dozens of brewpubs, microbrews, and wineries, as well as numerous BYOs scattered throughout the state, and 21 is the legal drinking age. New Jersey law allows for unfinished bottles of wine to be recorked, bagged, and carried out from restaurants, and for packaged goods to be sold by licensed retailers between 9 A.M. and 10 P.M. daily. The sale of liquor varies statewide, with some towns prohibiting alcohol sales before 1 P.M. on Sunday, and designated liquor stores replacing supermarket sales in the southern half of the state. If you want a six-pack after 10 P.M., you often have to purchase it directly from a bar.

Coffee shops are finally catching on in New Jersey, though they haven't yet made a clean sweep of the state (the convenience stores still occupy that business). To find one in the region you're planning to visit, try **The Delocator** (www.delocator.net), an online site that allows you to punch in a zip code and view a list of all the independent cafés in the area, alongside a separate list of nearby Starbucks. The point is to support local business while seeing the power of corporations to take over a neighborhood, but someone has to enter the cafés into the database, and so far states like New Jersey, especially in the more rural areas, are misrepresented. Still—it's a handy tool to use.

Shopping

In general New Jersey employs a six percent sales tax, though its 31 Urban Enterprise Zones, usually located in areas seeking revitalization, offer three percent sales tax. Clothes and shoes, as well as newspapers and magazines, are not taxed in New Jersey.

As many New Jerseyans can attest, shopping is a popular local pastime. Malls hold a prominent place within the state—in fact, New Jersey's reputation is as intricately tied with the shopping mall as it is with thick accents and big hair, and has been since the Cherry Hill Mall—the East Coast's first indoor climate-controlled shopping center—opened in 1961. Some of the state's best malls include the Mall at Short Hills, the aforementioned Cherry Hill Mall, Freehold Mall, the three-story Bridgewater Commons, and the more modern "lifestyle center" that features upscale shops each with a drive-up entrance, an example of which is Marlton's Promenade.

You'll find plenty of outlets, antique stores, flea markets, and independent boutiques throughout New Jersey as well. Mullica Hill, Chester, Long Beach Island, Lambertville, and along Route 9 in Cape May County are wonderful places to go exploring for antiques,

and twice a year the Atlantic City Convention Center hosts **Alantique City** (www.atlantique city.com). Flea markets are just as popular in New Jersey, and the state's finest can be found in Central Jersey (the Englishtown Auction), Lambertville (the Golden Nugget Antique & Collectible Flea Market), Berlin (the Berlin Market), and Woodstown (Cowtown).

Outlets are spread statewide, and include multiple locations in Flemington and Secaucus, as well as centers in Elizabeth and Jackson, and an Atlantic City shopping experience known as The Walk. The state's best street shopping, including independent boutiques and specialty shops, can be found in Haddonfield, Red Bank, Lambertville, Hoboken, Spring Lake, and Atlantic City's The Quarter.

Yard sales are posted in the paper come spring, and many New Jerseyans make a sport out of prowling the neighborhoods, scouting out exquisite deals. During the summer months, visit one of the state's roadside fruit and veggie stands—you'll find them all along back roads throughout South, Central, and northwest Jersey, and there's no better place to pick up a bushel of tomatoes and a few ears of sweet Jersey corn.

Tips For Travelers

The American Automobile Association, better known as **AAA** (www.aaa.com), offers members substantial benefits, including 24-hour emergency service, free and discounted maps, discounts on theater and sports tickets, and cheaper rates on hotels, to name a few.

A photo ID is required to get into many nightlife establishments, and you must be 21 years of age to purchase alcohol.

OPPORTUNITIES FOR EMPLOYMENT
Getting a seasonal job down the Jersey Shore is a rite of passage, and a great way to spend

the summer. International recruits, including Russians, French, Irish, Italians, and Canadians, have arrived in large numbers over the past decade, running the prize booths, staffing casino arcades, and working as servers and bar backs, but Shore employment is open to everyone. There is, however, one minor caveat: Seasonal housing is pricey, and it's not uncommon to find yourself in a rental situation with too many occupants and too few beds.

An organization that sets up jobs with Jersey Shore companies is Council Exchanges (www.councilexchanges.org).

ACCESS FOR TRAVELERS WITH DISABILITIES

These days it's required that any establishment making upgrades must be accessible to visitors with disabilities, and since New Jersey is constantly changing its appearance, it's becoming more infrequent to find a place not adhering to required standards. Generally speaking the state has made great progress, especially down the Shore, where some bicycle rental businesses have begun carrying electric wheelchairs, and towns such as Wildwood provide plastic chairs with large tires ideal for navigating through sand. Manasquan is the Shore town most accessible for travelers with disabilities, with a walkway that runs the length of the beach to its inlet waters. **Seniors on the Go** (35 S. Main St., Pleasantville, 609/569-0443) rents electric wheelchairs to visitors of the southern Shore towns, and does a large business in Atlantic City.

Though 99 percent of NJ Transit buses are wheelchair-accessible, only 61 of the state's 161 commuter platforms offer a convenient method of boarding, such as a ramp or elevator. To find out more go to www.njtransit.com/as.shtml. NJ Transit does offer reduced fares for travelers with disabilities.

TRAVELING WITH CHILDREN

New Jersey is a family-friendly state that has a ton to offer those traveling with children, most notably the Jersey Shore. One thing you should understand: Get a kid hooked on the Shore and they'll be hooked for life. In addition to the Shore's attractions, the state has numerous amusement parks, some specifically geared toward children such as Hope's Land of Make Believe and Atlantic County's Storybook Land, while others like Six Flags' Great Adventure have a plethora of family-friendly entertainment—in this case a drive-through safari where giraffes and monkeys have full run of the roads. There are a handful of zoos, a couple of aquariums, and plenty of educational facilities, including the Liberty Science Center in Jersey City's Liberty State Park, the Old Barracks in Trenton, and Morristown National Historic Park. And of course, kids score discounts at most places.

A few thing to note: Kids under one year of age are required to ride in a rear-facing car seat in the back seat of an auto, and are required by state law to continue use of a car seat until they are 40 pounds, at which time they switch to a booster until they're eight years old. Those under 12 years must wear a helmet while bicycling, inline skating, or skateboarding.

SENIOR TRAVELERS

Senior discounts are available at many of the state's parks, museums, and attractions, but it also benefits to be a member of the American Association of Retired Persons, or **AARP** (888/OUR-AARP or 888/687-2277, www.aarp.org), which provides additional hotel, auto, and travel discounts to those over 50 for a $12.50 annual fee. Seniors can also take advantage of national and local transit discount rates. Those 62 and older are eligible for free admission and parking at all of New Jersey's state parks, historic sites, and recreational facilities, as well as a $2 deduction on overnight fees at state camping facilities. However, you must first apply with the New Jersey Division of Parks & Forestry by calling 800/843-6420 or downloading a PDF application, available for print at www.state.nj.us/dep/parksandforests/parks/#discounts.

WOMEN TRAVELING ALONE

Women should use the same precautions they use elsewhere when traveling alone, including being aware of one's surroundings, steering clear of poorly lit areas, back stairs, and parking garages, and always using caution. Some women may feel uncomfortable traveling to certain cities alone, but while some areas of Camden, Jersey City, Newark, Trenton, Union City, Paterson, and even Asbury Park and Atlantic City are best to be avoided altogether, you'll have little trouble during the day as long as you stick to your destination. Know where you're going ahead of time—places like the Pinelands seem innocent enough, but many of its roads go on forever and lead nowhere. Having a map and a cell phone handy and traveling during daylight hours are ways to ease discomfort.

New Jersey is just like anywhere else—exercise good judgment and you'll be fine.

GAY AND LESBIAN TRAVELERS

Many may be surprised to find that New Jersey is at the country's forefront when it comes to gay rights. In 2004 the state signed a gay partnership law, and is one of six states in the country that currently recognize a form of same-sex union, along with Maine, Vermont, Massachusetts, California, and Hawaii. For a short while in February 2004, Asbury Park was one of the few nationwide cities allowing same-sex marriages to take place. Over the last decade the state has seen an influx of gay residents drawn by New Jersey's proximity to Philadelphia and New York City, affordable housing, and open space, and towns and cities with a noticeable gay population include Collingswood, Haddonfield, Moorestown, Trenton, Maplewood, Asbury Park, South Orange, and Jersey City. Local resources for gay and lesbian visitors include **New Jersey Gay Life** (www.njgay life.com), which hosts a directory to gay- and lesbian-friendly and gay- and lesbian-owned business throughout the state; **Gay Asbury Park** (www.gayasburypark.com); and **Out in the Neighborhood** (www.outintheneighbor-hood.org), a South Jersey resource geared toward events in Collingswood.

INTERNATIONAL TRAVELERS

International travelers to New Jersey must adhere to U.S. visa requirements. Canadians and citizens from 27 Visa Waiver Program countries do not need visas. Citizens from other countries are required to have a non-immigrant visa, which costs about $100 to process. Both visitor and student visas are issued, and the embassies and consulates of most countries are located in nearby New York City.

For those visiting the United States, I suggest carrying both travel insurance and an **International Student ID Card** (www.isic.org). The former is essential when visiting the United States, where the cost of healthcare is sky-high—shop around for a policy that best suits you. The latter holds the key to substantial savings for full-time students, teachers and professors, and those 26 and younger, can be used the world over (after your trek through the Garden State), and can be obtained at travel offices around the globe.

Health and Safety

Crime in New Jersey is similar to in other parts of the country, with the state's larger cities seeming to host the highest crime rates. Always be aware of your surroundings, especially when in such areas as Camden, Paterson, Newark, Trenton, Jersey City, and Atlantic City. Many shore towns can give you the feeling you're in la la land, and for the most part, you are, but just be aware. *Sopranos*-like organized crime is nothing for the average traveler to worry about, but there's no reason to be hanging around downtown Camden at night unless you're asking for trouble. If you have a cell phone, keep it on you—it's easy to get lost in the state, especially with all the recent roadwork that requires drivers to detour. Remember—Jersey's not that big, and head east, west, or south and you'll eventually hit water. Head north and once you reach New York State you'll know you've gone too far.

ROAD SAFETY HAZARDS AND WILDLIFE

New Jersey roads have a reputation for aggressive drivers. I'm not saying they're all state residents (many of the highways are overtaken by throughway traffic) but, especially in the Gateway Region, proceed with caution—roads can be downright hellish. While driving at night, especially in the Skylands region, be on the lookout for deer. I can't tell you the number of bright eyes and roadside carcasses I've passed while driving in the area, but it's more than I'd ever cared to see, and if that was what happened to the deer, I hate to think what happened to the cars and drivers.

Be aware of erratically acting wildlife. Species such as bats, skunk, raccoon, even dogs, are known to carry rabies, a fatal virus that results in death without treatment. If you're bitten by a wild animal call 911 immediately. Black bear primarily inhabit the state's northwest region, and have been making their way south through the Pinelands and even into Cape May County. Though many have grown accustomed to humans, they'll generally steer clear if they hear people approaching. It's a good idea to make noise while hiking, especially if you're alone (not recommended). According to the NJ Department of Fish and Wildlife brochure, if you do encounter a bear, yell, and use whatever you have handy to make noise. Never turn your back on a bear—if one's being aggressive, slowly back away, and report the incident immediately. You can further prevent bear encounters by keeping food, make-up, and anything that produces scent in a tightly sealed storage container. *Never* camp with food or drink in your tent, or cook in your tent, and always wash utensils immediately after use.

New Jersey is home to two species of poisonous snakes: northern copperheads and timber rattlesnakes. Northern copperheads live in the state's Skylands region, and are mostly found in Sussex, Warren, Hunterdon, and Passaic Counties. They are active from May to October and have a distinct reddish-brown color with hourglass bands, and according to the New Jersey state website, favor "rotting woodpiles in rocky, wooded areas that are usually mountainous." New Jersey's timber rattlesnakes are either yellow-colored with dark V-shaped crossbands, or entirely black or darkened. These snakes are also active May–October and exist in both the Pinelands and in the state's upper northwest corner.

INSECTS AND PLANTS

Mosquitoes are common to New Jersey, especially on summer evenings and near still bodies of water. Though malaria in the state has long been controlled, mosquitoes—besides being pesky and annoying—are now known to carry West Nile virus, an infection that increases risk of illness mostly in the elderly and those with weakened immune systems. To avoid contacting the virus, use bug spray and keep away from wetlands and marshes during summer months. Lyme disease, transmitted by deer ticks, is a problem in the Eastern United States, and New Jersey has one of the highest numbers of reported cases in America. If you notice a bull's-eye–like rash anywhere on your skin, see a doctor immediately. Lyme disease is treatable if cared for right away, but left on its own the symptoms are nasty, incurable, and will continue to worsen. May and June are the worst months for ticks, but if you are heading outside there are preventative measures you can take: dress in light-colored clothes to be able to see ticks more clearly, and a hat or a bandanna to protect your head, and if you're out for a hike, wear long pants and tuck them into your socks (I know, I know). Always stay on trails, keep away from tall grass, and avoid marshlands and wetlands during summer months—they're full-on breeding grounds for ticks and mosquitoes. It's also a good idea to use insect repellant, and to check yourself (or have someone check you) for ticks after being outside. Ticks are tiny, eight-legged arachnids that try to bury themselves in your skin—feel around for any unusual bumps and look for dark spots.

Another reason to avoid still water is green flies. These vile creatures have large, almost transparent green heads and a stinging bite, and they exist all along the East Coast and around to Texas. Green flies are best associated with the humid, sticky months of July and August. They breed in the salt marshes, which line much of the western side of the Jersey Shore, and they are not shy about coming in for the attack as you're relaxing on the beach.

Insect repellent is required to keep these buggers at bay, and it's when the wind blows east from the bay that you'll encounter the worst of them. One website cited Brigantine, just north of Atlantic City, as having the most green flies "on the planet."

Poison ivy is common throughout New Jersey. The old adage states "leaves of three, let it be."

SUN, TEMPERATURE, AND NEW JERSEY WATERS

Don't let the jokes about New Jersey smog fool you—the state gets plenty of sun. Cloudy days are oftentimes the worst because sunbathers along the Shore don't realize the sun is still shining down behind all that overcast. The hours between 10 A.M. and 2 P.M. are when the sun is at its strongest—avoid laying out during this time, and always use sunscreen, preferably SPF 30 or higher, re-applying it every few hours, especially after a dip in the ocean or a pool.

Summer months can be brutally hot and humid in New Jersey—always drink plenty of water and, when the sun is at its peak, find some shade (or at least wear a hat or a visor). Dehydration occurs more often than you may think, and is not worth the nausea. Winter temperatures often drop below freezing and it's important to be adequately prepared. If you're going out for a hike, always carry extra layers, bottled water, and some snacks, and tell someone where you'll going and when you plan to return. Freak snowstorms have been known to occur.

Swimming in the ocean is a favorite New Jersey pastime, and one where you should encounter few problems as long as you take a couple of precautions. Beaches employ lifeguards up and down the coast Memorial Day–Labor Day—swim in the designated areas only, as the ocean can have a mean undertow and before you know it you can be sucked out to sea without anyone knowing you were even in the water. Shark sightings are a rare, though not unheard-of, occurrence off the Jersey coast, and in 2005 a surfer was bitten in the foot off the coast from Long Beach Island's Surf City. If the lifeguard yells "shark," get out of the water, but otherwise don't think too much about it—it's a big ocean out there. Along the ocean floor you may run across the occasional crab, but the biggest problem are the populations of jellyfish that hover around the coastline and wash onto the beach in July and August. Occasionally a beach will close because of large numbers of jellyfish making it nearly impossible to walk a few feet without stepping on one. New Jersey jellyfish are not poisonous—but they do sting. Ouch!

SMOKING

As of April 15, 2006, New Jersey has banned smoking in bars and restaurants. The ban does not apply to casino floors but does include restaurants and bars in casinos. It's also against the law to smoke in the state's public buildings, and many boardwalks have declared designated smoking sections, though it's unclear how enforced these are.

HOSPITALS AND PHARMACIES

You'll find hospitals in all of New Jersey's counties, though the greatest concentrations lie within the two metropolitan regions of Philly and New York. Cape May County has only one hospital. The **New Jersey Hospital Association** provides a list of the state's hospital systems alphabetically, by county, or on a downloadable PDF map on its website, www.njha.com. For overseas visitors and those traveling without a provider, I highly recommend travel insurance—healthcare in the United States is overwhelmingly expensive, especially if you don't have good coverage. Your local travel agency can help you out with this—a good place to try is **STA Travel** (www.sta travel.com), with locations worldwide.

With its reputation as a pharmaceutical giant you'll have little trouble finding a pharmacy anywhere in-state. **Rite Aid** (www.rite aid.com), **Walgreens** (www.walgreens.com), and **CVS** (www.cvs.com) all offer 24-hour prescription-filling locations in New Jersey.

Information and Services

MONEY

ATMs (automatic teller machines) are readily available throughout New Jersey and accept most cards. Those that are located within Wawa convenience stores (which seem to multiply like bunnies throughout the southern half of the state), or Quick Chek in the Skylands region, don't charge a processing fee. Overseas travelers will have no trouble exchanging their currency at JFK, Philadelphia, or Newark Liberty International Airports, but for those already on the road, **American Express** (http://home.americanexpress.com) has travel offices throughout the state, including currency exchange centers in Newark (airport), Fort Lee, and Summit.

One bank with a large New Jersey presence is **Commerce Bank** (www.commerceonline.com), a Cherry Hill–based business whose perks include seven-day banking and longer hours for 9–5ers. Other banks existing in-state include **PNC Bank** (www.pncbank.com) and **Bank of America** (www.bankofamerica.com).

Credit Cards

You'll find that many establishments, especially along the beach towns, do not take credit cards. It's smart to always have a bit of cash on hand.

Tipping

Tipping is a common practice in the state's service industries, and many employees depend on the money they earn from tips to survive. At New Jersey restaurants, it is common to tip waitstaff 15–20 percent on top of your total bill, depending on the quality of service, and taxi drivers and hairdressers usually receive 15–20 percent as well. A couple of dollars is common to leave in your hotel room for the cleaning staff, and is also a common tip for valet parkers and airport porters. At cafés and coffee houses, spare change is customary for an espresso drink (just how much depends on its complexity), or a couple of dollars for a round of drinks or a pre-

pared meal. Bartenders usually receive a dollar for a mixed drink, or a few dollars for a round of drinks (though a round of beers would require less of a tip then a round of cosmopolitans). New Jersey's gas station attendants are paid per hour and are not usually tipped.

MAPS AND TOURIST INFORMATION
Tourist Information Offices

New Jersey has numerous information and welcome centers. State Welcome Centers are located in Jersey City (Liberty State Park, Central Railroad Terminal, NJ Turnpike exit 14B, 201/915-3400), Newark (Newark Liberty International Airport Terminal B, International Arrivals, 973/623-5052), Flemington (Liberty Village Premium Outlets, One Church St., 908/782-8550), and Jackson (Jackson Outlet Village Information Center, 537 Monmouth Rd., 732/833-0503, ext. 7). The greater tourism councils for regions divided by the NJ Office of Travel and Tourism (800/VISIT-NJ or 800/847-4865, www.visitnj.org) are the Greater Atlantic City Tourism Council (866/719-8687, www.actourism.org), Delaware River Regional Tourism Council (856/757-9400, www.visitsouthjersey.com), Gateway Regional Tourism Council (877/428-3930), Shore Regional Tourism Council (800/722-0201, ext. 200), Skylands Regional Tourism Council (800/4SKYLAND or 800/475-5263, www.skylandstourism.org), and Southern Shore Regional Tourism Council (800/277-2297, www.njsouthernshore.com). On New Jersey's official state website (www.state.nj.us) you'll find information regarding government, economy, and local flora and fauna.

COMMUNICATIONS AND MEDIA
Internet

Many—if not all—of New Jersey's public libraries offer Internet access of some form, whether hook-up or wireless, and most provide a number of computers for public use. To search for libraries in South Jersey that offer Wi-Fi connections log onto www.sjrlc.org/wireless. Many Burger Kings and McDonald's throughout the state offer wireless connections, but I'd recommend supporting the local cafés and coffee houses that also offer Internet—they're something that the state could use more of. Many hotels have wireless access in both guestrooms and public areas, and some will allow you to connect for a short bit even if you're not staying there (if you ask nicely). Other hotels features in-room data ports, and lobby computers that require a fee—these can add up quickly. The website www.wififreespot.com/nj.html provides up-to-date listings of wireless access throughout New Jersey.

Phones and Area Codes

New Jersey has six area codes currently in use: 201, covering much of the Gateway Region; 732, used for the Northern Shore and much of eastern Central Jersey; 973, covering the midportion of North Jersey where the Gateway and Skylands meet; 908, used for the greater western Skylands; 609, covering the Pinelands, the Cape, the Greater Atlantic City Region, Central Jersey's western portion, and a small part of the Skylands; and 856, covering the Philadelphia metropolitan region.

Cell Phones

Like elsewhere in the country, cell phone usage has run amok in New Jersey. Although it's illegal in the state to drive while talking on a handheld phone, this hasn't stopped the average citizen, nor is the law enforced on its own accord. The state's drivers have a bad enough rep as it is (though *we all know* it's really those Pennsylvania and New York drivers that are mucking up the roads) and the phone-to-hand-to-head doesn't help.

A number of New Jersey's restaurants have decided to ban cell phone usage in dining areas.

Radio and TV

Many of New Jersey's television stations are broadcast from either New York or Pennsylvania, and in-state offerings are slim. The state does have its own public television station, **NJN** (www.njn.net), which features shows pertaining to New Jersey history and culture, as well as Jersey-centric news coverage and is accessible state-wide.

Radio stations tend to broadcast only as far as regional boundaries (Gateway, South Jersey), and in some cases, sub-regions (Atlantic City and Vicinity, the Cape), before getting fuzzy. To cut down on the channel surfing log onto **www.radiolocator.com** before heading out—the website will tell you where to turn for the best in oldies or alternative tunes, based on the zip code you enter.

Magazines and Newspapers

New Jersey is home to dozens of publications, both newspapers and magazines, that cater to the state and its specific regions. Both Pennsylvania's *Philadelphia Inquirer* (www.philly.com) and Manhattan's *New York Times* (www.nytimes.com) are distributed in New Jersey as well, and feature local news sections pertaining to the state's greater metropolitan suburbs, as well as occasional stories on the Jersey Shore.

Some of New Jersey's best known newspapers include the Gateway's *Star-Ledger* (www.nj.com/starledger), the *Trenton Times* (www.njtimes.com), keeping readers up-to-date on New Jersey's capital city, and the *Press of Atlantic City* (www.pressofatlanticcity.com). For complete New Jersey news coverage log onto **www.nj.com.**

Booksellers find it difficult to keep issues of *Weird NJ* (www.weirdnj.com) in stock. This wonderful publication focuses on all that's odd and offbeat within the Garden State (there's plenty), and has developed quite a cult following. The magazine's readers are some its main story suppliers, and features range from in-depth on albino villages to coverage of haunted asylums.

New Jersey Monthly (www.njmonthly.com) is perhaps the state's most established publication, a well-written monthly filled with up-to-date restaurant info, local profiles, and in-depth articles pertaining to New Jersey culture, life, and politics. The magazine features an annual "Best of the Shore" issue each June.

Upstage Magazine (www.upstagemagazine.com) is a free publication listing local nightclubs and nightlife happenings, music venues—really anything to do with entertainment. Reviews and interviews are a substantial part of the print, which is distributed throughout Central Jersey and the northern Jersey Shore.

Though you have a better chance of finding it in New Jersey bookstores than elsewhere in the country, **Backstreets** (www.backstreets.com) is more of a subscription-type magazine. This is the ultimate Springsteen resource, a fan-based publication centered around the Boss that's been distributed since 1980. Backstreets updates its website daily with current set-lists, news, and the latest in possible Springsteen-centric purchases.

RESOURCES

Suggested Reading

GENERAL INFORMATION

Genovese, Peter. *Jersey Diners.* Rutgers University Press, 1996. While not its original birthplace, New Jersey has the largest number of diners of any U.S. state. Peter Genovese pays homage to this fact by visiting the structures, sitting on the stools, and speaking with the staff of these pop-culture icons—a fine book for any diner-lover or New Jerseyan.

Genovese, Peter. *The Jersey Shore Uncovered.* Rutgers University Press, 2003. Genovese focuses on the personalities and events that make the Jersey Shore oh-so-Jersey. This coffee-table book includes plenty of unique and often colorful photos sure to turn even a curmudgeon nostalgic for the shore.

Gillespie, Angus K., and Michael A. Rockland. *Looking for America on the New Jersey Turnpike.* Rutgers University Press, 1993. A fascinating historical ride along one of New Jersey's most infamous landmarks. Who knew it was illegal to snap a photo on the Turnpike? Anyone?

Lurie, Maxine N., and Marc Mappen. *Encyclopedia of New Jersey.* Rutgers University Press, 2004. A massive collection of New Jersey including everything you may want to know about the state's mob history or brick patterned architecture in Salem County. It's all here, and it's interesting.

Sceurman, Mark, and Mark Morean. *Weird N.J.: Your Travel Guide to New Jersey's Local Legends and Best Kept Secrets.* Barnes & Noble, 2003. The *Weird NJ* boys picked the best of the state's roadside superheroes, abandoned missile bases, and lizard creatures and brought them together in one hardcover book—a bible for the offbeat trip planner.

LITERATURE, FICTION, AND CULTURAL STUDIES

Capuzzo, Michael. *Close to Shore.* Broadway Books, 2001. Capuzzo uses a wealth of resources, including historic newspapers, magazines, and journals, to piece together the events of July 1916, when one of history's worst attacks by a single shark occurred in New Jersey waters—a fascinating read.

Evanovich, Janet. *Stephanie Plum* series. St. Martin's Press, 1995–2005. Janet Evanovich has conjured the ultimate Jersey Girl in Stephanie Plum: a big-haired, ill-fashioned bounty hunter who the world can't help but adore. So far Stephanie and her entourage have mishapped their way through 11 easy reads—here's hoping there's many more to come!

Kalita, S. Mitra. *Suburban Sahibs* Rutgers University Press, 2003. A modern-day cultural study of three Indian families living in the Central Jersey suburb of Edison.

McPhee, John. *The Pine Barrens.* Farrar, Straus, & Giroux, 1968. McPhee's groundbreaking work on the New Jersey Pinelands thrust this fragile ecosystem into the limelight and led to the establishment of the country's first National Reserve.

Roth, Phillip. *American Pastoral.* Houghton Mifflin Company, 1997. Roth's Pulitzer Prize–winning novel explores a fictional yet familiar America from the eyes of a Newark-based Swede.

Roth, Phillip. *Goodbye Columbus: And Five Short Stories.* New York, NY. Vintage, 1994. This early collection of Roth's short stories is set in Newark and the surrounding Gateway Region at a time when the Essex County suburbs were coming into their own.

Smith, Rosamond. *The Barrens.* Carroll & Graf Publishers, 2002. Under the Smith pseudonym New Jersey–based author Joyce Carol Oates writes one of the state's most chilling fictional tales—read it *after* your visit to the Pinelands.

Sullivan, Robert. *The Meadowlands: Wilderness Adventures on the Edge of a City.* Anchor, 1999. One man's passionate journey through the backwaters of New Jersey's Meadowlands, the oft-described "Armpit of America" is a humorous and educational account of New Jersey's famous swampland.

Talese, Gay. *Unto the Sons.* Alfred A. Knopf, 1992. This epic and potent novel intertwines the story of Talese's childhood in Ocean City with that of his Italian ancestors.

PHOTOGRAPHY, MUSIC, AND HISTORY

Buchholz, Margaret Thomas. *New Jersey Shipwrecks: 350 Years in the Graveyard of the Atlantic.* Down the Shore Publishing, 2004. This hardcover book tells the stories of New Jersey's hundreds of shipwrecks with strong text and captivating black and white photos.

Cunningham, John T. *Four Seasons at the Shore: Photographs of the Jersey Shore.* Down the Shore Publishing, 2004. A breathtaking look at the Jersey Shore as it travels through time—packed with gorgeous images.

Goldstein, Stan, and Jean Mickle. *Rock & Roll Tour of the Jersey Shore.* Hard to find outside the greater Asbury Park region, this book is a good resource of local music sites, and an excellent accompaniment for anyone who follows Jersey Shore music.

Kirst, Bob. *Down the Shore: A Photo Tour of the Jersey Coast.* Photo Tour Books, Inc., 2005. One of the most inspiring photo anthologies of the New Jersey Shore, this book captures the state's coastal spirit in a lovely still journey worth the price of admission.

Pike, Helen-Chantal. *Asbury Park's Glory Days: The Story of an American Resort.* Rutgers University Press, 2005. This hardcover book about Asbury Park's early history as a resort town is an interesting read. Vintage photos are spread throughout.

Springsteen, Bruce. *Songs.* Harper Paperbacks, 2003. A book of Springsteen's song lyrics interspersed with the Boss's own commentary on what was truly going on behind the music.

Wien, Gary. *Beyond the Palace.* Sage Publications, 2003. This well-researched book highlights the Asbury Park music scene and is written by one of the founders of the Jersey Shore Music Association.

OUTDOORS

Boyle Jr., William J. *A Guide to Bird Finding in New Jersey.* Rutgers University Press, 2002. An excellent birding guide that's easy to navigate and provides in-depth state coverage.

Kenley, Kathy. *Quiet Water New Jersey: Canoe and Kayak Guide.* Appalachian Mountain Club Books, second edition, 2004. Practical and insightful information on canoeing and kayaking New Jersey's lakes and ponds.

Santelli, Robert. *Short Bike Rides in New Jersey.* Globe Pequot, fourth edition, 1998. A pocket-size and easy-to-read book of the state's best bike rides, heavy on the Skylands and interspersed with factual tidbits.

Scherer, Glenn. *Nature Walks in New Jersey: AMC Guides to the Best Trails From the Highlands to Cape May.* Appalachian Mountain Club Books, second edition, 2003. New Jersey's a true hiker's paradise if you know where to look, and this book explores 40 of the state's best trails.

Internet Resources

GENERAL INFORMATION

New Jersey State Website
www.state.nj.us

New Jersey's official state website, with information on local transit, Jersey Fresh produce, state government, and tourism. The site offers free maps and travel guides, as well as interactive NJ-based games and trivia for kids.

NJ.com
www.nj.com

The ultimate New Jersey resource, with local and statewide news, sports, and weather, restaurant listings and reviews, and online access to a number of the state's newspaper publications.

New Jersey Motion Picture & Television Commission
www.njfilm.org

This site provides information on all New Jersey filming locations past and present, as well as a comprehensive list of all movies and TV shows shot in-state.

HISTORIC PRESERVATION

Doo Wop Preservation League
www.doowopusa.org

A site devoted to the preservation and utilization of the Wildwoods' wacky architectural contribution. If you're interested in learning more about Doo Wop, this is the place to get started.

Cinema Treasures
http://cinematreasures.org

This wonderful site is dedicated to old movie houses and theaters across the United States, providing a brief history and current status of all single screens (even those that have been demolished) and converted multiplexes, a message board, and often photos with each listing. It's *definitely* worth a visit, though you may find yourself browsing around here for hours.

New Jersey Lighthouse Society
njlhs.burlco.org

A non-profit committed to the preservation and longevity of New Jersey's lighthouses and sponsor of the annual Lighthouse Challenge.

Palace Museum Online
www.palaceamusements.com

Asbury Park's now-demolished Palace Amusements lives on in this well-crafted online museum, put together by **Save Tillie** (www.savetillie.com), a non-profit devoted to saving all of Asbury Park's landmarks.

Preservation New Jersey
www.preservationnj.org

This private organization focuses its efforts on saving New Jersey's endangered sights, and its home page features a list of the current year's top 10. Hope Village, Wildwood's Doo Wop motel district, and Asbury Park's Stone Pony all appeared in 2005.

OUTDOORS

New Jersey Audubon Society
www.njaudubon.org

New Jersey's top birding website provides information on Audubon centers throughout the state, local activities and events, and Cape May's annual World Series of Birding.

Tracker School
www.trackerschool.com

Wilderness survival guide Tom Brown, Jr. is no stranger to the Pinelands—he's been hosting courses here for years. The Tracker School website provides a listing of all current classes and prices. If you're going to find yourself lost in the Pines, this is the way to go.

Pinelands Preservation Alliance
www.pinelandsalliance.org

A non-profit committed to preserving the Pinelands for future generations, this group hosts a site that features an up-to-date newsletter and a schedule of the Alliance's upcoming events, including Jersey Devil hunts, Pineland ghost town tours, and wilderness survival training courses.

OFFBEAT SITES

NJ Diners
www.njdiners.com

Looking for a diner in New Jersey? This is the place to come—just click on a region and viola! The website brings up a list of all the nearby diners. Now you'll never be stuck without roadside assistance.

Roadside America
www.roadsideamerica.com

The website for all that's truly tacky and kitsch, and it's no secret that much of this lies within the Garden State. Muffler Men; storybook castles; giant stuffed grizzlies—if it's odd, you'll find it here.

Soprano Sue Sightings
www.sopranosuessightings.com

There's no better place to uncover the going-ons of New Jersey's favorite mob family. This site includes updated news, information on cast and characters, *Sopranos* trivia, and a listing of all local sights that have appeared in the show.

Index

Acknowledgments

I can't say enough about the wonderful people who assisted me in the writing, research, and completion of this book. To my parents, thank you for the use of your home and car and for your unwavering belief in my ability to get the job done. Dad—you are an excellent travel companion who, as always, went above and beyond my expectations. You can be my assistant any day. Mom—your knowledge of New Jersey is outstanding. Thanks for showing me the back routes and providing endless historical tidbits. I love you both. Drew and Alycia, I so appreciate you filling in the gaps on such short notice, and Bonnie Jones, that recorder was the perfect gift! To my cousin Jim Greenhalgh, thanks for allowing me the use of your Sea Isle City home. Can you really call it work if you're living down the Shore? Rebecca Marsh, I could never have tackled Camden without you—you are the best Jersey Girl and friend around—and Jim, your assistance that night in the coffee shop was key. Thanks Mike and Patti Simmons for the research materials, wonderful stories, and a life's worth of visits to the Pinelands. Let's say we take that boat of yours for a spin around L.B.I.? Alicia, thank you for the insider tips on Cape May (it helps to be related to a local). David, Tommy, and Patrick, you make my trips to New Jersey all the brighter. To Chris and Mary Borzell, who assured that my interest in the Garden State never waned, and Toshi Tanaka, who found us just when we needed you, thank you. Matthew, for the late nights and early mornings, critiques and encouragement, shoulders to cry on, and accompanying me 2,800 miles around the state, I can't offer enough gratitude. Regardless of what you say, I could have never done this without you—my love for you is immense.

I'd like to thank the entire Avalon staff, especially Kevin Anglin and the cartography department, Leslie Walters, Stefano Boni, and my superb editor Grace Fujimoto, who patiently allowed me to grow as a writer while working her endless magic—it's been an amazing experience. Rebecca Browning, Krista Lyons-Gould, and the Avalon execs: many thanks for the opportunity, and Amy Scott—copy editor extraordinaire—for keeping me on my toes.

The assistance I received from New Jersey businesses, agencies, tourism boards, and locals is indispensable, and though there are too many to name, I thank you all. Special acknowledgment goes out to Sea Isle City Public Relations Director Irene Jameson, the Gateway and Skylands Tourism Councils, the staff at Fort Mott State Park, Joshua and Diana Cutler at the Tibetan Buddhist Learning Center, Mary at Community Publications, the Burlington County Tourism Office, Rob and Linda Castagna of Milford's Chestnut Hill on the Delaware, the awesome women at the Cumberland County Library, Kathy at My Fair Lady Consignment Shoppe in Pitman, Atlantic City Tourism, Barbara Holmes at PAWS Nature Center, Roz Ressner at Earth Friendly Organic Farm, and to all those establishments who allowed me use of their photographic images.

Ken Whelan, wherever you are, this is for you.

MAP SYMBOLS

▨▨▨ Expressway	【 Highlight	✗ Airfield	⚲ Golf Course
▬▬ Primary Road	○ City/Town	✈ Airport	🅿 Parking Area
▬▬ Secondary Road	◉ State Capital	▲ Mountain	⬬ Archaeological Site
▭ ▭ ▭ Unpaved Road	⊛ National Capital	✛ Unique Natural Feature	♦ Church
- - - - Trail	★ Point of Interest		⛽ Gas Station
·············· Ferry	• Accommodation	☈ Waterfall	〰 Glacier
┼─┼─┼ Railroad	▾ Restaurant/Bar	♠ Park	▨ Mangrove
▨▨ Pedestrian Walkway	▪ Other Location	▣ Trailhead	▨ Reef
▥▥▥ Stairs	∆ Campground	⛷ Skiing Area	▨ Swamp

CONVERSION TABLES

°C = (°F - 32) / 1.8
°F = (°C x 1.8) + 32
1 inch = 2.54 centimeters (cm)
1 foot = 0.304 meters (m)
1 yard = 0.914 meters
1 mile = 1.6093 kilometers (km)
1 km = 0.6214 miles
1 fathom = 1.8288 m
1 chain = 20.1168 m
1 furlong = 201.168 m
1 acre = 0.4047 hectares
1 sq km = 100 hectares
1 sq mile = 2.59 square km
1 ounce = 28.35 grams
1 pound = 0.4536 kilograms
1 short ton = 0.90718 metric ton
1 short ton = 2000 pounds
1 long ton = 1.016 metric tons
1 long ton = 2240 pounds
1 metric ton = 1000 kilograms
1 quart = 0.94635 liters
1 US gallon = 3.7854 liters
1 Imperial gallon = 4.5459 liters
1 nautical mile = 1.852 km

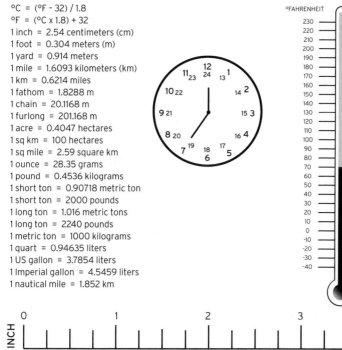

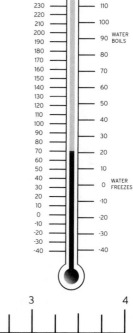

www.moon.com

For helpful advice on planning a trip, visit www.moon.com for the **TRAVEL PLANNER** and get access to useful travel strategies and valuable information about great places to visit. When you travel with Moon, expect an experience that is uncommon and truly unique.

MOON NEW JERSEY

Avalon Travel Publishing
An Imprint of
Avalon Publishing Group, Inc.

AVALON
publishing group incorporated

1400 65th Street, Suite 250
Emeryville, CA 94608, USA
www.moon.com

Editor: Grace Fujimoto
Series Manager: Kathryn Ettinger
Acquisitions Manager: Rebecca K. Browning
Copy Editor: Amy Scott
Graphics Coordinator: Stefano Boni
Production Coordinator: Tabitha Lahr
Cover & Interior Designer: Gerilyn Attebery
Map Editor: Kevin Anglin
Cartographers: Kat Bennett, Chris Markiewicz
Proofreader: Ellie Behrstock
Indexer: Judy Hunt

ISBN-10: 1-56691-949-5
ISBN-13: 978-1-56691-949-4
ISSN: 1930-2630

Printing History
1st Edition – May 2006
5 4 3 2 1

KEEPING CURRENT

If you have a favorite gem you'd like to see included in the next edition, or see anything that needs updating, clarification, or correction, please drop us a line. Send your comments via email to feedback@moon.com, or use the address above.